Parties and Elections in America

Parties and Elections in America

The Electoral Process

Third Edition

L. Sandy Maisel
Colby College

ROWMAN & LITTLEFIELD PUBLISHERS, INC.
Lanham • Boulder • New York • Oxford

ROWMAN & LITTLEFIELD PUBLISHERS, INC.

Published in the United States of America
by Rowman & Littlefield Publishers, Inc.
4720 Boston Way, Lanham, Maryland 20706
http://www.rowmanlittlefield.com

12 Hid's Copse Road
Cumnor Hill, Oxford OX2 9JJ, England

British Library Cataloguing in Publication Information Available

Library of Congress Cataloging-in-Publication Data

Maisel, Louis Sandy, 1945–
Parties and elections in America : the electoral process / L. Sandy Maisel. — 3rd ed.
p. cm.
Previously published: New York : McGraw-Hill, c1993.
Includes bibliographical references and index.
ISBN 0-8476-8549-7 (pbk. : alk. paper)
1. Elections—United States. 2. Electioneering—United States. 3. Political Parties—United States. I. Title.
JK1965.M35 1999
324.973—dc21 99-28825
CIP

Printed in the United States of America

⊗™The paper used in this publication meets the minimum requirements of American National Standard for Information Sciences—Permanence of Paper for Printed Library Materials, ANSI/NISO Z39.48-1992.

To Patrice
with my love

Contents

Tables and Figures

TABLES

FIGURES

Preface

I cannot remember a time when I was not interested in politics. My earliest political memory is of my father's excitement at being invited to a campaign breakfast with President Truman. I remember fighting with my first-grade friends over our candidates in the 1952 election. My enthusiasm grew as my knowledge and level of political sophistication grew. Those who knew me during my youth in Buffalo or during my college days could not have been surprised that I have become both a political scientist and a political activist. I am one of those fortunate few who can merge vocation and avocation.

For nearly three decades I have taught courses about various aspects of the U.S. electoral process to students at Colby College. Each time I plan a new syllabus, I face a new challenge. How do I excite a new generation of students in a subject that is for me a consuming interest? How can I communicate the reasons for my excitement to a generation that may have good reasons to be turned off to politics?

More specifically, I am concerned about helping students see two connections, first, the connection between things that are important in their lives and what goes on in the political realm and, second, the connection between real-world politics and their readings in political science books and articles. Political parties seem irrelevant to many students; the various theories of voting behavior and the means used to study that subject are often difficult for students to grasp, and the rules of the political game seem mysterious. Undergraduates, even those who are interested in politics, often do not understand how our political process actually works. They acquire their interest because they (and/or their families) favor one particular candidate or another. Their arguments are often highly emotional, and their factual understanding of how the political process functions is often flawed. A huge information gap needs to be bridged.

This book, which is about elections and political parties, represents my attempt to make both of the connections mentioned above and to bridge the information gap for students who are interested in politics. In the chapters that follow, readers will learn about the electoral process in America. They will learn not only the mechanics of how the system works and how it has worked in the past but will also learn about the impact of the way it works, and why it has come to work in that way. The book is written from the perspective of a political scientist who has run for office and has been actively involved in politics for more than thirty years.

I have been chastened by criticism from politicians who claim that most political scientists know nothing about how politics really work. Their criticism has not fallen on deaf ears. This book is about the political process as it is analyzed by political scientists and also as it is experienced by politicians. I think that students gain the best understanding of the political process when they are introduced to the academic study of the subject and to the thrill and excitement of the political game at the same time. My teaching experience has proven that mix of perspectives to be a happy one. Enthusiasm for the study of politics follows from a concern about the political world we all experience. And this conclusion follows as directly for those who are unhappy with the current state of politics as it does for those who agree with the direction our polities are taking, for those who oppose current officeholders as for those who favor them.

As I complete this preface, President Clinton has embarked on his last two years in office, with the impeachment trial, if not the scandal that preceded it, behind him. Vice President Gore seems primed to replace Clinton as the Democratic standard-bearer, though he will face at least one challenger, former senator and New York Knicks star Bill Bradley. No fewer than twelve Republicans have expressed active interest in their party's nomination. These include old candidates—magazine publisher Malcolm (Steve) Forbes, former vice president Dan Quayle, television commentator Pat Buchanan, and former Tennessee governor and secretary of education Lamar Alexander; new candidates—former Family Research Council leader Gary Bauer, Arizona senator, John McCain (R-Ariz.) and Orrin Hatch (R-Ut.), and Ohio congressman John Kasich; long shots—commentator Alan Keyes and New Hampshire senator Bob Smith; and putative front-runners—Elizabeth Dole, the first woman whose candidacy has been taken seriously even a year before the first primaries, and George W. Bush, Texas governor and son of the last Republican president. There ought to be someone for everyone, and surely watching will be great sport.

We have a new Speaker of the House of Representatives, Dennis Hastert (R-Ill.), and a veteran House minority leader, Dick Gephardt (D-Mo.). We have Senate leaders whose performance during the impeachment trial drew close public scrutiny. And we have intense competition for partisan control of Congress.

The same can be said for politics in many of the states. Term limits, imposed on legislators in some states, will be more and more evident in state politics in the years ahead. State legislative politics might well be as heated as any at the national level. And then we have Jesse (The Body) Ventura, the Reform party governor of Minnesota, clearly demonstrating for all to see that politics can be fun as well as serious. In the chapters ahead I attempt to engage students in our political process, showing them how exciting it can be and how colorful the characters are and also how important the process is. An understanding of the political process and the roles played by parties and elections can impact their lives.

Chapter 1 is a conceptual introduction to the study of political parties and elections. In it I define parties and clarify their role in the electoral process. The issues raised in chapter 1 go far toward structuring the rest of the book. The electoral process, which is under examination here, is a multidimensional phenomenon, not a simple one. Political parties form an important dimension of the electoral process, but only one dimension. All of these dimensions are examined in turn.

Chapter 2 recognizes the key role that parties play in the electoral process. Modern political parties are a distinctly American invention, yet politicians tend to have an ambivalent view of parties, playing a role in their development but also bemoaning their existence. In chapter 2 I examine the development of American political parties in two ways. First, I outline the history of the parties as a history of distinct party systems. Then I focus on the development of the institutions and structures of political parties as organizations, a development that sometimes has and sometimes has not run parallel to transformations in party alignment. Like every other chapter but the last one, chapter 2 ends with an assessment of how politicians view the topic under discussion.

Chapter 3 details how political parties are organized throughout the nation. Party as organization has evolved in important ways in recent years, responding to challenges to the roles that parties have traditionally played. I note the significant role played by organizations at state, county, and national levels.

Chapters 4–6 focus on different aspects of individual political activities. In chapter 4 I emphasize different levels of activity—who votes and who does not vote, and who participates in political activities of other kinds. This chapter includes a look at motives and incentives for participation and an initial assessment of the pleasures and pains that derive from political involvement.

Chapter 5 provides a detailed examination and careful review of the voluminous professional literature on voting behavior. No text on parties and elections would be complete without such a review. Students proceed from the early community-based studies through the most recent discussion of voting. As important as this literature is for its findings, it is also important for demonstrating how scientific knowledge accumulates progressively. Students will see how each study rests on the intellectual shoulders of preceding studies, and how each study in turn supports the work of succeeding generations. Concepts such as party identification are important not only in their own right but also as expressions of a discipline struggling with the difficulty of understanding complex phenomena and processes.

Political observers from Alexis de Tocqueville to V. O. Key Jr. have commented that Americans have a congenital tendency to join groups and to act as members of those groups. Individual voters often perceive themselves and relate to the electoral process as members of groups. In addition, organized group behavior has long had an impact on American politics. This phenomenon is perhaps more important today than at any other time in our history. It could even be argued that some interest groups fit our definition of political party almost as well as the Democratic and Republican parties do; indeed, better than some minor parties do. The only difference is that "they don't quack like a duck."

Chapter 6 examines the behavior and influence of organized groups in American politics, stressing the electoral activities of these groups and the extent to which they attempt to influence and succeed in influencing the voting behavior of their members.

Chapters 7–10 examine nominations and election campaigns in the United States. Chapters 7–8 deal with gubernatorial, senatorial, congressional, and state and local elections; chapters 9–10 with the presidential election. Chapter 7 begins with a discussion of common views on the nominating process and then examines how reality differs from these views. The development of the direct primary as a means of securing partisan nominations, the variety of primaries that exists in various jurisdictions, and the politics of securing party nominations are all explored at some length.

Chapter 8 examines general election campaigns below the presidential level. Conventional wisdom holds that politics has changed dramatically as the age of television and computers has evolved. In this chapter I argue that the "new politics" is very much in evidence in some campaigns, but the "old politics," the politics of personal contact and detailed organization, remains essential for many local politicians. In addition, I explore in some detail the important question of whether or not general election campaigns make a difference in who is elected, as well as the factors that determine whether or not third parties are likely to have an influence in elections at this level.

The presidential election process is so complex and so important in the American system of government that it is dealt with as a separate topic. Despite the prominent attention that presidential nominations receive in the national media, few truly understand them. In Chapter 9 I explore the nominating process, beginning with a review of recent changes and continuing with a review of recent nominating contests and the strategic considerations that determine how they were fought. I discuss national party conventions, the ultimate spectacle in American politics, in light of current criticism that they represent useless vestiges from a bygone era and are no longer worthy of serious consideration, and in light of contrary opinions that conventions remain an important element of the electoral process.

To many Americans, the term "election campaign" means the general election of the president. In chapter 10 I 1ook at how such an election is organized, at recent strategies and tactics for implementing those strategies, and at the impact of the campaigns. Although many readers may find the topic a familiar one, the nuances of presidential campaigns can be obscure except to the most practiced observer.

Throughout the chapters on nominations and elections, I stress the importance of money in electoral politics. Campaign financing is such an important topic that I devote an entire chapter to exploring the current situation. In chapter 11 I examine the campaign financing reforms of the 1970s and the current climate for further changes. I present data that summarize the costs of maintaining our democracy, and I examine the sources to which politicians turn for campaign funding, particularly political action committees. In this chapter, to an even greater extent than in some of the earlier ones, politicians' views are seen as going a long way toward determining how the process will function.

Chapter 12 highlights another separate aspect of the electoral process—the impact of the media on American elections. I explore the roles of unpaid and paid media separately. Constraints on newspaper and television coverage of politics explain some apparent shortcomings. The controversy over negative advertising makes up an important aspect of the discussion of paid media, as does the use and possible misuse of issue advocacy advertising.

The role of party in government has received considerable attention in the professional literature. In chapter 13 I turn to that topic. Ours is not a parliamentary system in which decisions by party members as party members have a direct impact on governmental policy. However, our governing institutions are structured by political parties; appointments tend to be made with due recognition of party affiliation. In short, despite the fact that parties are organized to help candidates win elections, they play a vital role in governing as well. I outline that role, and explore recent changes in it, in this chapter.

The concluding chapter returns to the themes raised in the introductory chapter. How well does the electoral process function? What roles do parties play? How do those roles differ from their traditional roles? What institutions have replaced parties in functional terms? What are the consequences for our political system of candidate-oriented campaigns? Of increased PAC influence? Of public financing? What does this view of the electoral process imply about the link between parties as the organizing structure of an election and parties as the organizing structure of our governmental institutions? Can this process be reformed? Should it be reformed?

I suppose that any author wants his or her readers to know what he or she thinks is most important about a new or newly revised book. I am no different. I stress a number of points in this text. First, as noted above, I think it vitally important that students see the excitement of politics and the connection of the political process to their own lives, even if they might be cynical about contemporary politicians. I hope that I succeed in conveying my excitement to my student audience.

Second, I think it is important for students to see the connection between the political science literature and the real-world politics they observe. Even some political scientists do not see this, and so it is crucial for students to do so. I have tried to emphasize this aspect in my discussions as well.

Third, political history is fascinating and absolutely crucial to an understanding of modern politics. This book, more than others, emphasizes political history. Students should not think that the parties they observe today, that the process they observe today, appeared all at once. What lessons can be learned from the past? From the politicians of the past? Who were these leaders and how did they "play the political game"? This text is full of historical examples—even of the history of studying politics—not just because I am "old" but because I hope students can see links to the past and thus learn lessons from our history.

And fourth, politics is to be studied, not just read about. This text is extensively documented. I have used in-text references to avoid interrupting the flow of the discussion. But I have used many references so that students interested in exploring further can find a place to start. Similarly, I have included many tables and figures, most of which illustrate the discussion. But some of them I have included because I think the data are interesting, again hoping to stimulate student excitement in research.

The chapters in this book are meant to instruct, to tell the reader how the process works and to explore its complexity. These chapters are also meant to cause the reader to empathize, to understand how it feels to be part of this process, to share the perspective of politicians and political activists, to become part of the system that affects all Americans' lives. This text can be deemed to be a success or a failure according to whether or not the reader gains an understanding of the American electoral process in not only an analytical but also a pragmatic and emotional way. And if that understanding leads the student reader to continued interest.

Acknowledgments

In preparing this third edition of the text, I have had an opportunity to reflect on comments made by those who used the first two editions and to study how the editions worked in various classrooms. I have also edited three editions of an anthology designed for a college course on parties and elections (Maisel 1998 is the most recent version) and have discussed topics for inclusion in works of this type with a wide range of scholars in political science and closely related fields. I am indebted to many colleagues for the advice about improving my work that they offered as we discussed mutual concerns about how to teach political parties and elections. The addition of a separate chapter in this text on the role of the media and the expansion of a number of other points are directly attributable to comments and reactions of my friends in this profession. I want to begin by thanking all of those who have aided this work in that way.

This book has also benefited from the comments of those for whom it is intended—student readers. I am grateful to generation after generation of Colby students and to students I have taught at the University of Melbourne, Monash University, Harvard, and Stanford. One of the real joys of teaching is to have the opportunity to test one's ideas on the palette of relatively unpainted young minds and to learn from the ways in which the colors are reflected. For nearly three decades I have tested my ideas about elections and politics on Colby students. Their insights have helped me to shape and refine those ideas; their reactions have led me to a better understanding of what works and what does not work in a teaching environment, of how complex ideas can be effectively communicated, of how concern and enthusiasm can be transmitted to those who will be carrying political banners in the years ahead. In a very real sense this book is written for my students and because of my students; any success it enjoys as a teaching tool is a direct result of what I have learned from them.

Of course, some students stand out. I could go back over twenty-eight years of rosters and name student after student who has had a direct impact on the concepts developed in this book; but I fear if I did so I would miss some people. The students with whom I have worked most closely know who they are and know how much I value the times we have spent together. In recent years Colby has developed a work-study program that allows faculty members to hire undergraduate students as research assistants, a liberal arts college equivalent of graduate assistants. In working on this edition, I was immensely helped by the efforts of Kendra Amman, Kara Falkenstein, Cathy Flemming, Lizzie Ivry, Ben Ling, Alex Quigley, and Rebecca Ryan. I am most grateful to each of these friends—the next generation of teacher-scholar-activists, I hope. I also want to thank the students who helped on earlier versions of this text, and Kara Chessman at the Brookings Institution, Chad Higgins, a former student now working at Arnold and Porter in Washington, and Anthony Talbott at Arizona State University for help solving particular problems as this project neared completion.

Others have made important contributions to this text. I especially want to thank Paul Herrnson, Stephen Hess, Malcolm Jewell, Michael Malbin, Tom Mann, David Rohde, and the anonymous reviewers for Roman & Littlefield. Each of these read all or parts of some version of this work and made important suggestions that saved me from errors.

As one finishes work on a text, one almost automatically thinks back to those who have influenced the book's development in less specific ways. I feel fortunate to be a member of two very special communities. First, I am part of the community of scholars, in this case the specific community of scholars of American politics. My work has been influenced over the years by conversations with and encouragement from literally scores of fellow political scientists. I cannot help mentioning my close friends and colleagues who have been important influences in my professional development—John Bibby, Dave Brady, Chuck Bullock, Joe Cooper, Linda Fowler, Paul Herrnson, Chuck Jones, Ruth Jones, the late Warren Miller, Ron Rapoport, and Walt Stone among others, and those who have led and contributed to two groups in which I have been active and from which I have gained a great deal: the Political Organizations and Parties and the Legislative Studies organized sections of the American Political Science Association. Much of the material in this book is derived from the ideas and research of colleagues and friends who have seen the importance of sharing ideas, working together, and growing as a cooperating community of scholars. I feel fortunate to work in a profession that so clearly sees growth as a community to be a critical common goal.

Second, I am part of a uniquely American phenomenon—the community of a small liberal arts college. And what a wonderful community that is in which to live and grow. Colby College as an institution has been enormously supportive of my work. Throughout the years I have benefited from discussions with my colleagues in the Government Department. I have team-taught a large number of courses with Tony Corrado, Cal Mackenzie, and Charles Bassett. Their influence on my thinking and my writing (especially Bassett's on the quality of my writing) is inestimable; I hope they are aware of how much I appreciate their efforts, support, and friendship. In preparing this book, I have called on Joe Reisert for advice and support; I want to thank him and the other members of my department for providing a wonderful environment in which to live and work.

Much of this book was written while I was on sabbatical leave from Colby. In the fall of 1999 I was fortunate enough to live and work in Manila, the Philippines, as the Philippine Centennial Distinguished Fulbright Lecturer. That opportunity was a most rich one. I was able to discuss American politics with those who view our system from a very great distance—and that perspective helped to shape my ideas. I am grateful to the Fulbright program and especially to Dr. Alex Calata for the Philippine-American Education Foundation, the Fulbright office in the Philippines, for that opportunity. For the winter and spring, I have been a Guest Scholar in the Governmental Studies Program at the Brookings Institution. It is difficult to imagine a better environment in which to work on topics in American politics. I want to thank Brookings, and especially Tom Mann, the director of the Governmental Studies Program, and the colleagues who have commented on my work—E. J. Dionne, Bill Frenzel, Stephen Hess, Michael Malbin, and Jennifer Steen.

This book reunites me with Jennifer Knerr, who is in my estimation the best political science editor in the country. Jennifer has been a good friend for many years. She is also a most esteemed colleague. As an editor, she has helped to shape every aspect of this book; any success it has is a reflection of her professionalism and dedication to quality publishing. As a friend, she has been tolerant of my idiosyncrasies as an author and generous of time and feelings when I have struggled to meet deadlines. I am most grateful to her for both her immense talents as an editor and her friendship. I also want to thank the others at Rowman & Littlefield who have worked on this book: Brenda Hadenfeldt, Jennifer's talented assistant, assistant managing editor Lynn Weber, copy editor Chrisona Schmidt, proofreader Susan Finkelstein, and photo editor Sallie Greenwood.

Finally, I want to thank my family and friends, who support me in all that I do. This book is dedicated to my wife, Patrice Franko. Patrice and I have been working toward completion of books on parallel paths; she finished slightly before I did. I only hope that, as she has finished her task, she has benefited half as much from my support, encouragement, and love as I have from hers. Each day I reflect on how very fortunate I am to have her as a wife, a partner, a colleague, and a friend. The dedication of this book comes with my deepest love.

L. Sandy Maisel
Spring 1999

Credits

Chapter 1: 1 Charles Schumer and Daniel Patrick Moynihan: Henry Ray Abrams, CORBIS/AFP. **4** "Yes, I really love you. . . . Now tell me a little about yourself." Jeff MacNelly, Chicago Tribune, © Tribune Media Services, Inc. All rights reserved. Reprinted with permission.

Chapter 2: 29 Johnson signing Civil Rights Act, July 2, 1964: Cecil Stoughton, Lyndon Baines Johnson Library Collection 276-10-64. **51** Lincoln and Douglas in a presidential footrace: Library of Congress LC-USZ62-14834.

Chapter 3: 65 Voter looking at sample ballot, Arlington, Virginia, 1992: Marcy Nighswander, AP/Wide World Photos.

Chapter 4: 91 AARP members lobbying on Medicare, Boston, 1997: Gail Oskin, AP/Wide World Photos. **114** "Are low voter turnouts due to ignorance or apathy? I don't know and I don't care." © 1998 Gary Markstein, Milwaukee Journal Sentinel.

Chapter 5: 125 Woman voting: CORBIS/Owen Franken. **132** Table 5.1: Reprinted by permission of the publisher from *The Responsible Electorate* by V. O. Key Jr., Cambridge, Mass.: The Belknap Press of Harvard University Press, Copyright © 1966 by the President and Fellows of Harvard College.

Chapter 6: 157 Pro-choice rally at the Missouri state capitol, 1989: CORBIS/Joseph Sohm, ChromoSohm Inc. **180** "You have reached the National Rifle Association. . . ." Jimmy Margulies, © 1999 The Record (New Jersey).

Chapter 7: 187 Roy Romer, Democratic Party Chair, at National Governors' Association press conference, 1993: Ron Edmonds, AP/Wide World Photos.

Chapter 8: 219 Jesse Ventura with George W. Bush: CORBIS/AFP, Paul J. Richards.

Chapter 9: 265 Steve Forbes and Jack Kemp, 1996: CORBIS/Robert Maass. **284** "Sit down, Bob. . . ." © 1999 Scott Willis, San Jose Mercury News.

Chapter 10: 319 Clinton supporters, Los Angeles, 1996: CORBIS/Catherine Karnow. **348** "Howdy! I'm Ross Perot. . . ." OLIPHANT © 1992 UNIVERSAL PRESS SYNDICATE. Reprinted with permission. All rights reserved.

Chapter 11: 371 John McCain and Russell Feingold, January 23, 1997: CORBIS/Wally McNamee. **412** "Show me the money!" © 1997 Mike Luckovich, Atlanta Constitution.

Chapter 12: 417 Clinton and media, October 1992: CORBIS/Robert Maass. 423 Bloom County: © Berkeley Breathed.

Chapter 13: 445 Henry Hyde, Barney Frank, and John Conyers Jr., December 9, 1998: CORBIS/AFP, Paul J. Richards. **453** "Newt's contract with America II." © 1997 Mike Luckovich, Atlanta Constitution.

Chapter 14: 483 Al Gore: AP Photo/The Palm Beach Post, Richard Graulich.

CHAPTER 1

Elections and Political Parties

Let's begin by talking about the electoral careers of four contemporary political figures, members of the U.S. Senate. Massachusetts's senior senator, Democrat Edward M. (Ted) Kennedy, was first elected to the Senate in 1962 in a special election to fill the remaining years of the term for the seat left vacant when his brother, John F. Kennedy, was elected president. Ted Kennedy won election to a full term in 1964 and has won reelection five times since then. Only once in that time did he poll less than 60 percent of the vote; his highest total was nearly 75 percent.

Alphonse M. D'Amato, New York's Republican senator for eighteen years, was elected in 1980, winning the general election with only 44.9 percent of the vote and a margin of approximately 1 percent. He won his party's nomination with a primary victory over four-term incumbent Jacob Javits. D'Amato won reelection quite handily in 1986, but in 1992 he was again held under 50 percent of the vote and won by about 1 percent. In 1998, he finally met his match, losing to Charles Schumer in one of the most hotly contested elections in that year.

In 1986 Alabamans elected Richard C. Shelby to the Senate. Shelby, a Democratic congressman from Birmingham, defeated one-termer Jeremiah Denton, who in 1980 had been the first Republican elected to the Senate from Alabama since the passage of the Seventeenth Amendment to the U.S. Constitution, calling for the direct election of senators.[1] After having beaten an incumbent in a very close election, Shelby went on to win reelection in 1992 by a margin of almost 2 to 1. In 1994, after Republicans won partisan control of the Senate, Shelby announced his intention to switch from the Democratic to the Republican party, a move welcomed by the Republicans because it strengthened their thin majority. He won reelection as a Republican handily in 1998.

Finally, Dianne Feinstein (D-Calif.) took a more circuitous route to the Senate. As president of the San Francisco board of supervisors, Feinstein succeeded to the position of mayor (which she had twice sought and lost) when the incumbent, George Moscone, was assassinated in 1978. Elected and reelected in her own right in 1979 and 1983 but ineligible to seek a third full term in 1987, Feinstein left city government and ran for governor of California in 1990, winning the Democratic primary and barely losing the general election to Republican Pete Wilson. To assume the governorship, Wilson had to vacate his seat in the Senate. He appointed a little-known Republican, John Seymour, to replace him; Feinstein immediately declared her candidacy to fill the remaining two years of Wilson's term. In 1992 she defeated Wilson's appointee quite easily, polling nearly 60 percent of the vote. Most political observers felt that she would have an easy contest in 1994 as she sought to win a full six-year term. But that was not to be. In 1994 she was opposed by Republican congressman Michael Huffington, who became a serious contender because of his willingness to spend millions of his own dollars to win the seat. Feinstein prevailed by 2 percent in an election in which she spent nearly $15 million; her opponent spent twice as much as she did. California Democrats hoped that Feinstein would seek their state's governorship again in 1998, but she elected to remain in the Senate, in part at least because half billionaire Al Checchi entered the Democratic primary and thereby raised the specter of another exorbitantly expensive campaign.[2]

These cases are presented as instructive places to begin an examination of elections and political parties in the United States. Four senators followed four very different routes to power and have had four very different careers. Kennedy essentially followed a family tradition, winning his first election largely on the power of his family name. Despite personal scandal, he has maintained a prominent place in his state's and the nation's political arena. Residing in a state dominated by his political party, he has been able to thwart even serious opponents with little difficulty. D'Amato worked his way up through a strong local political organization and had to fight to win his party's nomination over an entrenched incumbent who was somewhat out of sync with his constituents. In a state characterized by intense partisan battles, he had to fight constantly to keep himself on top of the political heap but finally was defeated. Richard Shelby changed with a changing political environment. As Republicans came to power in the once solidly Democratic South, Shelby judged that his politics were more in line with the rising power than with those whose power was fading. Finally, Dianne Feinstein came to prominence by being in the right place at the right time. In a two-party state, she has won and lost, has contested for office and has chosen to forgo contests, in the process building a personal following that makes her one of the state's most popular figures.

Under the American system of government, elections are used to assure popular support and **legitimacy** for those who make governmental decisions. In his classic study *The Theory and Practice of Modern Government,* Herman Finer (1949) summarized this connection between democracy and elections: "The real question . . . is not whether the government designs to take notice of popular criticisms and votes, but whether it can be voted out of office or forced by some machinery or procedures to change its policy, above all against its own will" (p. 219).

LEGITIMACY

Acceptance of the right of public officials to hold office and to promulgate policies because of the means by which they were chosen.

The examples cited above illustrate that the process is a most complex one. To even begin to understand American politics, one must know something about the political history and **political culture** not only of the nation but also of various regions. One must understand the kinds of choices that individuals make and the political contexts in which they make them. One must look at the role of political parties, individual voters, and money. And one must always remember that politics is not only about power but also about personalities; the importance of how different people react to situations should never be underestimated. For many, those personalities are what makes politics so

POLITICAL CULTURE

Norms, expectations, and values concerning political life in a particular polity or region.

interesting, but their role must be understood in terms of the process in which they participate.

I. An Examination of Elections in the United States

The contest for office is the machinery used by Americans to change policy and to change those who govern, often against their will. And the American electoral process is clearly different from that in other countries. A number of aspects distinguish how we use this machinery from how other countries do so. First, Americans are expected to go to the polls more frequently and to vote for more officeholders. Table 1.1 shows the elections in which citizens of four different cities had to vote in the eighteen months before the year 2000 presidential elections. Critics of American democracy complain about low turnout rates for our elections, but they rarely note how often we are asked to vote. The implication of this difference between the American system and those in most other countries is worth contemplating.

Second, our elections are held at regular intervals, regardless of the flow of world events, and are never changed because of particular national crises. President Clinton did not have the luxury that, say, Prime Minister Tony Blair of England has, to call for a reaffirming election at a time when his popularity was high nor to postpone a regularly scheduled election if his popularity were low. Our presidential elections are held on the first Tuesday after the first Monday in November of every fourth year, without exceptions. Period! No exceptions! For example, President Franklin D. Roosevelt won reelection twice during World War II, once on the eve of our entry into the war and once as the push to victory neared completion; the dates of American elections are never changed because of particular national crises.

Table 1.1 Examples of Elections Held, Selected Municipalities, 1999–2000

Montgomery, Alabama	
1999	
October	Municipal elections (mayor, council)
2000	
June	Statewide and presidential primaries with runoffs later in the month
November	Federal and state elections Judicial elections
Bangor, Maine	
1999	
November	Municipal elections and referenda (state and/or candidate)
2000	
February	Presidential preference primary
June	Primary elections for federal, state, and county offices
November	General election for federal, state, and county offices
Athens, Ohio	
1999	
November	County, township, and municipal elections Elections to school board
2000	
March	Presidential primary*
May	Congressional primary
November	Election of federal and state officials
Seattle, Washington	
1999	
February–May	Special elections (if necessary)
September	Primary elections for municipal offices (mayor, council, school board)
November	Municipal elections Statewide and local initiatives
2000	
February–May	Special elections (if necessary)
September	Primary elections for federal, state, and county offices
November	Election of federal and state offcials Statewide and local initiatives

Source: Data provided by the Office of the Registrar of Voters in each respective municipality.
*Date tentative.

Third, the terms of various offices in our system are not all the same; thus, though elections are held at regular intervals, exactly which offices are contested in any particular election varies, not only from election to election but also from state to state for the same election. All members of the U.S. House of Representatives are up for election every two years; only one-third of Senate seats (plus special elections to fill vacancies) are contested in any one national election.[3] The president is elected for a four-year term, as are most governors. Some governors, however, are elected for two-year terms, and most of the four-year gubernatorial terms do not end when the president's term ends. The complexity is accentuated by state legislatures and local offices. Table 1.2 summarizes the terms of office and election cycles for state governors and legislators.

EQUAL PROTECTION CLAUSE

The phrase in section 1 of the Fourteenth Amendment to the U.S. Constitution that guarantees that no state may deny any person within its jurisdiction the "equal protection of the laws."

LEGISLATIVE TERM LIMITS

Fixed limitations on the number of terms of office that members of a legislature may serve.

Fourth, the rules in different states and for different offices vary significantly. The Constitution specifies that states have the right to control the times and places of elections, even national elections, except for instances in which special provisions apply. The states also control most aspects of their own political systems, again with a few exceptions, as, for example, the "one man–one vote" provision imposed on drawing district lines through a Supreme Court interpretation of the **equal protection clause** of the Constitution.[4] One recent controversy that illustrates this point relates to **legislative term limits.** In an effort to limit the power of entrenched incumbents, a number of states have imposed lim-

Table 1.2 Terms of State Offices and Election Cycles

State	*Governor's Term (years)*	*Expiration of Current Term (date)*	*Senators' Terms (years)*	*Representatives' Terms (years)*
AL	4	Jan 03	4	4
AK	4	Jan 03	4	2
AZ	4	Jan 03	2	2
AR	4	Jan 03	4	2
CA	4	Jan 03	4	2
CO	4	Jan 03	4	2
CT	4	Jan 03	2	2
DE	4	Jan 01	4	2
FL	4	Jan 03	4	2
GA	4	Jan 03	2	2
HI	4	Jan 03	4	2
ID	4	Jan 01	2	2
IL	4	Jan 03	4	2
IN	4	Jan 03	4	2
IA	4	Jan 03	4	2
KS	4	Jan 03	4	2
KY	4	Dec 03	4	2
LA	4	Jan 00	4	4
ME	4	Jan 03	2	2
MD	4	Jan 03	4	4
MA	4	Jan 03	2	2
MI	4	Jan 03	4	2
MN	4	Jan 03	4	2
MS	4	Jan 00	4	4
MO	4	Jan 01	4	2
MT	4	Jan 01	4	2

continued

itations on the number of terms their state legislators can serve in office.[5] States that have imposed such limitations and the variation among states in how this concept has been implemented are shown in table 1.3. Of course, most states (though not all) restrict their governors to two terms, paralleling the federal example of the president.

In some states it has been possible to run for more than one office in the same election. Lloyd Bentsen (D) was reelected to the Senate from Texas on the same day in 1988 that he lost the election to be vice president of the United States as the running mate of Michael Dukakis (D-Mass.).[6] In Pennsylvania, one has been able to run for the party nomination for of more than one office on the same day. At the opposite extreme, in Hawaii, a state officeholder must resign if he or she seeks another office. Vacancies in some offices are filled through an automatic succession. On the national level the vice president becomes president upon the death, resignation, or declared disability of the president. Other vacancies are filled by appointment; governors appoint senators to fill vacant seats until the next general election. Still

Table 1.2 Terms of State Offices and Election Cycles *(continued)*

State	*Governor's Term (years)*	*Expiration of Current Term (date)*	*Senators' Terms (years)*	*Representatives' Terms (years)*
NE	4	Jan 03	4	(unicameral)
NV	4	Jan 03	4	2
NH	2	Jan 01	2	2
NJ	4	Jan 02	4	2
NM	4	Jan 03	4	2
NY	4	Jan 03	2	2
NC	4	Jan 01	2	2
ND	4	Dec 00	4	2
OH	4	Jan 03	4	2
OK	4	Jan 03	4	2
OR	4	Jan 03	4	2
PA	4	Jan 03	4	2
RI	4	Jan 03	2	2
SC	4	Jan 03	4	2
SD	4	Jan 03	4	2
TN	4	Jan 03	4	2
TX	4	Jan 03	4	2
UT	4	Jan 01	4	2
VT	2	Jan 01	2	2
VA	4	Jan 02	4	2
WA	4	Jan 01	4	2
WV	4	Jan 01	4	2
WI	4	Jan 03	4	2
WY	4	Jan 03	4	2

Source: Almanac of American Politics, Secretaries of State.

Table 1.3 Term-Limited States

		House		Senate	
State	*Year Enacted*	*Limit*	*Year of Impact*	*Limit*	*Year of Impact*
Arizona	1992	8	2000	8	2000
Arkansas	1992	6	1998	8	2002
California	1990	6	1996	8	1998
Colorado	1990	8	1998	8	2000
Florida	1992	8	1998	8	2000
Idaho	1994	8	2004	8	2004
Louisiana	1995	12	2007	12	2007
Maine	1993	8	1996	8	1996
Michigan	1992	6	1998	8	2002
Missouri*	1992	8	2002	8	2002
Montana	1992	8	2000	8	2000
Nevada	1994	12	2008	12	2008
Ohio	1992	8	2000	8	2000
Oklahoma	1990	12	2004	12	2004
Oregon	1992	6	1998	8	2002
South Dakota	1992	8	2000	8	2000
Utah	1994	12	2006	12	2006
Wyoming	1992	12	2006	12	2006

*Due to special elections, term limits will affect five representatives in 2001 and one senator in 1998.
Source: National Conference of State Legislatures.

other offices, such as U.S. Representative, can only be filled by election and remain vacant until a special election can be held if an incumbent dies, resigns, or is removed from office.

Generally speaking, well-known state laws and party rules structure most contests for office, but we will constantly reassess that situation. We will also ask whether the role that party plays is a good one or a bad one and will be concerned with what standards should be used to answer that question. This text also assumes that the electoral contest provides a mechanism for expressing **popular support** or disapproval and for granting legitimacy, as Finer posited. We will ask whether or not we are satisfied with how this part of our democracy is working.

POPULAR SUPPORT

Public approval of the officials running the government and, by implication, of the policies they are pursuing.

Do you remember the discussion of Senator Shelby at the beginning of this chapter? Recall that his predecessor was the first Republican ever to be popularly elected to the Senate from Alabama. In fact, most of the Democratic senators who preceded Senator Denton won with over 80 percent of the popular vote. In what sense, then, could it be said that political parties structured that contest for office? There was no contest for office. What possible interpretation could be given to those senators' mandates to govern? We will ask this question over and over again. How well does our system work? And, to the extent that we are not happy with its functioning, what can be done to make it more effective?

While the South is no longer solidly Democratic, intense partisan competition does not exist everywhere in the country. In 1998, 86 incumbent members of the House of Representatives faced no major party opposition in the November general election; that number reflects approximately one out of every five congressmen and is the highest in recent times.[7] How can the public express popular support in these "contests" for office?

And what happened when Democrat Shelby switched to the Republican party in 1994? If party membership is important in elections, as I have posited it is, shouldn't switching parties be anathema for elected officials? On the contrary, the Republicans embraced Shelby and gave him a position in their party's seniority as if he had been a Republican since he was first elected to the Senate. What does Shelby's experience say about the role of party? While party switching is not commonplace, eight members of the 106th Congress have switched parties since their original election. In addition to Shelby, three other senators serving in the 106th Congress—Campbell (R-Colo.), Gramm (R-Tex.), and Thurmond (R-S.C.)—were originally elected to office as members of the other party. Even former president Ronald Reagan was once a Democrat and an active member of the quintessentially liberal Americans for Democratic Action. Thus ample evidence exists for the proposition that the most basic assumptions about the role of party and even the role of elections themselves require careful study.

It is my goal is to examine the process through which **partisan elections** are contested in the United States.[8] While the examples adduced above call into question certain basic assumptions about the role of political parties, it would be naive to ignore the role that parties historically have played in American elections and continue to play.

PARTISAN ELECTIONS

Elections in which those on the ballot are identified by their political party affiliation; by contrast, in nonpartisan elections no designation appears next to a candidate's name.

This text addresses a tension as it emphasizes the role of political parties as well as the more broadly defined electoral process. Partisan elections are, by definition, elections contested by nominees of political parties. For much of our nation's history, the parties dominated the contest for office (see Silbey 1998). Citizens typically supported candidates of one party or the other with great loyalty. In order to understand elections in the contemporary contexts, we must understand this background.

Thus this text looks at the history and development of the role played by parties in structuring American elections. It also looks at the current role of parties in the contest for office. However, in the chapters to follow, we will also explore ways in which other groups may now be playing the role that parties once played and, if so, with what impact. That is, parties have played and continue to play an important role in elections. But parties do not constitute the sum total of the electoral process.

The clear theme of this book is that the contest for office is the most crucial element to be examined. Political parties play an important role in that process, but only one role. It is not possible to understand the contest for office without understanding parties. But merely understanding how parties function does not tell the student much about how elections are fought. Our goal is to reach that latter understanding.

II. The Role of Elections in Democratic Theory

Scholars are fond of pointing out that modern political parties are an American invention even though they are never mentioned in the Constitution. In *Federalist* 10 (1787) Madison warns of the mischief of faction, reasoning that many groups must be allowed to flourish so that no one group becomes too powerful. Such was the concept of "party" at the time the Constitution was drafted.

The Founding Fathers, moreover, defined democracy in a somewhat limited way: the masses were not to be trusted with political power. Thus, while the House of Representatives was to be popularly elected (certainly a necessity, given the history of our Revolution and its most famous slogan, "Taxation without representation is tyranny!"), the Senate was indirectly elected by state legislatures, and the president was even more indirectly elected through the cumbersome mechanism of the electoral college.

A. Modes of Elections

1. Direct Elections

What general principles guided these rules for contesting offices? For direct representation in the House of Representatives, two were primary: districts with small populations so that the voters could "know" their representatives, and frequent elections so that citizens had the opportunity to express their views on how the government was working. The Founding Fathers would have been appalled by twentieth-century recommendations to extend congressional terms to four years. They envisioned an intimate connection between a congressman and his constituents. He would be one of them, one who was just like his neighbors and thus best suited to serve them. He would do his duty and return home to be replaced by another. If he became too headstrong in support of his own alien ideas, frequent elections would guarantee that the violation of trust would not go on too long.

2. *Indirect Elections*

The other elected officials of the federal government were chosen through a filtering process. Only the "best of the best" were supposed to make the grade and be chosen to represent the interest of the people. Only those who really understood what was best for the masses would be chosen to serve in the Senate. Further, the elaborate mechanism for choosing the president can be understood best if one realizes that all those at the Constitutional Convention assumed that the towering figure of his time, the "father" of the new nation, George Washington, would be the first president. The mechanism was designed to pick the "right" leader, i.e., someone like Washington.

B. Implications for Representation

1. *Representatives' Perspectives*

However, this system of elected representatives—or any other system yet devised—faces an inherent conflict. On one hand, elected representatives should accurately represent the views of the people who choose them. On the other hand, they must have enough freedom to act on what they determine to be in the best interest of the people. One need not long debate the merits of the two theories of representation implied by these statements to see that a conflict exists. The American solution to this problem has been to give representatives a good deal of freedom to act but to hold elections frequently in order to keep them accountable for their actions. One of the basic questions raised in this text is, How does that system work?

2. *The Public's Perspective and the Role of Parties in Representation*

Democratic theory also requires a citizenry that has the ability to convert its views on the issues of the day—certainly the pressing, salient issues—into public policy. Frequent elections do not serve their intended purpose if the electorate is not given a choice, nor if, after that choice is expressed, public policy does not reflect that preference.

The role that political parties have traditionally played in this context has been to structure the contest for office so that elections can perform their role most effectively. One of the key questions facing the American polity concerns how effectively that role is played (Brady, Bullock, and Maisel 1988; Brady and Stewart 1986). Pomper (1972) and Fishel (1977), among others, have demonstrated that the Republican and Democratic parties differ from each other on major policy

PARTY IN THE ELECTORATE

Those who support a political party at the polls—the loyal followers.

PARTY ORGANIZATION

The formal structure of a political party's professional and volunteer workers.

PARTY IN GOVERNMENT

Members of a political party who are serving in an official capacity in the government.

PARTY UNITY SCORES

The percentage of time a legislator votes with his or her party on those votes on which a majority of one party votes against a majority of the other party.

PARTY UNITY VOTE

A vote in a legislature in which a majority of one party votes in opposition to a majority in the other party.

LINKAGE

That which connects one actor or set of actors in a polity with others.

REAGAN REVOLUTION

Changes in policy direction, reversing liberal policies with conservative alternatives, thought to follow from the election of President Reagan in 1980.

questions. But the links among differing party platforms, elections, and subsequent public policies are less clear in the American system than they are in parliamentary democracies.

V. O. Key Jr. (1964) highlighted the important distinctions among **party in the electorate, party organization,** and **party in government.** The term "party in the electorate" refers to voters who generally align themselves with a particular party, the party's supporters at the polls. "Party organization" is the formal structure of the party, the elite that leads the party in election campaigns. Finally, "party in government" is composed of the individuals who serve in the government as a result of having run on a party label or having been appointed by someone who ran on a party label.

This text is mainly concerned with party in the electorate (i.e., the extent to which party determines how citizens vote) and with party organization (i.e., how political parties are structured as institutions), but we cannot ignore the governmental context either. We elect members of Congress in individual districts and stress their electoral independence, but we should not forget that these individual representatives often consider the position of their party when deciding how to vote once in office.

For many years *Congressional Quarterly* has reported **party unity scores** for members of Congress each year. A **party unity vote** is one on which a majority of one party votes together against a majority of the other party. A member's party unity score is the percentage of time he or she votes with his or her party on those votes. Since President Clinton assumed office in 1993, more than half of the votes in each session in each house of the Congress have been party unity votes. And in each case the average party unity score for members of each party exceeded 80 percent. This period of extremely high party unity covers periods in which each party was in the majority. Thus it seems clear that party affiliation is far from unimportant as a **linkage** between citizens as they cast their votes and policies that are eventually adopted. (See chapter 13.)

Similarly, the extent to which recent presidents have imposed partisan tests on their principal appointees is without precedent. Presidents Reagan, Bush, and Clinton all replaced party recruiters with their own White House personnel offices, but those selected for important positions have almost all been members of the president's party (Mackenzie 1991; 1998). Thus, while the takeover of the national government by committed conservatives hailed as the **Reagan revolution** in 1980 might not have changed the role of government as completely as its perpetrators might have hoped, and while Clinton's recapturing of the White House for the Democrats might not have reversed all trends started in the previous twelve years of Republican rule, each of those elections did lead to significant changes in who populated the government. Just as surely they led to changes in the philosophy of governing espoused by those in appointive as well as elective office. For our purposes, the importance of those appointments is also that they demonstrate another link between elections and subsequent government policies.

That political parties would serve as the linkage mechanism between electorate and governing officials was not envisioned by the Founding Fathers and, in fact, evolved quite slowly (see chapter 2). Historically, the effectiveness of parties as the bridge between citizens and those they elect to govern has not been judged with universal acclaim, nor has that role remained constant in the face of a changing political environment. In order to understand this role, we must more carefully define what is meant by "political party" in the American political context.

III. DEFINITIONS OF "POLITICAL PARTY" AND "PARTY SYSTEMS"

French political scientist Maurice Duverger, in a classic study entitled *Political Parties,* drew an important sociological distinction between **cadre parties** and **mass membership parties** (1951, 62ff.). Duverger starts with a definition of party member in the European setting, one that most Americans would find restrictive. For Duverger "the concept 'member' of a party coincides with that of adherent. . . . The latter is distinguished from the 'supporter,' who declares his agreement with the doctrines of the party and sometimes lends it his support but who remains outside its organization and the community it forms" (1951, 62). Cadre parties, then, have relatively few *members;* mass membership parties tend to have a large number of dues-paying supporters.

CADRE PARTIES

Political parties in which a small committed group of leaders form the heart of the party organization; members are distinguished from mere supporters; primary purpose is electoral.

MASS MEMBERSHIP PARTIES

Political parties characterized by large memberships that determine party direction; tend to have ideological positions and play an educational role in the system; concern is with governing more than electing.

However, Duverger's distinction is broader than that. Cadre parties (most conservative European parties fit into this mold) are organizations whose primary goal is to obtain electoral success. They are subordinate to leaders in government and are basically inactive between elections. Not only are there not many members, but the staffs of these organizations are also small.

Mass membership parties, at the opposite extreme, are ideological and educational organizations. Their goal is to convince the working class of the desirability of their point of view and thus to change the system radically. To succeed, they must maintain a large, permanent, continuously active professional organization. When mass membership parties gain control over the government, the party organization maintains an influence unimagined in the case of cadre parties. Socialist parties in Europe meet most of Duverger's criteria for mass membership parties.

Duverger's definition is really a distinction among types of political parties. He never does arrive at a concise definition of what constitutes a political party, though he identifies a number of important considerations—membership, level of activity, type of activity, type of leadership, relationship to the government. On the other hand, several scholars studying American parties have attempted to define exactly what constitutes a political party:

> We may define "political party" generally as the articulate organization of society's active political agents, those who are concerned with the control of governmental power and who compete for popular support with another group or groups holding divergent views. (Sigmund Neumann 1956, 396)

> A political party is a team of men seeking to control the governing apparatus by gaining office in a duly constituted election. (Anthony Downs 1957, 25)

> Pat definitions may simplify discussion but they do not necessarily promote understanding. A search for the fundamental nature of party is complicated by the fact that "party" is a work of many meanings. . . . The nature of parties must be sought through an appreciation of their role in the process of governance. (V. O. Key Jr. 1964, 200)

> Any group, however loosely organized, seeking to elect governmental office-holders under a given label. (Leon D. Epstein 1967, 9)

> A party is any political group that presents at elections, and is capable of placing through elections, candidates for public office. (Giovanni Sartori 1976, 64)

> The major American political parties exist, as do other political organizations, to organize large numbers of individuals behind attempts to influence the selection of public officials and the decisions these officials subsequently make in office. . . . The differences between parties and other political organizations are often slender. (Frank J. Sorauf 1980, 17)

A number of themes emerge from this group of definitions. First, as Sartori claims, a minimal definition of contesting for office emerges. Second, as Neumann, Downs, and Epstein state, some type of organization is assumed. Third, as Key and Sorauf imply, "party" is a multidimensional term. Defining "party" too narrowly excludes organizations that ought to be included. Defining "party" too broadly takes in organizations that would be excluded by general consensus. The student almost has to fall back on the classic test, "If it looks like a duck, swims like a duck, flies like a duck, and quacks like a duck." . . . Thus the Republican party is a party; the AFL-CIO, despite the fact that it does many of the same things, is not.

THIRD PARTIES

Political parties that enter into electoral contests without having a realistic chance of winning an election; at times these parties do affect the outcome of the contest between the two major parties.

For most purposes this definition is sufficient, but for others, often very important ones, it is not. For instance, when John Anderson ran for president as an independent or **third party** candidate in 1980, the Federal Election Commission (FEC) had to rule on whether John Anderson's "party" in the 1980 presidential election constituted a party in any meaningful sense.[9] The FEC ruled that it did, thus making Anderson eligible for federal campaign financing in 1984.[10] The FEC ruled similarly on Ross Perot's "party" in the 1992 presidential election, even though the party under whose label he ran in 1996, the Reform party, did not exist in 1992. What definition is appropriate in that context?

This text adopts a fairly restrictive definition of political parties. Political parties are organizations, however loosely organized, that (1) have, for a period of time, run candidates for public office, (2) have earned the support of a significant following in the electorate for those candidates because of their allegiance to the organization, and (3) must be taken into account by other similar competing organizations. Did Anderson's party meet this definition in 1980? Remember it disappeared by 1984. It did not meet the definition, then, because it did not meet the test of time. Does Perot's Reform party meet the definition?

This definition also implies acceptance of the concept of **party systems**, at least in its simplified form.[11] In democracies, if parties are to contest for public office, they must take into account others who are also competing for office. William N. Chambers (1975, 6) defines a party system as "a pattern of interaction in which two or more political parties compete for office or power in government and for the support of the electorate, and must therefore take one another into account in their behavior in government and in election contests."

PARTY SYSTEMS

Electoral arrangements in which two or more parties compete for support of the electorate and control of the government and take each other into account as they set various electoral and governing strategies.

Party systems are characterized on two different axes. First, they are distinguished by the number of parties competing. Second, they are distinguished by the intensity of competition. The American national party system is generally classified as a **competitive two-party system.** The Democratic and Republican parties compete with each other for national offices; each has a chance of winning. Minor parties may be on the ballot from time to time, but they neither persist nor have a chance of winning. In the 1992 presidential election (and to a lesser extent in 1996 campaign) Ross Perot's third party threatened the hegemony of the Democratic and Republican parties. But in the final analysis his effort to undermine the two-party system fell short (Bibby and Maisel 1998). Thus our national system remains the competitive two-party system it has been since the election of 1828, though the parties have changed during that period.[12]

COMPETITIVE TWO-PARTY SYSTEM

An electoral system in which two, and only two, parties compete for dominance and have a realistic opportunity of controlling the government.

Tables 1.4, 1.5, and 1.6 show a number of different measures of national electoral competition in this century. The pattern is clear; Democrats compete with Republicans for control of our national government. Other parties may contest for some offices (fourteen minor parties appeared on at least one state's presidential ballot in 1996; more than thirty ran at least one candidate in the 1998 congressional elections), but real competition is restricted to two parties. It is in this sense of structuring the contest for national power that the role of parties in the electoral process must be evaluated.

Table 1.4 Two-Party Competition in 20th-Century Presidential Elections

	Percentage of Popular Vote			*Percentage of Popular Vote*	
Year	*Democratic*	*Republican*	*Year*	*Democratic*	*Republican*
1900	45.5	51.7	1952	44.4	55.1
1904	37.6	56.4	1956	42.0	57.4
1908	43.0	51.6	1960	49.8	49.5
1912	41.8	23.2	1964	61.0	38.5
1916	49.2	46.1	1968	42.7	43.2
1920	34.2	60.3	1972	37.5	60.7
1924	28.8	54.1	1976	50.1	48.0
1928	40.8	58.2	1980	41.0	50.7
1932	57.4	39.6	1984	40.6	58.8
1936	60.8	36.5	1988	45.6	53.4
1940	54.7	44.8	1992	43.0	37.4
1944	53.4	45.9	1996	49.2	40.7
1948	49.5	45.1			

*Percentages are of total vote; other parties not shown.
Source: Vital Statistics on American Politics, 1997–1998.

Table 1.5 Two-Party Competition in the 20th-Century Senate

		Seats Occupied by Party in the Senate		
Year	*Congress*	*Democratic*	*Republican*	*Other*
1899–1901	56th	26	53	8
1901–1903	57th	31	55	4
1903–1905	58th	33	57	
1905–1907	59th	33	57	
1907–1909	60th	31	61	
1909–1911	61st	32	61	
1911–1913	62d	41	51	
1913–1915	63d	51	44	1
1915–1917	64th	56	40	
1917–1919	65th	53	42	
1919–1921	66th	47	49	
1921–1923	67th	37	59	2
1923–1925	68th	43	51	1
1925–1927	69th	39	56	
1927–1929	70th	46	49	1
1929–1931	71st	39	56	1
1931–1933	72d	47	48	1
1933–1935	73d	60	35	2
1935–1937	74th	69	25	4
1937–1939	75th	76	16	4
1939–1941	76th	69	23	2
1941–1943	77th	66	28	1
1943–1945	78th	58	37	1
1945–1947	79th	56	38	

continued

For all that, it is very misleading to look only at national politics. American politics is perhaps most notably characterized by its **decentralization;** local and state politics are *not* totally controlled by national forces. An observer cannot stop after saying that the American party system is a competitive two-party system. At the very least, one must look at the fifty separate state party systems. For most of the twentieth century all of the South was solidly Democratic; even with the recent Republican resurgence in the South, most state legislatures remain firmly in Democratic hands. Similarly, much of the nation's heartland has long favored Republicans. While presidential politics may be hotly contested at the national level, Kansas has had two Republican senators in every Congress since 1939. At the other extreme, the Massachusetts state legislature has been under Democratic control for more than four decades. Thus the domination of a single party within certain

DECENTRALIZATION

Power and decision making are removed from the most central locus in a political system and spread to regional and local officials.

Table 1.5 Two-Party Competition in the 20th-Century Senate *(continued)*

	Seats Occupied by Party in the Senate			
Year	*Congress*	*Democratic*	*Republican*	*Other*
1947–1949	80th	45	15	
1949–1951	81st	54	42	
1951–1953	82d	49	47	1
1953–1955	83d	47	48	1
1955–1957	84th	48	47	
1957–1959	85th	49	47	
1959–1961	86th	64	34	
1961–1963	87th	65	35	
1963–1965	88th	67	33	
1965–1967	89th	68	32	
1967–1969	90th	64	36	
1969–1971	91st	57	43	
1971–1973	92d	54	44	2
1973–1975	93d	56	42	2
1975–1977	94th	60	37	2
1977–1979	95th	61	38	1
1979–1981	96th	58	41	1
1981–1983	97th	46	53	1
1983–1985	98th	45	55	
1985–1987	99th	47	53	
1987–1989	100th	55	45	
1989–1991	101st	55	45	
1991–1993	102d	56	44	
1993–1995	103d	57	43	
1995–1997	104th	47	53	
1997–1999	105th	45	55	
1999–2001	106th	45	55	

Source: Vital Statistics on American Politics, 1997–1998.

states can be veiled by a claim that we have a competitive two-party system nationally. Similarly, changes in national politics can reflect either trends across the entire nation in one direct or asymmetrical offsetting trends in a number of directions in a number of states or regions (Brunell and Grofman 1998).

Austin Ranney, perhaps the dean of this generation's scholars of American politics, has categorized American state party systems according to level of competition. Ranney has constructed an index of state party competitiveness consisting of four criteria: (1) popular vote for Democratic candidates for governor; (2) percentage of the seats in the state senate held by Democrats; (3) percentage of the seats in the state house of representatives held by Democrats; and (4) terms for governor, Senate, and House in which the Democrats held control (Ranney in Jacob and Vines 1971). State rankings, using the Ranney index of competitiveness, are presented in table 1.7.

Table 1.6 Two-Party Competition in the 20th-Century House of Representatives

	Seats Occupied by Party in the House			
Year	*Congress*	*Democratic*	*Republican*	*Other*
1899–1901	56th	163	185	9
1901–1903	57th	151	197	9
1903–1905	58th	178	208	
1905–1907	59th	136	250	
1907–1909	60th	164	222	
1909–1911	61st	172	219	
1911–1913	62d	228	161	1
1913–1915	63d	291	127	17
1915–1917	64th	230	196	9
1917–1919	65th	216	210	6
1919–1921	66th	190	240	3
1921–1923	67th	131	301	1
1923–1925	68th	205	225	5
1925–1927	69th	183	247	4
1927–1929	70th	195	237	3
1929–1931	71st	167	267	1
1931–1933	72d	220	214	1
1933–1935	73d	310	117	5
1935–1937	74th	319	103	10
1937–1939	75th	331	89	13
1939–1941	76th	261	164	4
1941–1943	77th	268	162	5
1943–1945	78th	218	208	4
1945–1947	79th	242	190	2
1947–1949	80th	188	245	1
1949–1951	81st	263	171	1

continued

A number of interpretations should be noted. First, Ranney's criteria have allowed him to divide the states into five possible categories, ranging from one-party Democratic through competitive two-party systems to one-party Republican. However, the one-party Republican cell was empty for the entire period covered; the modified one-party Republican grouping had shrunk to one state by the second period. Today no states would meet Ranney's one-party criteria.

Second, Ranney's categories, or any similar groupings, are time bound. Republican gains in the South or Democratic gains in states like Maine and New Hampshire demonstrate that movement is not only possible, but likely (see also Sundquist 1983, chaps. 11–12).

Third, and perhaps most important, Ranney's rankings depend on a number of research decisions that he made. He is concentrating only on state offices. His judgment in so choosing cannot be questioned, but one must recognize that in restricting himself in this way, he did not take into account two sets of variables: (1) the distorting idiosyncrasies

Table 1.6 Two-Party Competition in the 20th-Century House of Representatives *(continued)*

		Seats Occupied by Party in the House		
Year	*Congress*	*Democratic*	*Republican*	*Other*
1951–1953	82d	234	199	1
1953–1955	83d	211	221	1
1955–1957	84th	232	203	
1957–1959	85th	233	200	
1959–1961	86th	283	153	
1961–1963	87th	263	174	
1963–1965	88th	258	177	
1965–1967	89th	295	140	
1967–1969	90th	247	187	
1969–1971	91st	243	192	1
1971–1973	92d	254	180	
1973–1975	93d	239	192	
1975–1977	94th	291	144	
1977–1979	95th	292	143	
1979–1981	96th	273	159	
1981–1983	97th	243	192	
1983–1985	98th	267	168	
1985–1987	99th	252	182	
1987–1989	100th	258	177	
1989–1991	101st	259	174	
1991–1993	102d	267	167	1
1993–1995	103d	258	176	1
1995–1997	104th	204	230	1
1997–1999	105th	207	227	1
1999–2001	106th	211	223	1

Source: Vital Statistics on American Politics, 1997–1998.

Table 1.7 Measures of State Party Competition

1956–1970	*1974–1980*	*1965–1988*	*1989–1994*	
		One-Party Democratic		
Louisiana	Alabama	Mississippi		Louisiana
Alabama	Georgia	Georgia		Georgia
Mississippi	Louisiana	Alabama		Arkansas
South Carolina	Mississippi	Louisiana		Alabama
Texas	Arkansas	Arkansas		Mississippi
Georgia	North Carolina			Maryland
Arkansas	Maryland			Kentucky
	Rhode Island			Oklahoma
				Texas
				North Carolina
		Modified Democratic		
North Carolina	South Carolina	Hawaii	Arkansas	West Virginia
Virginia	West Virginia	Maryland	Louisiana	New Mexico
Florida	Texas	South Carolina	Hawaii	Massachusetts
Tennessee	Massachusetts	Texas	West Virginia	Minnesota
Maryland	Kentucky	Kentucky	Rhode Island	South Carolina
Oklahoma	Oklahoma	Florida	Maryland	Tennessee
Missouri	Nevada	New Mexico	Kentucky	Rhode Island
Kentucky	Hawaii	North Carolina	Georgia	Florida
West Virginia	Florida	Oklahoma	Mississippi	Nevada
New Mexico	Connecticut	Rhode Island	Alabama	Missouri
	New Jersey		Nebraska	Wyoming
	Virginia		Oklahoma	
	New Mexico		Massachusetts	
	California			
	Oregon			
	Missouri			
	Minnesota			
	Tennessee			
	Wisconsin			
	Rhode Island			
		Two-Party		
Alaska	Montana	Massachusetts	Tennessee	Virginia
California	Michigan	West Virginia	New Mexico	Washington
Nebraska	Ohio	Missouri	North Carolina	California
Washington	Washington	Tennessee	Missouri	Oregon
Minnesota	Alaska	Virginia	Texas	New Jersey
Nevada	Pennsylvania	Minnesota	Virginia	Wisconsin
Connecticut	Delaware	California	Minnesota	Delaware

continued

of "unusual" presidential candidacies such as Barry Goldwater's Republican campaign in 1964, George Wallace's third-party effort in 1968, George McGovern's campaign as a Democrat in 1972, or, if the analysis were extended, Ross Perot's 1992 and 1996 quests; and (2) the sometimes wide variation within state party systems.

Furthermore, Ranney's index only looks at winners of various elections for three of his four criteria; he does not consider margin of vic-

Table 1.7 Measures of State Party Competition *(continued)*

1956–1970	*1974–1980*	*1965–1988*	*1989–1994*	
		Two-Party		
Delaware	New York	Nevada	Florida	South Dakota
Arizona	Illinois	Washington	Washington	New York
Montana	Nebraska	Michigan	Vermont	Arizona
Oregon	Maine	Oregon	South Carolina	Connecticut
New Jersey	Kansas	Connecticut	Nevada	Illinois
Pennsylvania	Utah	New York	California	Pennsylvania
Colorado	Iowa	Arizona	Oregon	Ohio
Michigan	Arizona	Utah	New York	Montana
Utah	Colorado	Alaska	Maine	Michigan
Indiana	Indiana	Wisconsin	Delaware	Indiana
Illinois	New Hampshire	New Jersey	Indiana	Maine
Wisconsin	Idaho	Montana	Connecticut	Colorado
Idaho	Wyoming	Maine	Wisconsin	North Dakota
Iowa	Vermont	Delaware	Pennsylvania	Vermont
Ohio	South Dakota	Pennsylvania	Iowa	Iowa
New York		Ohio	Alaska	Kansas
Maine		Iowa	Illinois	New Hampshire
Wyoming		Illinois	Montana	
		North Dakota	Colorado	
		Indiana	Michigan	
		Idaho	New Jersey	
		Kansas	North Dakota	
		Colorado	Ohio	
		Vermont	Kansas	
		Wyoming		
		Modified Republican		
North Dakota	North Dakota	South Dakota	Idaho	Nebraska
Kansas		New Hampshire	South Dakota	Utah
New Hampshire			Arizona	Idaho
South Dakota			New Hampshire	
			Utah	

Sources:
1956–1970 measure taken from Ranney in Jacob and Vines 1971, 87.
1974–1980 measure taken from Bibby, Cotter, Gibson, and Huckshorn 1983, 66.
1965–1988 measure taken from Jewell and Olson 1988, 26–27.
1989–1994 measure taken from Gray and Jacob 1996, 105.
Party identification measure taken from Wright, Erikson, and McIver 1985, 469–489.

tory. But Holbrook and Van Dunk (1993) have pointed out that winning is not necessarily everything when one is interested in competition. For instance, if two elections were each decided by a very few votes, but the same party won both elections, Ranney's index would have those elections reflecting one-party control. One could equally well argue that they demonstrate intense competition. Conversely, if two elections were each decided by landslide margins, say with the winners polling over 80 percent, but the winners were not from the same party, they would contribute toward a measure of two-party competition in Ranney's terms, but one could also argue that little or no competition was present in either election. To demonstrate how different research decisions lead to different interpretations, and also to show changes over time, table 1.7 also includes two other means of characterizing state systems, one relying on governorships and state congressional delegations (Jewell and Olson 1988, 26–27) and one relying on party identification as provided by respondents to surveys (G. Wright, Erikson, and McIver 1985, 476–477).[13]

If the concept of party system is a valid one, the most crucial research decision involves defining the boundaries of that system. Pat answers will not suffice. Surely we can look at our national system and draw conclusions about parties and elections at that level. But even casual observers of politics will see that concentrating on the *national* scene masks important differences at the *state* level that must be understood if one is to understand how American politics really works.

Similarly, viewing state party systems is useful (and the data are easily obtained), but this perception also obscures important distinctions for the purpose of simplicity. For example, what purpose is served by trying to understand Illinois as a competitive two-party state without noting the differences among Cook County, the Chicago suburbs, and downstate Illinois? The same can be said of northern and southern California; New York City, the immediate suburbs, and upstate New York; and less well-known variations in states as widely separated as Massachusetts, Virginia, and Texas. In evaluating the role that party plays in structuring the contest for office, the careful student must draw these distinctions appropriately. What is the *dimension* of the party system that is under examination?

IV. POLITICIANS VIEW THE PARTY SYSTEM

This text is not intended to be a workbook. However, if one homework exercise were to be assigned, it would be to have each reader call his or her state representative and ask, "What is the dimension of the party system that I should examine in order to understand the role that party plays in structuring your own electoral contest?" Merely posing the question should be sufficient to demonstrate how ludicrous it is. While it is important to understand "the role of party," "structuring the contest for office," and "party systems" in order to analyze elections in America, these abstract terms are not in the working vocabulary of most politicians. Therefore this text regularly steps back from the analytical world of the student of politics to the practical world of the politician.

In that regard, it is important to understand that politicians only rarely look beyond the next election. Elections serve as their link to the people in a very concrete way. If the people vote for them, they are in office; if the people vote for someone else, they are out. The questions that politicians ask relate to what they must do in order to assure their continuation in office or advancement to the next office that they decide to seek.

Important questions immediately arise. Are elections in America an effective way for the citizenry to control politicians? That is, do politicians lose because of the dissatisfaction of their constituents? This question can be answered empirically by looking at incumbent losses and the reasons for them, at the knowledge that constituents have of their officeholders' position, and at major swings in the fortunes of the two parties (see Jacobson 1980; Maisel and Cooper 1981; Stokes and Miller 1962; Sundquist 1983).

However, equally important is how politicians think the electoral process works. Do politicians change their positions because they fear electoral reprisals? The late Senator Henry Jackson (D-Wash., 1952–1983), sometimes referred to as the senator from Boeing (because the aircraft manufacturer is located in Washington State and Jackson saw it as part of his job to represent the interests of the thousands of his constituents who were Boeing employees), early in his Senate career explained the apparent contradiction between his "liberal" views on social and economic policies and his "conservative" views of defense matters. Jackson contended, "I have to be a senator before I can be a statesman." His winning percentages in four reelection campaigns for the Senate were 72 percent, 82 percent, 72 percent, and 69 percent; consequently, his fear of electoral reprisal might have been slightly exaggerated. But it was real nonetheless.

Anyone who has worked closely with an elected officeholder facing another election knows that nearly all such officeholders consider public opinion very important.[14] Politicians panic if their margin of victory goes down from one election to the next; they fret over the effects on their popularity of votes on controversial, salient issues. Study after study has emphasized how safe most incumbent legislators are from electoral defeat, in both the Congress and in the state legislatures (Herrnson 1998; Jewell 1994; Jacobson 1992; Holbrook and Tidmarch 1991; Weber, Tucker, and Brace 1991). Although few incumbents are thrown out by constituents because of their stand on public policy issues, elections do work as a means of public control because politicians act as if they might be thrown out by the voters if they do not heed perceived voter opinion. In this case, a politician's perception of reality is more important than reality itself.

Similarly, just as it is important to understand how politicians view elections, it is important to know how they view party. In this case, the answer is very simple: It all depends.

Politicians may not understand abstract notions of party system and electoral environment, but they certainly do understand what the party—whether it is defined as the label or the formal organization—means for their election or reelection chances. In all but a very few cases, office seekers need a major party nomination in order to get on the ballot and stand any chance for success. However, that generalization is perhaps the only one that can be made.[15]

Beyond a means of access to the ballot and perhaps some legitimacy in the eyes of the voters, major party designation means different things to different politicians. The key variables are the office being sought and the strength of the party, in terms of both organizational resources and voter identification, in the particular district.

Thus in many major cities, such as Chicago or Philadelphia, the Democratic primary is tantamount to election; candidates worry a great deal about party in those cases. On the other hand, in many other cities, candidates know that their nomination is no guarantee of election. Furthermore, the help that the candidates can expect from party organization in terms of financial support or other campaign services varies widely.

Similarly, campaigns for state legislature vary widely from area to area. In Massachusetts in 1998 eighteen of the forty seats in the state senate were won without any major party opposition (45 percent); 68 out of 160 house members won reelection with no opponent (42.5 percent). In Florida in the 1998 elections for representative to the state house of representatives, Democratic candidates ran unopposed by Republican opponents in 37 of 120 races. Republican candidates faced no major party opposition in twenty races.

The role of party in funding legislative campaigns also varies significantly (Gierzynski 1992). In Maine organized parties rarely have enough strength to help state legislative candidates significantly; however, in states such as Minnesota (or in some areas in other states, such as Cook County in Illinois) party organizations practically run the campaign for candidates.

Congressional elections engender another set of problems. Congressional districts only occasionally share boundaries with other political units. Most American political organizations are based on the county as the organizing unit. In some states congressional districts span more than one county. Some of those counties may have strong parties, some weak; some may be heavily Republican, some competitive, some heavily Democratic. But in other states or areas within states, several congressional districts may be found in the same county. Only rarely is a U.S. congressman a key figure as a party leader; Henry Waxman (D-Calif.) distinguishes himself as one example. Similarly, party leaders do not play key roles in many congressional campaigns. But one cannot overgeneralize; certainly members of Congress as different as John LaFalce (D-N.Y.), Howard Berman (D-Calif.), David McIntosh (R-Ind.), and George Gekas (R-Pa.) would never deny the importance that party organization has played in their electoral careers.

Statewide party influence differs widely as well. Party nomination is often decisive in modified one-party states, though as politicians like former Republican governor William Weld of Massachusetts have shown, in no state is it impossible for the candidate of the weaker party to win. However, some of the strongest one-party states have the weakest party organizations; this was particularly true in the South when Democrats had total domination but were often split internally. It remains true in areas dominated by one party as different as Nebraska and Massachusetts. Thus candidates in those states must form their own organization and draw on their own resources in order to capture first the party nomination and subsequently the office they seek. On the other hand, party nomination guarantees considerable support in some of the more competitive states such as Illinois or New York due to the strength of the party organizations at work.

Finally, in the battle for the White House, only the two major party candidates really have a chance to win. Whether party organization is of any help to a candidate before the nominating convention varies with incumbency and intraparty competition. Bill Clinton, who as president had no challenger in his own party in 1996, was able to use the Democratic party apparatus to smooth his path through the nominating process and the convention. But George Bush, as a president with a challenger in his own party in 1992, or Mike Dukakis, as a nonincumbent dealing with defeated rivals who were not fully behind his candidacy even at the time of the 1988 Democratic national Convention, had to deal with party organizations that played more neutral roles.

Whatever the case prior to the nomination, merely winning the presidential nomination of either major party guarantees the successful candidate access to the ballot in nearly every state[16] and financial support through federal funding. Access to additional resources for the party nominee used to vary significantly from state to state, but recent national party fund-raising efforts and regulations that have allowed funneling of federal soft money through state committees have reduced that variation.[17]

What role do politicians see party playing in the elections? Again, it all depends. The biggest mistake a political analyst can make in writing about elections is to overgeneralize. We must distinguish election from election by constituency and by geography. Campaigns for local office are, for example, different from those for congressional or statewide offices. And no other election compares to a race for the presidency.

Those who are tremendously successful at one level often find that they fail miserably at another. Consider the experience of Democrat Wilbur Mills (Ark., U.S. House of Representatives, 1939–1977), the once powerful chairman of the House Ways and Means Committee, whose presidential campaign in 1972 was all but ignored by the voters; of Republican (but former Democrat) John Connally, a former governor of Texas and secretary of the Treasury, who spent more money to win fewer delegates to a nominating convention than anyone would have thought possible; of former Republican senator Howard Baker of Tennessee, who felt that a leadership position in the Senate would aid a bid for the Republican presidential nomination. Baker discovered that his duties in Washington left him too little time to campaign and that the voters were not in the least interested in the important role he played in senatorial debates, only in whether he cared enough to trudge through the snows of New Hampshire in that state's media-dominated primary election.

Demonstrating the lesson he learned, Baker declined to seek re-election to the Senate in 1984 in order to run for the presidency in 1988, a race he eventually passed up when he was asked to serve as White House chief of staff under Ronald Reagan. Or consider Bob Dole (R-Kans.). Senator Dole, perhaps the most respected Republican legislator of his generation, desperately wanted to be president. He ran unsuccessfully for vice president as Gerald Ford's running mate in 1976; he campaigned for his party's nomination and lost in 1988. He finally won the Republican nomination in 1996 and resigned his seat in the Senate, and thus his position as majority leader, to concentrate on his presidential bid. And he lost badly. Senator Dole never came to understand why the qualities that made him a successful candidate in rural Kansas and a respected leader in the Senate did not translate into presidential politics. (See chap. 10.)

The list of congressmen seeking to move to the Senate or of state legislators seeking to move to the House and failing repeatedly would fill volumes. Likewise, no modern mayor of the city of New York has ever successfully sought higher office, a lesson that must give Rudolph Giuliani, the immensely popular and politically ambitious Republican mayor of the city, some pause.

In much the same way, campaigns in the East are different from those in the Midwest, and each of these is different from campaigns in the South or the Far West. Significant variations exist among geographic areas within these regions. The history of a particular area—particularly its political history—must always be taken into account. As noted above, the single most salient feature of the American political system is its decentralized nature. Unfortunately for the social scientist, much more is lost in accumulating what should be kept separate than is gained by trying to generalize about a series of diverse experiences.

For a political analyst to state at the outset of a text that generalizations about the electoral process might prove imprecise seems blasphemous, but the key point is that practicing politicians do not base their judgments on such academic generalizations. They base them on instincts, often faulty ones, about individual situations in particular circumstances. It might be argued that politicians are foolish to do so, but that does not change the reality. All too often politicians and political scientists seem to be operating in different worlds.

WEBSITES

http://www.yahoo.com/Government/Politics/Elections

An extensive site of links to election websites. Contains listings for the 1998 election, international elections, and commercial products. Also links to elections by region, election archives, and voter information.

http://www.vote-smart.org/organizations/POLITICAL_PARTIES

Links to any active political party.

http://www.termlimits.org

The most up-to-date term-limits information. Includes information about states that currently impose term limits, as well as those that are pending legislation. Has excellent links to other term-limits sites.

http://politicaljunkie.com

An impressive list of links to many other websites dealing with all aspects of state and national politics.

KEY CONCEPTS

cadre parties
competitive two-party system
decentralization
equal protection clause
legislative term limits
legitimacy
linkage
mass membership parties
partisan elections
party in government
party in the electorate
party organization
party systems
party unity scores
party unity votes
political culture
popular support
Reagan revolution
third parties

DISCUSSION QUESTIONS

1. Concerning citizen input into government decisions through elections, do you think it is preferable to have more elections (with the electorate asked to decide fewer questions each time) or fewer elections (with more items on the ballot each time citizens are asked to vote)? What factors should you consider in making this judgment?

2. Ideally, would you prefer American political parties of the mass membership type or the cadre type as identified by Duverger? Why? What is it about a political system that would make one variety of party more appropriate?

3. How would you describe the level of party competition in your

hometown? In your state? What criteria did you use to come to this judgment?

4. How effective do you think elections are in "controlling" political officeholders? Do you think those who have been elected to represent you think about how their decisions will affect their chances for reelection? Do you know how your local representatives or those who represent you in Washington stand on the issues that you care most about?

CHAPTER 2

The Development of the American Parties

Modern political parties are a distinctly American invention. They did not appear fully formed; rather, they evolved slowly, the product of experimentation and innovation by the leaders of the nation's new form of government, at the end of the eighteenth and beginning of the nineteenth centuries. And who were the leaders who concocted this new form of political activity?

FEDERALIST PARTY

One of the first American political parties, composed of the followers of George Washington and the architect of his administration's policies, Alexander Hamilton.

The **Federalist party** was shaped during the administration of George Washington, largely by Treasury Secretary Alexander Hamilton, who is most often credited with drafting Washington's Farewell Address, the theme of which was to warn of the dangers of party:

> In contemplating the causes which may disturb our Union, it occurs as a matter of serious concern, that any ground should have been furnished for characterizing party by *geographical discriminations*. . . . To the efficacy and permanency of your Union, a Government of the whole is indispensable. . . . Let me now take a more comprehensive view, and warn you in the most solemn manner against the baneful effects of the spirit of party. (Sparks 1840, 221–224)

FACTIONS

Divisions within the population, forming at first over economic interests, that were the precursors of American political parties.

The opposition party was organized by both James Madison and Thomas Jefferson, who served as secretary of state in Washington's first administration. Madison, in *Federalist* 10, wrote in some detail of the evils of citizens forming **factions**, which by their very nature are "adverse to the rights of other citizens, and to the permanent and aggregate interest of the community." Madison pressured Jefferson into forming a political opposition. Jefferson himself was so wary of splitting the nation that, despite fervent opposition to many policy initiatives, he stayed in the Washington cabinet until 1793. In 1796, Jefferson had to be persuaded to oppose John Adams for the presidency, despite continuing disagreements with Washington's Federalist successor.

Why did these early political leaders, virtually all of whom took pride in their stand against the evil of party, play such critical roles in shaping modern political parties? Certainly part of the answer is found in the notion that the "parties" against which the founders railed were not the same as the "parties" we know today. American parties at the dawn of the twenty-first century are descendants, but distant descendants in important ways, of those first formed over two centuries ago.

This chapter deals with the history and development of American political parties. For many decades parties played a central role in the electoral process in America (Silbey 1998). Despite the fact that their role has been diminished in recent years, their history cannot be ignored. This historical analysis is important background for what follows.

The first section of this chapter traces the transition from "faction" to "party," from the evil that the early leaders reviled to the uniquely American institution that they invented. Subsequent sections describe how this institution has evolved over nearly two hundred years, how individual parties have come and gone, how the role that the parties have played in the American system has changed as the country has changed.

I. From Faction to Party

Giovanni Sartori (1976, 3–4) discusses the transition from faction to party in a detailed introduction to his study of party systems. He concludes that "party" came into use as a word less derogatory than "faction." According to Voltaire, "The term *party* is not in itself loathsome; the term *faction* always is" (Sartori 1976, 3).

"Faction" comes from the Latin *facere,* meaning "to act," and was used by conservative Latin writers to refer to political groups bent on acting in a harmful fashion. "Party" also comes from the Latin, *partire* "to divide"; however, the term has taken on another connotation, "to share or partake." Thus semantically "party" seems less a negative term than "faction" (Sartori 1976, 4).

The discussion of "party" by political philosophers dates back to English democratic conservative Lord Bolingbroke in 1732. Bolingbroke and those who wrote after him in the eighteenth century had difficulty distinguishing party from faction, or party in a negative sense from party in an acceptable sense. Bolingbroke concluded, for instance, "Governing by party . . . must always end in government of a faction. . . . Party is a political evil, and faction is the worst of all parties" (Bolingbroke 1976, 401; Sartori 1976, 6, 30).

David Hume, another British political philosopher of the eighteenth century, was not so antiparty as Bolingbroke, though on factions he was very hard. "Factions subvert government, render laws impotent, and beget the fiercest animosities among men of the same nation" (Hume 1976, 58; Sartori 1976, 7, 31). Hume concluded that parties, as coalitions, formed naturally in free governments; he accepted them, even if he did not favor them.

British statesman Edmund Burke learned from Hume and Bolingbroke but chose a different direction. In 1770 he defined party as "a body of men united, for promoting by their joint endeavors the national interest, upon some particular principle in which they are all agreed" (1976, 425–426). Note that by this point the divisive nature of party has disappeared; parties advance the national interest. They are *for* the common good and not for subversion of it. In essence, Burke proposed that parties play a role in doing the work of governing within an established set of rules for governing. Burke's definition of party was unique largely because he was describing a political entity that could in fact exist but did not exist until that time (Sartori 1976, 10).

Background information like this would be totally useless in an attempt to explain the behavior of mid- and late-twentieth-century politicians. Which of the modern presidents—Eisenhower, Kennedy, Johnson, Nixon, Ford, Carter, Reagan, Bush, or Clinton—has read and followed philosophical debates in Europe? Which of today's politicians deal in theoretical abstractions about political science? Forms of government? Economic theory? Would any contemporary politician be considered among the leading minds of the late twentieth century?

A comparison of the writing and thinking of today's politicians with those of two centuries ago is not edifying. President Kennedy's oft-quoted toast to the group of Nobel laureates he had invited to dine at the White House—"I think this is the most extraordinary collection of talent, of human knowledge, that has ever been gathered together at the White House—with the possible exception of when Thomas Jefferson dined alone" (Adler 1964, 73)—holds more truth than many of us would like to admit. By contrast with today's political leaders, the nation's founders, our early politicians, were an extraordinary group of political intellectuals and intellectual politicians. Their education, their reading, and their activism merged.

During their younger years—and it must be remembered that these leaders were relatively young at the time of the nation's founding—those who were to become the first leaders of this new nation read and thought about revolution, about rights, and about justice. Jefferson's Declaration of Independence marks the end of this phase. In the next phase of their amazing careers as public servants, these same leaders fought the Revolutionary War together and won for this nation those cherished rights of which they had written.

The period under the Articles of Confederation can be viewed as one in which these leaders experimented with forms of government and eventually noted that their experiment had failed. The Constitutional Convention took note of this failure and sought to correct the major flaws that had been revealed. The resulting mixed form of government, characterized by the separation of powers and a system of checks and balances, stands as testimony to the continuing influence of European experience and of European thinkers—of Montesquieu, Hobbes, Locke, and their contemporaries.

Knowledge of these philosophers and their views contributed to the skepticism of the founders about factions, the only types of parties they knew. This skepticism was equally strong among the leaders of the French Revolution. The factions and parties that divided the French citizenry formed on the basis of economic self-interest and were opposed to the common good. The American leaders wanted to prevent similar divisions, or failing that, to control their influence. Thus Washington, Hamilton, Jefferson, and Madison all followed Bolingbroke and Hume in denouncing parties.

But these American politicians were also extremely practical (see Roche 1961). For example, the Constitution was written because the Articles of Confederation did not work. And Hamilton was a democrat only so long as the popular opinion coincided with his own; when it did not, he sided with the elite. None of the founders remained consistent in their views throughout their careers. How could they be expected to? Too much was changing; they had a new country to run.

II. THE FIRST AMERICAN PARTIES

In the early years under the new Constitution, most political leaders did reverse their opinions of parties (see Beeman 1991). While they were loath to endorse the concept of political parties—because the concept they endorsed had yet to be devised—they did perceive the need to organize those who shared their views in order to succeed with this new form of government they had established. In their efforts to make our democracy work, they invented the political institution that suited their needs. But this gestation had difficulty coming to term; the birth was dangerous.

One commonly held view about the founding of American political parties is that the first parties grew out of the fight over the ratification of the Constitution. Surely that fight did divide the new nation, but once Washington's government took office, nearly all those involved worked for its success. As Washington said in addressing the First Congress, "The fight over the Constitution is over."

But other battles were to be fought, even among those who had previously sided together to gain ratification. The first session of the First Congress went smoothly as the mechanics of governing were worked out. By the time that Alexander Hamilton presented his economic program to the second session of that Congress, however, President Washington's "honeymoon" period had ended.

A. Funding and Assumption

The keystone of Hamilton's program, which Washington adopted, was funding of the federal debt and assumption of the various state debts by the federal government. Hamilton felt that the strength of the new government would depend on its ability to demonstrate economic stability. Thus he favored full funding of the entire federal debt and the assumption of all state debts by the national government.

Others disagreed. On the question of funding, Madison and his followers felt that only notes held by original lenders, the true patriots, should be fully paid off. Notes held by speculators should only be repaid in part so that individuals did not profit from the war effort.

How one stood on the question of assumption of the state debts came down to which states stood to gain and which states to lose, a division that paralleled that over the political and theoretical question of how one stood on the necessity of expansion of the central government.

These two issues—funding and assumption—led to new lines of division. The fight over the Constitution pitted large states against small states. Economic issues presented to Congress in 1790 in a similar fashion divided the nation on sectional lines. Broadly speaking, the North was for Hamilton's funding plan; the South opposed it. Similarly, the North was for assumption, but the southern states opposed it. According to political historian Joseph Charles (1956, 23):

> There were two votes against Assumption from New Hampshire but none from the other New England States. There were three against it from New York, none against it from New Jersey, and four against it from Pennsylvania. Thus from the Northern states there were nine votes against the measure, while there were twenty-four in favor of it. In the South . . . a total of ten [were] for the bill, while eighteen were against it, but we should remember that the four votes from Maryland and Virginia had to be arranged.

B. Continuing New Divisions

Certainly parties in the sense of permanent entities with well-developed organizational bases had not formed, but funding and assumption marked the start of enduring new divisions. The other major issues of Hamilton's economic program—the charter of the Bank of the United States and the imposition of an excise tax—crystallized and invigorated public opinion and hardened the lines that had been drawn over funding and assumption.

Leaders in Washington's administration were uncertain about how to deal with these political differences. The overriding factor for most was success of the new government. A close second was personal loyalty to Washington, who, it is said, reigned more than ruled. The first president allowed his cabinet secretaries considerable autonomy, intervening only when they disagreed. Hamilton aggressively took the initiative and gained Washington's support for his program of economic growth. Adams, who disliked Hamilton personally and opposed some of his programs (feeling, for instance, that banks helped only the moneyed class), went along for the good of the nation. Jefferson also felt that his hands were tied; despite his strong objection to Hamilton's program, he remained in the cabinet until 1793, demonstrating his intense loyalty to Washington.

JEFFERSONIAN (OR DEMOCRATIC) REPUBLICANS

The party of Thomas Jefferson that formed around opposition to many of the policies proposed by Alexander Hamilton.

These divisions carried over into Congress, reaching new heights with the debate over ratification of the Jay Treaty with Great Britain. Hamilton, the Anglophile, led the Federalist party in support of the treaty that Ambassador Jay had consummated, a treaty that those who would become the **Jeffersonian (or Democratic) Republicans** denounced as a complete concession to the British. The Senate ratified the treaty before the opposition had time to focus its efforts, but the battle carried over into the House consideration of appropriations to implement Jay's economic compromise with Great Britain. This battle marked the first—and perhaps only—time in our history in which the an issue of foreign policy divided the legislature strictly on party lines. Those politicians, headed by Madison and Jefferson, who also opposed the administration, realized that they had to organize their supporters if their vision of a new American society was to be fulfilled.

Thus each of the earlier political leaders in his own way contributed to the development of political parties. Alexander Hamilton developed an unpopular program, but he linked it to George Washington, who was too popular to oppose. John Adams stuck with that program out of loyalty to Washington, but he provided a target for the opposition. James Madison voiced the early opposition in Congress and corresponded with others who shared his views, but he felt he was too young to lead the opposition. Finally, Thomas Jefferson, overcoming his sense of loyalty to Washington and fear of dividing the nation, assumed the leadership of the opposition, presenting an alternative vision of how American society should evolve.

C. Organizing to Gain Supporters

But how could this alternative be established? The target was the policy of the administration. Jefferson hoped that Washington and his associates would see that their policies were unpopular and change; had they done so, no parties would have been necessary. In any event, because the policies did not change, it was necessary to change the officials who implemented them. Who knew enough about these policies and cared enough to take action? Only those involved closely with the national government, for the government was still small and remote from the people. Information could not be disseminated easily to voters. Thus it was largely the legislative leaders who met together, planned strategy, and sought and decided upon candidates. The **congressional caucus** came to be the scene of partisan maneuvering.

CONGRESSIONAL CAUCUS

The meeting of all members of Congress affiliated with one party; used during the early period to nominate candidates for president.

How were these leaders to act? They had to discuss the matters among themselves, form groups of like-minded individuals, and then try to affect the next election by taking the word back to their local constituents. Who were their local constituents? Their friends, those who had served with them in the Revolutionary War, the local politicians. These leaders, in Camden, New Jersey, or Portsmouth, New Hampshire, or Savannah, Georgia, had to take action in turn to elect a president and a Congress responsive to the people's wishes. But suffrage was limited; presidents and senators were not popularly elected; progress had to be slow.

From the perspective of the late twentieth century, this process all seems simple enough. But one must recall the times. The "loyal opposition" were not professional politicians; Jefferson was perfectly happy, even eager, to return to Monticello when he left Washington's cabinet in 1793. He did not need to spend his life solving these problems. But he and his cohorts were also concerned men, and so they fought on.

D. The Elections of 1796 and 1800

Two elections were critically important for our nation's development. In 1796 George Washington stepped down, declining to seek a third term, thus establishing the important two-term precedent, violated only once in our history and now written into the Constitution. Washington's action provided for orderly succession in a way virtually unknown until that time.

In 1796 John Adams defeated Thomas Jefferson. While partisan ties were strong enough to carry the day for Adams, the votes for vice president were widely scattered. Thus Jefferson finished second and, by virtue of the electoral system in place at that time, became vice president. Jefferson agreed to serve under Adams, who thus accepted the legitimacy of his political opposition.

ELECTORAL VOTE

The votes cast by electors in the indirect system used for choosing the president of the United States; each state is allotted a number of electors equivalent to the number of representatives in Congress plus the number of senators; states determine how the electors will be selected; the winner is the candidate with a majority of the electoral votes.

In 1800 the Federalists chose President Adams to seek reelection against the Republican's choice, Vice President Jefferson. By this time, partisan allegiance was much more firmly established. Jefferson and his running mate, Aaron Burr of New York, each received seventy-three **electoral votes**. Adams and his vice presidential nominee, Charles Cotesworth Pinckney of South Carolina, received sixty-five and sixty-four votes, respectively. Because Jefferson's copartisans each cast their two electoral votes for both of the party's candidates, the election ended in a tie and went to the House of Representatives, to the Federalist-controlled House. Rumors of possible Federalist action to prevent Jefferson's election were rife. Federalist Hamilton devised a strategy to secure concessions from Jefferson; Adams met with Jefferson for the same purpose. The House meanwhile cast thirty-five inconclusive ballots. Finally, after several desperate Federalist caucuses, Jefferson was elected (see Chambers 1963, 162–169, for a discussion of this infighting).

The new governmental system had thus demonstrated remarkable stability; the House had ratified as the new president the man the nation had elected, despite the fact that he epitomized the political opposition. The peaceful transfer of power from Adams to Jefferson marked a most critical step in legitimating our new system of government and the role of opposition parties within that government.

The election of 1800 marked the high point of partisan conflict during these early years. The Federalist party soon became largely a New

England sectional party. The Republicans dominated the political scene for twenty-four years, without serious opposition during the administrations of Jefferson, Madison, and Monroe. Recall William N. Chambers's (1975, 6) definition of a competitive party system: "A pattern of interaction in which two or more political parties compete for office or power in government and for the support of the electorate, and must therefore take one another into account in their behavior in government and in election contests."

With the advent of the "era of good feeling," with the virtual collapse of the Federalist party, the first American party system collapsed.

E. Contributions of the First Party System

However, many significant advances in building our nation's political system can be traced to this period. The most important contribution of the first party system was the provision of an orderly means of settling political disputes and legitimating the victory of the winner. The election of 1800 was critically important in this regard.

Second, modern political parties, distinctly different from any known before, were invented during this period. The American parties became an important part of the government; they were not antigovernment. Parties were the mechanism through which it became possible legitimately to oppose the policies of the government and the leaders of the government without seeming to oppose the form of government itself. They were, in fact, the kind of parties that Burke had hypothesized as possible some thirty years earlier.

Third, the leaders of these new parties, or at least of the Democratic Republican party, in order to be successful became extraordinarily sensitive to the will of the people in this broadening democracy. They realized that new situations required new responses, that competing demands had to be accommodated, that the American polity was changing, and that they had to respond specifically to the changing social situation.

Fourth, parties as political institutions developed as enduring organizations during this period. The first party system grew from the center out, the parties at first being elite associations without grassroots support. The Democratic Republican party began with an opposition to administration policy; then legislators realized that they had to find a means to induce the election of like-minded colleagues if their policy preferences were to be adopted. Voila! a functioning political party. (See Cunningham 1957; for other interpretations of this period on the history of American political parties, see Binkley 1963.)

The congressional caucus as a means of nominating candidates was unique to this early party system. It suited politicians and their needs particularly well. In addition these leaders developed means of gaining support for their candidates, through letters of correspondence, drawing on friendships and alliances formed during the colonial and Revolutionary years.

Fifth, the two parties in this period also developed clearly distinguishable national ideologies. As early as 1792, a noticeably partisan James Madison wrote of these differences in the Philadelphia *National Gazette.*

> One of the divisions consists of those, who from particular interest, from natural temper, or from the habits of life, are more partial to the opulent than to the other classes of society; and having debauched themselves into a persuasion that mankind are incapable of governing themselves, it follows with them, of course, that government can be carried on only by the pageantry of rank, the influence of money and emoluments, and the terror of military force. Men of those sentiments must naturally wish to point the measures of government less to the interest of the many than of a few. . . .
>
> The other division consists of those believing in the doctrine that mankind are capable of governing themselves, and hating hereditary power as an insult to the reason and an outrage to the rights of man, are naturally offended at any public measure that does not appeal to the understanding and to the general interest of the community, or that is not strictly conformable to the principles, and conducive to the preservation of republican government. (Cunningham 1965, 11)

Not only were the ideologies clear, but politicians were already beginning to bring the American art form of rhetorical overstatement into the public eye.

The development of parties in this early period went further. The Democratic Republicans began to develop a party structure, based on the congressional caucus, and to recruit candidates for all offices. State legislators had to be recruited to elect U.S. senators; congressional candidates were also needed, in addition to presidential candidates. In order to secure the election of these candidates, the parties had to develop popular followings. To do this, they had to enlist party workers, adherents who would carry their cause to the voters. The first quarter of the nineteenth century was not a period when the franchise was extended; but, among other priorities, the parties had to convince eligible voters that participation was worthwhile. In short, American politics was born at this time. During this relatively short period was laid the groundwork on which subsequent politicians were to build.

F. The Collapse of the First Party System

The Jeffersonians learned the lessons of cohesive politics in this early period. The first system collapsed because the Federalists never really learned those lessons; they split internally over matters of policy and personality. More than that, the Federalists never realized that their policy preferences were too conservative and appealed to too few people to be successful electorally. Never able to develop the national following that the Jeffersonians enjoyed, they became politically irrelevant.

Why did this happen? Why did a ruling party's leaders allow their organization to collapse so completely so quickly? While such a collapse may seem incredible from today's perspective, we must remember that parties were weak and fragile in the early years of the nineteenth century. Partisan loyalties were not well established; political leaders themselves shifted frequently. Even in Jefferson's administration, few legislators identified themselves according to party. James Young's renowned study of early American party politics (1966) demonstrates that boardinghouse ties were as strong as party, that President Jefferson's personal appeals through carefully planned dinners were necessary to gain supporters for his legislation. These coalitions were built from the center out, not from the grassroots into the political arena. Consequently, when the Federalists adopted unpopular policies, they did not respond to popular protest and quickly lost support. No stable organization saved them from their decline.

Finally, the patrician politicians of the Federalist party had few incentives to save their party. They viewed themselves as political amateurs, happy to return to their prosperous farms and businesses once their service was over. The first "professional" politicians did emerge in this era—lawyers like Aaron Burr and the first clerk of the House, John Beckley—but these men were thought to be morally inferior to such "true" leaders as Washington, Adams, and Hamilton.

Parties thrive on tension and conflict; they cannot grow if they are electorally irrelevant. Thus the Federalists faded, and the Democratic Republicans had no competition by the 1820s. The first competitive party system ended, but competition was soon to be restored.

III. The Second Party System

A. The Election of 1824 and Its Aftermath

Today's political analysts complain about the length of presidential campaigns, but long campaigns are not a strictly modern phenomenon. Campaigning for the 1824 presidential election began shortly after Monroe's reelection in 1820. John C. Calhoun, the secretary of war, declared himself a candidate in 1821. Within the next two years the names of Secretary of State John Quincy Adams, Secretary of the Treasury William H. Crawford, Speaker of the House Henry Clay, and the hero of the battle of New Orleans, General Andrew Jackson, had all been put forward by their supporters.

Crawford might well have been the front-runner, but he suffered a paralyzing stroke in the fall of 1823 and had to stop campaigning. Calhoun withdrew when he was promised the vice presidential nomination by both Adams and Jackson. In the election itself, Jackson led both the **popular vote** (in the eighteen states in which electors were chosen by popular vote) and the electoral vote, but he lacked the majority of the electoral vote needed to gain election. Once again, as had been the case in 1800, the election was thrown to the House of Representatives, where each state's delegation cast one vote.

POPULAR VOTE

An election in which the winner is decided by the number of citizens casting their votes directly for particular candidates.

The House had to choose among the top three finishers—Jackson with ninety-nine electoral votes, Adams with eighty-four, and Crawford with forty-one. Clay, whose power came from the House, had been eliminated by finishing fourth with thirty-seven electoral votes, but his allies in the House guaranteed him influence. After careful consideration, Clay threw his support behind Adams, who was then chosen. When the new president subsequently made Clay his secretary of state, cries of **"corrupt bargain"** were heard throughout the land. No clear evidence of such a trade-off exists, but the "coincidence" of events permanently scarred Clay's reputation. The results also angered Jackson, who felt he had been deprived of what was rightly his.

"CORRUPT BARGAIN"

The claim that Henry Clay threw his support in the House of Representatives in the 1824 presidential election to John Quincy Adams, thereby ensuring Adams's election, in exchange for Clay's appointment as secretary of state.

The election of 1824 created a violent split in the Jeffersonian Republican party between the backers of Adams (the National Republicans) and those of Jackson (the Democratic Republicans). Jackson's men organized furiously, and the personal competition increased national interest in politics. By 1828 all but two of the twenty-four states selected their electors by popular vote. The popular vote in 1828 more than tripled that of 1824, and Andrew Jackson had his revenge. He defeated King Caucus (as the congressional caucus came to be known) and elite rule with a populist "revolution." More importantly, Jackson's election marked the beginning of a series of maneuvers that were to solidify the shape of American politics from that date onward.

B. Electoral Phases in the Second Party Period

The so-called second party period can be broken down into different eras. The first phase, of critical importance for the future shape of American politics, was a period of intense grassroots organization by Jackson's supporters. It culminated in Jackson's victory in 1828.

The second phase, corresponding roughly to Jackson's presidency, was a time during which both parties worked diligently to mobilize the voters. As Jacksonian Democrats continued to build support, a new opposition party, the **Whigs**, was formed to oppose Jackson. The **national convention** as a means of nominating presidential candidates destroyed the power of Congress over this important part of the process. King Caucus was dead for good. Finally, new sectional voting patterns began to emerge.

WHIGS

Political party that succeeded the Federalists and competed with the Democratic Republicans through much of the pre-Civil War period.

NATIONAL CONVENTION

A means of nominating presidential candidates by delegates from each state; replaced the congressional caucus as part of democratizing reforms of the Jacksonian era.

By the election of 1836, competition between the Democrats (as the Jeffersonian or Democratic Republicans came to be called) and the Whigs was intense, and this level of competition lasted into the 1850s. The Democrats originally had been a coalition of southern agrarians and egalitarian New York City residents, but during this period their adherents seemed to live everywhere in the nation. For as long as possible they managed skillfully to skirt the slavery issue in favor of less divisive domestic issues. Democrats were nationalistic, insular, antielitist.

It is less easy to characterize the Whigs. The traditional view is that they represented the more prosperous classes or that the split echoed ethnic heritage, but such easy answers do not explain why New Hampshire was heavily Democratic and Vermont was heavily Whig, or why adjacent areas in New York State often differed in partisan allegiance. The simple truth is that the Whigs united those who opposed Jackson. Old Hickory had honed the **spoils system** to a fine point, rewarding legions of friends who helped him politically. Those who lost jobs (or sought and did not get jobs) became his enemies and organized as the political opposition.

SPOILS SYSTEM

Reward system under which the spoils of victory, that is, patronage, went to the party workers from the winning party, at the expense of workers for the losing party.

C. Innovations of the Second Party Period

The second party system was a period of true innovation in terms of party mechanisms and processes. As mentioned earlier, national conventions replaced the congressional caucus as the means of doing party business. But perhaps the key innovation of this period was the development of an elaborate, complex, and decentralized party organization. Parties began to organize followers and workers at the local, grassroots level.[1]

Why did they organize at this level? Because, unlike the first party system in which policy differences were critical, *the electoral aspects of party were critical in this second party system.* And the local level is where the voters are. Parties established autonomous local units, again decentralized, to see to the business of elections. National conventions drew on these local units, again emphasizing citizen participation. By the 1830s, politics involved true two-party competition in every region, in fact in every state except perhaps South Carolina.

Politicians sought votes as best they could. One means was to make politics fun for the people. Mid-nineteenth-century politicians raised the practice of their profession to an art. Political rhetoric incited the people, parades stoked their emotions, military heroes sought their allegiance, catchy slogans simplified their views. "Tippecanoe and Tyler Too" had a lot less to do with governing than had the earlier political debate over the Jay Treaty, but it was a lot easier for the average voter to relate to. Politics emerged as the true national pastime.

The changing attitude toward politics was accompanied by equally significant changes in the law, changes that encouraged the spread of popular participation. Presidential electors came to be chosen by popular vote, with a whole slate of electors running at large in each state. The Constitution leaves the method of choosing electors to the states (Article 2, Section 1). State politicians soon realized that their state's strength would be maximized if the winner received all the electoral votes, not just a share. Thus the "winner-take-all" system, still in place in every state except for Maine and Nebraska today, was born in order to magnify political advantage, not to serve some higher principle.

On the other hand, the laws in many states were rewritten so as to mandate the election of congressmen by district, rather than at large. Because the presidency is a singular office, states wanted to increase their influence on the presidential selection process. However, because each state numbered its congressmen in proportion to its size and because each was an autonomous actor, politicians deemed it important to elect congressmen by district, supposedly in order to keep them closer to the people who chose them. Election of congressmen by district was written into law as part of the reapportionment legislation following the Census Act of 1840;[2] the Constitution only requires that members of Congress reside in the state from which they are elected. But the need for a close link between a representative in Washington and the people who elected him was recognized and actuated by district elections as early as the Jacksonian period.

Similarly, the populace began to participate in other elections during this time. More and more governors came to be popularly elected, whereas they had once been selected by state legislatures. Many local officials, heretofore appointed, had to stand for election. And these elections were conducted according to new democratic rules designed to encourage increased participation. Some of these election procedures were basic, like the provision of printed ballots by the state. Some seem only logical, like drawing small voting districts to decrease unneeded, difficult travel or holding all elections on the same day. All these regularized procedures taken together had an enormous impact. Change came slowly during the second party period, but these changes were profound. By 1850, the basic features of the American political system were not very different from those in place today.

IV. THE COLLAPSE OF THE SECOND PARTY SYSTEM

REALIGNMENTS

Fundamental changes in the party system signaled by a new line of cleavage and significant shifting of individuals' party identification.

Why then did this highly developed, highly competitive party system collapse? One answer to this question is probably too simple: the party system failed to respond to the stress on the American polity caused by the slavery issue. A longer answer is that this change is a perfect example of how political **realignments** occur in the American system and of how that system adapts to significant change. We will view the collapse of the second party system in these terms.

A party realignment may be defined as a lasting change in established patterns of political behavior. A grossly elementary picture of any party system (fig. 2.1) shows the electorate as split by one major issue and voting accordingly (see Sundquist 1983, chaps. 1–2).[3] This picture can apply just as easily to a college campus (where the **line of cleavage** might be on a profraternity or antifraternity split) as to a national or state party system. A system is said to change fundamentally with a relocation of the line of cleavage, and hence a resplitting of the electorate (see fig. 2.2).

LINE OF CLEAVAGE

Dividing line that separates supporters of one party from those of another.

Systems can change in less dramatic ways, for example, when the voting age is changed and the electorate either expands or contracts, or simply when individuals change their views. James Sundquist (1983, 41–47) maintains that the interaction of five variables determines when and in what ways established patterns of political behavior will change. The five variables are

- the breadth and depth of the underlying grievance that is affecting the system,
- the capacity of those supporting the status quo to resist change,
- the skill of the political leaders,
- the pattern of division of the polar forces on the new issue between the existing parties, that is, does the new cleavage cut across existing differences or mirror them?
- the strength of existing party attachments.

With these factors in mind, it is possible to examine American politics in the 1850s.

Slavery was the issue that raised the passion of the country. In the prealignment period, as depicted in figure 2.3, the parties did not divide on this issue. Rather, in order to avoid making enemies and losing elections, they skirted the most important issue of the day. Issues in Congress that made the slavery issue become the most important item

Figure 2.1 Hypothetical Representation of Any Party System.

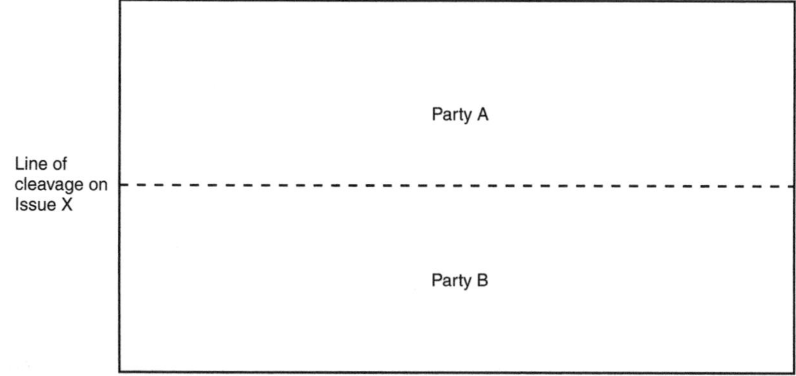

Figure 2.2 New Line of Cleavage Relocates Party Division.

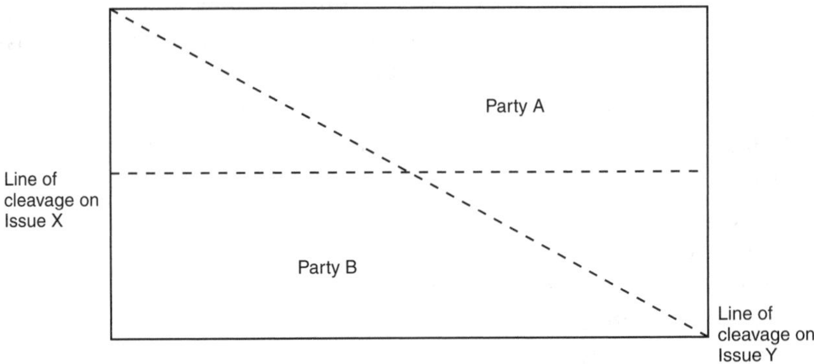

on the political agenda included the matter of whether or not to accept petitions (the gag rule), the abolition of slavery in the District of Columbia, the admission of Texas as a free or slave state, the prosecution of the Mexican war, the Wilmot Proviso, and the Compromise of 1850.

LIBERTY PARTY

One of the pre-Civil War parties that brought the issue of slavery into the forefront of the nation's political agenda.

While the major parties tried to skirt the most crucial question of the 1850s, other parties—third parties in a two-party system—were willing to stand or fall on that issue alone. One of the important roles that non-major parties play in two-party systems is to raise and debate the controversial issues of the day (Bibby and Maisel 1998; Sundquist 1983). New parties—first the **Liberty party** and then the **Free Soil party**—brought the slavery issue to the political forefront. Each of these antislavery factions drew significant numbers of votes in presidential elections and elected their supporters to Congress and the state legislatures. The shape of the political system was changing (fig. 2.4).

FREE SOIL PARTY

An important pre-Civil War third party that split adherents from the existing major parties on the issue of slavery.

The major parties tried to compromise on these slavery-oriented issues but could not. According to Sundquist, five responses to such stress were possible. The easiest solution would be for the issue to disappear. In this case no realignment would have occurred and the pre-

Figure 2.3 Party Division Prior to Realignment on Slavery Issue.

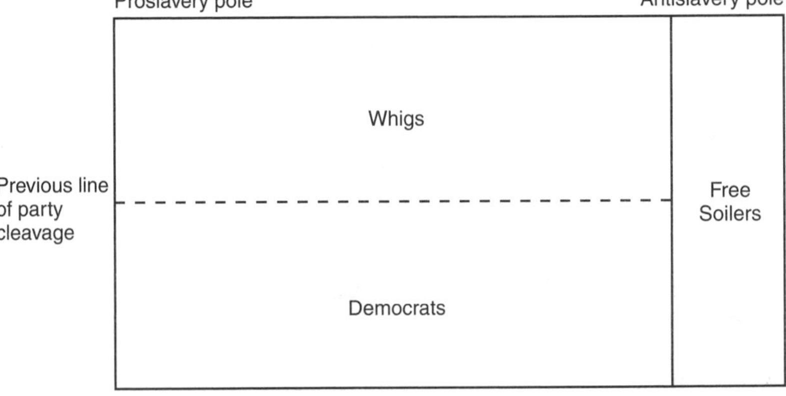

Figure 2.4 Stress on Party System Caused by Slavery Issue.

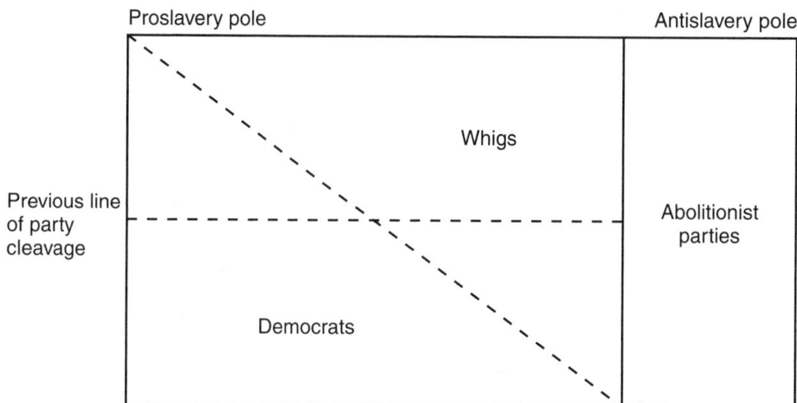

vious line of cleavage would have divided the electorate again. Slavery and the abolition movement refused to vanish, however.

Second, the two parties could have realigned along the new line, the slavery dimension. One party could have become the proslavery party, the other antislavery. Again, no such rearrangement took place because the leaders of each existing party tried to straddle an issue that cut squarely across existing party lines.

A third response would be for a third party to form and then be taken over by one of the existing parties, moving that party to take a stand on the new issue. Such ingestion was possible, but again existing party leadership did not move in that direction, each party's leaders hoping that passions aroused by the issue that brought the Liberty party and the Free Soil party into existence would eventually cool.

REPUBLICAN PARTY

The successor major party to the Whigs; the party of Lincoln that controlled the government after 1860 and led the nation through the Civil War, into Reconstruction, and beyond.

The fourth response would be for a third party to form and to replace one of the existing parties. This "small fish eats big fish" scenario did not happen with the Liberty party or with the Free Soilers, but the **Republican party** did absorb the Whig party, which had lost its appeal by the 1852 election, receiving a majority of the votes in only one state.

In 1856 the new Republican party held its first national nominating convention. The nominee, General John C. Fremont, called for the admission of Kansas to the Union as a free state and advocated a policy that upheld congressional authority over slavery in the territories. The Republican party was a sectional party from the start. Drawing on "conscience Whigs," antislavery Democrats, and old Free Soilers, Fremont got nearly 40 percent of the vote in 1856 (a majority in the North), but he was not even on the ballot in most of the southern states. The Whigs were gone, replaced by a new party that served virtually no "apprenticeship" as a third party but rather immediately achieved major-party status. Figure 2.5 depicts the realignment at the time of the Civil War. William E. Gienapp (1987, 1991) provides a detailed analysis of the formation of the Republican party. His account makes note of the importance of

Figure 2.5 Party System After Realignment on Slavery.

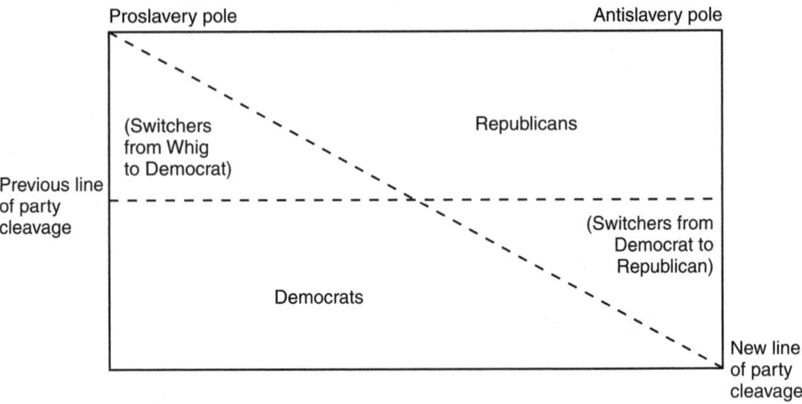

temperance and of nativism as well as of the antislavery movement in describing the demise of the Whigs and their replacement by the Republicans—as opposed to other anti-Democratic parties. While his discussion of realignment and the decomposition of the Whig coalition is consistent with that provided here, he gives a much more detailed, state-by-state account of the strategies followed by Republican politicians and of the role of pragmatic politics as well as ideology in the decisions they made.

The Civil War, of course, meant much more than a change in party system. Our entire political system was threatened and nearly collapsed. What emerged was a badly torn nation, divided on the issue of slavery, an issue that was resolved by bloodshed, not political debate. The politics of the post–Civil War period reflected the split of the nation and a whole new way of resolving debates.

The fifth possible response to stress was for both parties to be replaced by new major parties. This response did not eventuate, as the Democrats survived by embracing the southern cause.

V. Third Party System: Industrialization over Politics

Politicians who could not adapt to change failed to settle the conflict caused by the issue of slavery; they also did not regain their former prominence after the great battle that resolved that issue. The political system that emerged after the Civil War, while still characterized as a competitive two-party system, was vastly different from the one that preceded it.

The Republican party was the majority party during almost all of the third party period. But the leaders of American society during the last third of the nineteenth century were industrialists, not politicians, who once again were largely retired military leaders. America was dominated by men like Andrew Carnegie, Marshall Field, J. Pierpont Morgan, John D. Rockefeller, Leland Stanford, Cornelius Vanderbilt, and Aaron Montgomery Ward. No one doubts the importance of their reputations and accomplishments, particularly in comparison to those of politicians like Ulysses S. Grant, James Garfield, Chester Arthur, or Benjamin Harrison. Both national parties were captured by the industrialists, but it was the Republicans who dominated, sponsoring governmental programs favoring industrial growth and westward expansion.

The partisan split in this period was largely sectional. The Republicans dominated the East and the West. The Democrats, after Reconstruction, made political gains in the South, where resentment by whites toward Republican domination of their region after the Civil War was high. Southern blacks, moreover, were prohibited from active participation in politics by notorious Jim Crow laws.

While the nation as a whole was very competitive, rare was the state that was not dominated by one party or the other. For example, when Garfield won the election of 1880 or Cleveland the election of 1884, in each case with a popular plurality of less than 1 percent, the winning candidate had a 10 percent or larger margin in over half of the states. The Republicans would have dominated this period more convincingly had not a series of seemingly unrelated events hurt Republican political fortunes—a bad depression in 1873, the scandals of the Grant administration, a decline in agricultural production in 1884, and an economic downturn in 1890. Democrats may have gained some white votes by intimidating blacks in the South, but such action also served to characterize a party that had been on the losing side of a great struggle. The Democrats won some political skirmishes, but the Republicans were the well-financed and powerful party of the captains of American capitalism.

In addition to being a time of rapid industrialization, the last quarter of the nineteenth century was also a period of significant immigration. Newly arrived immigrants came to play an important role in the development of the most significant political innovation of this period, the urban **political machine**.[4] In many ways it is logical that political machines grew up during an era dominated by business growth. As Banfield and Wilson argue, the party organization of this period was essentially "a business organization in a particular field of business—getting votes and winning elections" (1963, 115). How was the politician to get what was desired in this context? Put simply, in business terms, American machine bosses bought the product needed. More precisely, they bought what was needed from whomever would sell the product most cheaply. For political leaders in an age of large-scale immigration, this formula implied giving material incentives to immigrant groups in exchange for their votes.

POLITICAL MACHINE

Hierarchically structured organization of political parties based largely on material incentives and patronage.

This formula was not as evil as it is often depicted. The political system was an effective means for immigrants to assimilate themselves into American society. The political machine provided jobs, lodging, extra groceries, and a means of socialization for new groups of citizens. In exchange, the immigrant groups provided votes for the machine. The bosses dominated politics; the industrialists dominated society. As immigrants found jobs in the expanding factories, their employment symbolized a period of transition in American life from an agricultural economy to an urban industrial economy. The political system reflected this shift.

But not everyone was satisfied. With the rapid industrialization of the country and the domination of politics and government by the business community, the farmers of the Midwest discovered that they were the consistent losers. As neither major party took up their cause, they soon set out on their own, forming a series of organizations to challenge the existing power structure. The **Granger movement** spread rapidly in the 1870s and 1880s and the **Farmers' Alliance** was politically active during much of this time as well. Finally, the **Populists** raised concerns that threatened the continuation of the existing two-party system. These groups signaled splits that were to lead to a significant change in the context of American partisan politics.

GRANGER MOVEMENT

Movement of farmers in the Midwest in the 1870s and 1880s that expressed discontent over the prominence of industrial policies to the detriment of farmers.

FARMERS' ALLIANCE

Separate but similar movement active at the same time.

POPULISTS

Leaders who took the discontent of the farmers into the political realm, threatening the hegemony of the two existing parties.

VI. THE CRITICAL ELECTION OF 1896 AND REPUBLICAN DOMINATION

America entered the last decade of the nineteenth century with a competitive two-party system at the national level. The election of 1876 had to be decided by a special commission, settling disputes over contested electoral votes and at the same time setting the course for the nation's industrial growth. Grover Cleveland won the elections of 1884 and 1892 by extremely close popular pluralities; he lost in the electoral college in 1888, despite his popular plurality of less than 1 percent. The Democrats won congressional majorities in 1890 and 1892. The country seemed to be turning away from the "bloody shirt"-waving Republican politics of the post–Civil War era.

All of that was to change quickly. The panic of 1893, during a Democratic administration, led to a huge Republican landslide in the congressional election of 1894; the Republicans gained 132 seats and completely controlled twenty-four state delegations. The debacle for the Democrats was a precursor of Republican William McKinley's defeat of quasi-Populist Democrat William Jennings Bryan, in 1896, an election that determined a new course for American politics, setting a pattern that would see the Democrats as the minority party for years to come.

A. The Critical Election of 1896

Political scientists refer to the election of 1896 as a realigning or **critical election** that marks the beginning of the fourth party system. The major parties did not change in 1896; Republicans still competed with Democrats. But the issues that separated the parties and the allegiances of large groups of voters did change.[5]

CRITICAL ELECTION

An election of particular importance to the party system because of the intensity of interest and the distinction between the two parties' views on the salient issues of the day; may lead to realignments.

Before 1896 both parties favored industrialization; both parties sought to appeal to urban populations. In 1896 not only did the Democratic party have to carry the burden of the 1893 economic downturn, but it also became associated with a charismatic leader who attacked business interests, called for softer money and a silver standard, and appealed to the farmers of the nation in a way that alienated urban workers. None could deny the power of Bryan's rhetoric:

> The humblest citizen of all the land, when clad in the armor of a righteous cause, is stronger than all the hosts of Error. . . . You shall not press down upon the brow of labor this crown of thorns. You shall not crucify mankind upon a cross of gold.

But many doubted the economic effectiveness of the cause. McKinley's campaign, led by perhaps the first modern campaign manager, Marcus A. Hanna, and financed by the nation's industrial leaders, was efficient and effective. Bryan was portrayed as a radical enemy of urban workers. Virtually all the cities came into the Republican fold. The new issue that divided the nation, the silver standard versus the gold standard, caused new regional splits—West versus East, rural areas versus urban—and the Democrats had defined for themselves a losing coalition.

The election of 1896 illustrates another important concept in the analysis of American electoral history, the critical election (Key 1955, 3–18). In a seminal article in 1959, V. O. Key Jr. maintained that some elections were more significant in electoral history than were others. Key defined a critical election as "a type of election in which there occurs a sharp and durable electoral cleavage between the parties" (1959, 198–210). That is, critical elections mark changes in party *systems* as we have defined them. These changes occur because of shifts, either temporary or permanent, in the line of cleavage. Key claimed that critical elections were marked by high levels of electoral involvement by the populace, depth of concern about the election's outcome by the voters, and profound readjustments in the power relationships within a community.

Key (1959, 198ff.) also qualified this theory with the concept of **secular realignment** (which he defined as gradual, rather than sudden and sharp), a long-term redistribution of party strength. He claimed that movement to a new party alignment might happen at different times in different regions and thus, when viewed nationally, appear almost imperceptible.

SECULAR REALIGNMENT

Realignment that occurs gradually over a period of elections, and perhaps at different times in different locales, rather than as a result of one critical election.

B. The Classification of Presidential Elections

Using Key's concepts, political scientists have been able to refine their classifications of various presidential elections. Angus Campbell and his associates classified elections according to whether or not the majority party won the election and whether or not the existing line

MAINTAINING ELECTIONS
Elections in which the coalitions supporting the major parties remain the same and the same party stays in control of the government.

DEVIATING ELECTIONS
Elections in which coalitions supporting the major parties remain the same but the minority party gains control of the government because of short-term forces.

REALIGNING ELECTIONS
Elections in which the coalitions supporting the two major parties shift as a new line of cleavage divides the electorate; the party that had been the minority party becomes the majority party.

CONVERTING ELECTIONS
Elections in which the coalitions supporting the two major parties shift on a new line of cleavage but the party that had been the majority party in the past remains in that position.

of cleavage prevailed or was changed (Campbell, Converse, Miller, and Stokes 1960, 531–538). They identified three types of elections—**maintaining elections**, **deviating elections**, and **realigning elections**. Seeing a logical gap in this reasoning and referring particularly to the election of 1896, Gerald Pomper (1973, 104) added a fourth category, the **converting election**. These concepts are shown in figure 2.6.

Thus the election of 1860, in which Abraham Lincoln, only the second Republican candidate to seek the presidency, defeated Democrat Stephen A. Douglas, as well as Southern Democrat candidate John C. Breckinridge and the Constitutional Union party's John Bell, was a realigning election, ushering in the third party system. In the election of 1896, however, the majority party from the previous electoral era remained the same. The election was a converting election, shifting the line of cleavage from old Civil War allegiances, which had weakened and led to more intense competition by the 1890s, to economic issues of gold versus silver. Geographically, urban and northern areas were aligned against rural, southern, and western areas. Even though the majority party remained the same, a new party system was in place.

The Republicans dominated the fourth party system, holding the White House for sixteen consecutive years and for twenty-eight of the next thirty-six years. The elections of 1912 and 1916 are, on the other hand, deviating elections. The electoral coalitions did not change; the Republicans remained the majority party. Democrat Woodrow Wilson won the 1912 election because Teddy Roosevelt split the Republican vote, running on his own third party ticket, that of the Bull Moose party. Wilson barely won again in 1916, as many old progressives marched back to the Republican party. By 1920 the Republican coalition had regained prominence.

Figure 2.6 Classification of Presidential Elections.

LINE OF CLEAVAGE \ MAJORITY PARTY	Same	Different
Same	Maintaining election (e.g., 1904, 1940)	Deviating election (e.g., 1912, 1952)
Different	Converting election (e.g., 1896)	Realigning election (e.g., 1860, 1932)

C. The Progressive Era: A Systemic Change

Whether the change in 1896 was as significant as others that were taking place during this period is open to question. By 1896 the issue that had divided the electorate before 1860, slavery, was resolved. After all, voters who were forty years old in 1896, men who had been voting for almost twenty years, had been only nine years old at the time of Lincoln's assassination. The issues of gold and silver and of the pace and cost of industrialization obviously were important to those interested in politics. But the techniques of politics were not changing; the party structure did not change in 1896; which parties had to be taken into account and how they interacted—the definition of a political system—did not change. Machines flourished; Mark Hanna transformed the role of a political boss into the ultimate, logical extension of the spoils system, the type of political organizations perfected by the Jacksonian Democrats.

PROGRESSIVE ERA

The period of time around the turn of the century in which political discourse centered on a series of reforms in the way in which government worked and related to the populace.

More fundamental changes in terms of how the political battle was fought occurred throughout the so-called **Progressive era**. These changes did not result in an electoral realignment because progressives belonged to both the Republican and the Democratic parties. But the reforms associated with the progressives caused fundamental changes in the ways the parties interacted, thus altering our entire political system in ways surely as profound as any electoral realignment.

The Progressive era had an impact on all aspects of American government. It was symbolized by the "sociological" briefs presented to the Supreme Court by Boston attorney (and later Supreme Court Associate Justice) Louis Brandeis, by the revolt against the dictatorial powers of the Speaker of the House exercised by "Uncle Joe" Cannon in the House of Representatives, by the "stewardship theory" under which Theodore Roosevelt expanded the powers of the presidency, and by the "New Freedom" of Woodrow Wilson.

CIVIL SERVICE SYSTEM

The system for appointing government officials based on merit, not patronage; an early progressive reform.

DIRECT PRIMARY ELECTIONS

Elections in which party members, variously defined, directly nominate candidates for office through voting at the ballot box; democratizing reform in opposition to party organization control of nominations through caucuses and conventions.

NONPARTISAN ELECTIONS

Elections in which party names do not appear on the ballot; instituted in many local elections as a progressive reform aimed at stripping parties of their influence.

In electoral terms, the rules of the game were dramatically changed. The first of these changes has been traced to Charles J. Guiteau, the deranged, disappointed office seeker who shot President Garfield and indirectly created the **civil service system**. The demise of the spoils system was the first step in the decline of the urban machines, a disintegrative process that went on for many years through the New Deal to modern reform clubs.

Other progressive changes had more immediate impacts. The invention of **direct primary elections** as a means to win party nominations took away from parties one key to their power—control over access to the ballot. No change could have had greater impact on the strength of parties. In 1913 the Seventeenth Amendment called for the direct election of U.S. senators. In this case one of the important stakes in the political game was changed. Again, party strength was weakened. When women won the right to vote in 1920, the political electorate was doubled. Although participation by women was not at the same level as men's, parties still had to contend with a whole new body of voters. Finally, to rid themselves of the evils of party bosses and machine corruption, many cities introduced **nonpartisan elections**. Once again the electoral system was greatly altered.

These innovations in the first decades of the twentieth century revised the shape of American politics most significantly. Although they are not associated with a new "party system" as traditionally defined by social scientists, the modifications represent changes as significant as those between the first and second party systems, changes much more fundamental than mere realignments. These shifts, when combined with the technological advancement that allowed for instantaneous political communication through radio, determined the parameters of political contests for more than four decades.

VII. The New Deal Coalition

The line drawn between Democrats and Republicans in 1896 remained in place for over thirty years. The context of electoral battles shifted during the Progressive era, but the line of cleavage dividing the American electorate did not. However, the Great Depression broke traditional allegiances and recast the shape of electoral coalitions. Some observers feel that a secular realignment may have been under way as early as the 1920s, but virtually all analysts agree that 1932 was a critical election that defined a new line of cleavage that became dominant in American elections.

In simplest terms, the American public blamed the Great Depression on Republican president Herbert Hoover and his party. Franklin Roosevelt gave hope to the millions who had been hurt by the Depression; they responded by giving their allegiance to the Democratic party.

A. Defining the New Deal Coalition

NEW DEAL COALITION

Electoral coalition forged by those favoring the policies of Franklin Delano Roosevelt; said to be composed of urban workers, ethnic Americans, Jews, blacks, the academic elite, and the traditionally Democratic South.

The **New Deal coalition** has been defined in many ways (see, e.g., Erikson, Lancaster, and Romero 1989; Ladd and Hadley 1975; Stanley, Bianco, and Niemi 1986). Journalists would say that the New Deal coalition included urban workers, ethnic Americans, Jews, blacks, the academic elite, and the traditionally Democratic South. Political scientist Robert Axelrod (1972) has defined this coalition more carefully. Axelrod maintains that a group's contribution to a political coalition is a product of three factors: the size of the group, the percentage of the group that turns out to vote, and the loyalty of the group's members to a political party (1972, 11–12). The interplay of these factors is crucial. For instance, blacks were very loyal to the Democratic party during the New Deal (and remain so). But because they represented a small percentage of the population (approximately 10 percent) and because many blacks either chose not to vote or were prevented from doing so by Jim Crow laws (average turnout of under 25 percent), they did not make up a very large component of the New Deal coalition.[6] According to Axelrod, the groups contributing most to the New Deal coalition were Roman Catholics and union members and their families (each accounting for approximately two in five Democratic voters). Significant, but smaller, contributions to the New Deal coalition were made by (1) the poor (defined as those with annual incomes under $3,000 at the time), (2) residents of the twelve largest metropolitan areas, (3) southerners, and (4) blacks (Axelrod 1972, 14).[7] With the exception of the poor and large-city residents, each of these groups was significantly more loyal to the Democratic party during the New Deal than was the country as a whole.

Although Axelrod was able to sort out members of a Republican coalition—nonunion members, nonpoor, whites, Protestants, residents of smaller cities and rural areas—significantly, none of these groups was much more loyal to the Republican party than was the nation as a whole (Axelrod 1972, 18). That is, the Republicans attracted voters disaffected by the Democratic party, but those disaffected were so few as to constitute only a losing coalition during the period of the New Deal and its immediate aftermath.

The division as outlined above defined the cleavage in the American political system for an unprecedented period of time. Most analysts feel that a description of electoral coalitions that was accurate in the mid-1930s would have been similarly accurate into the 1960s. Even though the Republicans won Congress in 1946, and despite President Eisenhower's defeat of Democrat Adlai Stevenson in 1952 and 1956, these elections were seen as deviations. The majority of Americans still owed allegiance to the Democratic party. The issues dividing the electorate were still the New Deal issues: whether the government had a responsibility to serve as the employer of last resort, to intervene actively in the economy, and to help those who were unable to help themselves. For more than three decades these issues defined the political agenda. For most of that time, the American public agreed with the Democrats' approach to the nation's problems.

Less consensus exists about whether the New Deal coalitions survived the turbulent 1960s and 1970s. A good deal of evidence suggests that the tie of parties is less strong and that the issues that are important to the electorate have changed. Wattenberg (1989; 1990a; 1991; 1994; 1996) for instance, points to issues such as women's rights, the environment, or the impact of drugs on American society, which concern citizens today much more than they did two decades ago. How these issues relate to the traditional appeal of the New Deal coalition is not clear (see Norputh 1987; Petrocik 1987a; Stanley et al. 1986). What is clear, however, is that one critically important part of that coalition, the South, has fallen away (see Aistrup 1996; Alt 1994; Bullock 1988; Brunell and Grofman 1998). Before looking at the shape of parties as we enter the twenty-first century, it is important to look at other changes in the current party system.

B. Changing Campaign Technology

VOTING RIGHTS ACT OF 1965

Civil rights reform that permitted federal government to intercede in those areas in which African-Americans had been hampered in exercising their right to vote.

Even during the early decades of the fifth party system, although the line of cleavage that divided the Democrats from the Republicans remained remarkably constant, the political system as a whole underwent changes that are as significant as those of the Progressive era, or the Jacksonian era. This time the changes have not involved the rules of the political game or expansion of the electorate whose allegiance has been sought, though party rules have changed and the electorate has expanded again with the granting of the franchise to eighteen-to-twenty-one-year-olds and the reenfranchisement of blacks and other minorities with the **Voting Rights Act of 1965** and its extensions. The important change in most recent years has involved rapidly changing campaign technology.

Earlier the impact of radio was briefly noted. Radio gave politicians the ability to communicate instantly and personally with large numbers of citizens. This advance, however, pales in comparison with the change in the ways politicians communicate with the electorate through television (see chap. 12). Campaign technology has changed rapidly and frequently during the fifth party period. The direction of all the changes has been away from party-centered campaigns toward candidate-centered ones (see Shea 1996; Aldrich 1995; Ferguson 1995; Herrnson 1995; Jacobson 1992; Wattenberg 1991).

Think about what you know, what even casual observers know, about today's campaigns. In most areas of the country, even candidates for local office reach the voters through television ads. The first television advertising for political candidates was done for Dwight Eisenhower and Adlai Stevenson in the 1952 presidential campaign. Nelson Rockefeller made the first extensive use of television for statewide candidates when he ran for governor of New York a decade later. As late as the 1970s many congressional candidates did not use television at all. Local candidates in much of the country did not begin to use this means of reaching voters until cable television became prevalent in your lifetime. Today campaigning and television advertising are synonymous.

Campaign strategists poll the electorate and follow polls conducted by news organizations to know what the voters are thinking and how their campaigns are faring. The first use of sophisticated polling by a political campaign organization was done by the Kennedy organization in the 1960 campaign—and even then Robert Kennedy, his brother's campaign manager, only wanted to hear the numbers, not the analysis of pollster Louis Harris. Even as the utility of scientific measures of public opinion came to be recognized by campaign professionals, in the 1970s and even early 1980s, the expense of polling meant that many campaigns below the statewide level and even at the level in smaller states made the decision to go without the information that could be provided so that scarce campaign resources could be used for advertising. Not until the late 1980s and 1990s, as innovations in sampling and polling techniques and in computer technology made polling less costly, did this technique of gauging what issues would play best with the voters come into widespread use for campaigns for all offices.

Every mailbox is filled with candidates' messages as an election approaches. "Mailing the district," like dropping literature at every doorstep, is a very old campaign technique. But again technology has made this tool much more sophisticated in recent years. Today's direct mail is not a scattershot to an entire area but is targeted to voters with specific views. Targeted mailings became possible when candidates could avail themselves of computers to keep track of lists of voters with certain specific characteristics, for example, union members, gun owners, or educators. It may be difficult to imagine, but as late as the 1970s, computers were only rarely used in any but the most expensive campaigns. Changes in information technology have radically altered the way in which campaigns communicate with voters (Bibby 1998; Herrnson 1998; Asher 1992).

These innovations go far to shape the context of the current political system. Many believe that the Internet, which came into use by political candidates in the 1990s, will change this context of campaigning as fundamentally as have television and computer technology (Selnow 1994, 1998; Rash 1997; Corrado 1996; Grossman 1995). Others, while not denying the importance of the Internet as an information source and a communications link, are more skeptical about its importance for campaigning because the extent and direction of Internet communication is determined by the user, not the provider. What is clear to all, however, is that the future of campaign technology is impossible to predict and that, whatever direction it takes, it will fundamentally affect the shape of the political system and how parties function within that system (Maisel 1998).

C. The Shape of the Party System at the Century's End

The New Deal coalition has eroded since the mid-1960s. Note that the word "eroded" was carefully chosen. Political journalists and political scientists have spent a substantial amount of time and effort defining whether the fifth party system has come to an end (see, e.g., Brunell and Grofman 1998; Ladd 1997; 1991; Silbey 1991; Burnham 1991; Aldrich and Niemi 1990). The best answer seems to be that no one critical election can be isolated as a point to define a major realignment. The American political system has been undergoing a gradual transformation, not a radical realignment (Abramowitz and Saunders 1998; Silbey 1991; Ladd 1991; Burnham 1991; Ladd 1978, 81–91; Ladd and Hadley 1975).

The current coalition in American politics is quite different from the coalition of two or three decades ago, not only in terms of partisan alignment but also in terms of the meaning of partisanship to the voters. Recall the definitions of political parties and of party systems presented in chapter 1. One key aspect of those definitions dealt with voter allegiance to parties and support for candidates at least in part because of that allegiance; related to that was the assertion that parties in an ongoing system competed with each other for the support of those voters.

The political system has undergone an important change in terms of the allegiance of voters to parties, and in some cases in terms of how the parties compete for voter support. A clue to this change can be found in voter attitudes toward the role of parties in American politics. Whereas once citizens voted for candidates *whom they viewed as candidates of political parties,* today the norm is to vote for the candidate, not the party. More than a decade ago Larry Sabato (1988, 133) noted that 92 percent of Americans agreed with the statement "I always vote for the person who I think is best, regardless of what party they belong to," whereas only 14 percent claimed they "always support the candidate of just one party." Those feelings have persisted. In a survey conducted by Hart and Teeter Research Companies for NBC News/Wall Street Journal in September of 1995, for instance, only 26 percent of voters said they cast their ballots for either all Republicans or all Democrats in the last few state and national elections in which they had voted (*Public Perspective* 1998).

Evidence of this change can be seen in a number of different ways. Voters are reflecting these attitudes at the polling place. Fewer and fewer are casting straight party votes. More and more are splitting their tickets, voting Democratic for Congress and Republican for president; Republican for Congress and Democratic for Senate; for one party for national office and the other for local office (see Wattenberg 1989, 23; 1990b, 162–166; 1991; 1994; 1996).

Furthermore, fewer and fewer voters claim strong allegiance to one party or the other (see *Public Perspective* 1997). The point is not that voters are alienated from the two parties, but rather that they are ambivalent toward the parties. Martin Wattenberg believes we are seeing a **dealignment** in American politics, a time in which citizen attachment to party is declining and the relevance of party for the vote has been greatly reduced (Wattenberg 1990a; 1991; 1994; 1996). Wattenberg (1991) notes that the concept of "dealignment" was first raised by Inglehart and Hochstein (1972) but that their discussion was preceded by two years by Walter Dean Burnham's (1970) discussion of "electoral disaggregation" and the "onward march of party decomposition." The term "dealignment," in the sense described first by Burnham, has become more commonly used.

DEALIGNMENT

The concept that citizens, instead of shifting their allegiance from one party to the other, have dropped allegiance to any political party and are more susceptible to election-to-election appeals.

It should be noted, however, that the consensus with which political scientists and journalists described the rise and composition of the New Deal coalition of the 1930s through the 1950s has not been matched in descriptions of the electorate in recent decades. Warren Miller (1998, 118–122; 1990; Miller and Shanks 1996, 163–165 and elsewhere), for instance, argues persuasively that partisanship remains strong among *voters* and that the trend toward dealignment appears most strongly among those who opt not to vote. He also notes generational changes (Miller 1990; 1994; 1998). Miller contends that the movement might be toward nonalignment among a new cohort of voters more than dealignment among those who already had exhibited party allegiance.

During the Reagan years, a large number of analyses, again by both political scientists and journalists, discussed a Reagan-led realignment, focusing at times on national trends and at other times on geographic and/or demographic trends (Edsall 1988; MacKuen, Erikson, and Stimson 1989; Norpoth 1987; Petrocik 1987; 1989; Petrocik and Steeper 1987; Schneider 1988). More recently the discussion has centered around **divided government** rather than realignment as the paradigm for understanding American government (Jacobson 1990; Cox and Kernell 1991; Mayhew 1991; Brady 1993; Fiorina 1996). Divided government refers to a pattern of governing in which one party controls one branch of government and the other party controls the other branch. This pattern has been common and often noted at the national level since the election of Dwight Eisenhower in 1952; Fiorina (1996) comments that it is a common pattern in an increasing number of states as well. The argument put forth is that divided government is not a random pattern but rather a willful one, in which citizens choose not to have the government all in the hands of one party.

DIVIDED GOVERNMENT

Description of a period in which one political party controls one elected branch of the government and the other political party controls the other elected branch.

The original discussions of critical elections and realignments, and the more recent discussions of divided government, grow out of the extensive literature on voting behavior, which I will discuss in chapter 5. At this point, however, it is important to put this discussion in the context of party development. Analysts agree that allegiance to political party originates with the ways in which the dominant parties respond to critical events, for example, the Civil War and the Great Depression. These allegiances are strongest in the generation that experienced those events and are passed on to later generations, though as the precipitating event fades further and further into distant memory, the allegiance itself becomes less and less strong.

At the national level, the last great event that "caused" partisan realignment happened nearly seventy years ago. Those who were young voters at the time of the Great Depression are today in their eighties or nineties; the youngest voters who can remember the Depression in any meaningful sense have reached retirement age. Their children are in their forties, and many of their grandchildren are voting. These "younger" voters' entire political experience has been with candidates using the modern campaign tools we noted above, appealing to the voters as individuals and not as representatives of political parties. It seems small wonder then that these voters respond to candidates, not parties. No event has drawn their allegiance to one party or the other; individual candidates have tailored campaigns to reach them.

Abundant evidence exists that a realignment has happened in the South in recent years (Abramson and Aldrich 1998; Abramowitz and Saunders 1998; Miller 1998; Frymer 1996; Glaser 1996; Jacobson 1996; 1998; Mattei 1996). Let's look at that realignment in these same terms. For much of the New Deal period, the South was an anomaly. Southern Democrats were conservative on a whole range of social issues. *Congressional Quarterly* annually computes a Conservative Coalition Support Score, measuring how often conservative Democrats (nearly all southerners) voted together with Republicans against a majority of the rest of the Democrats. Southern voters, nearly all of whom were white, were Democrats for a variety of reasons; but it is not too much of a stretch to say that this allegiance dated back to the Civil War and Reconstruction and was unaffected by the issues that lead to realignments in the rest of the nation in the 1890s and again in the 1930s. It is also accurate to say that the Republican party, as an ongoing organization that ran candidates and claimed the allegiance of a significant number of voters, did not exist in much of the South during the first decades of the New Deal party system.

But in the case of the South there has been a significant change, a change wrought by the civil rights movement. The presidential election of 1948 can be seen as a precursor of this change. In that campaign, southern Democrats walked out of their party's national convention in protest over the party platform plank on civil rights; South

Carolina governor Strom Thurmond, then a Democrat, ran for president under the label of the States' Rights party throughout the South and won enough states to garner thirty-nine electoral votes. At the presidential level, the South never returned to the Democratic party as a monolithic bloc. But for state and local offices, Democratic loyalties remained strong for two more decades.

In the case of the South, a realignment that occurred in the 1960s was precipitated by certain critical events: the lunch counter sit-ins that began in Greensboro, North Carolina, in 1960; the freedom rides in 1961; the forced integration of the state universities of Mississippi in 1962 and of Alabama in 1963; the protests in Birmingham, Alabama, and other southern cities; Martin Luther King's march on Washington, which was the stage for his powerful "I Have a Dream" speech in 1963; and the march from Selma to Montgomery, Alabama, in 1965. Responses by political leaders to those events included passage of the Civil Rights Act of 1964, which prohibited discrimination in employment and in public accommodations and penalized educational systems that discriminated against minorities. Also of great impact was the Voting Rights Act of 1965, which protected the voting rights of blacks by outlawing literacy tests and other methods of keeping blacks from voting (Weisbrot 1990). Those events accelerated a redefinition of voting allegiances among southern voters. Black voters registered and voted in numbers unseen before (see chap. 4). White voters began to look for conservative Republican alternatives. But they had difficulty finding them below the presidential level because the Republican party as an organization was so moribund throughout the South that they ran few credible candidates for any office.

In 1964, when virtually all of Barry Goldwater's electoral votes came from southern states, none of his fellow Republicans were serving as governor in a southern state, none was elected to the U.S. Senate, and only 17 of 106 representatives elected to the House from the South were Republicans. The Republican state legislator in the South was a rare breed indeed (Bullock and Brady 1983). By 1996, however, the picture had radically changed. The Republican party organization was flourishing throughout the South. After the 1996 election, eight of the eleven southern governors were Republicans. Eight of the ten senators up for reelection from the South in that year were Republicans; all were reelected. Of the 125 southerners elected to the House in that election, 71 were Republicans. Republican strength in state legislatures throughout the South reached new post-Reconstruction peaks.

It is difficult to argue, therefore, that the South has not realigned in recent decades. And some of the changes at the national level are a reflection of the change in this one region. For instance, if the Democrats still held all of the southern seats in Congress that they held in the 1960s or early 1970s, they would control the Congress and we would not have had divided government under the Clinton administration.

The current party system is a competitive one throughout the nation. No longer does one region stand apart from the politics that concerns the rest of the voters. These themes will be pursued further in later chapters.

VIII. POLITICIANS VIEW POLITICAL HISTORY

Two seemingly distinct strands have been interwoven in this brief history of the development of American political parties. One strand has been the traditional outline of American party systems. These are summarized in table 2.1. These party systems are defined by the lines of cleavage, the "issue clusters," that divide the political parties. Politicians understand these lines of division. They "cause" them by responding to problems facing the government in one way or another. They "respond" to them—often in their younger years—by joining one coalition or another. But they do not spend much time thinking about them. Does anyone think that many senators really care when our last realigning election was? How many members of Congress are concerned over why the second party system collapsed, or even whether the fifth party system is still intact? These concepts are important from an analytical point of view (and they do have practical consequences), but surely they are not the stuff of which politics is made.

The second strand running through this history has signaled systemic changes in a broader sense. What rules structure the political contest? How are political campaigns run? How do these areas relate to political parties? At times such changes have occurred while elec-

Table 2.1 Realigning Elections

	1860	*1896*	*1932*
Original parties	Whigs v Democrats	Republicans v Democrats	Republicans v Democrats
Issues	Slavery	Gold standard (economic)	Government involvement in domestic economic affairs
Third parties	Liberty party Free Soilers Conscience Whigs Cotton Whigs Barnburners Hunkers	Populists Greenbacks	League for Independent Political Actions
Resulting parties	Republicans v Democrats	Republicans v Democrats	Republicans v Democrats

toral coalitions were changing. Thus the second party system was different from the first both in terms of electoral coalitions and in terms of how political contests were fought. At other times systemic changes have taken place while electoral coalitions have remained intact; this was the case with the reformers of the Progressive era.

Practical politicians are aware of and very concerned about this aspect of electoral history. Even senators who neither knew nor cared about our last realigning election were all aware of the changes in campaign techniques, of what worked and what did not in the last election, *and of the impact these changes are having on political parties.* Members of Congress who could never define the fifth party system all know about the Republican advantage over the Democrats in the use of computerized mail for fund-raising; they also know what effect eliminating soft money for political parties will have on their campaigns (see chap. 11). These are not abstract questions to them. Patrick Kennedy (D-R.I.) wants to know how much money the Democratic Congressional Campaign Committee (DCCC), which he chairs, can raise, particularly in comparison to the Republicans. He wants to know how to get "ahead of the curve" on use of the Internet, to set new strategies for using new techniques, not to respond to them. Kennedy did not assume leadership of the DCCC because he is a political technician but because he understands how important it is to apply new techniques to congressional campaigns if his party is to reclaim the majority status it lost in 1994. And, of course, he was chosen in part at least because of his ability to raise money for Democratic candidates.

Joel Silbey (1990; 1991; 1998) has analyzed the history of American political parties in terms different from those discussed above. Silbey claims that American political history can be divided into four periods, distinguished by the importance of the role of political parties.

The justification for arranging American political history in this way grows out of the different kinds of political institutions, norms, and behavior that have *predominated* in each era. Thus, although two parties have always been on the scene, only once—from 1838 to 1893—did parties totally dominate the American political landscape (Silbey 1990, 4).

The period from the 1790s until the 1830s was a period of party development, but parties really did not predominate in electoral politics; in fact, they were resisted by many in politics. This was the preparty period (Formisano 1974). The period from the 1830s until the 1890s was one in which parties did dominate American politics (Silbey 1991). From the 1890s until the 1950s, parties were on the decline; this was the postparty period. And, according to Silbey, the most recent decades have been marked by candidate-centered politics; this is the nonparty period.

The intertwining of the strands discussed above and the separate analysis by Silbey is crucial. One learns from history. How politicians respond to systemic changes will determine the shape of politics in the years ahead. Those responses will determine whether we are indeed entering an era of politics without parties (as Silbey believes), whether the fifth party system will revive, or whether we will enter a sixth party system, and, if so, what its new shape might be. Throughout the rest of the book these questions will recur. How is the American political system responding to the changes it is undergoing? (See Maisel 1990c, 1998; Green and Shea 1996; Herrnson 1988; Sabato 1988).

Politicians are fond of recalling the names of the heroes from their party's past. "The party of Lincoln" does not forget its first successful presidential candidate—although Republicans rarely evoke the memory of Harding, Hoover, or Nixon. The names of Franklin D. Roosevelt, Harry Truman, and John Kennedy roll off Democratic politicians' tongues like marbles from a table—although Lyndon Johnson is mentioned somewhat less frequently. How many times have we all seen the picture of a teenaged Bill Clinton shaking hands with his hero and role model, President John Kennedy? But these evocations of the political past are purely rhetorical, and they should be treated as such. The true importance of the history of the great American political parties relates to the roles they have played in shaping electoral contests, in defining issues, in gaining voter allegiance, in governing—and in whether or not they can adapt to new political techniques, to a changing political system, and can continue to do so.

WEBSITES

http://www.library.advanced.org/12587/contents/parties/index.html

A list of any and all political parties throughout American history, including the Federalist, Whig, Free Soil, and all others. The site gives a history of each party, how and why it originated, its fundamental beliefs, major opposition, and links to important figures in each party.

http://www.abebooks.cm/home/HOOKEDONHISTORY/

Links to historical books, including those about the history of political parties.

http://www.usis-israel.org.il/publish/elections/bibby.htm

A history and background of U.S. political parties by John Bibby of the University of Wisconsin.

http://library.advanced.org/12587/contents/background/index.html

Detailed guide to the history of American politics—how American society has changed politics, and vice versa.

http://www.gallaudet.edu/~dpenna/Parties1.html

Political Parties: Definition and Evolution—briefly defines political parties, gives an account of their evolution, and lists roles they play in society.

KEY CONCEPTS

civil service system
congressional caucus
converting elections
"corrupt bargain"
critical election
dealignment
deviating elections
direct primary elections
divided government
electoral vote
factions
Farmers' Alliance
Federalist party
Free Soil party
Granger movement
Jeffersonian (or Democratic) Republicans
Liberty party
line of cleavage
maintaining elections
national convention
New Deal coalition
nonpartisan elections
political machine
popular vote
Populists
Progressive era
realigning elections
realignments
Republican party
secular realignment
spoils system
Voting Rights Act of 1965
Whigs

DISCUSSION QUESTIONS

1. Can you think of any issues that are so important to citizens today that they could divide the country in a critical election? What do you think would cause an issue to reach that level of importance?
2. Why do you think that today's politicians recall the past heroes of their parties so often? What relevance does that part of history have to them or to their audience?
3. Do you think that the politics of today is so fundamentally different from that of earlier eras that analyzing our electoral process using this same concepts, for example, party systems, critical elections, is of only limited use? Or do you think that there are lessons we all can learn about commonalities between earlier eras and our own?
4. Critical elections of the past have revolved around pressing issues of the day. In 1992 H. Ross Perot tried to make dissatisfaction with the way today's politicians were handling the business of governing a central issue in an election that would see the emergence of a new party. Why didn't his appeal work?

CHAPTER 3

Party Organization

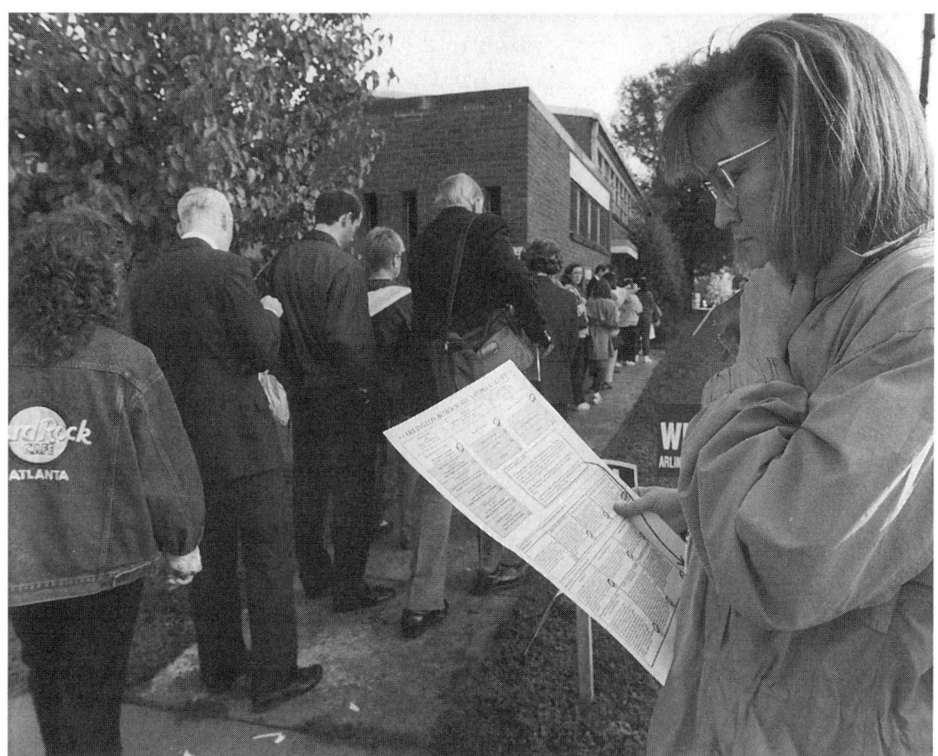

NATIONAL COMMITTEES
The pinnacle of the national party organizations, comprised of delegates from the states and from groups important to the political parties.

POLITICAL BOSSES
Derogatory characterization of the leaders of a local party organizations.

After the 1998 congressional elections, Republican party leaders expressed dissatisfaction with the job done by the chairman of the Republican National Committee, Jim Nicholson of Colorado. A number of state party leaders felt he should be replaced by another chair, preferably someone from the South. However, after intense lobbying and politicking, Nicholson was reelected. But then, you knew that, right? You follow the politics of the two **national committees** closely. Not!

What do you think of when you think of a "party organization"? **Political bosses**? City machines? Politicians? Are they all alike? Is the picture one of strength or of weakness? A modern office or a smoke-filled backroom? Or is there no picture?

These images are a metaphor for the problem involved in discussing party organization. We are tempted to ignore the subject; no one likes to discuss party organization. After all, the "real" party organizations—at least for those who conjure up images of big-city machines, local clubhouses as a hub of social life, and the like—went out of existence years ago. But modern party organizations exist, and they play an important and evolving role in the political process.

Recall the definition of political party developed in chapter 1. It said, in part, that "political parties are organizations, however loosely organized." The goal of this chapter is to describe the organizational aspects of political parties. We will begin with a road map, looking at different kinds of organizations and the formal relationships among them. Then we will turn to separate examinations of various types of organizations.

I. THE ORGANIZATIONAL FRAMEWORK

In the simplest terms, the organizational framework for political parties mirrors the geographic organization of the United States. That is, parties begin at the very local level and eventually emerge at the national level. However, specifying that structure says nothing about the relationships among the various parts. Party organization becomes clearer if one recalls that these organizations came into existence in order to help with election campaigns. Therefore, the organizational charts essentially parallel the ways in which elected offices are distributed across the country. It is interesting to note, however, that some elected officials represent areas for which there is no preexisting governmental unit, often because of mandated redistricting after each census. For example, congressional districts often cross city or even county lines. As a result, no party organizational structure necessarily parallels these districts.

A central feature of American political life has always involved decentralization. Political organization begins in the neighborhood. Generally, people who live in the same neighborhood vote in the same place. These polling places define precincts, the most local organizational level in American politics. In rural areas, frequently all the people in a town vote in one place; the town then is the functional equivalent of the precinct. Party organization begins at this level.

While the most local level of political organization is the precinct, many observers agree that the county is the more important level of party organization. Again, this significance follows from the fact that the county is the organizing unit for most governmental offices. Counties, of course, elect their own governments—and these governments often control jobs. While it is often more important than local organization, county party organizations are derived from the local level; that is, county committee members represent local units, reflecting the decentralized nature of the entire system.

Party organization at the state level parallels that at the county level. Each major political party has a central committee in each of the fifty states. Committee members are typically chosen by delegates to county (or sometimes congressional district) conventions. In some states, state committee members are elected in primary elections. Each state committee has a slate of officers. State chairs tend to be significant political figures in their states, and occasionally at the national level.

At the pinnacle of the party organizational hierarchy are the two national committees and the two **national chairs**. The two national committees do not directly parallel each other in composition (see section IV below); however, in each case representatives to the national committee come from the state committees and from others in the states. The national chairs are chosen by the committees, often with direct input from presidential candidates, particularly successful candidates. At mid-century, the seminal study of the parties' national committees was aptly entitled *Politics without Power* (Cotter and Hennessey 1964). Today the national parties play a prominent role in funding the activities of their constituent parts; national committees' supplying operating capital to state and local organizations implies power flowing in a way unthought of even twenty-five years ago.

NATIONAL CHAIRS

The heads of the national committees, charged with the day-to-day functioning of the national parties.

Despite the increased influence of the national (or central) party organizations over their geographically disbursed subunits, it still makes sense to look at parties as the decentralized bodies that their organizational structures define. The sections below describe the various types of party organizations and the patterns that exist in the relationships among them.

National party chairs whose party controls the White House, usually referred to as "in-party" chairs, speak for the president on party matters; "out-party" chairs tend to play a more independent role. While politicians and political analysts would agree that the chairs of the two national committees are important political figures, few of us would recognize Jim Nicholson, whom I mentioned at the beginning of this chapter, or Roy Romer, his counterpart at the Democratic National

Committee, if they stood in front of us in a line. Their influence is with other politicians and perhaps as spokespersons for their parties, but not as politicians who command the public's attention.

STRATARCHY

Description of the structure of party organization that implies that each level is a stratum separate and distinct from each other level.

Technically the national committees are at the pinnacle of party organizational hierarchy, but that status does not reflect relationships among these organizational units. Writing more than three decades ago, Samuel Eldersveld (1964) described party organization as a **stratarchy**, implying that each organizational level occupied a separate strata, distinct from the others. Connections existed across the various strata, but the organizations really coexisted under a code of "mutual deference." While Eldersveld based his conclusions on a study of political organization in the Detroit area in the 1960s, many felt it possible to generalize from this picture of the relationship among political organizational units.

PARTY REFORMS

The efforts to change the rules and proceedings of the political parties to make them more democratic and

SOFT MONEY

Money raised for political purposes that it outside of the constraints specified under the Federal Election Campaign Act, unregulated money not to be used directly for federal campaigns.

The picture seems less accurate in the 1990s. Many observers have noted the "nationalization" of party organizations, that is, more influence from the national level and less local color painting the organizational picture (Herrnson 1998; Bibby 1998). Variations exist within that pattern. Democratic **party reforms** in the presidential nominating process have nationalized party rules to a great extent (see chap. 10). Republicans have not followed this pattern and allow much more local autonomy; in fact, they favor autonomous local organizations as a matter of principle. However, the most significant change in the last decade has involved funding of party activities. For some time the Republicans have funded many of their state and local efforts with funds raised at the national level; the Democrats have emulated this pattern, though with less success. Still, in the most recent national elections, many state-level activities have been coordinated from the national level and funded with **soft money**, raised in Washington but spent throughout the land (see chap. 10).

II. LOCAL AND COUNTY ORGANIZATIONS

LOCAL PARTY ORGANIZATIONS

The level of party organization, composed of precinct and ward leaders, that is geographically closest to the voters; in age of strong parties such organizations were cemented together by material incentives controlled by powerful leaders.

The heyday of strong party organizations lasted roughly from the 1870s until the end of World War II (Mayhew 1986). Most frequently when muckrakers berated the political machines and the corrupt political bosses, they were criticizing **local party organizations**. And those bosses and their machines were legendary—Boss William Marcy Tweed of New York City's Tammany Hall, depicted as the very stereotype of a corrupt political boss in Thomas Nast's famous cartoons in *Harper's Weekly* in the 1870s; Frank Hague of Jersey City, New Jersey, and the four O'Connell brothers of Albany, New York, dominant bosses in their homes for most of the first half of this century; James Michael Curley of Boston, the engaging rogue on whom Edwin O'Connor patterned *The Last Hurrah*; Tom Pendergast of Kansas City,

Missouri, a local boss who started the career of President Harry Truman; Ed Crump of Memphis, Tennessee; Anton Cermak, Pat Nash, and Richard Daley of Chicago, Illinois. The list goes on and on. Their stories are the stuff of legend. (See Mayhew 1986; Steinberg 1972.)

The picture of these political machines is clear. Each had a dominant leader, the political boss. Each was organized as a structured hierarchy, with ward leaders beholden to the boss, precinct leaders beholden to their ward leader, and those who worked the streets beholden to those organizing the precinct. The glue that held these machines together was **material incentives**, tangible rewards for work well done (and the withdrawal of those rewards if the work was not done). **Patronage** jobs were the reward for electoral success. Aid—to the newly arrived immigrant, the unemployed, or the underemployed—ensured loyalty to the machine. The machines were also important socializing elements, helping immigrants adjust to American society; interpersonal ties added to the binding of followers to their party leaders. The names given to the organization leaders spoke wonders—the boss, the ward heeler, the precinct captain. Friends were rewarded and enemies were punished. Winners advanced; losers fell by the wayside. Results were what mattered, and methods were rarely questioned. The machine era was marked by charges of corruption and attempts at reform. The charges were not without foundation in many cases, and reformers succeeded only when party organizations strayed too far from accepted norms. These seventy-five years marked a time of colorful, if corrupt, politics in America (Banfield and Wilson 1963; Bridges 1984; Erie 1988; Rakove 1975; Riordan 1963; Tolchin and Tolchin 1971; Wilson 1973).

MATERIAL INCENTIVES

Tangible rewards for work well done.

PATRONAGE

Jobs or other material incentives given to party campaign workers after a successful election.

But a word of caution is in order. Even at their height, organized machine politics did not dominate all of American politics. About two-thirds of the largest American cities had some sort of political machine during at least part of this period. But they did not all exist at the same time, and they did not all maintain the same level of dominance. And many areas of the country were never under machine dominance. As David Mayhew (1986) has observed, machine politics was much more likely to exist in those states that had been settled by the beginning of the second party system, the Jacksonian party system, when the spoils system—"to the victor go the spoils"—came into existence. The spoils system established a base and gave rise to a political culture that persisted for some time. But other areas never followed suit. And surely, by the last quarter of the twentieth century, traditional political machines had been changed not only by new moralities but also by new styles of politics and political communications.

What then is the nature of political organization in the roughly 190,000 precincts in the 3,000 counties in the United States today? In terms of structure, that question is easy to answer. Towns or precincts are politically organized as town or precinct committees, with chairs and other officers. Theoretically, each political party has a committee at this level. But in practice, a wide variety is the norm. At the precinct or town level, organization is often minimal. Each party would like to have a functioning organization in each local precinct. But in actuality, if the parties can have a name on paper—a possible contact person who is interested—that is often a bonus. Do not try to look your local precinct committee up in the telephone book. Don't try to find its office. Throughout most of America, precinct or town committees "work" out of the kitchen of the committee's leader. One person—or sometimes a couple of people—has an interest in organizing the area for the political party he or she favors. That person then becomes the foundation of an organization; he or she attracts friends; the committee members communicate with other organizations; they work with candidates and help on campaigns. These people are not "politicians" in any meaningful sense of the word. They are citizens interested in politics.

It was not always that way, and it is not the same in every neighborhood even today. In the days of the classic political machine, precinct leaders were men (almost never women) deeply involved in politics. They frequently held patronage jobs, jobs that depended on their delivering votes. Precinct committees were active and vibrant; the clubhouse was a social center for the lives of many in the neighborhood. Politics was a critically important part of the lives of those who worked for the government—because their livelihood depended on the outcome of elections. Even today in a few urban centers with strong party organizations and patronage available to elected leaders, most notably in Chicago but to a lesser extent in other cities, precinct leaders, often called precinct captains, remain active and committed. (See Banfield and Wilson 1963; Gosnell 1939; Tolchin and Tolchin 1971.)

According to the structural model, in larger urban areas, members of precinct committees elect representatives to serve on ward committees. Wards are simply groupings of precincts. Often city council members are elected by ward. Thus an obvious connection exists between the organizing unit for the government and the political unit. Ward organizations are more active in those areas in which the political stakes are higher, for example, those in which politicians elected at the ward level have favors to confer. But it is rare that both parties have ongoing organizations within the same area; more often one party or the other dominates and maintains an ongoing organizational presence while the other struggles to remain viable.

RECRUITMENT

Effort by party officials to find candidates to run for various offices.

On the other hand, each party is organized, at least at some level, in most counties. County organizations tend to have formal rules and officers. One of the jobs of these officers is **recruitment** of candidates for county offices and leaders for precinct politics; part of their success is measured by their ability to fill these slots. County committees and county chairs are usually elected by meetings of the party faithful; in large part they are self-selected, with real competition a rarity. County leaders are mostly volunteers, and few officers are paid. Only the very wealthiest county organizations maintain a paid staff or a permanent headquarters.

But county organization remains an important building block in the overall party structure. Many officials are elected at the county level; what few patronage jobs remain in the nation are often county jobs. State legislative districts often fall within county lines. Furthermore, counties tend to be large enough that a "critical mass" of active politicians can form. Thus county committees, typically formed by elections from precinct, town, or ward committees, are often much more politically active than more local units. County chairs are often important political leaders, men (again, infrequently women) of influence with politicians in an area.

County organizations are most active during the campaign season. The most active and "professional" county organizations work year-round, building local organizations, recruiting desirable (or discouraging undesirable) candidates, and raising money. But during campaign season, activity heats up for all these organizations. They help register voters, work on get-out-the-vote drives, and coordinate field campaigns for all the candidates running within their jurisdiction. County committees focus their activities on candidates for local office or on local candidates for state office. These men and women are known commodities; many volunteer activists are involved because of their connections with individual candidates. Many of the candidates are themselves active in the organization. This kind of activity is the politics of the **grassroots**, the bread and butter of local politics. These party volunteers make it possible for local candidates to run credible campaigns, to distribute literature, and to woo voters.

GRASSROOTS
The rank-and-file voters or party members.

How important are these activities in the age of modern campaigns, with polling, television, computers, and relatively little grassroots campaigning (see chaps. 8, 10)? Two answers seem apparent. First, many races are far from "new style" campaigns. Often local candidates cannot afford the cost of modern campaigning, and their campaigns remain labor-intensive efforts. They still rely heavily on the foot soldiers of American politics—the organizational volunteers at the precinct and county levels.

Second, a good deal of evidence points to the conclusion that strong party organizations do indeed contribute to larger numbers of votes for the party (Bibby and Holbrook 1996; Frendeis, Gibson, and Vertz 1990; Gibson 1991). Party organizations help coordinate the various campaigns in an area. National parties have seen this kind of activity as important enough to fund much of it in many areas during presidential election years. By pooling resources (and because the national organizations have funded coordinated campaigns in local areas), political activity of this type allows some local candidates who could not otherwise afford to do so make use of modern campaign technology and thus improve their campaigns.

More important in this context is the role that party organizations play even before the campaign begins. Stronger party organizations are clearly better at recruiting candidates. Frendeis and colleagues (1990) demonstrate that slates of candidates are more likely to be full in those counties with actively functioning party organizations. If slates are not full, that is, if a party has no one running for certain offices, by definition voters cannot express support for that party's candidates. When this recruitment function is added to the more traditional grassroots roles that party organization plays, the total impact of a strong organization on vote totals—while not overwhelming—is still significant.

For local party organization to be successful, first, the organization must have a solid base. Grassroots politics is about people, and people need incentives to participate. Without the material incentives most often connected with patronage jobs, fewer and fewer people are becoming involved in local politics. The primary goal for those interested in maintaining organizational strength then involves energizing the activists and recruiting the volunteers.

Second, organizations need resources to do the work of politics: money remains high on the list of needed resources. In recent years the national parties have recognized this need and have seen that satisfying it meets their objectives as well. In presidential election years each party has invested millions of dollars in local and county organizations (see table 3.1). The Republicans particularly have set a real goal of building organization at the local level. Local party organizations will continue to seek and define new roles for themselves in an emerging political reality in the years ahead, but the importance of local connection to voters can never be denied.

III. STATE PARTY ORGANIZATIONS

Most casual observers cannot distinguish one level of political organization from another. And they don't spend much time thinking about any level of organization. Who is the chair of the Democratic state committee in your home state? Of the Republican state committee? Can you name any state committee members? What do they do? Where do they meet? What difference would it make if they did not exist?

A. The Age of Strong State Party Organizations

SENATORIAL COURTESY

The right of any U.S. senator to veto (and as a practical matter to approve) any appointee from that senator's state if the appointment requires senatorial confirmation.

Such cloudiness was not always so. In the early years of the twentieth century, state party organizations mattered. Generally the organization of the dominant party in a state was headed by one of its two U.S. senators. Why would a senator care about party organization? You must remember the political context of the time. First, **senatorial courtesy**

Table 3.1 Nonfederal Accounts of National Party Committees, 1995–1996

Democratic Party	*Transfers to State Party Organizations*	*Transfers to State and Local Candidates*	*Share of Joint Activity*	*Other*
National Committee	$54,193,497	$318,684	$27,592,503	$18,379,293
Democratic Senatorial Campaign Committee	$5,859,770	$3,049,918	$2,385,324	$2,766,261
Democratic Congressional Campaign Committee	$4,545,199	$1,070,500	$3,313,879	$2,893,212
Total	$64,598,466	$4,439,102	$33,291,706	$24,038,766

Republican Party	*Transfers to State Party Organizations*	*Transfers to State and Local Candidates*	*Share of Joint Activity*	*Other*
National Committee	$48,218,708	$1,349,882	$40,325,732	$24,507,651
Republican National Senatorial Committee	$1,641,800	$3,015,371	$7,668,704	$17,036,778
Republican National Congressional Committee	$385,000	$834,500	$9,180,754	$18,346,625
Total	$50,245,508	$5,199,753	$57,175,190	$59,891,054

Source: Federal Election Commission.

gave majority-party senators control of most federal patronage in their state at the time. Put simply, the practice of senatorial courtesy meant that if a senator in the president's party objected to an appointment, the other senators would refuse to confirm the prospective appointee. The existence of this potential veto thus made it possible for senators to determine who in their state would get federal appointments. Thus the material incentives to cement a party organization, at least those that emanated from Washington, were controlled by this particular senator.

SEVENTEENTH AMENDMENT

The amendment to the U.S. Constitution that calls for the direct election of U.S. senators; prior to its adoption in 1913, senators had been appointed by state legislatures.

Second, U.S. senators were appointed by state legislatures, not elected by the people, until the passage of the **Seventeenth Amendment** to the Constitution, which was passed in 1912 and ratified in 1913 as part of the Progressive agenda. Thus senators were motivated to involve themselves with state legislative politics, at the very least to assure their party the majority status that would lead to their own reelection.

Some of these senator-bosses were as powerful and almost as legendary as the urban machine leaders mentioned above—Republicans Simon Cameron, Matthew Quay, and Boies Penrose of Pennsylvania, Thomas Platt of New York, and Stephen B. Elkins of West Virginia; Democrats Arthur Pue Gorman of Maryland and Thomas Martin of Virginia. The power of state organizations seemed to wane after World War I, but some notable exceptions persisted—the Democratic machine begun by Huey Long and continued by his heirs in Louisiana, Eugene Talmadge's Democratic organization in Georgia,[1] and the Republican organization headed by J. Henry Roraback and the Democratic organization controlled by John M. Bailey, both of Connecticut.[2]

For a period of time, however, state party organizations seemed ready to disappear not only from public view but also from any place of significance in the political process (Key 1956). State party committees were largely shadow organizations, their only possible function being to serve the will and the cause of a few elected politicians. In the last quarter century, however, in terms of their role in the political system and the interest of political analysts, state-level organizations have made a remarkable comeback (Cotter, Gibson, Bibby, and Huckshorn 1984 1989; Huckshorn 1976).[3]

B. The Structure of State Committees

State party central committees operate for both parties in each of the fifty states; generally the means of choosing state party committee members is set by state law. In twenty-seven states, state committee members are chosen by other activists—by committee members at more local levels or delegates to state, congressional district, or county conventions. In fourteen other states, party rules determine the manner of selection, and again election by other party activists is the norm. In the remaining nine states voters choose state committee members in primary elections.

All of these means of selection are significant. Those who favor strong party organizations, such as the bipartisan Committee for Party Renewal (Epstein 1991; Mileur 1991), feel that the state should interfere as little as possible with the internal workings of political parties. Furthermore, party activists can, of course, have more to say about the direction toward which they chart organizational activity if they themselves select their leaders. That is, the further that selection of state committee members is removed from the public—though not from public view or accountability—the more likely it is that party leaders will maintain a firm hold on state committee priorities.

State committees vary in size from relatively few to several hundred members. Some operate as committees of the whole; others have strong executive committees. Some meet with relative frequency; others only a few times a year, especially in nonelection years. State committees usually have formal responsibility for calling party conventions, and they often choose some members of the state's delegation to national nominating conventions as well. In reality these decision are often made by paid party officials in consultation with elected party leaders. These committees are continuously engaged in fund-raising efforts for the support of party candidates throughout the state.

All these formal duties were in place during the period of state party organization decline and have not changed in the ascendancy. But two other factors have changed: the role of the state party chair and the role of the state party headquarters. In a very real sense the most important function of state committees has become to elect the state party chair and then (as individual members who are themselves influential political figures in their home communities, not so much as a committee) to support the state chair and the headquarters staff in the initiatives that they put forth.

C. The Role of the State Party Chair

Robert Huckshorn (1976, chap. 4) has developed a now familiar categorization of the types of party leadership exercised by party chairs. His categorization relates to the role played by the state chair, regardless of the formal means by which that leader was selected. About three quarters of the state chairs are chosen by the committees they lead; the remainder are elected at state conventions. But the choice and the role played are reflections of political realities well beyond the means of selection.

An **out-party independent** is a state party chair whose party does not control the governorship. Frequently these men (again infrequently women) are important politicians in their own right, elected from their own political base and serving as spokespersons and leaders for a party with few comparably placed politicians in the state.

OUT-PARTY INDEPENDENT

Chair of a state party committee whose party does not control the governorship and who therefore can act as a free agent.

Most state party chairs serving while their party is in control of the

POLITICAL AGENTS

State party chairs whose actions for the most part are at the behest of governors of their party.

governorship are classified as **political agents** of the governor. Many of these state chairs have had political careers tied closely to the incumbent chief executive; they have managed his or her campaign or have served the governor (or with the governor in another capacity). The state chair is frequently the governor's choice for that position. Power and influence flow to the state chair as a result of ties to the governor; the role of the state chair is to mold the party machinery to meet the governor's best interest. Some political agent–state chairs are highly visible and reputedly powerful political figures; others are obscure party technicians. But their goal remains the same: to serve the governor.

IN-PARTY INDEPENDENT

State party chairs who act without regard to the views of the governor, even though the governor is a member of their own party.

The third leadership style for state party chairs is the **in-party independent**. These leaders come to office in a variety of ways. Depending on the timing of the selection of the state party chair, they may well be in office before the governor is elected, perhaps even as a supporter of someone who has opposed the winning governor for nomination. Party rules do not require state chairs to resign if the candidate they support loses; norms for remaining in this position vary from state to state. More frequently in this age of personalized campaigning, governors have shown little interest in the state party chair (thus permitting state committees to select their own leaders) because the governor has his or her own, totally independent, campaign organization. In still other cases state party chairs serve for longer periods of time, remaining in office even though the governorship changes hands and, more seriously, the other party takes control. In any of these instances the state party chair and the committee work separately from the governor. The strength of the leader depends on his or her ability to run an organization that has a significant impact on the electoral process.

No matter how they are chosen, state party chairs must fulfill certain responsibilities. They must lead the state committee that they head, developing a relationship with its members, defining tasks that they can accomplish, and setting goals toward which they can strive. The chairs must also be a link to the grassroots—the county and local organizations. Effective chairs know that coordinated organizational effort results in more support for party candidates. But coordination among individuals, each with his or her own stake and priority, is not easy to achieve. State party leaders spend a good deal of time mending fences and stroking individuals with easily bruised egos. The third responsibility for the state chairs—and the one that has led to their increasingly important role in the electoral process—is to maintain and direct an increasingly complex and involved state headquarters. It is the state headquarters and the staff of the state headquarters, whose roles nominally are to support the state committee but who in fact are the engine that drives whatever gets done, that define the success or failure, the power or impotency of state organization.

D. The Ascendancy of the State Party Headquarters

Data on state party headquarters size and staff are difficult to come by for all but the most recent years. Surely state party machines of the pre–World War I period had headquarters and workers on a payroll. But for many years, from the administration of Franklin Roosevelt through that of Dwight Eisenhower, little was heard from or known about what went on in state headquarters.

The rejuvenation of state headquarters seems to have begun in the early 1960s. At that time only a few state chairs occupied full-time paid positions; as many as half of the state committees (far more for the Republicans than the Democrats) employed full-time professional staff members. By 1990, however, approximately 30 percent of the state chairs were paid for working full-time for the party; nearly every state party was administered by either a full-time paid chair or a full-time paid executive director or both. Whereas once the headquarters of the state committee "traveled" from city to city as the hometown of the state chair changed, now virtually all state committees are housed in permanent headquarters, almost always in the state capital. Some of the headquarters contain the most up-to-date campaign technology, allowing for sophisticated campaigning for candidates for state and local office (Appleton and Ward 1996; Reichley 1992; Bibby 1990; 1998; Sabato 1988).

Concomitant with this strengthened presence has come a sizable increase in the budgets for state headquarters. Again, data are difficult to come by. However, the Party Transformation Study revealed that the average budget for state parties rose nearly five times (to nearly $300,000 annually) between 1961 and 1979. By 1984, the average had risen to nearly $350,000, with the largest state budgets reaching $2.5 million and with only a quarter of the party committees operating with budgets of less than $100,000. Jumps in the ensuing decade apparently have been even larger, with Florida's Republican state party having a reported budget of $6 million in 1988 (Biersack 1996, 115–122; Bibby 1990, 28; 1998, 32–33).

Professional staffs, permanent headquarters, and increased budgets are taken as measures of enhanced and reputedly more significant electoral activity. Huckshorn (1991, 1061–1063) has outlined ten separate kinds of activities carried on by various state party committees. Observers note, of course, that all state committees do not engage in all these activities. Variety among the political experiences in the American states is still one of the defining characteristics of our body politic. In the states in which one party or the other dominates (recall table 1.7), minority-party organization is not very well developed. The Republicans in strongly Democratic Mississippi, for example, are involved in relatively few of these activities. Still, the list is instructive to demonstrate the kinds of activities that organizations carry on when they are functioning effectively.

Five of the activities deal with supporting the development of the party itself. First, state parties are involved in significant fund-raising activities to support the budgets referred to previously. Professionally generated fund-raising is not free: donor lists have to be developed, computers maintained, telephone campaigns managed, large contributors involved, and the like. A number of state party organizations maintain full-time, paid fund-raising staffs to support these activities.

Second, parties are involved in various efforts to mobilize their electorate. This mobilization is a traditional party activity, but state headquarters are involved in more and more sophisticated ways of identifying potential voters, registering new voters, maintaining lists of party supporters, and getting out the vote on election day. Whereas once the files for local communities were kept on three-by-five cards in a precinct leader's kitchen drawer, now state headquarters maintain, update, and distribute computer-generated lists of potential supporters in every community in a state.

Third, state headquarters with larger budgets are also involved in public opinion polling for the entire state party ticket. These activities are particularly important to candidates for local office who cannot afford to pay for polling. Data provided by these polls are often not specific about how one particular candidate or another is doing, or how one campaign technique or another is working, but they do give general information about the mood of the electorate, reactions to statewide or national events, and the like.

Fourth, a number of state committees make an ongoing effort to be involved in issue development. State party platforms are normally written at state conventions, but throughout the political cycle issues change and new issues emerge. State party headquarters try to keep abreast of these developments, monitor how the party is doing on its platform pledges, and react to changing situations. Once again, individual state and local candidates and officeholders do not always have the sophistication to keep up with all emerging issues. The coordinated efforts of a state headquarters can be very helpful in this regard.

Fifth, the final activity relating to support of party development is the publication of a newsletter or the development of other means of assuring communication throughout the party. Most party committees publish newsletters that provide a good forum for the party chair and a means for party members to know what others are thinking.

Five other state party activities outlined by Huckshorn relate more directly to candidates for office. First, many parties are involved in recruiting candidates to run for office. One test of the strength of a state party organization is the extent to which it is able to fill the slate of candidates running for state legislature and other state offices. In 1990, Massachusetts Republicans pointed with pride to the fact that they competed for over three-quarters of the seats in the lower house of the state legislature and all but two state senate seats. That would not seem noteworthy except for the fact that only four years earlier 103 (of 160) Democratic candidates for state representative and 25 (of 42) Democratic candidates for state senate had faced no Republican opposition. (See chap. 8 for variation across states and within states over a period of years.)

Second, not only do state parties recruit some candidates for office, but in roughly half of the states, state party officials are involved in endorsing candidates before primary elections are held (see chap. 7). At times endorsement is a **decruitment** function, convincing prospective candidates for a nomination that they are likely to lose because the party will support someone else. State party officials involve themselves this way when they believe that one candidate would clearly be stronger in the general election or when they believe that a primary would so divide the party as to make the one who received the party endorsement a weaker candidate in the general election. At other times, parties use a formal or informal mechanism for stating their preference among candidates competing in a primary. Endorsement by a strong and effective party organization can have a great deal of impact because primaries are typically characterized by low voter turnout.[4]

DECRUITMENT
The effort of party officials to discourage an individual from seeking a particular party nomination.

Third, closely related to this endorsement function is the role that state parties play in selecting delegates to national nominating conventions. Democratic state party chairs (and the highest-ranking officer of the opposite gender) are automatically members of the Democratic National Committee and delegates to the national convention. While Republican rules are less formal, party leaders play an equally important role. In some states, in both parties, state committees select other delegates to national conventions. And in all states, in both parties, state leaders to varying degrees are able to influence how the other delegates are chosen and which individuals are selected.

Fourth, the final two activities are more directly related to candidate campaigning in the general election. State parties make financial contributions to individual candidates. Again, the variety of experiences among the states is wide. State party financial contributions are probably least significant for candidates running for statewide office because of the relatively small proportion of the large campaign budgets that state parties can give to candidates for statewide posts. They are most significant for campaigns with smaller campaign expenditures, e.g., campaigns for state representative.

Finally, state party headquarters provide a range of services for campaigns. Depending on the sophistication of the state headquarters, the state party supplies different types and levels of services for the party's candidates. Frequently because of economies of scale, because of their ability to piggyback with statewide campaigns, and because of their willingness to coordinate messages for all of a party's candidates, state headquarters can provide candidates with assistance in dealing with the media, designing paid advertising, complying with financial disclosure regulations, polling, developing issue positions, telephoning, distributing literature, identifying and turning out voters, and conducting other common campaign activities.

State party organizations have grown and developed in recent decades, in part at least because of an infusion of funds and influence from the national level. At the same time, state organizations stand as a cogent reminder of an organization's ability to adapt to a changing environment (Maisel 1998; Bibby 1998). Three decades ago candidates could safely ignore most state party organizations if they were interested in running for office. Analysts could be ignorant of the functioning of the state party and miss little of what was important in a state's politics. Neither is true today. More and more, state party organizations are vibrant and growing, commanding increased attention from those running for office and those analyzing their campaigns.

IV. Party Organization at the National Level

In 1964 Cotter and Hennessey called their important study of the two national committees *Politics without Power.* Their title aptly caught the significance of what went on at the two national committee offices. Politics was everywhere; politicians were everywhere; intrigue was everywhere. But no one cared. The national committees had no resources, they had no influence, and they had no power.

Nearly three decades later Paul Herrnson (1990b, 41) wrote that "national party organizations in the United States are now financially secure, institutionally stable, and highly influential." And he too aptly captured the aspect of politics that he was observing. Virtually every aspect of party organization has been transformed in recent years, but in no case is this change more apparent than in the national party organizations.

A. The Structure of National Party Organizations

HILL COMMITTEES

The name applied to the four party committees, one for each party in each house, charged with aiding candidates for Congress.

Cotter and Hennessey's book dealt with the two national committees. When analysts discuss the federal nature of the American party system, they are naturally led to the national committees, for these committees stand atop the organizational pyramid whose base is the precinct worker.[5] In the politics of the 1990s, however, party organization at the national level must involve the so-called **Hill committees**—the congressional and senatorial campaign committees of the two parties—as well.

1. The National Committees

The Democratic National Committee has existed continuously since 1848; the Republican National Committee since 1856. Each was structured as a means of coordinating national election campaigns. (For an exhaustive history of the national committees and their chairs in addition to Cotter and Hennessey 1964, see Goldman 1990.) Formation of the national committees was an important step in changing the parties from loose and totally autonomous confederations of state party activists to more federalized organizations with a unified purpose (Herrnson 1990b, 41-42). For the first century of their existence, the two national committees were involved principally with presidential elections. Only in recent decades has their role expanded.

Membership. The two national committees have some similarities and some differences. For example, each party is composed of representatives from the various states. However, the Republican National Committee (RNC) has normally followed a principle of equality among the states and has come to be composed of three representatives from each state: a national committeeman, a national committeewoman, and the state party chair.[6]

On the other hand, the Democratic National Committee (DNC) begins with state representation—a national committeeman and national committeewoman, the state chair, and the highest-ranking officer of the opposite gender from each state—and expands from there. Two hundred additional members are apportioned among the states according to a formula weighing population and Democratic vote in the last presidential election. Others are added ex officio because of positions they hold—the officers of the DNC (who need not otherwise qualify as members); three governors, including the chair of the Democratic Governors' Association; the party leaders in the House and Senate and an additional member of each body; representatives of the Young Democrats, the National Federation of Democratic Women, and Democratic mayors, county officials, and state legislators; and up to twenty other at-large members to accommodate groups still underrepresented.[7] The total membership of the DNC in 1990 had reached over four hundred members.

Executive committees. Obviously each committee is too large and unwieldy to work as an efficiently functioning body. Each meets only twice a year but has an executive committee that meets between full committee meetings and is, in actuality, the decision-making organization. The RNC's Executive Council includes eleven members, three appointed by the chair and eight elected from regional caucuses; in addition it has a number of ex officio members—the RNC officers and chairs of the various committees.[8] The DNC's Executive Committee is chosen in a way that reflects the constituent groups that constitute the full committee.

Chairs. Obviously, the most visible members of the two national committees are their chairs. Each chair and the other officers of the national committees are formally elected by the committee members. For the Republicans the chairman (and the cochairman, who must be of the opposite gender) is elected by the full committee in January of each odd-numbered year for a two-year term.[9] The chairman and cochairman must be full-time paid employees of the RNC, according to committee rules. During the Reagan and Bush administrations, the chairs were "nominated" by the presidents and anointed by the RNC. After the Republicans lost the White House in 1992, they turned to Haley Barbour, a long-time party official from Mississippi, who was one of those credited with the rejuvenation of their party in the South, as the new chair. Barbour, a prodigious fund-raiser, spent much of his two-year term criticizing President Clinton and working with Republican leaders in Congress. Barbour did not seek a third term as chair in 1997 and was replaced by Jim Nicholson, who had served for a decade on the RNC representing Colorado. Whereas Barbour's selection had been without opposition, Nicholson emerged from an eight-person field, a clear demonstration that the office is one prized by party leaders.

Typically less precise, the Democratic party rules call for a chairperson, five vice chairpersons, a secretary, a treasurer, and "other appropriate officers." The DNC officers have traditionally been chosen at a committee meeting on the day following the adjournment of the national convention. When tradition was followed, the chair, who served for the length of the campaign, was the choice of the presidential nominee. However, in 1984, candidate Walter Mondale wanted to select Bert Lance, the chair of the Georgia State Democratic Party and an early and influential Mondale backer. Many committee members objected, citing Lance's forced resignation as budget director in the Carter administration. Mondale was forced to back down and go with the DNC's preference, incumbent chair Charles Manatt, who had played a key role in rebuilding the national headquarters during his term of office.

In January, after the presidential election, Democrats choose their leader. Again the "old tradition" allows for the successful presidential candidate to name his party leader; but competition is more open if the Republicans have prevailed in gaining the White House. After President Clinton was elected in 1992, he tapped DNC chair Ron Brown to be his secretary of commerce. Brown was succeeded by David Wilhelm, a thirty-six-year-old Midwest political operative who had run President Clinton's campaign in that area during the 1992 election. After the party's debacle in the 1994 congressional elections, the position of party leader was transformed. Wilhelm was replaced by two "chairs"—a general chair who was to become the public face of the party, Senator Chris Dodd of Connecticut, and a national chair, who was to administer the party apparatus, South Carolina political leader Don Fowler. The same pattern was followed after Clinton's 1996 reelection, when Dodd and Fowler were replaced by Colorado governor Roy Romer as general chair and Massachusetts party leader Steve Grossman as national chair. In 1999 Grossman, in turn, was replaced by Joseph Andrew, a party leader from Indiana, while Romer remained general chair. Once again each of these was the clear choice of the White House; the decision to split leadership between a visible public official and a more "nuts and bolts"-oriented party leader represents a new pattern for the party.

2. *The "Hill Committees"*

The **National Republican Congressional Committee (NRCC)** and the **Democratic Congressional Campaign Committee (DCCC, or D triple C)** have been in existence since the end of the Civil War, growing out of incumbents' typical insecurity concerning their parties' electoral chances. The **National Republican Senatorial Committee (NRSC)** and the **Democratic Senatorial Campaign Committee (DSCC)** were created by party leaders in the Senate after the passage of the Seventeenth Amendment, that is, as soon as senators came to be popularly elected. During most of their existence, however, these committees, composed of incumbent representatives and senators, have been of little consequence.

These Hill committees tried to aid their party candidates. However, in an age when strong party allegiance dominated voting patterns, the Hill committees had little impact. The situation changed, ironically, when candidate-centered campaigns became the norm. As candidates began to run their own personalized campaigns, the most important resource became money, not party workers. The role of the Hill committees followed logically, and the role of the national party organizations changed.

NATIONAL REPUBLICAN CONGRESSIONAL COMMITTEE (NRCC)

The Republicans' party committee that is charged with raising money for and aiding in the campaigns of candidates for the House of Representatives.

DEMOCRATIC CONGRESSIONAL CAMPAIGN COMMITTEE (DCCC OR D TRIPLE C)

The Democrats' party committee that is charged with raising money for and aiding in the campaigns of candidates for the House of Representatives.

NATIONAL REPUBLICAN SENATORIAL COMMITTEE (NRSC)

The Republican party committee that is charged with raising money for and aiding in the campaigns of candidates for the U.S. Senate.

DEMOCRATIC SENATORIAL CAMPAIGN COMMITTEE (DSCC)

The Democratic party committee that is charged with raising money for and aiding in the campaigns of candidates for the U.S. Senate.

B. The Enhanced Role of the National Party Organizations

Just as the two national committees differ in their composition, reflecting a philosophical difference between a Republican party that reflects geographic constituencies and a Democratic one that reflects both demographic and geographic constituencies, the functioning of the national organizations of the two parties reflects broader party differences.

Political parties as significant contributors to electoral politics were "threatened" by changes in how campaigns worked. At one point in time, campaigns were labor intensive, relying heavily on grassroots efforts and established party loyalty to draw voters. In recent years, however, campaigns have become more candidate centered than party centered; they have relied on the "wholesale" technique of reaching the voters—using radio, television, and computer-generated mailings—rather than the "retail" techniques involving personal relationships and loyalty. Party organization, for the Democrats and the Republicans, appeared to be heading toward obsolescence; parties were in danger of becoming the dinosaurs of American politics. But the parties did respond, looking for a new role to play in an evolving new political reality (Maisel 1990; 1998).

The parties' first responses were very different. The Democrats undertook a period of intense party reform after the 1968 party convention. (This aspect of change in the Democratic national party organization is described in detail in chap. 10.) The goal of the reform was to make the party more open, more representative, more democratic. The means to achieve this goal was a series of changes in party rules and the imposition of those rules on state and local parties by the national organization. The party thus became more centralized, with reform commissions operating out of national headquarters stipulating rules that governed state and local party procedures (for assessments of these reforms, see Polsby 1983; Polsby and Wildavsky 1996; Wayne 1996).

The Republicans were satisfied with their rules; philosophically they did not believe in the national organization working its will on state and local party units. Except for those situations in which state law required party rule change, the Republicans were firm in their belief that a decentralized federation of state parties best reflected their view of how a national organization should be governed.

But after Watergate, the disastrous 1974 congressional elections, and Jimmy Carter's defeat of Gerald Ford in the 1976 presidential election, the Republicans became dissatisfied with the outcome of electoral competition (see Klinckner 1994). Former Tennessee senator William Brock, an advocate of **party renewal**, won the election to head the Republican National Committee in 1977. At approximately the same time two other strong party men—Congressman Guy Vander Jagt of Michigan and Senator Robert Packwood of Oregon—were chosen to head the NRCC and the NRSC, respectively. These three leaders saw it as their mission to build their organizations into effective campaign support for Republican candidates. They did so through a rigorous program of building the party's financial base, of developing the party's organizational structure, and of hiring a sophisticated staff to serve the campaign needs of Republicans throughout the nation.

PARTY RENEWAL

The effort to change the way in which political parties operate so that they can play a more important role in the electoral process.

Table 3.2 shows that the Republican party's financial base increased dramatically after Brock, Vander Jagt, and Packwood took command. You will note the slight lag that existed before anyone realized the fruits of their efforts. Fund-raising is a slow process.

And what was done with this money? The Republicans moved all their national organizations into a party-owned national headquarters. They hired a large number of staff members. They worked with the states and with regions, appointing political directors, organizational consultants, and fund-raising directors who fanned out across the nation. They made computer services available for all party candidates, assisting, for instance, with fund-raising, compliance with campaign finance regulations, research on public opinion, compilation of voting lists, and analyses of opponents' records. They established local liaisons

Table 3.2 National Party Receipts, 1976–1998 (hard money only, in millions)

Party	*1976*	*1978*	*1980*	*1982*	*1984*	*1986*	*1988*	*1990*	*1992*	*1994*	*1996*	*1998**
Democrats												
DNC	$13.1	$11.3	$15.4	$16.5	$46.6	$17.2	$52.3	$14.5	$65.8	$41.8	$108.3	$61.4
DCCC	0.9	2.8	2.9	6.5	10.4	12.3	12.5	9.1	12.8	19.4	26.6	24.8
DSCC	1.0	0.3	1.7	5.6	8.9	13.4	16.3	17.5	25.5	26.4	30.7	35.1
Total	$15.0	$14.4	$20.0	$28.6	$64.9	$42.9	$81.1	$41.1	$104.1	$87.6	$165.6	$121.3
Republicans												
RNC	$29.1	$34.2	$77.8	$84.1	$105.9	$83.8	$91.0	$68.7	$85.4	$87.4	$193.0	$99.9
NRCC	12.2	14.1	20.3	58.0	58.3	39.8	34.5	33.8	34.4	28.7	74.2	69.7
NRSC	1.8	10.9	22.3	48.9	81.7	86.1	65.9	65.1	72.3	65.4	64.5	51.8
Total	$43.1	$59.2	$120.4	$191.0	$245.9	$209.7	$191.4	$167.6	$192.1	$181.5	$331.7	$221.4

*1998 figures represent reports filed 20 days after the election; others are year-end reports.

Source: Federal Election Commission.

to help recruit strong candidates and to train and assist local candidates and campaign managers. In short, they provided a full-service campaign consulting organization for Republican candidates (see Herrnson 1990; 1994; 1998).

The Republicans did not stop there. The RNC and their two Hill committees developed truly awesome fund-raising capabilities so that they could support Republican candidates for federal office to the full extent permitted by the law. The NRCC and the NSCC entered into "agency agreements" with state party organizations, empowering the national offices to pay the state parties' share of campaign contributions and coordinated expenditures in House and Senate races (Herrnson 1988; 1990b; 1998; Jacobson 1985a).

In the starkest terms, the Democrats were caught napping—and they fell far behind in their fund-raising and organizational efforts. While their party's reforms may have conformed to a philosophical need to democratize the party, party renewal was necessary before the DNC and the Democratic Hill committees could begin to aid their party's candidates in ways even remotely similar to those that the Republicans were using. The Democrats' effort began after their massive defeat in the 1980 election—an election that saw President Carter's landslide loss to Ronald Reagan, the loss of the Democratic majority in the Senate for the first time since 1954, and the loss of thirty-four House seats, half of the margin they held before the election.

Charles Manatt, a long-time Democratic activist and fund-raiser, was elected chair of the DNC after the 1980 debacle. At the same time, the enterprising and ambitious Representative Tony Coelho of California took over the DCCC (Herrnson 1988; B. Jackson 1988). And in rapid succession, two senators committed to party building—Lloyd Bentsen of Texas and George Mitchell of Maine—were elected to chair the DSCC. Tables 3.1 and 3.2 demonstrate how far behind the Republicans the Democrats really were.

But by the 1986 election, party efforts finally began to pay off. New DNC chair Paul Kirk established task forces of consultants to aid Democrats in about a third of the states with the same kinds of services the Republicans were supplying throughout the nation. By 1988 they had doubled these efforts. The Democrats too have moved all their organizations into a new party-owned building, complete with an impressive media studio.

Catch-up is a difficult game to play, however. Even though the Republican fund-raising advantage over the Democrats has diminished in the most recent electoral cycles, the Democrats still cannot match Republican efforts in terms either of supplying services or of helping candidates and parties with significant infusions of funds (Herrnson 1998). Refer back to table 3.1 to see the spending by party committees for congressional and senatorial candidates in 1996. A great deal of controversy has surrounded the ways in which this money was raised by both parties (see chap. 11), but there can be no doubt about two factors—that each raised and spent a great deal of money aiding their candidates for office and that the Republicans maintain an advantage over the Democrats in this regard.

Thus the national organizations of both parties have made major efforts to modernize and professionalize their operations. To paraphrase George Washington Plunkett of Tammany Hall, the Republicans saw their opportunities first and they took them. The Democrats have been swimming upstream ever since; while the gap between the parties' respective fund-raising ability narrowed, it had not disappeared as the last election cycle of the 1990s began.

Both parties have used knowledge and experience gained at the national level to improve state and local organization. While the national Democratic party has imposed rules on its local party units, "sticks" to compel action, the Republicans have refused to do so. On the other hand, the Republican party has used money and services as financial inducements to entice its state and local units to professionalize their operations, "carrots" also used by the Democrats but in much smaller amounts. Thus, though in different ways, the "nationalization" of party organization goes on in both parties, affected more by the recognition of the sources of funds and of expertise than by philosophical concerns. The parties have adjusted to new situations, realizing that they are primarily electoral institutions and that they have had to find a means to make their contribution significant to those running for office.

V. POLITICIANS VIEW PARTY ORGANIZATION

John S. Trinsey Jr., a Pennsylvania real estate developer, has a very clear view of party organization. He does not like it. Trinsey, a Republican, wanted to be a U.S. senator. When Pennsylvania Republican U.S. senator John Heinz was killed in a tragic airplane-helicopter accident on April 4, 1991, Trinsey wanted to run to succeed Heinz. The laws of the commonwealth of Pennsylvania at the time required the major parties to nominate candidates for office by primary elections, except in the case of special elections (to fill unexpectedly vacated seats). In those cases commonwealth law permits the state party committee to make the nomination.

The Republican state party committee in Pennsylvania was prepared to nominate former governor Richard Thornburgh, then serving as U.S. attorney general, as the party's candidate to succeed Heinz. Trinsey, bitter in his disappointment, interceded with a lawsuit, claiming that nomination by party organization violated the Seventeenth Amendment to the U.S. Constitution, which called for the direct election of senators. United States district court judge Edward N. Cahn ruled in favor of Trinsey in early June 1991, causing Thornburgh to delay the announcement of his candidacy and his resignation from the Bush cabinet, and throwing the election into disarray.[10] Finally in early August a three-judge panel of the U.S. Court of Appeals overruled Judge Cahn and allowed the nominations and special election to proceed. John Trinsey had lost; party organization had won.

The Pennsylvania case is probably unique and might seem somewhat dated. But the point is illustrative. When party organization is strong or state laws favor strong parties (as do those that allow nomination by caucus or formal endorsements before primaries; see chap. 7), politicians care a great deal about those organizations. The most important tool available to party organization was control over nominations. When that power was given to the ordinary voters by the spread of direct primary elections during the Progressive era, party organizations suffered (Key 1956). Those party organizations that rapidly adapted or were favored by state law retain power and remain important to the politicians in their areas.

In recent years, however, smart politicians have taken note of the increased importance of the role of party. The debate over reform of the federal campaign finance laws in the 105th Congress has largely been a debate over (1) the role of political action committees and (2) the role of political parties. The Republican party has a financial base that is much stronger than that of the Democrats. Congressional Democrats are certainly not going to permit any change that deprives them of their base of campaign support while leaving Republicans in an advantageous position. Candidates for office know that the new role for political parties is an important one that can powerfully affect their careers. What is most amazing to me is that I wrote that very same paragraph about campaign finance reform six years ago, for the second edition of this textbook. *Plus ça change, plus ça même chose.*

Similarly, the 1988 presidential candidates considered grassroots organizations crucial to their efforts. Both the Bush and the Dukakis campaigns turned their impressive fund-raising efforts toward raising money for state and local organizations' campaigns after their own nominations were secure. In large part this strategy was a recognition of campaign finance laws that permitted money in excess of the federal grant to presidential campaigns to be spent in this way. But the two candidates also recognized that their support for strong local efforts would result in higher vote totals for themselves (see chap. 10). These patterns were repeated in the 1992 and 1996 presidential elections. National party campaigns use state and local efforts to further their own efforts.

Thus, from the politicians' point of view, party organization is far from inconsequential. While party machines no longer exist, while elected politicians no longer pay undying homage to the political boss, today's candidates for office have taken cognizance of a new reality—the redefined and enhanced role that party organization is playing in the electoral process.

WEBSITES

Political Parties

Communist Party	http://www.hartford-hwp.com/cp-usa
Democratic Party	http://www.democrats.org
Green Party	http://www.greens.org
Libertarian Party	http://www.lp.org
Reform Party	http://www.reformparty.org
Republican Party	http://www.rnc.org
Socialist Party	http://www.socialist.org
U.S. Taxpayers Party	http://www.ustaxpayers.org

KEY CONCEPTS

Democratic Congressional Campaign Committee (DCCC, or D triple C)
Decruitment
Democratic Senatorial Campaign Committee (DSCC)
grassroots
in-party independent
issue development
Hill committees
local party organizations
material incentives
national chairs
national committees
National Republican Congressional Committee (NRCC)
National Republican Senatorial Committee (NRSC)
out-party independent
party reforms
party renewal
patronage
political agents
political bosses
recruitment
senatorial courtesy
Seventeenth Amendment
soft money
stratarchy

DISCUSSION QUESTIONS

1. When strong bosses ruled American cities, politics was more efficient but less democratic. That is, bosses nominated candidates who did their bidding and ran their cities with much controversy, but the people had little say. Today the people have more say, but cities are less well run. How would you evaluate the trade-off between democracy and efficiency? Who wins? Who loses?
2. State party organizations want more control over candidate selection so that they can run candidates with a better chance of winning. However, control by party leaders is essentially less democratic than

a system in which party followers select candidates in a primary not influenced by party leaders. Do you think party organization has a legitimate role in ensuring that the best candidates run, even if they are not the most popular with party members?

3. Distinguish between party reform and party renewal. What does each seek to accomplish? Are the two necessarily in conflict with each other?

4. Assume that you, like most citizens, cannot name *any* party officials and have no idea about who your national or state committeemen and committeewomen are. What difference does it make? Should volunteer party leaders simply be replaced by paid party staff members? Why or why not?

CHAPTER 4

Political Participation

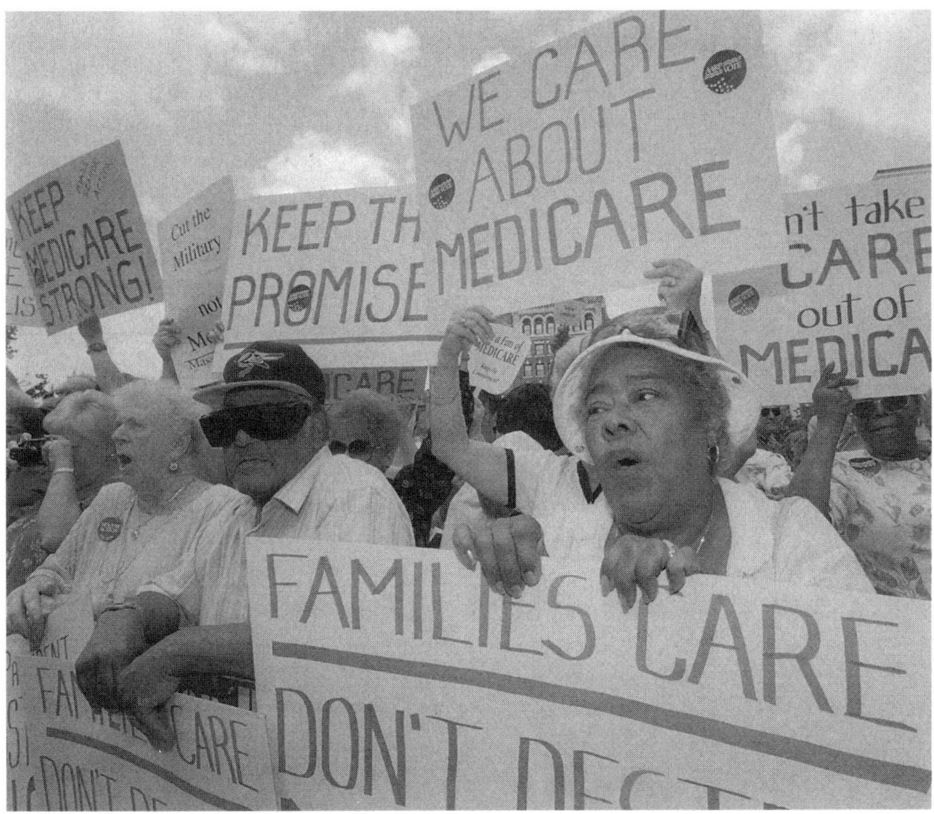

If you travel abroad and talk to your hosts about American elections, the most often heard complaint about our system of government is that so few citizens turn out to vote. In presidential elections only about half of the eligible voters bother to go to the polls. In congressional elections, only about one-third vote. So, President Clinton won reelection with fewer than a quarter of all eligible citizens actually voting for him. In the resounding Democratic victory in the 1998 congressional elections, only about 15 percent of those who could vote actually cast their ballots for Democratic candidates. Citizens of "less developed" democracies, often countries with voter turnout over 75 percent, ask incredulously, "How can you say the United States is a model we should follow when so few bother to take part in your democratic processes?"

Regarding the issue of political participation, some contend that America is a democracy and everyone should vote. Citizens who don't vote can't complain. The system is clearly in trouble if nearly half of the eligible voters stay home on election day. Others feel that those who care *do* vote. We don't want people who must be dragged to the polls, who vote for the candidate who looks best on television, to determine who will govern us. If citizens don't like what the government is doing, they will vote; low turnout shows satisfaction, not dissatisfaction. (For a discussion of this debate in the political science literature, see, e.g., Bennett and Resnick 1990; Gant and Luttbeg 1991, chap. 3; Piven and Cloward 1988.)

In the eyes of politicians, who votes is more than a theoretically interesting question. It is a matter of the most significant political consequence. Let's look at two examples from the 1996 election. In Orange County, California, one of the nation's most conservative areas, Loretta Sanchez (D) upset the incumbent Republican representative, Robert K. (Bob) Dornan, by only 984 votes, one vote in a hundred. Dornan challenged Sanchez's reelection because her margin of victory came from absentee ballots; he questioned whether fraudulent tactics had been used to "vote" people who did not actually cast their ballot. Dornan lost that challenge but won the Republican nomination to oppose Sanchez in 1998. In that election Sanchez won reelection comfortably, with no questions raised about who participated in the voting.

Extremely close races are not all that rare. Republican Connie Mack III defeated Democrat Buddy MacKay by fewer than 35,000 votes out of the more than 4 million votes cast in the Florida Senate race in 1988. Mack thought he had lost when the votes were counted on election night but awakened to find himself a winner, like Sanchez, because a vast majority of those who cast absentee ballots voted for him. Four years earlier, the congressional race in Indiana's Eighth District between incumbent Democrat Frank McCloskey and Republican challenger Richard McIntyre was determined by four votes out of nearly a quarter of a million cast. Because of a number of irregularities that occurred as the vote was counted, the election was disputed and eventually decided on a party-line vote in the House.[1]

The issue is not just how many turn out to vote, but which voters go to the polls. Consider this second example from 1996, this one from the U.S. Senate race in Iowa. Representative Jim Ross Lightfoot (R) challenged incumbent senator Tom Harkin (D), who was up for reelection. Harkin defeated Lightfoot by just over 62,000 votes out of more than one million votes cast. For Lightfoot it was a race of "what ifs?" For instance, Republican presidential candidate Bob Dole campaigned very infrequently in Iowa after the early nominating caucuses. Iowa's seven electoral votes were not considered important, and Dole was not considered popular in the state. Lightfoot was left to wonder: What if Dole had spent more time in Iowa? Would more Republicans have turned out and cast their votes for him as well as the presidential candidate? Would an increase in Republican turnout have changed his loss into a victory? Voting is only one aspect of political participation, albeit the only type of activity engaged in by most citizens (see Verba, Scholzman, and Brady 1996). It is perfectly legitimate to question whether other forms of participation are more important than voting or whether any participation at all is better than none. This chapter begins with an examination of voting, exploring the expansion of the **franchise** and the exercise of the right to vote. Then it looks at other forms of political participation, activities that require more commitment by citizens and are therefore the choice of fewer Americans. It also looks at nontraditional forms of participation, some of which are viewed as acceptable in other nations but not ours. I hope the discussion leads us to question why this disparity exists.

FRANCHISE
The right to vote.

Although many citizens vote out of a sense of civic responsibility, many others expend what political energy they have out of loyalty to a political party, concern about a particular issue, or belief in a specific candidate. Politicians want citizens to go to the polls, but they also want them to pull the "right" levers. In the next chapter we will turn to the issue of how individual citizens decide for whom to vote.

I. Who Votes; Who Doesn't

The discussion of voting in America can be broken down into two separate topics: who is eligible to vote and who exercises the franchise.

A. Expansion of the Franchise

In 1789, only white males who owned property were generally eligible to vote. According to Hugh Bone and Austin Ranney (1976, 35), the electorate was composed of only one in thirty Americans. Today, legal limitations keep very few citizens from voting. The history of this aspect of electoral reform in America has been one of continuous expansion of the franchise. This history has had four separate phases—increase in white male eligibility, enfranchisement of black citizens, enfranchisement of women, and enfranchisement of those between the ages of eighteen and twenty-one. More recently reformers have turned from asking who is eligible to vote to asking what impediments keep those who are eligible to vote from actually exercising that constitutionally mandated right. It is important to look at those efforts—and to examine the philosophical premise regarding democracy on which they are based—as well as at earlier successes in expanding the electorate through constitutional amendment.

1. Property Requirements

In colonial times only those who owned land were empowered to vote. The first step in expanding the franchise involved eliminating the property requirement for white males, often replacing it with the requirement that only taxpayers could vote. This reform happened on a state-by-state basis, starting even before the ratification of the Constitution, when Vermont granted universal male suffrage in 1777 and South Carolina substituted a taxpayer requirement for a property-holding requirement in 1778. The property qualification finally disappeared when Virginia eliminated it in 1850. A taxpayer requirement persisted for some years, often being fulfilled with the payment of a nominal **poll tax**. The poll tax was employed mainly in the South to keep blacks from voting, but poor whites were also affected. By the 1960s all but five states had eliminated even nominal poll taxes. Those remaining taxes were rendered void for national elections with the ratification of the **Twenty-fourth Amendment** in 1964; two years later, the Supreme Court held poll taxes to be unconstitutional in *any* election in the case of *Harper v. Virginia State Board of Elections,* 383 U.S. 663 (1966).

POLL TAX

A tax paid by each person as they exercised the right to vote; the tax weighed especially heavily on poorer citizens, as marginal dollars meant more to them.

TWENTY-FOURTH AMENDMENT

The amendment to the U.S. Constitution that prohibited the use of the poll tax or any other tax as a requirement for voting.

2. Black Suffrage

The extension of the franchise to black males was less unidirectional than it was for white males. The **Fifteenth Amendment** to the Constitution, ratified in 1870, was the culmination of a number of post–Civil War steps toward granting black males the right to vote. That amendment forbade states from denying or abridging the right to vote based on "race, color, or previous condition of servitude."

FIFTEENTH AMENDMENT

Amendment to the U.S. Constitution that explicitly states that individuals could not be denied the right the vote based on "race, color, or previous condition of servitude."

However, that seemingly broad prohibition did not end the problem of racial discrimination in voting. Post-Reconstruction southern legislators were extremely inventive in creating ways to prevent or at least discourage blacks from voting. These legal limitations, the so-called **Jim Crow laws**, included literacy tests, tests on interpreting the Constitution, **"whites only" primaries**, poll taxes, and **residency requirements**. Administrative decisions—such as locating polling places in remote areas or in areas that had been the site of black lynchings—and social and economic pressures further restricted black voting. The result was that the black vote was more apparent than real in most southern states during the first half of the twentieth century. For example, in 1960, fewer than 10 percent of the African-American citizens of Mississippi were registered to vote.

The first important attack against southern restrictions on black voting was the landmark Supreme Court decision in *Smith v. Allwright*, 321 U.S. 649 (1944). Southern states had established in law that political parties were private organizations; as such, they could determine their own membership and decided that these private organizations would be opened only to whites. According to the logic the southern states followed, because the parties were private organizations, party primary elections were private matters not regulated by state law. Since the Republican party was very weak throughout the South, receiving the Democratic party nomination in the primary was frequently tantamount to election. By setting party rules that limited the Democratic party primary to whites only, southern states effectively eliminated blacks from the political process. In *Smith v. Allwright* the Court ruled that the primaries were part of *one* electoral process and that, consequently, exclusion of blacks violated the Fifteenth Amendment. The "whites only" primary was thus ruled unconstitutional.

Black enfranchisement was an important goal of the civil rights movement of the 1950s and 1960s (see Weisbrot 1990; McClain and Stewart 1995; 1999). The Civil Rights Act of 1957 created the Civil Rights Commission and empowered it to investigate voting rights violations and to suggest appropriate legal remedies. The 1957 act also gave the U.S. attorney general the power to seek court relief from voting rights violations through the injunction process. The follow-up 1960 Civil Rights Act empowered the federal courts to appoint referees to help blacks register in areas in which discrimination had been found.

Thus the federal government was interceding to change the situation. But as table 4.1 shows, such efforts had little effect on black suffrage in many states until a full century after the passage of the Fifteenth Amendment. Many states used literacy tests or tests on the Constitution to keep blacks from the polls. Local officials exercised a good deal of leeway in administering these tests. In the Voting Rights Act of 1965 Congress suspended the use of such literacy tests. This suspension, renewed with the Voting Rights Act in 1970, was upheld by the Supreme Court in *Oregon v. Mitchell*, 400 U.S. 112 (1970). The 1965 Voting Rights Act empowered federal registrars to replace local or state officials in areas that had used literacy tests in the 1964 election and in ar-

JIM CROW LAWS

Laws designed to restrict the activities of former slaves in the South; included provisions that kept black citizens from voting.

"WHITES ONLY" PRIMARIES

An example of a Jim Crow law by which southern Democratic parties established themselves as private organizations open only to whites and then nominated candidates for office in elections normally not contested by Republicans, thus

RESIDENCY REQUIREMENTS

Requirement that a citizen live in a community for a specified period of time before becoming eligible to vote.

eas in which fewer than half of those eligible had registered and voted in 1964 (in a total of seven states). That act, which was renewed and expanded in 1970, 1975, and 1982,[2] has been credited with causing the dramatic impact on black registration that is shown in table 4.1.

The 1970 extension of the Voting Rights Act also dealt with the question of residency requirements. Local officials have long asserted that they have a legitimate need for some residency requirements so that they can maintain accurate voting lists and thus prevent people from casting ballots in more than one locality. However, in many areas, local officials used residency requirements to keep mobile populations (often blacks in the South, but certainly others such as young people) from voting. The 1970 Voting Rights Act set thirty days as the maximum residency requirement permissible for presidential elections. In *Dunn v. Blumstein,* 405 U.S. 330 (1972), the Supreme Court ruled that the thirty-day residency limit should be used for all elections.

Legal restrictions on black voting have been all but eliminated through a long series of constitutional amendments, congressional actions, and Supreme Court decisions. The path to this goal has been long, but *legal* limitations on black suffrage no longer keep black Americans out of polling places in the South or anywhere else in this country.

3. Women's Suffrage

In the early years of the abolition movement, the call for women's suffrage was closely linked to cries for black freedom and eventually black voting rights. However, male leaders of the abolition movement soon found it in their interest to separate the two causes (for a full history of the struggle for women's suffrage, see Catt and Shuler 1969). While not abandoning their participation in the movement to free those who were enslaved, women came together in the famous conference at Seneca Falls, New York, in 1848 to assert their own rights. From that point until the successful adoption of the **Nineteenth Amendment** in 1920, women **suffragists** waged a valiant, prolonged, often brilliant, frequently frustrating battle to win the right to vote.

NINETEENTH AMENDMENT

Amendment to the U.S. Constitution granting women the right to vote in all elections.

SUFFRAGISTS

The group of political leaders, mostly women, who campaigned for more than six decades at state and federal levels to gain the right to vote for women.

Arguments against women's suffrage were, in their own way, as illogical and immoral as arguments favoring slavery. Think about this statement from a Georgia state senator, Joseph E. Brown, citing opinions that he voiced in 1884, years after women had been granted the right to vote in many places on the frontier: "The Creator intended that the sphere of the males and females of our race be different. [Men] were qualified for those duties which required strength and the ability to combat with the sterner realities and difficulties of life. [Governing was] a laborious task, for which the male sex is infinitely better fitted than the female sex. . . . On the other hand, the Creator has assigned to women very laborious and responsible duties. . . . When the husband returns weary and worn in discharge of the difficult and laborious tasks

Table 4.1 Black Voter Registration in Southern States*

State	*1960*	*1964*	*1969*	*1970*	*1971*	*1976*	*1980*	*1982*	*1984*	*1986*	*1992*	*1994*
Alabama	13.7	19.3	61.3	66.0	54.7	58.4	55.8	69.7	71.4	68.9	71.8	66.3
Arkansas	38.0	40.4	77.9	82.3	80.9	94.0	57.2	63.9	71.2	57.9	62.4	56.0
Florida	39.4	51.2	67.0	55.3	53.2	61.1	58.3	59.7	57.3	58.2	54.7	47.7
Georgia	29.3	27.4	30.4	57.2	64.2	74.8	48.6	50.4	58.0	52.8	53.9	57.6
Louisiana	31.1	31.6	60.8	57.4	58.9	63.0	60.7	61.1	74.8	60.6	82.3	65.7
Mississippi	5.2	6.7	66.5	71.0	59.4	60.7	62.3	64.2	85.6	70.8	78.5	69.9
N. Carolina	39.1	46.8	53.7	51.3	49.8	54.8	51.3	50.9	59.5	58.4	64.0	53.1
S. Carolina	13.7	37.3	54.6	56.1	49.2	56.5	53.7	53.9	62.2	52.5	62.0	59.0
Tennessee	59.1	69.5	92.1	71.6	65.6	66.4	64.0	66.1	78.5	65.3	77.4	70.0
Texas	35.5	~	73.1	72.6	68.2	65.0	56.0	49.5	65.3	68.0	63.5	58.5
Virginia	23.1	35.5	64.8	57.0	52.0	54.7	53.2	49.5	62.1	56.2	64.5	51.1
Average of total	**29.7**	**33.2**	**63.8**	**63.4**	**59.6**	**64.5**	**56.5**	**58.1**	**67.8**	**60.9**	**66.8**	**59.5**

*All figures are percentages of the eligible voting-age population. Florida, Louisiana, North Carolina, South Carolina, and Georgia since 1980 have kept records of voter registration by race. The other state figures are based on estimates by state officials.

Source: U.S. Bureau of the Census, *Statistical Abstract of the United States: 1982–1983.* Data for 1984 taken from "Population Characteristics," *Current Population Reports,* series P-20, no. 397, issued January 1985. Note that the figures for 1964 and 1969 are based on the recorded voting-age population for 1960. Other data collected by Voter Education Project, Inc., Atlanta, Ga. 1992 data taken from "Voting and Registration in the Election of November 1992," *Current Population Reports,* series P-20, no. 471, issued Sept. 1993. 1994 data collected from U.S. Bureau of Census http://www.census.gov/population/socdemo/voting/work/tab04.txt

assigned to him, he finds in the good wife solace and consolation which is nowhere else afforded. [If woman were to engage in the affairs of state] who is to care for and train the children while she is absent in the discharge of these masculine duties?" (This argument is quoted from Key 1964, 613; Key in turn cites Anthony and Harper 1902, 4:93–100, for a fuller statement of the anti-women's suffrage argument and also Porter 1918, 141, for arguments on the other side.)

Women resisted these arguments, starting at the local and state levels. Women were first given the right to vote on school questions, presumably because these matters were closely related to "female" duties. By 1890 women could vote on educational matters in frontier states and territories (Key 1964, 614). Wyoming had granted women the right to vote on all matters in 1869, while still a territory. In applying for admission to the Union, Wyoming included women's suffrage in its constitution. When Congress first rejected this expansion of the franchise, Wyoming insisted on it. Congress ultimately had to relent, admitting Wyoming as the first state with universal female suffrage in 1890. Other western states followed Wyoming's lead, in at least partial recognition of the important and equal role women played in the settlement of the frontier. But the progress was slow and often frustrating.

The suffrage movement had to fight on a state-by-state basis while pursuing a national strategy. Campaign after campaign was fought on the state level as pressure was brought upon Congress. A variety of tactics were used. In states in which women had the right to vote, they pressured congressmen and senators to push for a national amendment. When the Democratic party proved recalcitrant, women organized a campaign against all Democratic congressmen in suffrage states to demonstrate their power. More than half of the Democratic candidates in the new suffrage states lost in the 1884 election; suffragists were credited with influencing this outcome.

Faced with this power, the parties began to listen. By 1916 women's suffrage was included in both party platforms, though the suffragists still wanted state action. In 1917 women turned to more militant actions, picketing the White House and delivering petitions to the president. Some were jailed; others replaced them. Those in jail demonstrated for the cause of prison reform; some engaged in hunger strikes. When female prisoners were force-fed, the press had a field day. More women came to Washington, and the jails became increasingly crowded. The effect of the pressure was telling.

The women's suffrage amendment passed the House in the second session of the Sixty-fifth Congress, but it failed to achieve the two-thirds vote necessary in the Senate. More women came to Washington, more picketed, more were jailed, and more hunger strikes ensued. Finally President Wilson was won over to the cause. When the Republican-controlled House repassed the measure in 1919, Wilson pressured his fellow Democrats in the Senate to enact women's suffrage. At long last, in August 1920, the Nineteenth Amendment was ratified by the requisite three quarters of the states, and women won the right to vote in all elections. No further *legal* barriers could be used to prevent women from voting.

This abbreviated description of the battle for women's suffrage points to a number of important conclusions. First, the tactics of the suffragists deserve much more attention than they are traditionally given. The suffragists' ability to gain their end, without the stimulus of a cataclysmic event like the Civil War or the benefit of the threat of electoral reprisal in most states, is a tribute to the skills of the women as politicians, skills seldom recognized by American scholars.

Second, political participation is most often defined as voting (or perhaps voting and other activities connected with the electoral process). The suffragists demonstrated that less traditional political participation (e.g., the hunger strike) can be equally effective in the American polity.

Third, the contrast with black suffrage is instructive. Black men won the right to vote through a constitutional amendment that forbade certain disenfranchisements by the states. Many states found ways around that amendment; it was nearly a century after the passage of the Fifteenth Amendment before black voting was successfully in place in states that resisted that movement, most notably southern states. Women won their right to vote first on a state-by-state basis, and only after decades of struggle at the national level. Yet once that battle was won, no further legal impediments stood in women's way. The South, for example, did not try to discourage women from voting; there was never an "all-male" primary there. However, as will be discussed below, social pressures did keep women from voting in numbers equal to men for many years; the difference between legal eligibility and actual voting requires further examination.

4. Lowering the Voting Age

As is the case with other eligibility standards for voting, the age at which a citizen can exercise his or her right to vote is determined by the constitution and laws of the state in which that citizen resides. For much of American history, twenty-one was the traditional voting age. During World War II, when eighteen-year-olds were conscripted into military service, many people felt that the voting age should be lowered to eighteen. In 1943 Georgia lowered its voting age to eighteen, but no other state followed suit. President Eisenhower expressed support for eighteen-year-old voters during his first term (1953–1957), but only Kentucky amended its constitution to effect that change. When Alaska and Hawaii were admitted to the Union in the late 1950s, their constitutions called for voting ages of nineteen and twenty, respectively.

No further changes ensued until the United States became embroiled in the Vietnam War. Once again, cries of "old men send young men to die in foreign wars" and "old enough to die but not old enough to vote" were heard. In response to this agitation and to the general public dissatisfaction with the war in Vietnam, Congress enacted the Voting Rights Act of 1970, one provision of which made eighteen-year-olds eligible to vote in all national, state, and local elections. In *Oregon v. Mitchell,* 400 U.S. 112 (1970), however, the Supreme Court struck down this provision, asserting that Congress could not constitutionally take such actions for state and local elections. As a response to this ruling, Congress passed—and the requisite thirty-seven states ratified—the **Twenty-sixth Amendment** to the Constitution, making eighteen the minimum voting age for all elections and expanding the electorate more than it had been expanded by any action other than the Nineteenth Amendment.

TWENTY-SIXTH AMENDMENT

Amendment to the U.S. Constitution setting eighteen as the minimum age for voting.

5. Additional Regulations: Residency and Registration

With few exceptions,[3] the potential voting population in the United States today includes all citizens over eighteen years of age. Even citizens who had once been prevented from voting because of their inability to read and understand English can now vote; the 1975 extension of the Voting Rights Act requires bilingual ballots in areas of the country with large non-English-speaking populations. A Native American tribe with no written language is even permitted to vote orally.

The other major barrier to voting involves the mobility of the American electorate. The 1970 Voting Rights Act extension established a maximum of thirty days for a residency requirement; it also established uniform state standards for absentee voting. But even this law did not answer all of the questions regarding who should be eligible to vote. Voting participation is actually a function of three different factors, To this point we have discussed eligibility requirements. The second factor involves registration laws, that is, how does one get his or her name on the roll of people who are permitted to vote in any community? The third factor is the decision of those who meet the requisite requirements and who have registered whether or not to turn out to cast their ballot on election day. Table 4.2 shows how each of these factors affects the number who actually vote. Turnout is usually expressed as a percentage of the voting-age population, that is, those who have reached the age of eighteen in a given area, who actually vote. But, as the table demonstrates, many of those who do not vote do not do so because they have never registered.

The Voting Rights Act of 1970 set some limits. But some feel these standards and requirements are still too strict. Four states—Maine, Minnesota, Oregon, and Wisconsin—allow so-called instant registration; citizens may register to vote up to and on the day of an election. Critics feel this procedure could lead to voter fraud, but no evidence of ef-

Table 4.2 Registered Voters and Percentage of Voter Turnout, 1992–1996

Year	*Population (in millions)*	*Voting-Age Population (VAP) (in millions)*	*Percentage of VAP Registered*	*Turnout as a Percentage of VAP*	*Turnout as a Percentage of Registered Voters*
1992	255,391	189,044	70.8	55.2	78.0
1994	260,682	193,650	68.8	36.6	53.1
1996	265,557	196,507	73.4	49.0	66.8

Source: Data from *America Votes* 1992, 1994, 1996; *Statistical Abstract of the United States*, 1997.

forts to subvert the system has been uncovered in states that use it. In any case, voter registration has increased in each such state. Table 4.3 shows turnout rates in selected states with reformed procedures; these relatively high rates are reflective, in part at least, of state laws that ease the burden on voters.

The debate over ease or difficulty of registration has been long and heated. Robert Erikson (1981) has demonstrated that the biggest reason citizens do not vote is that they are not registered. Richard Timpone (1998) has also shown that those with little or no history of political interest or participation are less likely to take the initial step toward participating—registering. A number of other studies have examined the relationship between registration laws and the number of people registered (Teixera 1992; 1993, 23–38; Powell 1986; Squire, Wolfinger, and Glass 1987; Wolfinger and Rosenstone 1978; 1980).

In the 101st Congress, the Democrats proposed legislation that would link voter registration to motor vehicle registration. The bill passed the House in February 1990, but it died when efforts to break a Republican filibuster in the Senate were unsuccessful as the session drew to a close in the fall of that year. Similar legislation passed in the 102d Congress in 1992 but failed to become law because of a veto by President Bush. The so-called **Motor Voter Bill** finally passed in 1993

MOTOR VOTER BILL

Legislation to increase the number of citizens who are registered to vote by expanding the availability of registration possibilities.

Table 4.3 Percentage of Voting-Age Population Registered to Vote in 8 States, 1996

State	*Voting-Age Population (in thousands)*	*Registered Voters as a Percentage of VAP*
Maine	909	81.6
Minnesota	3,296	80.9
Wisconsin	3,638	77.2
Michigan	6,921	73.7
Oregon	2,309	72.7
Iowa	2,059	71.7
Washington	3,924	66.8
New Hampshire	832	64.3

Source: Statistical Abstract of the United States, 1997, p. 289.

and was signed into law by President Clinton. As finally enacted, that Motor Voter Bill requires states to allow citizens to register to vote when applying for a driver's license, to permit mail-in registration, and to provide registration forms at certain public assistance agencies. Passage of this law will lead social scientists to reassess the impact of easier registration laws on voting turnout (see Knack 1995).

The debate on voter registration laws continues today. On the one hand, the issue poses a normative question about public policy: Shouldn't a democracy encourage its citizens to vote? Shouldn't all restrictions on voting be eliminated? On the other hand, the question is a pragmatic one: Is there evidence that restrictive voter registration laws significantly increase participation? Do those whose names are added to the rolls by eased registration requirements necessarily turn out to vote? (See Bennett 1990; Bennett and Resnick 1990; Cassel and Luskin 1988; Gans 1990; Jackman 1987; Piven and Cloward 1988; 1989; 1990; Powell 1986; Rosenstone and Wolfinger 1978; Squire et al. 1987; Texeira 1987; Wolfinger and Rosenstone 1980.)[4]

But the issue is also a political one. Surely Republicans and Democrats did not split on the motor vehicle registration bill because of differing views on the questions raised above. And surely the cost of this procedure for registering voters was not enough to cause such a complete partisan division. Further, the issue was not one of big federal government telling the states what to do—though each of these arguments was made. The crucial question was the political one: if people were encouraged to register and they turned out to vote, for whom would they cast their ballots? Democrats and Republicans alike believed that more of these newly registered voters would vote Democratic; thus each party dug in its heels and fought hard for its position on this seemingly innocuous change in electoral law.

Regardless of the impact made by changes in registration laws, it is clear that instant registration and even the thirty-day limit, and certainly registration tied to motor vehicle registration, cause problems for communities with large, transient student populations. Permanent residents of relatively small communities with large residential universities fear, with some cause, that students will dominate local governmental elections. This issue continues to spark controversy whenever a college student is elected to a city council. Although many students can point to cases in which this has occurred, to date it is mostly a problem that people worry about in theory, not one that has had a broad impact in practice.

B. Decline in Voter Participation

It has been noted that a lack of effort by the Republican presidential campaign in the 1996 Iowa Senate race may have resulted in a low turnout among likely supporters of the Republican candidate for the

Senate. Nonvoters were not kept from the polls by legal restrictions.[5] They simply were not motivated to exercise their right to vote.

The most egregious example of citizens not exercising their right to vote occurred in the 1980 presidential race. President Jimmy Carter conceded his defeat to Ronald Reagan before the polls closed on the West Coast. Local Democratic officials in many communities felt that many potential supporters who would have voted late in the day (e.g., on their return home from work) decided not to bother voting because they had already heard the presidential results. Democrats lost a number of very close races in California, including that of incumbent congressman James Corman, who was defeated by 864 votes of more than 145,000 cast. Many feel that these defeats were caused by the decision of potential supporters not to vote, a decision encouraged by President Carter's early concession.

Figure 4.1 shows that relatively low voter turnout is common in the United States. Turnout has actually been declining in recent years, with turnout for presidential elections reaching a high point in 1960; slight increases in the 1992 and 1994 elections encouraged some observers, but the low turnouts in 1996 and 1998 dampened their optimism. The decline has not been precipitous, but it has become a cause for concern among many political observers (Gant and Luttbeg 1991, 86–87). We know a great deal about voting turnout. Table 4.4, for instance, shows that voters in some states turn out in considerably higher numbers than those in other states. If the United States has become "one big country," with state and regional differences blurred because of our mobile population and our reliance on a national media for setting so many standards, why do states vary to the degree that they do?

The rather simple reason is that the degree of nationalization has

Figure 4.1 Turnout in National Elections, 1930–1998.

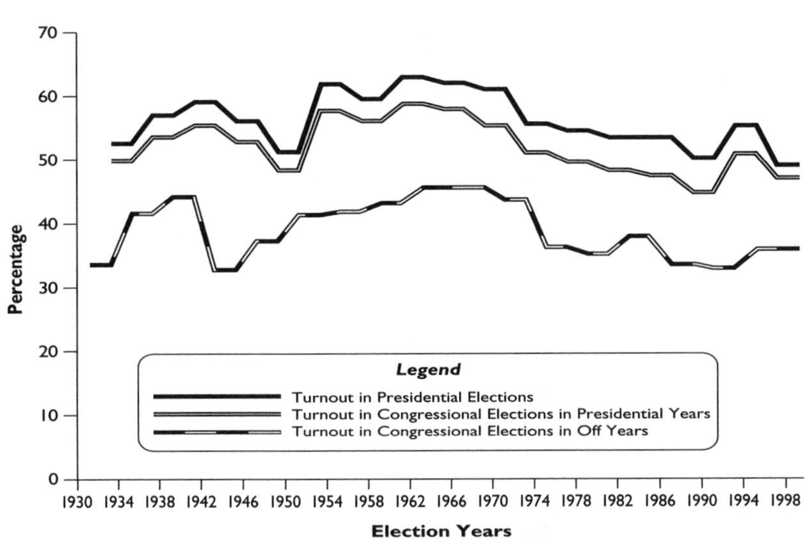

Source: Data from various Congressional Quarterly Service sources.

been overstated. States vary considerably in a number of easily discernible ways. For example, Utah is known as the state having the highest percentage of citizens who follow the Mormon religion. Utah is also the state that frequently has the highest percentage of voting turnout, though that was not true in the most recent election. Is the traditionally high rate in Utah merely a coincidence? I do not think so. One of the tenets of Mormonism is that followers should do their civic duty. What is a more basic civic duty than voting? While we do not have data on the "Mormon turnout rate" (nor the turnout rate for any religious group), it is not too much of a stretch to think that the hypothesized connection is real.

The populations of the fifty states vary in all sorts of ways, some of which have implications for voting turnout. In addition, state laws vary,

Table 4.4 Voter Turnout by State: 1994, 1996

	1994 (congressional election)	*1996 (presidential election)*
State	*Percentage of VAP Voting*	*Percentage of VAP Voting*
AL	35.5	47.7
AK	48.5	56.9
AZ	37.6	45.4
AR	39.0	47.5
CA	35.9	43.3
CO	38.9	53.1
CT	43.0	56.4
DE	36.5	49.6
FL	26.3	48.0
GA	29.0	42.6
HI	39.3	40.8
ID	49.0	58.2
IL	34.9	49.2
IN	36.0	48.9
IA	46.3	57.7
KS	43.3	56.6
KY	27.5	47.5
LA	26.7	56.9
ME	54.0	64.5
MD	35.9	46.7
MA	43.3	55.3
MI	43.0	54.5
MN	52.0	64.3
MS	32.6	45.6
MO	45.2	54.2
MT	56.5	62.9

continued

and these too impact voting turnout rates. We will explore some of these factors in the paragraphs below.

1. Voting by Blacks

Some aspects of the decline in voting turnout in recent decades can be easily observed. For example, despite intense registration efforts by federal officials, particularly in certain southern states, and despite the success of these efforts depicted in Table 4.1, turnout rates for black voters have actually fallen since 1966, and the difference between turnout for blacks and whites has not varied significantly since 1968 (see fig. 4.2).

These data make the registration and voter turnout efforts aimed at

Table 4.4 Voter Turnout by State: 1994, 1996 (*continued*)

	1994 (congressional election)	*1996 (presidential election)*
State	*Percentage of VAP Voting*	*Percentage of VAP Voting*
NE	47.9	56.1
NV	34.6	39.3
NH	36.7	58.0
NJ	33.6	51.2
NM	39.6	46.0
NY	33.8	46.5
NC	29.6	45.8
ND	50.4	56.3
OH	39.7	54.3
OK	40.5	49.9
OR	51.6	57.5
PA	36.6	49.0
RI	44.8	52.0
SC	31.7	41.5
SD	58.6	61.1
TN	36.2	47.1
TX	31.3	41.2
UT	40.5	50.3
VT	49.3	58.6
VA	38.4	47.5
WA	42.2	54.7
WV	29.3	45.0
WI	38.6	57.4
WY	57.2	60.1
Total	**36.6**	**49.0**

Source: Data from *America Votes* 1994, 1996.

Figure 4.2 Voter Turnout by Race.

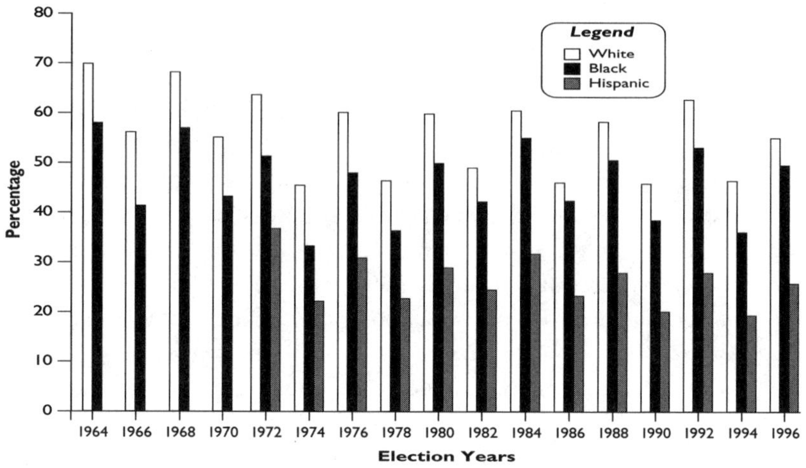

Source: Data from National Election Studies.

black voters, such as the one led by the Reverend Jesse Jackson and Operation PUSH (People United to Serve Humanity), all the more important. In 1984 Jackson demonstrated that efforts of this kind increase the black percentage of the vote and, as a consequence, the impact of the black vote on national elections. But results in more recent elections have been less encouraging. While the black percentage of the voting-age population has been increasing, there has not been a comparable rise in the black percentage of the vote.

Similarly, Hispanics are the fastest-growing group in the United States today. However, the Hispanic turnout is even lower than the black turnout, and it too has been decreasing recently, though not so noticeably as black turnout. In the case of Hispanic voters, the barriers to effective participation, including language and education level, remain serious obstacles. But in certain geographic areas, such as border districts in Texas and California, Hispanic voters have become powerful forces (McClain and Stewart 1995; 1999).

2. *Voting by Young Voters*

Furthermore, for many years political scientists have known that the youngest voters vote in the smallest proportion (Timpone 1998, 145–158; Miller and Shanks 1996; Wolfinger and Rosenstone 1980, 37; Converse and Niemi 1971; Campbell et al. 1960). (See fig. 4.3.) Since the passage of the Twenty-sixth Amendment, the young have constituted an increased portion of the total electorate; therefore, their unwillingness to vote contributes increasingly to the overall decline in voter turnout.

There has been some controversy in the professional literature concerning this trend. Basing their findings on data from the late 1970s and early 1980s, some scholars have suggested that voters who came

Figure 4.3 Voter Turnout by Age.

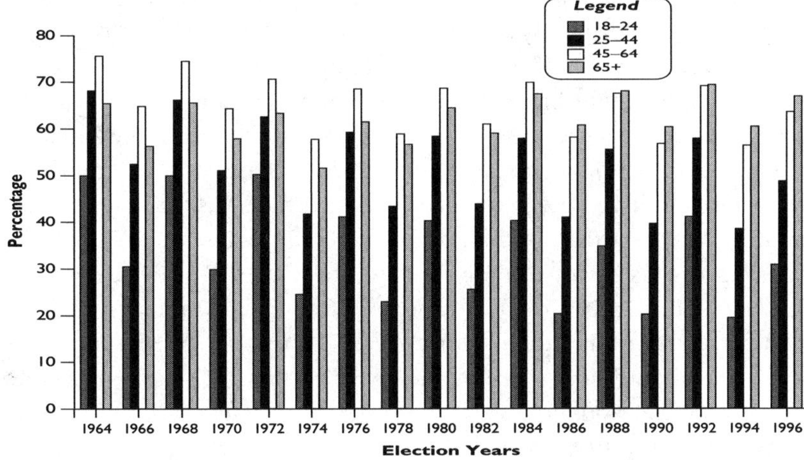

Source: Data from National Election Studies.

of political age in an era during which political activity was not an expected norm would not increase their participation rate with age, as had been the case in the past (Tarrance 1978, 12). The "negative" trend in overall voter participation, which was evident in the late 1970s, was attributed to a replacement of the age cohort that reached voting age before the New Deal with a cohort that first voted after the Great Society administration of Lyndon Johnson. The former, which is now dying out, consistently recorded high turnout rates. The latter constitutes an increasingly large part of the electorate but has a discouragingly low turnout rate (Miller 1992; Teixeira 1987). The fear was that this younger cohort of voters would never increase in participation rates as had the generation before them.

However, this fear seems to be unfounded. In recent years the pattern of youthful voters participating in numbers much lower than their elders has continued. As each cohort has aged, their participation rate has increased (Miler and Shanks 1996). The pattern of greatest interest at the end of the twentieth century involves older voters, those over sixty-five, who have traditionally participated at rates higher than the general population. With an increase in age expectancy, and with older Americans constituting a larger share of the population as the baby boomer generation ages, it seems apparent that this segment of the population will be overrepresented among the voting public. To the extent that they share opinions on the issues of the day, their views might well also be overrepresented by those whom they elect.

3. Voting by Women

If blacks and young voters have contributed to the decline in voter turnout, the opposite conclusion holds for women. Turnout among women was quite low in the years immediately after enfranchisement. However, the number of female voters steadily increased until it leveled off at a turnout level only slightly below that of men by 1972 (fig. 4.4).

The rejuvenation of political awareness by women spurred by the women's movement in the 1970s led to another increase in participation, and turnout rates of women voters have exceeded the rates for men in every national election since 1984. Because more women than men are eligible to vote, women now constitute a majority of the electorate. Women in the South participate in politics less than do women in other regions because of regional cultural norms. Therefore it is clear that women in other regions now participate in significantly higher percentages than do men in those areas (Pomper 1975, 88).

Certainly politicians and political analysts feel this to be the case. In the 1996 election, political strategists explored how issue after issue would appeal to the so-called soccer moms, a subgroup never before seriously considered. If participating in politics once constituted "a laborious task, for which the male sex is infinitely better fitted than the female sex," as Senator Brown so quaintly put it, no one can doubt that much has changed. Nevertheless, we must go beyond mere demographic characteristics in distinguishing voters from nonvoters.

4. What Distinguishes Voters from Nonvoters?

For more than three decades social scientists have been examining the American electorate in some depth. Despite a variety of research techniques, scholars have come to a remarkable consensus on what distinguishes voters from nonvoters. None of these conclusions is surprising, but some of the more important ones should be noted.

First, voting is a function of the "rules of the game." If it is easier to

Figure 4.4 Voter Turnout by Gender.

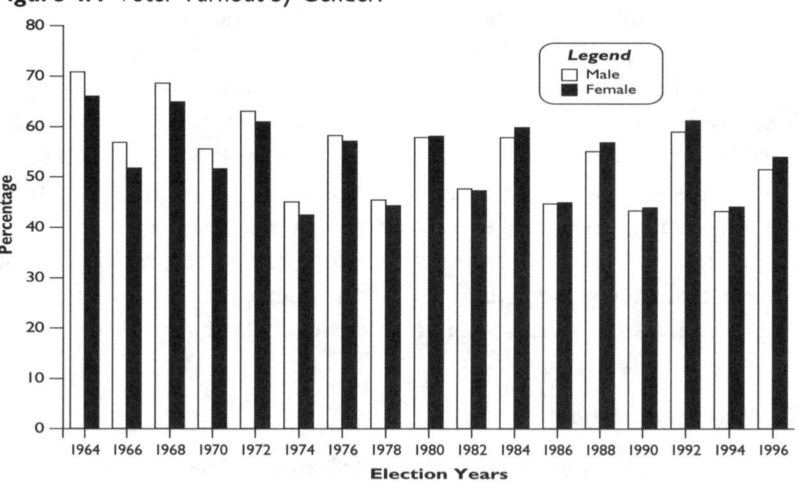

Source: Data from National Election Studies.

vote, if fewer roadblocks are put in the voter's way, more people vote. Thus the expansion of the franchise, the easing of registration requirements, and continued efforts to open the doors to black and Hispanic voters have increased the number of individuals voting. Those who still face legal roadblocks or racist hassles vote less frequently than do those in areas in which voting is easier (Campbell et al. 1960; Milbrath and Goel 1977, chap. 5).

Again, state experiences demonstrate this point. One claim is that requiring citizens to go to a voting booth during set hours on election day decreases turnout and unfairly disadvantages some citizens. Proposals have been floated to have twenty-four hour voting days and to make election day a national holiday (or to hold elections on Sundays, when fewer people are at work). These proposals have been rejected for a variety of reasons, including expense and legitimate questions of whether they would have the desired impact.[6] Two states, however, have tried interesting experiments, with positive results in terms of increasing turnout.

In Texas, since 1991, citizens have been permitted to cast ballots in their local polling place on election day or at any time from seventeen days prior to the election up until four days before at a designated site in their community. Votes are not tallied until the polls close on election day, but citizens are given many more options about when to cast their vote. Whether or not this reform increases turnout has not been conclusively demonstrated, but nearly a quarter of the votes cast in the 1992 Texas presidential election were cast prior to the election, and counties with a higher proportion of the vote cast early had significantly higher total voter participation in the 1992 presidential election (Stein and Garcia-Monet 1997, 657–671).

In Oregon, state officials began experimenting with mail ballots for certain elections as early as 1987. Those monitoring this experience have been very impressed with its impact. Citizens can vote from their own home; they can review material carefully before they vote. Turnout for referenda has increased with the use of mail ballots. In a special election to replace Robert Packwood (R) in the U.S. Senate, mail ballots were used for the first time for statewide elective office. While this voting technique caused considerable difficulty for campaign strategists (see chap. 8), the turnout rate of 57 percent in the primary for the special election was the highest for a nonpresidential primary since the state started keeping records and was an extraordinary showing for a special election (Southwell and Burchett 1997, 53–57).

Second, social position distinguishes voters from nonvoters. "Citizens of higher social and economic status participate more in politics. This generalization . . . holds true whether one uses level of education, income, or occupation to measure social status" (Verba and Nie 1972, 125; see also Berelson, Lazarsfeld, and McPhee 1954; Campbell et al. 1960; Dahl 1961; Lane 1959; Milbrath and Goel 1977). Wolfinger and Rosenstone have refined this commonplace notion by isolating the effect of the various components of a voter's socioeconomic status. They conclude that "even after controlling for all other variables, education has a very powerful independent effect on the likelihood of voting" (Wolfinger and Rosenstone 1980, 24). Education has the greatest effect on those with low-income or low-status jobs, but it has a continuing effect at all levels. Neither income nor occupation was found to affect voting turnout to the same extent. The obvious importance of this hypothesis is that it helps explain the finding that socioeconomic status affects turnout. Wolfinger and Rosenstone attribute that finding to increased information, ease of acquiring more information, and decline in anxiety because of greater political knowledge more than to economic variables that affect wealthier individuals (Wolfinger and Rosenstone 1980, 18–22).

Third, certain attitudes about politics distinguish voters from nonvoters. These attitudes are obviously interrelated, but they can be dealt with separately. For example, those who have the strongest feelings toward one political party or the other are much more likely to vote than are those without such intense partisan affiliation. This finding has held for every election since modern survey research began to be used extensively. It becomes particularly significant when combined with the finding (discussed later) that fewer and fewer Americans have strong partisan affiliation.

Figure 4.5 reveals a number of other interesting variations, for example, that the voting gap between independents and partisans is not consistent. On the one hand, the gap seems to be widening, a finding that grows in significance as the number of independent voters grows. On the other hand, peaks and valleys are evident. The fluctuations reflect another factor that distinguishes voters from nonvoters. People who are more interested in politics tend to vote more frequently. Partisans tend to be more interested than nonpartisans and hence to vote in higher percentages. Even in the 1992 and 1996 presidential elections, when third-party candidate Ross Perot attracted attention with his rhetoric decrying politicians in the two major parties, self-proclaimed independents voted at a lower rate than did Republicans or Democrats.

However, certain elections stimulate interest among more voters (fig. 4.5). When Dwight Eisenhower, commander of the Allied forces in the European theater in World War II, first ran in 1952, he was seen as the conquering hero returning to lead his nation. The strong appeal of his persona attracted a higher turnout. In 1960 Democrats nominated John F. Kennedy, only the second Roman Catholic ever to receive a major-party presidential nomination; Kennedy's Catholicism stimulated turnout among Catholics (and presumably anti-Catholics). The elections of 1948 and 1968 featured serious minor-party challengers to the Democrats and Republicans and were each thought to be closely contested elections. Elections in which the outcome is in doubt stimulate turnout as well. Of course, some elections meet many of these criteria and are categorized as critical elections, as was noted in chapter 2. Elections that meet none or few of these criteria, such as those of 1976, 1984, or

Figure 4.5 Voting by People of Differing Commitment to Party.

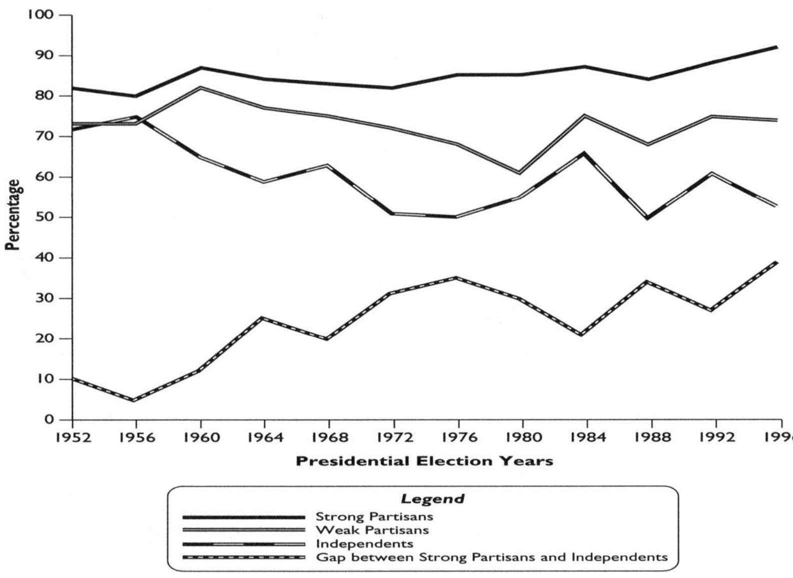

Source: Data from National Election Studies.

1996 stimulate the least interest and have the lowest turnouts (Berelson et al. 1954; Campbell et al. 1960; Hill and Luttbeg 1980, chap. 3; Milbrath and Goel 1977, chap. 3; Verba and Nie 1972).

So far the discussion has focused on turnout in presidential elections. As noted in table 1.1, Americans are asked to go to the polls very frequently. Turnout is much lower for elections that do not include a presidential race. Congressional elections are held every two years, whereas presidential elections take place every four years. Thus half of the congressional elections take place in off-presidential years (e.g., 1994, 1998). Turnout in these years is typically under 40 percent; it has always been lower than in adjacent presidential election years.

A few states still hold statewide elections in odd-numbered years that do not include either presidential or congressional elections. Many cities hold municipal elections in those years as well. Turnouts for them are typically lower than congressional elections—though highly salient state or local issues can stimulate larger turnout from time to time. Finally, primary elections see the lowest turnouts of all. For example, although Maine typically comes close to leading the nation in turnout in presidential and off-year general elections, in the Maine primary elections in 1998, fewer than 12 percent of the electorate turned out to vote.

Obviously a number of factors contribute to low turnout in these elections. First, potential voters are not stimulated by a highly visible presidential campaign to get them thinking about politics. Second, the candidates and issues are often not as important to the average voter as are the candidates and issues in presidential campaigns. These campaigns typically have a lower budget and thus buy fewer of the advertisements that stimulate citizen involvement. In the case of primaries, all of the elections are not held on the same day everywhere in the nation. The rules are not always the same and voters may be confused about their eligibility. Finally, many more of these races are uncontested, leading citizens to think voting is not worth their time. The point should not be lost, however, that in each of these races below the presidential level, except in extraordinary cases, a majority of the eligible citizenry opts not to vote.

In addition to partisanship and interest in a campaign, researchers have found that voters are distinguished from nonvoters by the number of political stimuli to which they are exposed. This finding is not surprising, but it has interesting implications. We would expect those most interested in politics to receive the most political communication, in fact, to seek out such contacts. This expectation is particularly apt for those highly involved with political parties. And both of these expectations are supported by a good deal of evidence.

Similarly, those less interested would doubtless not go out of their way to look for political information. Yet we do not always control the information we receive, and campaign managers know that those who receive more information vote more frequently. Therefore, one of their goals is to bombard citizens with political messages, trying to penetrate the defenses of those who seek to avoid politics. Why? The more people are reminded about politics, the more they are reminded of their civic duty to vote and the more they feel guilty about not voting. Thus one clear campaign strategy is to work hard to stimulate the participation of those most likely to support one's cause. If people are not interested in politics because of their own predilection or because of campaign-related factors, the office seeker must stimulate that interest among his likely supporters, must appeal to their sense of civic duty, and must turn nonvoters into voters (Almond and Verba 1965; Berelson et al. 1954; A. Campbell et al. 1960; Lazarsfeld, Berelson, and Gaudet 1944; Milbrath and Goel 1977, chap. 2). There is ample evidence that candidates running in nonpresidential years find it difficult to penetrate citizen apathy.

Finally, in a number of different ways scholars have demonstrated that those who are more knowledgeable about politics participate in greater numbers than those less knowledgeable. Tables 4.5 and 4.6 divide the electorate according to how voters evaluate candidates for the presidency. Ideologues look at candidates' views on issues from a broad perspective. Those who are issue-oriented or group-oriented view the candidates according to their stand on particular issues or their relationship to groups in society with which the voters associate themselves. Partisan evaluators use the lens of political party, and those who rely on image tend to focus on a more general perception of the candidates.

Table 4.5 clearly demonstrates a trend toward a more issue-oriented and ideological electorate. Certainly the modern electorate is more knowledgeable than one casting votes based on image or empty

Table 4.5 Mode of Candidate Evaluations by American Voters*

Year	*Ideologue*	*Issue Oriented*	*Group Benefit*	*Partisan*	*Image*	*No Content*
1952	1	16	5	1	62	15
1956	1	19	6	~	64	10
1960	1	20	5	~	62	12
1964	6	35	5	~	44	9
1968	3	23	5	19	36	15
1972	7	44	5	6	28	10
1976	7	35	9	13	27	9
1980	10	48	3	5	22	12
1984	6	67	5	5	8	10
1988	7	48	5	12	13	16

*Cell entries are percentages of the total sample who evaluated by each means.
Source: Data from National Election Studies.

Table 4.6 Voting by Different Types of Candidate Evaluators*

Year	*Ideologue*	*Issue Oriented*	*Group Benefit*	*Partisan*	*Image*	*No Content*
1952	87	76	63	71	79	48
1956	87	72	73	—	78	42
1960	100	87	84	—	85	50
1964	81	80	69	7	81	51
1968	93	79	64	77	79	54
1972	87	73	79	61	72	43
1976	77	74	70	72	67	33
1980	87	74	60	80	68	53
1984	88	76	73	77	70	45
1988	92	75	75	76	67	35

*Cell entries are percentage in each category of those who reported having voted.
Source: Data from National Election Studies.

rhetoric, and arguably more knowledgeable than one basing evaluations simply on group benefits or partisan appeal. Table 4.6 shows that those who base evaluations on ideology or issues vote in higher proportions than those relying on image or rhetoric. The clear implication of these data is that frequent voters are becoming more knowledgeable and distinguishing themselves more from nonvoters who are less informed (Gant and Luttbeg, 1991, chap. 2).[7]

C. Voters and Nonvoters Revisited

Citizen participation is central to the functioning of the American political system. Theorists of democracy know this, social scientists know this, and politicians know this. A politician can be the most brilliant, best informed, most skilled and socially committed citizen in a community, but, as a candidate, that politician is a loser if the votes are not there. Who votes, therefore, is critical.

This review of voter participation has had two rather elementary themes. First, the eligible electorate has been expanding. Second, the actual electorate has not been growing proportionately. Legal barriers that once prevented certain groups from voting have been removed, but, at least in the case of black and young voters, these changes in law have not always led to mass marches to the polls. To the contrary, participation by these groups has not increased as much as reformers would have liked.

Analysts have postulated other distinctions among voters and nonvoters as well. Among the voters is a broadening group of educated, concerned, issue-oriented, or ideological balloters, who often express preferences among candidates based on the considerable store of knowledge that they have obtained and evaluated, not simply because of partisan or image-related appeals.

At the other extreme is a considerable number of nonvoters—individuals who are not interested in politics, do not associate themselves with either party, and are not informed about political matters. They avoid political stimuli and ignore claims that they have a civic duty to vote.

What does this polarity say about the health of the American polity? Obviously, the fact that the voting electorate is informed is a positive sign, though an observer must at least inquire about the implications of the voting patterns of these superbrights for political parties and then determine if these implications are meaningful. But what about the nonvoters? Does America need "charismatic" candidates, lowest-common-denominator advertising, and divisive issues in order to stimulate participation? Or should anyone care that so many Americans stay home, disinterested? If their lives were full of unbearable suffering,

they would indeed become involved, so perhaps inactivity is a sign of health. Either side of this position can be argued convincingly. Do these people participate in some other form of political activity? Before we turn to an examination of individual voting behavior, we will look at varieties of political participation other than voting.

II. Participation in Politics in America

Social science research into political participation has consistently emphasized voting, since it can be measured easily. Official returns show how many go to the polls, census data provide a demographic breakdown of the electorate, and survey research reveals something about the opinions, attitudes, motivations, backgrounds, affiliations, and other characteristics of voters.[8]

Finding out about other activities involves carefully identifying them, grouping them, and then analyzing them. Few are dichotomous variables. An individual either votes or not. But what about talking about politics? Or trying to tell others how to vote? If a woman casually complained to a friend that Ross Perot's television infomercials offended her, was that discussing politics? How should we measure that activity against a long discussion comparing President Clinton's policy on Bosnia or Kosovo with the policy that Dole might have pursued had he been elected? There are other more difficult research questions. Should an individual who gives $25 to a friend running for school board be grouped with another individual who gives $1,000 to each of ten congressional candidates, listing both as "those who contribute to campaigns"? What could be learned from such a combination?

Finding out about political "passivists" is also difficult. Probably half of the nonvoters in this country tell survey analysts that they vote. Who are they? Why don't they vote? Why do they lie about it? Scholars do not really know. If it is not easy to ascertain what low voter turnout means for the American system, it is even more difficult to evaluate political behavior that is nonconventional or even illegal. How many individuals who have been involved in burning abortion clinics would discuss their reasons for doing so in response to a scholar's open-ended questions?

Thus our knowledge about political participation is not as extensive as we would like. On the other hand, we do know a good deal. The most recent work on this subject is found in an important study by Sidney Verba, Kay Lehman Schlozman, and Henry Brady (1995). Verba, Schlozman, and Brady have studied political and other voluntary activities engaged in by an extremely large sample of American citizens. Although their conclusions cannot be summarized in a brief paragraph, some of their findings can be highlighted. Social and economic resources influence both the ways in which citizens participate in political and other voluntary organizations and the extent to which they participate. The views of those who are active in these types of organizations are not representative of the views of inactive racial and ethnic minority group members. Furthermore, activity in politics is more skewed by demographic and socioeconomic factors than is activity in either religious or community organizations. The implication of these conclusions is stated in the title of the book *Voice and Equality*; those who are not equal in other ways are not heard equally through participation in voluntary groups in our society, particularly not in political activities.

Two earlier studies, one by Sidney Verba and Norman Nie and associates (part of a very extensive multination study) and one by Lester Milbrath and associates (conducted in Buffalo, New York, but viewed as generally pertinent because of the similarity of its results to the other study) long dominated this field. They dealt extensively with varieties of political activity.

These studies found that it is possible to break the American electorate's political behavior down into certain modes of participation. Citizens were classified as active, passive but supportive, and inactive. The active group includes those who are identified as party and campaign workers, those who are community activists, those who frequently contact officials about particular problems, and those who are involved in a communications network that discusses political matters (a group identified only by Milbrath). Not many Americans fit into these groups; the numbers cited by Verba and Nie and/or Milbrath range from about 4 percent who contact officials about particular problems to 20 percent who are community activists to over 30 percent who engage in some form of campaign activity—such as running a campaign, contributing money, or wearing a button or putting a bumper sticker on the car. These groups are not mutually exclusive, nor is it essential that an individual participate in one kind of activity in order to acquire enough sophistication to participate in another. We can identify separate styles of participating in politics. Although most of these "active" individuals also vote, voting is a separate style of participation. In fact, the "contact specialists" identified by Verba and Nie frequently participate in no other form of political activity.

By far the largest group consists of those identified as passive supporters—individuals who pay taxes, who rise and sing the national anthem at ball games, but whose active involvement in politics is limited to voting. Large numbers of Americans support the system, at least passively—nearly everyone stands for the flag and over 90 percent pay the taxes they owe. More than three in five Americans claim to vote regularly; the number who actually vote is less than that, but voting occasionally is not viewed as an onerous task by most Americans.

The group of citizens defined as inactive or apathetic is the smallest group, constituting less than a quarter of the population. We know little about why they are not involved. We do know that they are uninterested, uninformed, and alienated from the system. Nevertheless, these individuals who engage in no political activity rally 'round the flag. They are supportive of the system and are patriotic enough to fly the flag on the Fourth of July. They cheered for star-spangled gymnast Kerry Strug and grieved for the victims of the Oklahoma City bombing. If these citizens maintain their love of country, even though they do not participate in politics, perhaps their apathy really does not hurt the political system.

They can be compared with a group of unconventional activists labeled as "protesters."[9] Lester Milbrath (Milbrath and Goel 1977, 14–19) gathers into this category those who would "protest vigorously if the government does something morally wrong (26 percent)," "refuse to obey laws (16 percent)," "attend protest meetings (6 percent)," "join a public street demonstration (3 percent)," and "riot if necessary (2 percent)." These findings should be viewed as tentative because they were derived from one city at a time of considerable urban unrest (1968), but they also reinforce the conclusion drawn above, because protesters, by and large, participate in all forms of political activity. They did not withdraw from politics and thus "vote with their feet." They were active in politics and saw protesting as an extension of their activity.[10]

One could look at the American experience through a slightly different lens, however. Protesting against the government, that is, trying to "redress grievances" through nontraditional means, has a long history in this country. After all, what were our nation's founders if not violent protestors against the British? The Civil War, the bloodiest chapter in our country's history, resulted from the government's unwillingness to accept the ultimate form of protest—secession by the southern states. Earlier in this chapter we discussed the nonviolent protests of the civil rights movement that led to the Civil Rights Act of 1964 and the Voting Rights Act of 1965. Urban protests in the 1960s in Los Angeles, Detroit, Newark, New York, Washington, and other major cities often turned to violence as a means of expressing dissatisfaction with the policies of local, state, and national public officials. Student protestors on college campuses throughout the land were instrumental in changing the nation's policy in regard to the Vietnam War.

Although the number of citizens involved in protests of these types is typically small, especially compared with the number who vote, their commitment to their causes has been passionate and the impact of their actions has been far-reaching. Critics of the American political system say that our politics are ineffective because, to use an analogy from football, everything happens between the forty-yard lines. When people want to change a situation drastically, they have to act in a totally different way. These means are nontraditional and are not much discussed in books on elections and the electoral process. But look back at the list I compiled previously—and note that it is meant to be illustrative, not inclusive. Shouldn't we be concerned about a system that often fails to address such important problems in a way that defuses these kinds of protests?

What about today? Are there signs that the system is not working for a significant group of citizens? Susan Tolchin, in a book entitled *The Angry American* (1996), presents evidence that the electorate is angry. Others disagree, citing reelection rates for incumbents as a sign that voters at least are not discontent. How many of you live in states with active militia movements? The militia movements generally are composed of Americans who are extremely unhappy with the system, with the intrusion of government into their lives, with the loss of independence and individual freedom. They express these views in various ways. Some have taken their protests to an extreme, arming themselves and resisting all forms of government intervention. Government intervention, for example, at Ruby Ridge, Idaho, resulted in violence and death. In this case, government officials confronted a group that was resisting their authority; the confrontation ended with a shoot-out in which innocent people were killed.

Are these protestors so far outside of the mainstream that they should be ignored? Congress does not think so. In October 1995 the Senate Judiciary Committee held hearings on the shoot-out at Ruby Ridge and heard testimony from militia leaders. Critics in Congress felt that these hearings were inappropriate because they lent credibility to those at the fringe of American politics, who might well want to change the system so drastically as to bring it down. Do you think that makes them so anathema that they should be ignored? Might ignoring them play into their hands? How should our system treat those who hold extreme views and choose to participate in the most nontraditional ways? This question is not an easy one to answer. It has confounded elected officials throughout our nation's first two centuries.

Consider Operation Rescue, a small group headed by Randall Terry. Its members firmly believe that abortion is murder and are dedicated to closing down abortion clinics. Their position is based on their moral views. They believe that other citizens' rights are less important than the right to life that they are defending. Of course, other people disagree with their views, feeling that abortion should be permitted and that the decision to abort a fetus or not should be made primarily by the woman carrying that fetus. These citizens' rights are abrogated by the actions of Operation Rescue. When rights clash, the government generally intervenes. The question becomes, What level of protesting at abortion clinics is permissible? Again, some agreement can be reached. Most would agree that marching outside a clinic is a permissible exercise of First Amendment free speech rights. What about blocking clinic entrances? Some might claim that preventing abortions is so important that restricting other people's freedom of access, requiring intervention by local police to open the doors, is an action that firm believers can legitimately take. Others would disagree. What about bombing an empty clinic? That would shut it down without hurting anyone. What about bombing a clinic that is open? Some people might be hurt, but abortion protestors might find that price acceptable for ending abortion. What about shooting a physician who performs abortions? Is that level of violence permissible? Probably most people would not think so; most would draw a line well short of this type of violence. But clearly others disagree. And it is important to understand that their actions, while not traditional political participation as we usually think of it, is participation of an important kind that cannot be ignored.

Is it possible, then, to draw a profile of political participation among Americans? First, most Americans only engage in voting, not in any other political activities. In any given election 30–80 percent of the electorate does not vote, but these nonvoters do not make up a stable group. Over three-quarters of all American citizens consider themselves regular voters.

Beyond voting, political participation falls way off. Only one in ten Americans belongs to a political club or organization or contributes money to political campaigns; only a slightly larger number ever wear a button or display a sticker; only one in four tries to convince others to vote for specific candidates.

Other modes of behavior have been distinguished from those that some believe are in political decline. Nearly a third of all Americans are involved in community activities, and many more make certain they are involved in communicating about politics. A much smaller number contact public officials about their personal problems with the government, whether they participate fully or not. Furthermore, some evidence points to the thesis that a small group of people are very actively involved in political life in an unconventional way—people willing to protest (and even riot) if necessary to accomplish their political ends. These protesters do not view their activity as illegitimate but as the ultimate expression of their patriotism.

Finally, a small, but not insignificant, number of Americans are inactive and apathetic. They rarely even vote; however, they remain patriotic citizens. It appears that they truly are unconcerned, not turned against the system.

III. Politicians View Political Participants

A county chairman, along with his friend, walked up the stairs and into the first meeting of the county committee after the state convention. The chairman had been something of a hero at that convention, defending a gay rights plank against an attack from the religious right. This meeting would be a mere formality; he would be reelected, discuss plans for the upcoming election year, and adjourn the meeting in time to catch the last few innings of the Red Sox game. As he opened the door into the meeting room packed with people, he turned to his friend and said, "We're in for a long evening."

His friend viewed the packed room. "What do you mean? Who are these people?"

"I don't know, but they sure didn't get elected to the county committee to come to vote for me." The about-to-be-ex-county chairman had learned an important political lesson.

For practicing politicians, the most important part of citizen political participation is predictability. If only 50 percent turn out to vote, no one is bothered, as long as it is always more or less the same 50 percent. If attendance at county committee meetings is sparse, the chairman breathes easily as long as he knows who will be there. If a few people complain when an officeholder takes a controversial stand, he will not get upset—if that reaction was expected. But the unpredictable reaction—the large turnout, the new faces, the massive protests—doesn't just worry politicians. Worry is too calm a word. Unpredictable participation gives politicians nightmares.

The county chairman mentioned above lost his seat because he took a stand that caused people who had never been concerned before to pay attention to him, to take an interest in party politics. He didn't bring his supporters out to help reelect him because he didn't know he was in a contest. When he saw a sea of unfamiliar faces, he knew only too well why they were there. Others cared greatly about his stand at the state convention; they did not view him as a hero. The county chairman was a scapegoat. His opponents took advantage of the meeting to get rid of an unacceptable "radical."

The same scenario is repeated often. Voter turnout, particularly in primary elections, is difficult for politicians to predict accurately. Figure 4.6 shows the turnout in Iowa presidential caucuses from 1968 to 1996. A campaign manager looking at the data up to 1976 and planning for the 1980 caucuses would know how many votes his candidate needed to win. Using well-tested and sophisticated techniques for identifying supporters and getting them to the polls, such a manager could judge quite accurately how his candidate would do on the eve of the caucuses. Then he would be faced with the 1980 turnout figures: an estimated 100,000 Democrats voted. He throws out all previous assumptions. Who can judge who these new participants are and how they will react? More nightmares. He tries planning for 1984. How many will turn out? How many supporters does a candidate need to win? To make a good showing? About 75,000 Democrats participated in the Iowa caucuses in 1984; in 1988 the number jumped again, to about 126,000. Again, it was hard to know how many supporters would have to be mobilized to do well. To extend this point, the number decreased in 1992. The Iowa Democratic caucuses were not seen as pivotal in the nominating contest because the candidacy of Iowa senator Tom Harkin (D) discouraged others from making the state a pri-

Figure 4.6 Estimated Turnout in Iowa Democratic Caucuses, 1968–1996.

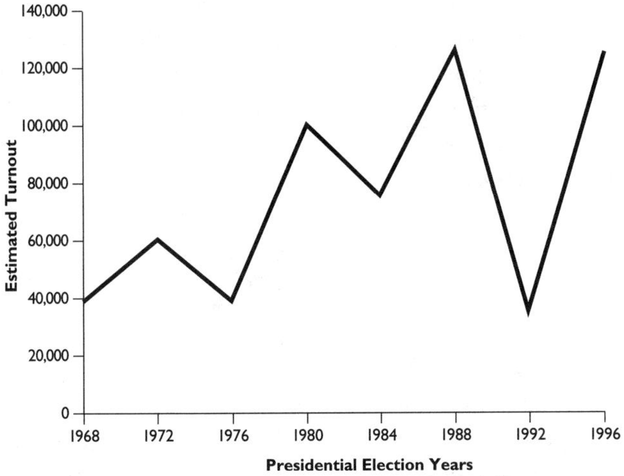

Source: Data from various Congressional Quarterly Service sources.

ority. In 1996, of course, President Clinton faced no opposition, but voters still turned out. None of these figures help those who must plan for the caucuses in the year 2000.

The same process can be used to examine reactions to governmental policies. History seeks to tell us how people react. But history did not predict the urban riots of the late 1960s or the campus riots following the Cambodian incursion during the Vietnam War in 1970. What could history have told Attorney General Janet Reno about how to react to the Branch Davidian siege in Waco in 1993? How should politicians react to those events? They do not know. Worse still, our political system has always been based on predictability. Political planning has to follow from what has happened before.

How then have practicing politicians viewed the changes in the electorate presented earlier in this chapter? First and foremost, as unfamiliar terrain they have to cross. When the electorate has expanded, they have dealt with that expansion, making appeals to new voters as they have seen fit. Those who have predicted accurately how the new voters would react, like the southern politicians who have softened their formerly racist rhetoric, have prospered. Those who have guessed wrong—like George McGovern, who assumed that masses of young voters against the war in Vietnam would rush to the polls in 1972—have lost, often badly. Others learn for the next electoral round. Today's politicians are faced with an expanding Hispanic electorate. How do they appeal to those voters? Some will strike a responsive chord and succeed. Others will not be so fortunate—or prescient.

When the electorate is not expanding unpredictably, politicians still proceed with caution. They know more or less what to expect, but they must avoid tearing up the pea patch, arousing opponents who do not normally participate. Politicians always prefer to remain on familiar terrain. Conjointly, their understanding of the electorate has become more and more sophisticated as polling techniques have improved. They know to whom they must appeal to win and how to base that appeal, as do their opponents. Elections, then, turn on the political skill and understanding of both aspirants and officeholders. The discussion in this the next chapter now turns to the behavior of the electorate, which these politicians seek to understand.

WEBSITES

http://www.census.gov

The U.S. Census Bureau provides information not only on population statistics but also on citizen responses to a detailed survey regarding political participation and many other areas of interest.

http://www.umich.edu/~nes

The National Election Studies (NES), conducted by the Center for Political Studies of the Institute for Social Research at the University of Michigan, have polled the American electorate for many decades. Data is available from surveys maintained by the Inter-University Consortium for Political and Social Research.

http://tap.epn.org/csae

The Center for the Study of the American Electorate maintains this website to publicize studies on how often Americans turn out to vote.

KEY CONCEPTS

Fifteenth Amendment
franchise
Jim Crow laws
Motor Voter Bill
Nineteenth Amendment
poll tax
residency requirements
suffragists
Twenty-fourth Amendment
Twenty-sixth Amendment
Voting Rights Act of 1965
"whites only" primaries

DISCUSSION QUESTIONS

1. Why wouldn't everyone favor a system in which every citizen automatically had the right to vote? Given today's computer technology that presumably can detect those who try to vote more than once, should we favor a law that permits any citizen with proof of age to vote anywhere?

2. How do you evaluate the low turnout rate in the United States? Some countries have compulsory voting. Should we require citizens to vote? If so, why? If not, why not?
3. What is implied by lower voting rates among members of racial minority groups? Does that make our democracy less legitimate?
4. Why don't young citizens turn out to vote? What could be done to stimulate turnout by people of your age? Does the government have an obligation to take such steps? Does it have an interest in doing so?
5. Are there forms of political participation that you believe are unacceptable? What are they? Why are they so tainted in your view? How would you have reacted to the type of political participation engaged in by those who dumped tea into Boston Harbor in 1775?

CHAPTER 5

Theories of Voting Behavior

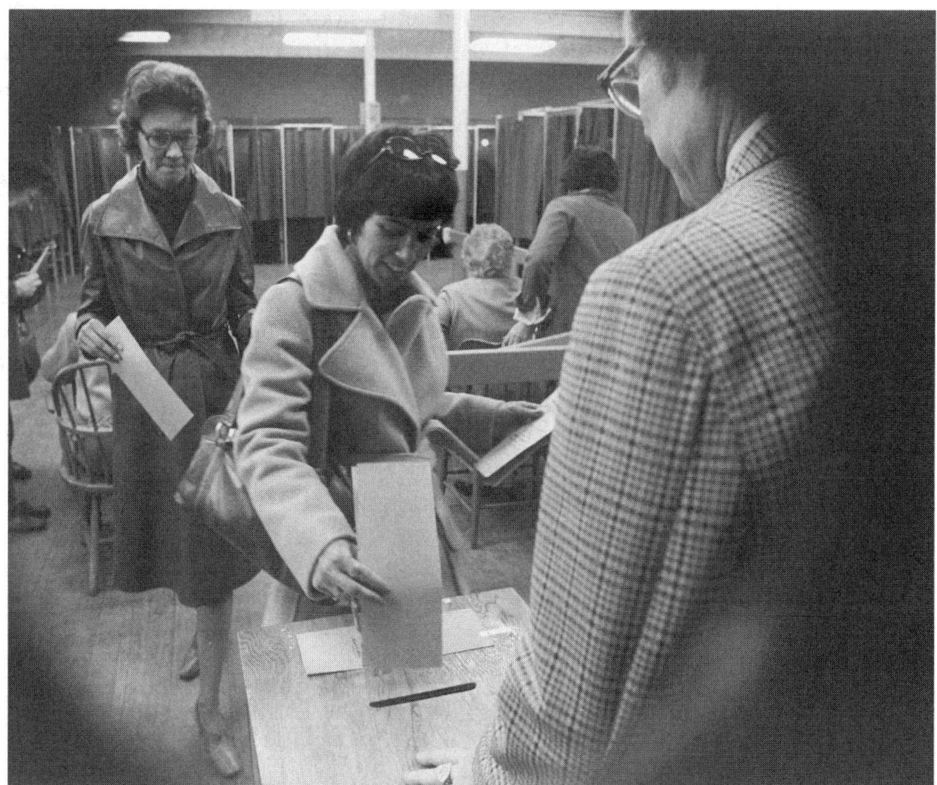

"I am not a Republican or a Democrat; I vote for the person." How many times have we heard this statement used to rationalize an individual's vote? What does it mean?

When you ask friends about their choice for a certain office, say, whether they supported President Clinton for reelection or how they decided to vote for any particular candidate, how do they normally respond? Do they begin elaborate discussions of different candidates' stands on different issues? Do they talk of one issue that is most important to them? Do they talk about party only? Or do they talk about a candidate's personal characteristics? What is it that makes someone decide how to exercise the right to vote, once the decision to vote has been made?

The individual voter is, after all, the basic building block of the political world. We really want to know how each *individual* votes, but we cannot know this about millions. And so we often group individuals together and look at their voting patterns in that way. In this chapter we will begin by looking at the individual's voting decision.

I. VOTERS IN PRESIDENTIAL ELECTIONS

Too often students of political science are aware of what current professional literature says but are ignorant of earlier writings that laid the groundwork for current studies. Much is lost by ignoring the work of scholars writing a generation ago, especially in the study of voting behavior. Moreover, it is always beneficial for students to see how a discipline progresses; in political science this progression, from the work of one group of scholars to the next, from one generation of scholars to the work of their students and even their students' students, is evident in a brief overview of what is known about the voting behavior of our citizenry and how it came to be known.

A. Models of Voting Behavior: *The American Voter*

THE AMERICAN VOTER

The classic study of American voting behavior.

Few books have dominated an area of study in the way that ***The American Voter*** (Campbell et al. 1960) has influenced the study of electoral behavior for a period of four decades. Angus Campbell, Philip Converse, Warren Miller, and Donald Stokes, the authors of this classic study, were not the first to study voting behavior in depth. They owed and acknowledged a debt to earlier students of voting behavior in local communities, particularly to Bernard Berelson, Paul Lazarsfeld, and their associates at Columbia University (Berelson et al. 1954; Lazarsfeld et al. 1944), who had earlier hypothesized that social characteristics determine political preference. Campbell, Converse, Miller, and Stokes drew on some of the findings of these earlier studies and clearly used them as a baseline from which to move. In so doing they focused the attention of a good segment of the research community on two questions: Who decides to vote and who opts not to participate in this way? Once a citizen has decided that he or she will vote, how does that citizen decide for whom to cast a ballot?

The authors of *The American Voter* and their colleagues at the University of Michigan Survey Research Center refined the national survey as a research instrument for social scientists and presented their findings in such a clear and coherent way that their work essentially became the model against which all others compared their results.

Their work was so influential that all students of electoral behavior need to be aware of its conclusions. The difficulty in presenting the findings of *The American Voter* in a brief summary like this one is that oversimplification masks the richness of the analysis and the sophistication of the presentation. However, as with many such classics, what people believe Campbell and his associates said is in many ways more important than what they actually did say. It is, after all, this oversimplified view of *The American Voter*—and not a detailed, careful analysis—that has determined the influence of this book. Having announced this caveat, I will attempt to summarize the book's conclusions.

Campbell and his associates were engaged in a study of the psychological and sociological determinants of voting behavior. They looked to the end of what they called a **funnel of causality**; at the narrow end of the funnel was the vote, the **variable** they sought to understand. Leading into the funnel were factors that caused the individual to vote or not, and, if that individual did vote, to vote for a certain candidate; these factors were deemed to be the determinants of voting behavior. But there were intermediate steps along the way. The authors of *The American Voter* studied how voters perceived parties, candidates, and issues and why they perceived them as they did. By cumulating the experiences of individual voters, they were able to draw conclusions about how the American electorate as a whole came to perceive the political world and to make their own political decisions.

FUNNEL OF CAUSALITY

Symbolic depiction of discussion of why Americans vote as they do.

VARIABLE

The measure used to capture the variation in observations of a concept one is interested in studying.

Their first conclusion was that voter perception is a mixture of cognition and evaluation, of perception and affect. How the voter perceives politics is a mixture of what that voter chooses to know and how that voter feels about a political situation. The average voter is concerned about politics, but not all *that* concerned. While the average American does vote, he or she does not think about politics a great deal, does not become involved in many other political acts, and does not spend a good deal of time keeping informed about politics.

A number of conclusions follow from this finding. First, the average American has an extremely unsophisticated view of politics. Campbell and his associates note the inability of the voter to view politics in abstract terms, to develop a coherent **ideology**. Rather than make judgments based on a sophisticated view of the issues, voters view can-

IDEOLOGY

A coherent set of beliefs that structure one's thinking about political issues.

didates as representatives of the two major parties; the parties in turn are viewed as feeling certain ways on issues and toward certain groups in society. Whether or not these views are accurate, the voters use their perceptions in making decisions by fitting or ordering their view of politics to the outlines of the perceptions. Because most people do not care much about politics, it is fairly easy to manipulate their views.

According to *The American Voter* model, most Americans have developed a strong, long-term commitment to one or the other of the major political parties, and this commitment is a most significant guide to voting behavior. How is this tie to a political party developed? Campbell and his associates review a good deal of social science literature as well as their own survey findings in order to conclude that the individual's home is the most important source of partisan affiliation. The two most influential factors seem to be the parents' partisanship and their level of political activity. If both parents are strongly involved with one party, the children are likely to follow the same course. If the parents' **party identification** is not the same, or if the commitment of the respondent's parents to politics is not strong, then the likelihood of the children affiliating with one of the parties declines commensurably. In fact, the likelihood of children in those households becoming significantly involved in politics is also low.

PARTY IDENTIFICATION

Self-assessment of a person's allegiance to one or the other of the major political parties.

Other elements also influence the choice of party, particularly when parental pressure is not strong. Among these influences are other important **socializing elements of American society**—the school, the work group, the church. Once partisan affiliation is confirmed, it is quite difficult to change; however, factors such as marriage, increased education, changes in job, social status, and/or neighborhood can have an impact. More significantly, cataclysmic events such as the Great Depression can affect the partisan political affiliation of entire generations.

SOCIALIZING ELEMENTS OF AMERICAN SOCIETY

Institutions that teach those in a social grouping its norms, expectations, values, ideas, and so on.

Most important to remember is what this view says about the role that the voter plays in democratic theory. This is essentially a pessimistic view of the American electorate's ability to control its own destiny. Voters are not capable of making decisions based on a rational consideration of issues. In order to cast "issue-oriented" votes, the citizen must have an opinion on an issue ("cognize" the issue, in *The American Voter's* term), must have knowledge of current governmental policy on the issue, must have some information about competing party stands on the question, and then must feel strongly enough to vote according to the perceived differences between the parties on that issue.

According to Campbell and his associates, voters meet none of these criteria. Rather, partisanship is determined by socializing instruments in society. Voters follow partisan cues for voting. When they stray from these partisan predilections, it is not because of opinions on issues, but because of appeals based on the personality or media image of the particular candidate or because of a particularly compelling short-range issue—such as a scandal or the appeal of a demagogue.

Looking further into *The American Voter*, one reads that **independents**, those without a strong partisan affiliation, tend to be those least involved in politics, least interested, least committed. Independents are the voters most likely to be swayed by emotional appeals, by charismatic candidates. Given that the Democrats' lead in voter allegiance constituted less than a majority in the 1950s, at the time this study was done, these least attractive voters—in terms of a democratic model—are often the ones who determine election results.

INDEPENDENTS

Those who do not identify with one major party or the other.

Not a very optimistic picture. Remember, this summary is an exaggeration of what Campbell and his associates actually wrote. After analyzing the American electorate in great depth, they did not set out to paint such a bleak picture. Rather, they seemed to predicate standards for performance that the electorate, taken as a whole, was unable to meet. Campbell et al. asked for an electorate that was able to order complex political issues, one that was able to make voting decisions based on comparative stands on particular issues, and one that demonstrated qualities such that elections were in fact viewable as **mandates** for the policies proposed by opposing candidates.

MANDATES

Instructions or directions from the electorate to adopt certain policy alternatives based on what the electorate meant to say in an election.

They found instead an uninvolved, unconcerned, unsophisticated electorate, voters making decisions based largely on partisan affiliations, which in turn were handed down from generation to generation. This partisanship was in the first place often based on issues that were perhaps no longer relevant, an oversimplification that led citizens to view American political dialogue in often unrealistic ways. The element of this electorate that often held the balance of power between the two parties was the group that met the tests of "good" citizens least well, that was most responsive to emotional appeals, that was least well informed, least concerned, and least involved.

B. Critics of *The American Voter* Model

Just as it is important for students of political science to know the foundations for current research, so too is it important for them to realize that even basic understandings of significant aspects of American political behavior can and do change over time. The fact that "revealed wisdom" of political analysis is overhauled is not a negative comment on those who have explicated the original model; rather it is a testament to the progressive way in which we learn, drawing on and going further than those who preceded us.

The view presented in *The American Voter* has not been accepted without controversy. Two schools of criticism stand out. The first group of experts, typified by V. O. Key Jr., maintained that Campbell and his associates had placed too heavy a burden on the American electorate and that the view presented was far more negative than the actual situation warranted. The second group claimed that the heavy reliance on data from the 1950s in *The American Voter* led the authors of that book to draw certain conclusions about the electorate that would not hold true over longer periods of time, even when applying the same theories to data gathered in the same manner but at a different time. The two schools will be discussed in turn.

1. Criticism by V. O. Key Jr. and His Followers

V. O. Key Jr. was perhaps the political science profession's consummate believer in American democracy. While not refuting the data presented by Campbell and his associates, Key insisted that an expert could reinterpret those data and still arrive at the conclusion that the American electorate was a responsible and trustworthy body. Key dedicated his slim volume, *The Responsible Electorate,* published with the assistance of Milton Cummings after Key's death, to the theme that the "voters are not fools" (Key 1966, 7).

STANDPATTERS

V. O. Key Jr.'s terms for those voters who support the candidate of the same party for two successive elections.

SWITCHERS

V. O. Key Jr.'s terms for those voters who vote for the candidate of one major party in one election and the candidate of the other party in the next election.

Rather than divide the population by partisan affiliation, awareness of issues, concern over politics, and ability to conceptualize ideology, Key used survey data to categorize citizens according to how they voted in sets of elections. Looking at presidential elections, Key characterized those who voted for the same political party in two consecutive elections as **standpatters**, those who voted for one party in one election and the other party in the subsequent election as **switchers**, and those who voted in one election after not having voted in the preceding one as "new voters."

Key then examined the behavior of voters in each of these categories, trying to determine if their behavior could be understood as rational. Most of the voters in any election were standpatters, those who voted the same way in two consecutive elections. However, these voters were rarely numerous enough to determine a winner. The next largest group was the new voters, reaching 30 percent in the election of 1952. These voters tended to side heavily with the winner. Switchers constituted between 13 and 20 percent of the electorate in the time Key studied.

Key's findings about the relative positions of the two parties is important, particularly given *The American Voter*'s conclusion about party affiliation and its determining effect on vote. Key discovered some shifting between elections even though most voters maintained stable party allegiance. Although the maintenance of the relative strength of the two parties between elections leads us to believe that a static situation exists, the supposed immobility is in fact the net result of a dynamic flow.

> A series of maintaining elections occurs only in consequence of a complex process of interaction between government and populace in which old friends are sustained, old enemies are converted into new friends, old friends become even bitter opponents, and new voters are attracted to the cause. (Key 1966, 30)

Key further maintains that membership in certain cultural, economic, and social groups is an important factor in deciding how an American votes, again as Campbell and his associates have maintained, but not in an irrational or predeterministic way. Group pressure or membership becomes important only for issues affecting that particular group. The fact that a voter is a member of a racial or religious group only affects that person's vote if and when that person believes that his or her racial or religious affiliation has an impact on how one distinguishes among candidates. This kind of analysis is significant in viewing the high percentage of blacks who vote Democratic or the switch to Kennedy among Catholic voters in 1960.

Perhaps Key's preeminent conclusion is that the most admirable, most rational voters are the switchers. He maintains that individuals switch because of the way that they perceive the government as treating them in the intervening period between elections. If they are happy with what the incumbent has done, regardless of whether they voted against him in the past, they will support him in the next election. In a parallel way, supporters of an incumbent in one election will turn against him—and importantly against a subsequent nominee of his party—if those voters are unhappy with the effects of policies adopted during the intervening four years.

Similarly, Key maintains that standpatters are rational voters. Those voters who support the same party in consecutive elections do so either because they like what a winner whom they have supported has done or because they dislike what a winner whom they have opposed has done. "Like" and "dislike" in this context are defined according to how those policies affect the individual in the areas that are of most concern to him.

Key's view of the new voters is not so sanguine. Actually, new voters fall into two categories—first-time voters and "in-and-outers," who vote in one election but not in the next. According to Key, new voters tend to go along with the tide. Those who are infrequent and not consistent participants are similar to the independents described in *The American Voter*: uninformed, unconcerned, uninvolved voters. While this group is large and tends toward trendiness, it is not the group that ultimately determines the winner in elections. Key maintains that the switchers play this role in American politics. (See table 5.1.) Note, for instance, that when Franklin Delano Roosevelt won reelection in 1940, most of his support came from those who had supported him in 1936; thus they were standpatters. By way of contrast, much of President Kennedy's support in 1960 came from switchers—and a very high percentage of those who switched in 1960 from how they had voted in 1956 went from Republican to Democratic, not the other way around.

Two other conclusions follow from Key's analysis. First, he explicitly rejects the cult of personality. One need not have been a charismatic figure like Franklin Roosevelt in order to convince the Republi-

Table 5.1 Voter Patterns in Supporting Major-Party PresidentialCandidates*

Year		*Democratic Candidates (%)*			*Republican Candidates (%)*		
		Standpatters	*Switchers*	*New Voters*	*Standpatters*	*Switchers*	*New Voters*
1940	Preelection	80	2	18	58	28	14
	Postelection	80	3	17	61	25	14
1944	Preelection	80	4	16	64	22	14
	Postelection	79	6	15	74	14	12
1948	Preelection	73	3	24	58	23	19
	Postelection	77	5	18	69	18	13
1952	Preelection	65	4	31	52	19	29
	Postelection	74	5	21	57	23	13
1956	Preelection	52	17	31	72	4	24
	Postelection**	n.a.	n.a.	n.a.	n.a.	n.a.	n.a.
1960	Preelection	46	24	30	71	6	23
	Postelection	56	30	14	78	8	14

*For a description of the data used in this table, see Key 1966, 22.
**No postelection poll was reported in 1956.
Source: Key 1966, 27.

can voters of 1928 to vote Democratic in 1932. Voters switched because of how they felt about the policies of the Hoover administration. Eisenhower's personality was not the critical element in the presidential race of 1952; the more important factor was that Adlai Stevenson was tied, in the voters' minds, to the policies of Harry Truman, who was perceived to have embroiled America in the Korean War. Truman supposedly had only a certain response to communism. Voters rejected Truman's policies. New voters rejected them in large numbers, but many who voted for Truman in 1948 also rejected them and switched to Eisenhower in 1952.

The other conclusion that follows from Key's analysis has served to structure much of the debate over voting behavior in the last two decades. *Key maintains that voters respond to the past, not the future* (1966, xii). He draws an explicit distinction between **prospective (future)** and **retrospective (past) voting**.

PROSPECTIVE (FUTURE) VOTING

Casting a vote based on what the voter thinks candidates for office are likely to do after the election.

RETROSPECTIVE (PAST) VOTING

Casting a vote based on the records that candidates have built prior to the time of an election.

Modern scholars, for all that, are quick to criticize Key's methods. His reliance of recall data (voters remembering their past actions) is particularly questionable. However, no one should underestimate his instinctive knowledge of politics and of the important questions to be examined. Key's influence persists more than three decades after his death.

The American Voter maintains that voters fail to vote prospectively because they are not well-enough informed or concerned. Consequently, they are left to cast their votes irrationally, basing them on party ties; theirs is a retrospective vote, but not an informed one.

Key claims that evaluation is the most important element in rational voting. Key's responsible voters evaluate what has happened in the past four years and make judgments. They are concerned with results only, not with policy promises. They do not give mandates; rather, they respond to results of past performance. To vote rationally in this context, one does not need to understand issues thoroughly, nor to recall where the party stands on those issues, nor to know precisely what the government has been doing. To vote rationally in this context, an American only needs to know if "the shoe is pinching" and, if so, who is causing it to pinch. This is a much easier test for the electorate to meet. According to Key, it is also a perfectly appropriate test.

More recently, scholars have expanded on Key's concept of retrospective voting. Drawing on the theoretical writing of Anthony Downs (1957), Morris Fiorina has developed a carefully crafted conceptual model of individual voting behavior (Fiorina 1977b; 1981; see also Franklin 1984; Franklin and Jackson 1983; Jackson 1975). Fiorina claims that the electorate makes rational choices. Citizens vote retrospectively because doing so is patently more manageable. Human beings simply find it easier to get information about what has gone on in the past than to evaluate what may happen in the future. Retrospective information, in fact, is acquired without effort. Furthermore, it is much more reliable than evaluative projections. Who, as a rational actor, believes politicians' promises today? Who ever did?

In order for retrospective voting to be rational, voting citizens must see some tie between candidates and parties; they must understand that parties are consistent on the issues that most affect them. Thus a vote for George Bush in 1988 was a rational vote, in this context, if one believes that voters favored Ronald Reagan's policies and linked Bush with those policies. An extension of this logic also holds that it is perfectly rational for a citizen to vote for a presidential candidate of one party and a congressional candidate of the other—if one does not want policy to move too far toward one party's view or to the other, or if one was satisfied with the policies produced by divided government (Fiorina 1996). Policy implications determine voting decisions only in a very few instances—those that touch many people, those in which there is a clear link between means and ends, and those that are tied to the parties by the electorate.

2. Criticism from Successors in the Michigan School

Before turning to a discussion of retrospective voting in the context of politics today, I want to evaluate the other criticism of *The American Voter*, the one that maintains that even though the study is time-bound, the model of expected behavior is an appropriate one.

NATIONAL ELECTION STUDIES (NES)

Series of studies of the American electorate carried out over the last half-century under the direction of a national board of scholars by the Survey Research Center at the University of Michigan.

Scholars at the Survey Research Center, analyzing the series of **National Election Studies (NES)** subsequent to the ones on which *The American Voter* was based, noticed a change in voter behavior. They began to look for reasons to explain these changes. Many articles published in the 1970s provided new interpretations of theAmerican electorate's behavior (Brody and Page 1972; Miller 1978; Miller and Miller 1977; Miller, Miller, Raine, and Brown 1976), but it was left to another group of scholars, using National Election Studies data from the 1960s and 1970s, to question some of the basic findings of *The American Voter.*

THE CHANGING AMERICAN VOTER

Study that built on the findings of *The American Voter* while criticizing the original study as time-bound.

In ***The Changing American Voter***, Norman Nie, Sidney Verba, and John Petrocik explicitly acknowledge their debt to the authors of the earlier classic work. In fact, in the dedication to *The Changing American Voter*, Nie, Verba, and Petrocik acknowledge Campbell, Converse, Miller, and Stokes, "on whose coattails we ride." In calling the paradigm laid out in *The American Voter* into question, the authors of *The Changing American Voter* state that such criticism "does not imply criticism of the paradigm makers" (1979, 8). However, they most definitely do call the conclusions into question.

The basic criticism is that the model constructed by the authors of *The American Voter* was based largely on the NES 1956 survey, and according to Nie and his associates 1956 was hardly a baseline on which to construct a sound hypothesis; that year had some peculiar and problematic characteristics. The task of *The Changing American Voter* is "to separate the time-bound from the timeless in political attitudes" (1979, 7). If the year 1956 was too placid to use as a baseline, which characteristics of voting behavior are indeed truly timeless, and which are time-bound and therefore in need of reinterpretation? Merely posing that question demonstrates how knowledge accrues.

The major finding of *The Changing American Voter*, one that differs from the conclusions in *The American Voter*, is that the electorate is much less committed to party. This is seen in a rise in the number of independent voters, in a decline in strong partisans, and in an increase in ticket splitting. Many more of the respondents to the quadrennial survey of voters expressed dissatisfaction with the two parties than was the case of the surveys done in the 1950s.

Further, Nie and his associates found that voters use two kinds of measures in presidential voting. The first of these is the personal characteristics of the candidates. The second, and this is the one emphasized, is *issues.*

This group of scholars claims that parties have become increasingly weak in the time since *The American Voter* was published. With Walter Burnham (1970) they argue that this party weakness may well represent a long-term trend. Whatever the length of the trend, its significance is clear. Parties as organizations are feebler; citizens might not oppose parties, but their commitment to parties is wavering; therefore, parties are less relevant to electoral behavior.

The authors of *The Changing American Voter* go further. They also argue that the new independent voters, whom they have identified in increasing numbers, fall into two groups. One group is the same as the independents identified by Campbell and his associates nearly twenty years earlier. The other group, however, is very different. While the original group of independents constituted the least involved, least concerned, and least informed voters, Nie et al. found that the new group is just the opposite. The new independent voter is very well informed, very concerned about politics, very involved in every way. These voters are people who charge the two major parties with irrelevance but take politics very seriously and choose a candidate based on their perception of his or her stand on issues (see also Miller and Wattenberg 1985; Wattenberg 1984; 1986; 1990b; 1994). Thus these authors claim that the way in which Americans decide how to vote has changed because, they claim, the times have changed. Issues have become more important in people's lives.

What issues? The new and important issues of the day, a new set of issues that distinguish this time from the 1950s. War and peace in Vietnam, lifestyle, and race relations were important concerns for the new American electorate of the late 1960s and early 1970s. These are issues on which voters were able to form a coherent political ideology, to distinguish the two parties, and to vote based on issue preference.

Nie, Verba, and Petrocik also show us why these issues have not

Figure 5.1 Split-Ticket Voting.

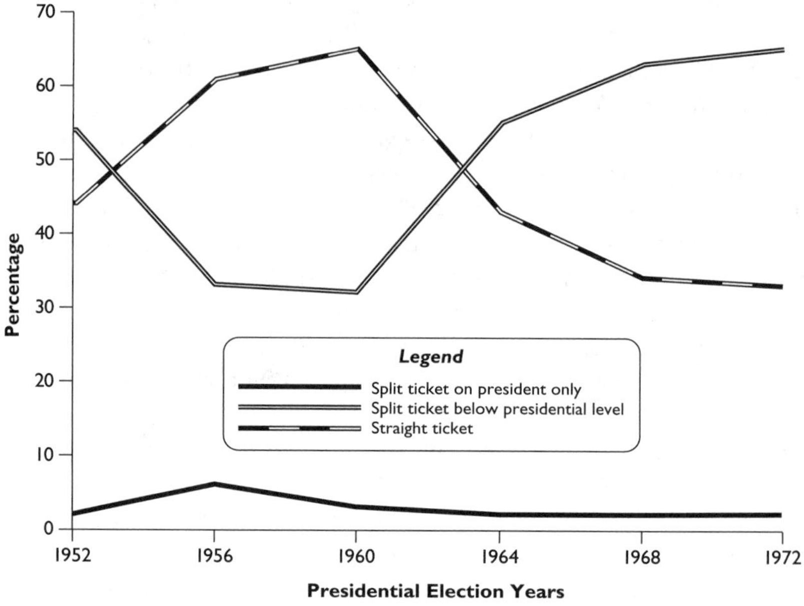

led to a new realignment. Rejecting retrospective voting, they argue that the parties are so weak and inconsistent in policy that retrospective voting is impossible.

> The individual candidates are more independent of party; they run on the basis of their own characteristics and programs, not as representatives of continuing party institutions. Insofar as this is the case, electoral choice can no longer be retrospective. Voters are less able to vote on the basis of past performance (as V. O. Key Jr. and others have argued they did), since the candidate cannot be held responsible for what others in his party have done while in office—unless, of course, the incumbent is the candidate. (Nie, Verba, and Petrocik 1979, 346–347; see fig. 5.2)

The Changing American Voter is based on the analysis of the National Election Studies surveys conducted at the time of the 1964, 1968, and 1972 elections. These presidential elections—and this study is only based on presidential voting—might be atypical in terms of being elections determined by highly salient issues, just as 1956 was atypical in terms of being a low-saliency election.

The election of 1964 is the one that best defines the parties in terms of issues, according to Nie, Verba, and Petrocik. This election was perhaps the most ideological of our recent elections. Senator Barry Goldwater (Ariz.), the Republican candidate, was referred to as "Mr. Conservative" by friend and foe alike.

During the election of 1968, the nation was torn apart by the Vietnam War. Try as he might, Hubert Humphrey, the Democratic candidate, could not separate himself from Lyndon Johnson, whom he had served

Figure 5.2 Voters' Evaluations of the Political Parties.

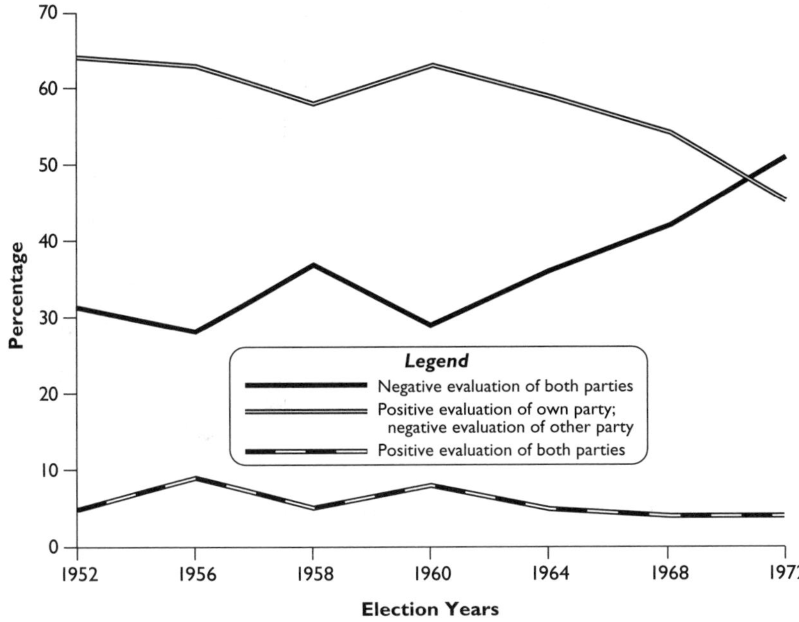

Source: Data from National Elections Studies.

with utmost loyalty as vice president. Johnson was generally perceived to be the architect of our military involvement in Vietnam.

Finally, the election of 1972 was the one in which the Democrats chose an extremist candidate, perhaps more in appearance than reality, but certainly in the perception of the voting public. Senator George McGovern (S.D.) was viewed by many as a radical, the candidate of "acid, amnesty, and abortion." The fact that the McGovern election was tainted on the Republican side by Watergate and dirty tricks and that McGovern was not so far to the left as he was often depicted does not negate how easy it was for the public to see this election in ideological terms as well.

When the authors of *The Changing American Voter* enlarged their book to include the 1976 election, they began to see a trend that called some of their findings into question. They assumed that an election like 1976, which pitted as opponents two centrist candidates, Gerald Ford, the Republican incumbent who had succeeded to the presidency when Richard Nixon resigned amidst the Watergate scandal, and former Georgia governor Jimmy Carter, would be different. But some of the differences turned out to deserve further analysis. This was particularly true of a tendency away from increased independence of voters and back to allegiance to political parties (see table 5.2). Again, we are left asking which of the findings are timeless and which are time-bound.

At this point it might be worthwhile to go back to Nie, Verba, and Petrocik's rejection of retrospective voting (quoted earlier). Two phrases stand out: "Insofar as this is the case" and "unless, of course, the incumbent is the candidate." A third phrase might have been necessary: "If the electorate sees that the candidates are rejecting party." The evi-

Table 5.2 Party Identification, 1952–1996

Identification	*1952*	*1956*	*1960*	*1964*	*1968*	*1972*	*1976*	*1980*	*1984*	*1988*	*1992*	*1996*
Strong Dem	22	21	20	27	20	15	15	18	17	17	18	18
Weak Dem	25	23	25	25	25	26	25	23	20	18	18	19
Ind. Dem	10	6	6	9	10	11	12	11	11	12	14	14
Ind. Ind	6	9	10	8	11	13	15	13	11	11	12	9
Ind. Rep	7	8	7	6	9	10	10	10	12	13	12	12
Weak Rep.	14	14	14	14	15	13	14	14	15	14	14	15
Strong Rep	14	15	16	11	10	10	9	9	12	14	11	12
Apolitical	3	4	2	1	1	1	1	2	2	2	1	1

Source: Data from National Election Studies.

Note: Entries represent percentage of survey respondents self-reporting in each category.

dence really is not clear on these issues (Wattenberg 1984; 1986; 1990b; 1994). The electorate seems to be linking together candidates of the same party, whether the candidates want to be linked or not. Even in the 1968 election, on which *The Changing American Voter* is based in part, Hubert Humphrey did all he could to separate himself from Lyndon Johnson but failed. Often one of the candidates is the incumbent, as Ronald Reagan was in 1984, George Bush in 1992, and Bill Clinton in 1996—or closely tied to the incumbent, as Bush was to Reagan when he captured the presidency in 1988. That link is all that is necessary for retrospective voting at the presidential level to be possible.

Sometimes political scientists become too involved in their own struggles over methods. The controversy over how one decides if the American public votes prospectively or retrospectively, over how much issues matter, in what circumstances, over whose interpretation of the same data is correct may well be one such parochial involvement. At times it may be appropriate to reject the most sophisticated research methodology and go with one's instincts, to use the old Studs Terkel method—sit down in an Irish pub and ask people how they decided. If an analyst did that for the 1980 election, the answer, at least for that election, should be clear. Ronald Reagan had his finger on the pulse of the people. He asked them one question—or rather asked them to ask themselves one question:

> Next Tuesday is election day. Next Tuesday all of you will go to the polls; you'll stand there in the polling place and make a decision. I think when you make that decision, it might be well if you would ask yourself, are you better off than you were 4 years ago? Is it easier for you to go and buy things in the stores than it was 4 years ago? Is there more or less unemployment in the country than there was 4 years ago? Is America as respected throughout the world as it was? Do we feel that our security is as safe, that we're as strong as we were 4 years ago? And if you answer all of those questions yes, why then I think your choice is very obvious as to who you'll vote for. If you don't agree, if you don't think that this course that we've been on for the last 4 years is what you would like to see us follow for the next 4, then I could suggest another choice that you have. (Carter 1982b, 250–251)

C. Presidential Voting Reviewed

Where does this review leave the question of how Americans decide for whom to vote? Certainly the professional social science community is not of one mind. Parts of the model developed by Campbell, Converse, Miller, and Stokes have been rejected; other parts remain intact. Portions of the criticism of Nie, Verba, and Petrocik have been accepted. Other portions might well need reexamination. The theory of retrospective voting, propounded by V. O. Key Jr. as a defense of the American electorate against the implied view of *The American Voter* and amplified by Morris Fiorina and others, has attracted some strong adherents.

THE NEW AMERICAN VOTER

Last major work by political scientist Warren Miller, reaffirming his belief in the basic findings of *The American Voter.*

The concepts under consideration are extremely complex. Generations of scholars have devoted their professional lives to studying party identification, with the basic concept being challenged, refined, reexamined, operationalized in various ways, and defended in various forms. Recently, Warren Miller and Merrill Shanks revisited the entire question of determinants of individual voting behavior in a magisterial new book, ***The New American Voter*** (Miller and Shanks 1996; see also Miller 1991b). While we cannot review the findings of this entire book, it is important to note that Miller and Shanks reaffirm the importance of party identification in determining voters' choices. They claim that the much-discussed dealignment of the American electorate misrepresents the actual situation. According to the Miller and Shanks analysis, younger voters entering the electorate are not aligning with either party, but voters in older age cohorts have maintained their party identification, with certain caveats regarding southern white voters stipulated.

What is impressive about *The New American Voter* is the extent to which it draws scholars back to a reexamination of a fundamental set of questions—who votes or who does not and how do the voters decide for whom they will vote? Presumably, Miller and Shanks and the others working to understand voting behavior will continue to grapple with these difficult questions.

The link between party identification and voting—and rationality of voters—has consumed political scientists' attention for decades. Human behavior is complex and difficult to comprehend. No clear consensus has emerged as research controversies abound (see Gant and Luttbeg 1991, 29–82, for a review of this literature; see also Niemi and Weisberg 1993). The necessity of examining the context of each particular election is absolutely clear (see Miller and Wattenberg 1985). And in the final analysis, it is important to supplement scientific examinations with common sense, with the knowledge of politics, and with a feel for people, not just numbers.

To this point we have considered only presidential voting. Only the president and vice president run in elections that have a visibility approaching that discussed in the literature reviewed to this point. What goes on in other elections? How do voters decide in cases different from those at the presidential level?

II. Voters in Congressional and Senatorial Elections

Almost all the research into American voting behavior has been research into presidential voting. This follows naturally from the fact that scientific survey research is extremely expensive and that the community of scholars have drawn heavily on the data collected by the Survey Research Center and the Center for Political Studies of the Institute for Social Research at the University of Michigan, made available to a large number of scholars through the Inter-University Consortium for Political and Social Research. The Survey Research Center has received a series of substantial grants to study voting behavior as an important factor to understanding the functioning of American democracy. Their original studies focused on presidential voting; it made a good deal of sense to continue a series of studies exploring the same phenomenon. At the same time, studies of voting behavior in nonpresidential elections, while certainly also of importance, have been conducted less frequently.

The Survey Research Center analyzed the electorate during the 1958 congressional elections and has asked questions about congressional elections on quadrennial presidential surveys; on other occasions it has conducted studies in nonpresidential years. The most often cited analyses of the data generated by that initial study of congressional voters describe an electorate not very concerned or knowledgeable about congressional politics (Miller and Stokes 1963; Stokes and Miller 1962). Nearly half of the respondents replied that they had neither read nor heard anything about *either* candidate. More than twice as many knew something about the incumbent than knew anything about the challenger, but few had any sense of how their representative stood on issues.

With so little knowledge, voters relied heavily on party affiliation to determine their congressional choice. Those who did not support the party's nominee deserted their party not because they were concerned over issues but because they had heard of the other party's candidate and not their own. Virtually all the voters who knew anything about their party's nominee supported him or her. Voting, then, seemed to be the product of blind party loyalty, not of party loyalty as a statement of issue positions. The 1958 respondents knew very little about who organized Congress or how issues distinguished the parties in Congress.

This view of electoral behavior should be recognized as consistent with the *American Voter* model, only more so. The Miller and Stokes analysis reveals an electorate in congressional elections that has virtually none of the characteristics necessary for rational prospective voting or retrospective voting. Rather, voters were almost totally uninformed and voted on the basis of party affiliation and the slightest degree of candidate recognition.

This perception of congressional voting behavior was not seriously reexamined in a systematic way until the Survey Research Center undertook an examination of the electoral behavior in the 1978 congressional elections. This study, tangible evidence of renewed interest by scholars in voting behavior below the presidential level, produced a wealth of literature on congressional elections that reevaluates the Stokes and Miller view (see Abramowitz 1981; Hinckley 1981; Jacobson 1980; Maisel and Cooper 1981; Mann and Wolfinger 1980).

The most noticeable change is that most voters have an increased awareness of congressional candidates. Depending on the measure used, voters were able to express an opinion on over 90 percent of the incumbent candidates and nearly half of the challengers. Further, examinations of highly competitive elections show that very high percentages of voters were able to evaluate both candidates.

For some years scholars had noted that an extremely high percentage of members of Congress seeking reelection were reelected (see, e.g., Fiorina 1978; Mayhew 1974a; 1974b). The 1978 data afforded scholars the opportunity to explore the reasons for this phenomenon. They found that partisanship had been replaced by incumbency as the key voting cue. Further, voters supported incumbents because they had more positive information about them, resulting in large part from the incumbents' skillful use of the resources available through their offices.

Some of the data are particularly striking. Nearly 90 percent of the respondents reported having had some contact with their congressmen; almost a quarter had personally met their congressmen; almost three quarters had received mail from their representative in Washington. These associations, all structured by the incumbent and virtually all positive in content, built a base of a favorable image that was all but impossible to overcome. Typically, challengers were not known at all; voters did not choose between two candidates on equal footing but between one who was well known and positively viewed and another who had to fight to be viewed at all. The electoral success of the incumbents should not be surprising. (See fig. 5.3.)

Note that issues were not mentioned as instruments that contribute to an incumbent's popularity. The 1978 data confirm the 1958 findings that citizens know very little about how their members of Congress stand on issues and that Congress members build their reputation

Figure 5.3 Electoral Success of House Incumbents.

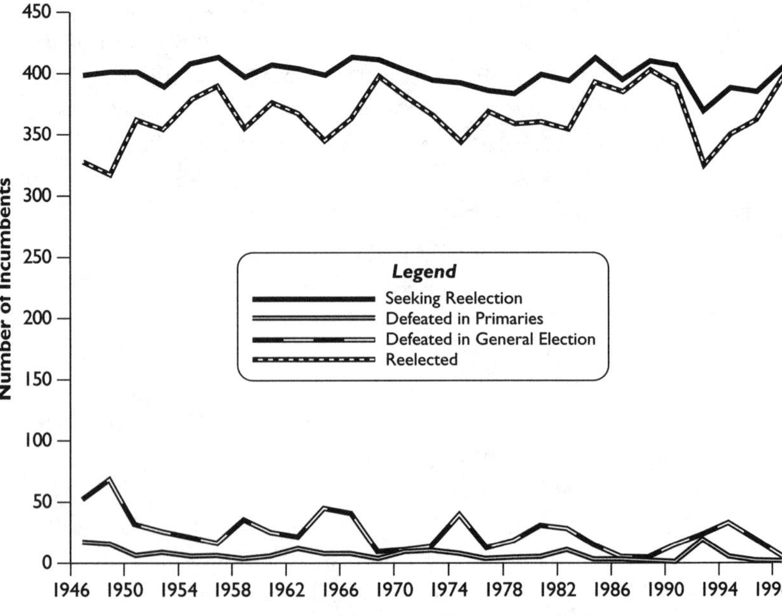

Source: Data from various Congressional Quarterly Service sources.

through constituent service, frequent communication, and positive publicity on popular causes.

Just as scholars were interested in incumbent advantages in House elections, they were also interested in why incumbent U.S. senators were frequently defeated. The data from 1978 show that senatorial incumbents did not have the advantages over their challengers that House incumbents had. Senatorial challengers were more well-known and contacted voters more frequently. Incumbents also could not "control" all their contacts with constituents as well as members of Congress were able to do. Senators were more frequently covered by the news media in situations they could not control; their jobs made them more prominent politicians in most states. Most senators could not build the personal relationships with constituents that congressmen could because of the size of their constituency. That combination—"balanced" image building, challengers who start out with better name recognition, and challengers' ability to spend money to become even more widely known—has significantly reduced the advantage of the incumbent in Senate races. The variation in the number of incumbents defeated revealed in table 5.3 demonstrates that other factors are clearly at work in these elections.

Some of you reading this analysis of how citizens vote in congressional and senatorial elections might well be asking: wasn't that all changed in 1994 when the Republicans took over Congress running on the Contract with America? The short answer to that question is that the theories of voting behavior still held in that election. Look at the data for the 1992, 1994, and 1996 congressional elections. At first glance, you notice that there has been more turnover; you also might notice that the incumbent return rate has decreased from the very high levels achieved in the elections immediately preceding those.

But you should also be reminded of a number of special factors. First, these elections were not "normal" elections. Incumbent advantage in 1992 was offset in large part by a widely publicized scandal about abuse of the House bank by certain incumbents. There is evidence to suggest that the scandal got so much publicity that members not implicated in any way were tainted by the actions of their colleagues. For instance, exit polls in one Illinois district revealed that a House member had lost a primary because of the bank scandal even though he had not been accused of any wrongdoing. Second, much of the turnover was caused by retirements, not by defeats. Surely some of these retirements were hastened by fear of potential defeat; more were caused by fear of a difficult campaign to win reelection on the part of incumbents who had not had to campaign hard in many years. There is no conclusive evidence that those who retired would necessarily have been defeated. Third, the incumbent return rates in the 1992 and 1994 elections are not far out of line from those a decade earlier; they only seem low because of the extraordinarily high rates of the immediately preceding elections. And fourth, the 1996 election looks a lot like a return to a more normal pattern.

Table 5.3 Electoral Success of Incumbents Seeking Reelection

Year	*Office*	*Number Running*	*Number Winning*	*Number Losing*	*Percent Winning*	*Percent with >60%*
1960	House	400	374	26	93.5	58.9
	Senate	29	28	1	96.6	41.3
	Governor	13	7	6	53.8	15.4
1962	House	396	381	15	94.3	63.6
	Senate	34	29	5	85.3	26.4
	Governor	24	15	9	62.5	12.5
1964	House	389	344	45	88.4	58.5
	Senate	32	28	4	87.5	46.8
	Governor	14	12	2	85.7	42.9
1966	House	402	362	40	90.1	67.7
	Senate	29	28	1	96.6	41.3
	Governor	21	14	7	66.7	23.8
1968	House	401	396	5	98.8	72.2
	Senate	24	20	4	83.3	37.5
	Governor	13	9	4	69.2	15.4
1970	House	391	379	12	96.9	77.3
	Senate	29	23	6	79.3	31.0
	Governor	24	17	7	70.8	4.2
1972	House	380	367	13	95.6	77.8
	Senate	25	20	5	80.0	52.0
	Governor	9	7	2	77.8	44.5
1974	House	383	343	40	89.6	66.4
	Senate	25	23	2	92.0	40.0
	Governor	22	17	5	77.3	36.4
1976	House	381	368	13	96.6	69.2
	Senate	25	16	9	64.0	40.0
	Governor	7	5	2	71.4	28.6
1978	House	378	359	19	95.0	76.6
	Senate	22	15	7	68.1	31.8
	Governor	21	17	5	76.2	28.6

continued

But what about the Contract with America? Wasn't the electorate saying that it was time for a change? Weren't they voting for Republicans specifically because they were tired of what the Democrats were doing? Certainly the Republicans felt that way when they took over as majority party in the 104th Congress. But the evidence is less than compelling. Most citizens could not name the items in the Contract with America. The Contract itself was composed of items that polling data revealed were supported by most citizens and that had traditionally been part of the Republican agenda (Pitney and Connelly 1996). In chapter 8 I discuss the Contract with America as an example of a successful campaign technique, but its impact on the 1994 congressional election does not call previous theories of how the electorate deter-

Table 5.3 Electoral Success of Incumbents Seeking Reelection (*continued*)

Year	*Office*	*Number Running*	*Number Winning*	*Number Losing*	*Percent Winning*	*Percent with >60%*
1980	House	392	361	31	90.7	72.9
	Senate	25	16	9	55.2	40.0
	Governor	10	7	3	70.0	30.0
1982	House	381	352	29	92.4	68.9
	Senate	30	28	2	93.3	56.7
	Governor	24	19	5	79.2	41.7
1984	House	407	391	16	96.1	78.9
	Senate	29	26	3	89.7	65.5
	Governor	6	4	2	66.7	50.0
1986	House	391	385	6	98.5	84.5
	Senate	28	21	7	75.0	50.0
	Governor	17	15	2	88.2	52.9
1988	House	409	402	6	98.3	87.3
	Senate	27	23	4	85.0	60.9
	Governor	9	8	1	89.0	37.5
1990	House	406	391	15	96.3	79.5
	Senate	32	31	1	96.9	66.7
	Governor	23	17	6	73.9	64.7
1992	House	349	325	24	93.1	65.0
	Senate	28	24	4	85.7	46.4
	Governor	4	4	0	100.0	100.0
1994	House	384	349	35	90.9	63.0
	Senate	25	23	2	92.0	48.0
	Governor	4	4	0	100.0	100.0
1996	House	382	361	21	94.5	59.9
	Senate	20	19	1	95.0	30.0
	Governor	7	7	0	100.0	71.4
1998	House	404	397	7	98.5	78.3
	Senate	29	26	3	89.7	73.1
	Governor	25	23	2	92.0	39.1

Source: Compiled by author from Congressional Quarterly Service sources.

mines for whom it will vote in congressional elections into question (Jacobson 1996).

What of electoral behavior in elections for statewide or local offices? Until very recently, political scientists have not produced systematic studies of elections at these levels (for recent examples, see Cox and Morgensten 1993; 1995; Garand 1991; Gierzynski and Breaux 1991; Jewell and Breaux 1991; and Weber, Tucker, and Brace 1991). However, some conclusions are inescapable. Races for governor, for instance, probably feature voting behavior parallel to that for senator. Governors are well known, but so are their opponents. Their accomplishments in office are examined in detail in the press. Gubernatorial opponents spend a good deal of money portraying the negative parts of incumbents' records. Voters decide based on these appeals—on party, image, record. Table 5.3 shows the electoral success of incumbent governors seeking reelection in the last decade. And one would expect a similar pattern for big-city mayors.

State legislators and others running in smaller constituencies face an electoral environment similar to the one that members of Congress face, with one notable exception. Again, few citizens know how a state legislator stands on key issues. In this case, however (and we note significant variation here from state to state), districts are often small enough that a significant percentage of the voters not only have had personal contact with the official but also know the official on a personal basis. When this is the case, partisanship and issues probably become less important; when the personal relationship does not exist, partisanship and name familiarity again dominate (Hogan 1997; Squire 1992; Garand 1991; Weber et al. 1991).

III. Voting Behavior Theory Revisited

The picture that emerges of the American electorate in the 1980s is not a clear one. As table 5.2 shows, most Americans do identify with one major party or the other. The number so identifying themselves declined during the 1960s and early 1970s. Some of that decline seems to have been reversed in the 1980s, but a movement toward more independents and fewer party identifiers, particularly fewer with strong party identification, is evident. Questions have arisen about the strength of party allegiance—and about the significance of that strength (see Converse and Pierce 1987 for a discussion of means of measuring partisanship; Miller 1998; Mattei and Niemi 1991; Finkel and Opp 1991).

Recall the discussion of party systems in chapter 2. Political scientists concur that the New Deal era ushered in a new party system, the fifth, in which the political line of cleavage dealt with responsibility of the federal government to aid citizens in times of economic crisis. But much less consensus exists concerning what has happened since that realignment.

The research community has been watching elections for signs of a new partisan realignment since 1968. During the Reagan years, National Elections Studies data revealed a decided move toward the Republican party, so that the gap between those considering themselves Democrats and those aligning with the Republicans narrowed to 7 percent by 1988. The major question challenging scholars has been whether we were witnessing a new realignment or a continuing "dealignment," a period in which citizens relate less positively to and are less influenced by political parties.

The debate continued as political scientists searched for meaning in the NES studies of the electorate. Merrill Shanks and Warren Miller

(1990) and Miller (Miller 1985a, 1) writing alone claim that "the election of 1984 brought the first substantial indications that such a realignment may be occurring along ideological fault lines." Developing the argument further, Miller (1985a, 14) writes:

> The fact that party identification provided somewhat less net support for the Democratic candidate, Mondale, in 1984 was not the consequence of the reduction in its centrality for individual voters' decisions. It was the result of a shift in the partisan balance, the ratio of Democratic to Republican identifications. That shift, in turn, was the product of a large realignment of party identifications which brought party loyalties closer into alignment with voters' ideological perspectives.

Studies of the 1988 presidential election tended to confirm the belief that a realignment was occurring. According to Miller (1990, 110–115) the realignment was a two-stage realignment:

> My analysis of the 1988 elections thus supports the thesis that a significant first phase of the 1980–1988 realignment occurred between 1980 and 1984 among the less experienced and less sophisticated voters who responded to Reagan's personal leadership with an increase in Republicanism. A smaller but perhaps more meaningful second phase then occurred between 1984 and 1988, particularly among the older and better-educated voters who ultimately responded favorably to the Reagan administration's emphasis on conservatism. (Miller 1990, 114; see also Miller 1991b; Shanks and Miller 1989; 1990)

But those conclusions did not go unchallenged. And into the 1990s scholars continue to debate topics such as the extent to which the most recent realignment is regional rather than national in scope (Black and Black 1987), that voters' identification with party is different at the national and state levels (Hadley 1985; Niemi, Wright, and Powell 1987), the group composition of the two parties and its significance (Stanley et al. 1986), the extent to which dealignment is merely a reflection of "unrealized partisanship" (Carmines, McIver, and Stimson 1987), or the degree to which the apparent dealignment is in fact a reflection of the nonalignment of the newest voters (Miller and Shanks 1996). The research plate stays full, and scholars, fascinated by the interplay of these factors, remain hard at work.

Two concerns drive this research. At the most basic level, political scientists remain concerned with how citizens make voting choices. That has been the central inquiry driving data collection and analysis by voting-behavior scholars. At a more practical level, scholars are also concerned with describing what is happening to the American political system as a whole. Some have begun to ask whether the realignment paradigm is no longer appropriate and whether another, perhaps based on divided government as the defining feature of American electoral behavior at the turn of the century, should replace it (Fiorina 1996).

Politicians and political journalists observing the same phenomena are no more certain of their meaning. All these analysts are now relying on an increasing number of sophisticated opinion surveys, those carried out by partisan pollsters and/or those conducted on behalf of major newspapers and television networks. In the aftermath of the 1984 election, much was made of the margin of the "youth" vote for Reagan. Although Shanks and Miller (1990, table 2) discounted the impact of the youngest age cohort on the shift toward the Republicans in 1984, many politicians and political journalists pointed to this vote as evidence that a major realignment was under way. Richard Wirthlin, a leading Republican pollster, has said, "If we see young people staying the most Republican group of the electorate, if we see first voters registering Republican, . . . then we'll have a good chance to . . . become the majority party of the 1990s" (Broder 1986, 6).

But Ronald Reagan's popularity did not result in a whole generation of young Republican voters. In 1992 Bill Clinton, the first baby boomer to run for president, unseated George Bush, who will undoubtedly be the last World War II veteran to serve in the White House. Clinton made a direct appeal to the youngest age cohort. His success came from his own relative youth and from his recognition that young voters listened to different appeals. Thus he campaigned on MTV and played his saxophone on the *Arsenio Hall Show,* strategies that would not have occurred to the more traditional Republicans.

How one views the role of party in the electoral decisions reached by voters in the 1980s and 1990s depends on what theory one espouses. We know that the parties are still important to many, that the major parties are now closer to each other in terms of voters identifying with them, but also that many people eschew party allegiance, identify with neither party, and vote based on other cues.

What else enters into that decision? When issues seem to play a crucial role in election races or when the parties clearly differentiate themselves on ideological grounds, issues and ideology can have a large impact on voting behavior. The authors of *The Changing American Voter* explicitly demonstrate that impact in their book.

It could be argued that "issue voting" led to the defeat of a certain number of senatorial incumbents in 1978 and 1980. In those campaigns, the records of liberal Democratic senators like John Culver and Dick Clark of Iowa, George McGovern of South Dakota, and Frank Church of Idaho were systematically attacked, not only by their challengers but also by organized conservative groups who orchestrated campaigns emphasizing key emotional issues (see chap. 6). Significantly, incumbent members of Congress were winning in these same states in which incumbent senators were losing; voters were splitting their tickets because their votes were based on different criteria.

On the other hand, often voters do not seem to care about the details of issues; they appear to be more concerned about their overall well-being and how politicians—in their role as government officials—have contributed to that well-being. Voting based on the evaluation of an incumbent's performance, rather than promises of future action, is the most common explanation of President Reagan's 1980 victory (Pomper 1981a, 97), of his reelection in 1984, and even of the Bush victory in 1988 (because he was viewed as an heir to the still-popular Reagan). More compelling is the fact the President Clinton's victory in 1992 is also attributable to the public's evaluation of the incumbent, in this case to the negative evaluation of the performance of the Bush administration in the year leading up to the 1992 election. Few who followed that election have forgotten the sign prominently displayed in Clinton's Little Rock campaign headquarters, "It's the economy, stupid!" (Arterton 1993; Quirk and Dalager 1993). Clinton's reelection in 1996, despite the Republican congressional victory in 1994 and continuing attacks on the president's character, can best be interpreted as the voters expressing satisfaction with his performance as president. Thus voters turned out the Democrats from majority status in the Congress in 1994 and kept the Republicans as the majority party in Congress in 1996. But they voted for Democrat Clinton as president because they positively evaluated his performance in the White House, his handling of the economy, and his conduct of foreign affairs (Elshtain and Beem 1997).

One school of thought claims that voters are casting rational, considered votes when they choose to support a presidential candidate of one party and a congressional or senatorial candidate of the other. These scholars say that voters want to hedge their bets. They might favor one candidate for president, but he or she might be a little too liberal than they really want; they will thus temper their vote by choosing a congressional candidate who is more conservative to keep the president from going too far (Fiorina 1996; Jacobson 1996). Given what we know about the level of information citizens have concerning their representatives in Washington or the issues of the day, it is difficult to imagine citizens sitting down and thinking in this way. But perhaps it is not too difficult to imagine them doing so intuitively. Voters might not have sophisticated views about issues or political ideology, but they generally can place themselves somewhere on an ideological scale and have a perception of where prominent politicians fit. If they believe the government has gone too far in one direction or not far enough in another, they can cast their vote accordingly.

But even this retrospective evaluative voting is not always in evidence. Below the presidential (and perhaps senatorial and gubernatorial) level, citizens know little of incumbents' records or the issues with which they are concerned. They might blame Congress for the mess the country is in (Fenno 1972) or might not have much faith in government and politicians generally, but they rarely blame *their own* representatives. Voters know these local politicians, view them positively, and frequently reelect the ones who seek reelection. Voters distinguish between the individual they know and trust and the impersonal institution—far removed from their daily lives—causing trouble.

IV. POLITICIANS VIEW POLITICAL BEHAVIOR THEORY

Politicians look upon the American electorate as consumers. They, the politicians, are the products that have to be sold. And they are sold in any way that is effective in getting the most people to vote for a candidate.

An oft-stated theoretical argument is that politicians seek only a plurality of the votes while making as few commitments and/or concessions as possible in order to guarantee a winning coalition. Nothing so badly misreads politicians as does this argument. Politicians fear losing; they do not fear commitments or concessions. Officeholders never feel secure; they have too much to lose if they are wrong. Consequently, in setting electoral strategy, they seek to generate maximum support, not merely win. In fact, one of the consequences of failing to win by a wide margin is appearing vulnerable and attracting more serious opposition in the next election (Herrnson 1998; Jacobson; 1980; 1992; Goldenberg and Traugott 1984). Thus politicians seek to maximize their winning margin, to attract as many voters to their side as is possible. To do so, they have to make assumptions about how voters decide.

It is also evident to most politicians that an individualized sales approach is the most effective. As one member of Congress put it, "I love going door-to-door. When I talk to someone in their living room, and when they say they'll support me, *I know* I have their vote. No question about it."

Door-to-door campaigning, that famous one-on-one sale of self, has proven successful in campaign after campaign. Eugene McCarthy (D-Minn., 1949–1971), George McGovern, Jimmy Carter, and Gary Hart (D-Colo., 1975–1987) all used that approach successfully in the New Hampshire Democratic presidential primaries. "Walking Dan" Walker, Democratic governor of Illinois (1973–1977), and Lawton Chiles, Democratic senator (1971–1989) and governor (1991–1999) of Florida, spent months walking the length of their state to greet voters personally. Many members of Congress have followed a similar strategy, though the publicity that initially accompanied such walks and added to their effectiveness as a campaign technique has lessened considerably as campaign "walks" have become commonplace.

But consider the problems of bringing one's campaigning to individual voters. The average congressional district, for example, has approximately 650,000 citizens. Maybe 450,000 of those are potential voters, who live in 200,000 households. If a candidate spent twenty minutes in each living room, assuming everyone was home and no time was needed in between stops, that candidate would have to have put in nearly 5,500 twelve-hour campaign days. Candidates accomplishing one one-hundredth of such a schedule in a two-year cycle feel that they have developed the common touch. Even with surrogates and volunteers, the enormity of "personal" effort becomes apparent. And the effort must be multiplied many times over for senatorial, gubernatorial, or presidential campaigns. Campaigning for individual votes might well work in local elections, and it is used to good effect for some offices in larger districts, but most politicians must use other means to approach the electorate.

Rather than see voters as individuals, politicians tend to see them as members of groups to whom appeals can be made. Once the decision has been made to group individuals, a number of options are open, some of which can complement each other. Some others, however, seem to preclude possible strategies.

One of the most influential groups in the Republican party today is the so-called **religious right** (see Wilcox 1996). This group of citizens, defined in various ways, agrees that certain moral principles they share should be important in political decision making (see chap. 6). Among the issues most important to this group are outlawing abortion and permitting prayer in schools. In some areas of the country those who adhere to these principles and feel that they are the most important issues on the political agenda constitute a majority, or a near majority, of the Republican party. Republican candidates must decide if they are going to appeal directly to these voters. If they do, they might well be hindering their chances of reaching other voters who are less committed on the issues of concern to the religious right or oppose these positions but favor Republican positions on economic issues.

RELIGIOUS RIGHT

Group that believes that adherence to certain moral principles constitutes an important aspect of political life.

In seeking the Republican presidential nomination in 1996, magazine publisher Malcolm "Steve" Forbes stressed his economic platform, calling for replacement of the Internal Revenue Service code with a flat tax. He tried to avoid the litmus test issues on the religious right's social agenda. He fared poorly in Republican primaries in states dominated by this group. After 1996 Forbes made a determined effort to appeal to the religious right, clearly acknowledging that his 1996 strategy had failed. What he could not know, however, was whether his new approach would alienate the economically conservative but socially moderate voters who had favored him earlier.

Many Republicans consciously appealed for the support of those hurt by waves of illegal immigrants in states such as California, Texas, and Florida in 1996. They called for stricter immigration laws, increased use of the Border Patrol, and denial of benefits to those who entered the country illegally and to their children. Although some voters responded to these appeals, Hispanic voters reacted negatively. An appeal to one group precluded an appeal to another.

Democratic candidates face similar dilemmas. An appeal to the least-advantaged elements in society might alienate Democrats who feel that the welfare system has run amuck or that government is too inefficient. Democrats taking a strong pro-choice position on abortion, a position favored by a majority in their party, might alienate anti-abortion elements whose votes they will need in the general election.

Each candidate must define his or her constituency by grouping the potential electorate in ways that were meaningful to his or her campaign. Some groupings preclude others; it is not possible to appeal to both the religious right and activist women's groups. Other strategies are less limiting; a candidate can appeal to the elderly on social security or health care issues without ruling ardent environmentalists in or out of his likely supporters.

But politicians can also look at their constituency as a whole and break it down into groups of people who are concerned with particular issues. Which groups seemed to favor President Clinton in 1996? How did he get their support? He concentrated his campaign remarks on general economic conditions, appealing to people who had benefited from his first four years in office. He stressed his position as a moderate Democrat, having cut the size of the federal deficit and having produced a robust economy with low unemployment and low interest rates. He talked about making the welfare system work, not about helping people on welfare. He sought to capture the middle of the political spectrum and to isolate the Republican candidate, former senator Bob Dole (Kans.) on the extreme right. Clinton's appeal seemed to be a national appeal. He rarely stressed local issues. Similarly, candidates for governor or U.S. senator or those for seats in the House of Representatives often look at their states or districts as a whole and campaign to specifically identifiable interests.

A second strategic approach groups voters by geographic region, not by interests or similar categorizations. According to this view, the West votes as one bloc in a presidential election, the South as another. The map of the nation is drawn in terms of electoral votes. Where can a candidate win the 270 electoral votes needed for election (see chap. 10)? This strategy uses a different arithmetic; it is based on winning states, not groups of votes. If a Democratic candidate can hold states in the Northeast and the Midwest that went for President Clinton in 1992 and 1996, he will have nearly half of the electoral votes needed for victory. Where can he get the rest? He had better concentrate his campaign in those crucial areas.

Similarly, candidates for statewide office in Massachusetts look at how their campaign is doing in Boston—and then the rest of the state. In New York, they look at New York City, the suburbs, and upstate. In Illinois, at Chicago and downstate. In Colorado, at Denver, those areas on the western slopes of the continental divide and the arid planes on the eastern slopes. In California, at liberal northern versus conservative southern California. In some congressional districts the geographic distinctions are almost as pronounced. Representative Jim Maloney (D) represents Connecticut's Fifth District, divided between poor mill towns and affluent bedroom suburbs of New York City. Republican Mary Bono (Calif.) succeeded her late husband, Sonny Bono, as the representative from their state's Forty-fourth District, which includes not only her hometown of Palm Springs and other wealthy suburbs of Los Angeles but also lush farmlands and nearly unirrigatable desert. When politicians in any of these areas campaign, they are always acutely aware of their geographic surrounds.

Note the distinction. In this case the politicians are appealing to those who live in a certain area because they assume that citizens relate to others in that area. This strategy is quite different from appealing to groups based on shared issue concerns. But in a broader sense, the theory is the same. Electoral strategies do not normally involve appeals to individuals. Individuals vote, but candidates appeal to them in groups, groups defined by the candidates and their strategists according to their strengths and perceptions of what will work. The larger the constituency, the more this is the case.

Tip O'Neill (D-Mass., 1953–1987; Speaker of the House 1977–1987) has been quoted as saying, "In the final analysis, all politics is local." Politicians still believe Tip, decades after his retirement, years after his death. Many started out as local politicians, and they know the effectiveness of one-on-one campaigns. Their goal, accordingly, is to make national or statewide politics local. They do this by defining smaller groups into which voters fall and then seeking to appeal to these groups. Many techniques are available for these appeals—mass media directed at a certain audience, targeted mailings, speeches to certain groups. But in the end, the political strategy is the same: make an appeal, in any way possible, to the largest number of people, so that it will seem personal to each one. Campaigners sell the product by figuring out what the voters want to buy.

Whereas political scientists seek to explain voting behavior with some precision, politicians—with the souls of artists, not scientists—try to mold the electorate into the shape they want. The skill of both the scientist and the artist deserves attention.

WEBSITES

http://www.umich.edu/~nes

The National Election Studies (NES), conducted by the Center for Political Studies of the Institute for Social Research at the University of Michigan, has polled the American electorate for many decades. Data is available from surveys maintained by the Inter-University Consortium for Political and Social Research.

http://www.ropercenter.uconn.edu

The Roper Center for Public Opinion Research holds the largest library of public opinion data in the world. Much of this data is available on-line, as are its publications *America at the Polls* and *Public Perspective*.

http://www.pollingreport.com/

An independent, nonpartisan resource on contemporary public opinion.

http://www.people-press.org/

The Pew Research Center for the People and the Press is an independent public opinion research organization that also focuses on contemporary views of the American electorate.

KEY CONCEPTS

The American Voter
The Changing American Voter
funnel of causality
ideology
independents
mandates
National Election Studies (NES)
The New American Voter
prospective future voting
religious right
retrospective past voting
socializing elements of American society
standpatters
switchers
variable

DISCUSSION QUESTIONS

1. How would you describe your own party identification? Would you call yourself a Democrat? A Republican? An independent? How strongly do you hold to that party affiliation? Where do you think it came from?

2. How would you answer the questions above about your parents? How interested are they in politics? Has their involvement or lack of involvement had an impact on your own views?

3. Have you ever voted? If you were eligible to vote and did not, why not? If you did vote, how did you decide for whom you would vote? Can you think about that question for different offices?

4. Do you think it is "better" if citizens vote prospectively or retrospectively? How did you define "better" in answering that question? How do you think most citizens vote in these terms?

5. Do you think it is appropriate for citizens to split their ticket or should they vote for politicians from the same party? If you think they should split their ticket, how should politicians interpret those votes when they go to make public policy? If you think they should vote a straight ticket, what role do individual legislators play?
6. What do you make of the current era of divided government? What are the citizens saying, if anything, when they vote in a Democratic president and a Republican Congress?

CHAPTER 6

Organized Groups in the Political Process

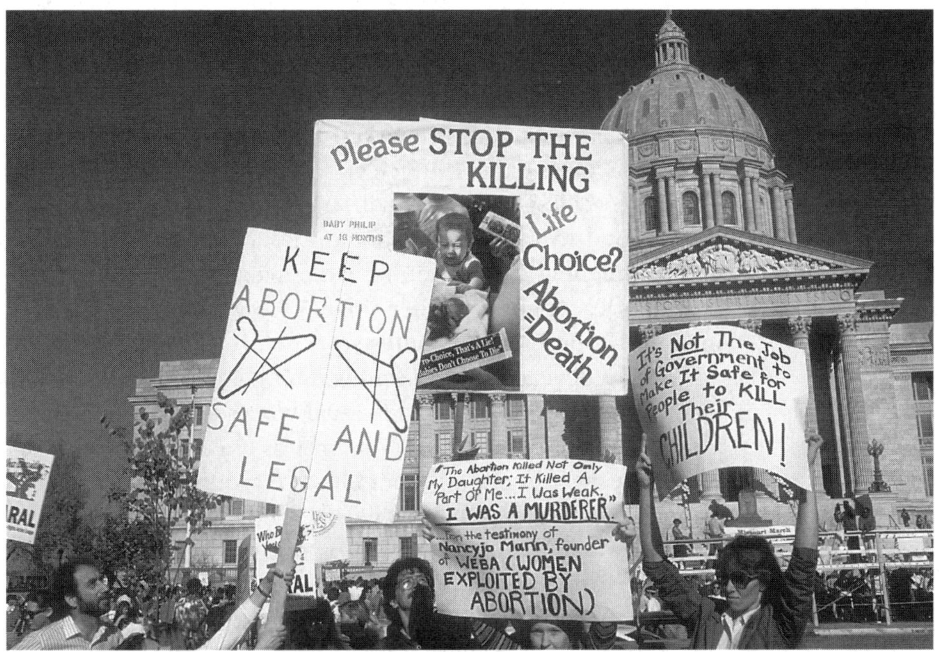

A recent National Election Study survey from the Survey Research Center at the University of Michigan asked a series of questions about groups, including the following:

> There's been some talk these days about different social classes. Most people say they belong either to the MIDDLE CLASS or the WORKING CLASS. Do you think of yourself as belonging to one of these classes?

> In addition to being an American, what do you consider your main ethnic group or nationality group?

The question "How would you rate the following groups?" was followed by a list: labor unions, feminists, civil rights leaders, people on welfare, women, conservatives, poor people, Catholics, big business, blacks, evangelical groups active in politics, the federal government in Washington, liberals. Obviously, the designers of this question believe that Americans respond to political messages by filtering those messages through reactions that they have as members of a group.

A similar perspective marked the analysis of candidate appeal by journalists during the 1996 elections. How would the Republican position on social security play with the elderly? How would Hispanic voters respond to various immigration policy proposals? Could Republican presidential candidate Bob Dole make any inroads into President Clinton's lead among "soccer moms"? How would organized labor vote in closed congressional contests?

A careful reading of the preceding paragraphs and my analysis of how politicians appeal to individual voters in chapter 5 should reveal a conceptual inconsistency. The groups cited in the National Election Study questions were different kinds of groups—social groups, ethnic groups, racial groups, ideological groups, occupational groups, and others. Not only are these groups not mutually exclusive (e.g., one could certainly be a black teacher who is a union member) but they are also generically different. The first NES questions seek to find out how the respondent perceives himself or herself. The questions allow for more than one answer and then probe for primary **self-identification**. In analyzing the influence of groups on the electoral process, however, a researcher must distinguish among types of groups and the effect these groups have on politics.

SELF-IDENTIFICATION

Responses that individuals give about their own sense of whom they are or to what groups they belong.

Americans, like citizens of any other nation, divide themselves "automatically" into certain types of groups. The electorate can be divided racially (blacks, whites, Hispanics, Asians, etc.), religiously (Protestants, Catholics, Jews, etc.), by age (the elderly, the middle-aged, young adults, etc.), or by occupation (farmers, teachers, construction workers, lawyers, etc.). Other similar groupings could be added to this list. As mentioned in chapter 5, politicians often treat the electorate as a collection of such groups, appealing to voters to react through their **group consciousness**. In this regard it is important to find out which groups with which voters principally self-identify (as the survey asks) and how candidates will appeal to their rivals' social groups"—as journalists wondered in trying to predict the 1996 elections.

GROUP CONSCIOUSNESS

Concept that certain attitudes and opinions are adopted because they reflect the views of those in a group with which one associates.

What commentators for centuries have noted as a distinguishing characteristic of the American populace is not the ability to identify with demographic, occupational, or social groups but rather a long-lived tendency to join organized groups. Until very recent times, analysts, from the authors of the *Federalist* papers through V. O. Key Jr., have focused their attention on the impact of organized groups on the policy-making process, not the electoral process. In the last edition of his classic text *Politics, Parties, and Pressure Groups*, published in 1964 (p. 18), Key wrote:

> A striking feature of American politics is the extent to which political parties are supplemented by private associations formed to influence public policy. These organizations, commonly called **pressure groups**, promote their interests by attempting to influence government rather than by nominating candidates and seeking responsibility for the management of government. Such groups, while they may call themselves non-political, are engaged in politics; in the main theirs is a politics of policy.

PRESSURE GROUPS

Descriptive name by which interest groups were known in the past.

Key (1964, 19) acknowledges that "pressure groups may campaign for party candidates and may even become, in fact if not in form, allied with one or the other of the parties." However, the emphasis in his five chapters on pressure groups is most decidedly on how these organizations seek to effect policy changes *after* elections have been held.

Within a decade of Key's death in 1963, even much less perceptive observers of American politics had come to realize that the role of interest groups (the term "pressure groups" has been all but dropped because of its pejorative connotation) has been drastically altered. Although they continue to play an important role in all aspects of the policy-making process, organized interest groups acting as organizations, not merely associations with which voters identify, now play a central role in the electoral process as well. (See, e.g., Berry 1997; Wright 1996; the articles in Herrnson, Shaiko, and Wilcox 1998, and those in Cigler and Loomis 1995; and Schlozman and Tierney 1986.) When Democratic candidates challenging freshman Republicans in the 1996 election were dubbed as "the tools of organized labor," the appellation stemmed from endorsement and support by organizations *as* organizations, not because individual voters who were members of those groups supported him.

This chapter focuses on the role of organized groups in the electoral process. Two aspects of this role will be examined separately: (1)

the ways in which these organizations enter into the campaigns of various candidates and (2) the effectiveness of these groups in controlling their members' votes. As you read these sections you should be asking yourself about what role you think groups should be playing in the process. What were once referred to as "pressure groups" have become "interest groups." But political journalists talk all the time about the pressure put on politicians by those groups whose support they seek. Is that good or bad in your view? What is the relationship between interest groups and political parties? The Democrats are often viewed as the party of the labor unions, and the Republicans as the party of big business. What do those connections entail? How often do parties and interest groups work together? When are they at odds? Before turning to these questions, however, we need an explicit understanding of types of groups to be examined.

I. Organized Groups in American Politics

Table 6.1 lists a sampling of organized groups in the United States today. They cover a wide array of interests, from those concerned with more general topics, like the AFL-CIO, to those concerned with very specific subjects, like the National Abortion Rights Action League. They come in a variety of sizes, from a few hundred members, like the National Football League Players' Association, to tens of millions, like the American Association of Retired People (AARP). They engage in a variety of activities, from sponsoring agricultural fairs like 4-H Clubs to sponsoring presidential candidate debates like the League of Women Voters. Only some of these groups are involved in the political process as groups, though members of virtually every group are involved in politics.

A. Political and Nonpolitical Associations

Americans form associations for various reasons: camaraderie, education, charitable work, economic advancement (Walker 1983; Verba, Schlozman, and Brady 1995). Some of these groups have an obvious stake in the political process. For example, the National Federation of Independent Businesses clearly is concerned with legislation affecting small business establishments. Some of these organizations were formed for political purposes, the liberal Americans for Democratic Action standing as one such group. Other groups were formed for purposes unrelated to politics, but they became politically involved as the government began to involve itself in matters relating to that group's purpose. For most of its first hundred years, the American Medical Association tried to stay out of organized politics. But for the last fifty years or so, the AMA has monitored national legislative action and has frequently lobbied and

Table 6.1 Types of Organizations and Examples of Associations

Health and Medical Organizations
Aerospace Medical Association
American Board of Allergy and Immunology
American Council on Pharmaceutical Education
International Association for Accidental and Traffic Medicine
March of Dimes Birth Defects Foundation
National Geriatrics Society
Society of Behavioral Medicine
Religious Organizations
American Zionist Federation
Christian Coalition
Christian Women's Fellowship
Fellowship of Concerned Churchmen
International Conference of Police Chaplains
National Association of Church Personnel Administrators
Society of the Bible in the Hands of Its Creators
Cultural Organizations
Afghanistan Studies Association
Association of Aviation and Space Museums
Authors Guild
Business Committee for the Arts
Creative Artists Public Service Program
Drawing Society
Friends of the American Museum in Britain
Virgil Society
Scientific, Engineering, and Technical Organizations
American Board of Clinical Chemistry
American Political Science Association
American Society of Landscape Architects
Herb Society of America
Musser International Turfgrass Foundation
Roller Bearing Engineers Committee
Stonehenge Study Group

Source: Encyclopedia of Associations.

campaigned to protect its perceived interest. Finally, some groups have stayed above the political fray, despite the expanding role of government. Phi Beta Kappa, the academic honor society formed in the year of our Revolution, has never entered the political realm in over two hundred years and remains removed from politics today.

The decision of whether or not to become involved in politics—through either the policy-making process or the electoral process, or both—is a significant one for an organization. As the leaders of an organization see that their group's interest is affected by governmental action, they must decide on the role they wish to play. If they decide to become politically involved, they take on a new status. If they decide to

LOBBYING

Taking actions to persuade legislators or those in government to pursue policies favored by one's group.

POLITICAL ACTION COMMITTEES

Organizations that receive contributions from fifty or more individuals and contribute money to at least ten candidates for federal office; often, but not always, affiliated with lobbying organizations.

lobby the Congress for legislation, they must register as a **lobbying** organization. If they decide to support candidates for office, they must form a separate **political action committee**. In any case, if they were ever granted tax-exempt status by the Internal Revenue Service, they will likely forfeit that status. Politicization may make fund-raising more difficult. However, if they stay out of politics, the group's members may decide that the group has become irrelevant to the issues around which it formed; this perception may erode the group's membership and support as well.

At times these decisions are easy for leaders to make; at other times they are not. Environmental groups are an interesting example. In the early years of its existence, the only political activities engaged in by the Sierra Club involved efforts to create more national parks. In the late 1960s, however, as environmental concerns heightened, the club became involved with lobbying on more issues. In 1975, for the first time, the Sierra Club opened a Washington office in order to focus its political efforts. It began to use paid advertising to extend its message of environmental concern to a wider audience. Because the Sierra Club spent more than 10 percent of its revenues for political purposes, the Internal Revenue Service revoked its status as a tax-exempt foundation.

Obviously, the leadership of the Sierra Club was aware of the implications of the decision to expand its political activities. The Audubon Society, an organization with a similar perspective, has decided to forgo this approach and has remained a foundation exempt from federal taxes and eligible for tax-deductible contributions.

B. Politically Active Groups

Our concern is with groups (or individuals representing groups) that have decided to become involved politically. The number of such groups is staggering: over 12,500 individuals were listed in a recent directory of Washington lobbyists. Over 1,600 political action committees contributed to candidates in the 1978 congressional elections; more than 4,000 had registered with the Federal Election Commission by the end of 1988; nearly 4,300 by 1998. In the face of these awesome numbers, we should look carefully at the rationale behind the formation of such a farrago of interest groups.

1. Economic or Noneconomic Interests

One way to analyze interest groups is on the basis of their membership. If the members are motivated by *primarily* economic interests, they can be distinguished from other groups whose members have fewer (or at least less obvious) immediate tangible concerns.

A preponderance of the groups active today exist in order to defend their members' economic interests. Why do people find this economic defense so crucial? As the American economy diversified, our citizens increasingly felt that they needed to band together with people of similar interests to defend themselves against those who seemed to be more powerful. Thus farmers' cooperatives and labor organizing began at various times in the 1800s. As these groups diversified further—and thus developed separate interests—more groups were formed. At present, groups with very specific interests have registered themselves with the Federal Election Commission. For example, groups that are active politically include the Florida Tomato Exchange Committee for Responsive Government, the Missouri Soybean Association, and the Ice Cream, Milk, and Cheese Political Action Committee.[1]

The number of economic interest groups also increased rapidly when the federal government became more and more involved in regulating the daily life of most Americans. As government played an increasingly intrusive role in regulating economic matters, greater numbers of Americans came together to advance or defend those interests. Similarly, as the American economy became more and more diversified, the associations became more and more specialized. Many Americans have strong feelings about the overall tax rates in the country, but one group, called the "Beer Drinkers of America," lobbies specifically to keep Congress from raising the alcohol tax. The group is made up mostly of friends and family of brewery owners and employees. They also have a wide representation of regular citizens, though, who really like beer and feel very strongly that a higher tax should not be imposed on an item that gives them pleasure.

Examples of economic interest groups abound. Some are quite well known, such as the United Auto Workers or the National Association of Manufacturers. Others are considerably more obscure, like the Coalition for Common Sense in Government Procurement or the Joint Labor Management Committee of the Retail Food Industry.

Noneconomic groups, sometimes called **public interest groups**, pursue goals that their members view as good for the entire society, even if those goals do not serve the economic interest of one particular segment of society. The individual most closely associated with the formation of public interest groups is **Ralph Nader**. He first made his reputation by crusading against General Motors for producing unsafe automobiles (Nader 1991). He was instrumental in forming a cadre of public interest groups concerned with consumer issues, government reform, health care, and other issues. Currently active "Naderite" organizations include Public Citizen, Congress Watch, Critical Mass, Public Citizen Litigation Group, Tax Reform Research Group, Health Research Group, and various state and local public interest research groups (PIRGs).

PUBLIC INTEREST GROUPS

Organizations that lobby the government and work for a political agenda that is not defined by economic or other narrowly defined interests.

RALPH NADER

Consumer advocate who has pressured government for reform agenda since the 1960s.

Others associate public interest groups with Common Cause, an organization of nearly a quarter-million members formed by former

Health, Education, and Welfare Secretary John Gardner in 1970 (McFarland 1984). Common Cause bills itself as the "citizens' lobby" and concentrates heavily on issues of government reform.

However, many other groups—some older, some younger; some larger, some smaller; some more effective, some less effective—have formed around noneconomic issues and remain active in politics today. These include the environmental groups mentioned earlier, civil rights organizations, ideological groups of the left and the right, religious groups, groups interested in government reform, and many more. Their impact on public policy and on elections is often just as great as the ones made by their economic counterparts.

Although the distinction between economic and noneconomic groups is a useful one, it should not be overemphasized. The line can become blurred and can change over time. The organized women's groups that formed around the issue of suffrage are a good example. Suffrage, once achieved, gave way to certain other rights, culminating in the unsuccessful drive for ratification of the Equal Rights Amendment. Along the way, however, women's economic rights were recognized as being as clearly involved as their other rights. One important goal of the women's movement became "equal pay for equal work." The goal was symbolized by the "59 cents" button, signifying that women earned only fifty-nine cents for every dollar a man earned. Although equal pay is now mandated by law, "equal pay for comparable work" has remained a goal of the women's movement. The economic concerns of organizations like the National Organization for Women (NOW) have spread to include the allegedly discriminatory practices of the insurance industry, compensatory pay for past discrimination, and many other important issues. NOW is not primarily an economic interest group, but it cannot ignore women's economic concerns.

2. Multipurpose or Single-Purpose Groups

SINGLE-PURPOSE GROUPS

Interest groups that concentrate their efforts on one particular issue.

MULTIPURPOSE GROUPS

Interest groups that reflect the views on a variety of issues on which their members express concern.

The discussion of the women's movement raises another possibility for categorizing groups active today. Some groups—**single-purpose groups**—are organized for a single purpose; others—**multipurpose groups**—lobby on a whole range of issues of interest to their membership. The size of each division depends on how narrowly or widely the term "single interest" is defined. Again, some examples are self-evident; others, however, cannot be so clearly defined.

During the first two decades of this century, the Congressional Committee of the National American Women's Suffrage Association was organized for the sole purpose of achieving women's right to vote. Similarly, today's Pro-Life Association and National Abortion Rights Action League (NARAL) are associations whose purpose relates to only one issue—the existence or nonexistence a woman's right to choose. On the other hand, groups such as NOW, the League of Women Voters, and the American Association of University Women are concerned with a whole array of women's issues.

The distinction between single-purpose and multipurpose organizations has important implications for the effectiveness of these groups. When Kate Michelman, the leader of NARAL, speaks on the question of abortion, she speaks authoritatively for the approximately 500,000 dues-paying members of her group. They joined the group, combining their financial investment often with a personal investment of time, because they feel a strong commitment to one side of the issue of abortion. No one can question the firmness of their stand on this issue.

On the other hand, if Susan Dailey, the leader of the Business and Professional Women's (BPW) Foundation of America, were to speak on the same question, despite the fact that she "represents" that group's members (70,000 members in 2,000 local organizations), her audience could certainly question the commitment of her members to a strong stand on this particular issue. BPW's views are not self-evident. The same questions regarding commitment are also important in trying to determine how important membership in a group is to the member's other political activities.

3. Federal or National Groups

A distinction like the one made above differentiates **federal groups** from **national groups**. National organizations are ones in which members, be they individuals or groups, belong directly to the national organizations. The National Association of Manufacturers is a national organization to which various corporations belong individually. Decisions in these organizations are made directly, with the leaders of the national organization responsible (in ways that are often difficult to define) to their members (see Eismeier and Pollock 1984).

FEDERAL GROUPS

Interest groups whose structure reflects a decentralized organization with local, state, or regional units contributing policy views to the federal unit.

NATIONAL GROUPS

Interest groups whose structure is centralized, without powerful local, state, or regional component units.

Federal organizations are ones whose national organization is a joining together of state or local organizations, each of which is itself autonomous or semiautonomous. The AFL-CIO is the obvious example of such a group, but it is only one of many that could be given. In organizations of this type, lines of authority are much less distinct. If the various constituent units split on a particular issue, how can the federal leadership speak authoritatively, particularly if the local units are permitted to retain their autonomy? Thus federal organizations may spend a good deal of time on internal politics, assuring that stands taken in Washington do not cause problems out in Pocatello.

The same distinction between national and federal organizations affects the input they make to the electoral process. When the Grocery Manufacturers of America, a national organization, decides to back a candidate for U.S. Senate in Illinois, it is clear that the organization has spoken. However, before the Americans for Democratic Action decides to take a similar stand, the leadership in Washington has to consult with the local Illinois affiliate. The problems of federal organizations multiply when the autonomous members disagree. The power of such a group is diminished when politicians perceive that it does not speak for "all."

II. ELECTORAL ACTIVITIES OF ORGANIZED GROUPS

The purpose of drawing the distinctions noted above relates to the varying impact that groups have on the electoral process. The groups became involved in electoral politics in the first place in order to effect changes in public policy. For many years "interest group" or "pressure group" was used as a synonym for "lobbyist." The primary means used by these groups was lobbying legislators and, to a lesser extent, administrators (Key 1964, chaps. 2-6). Only *after* the lobbying role was firmly established did organized interest groups become involved in the electoral process in a meaningful way. Today it is not far from the truth to assert that most people who think of interest groups assume that they are synonymous with political action committees. Although this connection is not absolute, the role of interest groups in campaigning has indeed become prominent.

Even as their role has expanded, however, it is distinct from the role played by political parties. Parties run candidates for office and seek control in order to organize the governing process. The parties stand for certain principles, but they use these principles chiefly as a means to attract adherents. Interest groups, contrarily, became involved in the electoral arena *only* to forward their policy preferences. Put simply, instead of taking positions to attract followers, they support candidates who support their positions—or oppose candidates who do not favor their positions. This last point is important. Political parties field candidates in order to *win* positions; interest groups at times support one candidate simply to bring about the defeat of another.

In the 1996 congressional election, for example, the AFL-CIO, the main arm of organized labor, opposed a group of freshman Republicans who had taken stands opposed by labor in the 104th Congress. The AFL-CIO was against these incumbents; the quality of the challengers in these districts was almost completely inconsequential, though their views on the key issues were not. Political parties, conversely, would not be so concerned with policy positions as they would be with a partisan label.

How do interest groups affect the electoral arena? In the following section, which deals with the group's impact on the voting behavior of group members, we will examine the activities through which these groups seek to have an impact in the broadly defined political environment. (See Gimpel 1998; Berry 1997; Wolpe and Levine 1997, 48-54; Wright 1996; and Schlozman and Tierney 1986, 200-220.)

A. Working within the Party

Most interest groups attempt to maintain some degree of bipartisanship because they do not want to alienate, in either party, public officials who favor their policy preferences. However, remaining "above" the partisan battle does not mean removing themselves wholly from the internal operations of both parties. Traditionally, interest groups have attempted to effect changes in the two party platforms.

It has already been noted that the suffragists defined platform support for the women's vote as one of their goals earlier in this century. Similarly, those favoring passage of the Equal Rights Amendment fought to have it included in both parties' platforms. Republicans first expressed support for the ERA when they were seeking to build opposition to four-term president Franklin Roosevelt. One of the most interesting aspects of the 1980 Republican Convention was the successful effort by anti-ERA groups to keep support for that amendment out of the GOP platform. Similarly, the Pro-Life Impact Committee was successful in having an anti-abortion plank inserted into that platform. In both cases, the debate before the Republican Platform Committee was structured by interest groups (Malbin 1981, 100–110).

Many groups have been actively involved in the platform-writing process. Before most recent conventions, each party has held a series of platform hearings. The stated goal has been to reach out for the opinions of rank-and-file Republicans and Democrats. To a great extent the effect was to reach out for the views of organized groups. The groups send their leaders to testify; they prepare their own "miniplatforms," and they "lobby" with members of the platform committee. The most involved groups even campaign, often successfully, to have their followers made members of platform committees. Certainly this has been the case with the religious right, which has been most successful at capturing control over Republican delegations in states with permeable delegate-selection rules, rules that make it relatively easy for those not normally involved with a political party to take part in its work (Usher 1998). Although debate continues over the importance of platforms in the making process (see Pomper with Lederman 1980, chap. 8; Wayne 1988, 147–151), interest-group leaders unquestionably see the platform as one place in which they can have an impact.

In the 1998 election cycle, anti-abortion forces went one step further in trying to influence the Republican party. Instead of seeking to have their position inserted in party platforms, they attempted to make adherence to their position a sine qua non for receiving campaign funding support from the national Republican party, essentially applying a litmus test that GOP candidates had to pass in order to receive support. The effort, put forth at a Republican National Committee meeting by committee members from states with strong religious-right delegations, was narrowly defeated after the intercession of RNC chair Jim

Nicholson, who argued that he did not want to exclude candidates from the party who would be potentially strong in some regions. This example also demonstrates the sometimes conflicting needs of interest groups and of parties. Parties certainly want the support of members of important interest groups (and party leaders court the leaders of various groups who are thought to be influential in gaining that support), but at the same time, the parties do not want to be captured by the interest groups. Party leaders must look to a broader audience with a wider range of views than is true of group leaders.

While groups try to maintain ties in both parties, no one doubts that many groups are closer to one party than the other. The more feminist-oriented women's groups—NOW, NARAL, ERAmerica—certainly feel more at home in Democratic party circles then they do in Republican circles. The same can generally be said for black organizations. While these groups maintain contact with Republicans and attempt to influence the positions of Republican party candidates, they have been more successful with the Democrats. And, of course, the opposite can be said for groups such as the Christian Coalition, whose allies are mostly Republicans.

The relationship between organized labor and the Democratic parties brings this tie to the extreme. While labor has traditionally been close to the Democratic party, labor's loyalty was strained at the 1972 National Convention when the AFL-CIO—as well as many other groups traditionally part of the New Deal coalition—felt excluded. After its overwhelming electoral defeat in 1972, the Democratic party needed once more to appeal especially to labor. Party chairman Robert Strauss appointed a new Commission on Delegate Selection and Party Structure, to be chaired by United Auto Workers president Leonard Woodcock. Five other prominent labor leaders were appointed to the panel. When Woodcock resigned, claiming he did not have time to devote to the task, the leadership fell to the vice chair, Barbara Mikulski, then a little-known Baltimore city councilwoman. Mikulski, appointed as a representative of ethnics and women, proved to be a feisty and outspoken chair. Labor received less than it wanted from the Mikulski Commission, but a foot was back in the Democrats' door (Crotty 1983; see chap. 9).

Labor has continued its active involvement in the Democratic party. When the Democratic National Committee was elected in 1980, party leaders felt that too few of the members were labor leaders. Consequently, the chair of the DNC used fifteen of his twenty-five at-large appointments to name union officials to the party's ruling body. In addition, four of these union leaders were appointed to the Executive Committee of the DNC, the most important decision-making group (see chap. 3).

To cement its ties with the Democratic party further, organized labor formed an advisory committee to help with party fund-raising and strategy setting immediately before the 1982 elections. Union-represented groups have contributed substantially to the DNC each year since. As a final step in reasserting its role in the Democratic party, and in order to guarantee an impact on the internal workings of the party, the AFL-CIO Executive Committee decided that labor leaders would gather in advance of the 1984 presidential primaries to endorse the candidate they felt should be supported as the opponent of President Reagan. They tapped Walter Mondale and then faced the test of delivering their members' votes in the subsequent primaries and caucuses. A divergence of opinion between union leaders and their membership is a fairly recent phenomenon that reduces the influence of labor leaders in today's politics. Regardless of the impact of this endorsement, its intent was clear.

Organized labor was saying that union members had a home in the Democratic party. And one way they intended to effect the public policy changes they desired was through a continuing influence over the internal operations of the party. In 1988 labor leaders backed away from a preprimary endorsement of a presidential candidate, but again many labor leaders were active in candidate organizations. As the 1992 nomination approached, with few Democrats out front looking to be tapped (see chap. 9), labor leaders played a more low-key role. However, even early in the process they made it known that they stood ready as a group to support New York governor Mario Cuomo should he decide to advance his candidacy. When Cuomo opted out, labor did not come down strongly in any one camp. However, it remained a force in the party by assuring that each potential nominee had labor leaders among their top supporters.

Labor leaders have also been important in the internal functioning of many state and local Democratic organizations. They have played key roles as Democrats plotted strategies for congressional and senatorial elections. And, as noted earlier, they took the lead in the effort to recapture the House of Representatives after the Republican takeover in 1994. They did this not only through financial contributions, but through working with Democratic strategists in planning attacks on the freshman Republicans seeking reelection throughout the nation.

The extent and openness of organized labor's commitment to the Democrats is unique. At the same time, women and minorities, despite the fact that both groups were also given positions of privilege within the Democratic party, still maintain ties with the Republicans. The National Women's Political Caucus has cochairs of different parties, for instance. Attempting to bring influence to bear on internal party matters is clearly one technique that interest groups use to reach their goals.

B. Group Ratings

Increasingly, organized groups are "rating" representatives and senators in terms of the degree to which they support or oppose legislation favored by those groups. These ratings, which usually range from zero (no support) to one hundred (total support), are computed by the groups after they select the issues most important to them (Fowler 1982).

Group ratings differ in terms of which issues are chosen (those deemed appropriate to the group's concern), how many votes are chosen (all or only the most important on the selected issues), and how scores are computed (how absentee or proxy votes are counted). For example, the Chamber of Commerce of the United States constructs an index of how members vote on a series of issues on which they take a position and communicates that position to members in advance of a vote (Gugliotta 1998). Other groups choose issues after the session is over and rate members without regard to whether the group's position was known in advance. Whatever means are chosen, the ratings are identical in intent: they identify friends and enemies of the groups for the group members to see and for others interested in the group's opinions to weigh in judging incumbents.

Some of the ratings are more prominent than others. *The Almanac of American Politics* and *Politics in America,* two widely circulated books that give basic information on every representative and senator, list how various groups rate the officeholders. *The Almanac of American Politics* uses ten different group ratings, whereas *Politics in America* restricts itself to four. Two of the more widely used scores are attempts to rate legislators ideologically across a range of issues. Americans for Democratic Action uses a series of votes—on both domestic and foreign policy issues—which it asserts are litmus tests for liberals. In 1998 three senators—Bumpers (D-Ark.), Wellstone (D-Minn.), and Wyden (D-Ore.)—scored a perfect one hundred, as did nearly fifty members of the House; the number of members with perfect ADA ratings has steadily increased in recent years.

At the other ideological extreme, the American Conservative Union uses a sophisticated system to show how frequently members of Congress vote "for safeguarding the God-given rights of the individual" (Malbin 1981, 126), that is, to determine how conservative legislators are, according to the ACU's definition. Unsurprisingly, those who score high on the ADA scale frequently score low on the ACU scale, though the two scales are not exact opposites because of different issues chosen and different ways of handling absences. In 1998 the ACU gave perfect scores to eight senators, all Republicans: Allard (Colo.), Ashcroft (Mo.), Faircloth (N.C.), Helms (N.C.), Hutchinson (Ark.), Inhofe (Okla.), Sessions (Ala.), and Smith (N.H.). In addition, fifty-five representatives received perfect scores. Although this number is more than double the twenty-seven members of Congress who received perfect scores in 1997, scores for Congress as a whole were on average lower than in previous years, indicating a more liberal group of elected officials.

Similarly, those who do well on the AFL-CIO Committee on Political Education (COPE) rating often do not do well on ratings published by the Chamber of Commerce of the United States. Each of these groups, as well as the more than a dozen others that issue ratings, try to inform voters on how legislators stand on issues of particular relevance to group member sympathizers.

The exploding number of ratings can confuse even the most sophisticated political observer. Groups often change their method of computing an incumbent's scores, making comparisons over time difficult. Frequently two groups representing variant elements of the same "constituency" define important issues differently, leading to different ratings of incumbents. This dissimilarity has been the case in recent years with the National Tax-Limitation Committee and the National Taxpayers Union. The National Tax-Limitation Committee seeks to limit government spending and taxation by campaigning for federal and state constitutional amendments designed for those purposes. Taking a different approach, the National Taxpayers Union wants to limit taxes through specific cuts, not a constitutional restriction.

The ratings of incumbents often have direct electoral implications. Although few citizens, and not even most members of the involved groups, monitor these group ratings closely, many interest groups weigh them heavily in determining whom to help financially in upcoming campaigns. In addition, groups take particular care to identify those on the "extreme" as special friends or enemies, of whom members should be aware.

Since the 1970s one group, the League of Conservation Voters (LCV), each election year has identified the twelve "worst" members of Congress according to their rating on environmental concerns. The group dubs these representatives the "dirty dozen" and targets them for defeat. Of fifty-two incumbents given the label over the course of the five elections ending with the election of 1978, twenty-five were defeated in the same year they were targeted, giving increased credibility the power of this group (*Congressional Quarterly Weekly Report* 1981, 510). Since the 1980s, the LCV has combined its legislative rating with a compilation of how much political action committee money incumbent candidates had accepted in the previous election cycle from PACs representing corporations it dubbed the "filthy five"; the LCV list has included senators and nonincumbents in more recent rankings. While a lower percentage of the identified incumbents have lost in more recent elections, the impact of the group remains impressive (Friedman 1990). Besides wishing to avoid being dubbed one of the twelve "worst" legislators on environmental issues, incumbents want to avoid being targeted for defeat by this particular group.

In 1998, the League of Conservation Voters directed their efforts at six incumbent representatives and one senator seeking reelection, at three members of the House seeking seats in the Senate, and at two congressional challengers—one a former member. Seven of these twelve—Senator Lauch Faircloth (R-N.C.); Representatives John Ensign (R-Nev.), Mark Neumann (R-Wis.), and Linda Smith (R-Ore.), who were each running for the Senate; Representative Bill Redmond (R-N.M.); Bob Dornan (R-Calif.), a former member of congress who was seeking to recapture his old seat; and California state senator Tom Bordonaro (R), who was challenging a first-term Democrat—were defeated on November 3, 1998. Clearly, the rating systems perform an important function for the politically involved interest groups and by implication for legislators as well.

C. Political Action Committees

Although some politicians complain about the impact of group activity on the political parties themselves, and many think that the various rating systems portray them unfairly, neither approach has had the influence or has caused the controversy of groups participating in the electoral process through political action committees.

The financing of campaigns is considered at length in chapter 11, but a short history of the rise of political action committees is appropriate at this point (see Alexander and Haggerty 1981, chaps. 1–4; Epstein 1980; Magleby and Nelson 1990; Sorauf 1988, chap. 2). The year 1974 was critical in terms of changes in campaign finance laws affecting groups. Before that year (or, more accurately, before 1971, when the Federal Election Campaign Act was passed, even though that year's provision did not affect groups), the difference between legality and reality was extreme.

The financing of federal elections was governed by a series of outmoded and largely ignored laws—the 1907 Tillman Act, which prohibited corporate contributions; the 1925 Corrupt Practices Campaign Act, which set limits on expenditures in House ($2,500 to $5,000) and Senate ($10,000 to $25,000) but not on presidential campaigns; the 1939 and 1940 Hatch Acts, which put limits on contributions and involvement of federal employees; and the 1944 Smith-Connally and 1947 Taft-Hartley Acts, which prohibited labor unions from contributing directly to campaigns. The most significant aspects of these laws were the ease and impunity with which they were ignored (Epstein 1980; Sorauf 1988, 28–33).

Candidates set up multiple committees to avoid the campaign spending limits. Corporations were notorious for giving election-year "bonuses," which were then passed on by obedient executives to deserving candidates. According to a *Congressional Quarterly* study of corporate executive giving in 1968, these contributions may have totaled millions of dollars (*Congressional Quarterly Weekly Report* 1971, 35). Labor unions set up committees on political education (COPE) that were used to solicit "voluntary" contributions from union members, funds that were then used to "educate" members about the issues of the day and the candidates most deserving of support. COPE sought to "interest" members in the political process through registration drives, get-out-the-vote drives, and poll watching. COPE activities were also worth millions of dollars, largely to Democrats.

The reality of campaign financing as America entered the decade of the 1970s revealed a picture of significantly increasing expenditures, corporate influence, and union activity, all sidestepping the intent, if not the letter, of the law, and all far removed from public view. The Federal Election Campaign Act (FECA) of 1971 marked the first step in reforming these practices. The major provisions of this act put a limit on media expenditures, deemed to be the major source of drastically escalating campaign costs. The FECA called for disclosing the source of campaign contributions, identifying them by occupation and business as well as by name and address. The theory was that disclosure was the best means of control (Corrado 1991a).

The 1974 amendments to the FECA of 1971 have led to a tremendous change in the role played by organized interest groups. The 1974 amendments limited individual contributions to $1,000 per campaign but permitted the establishment of political action committees, which could contribute up to $5,000 in each campaign. The amendments specifically allowed corporations or unions to use money for the "establishment, administration, and solicitation of contributions to a separate, segregated fund" (*Congressional Quarterly Report* 1982, 43). The weight carried by this action was made all the more clear when, in a 1975 case involving Sun Oil Company, the Federal Election Commission ruled that corporations could use general Treasury funds to establish political action committees. This ruling was opposed by organized labor, since the AFL-CIO foresaw the rapid expansion of corporate PACs (Epstein 1980). Table 6.2 shows that union fears had a firm foundation.

Organized labor unions formed PACs shortly after they were legalized; the number peaked at 394 in 1984 and has declined somewhat since that time. Similarly, trade, membership, and health associations—the organized interest groups with which we are concerned—saw the opportunity quickly. While we can list many more PACs in this category than in the labor category, their growth also slowed after the early 1980s, though nearly seventy new PACs in this category were added between 1992 and 1996, the first substantial growth in more than a decade. Corporate PACs, to the contrary, are another phenomenon. From the time of the SUNPAC decision in 1975 until the election of 1988, the number of corporate PACs expanded more than twenty-fold, though the peak seems to have been reached. In absolute numbers, there are approximately five times as many corporate PACs as labor PACs, and twice as many as PACs representing trade associations, membership groups, or health associations.

Table 6.2 Growth of Political Action Committees, 1974–1998

Year	*Corporate*	*Labor*	*Trade/ Membership/ Health*	*Cooperative*	*Corporation without Stock*	*Nonconnected*	*Total*	*Contributions to Congressional Candidates (in millions)*
1974	89	201	318	—	—	—	608	$12.5
1976	433	224	489	—	—	—	1,146	22.6
1978	785	217	453	12	24	162	1,653	34.1
1980	1,206	297	576	42	56	374	2,551	60.2
1982	1,469	380	649	47	103	723	3,371	87.6
1984	1,682	394	698	52	130	1,053	4,009	113.0
1986	1,744	384	745	56	151	1,077	4,157	139.8
1988	1,816	354	786	59	138	1,115	4,268	159.2
1990	1,795	346	774	59	136	1,062	4,172	159.1
1992	1,735	347	770	56	142	1,145	4,195	188.9
1994	1,660	333	792	53	136	980	3,954	189.6
1996	1,642	332	838	41	123	1,103	4,079	217.8
1998	1,567	321	821	39	115	935	3,798*	—

*In 1997 the FEC stopped listing 227 PACs that were deemed to be inactive.

Source: Data from Federal Election Commission.

Why do we discuss corporate PACs in a chapter on organized group activity? The answer should be evident. To a large extent corporate PACs are an extension of trade association PACs. Each PAC is limited in the amount it can contribute to any one campaign. However, corporate members of trade associations can form their own PACs and then give as separate entities, thus becoming the functional equivalents of interest groups (Schlozman and Tierney 1986, 9-12).

Table 6.3 lists the ten largest PACs in the 1995-1996 election cycle in terms of dollar contributions made to candidates. Five of the ten are labor PACs—the State, County, and Municipal Employees; the United Auto Workers; the NEA; the Electrical Workers; and the Food and Commercial Workers. The other five top contributors are all membership or trade associations, some of which have their own component units. However, while no individual corporate PACs made the top of the list, taken cumulatively, their power seems evident. In the 1995-1996 election cycle, corporate PACs contributed over $69.7 million to House and Senate candidates, according to Federal Election Commission records. Membership and trade association PACs contributed a total of $56.2 million. Labor PACs contributed $46.5 million.

Another type of political action committee is the so-called independent, or nonconnected, PAC. These PACs do not grow out of a parent

Table 6.3 Top Ten PACs in Contributions to Federal Candidates, 1995–1996

Rank	*PAC Name*	*Contributions*
1	Democratic Republican Independent Voter Education Committee	$2,611,140
2	American Federation of State, County, and Municipal Employees	2,505,021
3	UAW-V-CAP (UAW Voluntary Community Action Program)	2,467,319
4	Association of Trial Lawyers of America Political Action Committee	2,362,938
5	Dealers Election Action Committee of the National Automobile Dealers Association (NADA)	2,351,925
6	National Education Association Political Action Committee	2,326,830
7	American Medical Association Political Action Committee	2,319,197
8	Realtors Political Action Committee	2,099,683
9	International Brotherhood of Electrical Workers Committee on Political Education	2,080,587
10	Active Ballot Club, a dept. of United Food & Commercial Workers International Union	2,030,795

Source: Federal Election Commission.

organization but are formed for specifically political purposes. The prototype of this form of organization is the National Conservative Political Action Committee (NCPAC). These PACs can contribute to individual campaigns, and they also take advantage of a provision in the Federal Election Campaign Act that maintains that PACs can make independent political expenditures as long as they are not coordinated with a particular candidate. The Supreme Court in *Buckley v. Valeo,* 424 U.S. 1 (1976), the suit that challenged the constitutionality of the Federal Election Campaign Act, had ruled that limitations on such independent expenditures was an abridgment of the freedom of speech. In 1976 the FECA was amended to correct this constitutional fault; nonconnected PACs were first registered with the FEC in 1978; today more than 1,000 such PACs register and contribute to federal campaigns.

Using sophisticated direct-mail techniques, independent PACs have raised a substantial amount of money. As early as the 1981–1982 election cycle, NCPAC raised over $7 million. By the 1995–1996 cycle, the amount spent by nonconnected PACs had reached $22 million. How was this money spent? On whose behalf? It was spent as the directors of the fund wished, on behalf of or against any candidates they chose. As John T. Dolan, head of NCPAC said, "I am responsible to absolutely no one." NCPAC and other nonconnected PACs have run extensive campaigns *against* particular candidates. At times they have advertised against certain incumbents well before the surfacing of an opponent. In 1980 NCPAC's use of this technique was deemed successful in contributing to the defeat of liberal senators Birch Bayh (D-Ind.), John Culver (D-Iowa), Frank Church (D-Idaho), and George McGovern (D-S.D.). NCPAC was a feared opponent and an actor others sought to emulate as well. Now independent PACs cover the entire political spectrum.

The success or failure of specific interest groups does not alter the two most important basic questions about independent PACs: (1) unlike labor unions, trade associations, or even corporations, these groups represent leaders who are not held accountable in any way to their constituency and (2) these groups influence elections in ways that are by their very nature not connected with the candidates who are running but are very influential. Let's deal with these two points separately.

First, these PACs have no members per se. Individuals are contributors; they can fail to contribute again. But talented fund-raisers will tell you that there is no dearth of small contributors, which raises the key defense for independent PACs and political action committees generally and relates to participation in politics, by individuals and individuals acting as groups. A salient goal of campaign reform has always been to increase the number of small contributors. The objective is to get "big money" out of politics. PACs do indeed increase the number of small contributions. These contributors know the causes they are supporting. But do PACs get the big money out of politics? That conclusion is more doubtful. For years Common Cause and other reform-minded interest groups have waged a vigorous (but so far unsuccessful) campaign against PACs. Those who oppose the ability of PACs to contribute to campaigns, at least without further restrictions, argue that PACs hinder the political process by giving undue influence to powerful groups. PAC defenders argue that these organizations get individuals involved—just as has always been desired. To a large extent one's stand on this debate depends on where one sits. If you sit in Congress as a recipient of PAC money, you are unlikely to oppose PACs. But if you are a challenger on the outside—or one who is not like receive PAC money—PACs look much more evil.

Second, these groups use independent expenditures to influence elections. Figure 6.1 depicts the amount of money spent on congressional and senatorial campaigns through independent expenditures in the last twenty years. Even casual observers of American politics noticed the "spike" that is represented by expenditures in the 1995-1996 election cycle. First organized labor and then interest groups representing more conservative causes, such as the National Federal of Independent Business, spent millions of dollars in attempts to influence congressional campaigns. They did so by targeting individual representatives and attacking their records, often pointedly and sometimes (some would claim) unfairly. The result was the creation of a negative impression of the candidates under attack; their opponents, however, did not bear responsibility for the attacks. NCPAC's successful technique of twenty years ago has been used by other PACs—labor, association, and corporate PACs as well as nonconnected PACs. Many observers felt that the extent of these expenditures in 1995-1996 fundamentally altered the political process in a deleterious way.

The proliferation of PACs and the ever-increasing amounts of money that they contribute have caused many to question the conse-

Figure 6.1 Independent Expenditures in Congressional Elections, 1978-1996.

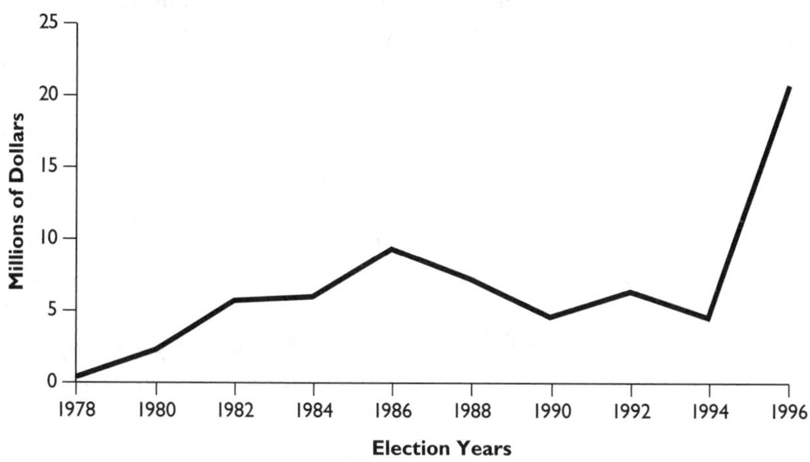

Source: Data From Federal Election Commission.

quences of campaign finance reforms. These issues will be discussed at length in chapter 11.

III. Interest Groups' Influence on Their Members

As stated above, interest groups try to affect the electoral process in two distinct ways. In addition to attempting to influence the ways in which candidates and parties present themselves, and the ways in which those campaigns are perceived by the electorate at large, interest groups try to influence the voting behavior of their own members.

Leaders of interest groups try to exert this influence for two distinct reasons. The simplest, most direct reason is that they believe their choice of candidates is the best for those sharing their interest; it is logical to try to convince others that Senator X is *their* candidate. A less direct reason is that the influence of interest-group leaders with political figures varies with the extent to which politicians feel that the group leaders have influence with their members. That influence is demonstrated in two ways—getting members to give money to a campaign and convincing members to support a candidate with their votes.

In this context we should separate interest groups in a way distinct from those already mentioned. Some interest groups—referred to as trade associations earlier—are actually confederations of other *organizations,* most frequently corporations. The leaders of these parent groups can speak to the leader of their member groups; they can convince lesser officials to support candidates with their dollars, but in fact few votes are involved. This type of association is, however, not unimportant. In fact, the unanimity of corporate PAC support for candidates who are also favored by their trade associations is a testimony to the effectiveness of this kind of network. However, the influence of this partnership is different from that of a union leader who claims to speak for tens of thousands of his members. In the latter case, politicians are increasingly distrustful of the effectiveness of these spokespeople. It is important, therefore, for interest-group leaders to demonstrate that they can distinctly influence their members.

How is this influence achieved? Interest groups use a number of techniques to persuade their members to support the candidates their leaders have identified. One technique has already been identified: the group rating. Interest-group leaders make certain that their members know the politician who supported them in the past and the one who did not. They clearly identify friends and enemies for their members. But few citizens follow politics closely enough to keep up on group ratings. These ratings can be used as evidence for identifying friends and enemies, but persuasion must come about through other means.

A second technique is producing a newsletter. Various groups use newsletters of varying levels of sophistication. The express purpose of communicating with group members through a newsletter is educational. The staff of an interest group wants the members to know what and how much they have been doing for the group, how various issues affect the group's interests, and which political officials have been helpful in their efforts to support favorable legislation or oppose that which is harmful. Using this technique, interest-group leaders frequently try to counter the "generalizing" effects of the mass media. The popular media give a general audience a particular view of a political issue and/or a political leader. Through interest-group mailing, interest-group leaders try to teach their members that they are a specific segment of the public and that issues and leaders affect them in a *particular* way.

Specialized approaches to a particular audience distinguish other techniques used by group leaders as well. Many groups use direct-mail and/or telephone campaigns to inform their members about specific pending issues in which they have a stake. Similarly, they make certain that their members know when the leaders feel that they have a pressing interest in a particular candidate, when one of their favorites is in trouble, or when they have an opportunity to beat one of their enemies.

Groups vary tremendously in terms of their effectiveness in reaching members. Some groups, like realtors, have a reputation of reaching members with persuasive messages in a very short time. Some labor union leaders, on the other hand, seem to be increasingly far removed from the opinions of the rank and file. Certainly during the Reagan years the leaders were more liberal and more clearly tied to the Democratic party than were their members; much of this disparity has been reduced because of confrontations between the Gingrich-led Republican-controlled Congress and labor leaders during the 104th and 105th Congresses.

In the last few years, more and more groups have concentrated their efforts on educating their members. Labor unions began to use cable television as a means of reaching their constituencies in the 1980s; other groups soon followed suit. Teleconferencing has become a common means of bringing group leaders in Washington into touch with their constituents across the nation. The Internet marks the latest phase of the communications revolution to attract widespread interest-group attention (Berry 1997; Patterson 1990; Coval 1984).

The effectiveness of interest groups in influencing the political opinion of their members has frequently been explored by political scientists. Nearly five decades ago, David B. Truman published his seminal interpretation of American politics based largely on group influence (Truman 1951). Truman's book *The Governmental Process* dealt with much more than the influence of organized groups. Truman's explanation of competing group influences is as persuasive today as it was when first presented.

Imagine the predicament of a certain hypothetical citizen: a Catholic woman who is a union member and an ardent hunter, along

with her husband. Many years ago they joined the National Rifle Association and have become active members. Their children have learned about gun safety at NRA workshops. She is faced with a choice in a congressional election between a Democrat who is very much a union supporter but a firm advocate of gun control, and his Republican opponent, a woman who is supported by the local business community for her economic stands and backed by the NRA because she opposes any further restrictions on handgun ownership. Our hypothetical voter is urged by her union leaders to support the Democrat; her economic interest seems to lie in that direction and, after all, good union members *should* vote for prolabor Democrats. But she is torn. Her NRA friends are for the Republican because of the contrast between that candidate's stand on gun-related issues and the Democrat's hard-line approach, which they see as a step toward taking their guns away. She is puzzled and confused. Clearly, neither the union leader nor the NRA leader can speak authoritatively as her representative.

The issue gets even more complicated. Let us suppose that our hypothetical voter has become something of a feminist as a reaction to the way women are treated in the workplace; in fact, she has become active in certain women's organizations. Her deep religious beliefs lead her to oppose abortion. Her feminist friends urge her to look at the predicament in which many working women, facing unwanted pregnancies, find themselves. She is frankly not certain about her own feelings on the abortion issue. The Democratic candidate is also a Catholic and states quite frankly that he is morally opposed to abortion. She agrees. The Republican candidate says that women often find themselves in untenable situations, that abortion is a terrible alternative, but it is one that many women need. Our hypothetical voter agrees with that assessment as well.

Truman presents exemplary cases of competing group demands, and his book demonstrates that group membership does not always determine a voter's choice on election day. Our hypothetical voter's dilemma reflects these competing influences. The position in which she finds herself, although exaggerated, is typical of many real situations. Her quandary shows us how difficult it is for group leaders to claim that they can speak for all the members of their association.

One case stands out, however, in which group membership seems to be a determining factor. Let us assume that our female Catholic union member is not just interested in women's issues but is a member of the National Abortion Rights Action League. She has had an unwanted pregnancy and has gone through the painful process of examining her own beliefs. She has emerged from this examination with the firm view that a woman must be able to control her own body, that her religious doctrine must be put aside in this instance, and that it is wrong for others to let their moral convictions dictate her actions. She did not arrive at these decisions lightly. The process that led to her decision was the most difficult she ever had to undertake. Further, she had to back up her conviction with action, undergoing an abortion, a step she had always been taught was against the law of God. In reaching the decision that an abortion was right for her, she also reached the very strong conclusion that no one should dictate what another may do. After all, anyone who asserted the right to make those decisions for all in society was directly calling into question the very process and the very decision in which she had been so intimately involved.

For this voter, only the candidates' stand on the abortion issue mattered. If the Democrat was pro-choice and the Republican was for restricting a woman's right to have an abortion, our hypothetical voter would have cast her vote for the Democrat. If the candidates held the opposite opinions, her vote would have changed accordingly.

The interest-group leaders who are most effective at claiming to represent their members' views and the leaders who are most effective at convincing their members how to vote are the leaders of single-issue groups whose members care more about that one issue than any other. These groups are few and far between. In recent years, in some geographic areas, the groups representing the two sides of the abortion question or the gun control issue have been in that situation. In close elections, those who vote on the basis of only one issue may in fact determine the result. Certainly it is in the interest of the group leaders to make it appear that they and their members can tip the balance. Single-interest groups seem to be most effective in multicandidate primary fields (Maisel 1986). However, in closely contested elections, no candidate can ignore the appeal of these groups with impunity.

IV. POLITICIANS VIEW INTEREST GROUPS

In a very real sense, interest-group leaders are politicians. They try to influence who is elected to office, attempt to affect policy outcomes, and deal with other politicians in striving for these goals. But they themselves do not seek office and do not vote on policy outcomes; the effectiveness of their advocacy for the interests they represent depends on how they are perceived by elected and appointed government officials.

ISSUE ADVOCACY ADVERTISEMENTS
Advertisements in which the sponsor's primary interest is in forwarding an issue position, not supporting a particular candidate; money spent in this way is unregulated as long as it is separate and distinct from candidate efforts.

Let's look at some recent examples. In the 1996 congressional elections, labor, business, and environmental groups spent more than $100 million in excess of what candidates had spent on campaign expenses (including the money candidates received from political action committees). Most of this money was spent on so-called **issue advocacy advertisements**, advertisements that are permitted because the group expressing its view is exercising its First Amendment right of free speech and thus cannot be restricted.

Labor began this barrage in 1996, aiming its attack at Republican freshman congressmen, most of whom had backed the Contract with America and other legislation opposed by labor. How did politicians respond? In two ways. First, those under attack found allies to counter these attacks. Pro-Republican groups responded by defending some of their allies under attack. The level of rhetoric escalated throughout the land. But second, many of those under attack responded by softening their records, by looking for some votes they could use to counter the attacks on their records. They did this because they did not want to be deemed as antilabor or antienvironment. No politician wants to be painted with a broad brush as controlled by one group or another.

Undeniably, politicians respond to organized interests. In 1990 Congress passed a tax bill that doubled the excise tax on beer, the first increase in that tax in more than four decades (McCarthy 1997, B1). The beer industry was caught by surprise but responded quickly. The association that represents the beer distributors is called the National Beer Wholesalers Association and has a very active political action committee, appropriately called Six-PAC. After the excise tax increase, the NBWA geared up its lobbying effort in Washington and targeted appropriate legislators for campaign contributions. By the 1995–1996 election cycle, Six-PAC had contributed more than $1.3 million to federal campaigns.

In addition, beer executives sought influence where they could. The nation's largest beer company, Anheuser-Busch, is located in the St. Louis area; a local member of Congress is Richard A. Gephardt, House Democratic leader. After the 1992 election Gephardt arranged for Anheuser-Busch's chief executive officer, August A. Busch III, to meet with President Clinton. Busch became one of the first of the nation's business leaders to back Clinton's economic recovery plan in 1993. Interestingly, when the administration announced its so-called sin tax to pay for its proposed health care plan, tobacco was included but beer was not. No one claims that there is a one-to-one relationship between campaign contributions and the connections of interest-group leaders, on the one hand, and policy outcomes, on the other. But political leaders clearly listen. When asked why he did not list beer as one of the targets of his sin tax, an announcement made with Mr. Busch standing at his side, Clinton responded, "I specifically passed up a chance to say that today" (McCarthy 1997, B1).

It is not always easy for politicians to know how to view interest groups. Consider the National Rifle Association as an example. The NRA has approximately 3 million members and chapters in every congressional district in every state. The organization's overall expenditure, including funds for lobbying the Congress, is approximately $120 million annually. In the 1992 and 1994 elections, the NRA spent an additional $3.9 million on candidate endorsements and political contributions. They are adamantly opposed to any form of gun control and state publicly that their members will punish those who favor gun control.

But will they? Do all NRA members really feel that every citizen has a right to own an automatic pistol? Will all NRA members vote against a Congress member who favors handgun registration laws? Especially after the devastation in Littleton, Colorado? The simple answer is that politicians do not know. Politicians must get a feel for their district and have a sense of their constituents' feelings. Interest group leaders try to "educate" politicians about the allegiance of their followers, but in the final analysis, it is the elected officials who must know their own districts or suffer the consequences.

One more example can demonstrate how interest-group leaders at times misrepresent the views of their members. In 1988, Congress passed and President Reagan signed into law the Medicare Catastrophic Coverage Act. Congress had acted after the AARP, which claims to be the nation's largest interest group representing senior citizens, lobbied long and hard for the legislation. The new policy extended supplemental health insurance benefits for catastrophic illnesses, paying for that coverage with a surtax on middle- and upper-income senior citizens. When legislators returned to their districts after the law was implemented and those affected saw the increase in their taxes, those very same senior citizens who were supposed to be the beneficiaries of the policy—and on whose behalf the AARP claimed to speak—were in an uproar. Protests were so vociferous that Congress repealed the program in 1989. One lesson clearly learned by members of Congress was that the AARP might be the largest senior citizens' lobby, but its leaders certainly did not speak for their members (Daley and Worthington 1989; McKibben 1989).

In the final analysis the question of how politicians view interest groups and their leaders becomes a question of how effective these leaders are at representing the views of their members. It is clear that the more specialized a group is, the more accurately its leadership can reflect members' views; but such groups are often quite small. As groups become larger and larger, their leaders claim to reflect the views of more and more voters. However, politicians have come to realize that these large groups often have diverse memberships and that people join for various reasons. Many of the AARP's millions become members to obtain the discounts the organization has negotiated from merchants to entice new members to join. The leadership does not necessarily reflect their political views. For politicians, the need is to weigh influence when deciding how to respond to interest-group demands.

WEBSITES

http://www.fec.gov

The Federal Election Commission website provides historical and contemporary information on political action committees and their contributions to federal candidates.

http://www.nra.org

The National Rifle Association is the largest progun interest group in the country.

http://www.handguncontrol.org

Handgun Control, Inc., is an organization dedicated to limiting the availability of handguns through legislative initiatives and educational campaigns.

http://www.aflcio.com

The AFL-CIO is the umbrella organization for many labor unions in the country. It has been very active in political campaigns through its Committee on Political Education and active PAC contributing.

http://www.nfibonline.com/

The National Association of Independent Businesses is an advocacy group for small and independent businesses. It has campaigned quite actively in recent election cycles.

KEY CONCEPTS

federal groups
group consciousness
issue advocacy advertisements
lobbying
multipurpose groups
national groups
political action committees
pressure groups
public interest groups
Ralph Nader
self-identification
single-purpose groups

DISCUSSION QUESTIONS

1. What groups do you consider yourself to be a member of? Is there formal membership in these groups? How did you get to be a member?

2. Interest-group leaders claim that they represent their members in the political process. Are there particular interest-group leaders who you think represent you? How do they know what you think?
3. Do you believe that PAC leaders should have to poll those who contribute to a PAC before they determine whom they will support? If so, why? If not, how should they decide who will receive their money?
4. How much pressure do you think legislators feel to vote along interest-group lines? How is the pressure exerted? Do you think it is a positive or a negative influence on American politics and/or on the legislative process?

CHAPTER 7

State and Local Nominations

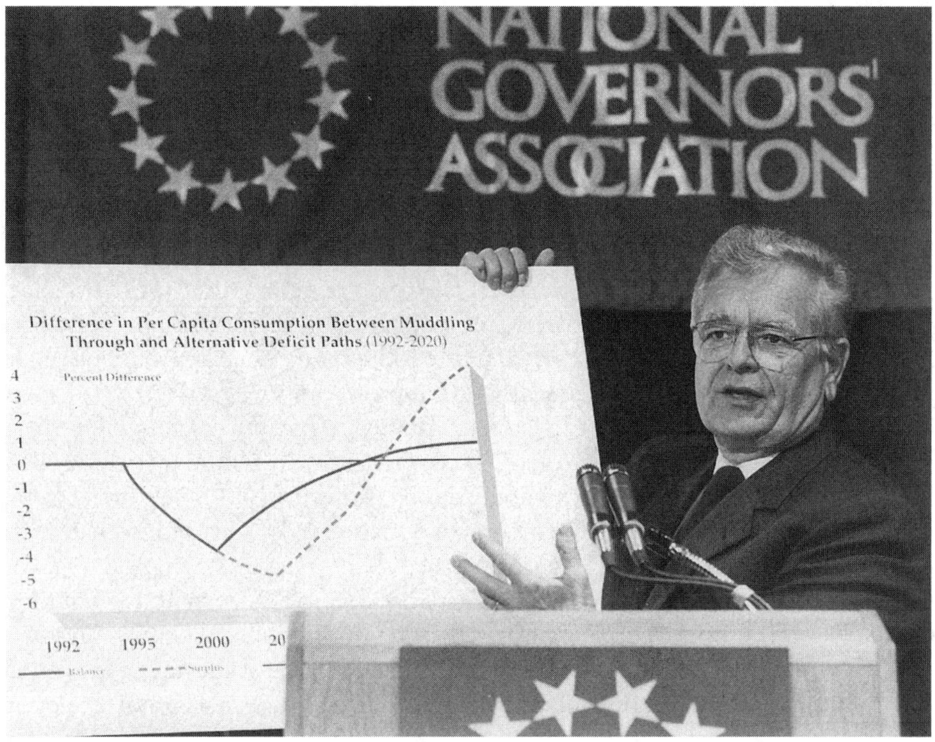

We elect one president of the United States. We elect fifty governors, one hundred senators, 435 members of Congress, 1,984 state senators, 5,440 state representatives, and literally thousands and thousands of mayors, city council members, county commissioners, judges of probate, clerks of court, water district commissioners, and other public officeholders. Although federal officeholders get most of the attention, state and local officials often make decisions that have more direct impact on our daily lives. It seems appropriate, therefore, to begin this discussion of nominations and elections with them.

CONVENTIONS

Meetings of party members to endorse or nominate candidates for office, adopt platforms, and establish party rules.

CAUCUSES

Local meetings of party members, often used to elect delegates to conventions; used to endorse or nominate candidates in some states.

We know a great deal about how presidents receive their party's nomination (chap. 9). For months on end we follow the candidate parade through the snows of New Hampshire all the way to the national party **conventions** in late summer. We complain that the process is too long. But when the Democrats did not have an array of candidates on the hustings in the summer of 1991, political pundits wondered whether Democratic politicians were conceding the 1992 election. Of course, Democratic contenders did emerge before the winter **caucuses** and primaries; far from conceding the November election, the Democrats won it. As the year 2000 campaign approached, journalists seemed to worry that the Democratic nomination would go by default to Vice President Gore; then they trumpeted the chances of former New Jersey senator Bill Bradley. They speculated about the presence of a number of well-known candidates with large bankrolls vying for the Republican nomination (Shribman 1999). But few stories appeared about possible nominating contests for governor, senator, U.S. representative, or state legislator.

The presidential nominating process is complex, but much of it is public and open. Anyone who wants to read about the presidential nominations need only look at the front page of any newspaper on almost any day during the year before the nomination is secured. Readers interested in more analytical views can find magazine articles, journal essays, and a large number of books dedicated to the subject (e.g., Aldrich 1980; Buell and Sigelman 1991; Kessel 1992; Lengle and Shafer 1980; Orren and Polsby 1987; Polsby and Wildavsky 1997; Wayne 1996). The Democratic National Committee has funded blue-ribbon commission after blue-ribbon commission, the goals of which have been to improve the process. The Republican party, with less publicity and controversy, has also focused on the quality of the presidential nominating process.

Still, what do we know about the ways in which the thousands of other elected public officials are nominated for office by their parties? Back in the days of party bosses and dominating political machines, Boss Tweed of Tammany Hall is reported to have claimed, "I don't care who does the electing, just so I do the nominating." When machines dominated American politics, one of the most important aspects of their control was the ability to control political nominations. We know that machines no longer dominate our politics as they once did. But what has replaced them?

Ask yourself! What do you know about how your U.S. senators were nominated? Your representative in Congress? Your state representative (do you honestly even know whom he or she is)? What about county commissioners? How do all these people receive their party's nod for the nomination? Where do they come from?

These questions are particularly important when we realize the significance of the decisions that many of these individuals make. They are also important when we remember that many holders of more prestigious positions have used lower offices as stepping-stones for higher, more visible public office. This chapter will look at the decision to run for office and how potential candidates view the political scene. It will then turn to the question of how state and local officials gain party nomination and thus access to the general election ballot. Finally, it will move to an examination of the politics of the nomination process.

I. POLITICAL CONTEXT AND POLITICIANS' DECISIONS TO RUN

Politicians think in terms of career progression. Is this the time for me to move up? How one defines "up" in this context is not absolute, but some definitions are pretty well accepted. For instance, a seat in the House of Representatives is generally considered a step up from a seat in a state legislature. A seat in the U.S. Senate is a "promotion" from serving as a member of the House (Schlesinger 1966).[1]

How do politicians decide to risk seeking a higher office? Jacobson and Kernell (1983) have posited an important theory—that politicians weigh the value of the office for which they strive and the probability of winning against the risk involved in giving up the office they currently hold. Politicians weigh the public climate in determining whether or not they will run. The decisions made by **qualified candidates** (who for these purposes are defined as politicians already holding some elective office) about whether or not they will seek a higher office are very important (see Maisel, Stone, and Maestas 1999).

QUALIFIED CANDIDATES
Generally defined as candidates for office who have previously run for and won elective office.

One reason for incumbent reelection success, at least in House elections, is that qualified candidates, in the aggregate, decide that the political climate is not right for moving up. When candidates with the greatest likelihood of winning decide not to run, challengers of lesser quality frequently step up to fill the void (Abramowitz 1981; Hinckley 1981; Jacobson 1981; Maisel and Cooper 1981).

Looking more deeply into the reasoning of individual candidates, Jacobson and Kernell review two competing sets of theories that are used to explain electoral results. One body of speculation stresses the impact of economic conditions on electoral outcome (most of this scholarship examines congressional campaigns because of the availability of data, but the conclusions can be generalized to other offices [Bloom and Price 1975; Kramer 1971; Tufte 1975; 1978]). The other theory uses survey data to explain electoral results in terms of individual voter attitudes (Arsenau and Wolfinger 1973; Fiorina 1978; 1981; Kernell 1977; Kinder and Kiewiet 1979; Mann and Wolfinger 1980). In either case the operating assumption is that voters cast their votes for *some* offices based on their overall assessment of the political and economic situation in which they find themselves. Politicians certainly think in these terms, but they also think in terms of separating themselves from such broader issues as Central America and the International Monetary Fund.

In making the decision about whether or not to run for higher office, politicians are very concerned about what else is going on at the time of that election. Potential candidates are aware that voters give most attention to the top of the ballot. In a presidential election year, electoral hopefuls must consider whether their party's presidential candidate is going to help or hurt them. Will they derive support from a popular candidate? Will they be able to separate themselves from an unpopular candidate? If it is an off-year election, one in which no presidential election is being held, what other elections are most likely to capture the voter interest (e.g., senator, governor)?

How will voters be affected by these elections, if at all? Political scientists argue persuasively that party influence on voting has declined, that voters are splitting their tickets much more frequently than they did in the past, and that politicians' coattails are shorter than they once were (DeVries and Tarrance 1972; Ferejohn and Calvert 1984; Wattenberg 1990b; 1991). Undoubtedly all these conclusions are true; however, practicing politicians are still very concerned about insulating themselves from the fate of other politicians or taking advantage of remaining coattails.

Recent changes in state election laws demonstrate this trend. In the early 1950s, the governors of nineteen states were elected for two-year terms. As states have changed their two-year terms to four-year terms, virtually every one of them has decided to hold gubernatorial elections in nonpresidential election years, thus insulating state elections from national politics. Rhode Island was the most recent state to make this switch, leaving only New England neighbors New Hampshire and Vermont with governors serving two-year terms (see table 7.1).

Candidates for office below governor are aware of this trend as well. In considering a run for the state senate, for instance, a political candidate is confronted with one political environment if the upcoming election year is a presidential election year in which there is also a gubernatorial and senatorial race in his or her state; that potential candidate faces a very different set of variables if it is a nonpresidential election year that features neither a senatorial nor a gubernatorial election.

Table 7.1 Electoral Context of Gubernatorial Elections

	4-Year Terms			*2-Year Terms*
Years	*Elected with President*	*Elected in Off Year*	*Elected in Odd Year*	
1951–1952	10	14	5	19
1999–2000	9	34	5	2

Source: Data from National Governors' Association.

Table 7.2 lists the various electoral environments that might confront potential candidates. These combinations are all possible because U.S. senators serve six-year terms and thus no senatorial seat is contested in any state in one out of three national elections (barring vacancies due to death, resignation, etc.).

These factors were not so important when all politicians for all offices campaigned in the same way. However, they become critically important when different types of campaigns are run for different offices. In this context politicians must evaluate how their careers are going to be affected, not only by the political climate of the times but also by their ability to campaign using different techniques.

II. COMMON VIEWS OF THE NOMINATING PROCESS

What is the conventional wisdom? How are nominations decided? One view is that a couple of guys (almost never women) sit in a smoke-filled backroom and choose the nominee. They then anoint that person and dissuade other potential candidates. Who are these people? They are

Table 7.2 Offices at the Top of the Ballot

	Number of States			
Combination of Offices	*1994*	*1996*	*1998*	*2000**
President/Governor/ Senator/Representative	x	5	x	9
President/Governor/ Representative	x	4	x	2
President/Senator/ Representative	x	29	x	29
President/Representative	x	12	x	10
Governor/Senator/ Representative	23	x	26	x
Governor/Representative	13	x	10	x
Senator/Representative	11	x	8	x
Representative	3	x	6	x

*These numbers assume no additional vacancies in the Senate due to death or resignation.
Source: Compiled by the author.

the party leaders, not necessarily in a formal sense, but the people who make the party go. These kingmakers have at least three things in common: party loyalty, intense interest, and money.

Another view is that the nominating process represents the purest form of democracy. Candidates can present themselves to the people, and the people will choose. A person does not have to be tapped by anyone. Potential candidates declare their availability, and people choose from among those presenting themselves. No one is in control, and everyone is eligible.

A few hold yet a third view: the chairman of the local party organization meets with an official committee, and together they decide on the party nominees. This view suggests that the process is more open than the smoke-filled room but falls short of the purest democratic ideals. Curiously, all three views are accurate—in part.

As with so much in American politics, what one sees depends on where one looks. In the case of nominating politics, the factors to be examined include the locality and the office sought. How nominations are decided varies from state to state and from locality to locality within a given state. The process is also quite different for the most visible and hotly contested offices—governor, senator, congressman, state legislator in some states but not others, mayor in some cities but not others (one can see the variations by locality at work)—than it is for offices that are seemingly less important.

In the sections that follow, we will sort out some of the more important questions about our nominating process. Keeping in mind the differences among localities and offices, we will look at the variety of nominating systems, exploring the question of who participates in the process—as candidates and as voters—and the more general question of how an ideal nominating system for the American political system might be structured.

III. Development of the Direct Primary System

The most common means of nomination in American politics today is the direct primary election. In a direct primary system, the citizens of a particular area who are permitted to vote in a party's primary election vote directly to choose the party's nominee. The direct primary is distinguished from any indirect means of nominating, the most notable example being the presidential nomination, which is decided upon in conventions by **delegates**—some chosen directly and some indirectly in caucuses, but delegates in either case.

DELEGATES

Party members who are elected to a convention to participate in doing the party's business.

Direct primaries were not always the most common means used for nominating in the American system. Chapter 2 traced the history of party systems in the United States and made the point that in the second party system the nominating system moved away from a legislative caucus system to a convention system; this move was seen as a democratizing reform. The further movement from the convention system to the direct primary system had two distinct impetuses.

A. Primaries as a Response to One-Party Domination

At the end of the Reconstruction era, following the Civil War, the Democratic party totally dominated southern politics. The Republican party for all intents and purposes did not exist in the South. In an era of one-party polities, when nominations were determined only by party officials, no mass participatory democracy existed. Citizens were given the opportunity to vote for only one candidate nominated by an elite faction of the dominant party. The primary election was first used, in the Democratic party, as a means to extend some modicum of democracy into this heavily one-party system.

B. Primaries as an Item on the Progressive Agenda

For more philosophical and ideological reasons, the members of the Progressive party included the direct primary election as part of their party platform. Shortly after the turn of the century, primaries began to appear as part of the nominating process in states with Progressive party influence. Seen as a response to boss domination of the political process in many northern cities and states, primaries spread rapidly; the direct primary was used to nominate candidates for at least some offices in all but a few states by the end of the second Wilson administration in 1920.

In contrast to the ebb and flow of the use of primaries in the presidential nominating process (see chap. 9), direct primaries as a means for choosing nominees for state and local office have had a more steady history of development and expansion. Few states that adopted direct primaries as the means for nominating candidates in the early years of this century have taken the nominating process out of the hands of the voter, even for short periods of time; today direct primaries are used as the means for nominating candidates for some offices in all states and for *all* offices in over forty states (Silbey 1991, 11–14).

It should be noted, however, that nominating conventions have not totally disappeared. A number of southern states give party committees the option of having a primary or of nominating by convention. The Republican party in a number of states has used the convention option, since until recently the party nod was not valued enough to merit a primary contest (of course that justification has disappeared with the reemergence of the Republicans as viable contenders throughout the region).

In Virginia, both parties have used the means of nominating

candidates as an instrument in guaranteeing the desired result. For instance, convention nominations have permitted "backroom" politicians to achieve geographically and racially balanced tickets. The Virginia law is indeed unique, allowing incumbent officeholders to choose the means through which they will be renominated. In 1996, Republican senator John Warner opted for a primary, rather than a convention, as was his right under the commonwealth's law. His opponent for the nomination, the much more conservative James C. Miller III, challenged the law but conceded after the commonwealth's attorney general ruled that the procedure should stand. Miller wanted a convention because his ideological supporters were more likely to dominate a convention than a primary, with its broader participation. Warner favored a primary, following the same logic but approaching it from a different perspective. This example shows how important the means of nominating can be in a particular case.[2] While nominating conventions are a rarer and rarer phenomenon, they remain among the most interesting aspects of politics for those able to participate in or observe them.

IV. Varieties Of Primaries

Stating that the direct primary is the means used for nominating party candidates in most states is not the same as saying that the identical system is used in all states. Some state laws mandate that a primary will be used and set very specific rules for that primary. In other states the decision on how to nominate is left to the parties. Therefore, it is not really uncommon for a primary to be used in one party and not in the other; if a primary is used, the rules for that primary may be determined by the party, not by state law. As noted previously, in some states the primary is used for all offices; in others it is used for only the more prominent offices (see Epstein 1989; 1991).

A systematic examination of the state and local nominating process is difficult because of the variety of systems in place. The complexity is less troublesome for candidates for statewide office, however, than it is for candidates for the presidency for one very simple reason: whatever particular system is in place for a particular political party in any one state is the only system relevant for state and local candidates for that party's nomination. Candidates for the presidency and their strategists have to be aware of fifty separate and often different systems, which are given different weights both in the nominating process and in media coverage of that process (see chap. 9). On the other hand, candidates for state and local office can plan their strategy to aim at only one event, the primary that will determine whether or not they are the party's nominee. Still, they must be acutely aware of how their state's system works.

States using the direct primary also differ in many other ways. For example, they differ in terms of who is eligible to vote in a particular primary, of whether parties can endorse—in an official way—in advance of the primary, of how such endorsements are made if they are permitted, and of whether a **plurality** or a **majority** is necessary to nominate. The variations among primary systems are explored in the following sections. (For further discussion of this material, see Jewell 1984; Jewell and Olson 1988.)

PLURALITY

Receiving more votes than any other candidate.

MAJORITY

Receiving one half plus at least one of the votes cast.

A. Who May Run

One would think that the question of who may run in a party's primary would be a simple one to answer. Democrats run in Democratic party primaries; Republicans run in Republican party primaries. If only it were that simple!

1. Party Membership and Petition Requirements

The most prevalent rules call for candidates to run in their party's primary if they meet certain fairly simple criteria. First, the prospective candidate must be a registered member of the political party whose nomination he or she seeks (or in some other way demonstrate allegiance to that party in states that do not have official party registration).

Second, candidates must meet some sort of "test" to gain access to the ballot. Often this test involves gathering a certain number of signatures on a petition, but the ease or difficulty candidates have in meeting this requirement is significant. The number of signatures necessary and who is eligible to sign are important factors. If the number is small and if anyone can sign any number of petitions, then access to the ballot is quite simple. For example, in Tennessee only twenty-five signatures are required for most offices. By contrast, if the number of signatures required is large and if some restrictions apply as to who may sign petitions, then access to the ballot is more restricted. In Maine, candidates must acquire a fairly large number of signatures, only registered party members may sign petitions, and they must sign a petition that only contains the names of party members from their hometown.

In states with easier requirements many more candidates frequently qualify for the primary ballot for the same office. Is this good or bad? "Good," one hears often, "because anyone can run." But what if one candidate appeals to a relatively small, but extremely dedicated, group of voters whose views are on the fringe of public opinion, and election law requires only a plurality to nominate?[3] Would the extremist nominee represent the voters' opinions in these districts? Is democracy served?

On the other hand, if access to the ballot is relatively restricted, as when a large number of signatures is required, or when only certain voters can sign petitions (e.g., statewide office in New York requires signatures by 15,000 or 5 percent of enrolled party registrants, of whom not less than 100 or 5 percent, whichever is less, must live in each of one-half of the state's thirty-one congressional districts), then fields of candidates tend to be smaller. All the candidates tend to be serious contenders, but groups out of the mainstream have less influence. Moreover, lesser-known individuals are prevented from testing their views in primary campaigns. Is democracy better served?

2. The Role of Parties

Access to the ballot can be even more restricted in some states than it is in those states that require a large number of signatures from a select group of voters. Six states—Colorado, Connecticut, New Mexico, New York, North Dakota, and Utah—have party conventions that play a significant role in determining access to the primary ballot for at least some offices. The philosophy behind systems like these is that, while the party voters in the state should have the final say, those most involved with party affairs, that is, those willing to go through the process of selection as delegate to a convention, should have increased influence.

How do these systems work? In Utah, the top two finishers at the state convention are on the party's statewide primary ballot, unless one candidate wins 70 percent of the convention votes; in that case, he or she is declared the nominee without a primary. In Colorado, New Mexico, and New York anyone who receives a specified percentage of the votes at the state convention has his or her name placed on the primary ballot. In Delaware, North Dakota, and Rhode Island, the person endorsed at the state convention—or by local committees for local offices—automatically appears on the primary ballot, but others must follow the petition route.[4] **Preprimary conventions** tend to be used in competitive two-party states with relatively strong party systems.

PREPRIMARY CONVENTIONS

Party conventions held in advance of a primary to endorse one of the candidates running in that primary.

Connecticut, which was the last state to adopt a direct primary, implemented a system called a **challenge primary** in 1955. New York State adopted a similar system, for statewide offices only, in 1967. In the challenge primary system, the convention nominee is automatically the party nominee unless he or she is challenged in a primary after the convention is over. The assumption that there has to be a primary election is reversed. Losers at the convention with a certain percentage of the delegate votes have an automatic right to challenge, but they have no obligation to do so. In Connecticut in 1998, only one Democratic party endorsee for Congress and none of the Republican endorsees was challenged in a primary. Those endorsed for governor were not challenged in either party, nor were most of the candidates for lesser state offices. While party endorsement has official status in the eight states mentioned above and a "semiofficial" status in Massachusetts, in a number of other states (e.g., Illinois, Minnesota, and Wisconsin) party organiza-

CHALLENGE PRIMARY

Primary election held after a nominating convention at which the convention's nominee can be challenged by a defeated candidate who must meet some specified criteria.

tion or other party groups endorse candidates and work for their election without that action having any official role in the primary process.

The quintessential example of this would be Cook County, Illinois, the Greater Chicago area. For many years the vaunted Cook County Democratic party machine was headed by "Hizzonah" the mayor, Richard J. Daley; today his son, also the mayor of the city, carries on that tradition, though to a much lesser degree. The first Mayor Daley's organization stands as the last of the classic urban machines (see Rakove 1975; Royko 1971; Tolchin and Tolchin 1971). When Daley endorsed a candidate, that candidate became a prohibitive favorite. The machine worked the streets. Few challenged the machine because a challenge was fruitless. However, reform clubs did eventually emerge in Chicago (Wilson 1962) to present an alternative to Daley. These clubs served as a base for political activists interested in a different type of politics in Chicago. Although they stood outside of the formal political system, these clubs helped structure politics in Chicago. They did not play an official role, but their influence was important nonetheless.

Can one generalize about how effective party endorsements have been? As is so often the case, the experience among the states varies widely. The ultimate statement of success is if the endorsed candidate is not challenged in a primary. In Connecticut the assumption has been that a challenge will not be held. Between 1956 and 1998 only 23 of 270 individuals nominated for the House of Representatives by congressional district conventions were forced to face challenge primaries. Challenges are more common for statewide offices, in both Connecticut and New York, two states with similar systems, but there the similarity ends. In Connecticut, the party endorsement is considered an important advantage, although Democratic candidates try to avoid being labeled as the candidate of the legendary party bosses.[5] In New York, to the contrary, many Democratic candidates view the official party endorsement as the kiss of death.

Malcolm Jewell and David Olson (1988, 96–98) have examined the recent history of party endorsements. Between 1960 and 1986, 57 percent of the endorsees in states with legal endorsement procedures were nominated without opposition; this figure compares with 28 percent in those states with informal endorsement procedures and 20 percent in all elections in northern states during this period. Jewell and Olson (1988, 96, table 4.2) note that some state parties are most effective, with endorsees rarely challenged (e.g., Connecticut and Delaware, Democrats and Republicans; Colorado, Democrats; New York, Republicans); other states' endorsees are sometimes challenged but rarely upset (e.g., North Dakota, Republicans; Utah, Democrats); and still other states' endorsees are usually challenged and sometimes upset (e.g., New York, Democrats; Utah, Republicans). The history of the party organizations helps explain this difference, as it does many such discrepancies among states.

3. Louisiana: An Exception

NONPARTISAN PRIMARY

Primary used only in Louisiana in which all of the candidates appear on one primary ballot and any candidate who polls a majority of the votes is declared the winner without competition in the general election.

Membership or allegiance to a political party has already been cited as one criterion for access to the ballot in almost all cases. Even that most basic rule has exceptions. In 1978 the state of Louisiana adopted a system called a **nonpartisan primary**, which sounds like a contradiction in terms. A primary, except when party labels are not used, is supposed to determine who a party's nominee will be. How can a "nonpartisan" primary determine a partisan nominee? In fact, Louisiana has changed the entire system around, and Republicans and Democrats appear on the same ballot. All candidates run on one ballot in the primary election. Each citizen is allowed one vote. If any one candidate receives a majority of the votes cast, that person is declared elected. If no one receives a majority on the first ballot, the general election is held between the top two finishers, regardless of their party affiliation.

Obviously, party officials do not favor this system. Further, its implications for state politics are not at all clear. When Mississippi tried to adopt a similar system, the changes in the state's election laws were challenged under the provisions of the Voting Rights Act, and the proposed system was disallowed as being disadvantageous to black voters. One problem with assessing the impact of a change as fundamental as this one is that politicians need a certain amount of time to adjust to a new political reality.

In Louisiana the effect of the new system has been to protect incumbents. Of the sixty-nine incumbents running for reelection to Congress from the time the system began through the 1998 election, sixty-six have been "reelected" at the primary election.[6] Of the remaining three incumbents, all won the general election, with two of the three victories coming by substantial margins. Most of the **open seats** were also uncontested beyond the primary. Party officials in other states are certainly watching the impact of this system closely.

OPEN SEATS

Seats in which no incumbent is running for reelection.

4. Cross-Filing: Another Exception to Party Allegiance

CROSS-FILING

Nominating system that permits a candidate to seek the nomination of more than one political party.

Cross-filing represents another exception to the rule that party nominees must be registered in or hold allegiance to the party whose nomination they seek. In New York State, a candidate may be the nominee of more than one party if the state party committee of the second party accepts that nominee. New York State has a tradition of strong third, fourth, and even fifth parties. While these parties do not win many offices on their own, they frequently hold the balance of power between the Democrats and Republicans.

One tactic used by the Conservative, Liberal, and Right-to-Life parties in New York is to endorse the candidate of one of the major parties. What is the strategy involved? What are the trade-offs? The minor parties know that they will not win office; however, they are very concerned about certain issues. Similarly, the candidates of the major parties know that minor-party candidates will not win. However, they are concerned that these minor-party candidates might draw votes from them and swing the election to their opponents. Thus the major-party candidates are willing to accept certain issue positions of the minor parties in exchange for that party's nomination and another line—literally another listing—on the ballot and some advertising and organizational support from the minor party's followers.

Frequently the trade-offs are not as explicit as the scenario just outlined. However, the implicit understandings are clear. If a major-party candidate in office offends a minor party, then the minor party will run its own candidate in the next election. Officeholders do not like to offend constituents who have that potential. Thus in congressional elections in New York in 1998, thirteen of the thirty Democratic nominees had Liberal party backing; and the same number of the thirty Republican party candidates had the Conservative party nomination (three of these were endorsed by Right-to-Life party).[7] In 1996, one nominee, Michael P. Forbes (First Congressional District), was endorsed by five parties: Republican, Conservative, Independence, Right-to-Life, and the Property Tax Cut.

Because of the way in which the New York State law is written, a candidate may even be nominated by both the Republican and Democratic parties. All that candidates need is the approval of the appropriate party committees to run in their respective primaries. For example, Mayor Koch of New York City ran in the Republican as well as the Democratic party primary in 1981 and won both party nominations by enormous margins. Consequently, he faced only minor-party opposition in the general election. When Republicans nominated Edward Adams to run against incumbent Democratic congressman Charles Rangel in 1996 and David Cunningham to run in 1998, those candidacies broke a pattern in which, more often than not since his first election in 1970, Rangel's name appeared as the endorsee of both major parties.[8] This kind of situation demonstrates the problems inherent in cross-filing. Popular incumbents can sew up the entire electoral process and eliminate any semblance of a competitive democratic election.

B. Who May Vote

Just as states and localities differ in who may run in partisan primaries, so too do they differ in who may vote in primary elections.

1. Closed, Open, and Blanket Primaries

Thirty-seven states use some form of **closed primaries**. Closed primaries are defined as primary elections in which only those who declare

CLOSED PRIMARIES

Primaries in which only voters enrolled in a particular party may participate.

allegiance to a party in advance may vote. However, the manner in which citizens are required to declare allegiance is not uniform across states.

At one extreme are states that require citizens to enroll in a political party in a formal sense. Official lists of Democrats and Republicans (and members of minor parties) are maintained by the state. These lists are public information, and thus a registered voter's party affiliation can be found out by others.

States that fall into this category often have specific requirements for changing party affiliation from one party to another or from independent status to party membership. Eleven of these states prohibit voters from changing party identification after the date on which candidates must declare themselves for the upcoming primaries.[9] These and the other states that maintain formal party enrollment lists also differ in the length of time between when a voter must declare party affiliation and when the primary is held, time spans varying from approximately one year to primary-day changes in Iowa, Ohio, Wyoming, and other states.[10] Further, we find variations in how state law applies to those previously unenrolled in a party—normally referred to as independents—as opposed to those who want to switch from one party to another.

At the other extreme among closed-primary states are those in which citizens openly choose one party or another on primary day, but those choices are not formally recorded by state officials. In some states (e.g., Missouri) this choice involves nothing more than publicly selecting one party's ballot as the voter enters the voting booth. In other states (e.g., Illinois) it involves a public declaration of intent to support a party's nominees or of having supported them in the past. Records are not kept of these choices. Only those actually present at the time that the choice was made are aware of the partisan preference of the voter.[11]

A thin line separates closed primaries of this latter type from open primaries. In open primaries, those voting in the primary elections are not required to publicly choose one party or the other. Rather, they enter the voting booth and choose the party ballot on which they will vote in secret. Obviously, once again, no records are kept of these decisions.[12]

OPEN PRIMARY

Primary in which each voter may choose one party's ballot or the other.

Washington and Alaska have used a unique derivative of the **open primary** called the **blanket primary** for some time; California moved to this system beginning with the 1998 election.[13] The blanket-primary ballot carries the theory of the open primary to its logical extreme. Citizens voting in a blanket primary can cast votes in the Republican primary for one office, the Democratic primary for a second and third office, the Republican primary for a fourth office, and so on. The only restriction is that they can only vote in one party's primary for each office. The winners of the primary are those affiliated with each party who draw the largest number of votes. Thus it would be possible for two Democrats to poll more votes than any Republican, but the party nominees for the November ballot would still be the one Democrat and the one Republican with the highest totals.

BLANKET PRIMARY

Primary election in which all names appear on one ballot, and each voter selects one candidate running for each race on the ballot; the candidates with the highest totals in each party qualify for the general election ballot.

The rules governing state elections are generally specified in state law; those wanting to change the rules of the political game have to work through state legislatures (or in the case of California through a ballot initiative) to alter state law. However, in 1984, the Republican party of Connecticut challenged that norm, not for philosophical reasons but for purely political ones. For some time Connecticut has been a heavily Democratic state and has had a closed-primary system. Independents, a large group in Connecticut, have not been permitted to participate in primaries. By allowing them to vote in Republican primaries, Republicans hoped to attract the allegiance of independents to Republican nominees. After unsuccessful attempts at changing state law, the state's Republican party challenged the closed-primary law in the courts. In the case of *Tashjian v. Republican Party of Connecticut*, 479 U.S. 208 (1986), the Supreme Court ruled that the Connecticut law failed to meet the First Amendment guarantee of freedom of association because it did not permit the Republican party to define its own membership. The law was thus ruled unconstitutional. Connecticut Republicans—and potentially other state parties—were permitted to define their own membership and have an open primary if they decided to do so (Epstein 1989; Maisel et al. 1990). The implications for this change in the ability of parties to define who can participate in their nominating process remains unclear, since further action by state parties has not followed that seen in Connecticut.

Political scientists use the traditional categories—closed, open, or blanket—to distinguish among primaries. In truth, it is more meaningful to view the variety of primaries as constituting a continuum from those in which party affiliation is the most fixed to those in which it is the least fixed. These distinctions have important consequences, whether they are viewed in terms of the theory of how politics should work or in the most practical political terms, as the Connecticut example demonstrates (Carr and Scott 1984; Finkel and Scarrow 1985).

2. Theoretical Arguments Regarding Primary Voter Eligibility

The question of who should be eligible to vote in a primary revolves around the theoretical debate over what role political party should play in the electoral process. The more restrictive primary eligibility is, the greater the role that party plays.

If the major political parties are viewed as distinct, as presenting differing philosophies from among which citizens should choose, then it follows that adherents of those philosophies should make the choice of who will carry their banner into the general election. Thus only those to whom the party is important and truly meaningful should decide the party's nominee.

If, on the other hand, one feels that the parties are really two sides of the same philosophical coin, then the primary is merely a way to pare down the field of eligible candidates. In this case, voters should be able to support the candidate most closely linked with their views.

This assertion is an extension of the argument about who should be able to run. Those who favor stronger parties want more of a role for party organization in determining who can seek a party's nomination; they favor systems that call for preprimary conventions and endorsements of one sort or another. On the other hand, those who view party as an unnecessary intermediary between citizens and their elected servants want anyone to be able to run; they favor no role for party regulars in determining primary contestants.

3. Pragmatic Considerations Regarding Primary Voter Eligibility

The student of politics who looks at the systems in place in various states and then talks to politicians in those states is led to conclude that politicians generally feel that their state systems reflect the needs of their constituents quite well. Few call for change. Many, indeed, cannot understand why other states do not do things the way they do. Two conclusions follow from this observation: Either state politicians have been incredibly astute in creating systems that correctly match the political culture of their state, or politicians are happy with a system they understand.

Very few politicians in the United States have expert knowledge of campaign laws beyond the boundary of the state in which they are working. Why should they? What they need to know is how to play the game in which they are currently involved. They approve of the rules that are in effect because they know how to play by and win under those rules. Reformers, conversely, tend to be those who are out of power, who have not managed to win with the rules in place. The efforts by Connecticut Republicans to open their primary stands as a case in point. More recently, both Democratic and Republican party leaders in California opposed the ballot initiative that led to the creation of that state's blanket primary. They knew how to play the political game under the old rules and were uncertain of the consequences of the new.

4. Strategic Consequences of Different Primary Rules

These comments about the views of working politicians point to the practical consequences of various primary systems. Regardless of how one evaluates a system, the details of that system determine how one will run a campaign.

Imagine the most basic problem facing a candidate in a primary: To whom must I appeal for votes? In a closed-primary state, with recorded party enrollment, the constituency seems easy to determine. Candidates and their campaign managers simply obtain lists of potential voters, that is, lists of people who are enrolled in their party and are eligible to vote in their party's primary.

In a closed-primary state without permanent enrollment, the only comparably available lists are rosters of those who voted in the party's last primary (if the party had workers collecting such a list at the poll in that last primary). Even where such lists are kept, they tend to be highly inaccurate, ignoring those who think of themselves as members of the party but did not vote in the last primary. And the lists have no way of accounting for new voters.

But those lists, as flawed as they are, are preferable to the lists that can be obtained in open-primary states. The only official lists that candidates can collect in open-primary states are lists of eligible voters and/or lists of those who did in fact vote in the last primary. Candidates have no way of knowing with certainty which ballot a particular voter marked.

Think of the consequences of these differences for campaign strategy. In the first case direct-mail and/or door-to-door campaigning is possible and efficient. Campaigns can reach those who are eligible to vote. In the second case these techniques of contacting voters are much less efficient, though still possible. In the open-primary scenario, if one does not want to contact all voters, it is necessary to rely on much less accurate methods of deciding on whom to concentrate, for example, targeting areas in which a high percentage of the voters seem to favor one's own party.

5. Crossover Voting

Politicians are also very concerned about **crossover voting**; let us assume that a Democratic incumbent is running unopposed for his party's nomination in an open-primary state. We further assume that there is a contested primary in the Republican party. No legal barrier prevents supporters of the Democratic incumbent from crossing over to the Republican primary and voting for the weaker of the two contestants in that primary, in an effort to nominate a weaker opponent for their favorite in the general election.

CROSSOVER VOTING

Practice of members of one political party voting in the other party's primary, presumably to nominate the weaker candidate.

Hypothetically this scenario could happen easily enough. In practice, however, it is difficult to document instances of this kind of perfidy. First, an orchestrated campaign to nominate the weaker candidate in the other party would require a sophistication unknown to most American political organizations. Raiding the other party's primary could not happen without such orchestration because the American electorate is not sufficiently involved in the nuances of electoral politics to employ such a strategy.

Second, voters who participate in primaries most often are concerned about more than one race. Even if an incumbent lacked a Democratic opponent in one race, still other offices would very likely feature contested Democratic primaries. In open primary states, Democrats crossing over to influence the outcome of a Republican primary would forfeit their rights to vote in these Democratic races, which presumably would be of more interest to them than other Republican primaries (some of which might even be uncontested). However, it is important to note that this "problem" does not exist for voters in blanket primary states. For instance, in California in 1998, the Democratic gubernatorial primary featured three strong candidates thought to have realistic chances for the nomination, Lieutenant Governor Gray Davis, Congresswoman Jane Harman, and former airline executive Al Checchi; the Republican nomination was conceded to Attorney General Dan Lundgren. Citizens who were strong Republicans could vote for one of the Democratic candidates—either their personal favorite or the one they thought would fare least well against Lundgren—and still vote in other contests in which Republicans were competing against one another.[14]

Third, the American voting public believes in fair play. It is very unlikely that enough voters would engage in this type of behavior to have an impact on any particular election. A political party that openly promoted such a strategy would run the risk of a moral backlash and thus lose more than it hoped to gain.

The fact that behavior of this type is unlikely to happen does not diminish the paranoia of politicians who worry about perfidy. Be that as it may, the true importance of voter eligibility rules relates much more closely to impact on election strategy than it does to the loyalty of the voters to the party in whose primary they participate.

C. Who Wins

1. Plurality Rule

MAJORITY RULE

An election system in which a candidate must receive one half plus at least one of the votes cast in order to be declared the victor.

PLURALITY RULE

An election system in which a candidate receiving a plurality of the votes is declared the winner.

Despite the lip service given to our "basic principle" of **majority rule**, majority rule is the exception in American politics. Most elections in America—and certainly most primaries—are determined by **plurality rule**. That is, the person with the most votes (not necessarily 50 percent plus at least one in the primary wins the nomination.

Plurality rule has important consequences, particularly in elections with large fields of candidates. For example, in Pennsylvania's Fifteenth Congressional District in 1998, six candidates competed in the Republican primary for the right to be the nominee to succeed the retiring representative, Paul McHale (R-Pa., 1992–1996). Restauranteur Pat Toomey won the nomination with under 27 percent of the vote, edging the next two finishers by fewer than 800 and 1,100 votes, respectively, out of almost 30,000 votes cast. Perhaps Toomey was the one most Republicans would have supported to succeed McHale in this heavily Republican district, but we will never really know. It might even be speculated that plurality nominee Toomey could command only a maximum of 27 percent of the Republican votes; perhaps those who voted against him would have supported any Republican other than Toomey. We do know that Toomey beat the Democratic nominee, state senator Roy Afflerbach, in the November election by a much narrower margin than typically enjoyed by McHale.

2. Variations from Plurality Rule: Runoff Primaries

Plurality rule is not in effect in every electoral jurisdiction. The major exception to the plurality winner rule is in the South, where nine states require a majority vote to receive the nomination; if no candidate wins a majority, a runoff or second primary is held. During his 1984 presidential campaign, Jesse Jackson drew a great deal of attention to runoff primaries, claiming that they discriminated against black candidates.

Runoff primaries were instituted in the South shortly after the beginning of this century, during a period of Democratic dominance in the South. Party officials viewed the **runoff primary** as a means of guaranteeing continued party strength, of assuring that the party was united behind one candidate and could thwart any independent challengers.

RUNOFF PRIMARY

Primary between the top two finishers in states that require majority votes in order to nominate.

Analysts differ over whether racial discrimination was a factor in creating runoff primaries. On the one hand, blacks were denied the right to vote through a whole series of Jim Crow laws and rules at this time; adding one more discriminatory obstacle to effective black participation would seem superfluous. On the other hand, almost all legislative action dealing with elections at the time was undertaken with an awareness of racial implications. It is difficult to imagine that those involved in establishing runoff primaries were incognizant of the fact that they could have an effect on the chances of blacks seeking office.

But let us put historical arguments aside and examine the effect that runoff primaries have today. Jesse Jackson's attention was directed to this issue by H. M. "Mickey" Michaux Jr., a black who lost the Democratic party nomination in North Carolina's Second Congressional District in 1982 after having captured 44 percent of the vote against two white candidates in the first primary. In the runoff Michaux polled 46 percent and lost to Tim Valentine, who went on to capture the seat. Using the Michaux contest as an example, some have claimed that blacks and other minorities would have ten to fifteen more seats in the Congress if the runoff primary were eliminated. This claim is based on two premises. First is the assumption that whites vote for whites and blacks for blacks in primary elections. Thus in districts with large black populations but not black majorities, blacks can lead in the first primary but lose when the whites all vote together in the runoff. The second premise is that voters stick to party lines in the general election, regardless of the candidates. These two assumptions seem to be at odds with each other and with recent experience.

If the first assumption is accurate, then runoff primaries are discriminatory against minority groups only in those districts in which they constitute a large bloc but not a majority. In districts in which blacks or Hispanics constitute a majority, the runoff primary would seem to work in their favor. For instance, African-American candidates can be helped in districts with African-American majorities.[15] In neither case is it evident that the system is discriminatory, only that one electoral system out of several possible ones has been chosen.

Turning to the second assumption, would it help minority candidates to get the nomination if they were then to lose in the general election? If voters follow racial lines, wouldn't it be logical for white voters to desert the Democratic party in the general election and support white Republicans? As the South becomes more and more a two-party region, wouldn't the elimination of the runoff primary accelerate the growth of the Republicans and lead to victories by even fewer "progressive" candidates than is now the case (see Bullock and Johnson 1985; Lamis 1984; Stanley 1985)?

MAJORITY MINORITY DISTRICTS

Districts in which a majority of the citizens or voters are members of a minority race.

These issues have all come into play in more recent congressional elections in so-called **majority minority districts**, congressional districts in which a majority of the voters are members of a racial minority. A number of majority minority districts were drawn after the 1990 census in order to increase the likelihood of black representation from southern states.

REDISTRICTING

The redrawing of the lines for legislative districts that takes place after decennial censuses.

REAPPORTIONMENT

The reallocation of districts among the states after each census so that each state receives at least one representative in Congress and all other state delegation sizes reflect population.

It is important to put this discussion into context, in this case the constitutionally mandated context of **redistricting** and **reapportionment**. Article 1, Section 2, of the Constitution says in part:

> Representatives shall be apportioned among the several States which may be included within this Union, according to their respective Numbers. . . . The actual Enumeration shall be made within three Years after the First Meeting of the Congress of the United States, and within every subsequent Term of ten Years, in such Manner as they shall by law direct.

Congress has ordered a census every ten years, as the Constitution stipulates. Actually, two processes are involved. Not only is the number of seats that each state is allocated in the House determined by the census (the process of reapportionment), but the boundaries of individual districts and of state legislative districts are also redrawn to reflect shifting population patterns (the process of legislative redistricting).

During much of the nation's history, the process of reapportionment was politically painless because Congress continuously voted to expand the size of the House of Representatives. Thus the House grew from its original 106 members to nearly 400 by 1900. In 1910, however, in part at least because of the size of the chamber, Congress voted to set the size of the House permanently at 435. Since that time this number has only been exceeded for the brief period of time between the admission of Alaska and Hawaii into the Union and the reapportionment following the 1960 census. As a result of the cap on the size of the House and of shifting population panels, reapportionment has become costly to some states after every census, with some delegations shrinking to accommodate growth in others. Since the 1930 reapportionment, a formula has been used, which removes the politics from reapportioning decisions.

The same cannot be said for decisions regarding legislative redistricting once apportionment is known. Traditionally, district lines have been drawn to accomplish political purposes. **Gerrymandering** is a revered part of American political folklore. Gerrymandering involves drawing districts, often of strange shapes, to suit the drawer's particular purposes.

GERRYMANDERING

Drawing district lines to achieve certain political purposes.

In the last fifty years, judicial intervention has led to less blatant gerrymandering when district lines are redrawn. In *Colegrove v. Green*, 328 U.S. 549 (1946), the Supreme Court refused to intervene in a challenge that claimed that congressional districts in Illinois needed to be redrawn because they were of unusual size. The Court held that legislative apportionment was a political question and thus not justiciable. However, in *Baker v. Carr*, 369 U.S. 186 (1962), the Court decided that redistricting was not beyond its purview in all circumstances. The Court was responding to extreme cases of malapportionment; in Tennessee; for instance, state legislative district lines had not been redrawn in sixty years, despite massive population shifts that resulted in some legislators representing a hundred times as many citizens as others.

In subsequent rulings (especially *Gray v. Sanders*, 372 U.S. 368 [1963] and *Wesberry v. Sanders*, 376 U.S. 1 [1964]) the Court established a criterion of **one person–one vote** against which apportionment schemes would be measured (Butler and Cain 1991; Cain 1984; Cain and Butler 1991; Grofman 1990; Lowenstein l991b; Polsby 1971; Schuck 1987).

ONE PERSON-ONE VOTE

Principle that reapportionment and redistricting must be accomplished in such a manner that each district has, to the extent possible, the same population and, therefore, each person's vote counts equally.

However, judicial regulation does not mean that reapportionment has become apolitical. Political scientists have spent a good deal of time and effort looking at the extent to which redistricting favors incumbents and impacts on subsequent electoral chances (Basehart and Comer 1991; Born 1985; Cain 1985; Gelman and King 1990; Glazer, Grofman, and Robbins 1987; King 1989; Niemi and Jackson 1991). The conclusions reached by these scholars convincingly demonstrate that redistricting does not affect one party adversely and does not make the ultimate difference in reelection bids by incumbents. Yet there can be no doubt that politicians work very hard to be certain that district boundaries are redrawn so as in a way that meets the judicial criteria but also brings as much benefit as possible to those drawing the lines. The Court has moved cautiously into the area of reviewing partisan gerrymandering. In *Davis v. Bandemer*, 478 U.S. 109 (1986), the Court seemed to rule that partisan gerrymandering could be a violation of the equal protection clause of the Constitution but that the case before the

Court did not appear sufficiently egregious to merit judicial intervention (Cain and Butler 1991, 32; Lowenstein 1991; Schuck 1987).

Similarly, the Court has stepped gingerly into the area of racial vote dilution by gerrymandering. In these cases the Court was applying the criteria of the Voting Rights Act of 1965 as well as that of the equal protection clause of the Constitution. The Court has wavered between examining whether the *intent* of the redistricting was to dilute racial minorities' power (the standard before the 1982 amendments to the Voting Rights Act) and examining the *effect* of the redistricting, regardless of the intent. Since the Court laid out criteria for examination of unconstitutional dilution of racial minorities' voting power in *Thornburg v. Gingles*, 478 U.S. 30 (1986), state legislatures have looked very carefully at whether the courts might respond that any proposed legislative redistricting plan violated minority rights according to these criteria (Perry 1991).

The 1990 census seems to have caused particular problems. First, a number of states (and large cities) claimed that the census takers undercounted up to 5 million citizens, most of them minorities living in urban centers. If the Bush administration altered the census count in line with any of the proposed estimates of error, various states stood to gain or lose seats.[16] In fact, the census count was accepted as originally tabulated (though various states challenged that count in court to no avail).

The stakes were so high that lawmakers in state capitols, those charged with redrawing district lines, went about their work very slowly. As late as August 1991, less than seven months before the first congressional primaries, only seven of the forty-three states with more than one congressional district had drawn their district lines. *Congressional Quarterly*'s commentary on the politics of redistricting used phrases like "both parties have enough power to gum up the redistricting process" in Louisiana, or Illinois Democrats "were ready to throw the politically sensitive chore to the courts" (Donovan 1991, 1776).

The chore was indeed sensitive and led to some bizarre results. Legislatures are charged with the task of redistricting, sometimes with governors having veto powers and sometimes not,[17] but the actual task of suggesting district lines falls to computer experts who have programmed their machines to draw maps according to certain agreed-upon criteria. Generally the computers have been fed information on the racial composition of each voting precinct, past electoral behavior, and party registration if available. With that information, the computers can draw districts to meet virtually any agreed-upon criteria.

In North Carolina in 1991, the criteria included protecting the seat of each incumbent to the extent possible and creating a new black majority seat and a new Republican seat, as well as meeting the Court's criteria of populations in each district being as equal as possible (called for in the case of *Karcher v. Daggett*, 462 U.S. 725 [1983]). The resulting districts surely do not meet the criteria of being "compact and

Figure 7.1 North Carolina Districts after 1990 Redistricting.

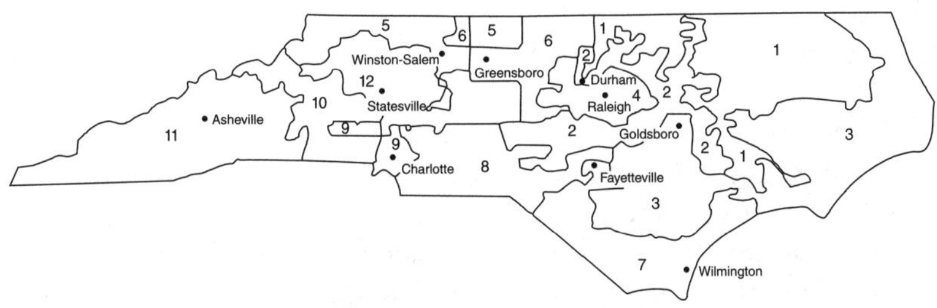

contiguous." In fact, the Second District looked remarkably like the very district after which gerrymandering was named.

That district, as well as other "majority minority districts," was challenged in the courts and found not to meet the judicial tests (see *Shaw v. Reno*, 509 U.S. 630 [1993]; *Miller v. Johnson*, 515 U.S. 900 [1995]; *Bush v. Vera*, 517 U.S. 952 [1996], *Abrams v. Johnson*, 117 S. Ct. 125 [1997], among other cases). The controversy lasted throughout the decade, with district lines in question right up to the elections of 1998. Some of these districts were challenged on the grounds that racial gerrymandering violated the equal protection clause of the Constitution. In other cases, the challenge was that the Voting Rights Act was being violated. In the cases in which the Supreme Court ruled the districts unacceptable, new lines were drawn, at times by courts because legislators were unable to reach agreement. In a number of cases the new plans created districts in which the black member of Congress who had been elected when the lines were first drawn now represented a district without a minority racial majority. And none of the incumbents so affected lost reelection bids.

All of this is to say that redistricting may be a more exact art than it once was, and certain democratic principles must be considered. But in essence the act of redistricting in the 1990s is just as political as it ever was.

This discussion of alternatives to plurality rule—and drawing district lines as another means to effect outcomes—should be viewed from a broader perspective. Thus it could be argued that plurality elections are not a good mechanism for guaranteeing popular rule in the case of factionalized electorates. Both Iowa and South Dakota have provisions in their electoral laws that require a primary winner to receive at least 35 percent of the vote in order to be declared the nominee. If no candidate reaches that threshold in South Dakota, runoffs are held for the offices of governor, state senator, and state representative. For the other offices, as well as for all offices in Iowa, a state party convention meets to select the candidates.[18] Clearly, there are many distinctions among primaries. In the next section we will explore the ways in which the various primary systems shape the politics of the nominating process.

V. THE POLITICS OF NOMINATIONS

A. Uncontested Nominations

Recall the offices listed at the beginning of this chapter. How much competition is there for clerk of courts? For water district commissioner? Compare the interest in those offices with interest in U.S. senator or governor. Or compare the attractiveness of serving as a state representative in Vermont, where the legislature sits for four to five months a year, there are 150 state representatives, and the approximate average annual salary is $6,750, with the attractiveness of the same position in California, where serving in the state assembly is a full-time job, the eighty assembly members each represent approximately 375,000 people, and the base annual salary is $54,800.

These kinds of comparisons point to the difficulty in analyzing nominations at the state and local level. The situation varies from office to office and from state to state. Obviously, more seats are contested for the more prestigious offices. Nominations for the U.S. Senate are uncontested much less frequently than nominations for state assembly. Further, state offices in larger states are more likely to attract contested primaries than are similar offices in smaller states.[19] This thesis follows quite naturally from the fact that such offices are more likely to be full-time, highly paid, and prestigious in larger states.

Other conclusions about contested primaries have been found to be similarly predictable. Incumbents win nominations without the necessity of contesting a primary more often than do challengers. Contested primaries are more likely to occur for open seats, those without an incumbent running, particularly in the party of the retiring incumbent, than for seats in which incumbents are running. Primaries are always more likely to occur in dominant parties than in minority parties. One basic rule seems to apply: the more valuable the party nomination, the greater the likelihood of a contested primary. The value of the party nomination, in turn, relates to two variables—the prestige of the office sought and the likelihood that the party's nomination will result in victory in the general election.

How do candidates get nominated in situations in which there is no contested primary? No systematic research has addressed this question, and most students of politics would answer it based on their personal experiences. The process is seemingly simple. Each candidate follows whatever procedure is necessary to have his or her name placed on the primary ballot. No one else does so. The nomination then goes by default. But that analysis begs the question. Who is the individual who presents himself or herself as a candidate?

One working assumption is that incumbents normally want to succeed themselves, even for the less prestigious offices. Few people desire or are more qualified to serve as water district commissioner than the individual holding that position; more often than not that individual will continue to hold the position.

If no incumbent is running, or if the incumbent is in the other party, then party officials have the responsibility of finding candidates for office.[20] For prestigious offices this search is not difficult. For less prestigious offices, however, the role of the party official is very different. In these cases, officials must identify potential candidates for office and convince them to run.

Party organization traditionally controlled access to the ballot. This power was lost for prestigious offices with the advent of the direct primary and with increased popular participation. However, the party's role persists for lesser offices. Some party organizations are quite successful in playing this role; others much less so.

In congressional elections in the 1980s, one major party or the other did not field a candidate for the House of Representatives in about one district in six. The parties each did somewhat better in the 1992 and 1996 congressional elections, but in 1998, one party or the other did not field a candidate for the House in eighty-six districts, the most since World War II. On the other hand, all eligible gubernatorial and all save for a very few Senate seats have been contested by both parties in all recent elections. Success in structuring the contest for office is one measure of success of the ways that party organizations do their jobs.

B. Contested Nominations

When most analysts talk about primary elections, they are actually concerned with *contested* primary elections, a subgroup that is a minority of all primaries.[21] Contested primaries receive the most attention because they provide campaign watchers with something to watch. They also play an important role in weeding out contestants for office. Any discussion of contested primaries needs to emphasize differences by office and locale.

1. Incumbent Advantage

Political observers have again been able to make some generalizations about these contested primaries. The first generalization is that incumbents win a high proportion of the primaries in which they are challenged (fig. 5.3; table 5.3). Second, incumbent victories are increasingly the rule for lesser or more local offices. Incumbents have an advantage over opponents in that they have already built up support within the party (Fenno 1978). Unless they have acted in a way that undercuts their own support, they are rarely beaten in a primary.

Incumbent losers are so few that analysts can almost always explain each case as idiosyncratic. Only two U.S. senators have lost primaries since 1980. In 1992, Democratic senator Alan Dixon of Illinois lost to Carol Moseley-Braun, who went on to become the first black woman elected to the Senate. Dixon had no declared opposition until he cast one of the few Democratic votes in favor of confirming Clarence Thomas to the Supreme Court. That vote enraged feminists and liberals and led directly to Moseley-Braun's candidacy. A third candidate in the race attacked Dixon as representing an unresponsive Congress removed from the people and dominated by special interests. There is even some evidence that Dixon was tainted by the House bank scandal, not because he himself was involved in any way but more as guilt by association. The combination of these factors led to his unexpected defeat.

In 1996 Shiela Frahm (R-Kans.) was appointed to fill the Senate seat vacated when majority leader Robert Dole resigned to run for the presidency full-time. Frahm was beaten in a primary a few short months later; she had had little time to make a legislative or constituent service record for herself before she had to face the voters. Similarly, she had been unable to build a campaign organization or a financial war chest to hold off primary challenger Sam Brownbeck, a House member at the time.

Similarly, House defeats are few and far between, but the 1992 election stands as an exception as nineteen House members lost primaries. However, this exception can also be explained. As noted previously, every ten years House districts change. After reapportionment, which determines the size of each state's delegation, the states must undergo redistricting to account for added or subtracted seats when their relative population has changed significantly or to account for population shifts within the state, so that each district contains the same population, meeting the constitutional mandate of one person–one vote. As a result of reapportionment and redistricting, many House members faced substantially new districts in 1992; in fact, in a number of cases two members found themselves representing the same district. When this decennial phenomenon was combined with the House bank scandal, in which many members were tainted as frequent abusers of a congressional privilege, the result was an unusual number of incumbents defeated in primaries. Even in that record year, however, 95 percent of the incumbents seeking renomination to the House were chosen by their party.[22]

The experience of 1998 is more common. Only one House incumbent, first-term California Republican Jay C. Kim, lost a primary election. Kim had been convicted of campaign fundraising abuses in his 1996 election and was forbidden by the courts from returning to his district to campaign for renomination. Obviously, his conviction and his inability to serve his district effectively were used successfully by his opponent.

2. *Contests without Incumbents*

What about races in which incumbents are not running? Conclusions in these cases are more tentative. Winners tend to be those who make best use of the resources necessary to win elections. Although the important resources may vary from race to race, key among them is name recognition. The candidate who is much more widely known than his or her opponent(s) is likely to win. How is such recognition achieved?

Some candidates have it when they enter a race. For instance, a state senator who is entering a congressional primary may have represented many of those who are eligible to vote in the primary, an eventuality likely to happen in large states with sizable state senate districts, such as California or Florida. Such a candidate would start with an advantage over a political neophyte.

Or a candidate may be known for other reasons. Two representatives to Congress from Oklahoma in the 1990s, Republicans Steve Largent and J. C. Watts, were extremely well known as football players before they became politicians. Athletes, actors, media personalities, astronauts, and others with similar fame start with a name recognition advantage when they enter the political arena (Canon 1990). They may even become president!

Yet many candidates do not start with these advantages, particularly candidates for local offices. How do they get known? Three key ingredients contribute to successful campaigns—candidate effort, campaign organization, and money. In smaller districts candidates themselves may well be able to "get around," to shake hands with a large portion of the potential electorate. Candidates for sheriff go into high schools and talk about drug and alcohol abuse. Candidates for state representative address the Rotary or the Lions in town after town. All candidates for these offices attend party meetings and picnics, town meetings, PTA meetings—any meeting at which they can be certain that they will be introduced. They go door-to-door and discuss mutual concerns with voters. Candidate after candidate will attest that there is no better campaign technique than actually talking to a potential voter. If a district is small enough and if a candidate can commit enough time, nothing is more effective.

Many districts (e.g., congressional districts, state senatorial districts) are too large, however, for a candidate to have any chance of meeting even a sizable proportion of the potential electorate. Although candidates campaign personally to the extent possible, they must rely on an organization to extend their outreach. A candidate's campaign organization uses various techniques to serve as surrogates for personal contact. Workers go door-to-door seeking support for their candidate. They carry literature that describes the candidate's views and qualifications. They telephone potential voters and discuss why they favor the candidate for whom they are working. They put up lawn signs, hand out buttons and bumper stickers, speak on behalf of their candidate at functions she or he cannot attend. An effective organization reaches out for candidates further than they themselves can reach. Such organizations frequently give the appearance of widespread support, which itself leads to more recognition and eventually to more support.

Campaign organizations in smaller districts are frequently volunteer organizations. Friends and neighbors of a candidate will offer their assistance. But even these campaigns need some money in order to function effectively. Buttons and bumper stickers, brochures and balloons—all the paraphernalia of a campaign—cost money. As the size of the district expands, the cost of the campaign rises. In many of today's primaries money has become a sine non qua for success. As recently as 1974, when the FEC began keeping these records, only ten congressional campaigns spent $200,000 in the primary and general elections combined, and expenditures of $100,000 in primaries were all but unknown. A decade later a congressional primary that was won on a budget of $100,000 has been cited as evidence that "a congressional seat can still be won without spending a fortune" (*Congressional Quarterly Weekly Report* 1984, 1119). In the last two election cycles, particularly in open seats in the party with a partisan electoral advantage, spending half a million dollars in a primary in no longer considered unusual (see chap. 11).

The precise combination of candidate effort, organization, and money that is necessary to win any primary is difficult to ascertain with precision. The ability to arrive at that combination is what separates winners from losers. Still, the imprecision of the calculation is why politics remains more art than science. If one formula worked for every campaign, then every campaign manager and every candidate would do the same thing. Candidates and their campaign managers start with a certain amount of knowledge of how to campaign (most of it gained from experience), with an understanding of their districts, their candidacies, etc., and with a certain amount of resources. Working with these, they devise tactics and strategies. They play on their strengths and try to exploit the weaknesses of their opponents. They play down their weaknesses and try to undercut the strengths of their opponents. Politicians seek to find the formula that will give them the largest number of votes in the primary while doing the least harm to their chances in the general election, ultimately hoping to appear invincible and not worth challenging (Jacobson 1983). That, after all, is what the primary campaign is all about (Maisel 1982; 1986).

VI. Politicians View the Nominating Process

How do politicians view all of this? No surprises here: it all depends on their situation. The means through which a candidate achieves a party's nomination can either help or hurt that candidate's chances in the general election. The same route to nomination can have differing impact in different years. Contested primaries can be divisive or they can help winning candidates gain name recognition. Uncontested primaries can save candidate resources for a general election, but they can also leave a candidate virtually unknown when he or she runs against a well-established incumbent.

Politicians generally like to avoid hotly contested primaries. However, under certain circumstances, such as when a candidate is not well known and/or a candidate's organization has not been tested, "a little primary can be a good thing." Primaries can be see as battles for the heart and soul of a party. Rather than look at individual experiences, some politicians view primaries from the "macro" level: what is happening to the party? Perhaps the 1998 Republican primaries as a whole are best viewed in this light.

In state after state, Republican primaries featured doctrinaire conservative Republicans against more mainstream office seekers. The argument of the more moderate candidates was that they could appeal to a wider range of voters in the general election and would thus be more likely to win in November. In the Illinois U.S. Senate primary to oppose Democrat Carol Moseley-Braun, for instance, candidate Loleta Didrickson claimed that she should be supported because "people know me," with reference to her statewide victory as comptroller. Her opponent, state senator Peter Fitzgerald, countered, "Stand up for your convictions. . . . Don't back down. Articulate our conservative principles as Ronald Reagan did, and you can win in Illinois" (Broder 1998, 3C).[23]

More conservative Republicans assert that their party has to stand on principles that many associate with Ronald Reagan. Battles along these lines were fought in statewide Republican primaries in states as widely separated as Alabama and Washington, Kansas and California.

The Republican party is divided in ways more typical of Democrats in years past. On the one hand, there is a split between moderates and ideological conservatives. On the other hand, avowed conservatives are not all of one mind. Some are deeply committed cultural or religious conservatives, many followers of the Christian Coalition and related groups; others are more traditional economic conservatives. And intraparty primaries have been the scene of these battles as well. They cause real problems within the party. As Representative Charles Bass (N.H.) has stated, "Their [Christian conservatives'] concerns and problems need to be taken very seriously and attended to with an open mind and open ears. . . . But there has to be a realization on their part that splitting from Republicans is basically the equivalent of political cannibalism. The result will be no winners at all" (Edsall and Connolly 1998, 14). In these cases politicians view the primaries as a means to power within the party, asserting the dominance of one wing over another. Or they view them as a chance that opportunities for victories will be lost in intraparty bickering.

How politicians view primaries depends very much on their political situation. They may view them from a personal point of view or from a broader perspective. But rarely do politicians lose sight of the ultimate goal—winning the general election in November.

WEBSITES

http://www.vote-smart.org

Project Vote Smart maintains an excellent website that highlights performance in office and election campaigns of candidates for president, other federal offices, governor, and other state offices.

http://www.cq.com

Congressional Quarterly Service's website follows congressional, senatorial, and presidential elections all the way through the process. Historical background is also available.

http://cnn.com/ALLPOLITICS/

This CNN political website does an excellent job of monitoring ongoing campaigns.

http://www.rollcall.com

Roll Call is one of two newspapers that specialize in covering Capitol Hill. During election years, their coverage of primaries and elections gives inside details.

http://www.hillnews.com

The Hill is the other Capitol Hill newspaper. While somewhat less well-known than *Roll Call*, *The Hill* also provides excellent inside views.

KEY CONCEPTS

blanket primary
caucuses
challenge primary
closed primaries
conventions
cross-filing
crossover voting
delegates
gerrymandering
majority
majority minority districts
majority rule
nonpartisan primary
one person–one vote
open primary
open seats
plurality rule
preprimary conventions
qualified candidates
reapportionment
redistricting
runoff primary

DISCUSSION QUESTIONS

1. Who benefits from open primaries as opposed to closed primaries? Blanket primaries? What do you see as the advantages and disadvantages of each system?
2. Describe the nominating process in your state. Why do you think your state has developed that kind of system as opposed to one of the others? What do you think would happen if the system were drastically changed?
3. The Republican U.S. Senate primary in California pitted an ideological conservative against a more moderate candidate in a contest to face the very liberal Democratic incumbent, Barbara Boxer. Do you believe that California's blanket primary system helped the Republicans field the candidate with the best opportunity to beat Boxer? Do you think the system was best designed to help Republicans settle internal ideological conflicts?
4. New York State law was recently amended to make access to the ballot somewhat easier. An opponent of stringent ballot access requirements claimed proudly that he used to live in a state in which all one needed was fifty signatures to get on the ballot. What are the advantages and disadvantages of easier versus harder requirements to get on the primary ballot?
5. In states as diverse as Rhode Island, Virginia, and Utah, political parties play an important formal role in winning a primary election. In other states, like New Hampshire, Maryland, and Wyoming, that role is much less important. What role does party play in your state? What are the advantages and disadvantages of an increased party role?
6. Most incumbents win renomination either without opposition or quite easily. Thus it could be argued that the system is stacked in their favor—and thus is undemocratic. It could also be argued that the system merely gives popular officeholders a chance to retain their position. What do you think?

CHAPTER 8

State and Local Elections

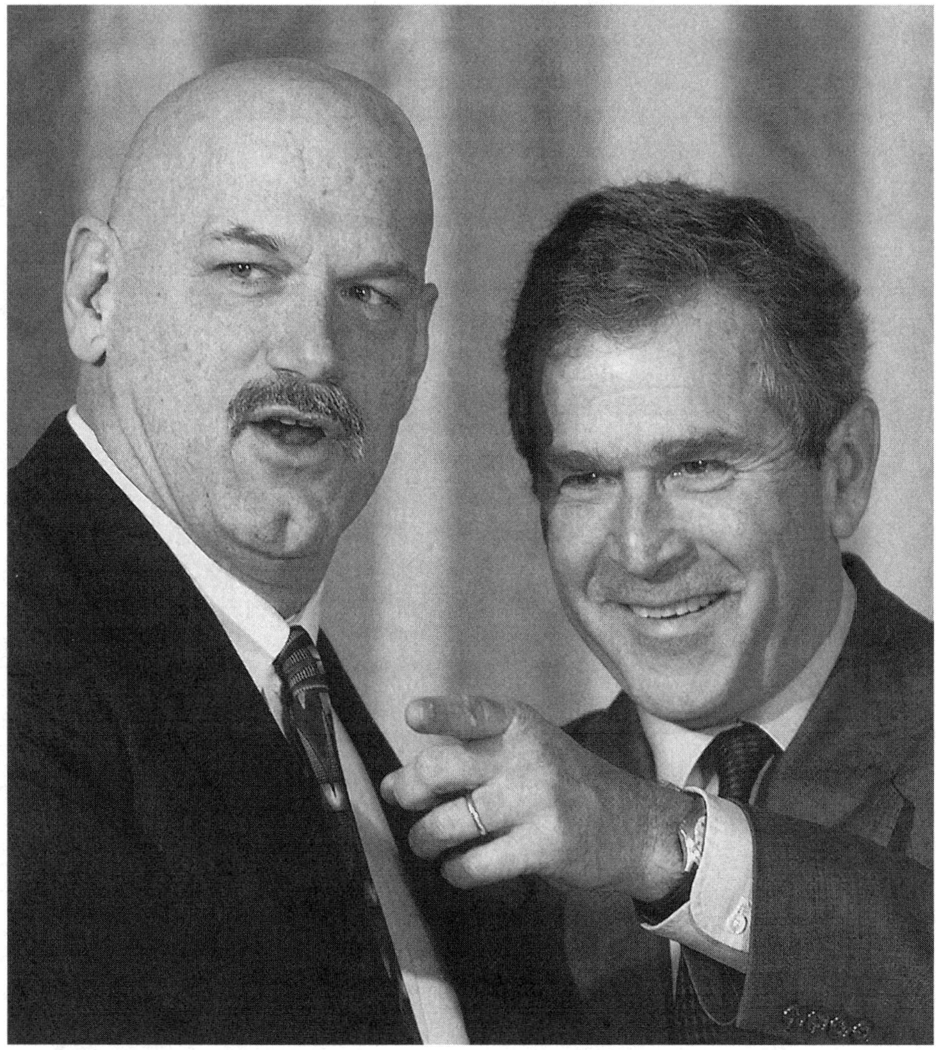

I. The Conventional Wisdom: Old versus New Politics
II. The New Politics: Campaigning in a Media Age
   A. The Role of Political Parties
   B. The Role of Organized Groups
   C. Media Politics
   D. The Candidate's Organization
   E. The Structure of a Modern Campaign
      1. Public Opinion Polling
      2. Media Consultants
      3. Fund-Raisers

Compare the experiences of two politicians at the Washington County Fair. Thirty-one states in the Union have Washington counties. Their experiences could happen in any of them. The first politician is a candidate for the county board of supervisors. His district encompasses about one-fifteenth of the county. He has been active in county politics and county government for some years. The second candidate is a member of Congress running for U.S. senator. Washington County is one of over sixty counties in the state; she is from the other end of the state and has been in Washington County perhaps twice.

The candidate for board of supervisors has been looking forward to the county fair for months. The fair is one of the most important social events on his annual calendar. Since most of the people in the county attend the fair at least once during fair week, this is also an important political event. Our candidate is in charge of the voter registration booth at the fair, making sure that the decorations are in place and that the booth is always open. He sees to it that his signs are in evidence. He has set the entire week aside so that he can spend as much time at the fair as is possible. After all, what could be a better way to campaign among likely voters?

The Senate candidate will attend the fair too. She will put in one appearance, for about an hour, at a time that the local people tell her will be quite busy. She is not looking forward to the fair with eagerness. In fact, one day before, she is not even aware that she will be attending. Her staff arranged for the visit. Someone else will be certain that her signs are in place, that she is introduced to the right people, and, most importantly, that the media know she is there. She probably will attend every county fair in the state.

The board of supervisors candidate's fair visit is one of the truly major events of his entire campaign. He is filmed introducing the Senate candidate to some of the local folks; that scene is on television at eleven, and everyone sees it. He makes sure that someone takes candid pictures to use in his campaign flyer; maybe the photographer will even get the best one autographed.

The Senate candidate squeezed the visit to the fair into a busy day. She was up at dawn, shaking hands at a factory gate. She flew halfway across the state to have lunch with a union leader whose PAC had promised, but not delivered, financial support. After lunch she did a brief radio interview and stopped in at the local newspaper to talk with the editor. On the flight into Washington County Airport she conferred with her campaign manager and her pollster about the impact of her recent statements on aid to victims of Hurricane Mitch in Central America. After the appearance at the fair, she was driven a hundred miles south for a fund-raising dinner. She did not even see the speech she was to give until an hour before the dinner. She did not know where she was staying that night but hoped she would have time to make some calls before she went to bed. One call would be to dictate some letters to her secretary; she would remember to tell her to write a note thanking that guy who introduced her at the fair. "Can't remember his name or where he's from. Find out from someone."

These two politicians seem to be engaged in the same enterprise—winning the votes of enough people to gain election. To win these votes, they must identify likely supporters and figure out some way to get those supporters to the polls. Both candidates have to set strategies aimed at accomplishing these goals. They must devise a strategy that involves identifying likely supporters and determining how they can structure a candidacy that will reach these voters. Each candidate must also come up with tactics aimed at carrying out the strategy.

But what do they do on a day-to-day basis? How do they structure an organization and what does that organization do? As the hypothetical scenario just depicted demonstrates, these two candidates on a day-to-day basis are actually involved in very different enterprises.

I. THE CONVENTIONAL WISDOM: OLD VERSUS NEW POLITICS

Under the old politics, campaigning was person-to-person and door-to-door; candidates were individuals representing the political parties that structured both the campaigns for office and the institutions of government. Supporters gave allegiance to the parties because they agreed with their stand on issues or because the parties' candidates would do certain things for voters if elected. The candidates of the party in control of government, as a group, were held accountable for the performance of the government.

New politics, however, is media and image oriented, not person-to-person. It is the politics of television and mass media (see chap. 12). Political party organization has been replaced by **candidate-centered**

CANDIDATE-CENTERED
The focus of a campaign or an organization is on a particular candidate, not on a party or a group of candidates running together.

organization. The link between campaigning and governing is difficult to document; institutional accountability has declined as individual candidates win or lose based on the strength of their own efforts, not those of the party (Fiorina 1990).

The reality of campaigning for office in the last decades of the twentieth century is, like so much else in this text, dependent on context. New politics has replaced old politics, in some areas, for some offices. Often the change is more subtle than bold. Consider again the Washington County Fair. The Senate candidate was running a "new politics," candidate-centered campaign. She was concerned about the perception of *her* position on foreign aid, about raising money for *her* campaign from the union PAC, about the media coverage of *her* appearance at the Washington County Fair.

But the candidate for county supervisor was involved in an "old politics" campaign. The booth at the county fair was a party organization activity; it was part of a voter registration drive run by the party. All the party candidates together put up their posters. He took time out of his normal campaign pattern to "interact" with the senatorial campaign, to "use" it for party and personal publicity, but such events were not part of his overall tactics or strategy. He spent much of the week at the fair because that was where he could greet and talk to the greatest number of people.

Old politics and new politics exist hand in hand in America today. New politics gets more attention because it is designed for getting attention—and because the bigger campaigns, for more visible offices, are often run using state-of-the-art new politics techniques. But that does not mean that all campaigning has changed. In this chapter I will show how the two coexist—and how Tip O'Neill's famous adage that "all politics is local" continues to contain a good deal of truth.

II. The New Politics: Campaigning in a Media Age

Let us assume that a politician is making a fully rational decision about seeking office.[1] A politician considering stepping up to a larger constituency, a more prestigious office, will seek some information:

1. What voters am I going to need to appeal to?
2. What is the partisan distribution of voters within the new district?
3. What is the normal voting strength for candidates of my party in this district? Conversely, what are the strengths of the opposition candidate and his or her party?
4. What kinds of techniques will work in appealing to the voters whose support I will need?

That list could easily be expanded, but it serves as a starting point for the discussion of so-called new politics. Candidates for all offices ask the same questions about how to get the support of a plurality of all voters. They ask the same questions about their party and/or personal support and that of their opponents.

Based on an analysis of the district (often a very impressionistic analysis of the district), they decide if they can win the election they are considering. Rarely does victory seem certain. If victory were certain, others with similar qualifications would be seeking the office, thereby removing the apparent certainty because of a primary election. If a politician believes that victory in moving up to a higher elective office is indeed certain, the assumptions on which that prediction was made should be reexamined.

If preliminary analysis leads to a conclusion that victory is unlikely, experienced politicians, holding other elective office, generally stay put.[2] It is almost always easier to retain a seat than to move up the ladder (Jacobson and Kernell 1983, chap. 3).[3] If, however, they feel that victory is possible, that they have a legitimate chance, then they begin to analyze how to get the votes.

At this stage, they must look at party strength in detail, at the potential for a personal organization, and at the potential for a media campaign (Gibson et al. 1983; 1985). A candidate who is considering a campaign for Congress or for statewide office, or even for state senate in some of the larger states, must realize that he or she cannot personally reach all the voters. Also, voters no longer use party affiliation as the only cue in deciding how to vote. What techniques will be successful in convincing voters that they should cast their ballot for this particular candidate?

Let us now assume that the candidate, a nonincumbent, has decided to run.[4] Our candidate is either challenging an incumbent or running in an open seat. In either case the tactical problems are the same, though the difficulty of the task may be more exaggerated in the first instance. The candidate has certain resources to utilize and certain tasks to accomplish. The problem is to match resources with tasks in the most effective way.

The first job is to identify likely supporters. The second is to ascertain what other voters are possible converts to the candidate's side. After identifying these two groups, the candidate must set a strategy for reaching both of these groups in a way that will solidify their support and increase the possibility that they will turn out to vote in droves. That might sound simple, but it certainly is not.

The most important resource that any candidate has is personal time (Mann and Wolfinger 1980). In some races nothing more is necessary. The candidate can identify supporters and potential supporters and go out and talk to them all. Many politicians started in that way for their first campaign. They are used to personal contact and have difficulty realizing that that will not work for all campaigns.

However, "pressing the flesh" of all the voters is not possible in a campaign for the House of Representatives, in which the average member represents over 650,000 people; nor is it possible in a campaign for statewide office, when over forty states have populations exceeding a million. Thus the candidate must learn how to use personal time in a new way, not merely contacting individual voters but maximizing the number of voters on whom that candidate can have an impact. Surrogates for the candidate are necessary in order to best use the results of time spent, essentially by "expanding" the amount of personal time.

A. The Role of Political Parties

Many candidates have experience in using party as a surrogate. Some voters will vote for a candidate because of party affiliation. For these voters, the candidate need only be certain that party affiliation is well known. Little candidate time is necessary to make this connection. Party, then, is one resource on which politicians are used to relying.

But political party is not a resource that is equally available to all candidates, nor is it a resource with which all candidates are equally comfortable. Candidates must weigh the impact of party in the new district. Is the organization efficient? Is the degree of partisan affiliation strong among voters? Is the candidate perceived to be in line with most of the others in the party? Or is the candidate an outsider to whom party people will not automatically flock? Is the candidate's party a majority or not? Is party strength spread equally throughout the district, or is it concentrated in some areas? What does the campaign do about the other areas? What is it that party organization can and cannot do in a particular campaign? How important is the campaign for the party organization? Are party activists likely to work hard for this campaign, or are they more concerned about another candidate or another race?

Merely posing these questions demonstrates how complex tactical campaign planning can be. Return for a moment to the question of what other offices are on the ballot. If John Doe is a candidate for Congress, in all likelihood his congressional district does not have the same boundaries that districts designed for other elective offices have. Most party organizations are structured around the county unit. In rural states, and in rural districts in some of the more urban states, congressional districts tend to encompass a large number of counties. For example, the First Congressional District in West Virginia includes all or part of ten counties; the First Congressional District in California, in the northeastern corner of the state, includes all or part of thirteen counties. On the other hand, in urban areas many congressional districts fall into single counties. The five counties that compose New York City, as an extreme example, contain all or part of twenty-one congressional districts; Harris County (Houston), Texas, contains all or part of five congressional districts.

For all that, county organizations are notoriously unconcerned about congressional politics. Members of Congress, and senators for that matter, deal with issues far away in Washington. Party people care more about issues closer to home because ultimately their concern involves those who can be counted on to do something tangible for them.

The local sheriff may have more immediate impact on these politicians than do their representatives in Washington. Consequently, local pols are more likely to work hard for local candidates. Similarly, they are more likely to work hard for candidates for executive office than they are for candidates for legislative office. All this theorizing assumes, of course, that the party organization exists and is capable of doing effective campaign work at all, an assumption that is far from clear in many areas of the country (Eldersveld 1982; Epstein 1986; for a more positive view of the role of county organizations, see Gibson 1991).

On the other hand, in recent years the national parties, particularly the Republican party, have become more active in local campaigns. Under the leadership of Bill Brock, who became Republican national chairman in 1977, and his successors, the Republicans have built a professional campaign organization at the national level. This organization concentrates on recruiting good candidates for office—at the congressional level and even at the level of state senator and state representative in some instances—training local candidates and their staffs in basic campaign techniques, and supplying certain technical support services, such as survey research, for their candidates. The Local Elections Division of the Republican National Committee has been active and effective for nearly twenty years. The Democrats, although way behind the Republicans in this regard, have emulated their opponents' techniques. Furthermore, both parties, again with the Republicans in the lead, are seeking means to persuade and mobilize voters, on a national or at least regional basis, to back party candidates (see Adamany 1984, 78–92; Bibby 1986; 1991; Herrnson 1988; Reichley 1985; Stewart 1991; and the discussion in chap. 3).

With all these caveats, what can be expected from party as a resource? First, in any geographic area some citizens will vote for a candidate because of party label. The number of diehard party loyalists varies from area to area, but candidates should know the history of party loyalty in a district. Similarly, some citizens use party label as a negative voting cue ("I could never vote for a Republican"). A candidate should know the history of antiparty voting as well (Sabato 1988, chap. 4).

Second, some jobs are better accomplished by party than by any other political organization. Some tasks benefit all candidates who are running under a party label. Thus candidates frequently call upon party organization to run voter registration drives, especially in areas or among groups that are likely to support candidates of that party. Party organizations can often be counted on to organize get-out-the-vote drives on election day, checking which of their regular supporters have voted and urging those who have not voted to do so. At the very least, the party can be counted on to monitor the polls on election day, to be certain that votes are not lost owing to error or fraud.

As the 1998 congressional election drew to a close, most observers felt that the outcome in many key districts would depend on voter turnout. Put in the most blunt terms, the question came down to whether more loyal Republicans would vote because they were disgusted with President Clinton and wanted to send a message or whether more loyal Democrats would turn out because they were repulsed with the partisan manner in which the Republican-controlled House of Representatives was conducting the inquiry into President Clinton's behavior. Many races were in doubt as election day approached. The final appeals were by party leaders to "rally the troops." In Wisconsin, Republican governor Tommy Thompson faced an easy reelection contest, but he knew that the race for U.S. Senate was one of the closest in the nation. He urged his copartisans to identify ten other Republicans and to "keep calling them until they get to the polls." For his part, Vice President Gore flew coast to coast, chanting his campaign mantra: "We've heard the word—it's November third! We've got a note—it's get out the vote!" (Connolly and Neal 1998, A1). Party leaders clearly understood that the most help they could give to embattled candidates was assurance that likely supporters turned out at the polls.

In New York State, site of an extremely close and bitter Senate race between incumbent Republican Alphonse D'Amato and his challenger (and eventual conqueror) Charles Schumer, both political parties had literally thousands of volunteers working on election-day efforts to get out the vote. According to Judith Hope, the state's Democratic party chair, "With the Senate race as tight as it is, both sides realize that the election will be decided by Election Day operations. . . . The question for each side is whether we can get our people inside the voting booths. We are putting everything we've got into that effort." For the Republicans, Nassau County chair Joseph Mondello, leader of one of the strongest political organizations in the country, was equally adamant. "They [Republican party volunteers] are going to get out across the length and breadth of this county and place these sample ballots in every home" (Hicks 1998).

In sum, party is a resource that candidates have to be aware of but must also beware of. One cannot expect too much from an organization that is probably not strong and may have interests that differ from those of a single candidate. But candidates must use each resource for all that it has to offer.

B. The Role of Organized Groups

Organized groups often work hard in a particular candidate's campaign. Group involvement in political campaigns was discussed in chapter 6. From a candidate's perspective, questions involving organized groups are like those that must be asked of political parties. Which groups can provide active support? How can they help reach out to supporters or potential supporters? How effective are they going to be at that task? How concerned are they going to be about supporting this candidate as opposed to other candidates?

Groups can be very effective surrogates for candidates. The techniques that groups use in the political arena have already been noted (chap. 6). All of the techniques that attempt to influence the voting behavior of group members are important for candidates because the group replaces the candidate as the prime contact to the voter. Groups attempt to assure that the supporter remains a supporter and actually votes and that the potential supporter comes over to the candidate's side.

However, group support does not come automatically to a candidate. Our hypothetical candidate must expend blocks of time to garner group support and more time to assure that group support stays firm and is mobilized in the most effective way. Furthermore, candidates must recognize that groups have multiple interests that extend beyond any one campaign, and that, by definition, these groups are engaged in activities other than politics. Thus group activity can help in a campaign, but it too is a limited resource.[5]

Even more to the point, candidates must recognize that the very same groups that are most likely to generate a good deal of support for a candidacy from their followers are the ones that also alienate other voters. A candidate who is not firmly committed to the views of a particularly controversial group might view that group's support as something of a mixed blessing. For many years Democratic candidates worried whether vocal support for very liberal groups hurt their chances; of course, repudiating that support would have a deleterious impact as well. In recent campaigns, the Republicans have asked the same questions about vocal advocacy by culturally and religiously conservative groups.

In a special election in California in March 1998, the Family Research Council, headed by the extremely conservative and extremely combative Gary Bauer, campaigned heavily for GOP candidate Tom Bordonaro. After he lost that election, a National Republican Congressional Committee poll showed a severe backlash against the campaigning and a perception that Bordonaro was an extremist as a result. Bordonaro is an extremely conservative candidate who shares the views of cultural conservatives like Bauer, but the focal support of those groups might well have hurt and not helped his chances for reelection (Edsall and Connolly 1998, 13).

Like political parties, special interest groups can be very effective at convincing their members to turn out to vote, when voting for a particular candidate is clearly perceived as in the members' interest.

C. Media Politics

The discussion to this point has purposefully avoided the major surrogate for personal contact by a candidate, media campaigning. A candidate who cannot reach the voters personally can surely reach them through the media. As the twentieth century draws to a close, media campaigning has become a way of life for all of us. Shouldn't that be obvious? Don't all successful candidates use television—and even radio—to reach voters?

Again, reality is not quite what it might appear. Certainly television and politics have blended in familiar ways in recent years. Using the media to carry political messages has become familiar to all viewers; a vast majority of Americans, moreover, receive most of their political information from television. But that does not end the discussion.

A number of different cases suggest themselves. First, look at a candidate for Congress from the Fourth Congressional District in Nassau County on Long Island in New York in 1998. Incumbent Democrat Carolyn McCarthy was defending her seat in a formerly Republican district against a strong challenge from Gregory Becker. A third-party candidate was also on the ballot.[6] The voters in the district were most concerned about the race for the U.S. Senate, in which Long Island native Senator Alphonse D'Amato was being challenged by Congressman Charles Schumer. The voters were also following Governor George Pataki's race for reelection and a most hotly contested statewide contest for attorney general. And, of course, there was the small matter of President Clinton, Monica Lewinsky, and potential impeachment hearings by the House Judiciary Committee. Most of the voters in the district watch New York television stations. Most listen to New York radio, and many read the New York newspapers, in addition to Long Island's *Newsday*. Many work in New York, as part of the district is a bedroom suburb of New York City. How could a Long Island candidate effectively attract attention in the New York City media market? Advertise effectively? Use the media as a surrogate for person-to-person campaigning or for the other techniques already discussed?

For a second scenario, imagine a candidate running for state senate from a district in Portland, Maine, in 1996. Of course, most voter attention is centered on the top of the ticket, with President Clinton seeking reelection. But Maine politics in 1996 also featured two hotly contested, very visible races. Portland native and former governor Joseph Brennan (D) was seeking a political comeback in the race for the U.S. Senate seat unexpectedly vacated by William Cohen; Brennan was challenged by Susan Collins (R), who along with Brennan had lost a 1994 bid for the governorship to independent candidate Angus King. Two lesser-known candidates were also on the Senate ballot. In the First Congressional District, which is centered in Portland, incumbent freshman James Longley Jr., who had won office in the Republican landslide of 1994, was targeted for defeat by the Democrats, whose well-funded candidate, Tom Allen, was a former mayor of Portland. Political activists had a lot on their minds before they began to focus on state senate races. The local media blankets the Portland state senatorial districts, but over ninety cents of every television advertising dollar for state senate candidates is wasted because messages are also beamed to voters who reside in other districts. The same is true of radio and newspaper advertising. What role, then, should the media play in this state senate campaign?

Contrast these two cases with a third scenario, a campaign for a U.S. Senate seat from Arkansas in 1998. The Senate race was the most visible contest on the Arkansas ballot in 1998, as Governor Mike Huckabee (R) faced only token opposition. Moreover, in a state with a population of over 2.25 million, with more than 1.2 million registered voters and with approximately 60 percent of the voters living in rural areas, it is impossible for a candidate to reach a significant proportion of the population personally. Little Rock is centrally located, and that city's media dominates the state. This situation is prime for a media campaign. It does not take a crystal ball to see that the two candidates, former Democratic congresswoman Blanche Lambert Lincoln, and Republican state senator Fay Boozman, would both use the media, particularly television, as a way to reach voters.

These three examples point to the first conclusion about the role of media in general, and television in particular, in modern campaigns. (See chap. 12 for a more complete discussion of the role of the media in modern campaigning.) Media advertising as a surrogate for personal contact is very important in today's campaigns. However, the electoral context determines the extent to which media campaigning can replace personal campaigning as a way to reach the voters.

An increasing amount of money has been spent on television advertising in recent campaigns for the U.S. Senate and House of Representatives. In 1998, more and more candidates went on television early, using the medium to define their image. For instance, Connecticut congresswoman Nancy Johnson (R), who had a tough race in 1996, started her ad campaign in the spring of 1998, hoping to create a positive image through early, unanswered advertising (Mitchell 1998, 1). The downside of this strategy is that much of the money spent in this way might be wasted because the voters are not yet paying attention.

Moreover, ample television money is not a resource that is equally available to all candidates. Candidates must determine how much of their financial resources should be spent on media advertising and how much is better spent in other ways. Some districts will be dominated by television campaigns. In other congressional districts television advertising is all but unknown. Although media campaigns are more common in statewide races, here too analysts have noted a great variety (Goldenberg and Traugott 1984).

The second conclusion about the role of media in modern campaigning relates specifically to districts in which media advertising plays a dominant role. Only certain kinds of messages can be transmitted through sixty-second or thirty-second commercials. These messages can convey impressions and images, but they cannot present and analyze issue positions very well. Nonetheless, such advertisements play a crucial, perhaps even critical, role in many campaigns. Candidates who are virtually unknown become familiar household friends through repeated appearances on television. In districts and states in which media advertising is an expected part of campaigning, citizens use television and radio presentations as a prime means of evaluating candidates.

In 1996 and in 1998, even more than in previous years, political parties and interest groups (through so-called issue advocacy advertisements [chap. 6]) used the media to convey pointed messages to the electorate. These supplemented the candidates' own media campaigns but were often intense enough to overwhelm the candidates' own efforts. In 1996 organized labor targeted a group of Republican congressmen who had first been elected running on the Contract with America in 1994. In the race in Maine's first district alluded to earlier, for example, Congressman Longley was portrayed as anti–social security and anti–middle class. The accuracy of these advertisements is debatable, but their impact is not. Despite responses by Republican-supporting interest groups, like the National Federation of Independent Businessmen, the labor ads were successful in creating negative images that the Republican freshmen had to overcome. Maine analysts attribute Tom Allen's victory over Longley to the effectiveness of the independent attacks on his image. Across the nation, in districts in which Republican freshmen lost and in those in which they narrowly won, similar scenarios were repeated.

In the closing days of the 1998 midterm election, the Republican party launched a $10-million advertising blitz in selected congressional districts (many of which were in states holding U.S. Senate elections as well). This last-minute advertising campaign targeted President Clinton and asked whether he should be rewarded with more Democrats in Congress. The effort was to link the tarnished image of an embattled president to congressional candidates in his party. The effort apparently failed, as the Democrats won close races in many of the areas in which the advertisements were aired. But again, there is no question that the campaign met its goal—keeping the president's problems in the forefront of voters' minds as they went to the polls for congressional elections. Their failure lay in interpreting how the voters would respond to this stimulus.

The charge is often made that the media consultant, the political equivalent of a Madison Avenue adman, makes or breaks a candidate. The implications of this charge for the role of campaigning in the political process are obvious and serious (cf. McGinniss 1969). Candidates must consider whether media advertising is appropriate for their particular campaign and must determine whether an impersonal message, often quick and slick, is the vehicle they want to use for presenting themselves to those whose support they seek.

D. The Candidate's Organization

Parties, groups, and media are frequently used as surrogates for personal campaigning in races for higher office. The fourth surrogate, the most common one, is the candidate's personal organization. When commentators speak of candidate organizations, they mean a number of different things. For the purposes of this discussion, they are volunteers who go out and campaign on behalf of a candidate. They function as the candidate's eyes, ears, and mouth. The candidate cannot personally contact every voter, but it is possible for others campaigning on the candidate's behalf to do so.

This type of campaigning is done in a number of different ways. Where possible, campaigners go door-to-door, talking to individual voters and seeking their support for a particular candidate. If an organization is sophisticated enough, these volunteers then compile lists of the voters they have visited, commenting on the likelihood that those voters will support the candidate. On election day the likely supporters are called again and urged to go to the polls. The voters who are likely to vote for another candidate are left alone. One congressional candidate claims to have contacted 31,000 households in this way during the fifteen weeks before the 1998 election (Moberg 1998), but analysis and follow-up of this sort require a sophisticated organization with a large number of trained volunteers.

Other campaigns use volunteers in less complex ways. Some campaigns merely "drop" literature at every door, letting the brochures speak for themselves. Still other campaigns use volunteers, usually young volunteers, to distribute leaflets at shopping centers, malls, ball games, or other locations where large numbers of potential voters are to be found. Many areas have their own typical modes of reaching voters—"human billboards" along congested commuter routes, door holders at subway stations, refreshment providers at factory gates, and so on.

Still other campaigns employ telephone banks, phoning perspective voters with messages about the candidate. Telephone campaigns vary tremendously in sophistication, depending on how well trained the callers are and how organized the entire operation is. At one extreme these campaigns can be as effective as door-to-door campaigning, especially for rural districts; at the other extreme they resemble the scattershot technique of shopping-mall leafleting.

One of the keys to establishing a volunteer organization is to have workers who will campaign for just one candidate. In some ways this service is inefficient. If a volunteer is to go door-to-door, why not carry propaganda for a group of candidates? Many volunteers will do this. The marginal difference in effort extended is minimal. However, from a candidate's perspective, the difference is important.

If a worker carries material or campaigns for more than one candidate, the potential effect of the volunteer contact on the voter is certainly diminished, and it might even be negated. What if the voter has not heard about one candidate but has a negative view of the other candidate, and, using only that opinion, discounts both candidates? The call has been dysfunctional. What if the voter has a negative view of politicians in general but might be persuaded because someone cares enough to go door-to-door on behalf of one very special politician in whom that volunteer truly believes? A New Hampshire candidate for state representative reported that one voter told her on election day 1998 that the only reason he bothered to vote at all was because of a call he received on the Sunday night before the election. He voted for one candidate on the whole ballot, the candidate from whose organization he received that call (Crosby 1998). Again, a positive response would be lost by combining campaign efforts.

Although scenarios can be imagined in which combined efforts would help a candidate, if they had their choice, most candidates would want volunteers to work for them and them alone, a far cry from the days when political parties did this kind of campaigning on behalf of an entire ticket.[7] Strong individual candidates who are supported by large numbers of dedicated volunteers eschew combined campaign efforts; weaker candidates with fewer supporters are the most eager to have a "team" approach to campaigning.

In the 1988 presidential election, a new twist emerged. Presidential campaigns are publicly financed, that is, the money to run these campaigns comes from a federal fund, and no more money can be spent if the federal grant is accepted (see chaps. 10–11). However, presidential campaigns also have the greatest ability to raise money. They developed the networks to do so during the primary, and the election stakes are highest for them. Campaign finance laws permit money to be raised at the national level and then spent locally, if it is spent in a coordinated manner on all the party's campaigns. Thus the Dukakis and Bush campaigns raised money during the general election phase of the 1988 presidential campaign and organized field campaigns for the entire ticket, as this was the only legal way in which they could raise and spend money on behalf of their candidates. The result was an interesting reversion to the days of party-centered field campaigns. (See Corrado 1992.) In the 1992 and 1996 presidential campaigns, this technique was repeated with greater sums of money, more of which was spent for coordinated advertising campaigns, but the coordinated field campaigns with staff from national party headquarters remained an important feature (see chap. 11).

The ability of candidates to form their own volunteer organization is another factor that varies with what other races are being held at the same time. However, once a winning candidate has a personal organization in place, maintaining it over a period of years is not difficult. Some supporters drop out; new supporters are recruited for each new campaign. But a core of candidate-inspired activists remains as a powerful resource (Fenno 1978).

E. The Structure of a Modern Campaign

Volunteer organizations such as the one just described have been an important part of American politics for some time, at least since the spread of direct primaries. In recent years, however, as campaigns have become more expensive and more complex, candidate organizations have taken on a different meaning.

Figure 8.1 depicts a possible organizational chart for a modern general election campaign. The coordination of various means of contacting voters, using traditional and modern techniques, defines the extent to which the new politics has come to dominate campaigns for many offices.

The candidate sits atop the organization. Or at least one hopes the candidate does. Too often campaigns run so efficiently that the candidates seem to be all but unimportant, merely the product to be packaged. However, in this case, let us assume that the candidate is in charge, selecting the campaign manager and coordinating strategy and tactics. (See Agranoff 1972; 1976; Hershey 1984; Johnson-Cartee and Copeland 1997; Kayden 1978; Luntz 1988; Maisel 1986; Rothenberg 1983; Salmore and Salmore 1985; and Shea 1996.)

The campaign manager runs the day-to-day campaign. Campaigns for statewide office routinely require budgets in the millions of dollars. This is a major enterprise that requires professional management. In the last two decades a corps of "professional" campaign managers has emerged.

Some work as individual entrepreneurs, working one campaign at a time and then waiting for the next biennium to begin again. More and more, however, the pattern is for political managers to form companies that take over the management of a number of campaigns at the same time, handling many of the tasks from a central headquarters. Political campaign management is indeed a growth industry these days.[8]

Firms tend to specialize in either Republican or Democratic

Figure 8.1 Structure of a Modern Campaign.

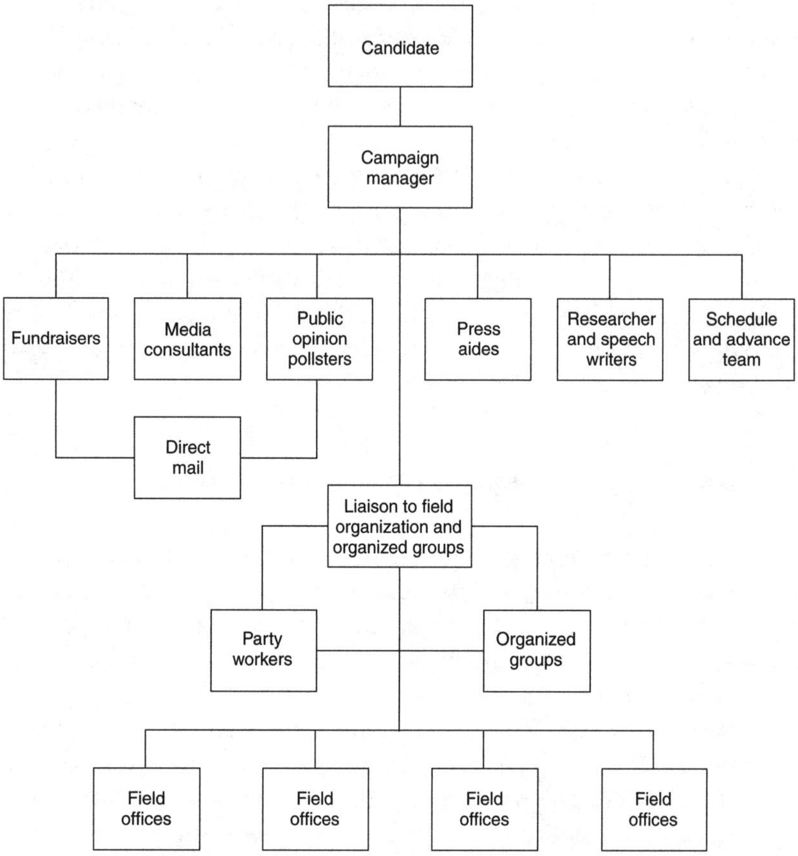

campaigns. Ralph Reed, former head of the Christian Coalition, has opened his own consulting firm catering to Republican candidates who carry a message of social conservatism to the electorate. In 1998 he worked for candidates for governor in Alabama, lieutenant governor in Georgia, and Congress in Kentucky, among others. Clients of the Democratic firm of Shrum, Devine included Senate candidates from four states—Connecticut, Maryland, North Carolina, and Georgia—and congressional candidates from four others. Different firms have different expertise and/or are willing to handle different aspects of a campaign. But they all combine some of the functions I will now describe, with advice on how the campaign should proceed. (See Luntz 1988; Sabato 1981.)

1. Public Opinion Polling

Most modern campaigns do not rely on hunches to determine what the public is thinking or to evaluate how different approaches to campaigning are working. Public opinion polling has acquired a prominent role in modern campaigns. In some cases the campaign management firm handles the public opinion polling; in other cases a polling firm plays a major role in campaign management; in still other cases two firms work together. Prominent pollsters like Garin-Hart-Yang Strategic Research Group; the Tarrance Group; Penn, Schoen, & Berland; Fairbank, Maslin, Maullin, & Associates are sought after as key figures in major campaigns. In any event, pollsters play major roles in ascertaining what issues concern the public, how the candidate is perceived, how the opponent in perceived, and what approaches will and will not work.

More elaborate campaigns do continuous polling during the campaign period. In other campaigns, a pollster takes a first poll, called a benchmark poll, to determine a candidate's position and the views of the public at the beginning of the campaign and then polls occasionally throughout the campaign, to measure attitudes and changes in opinions in response to specific events or to determine the impact of specific strategies. Pollsters for state and local campaigns have all of the tools at their disposal that are used in presidential campaigns (see chap. 10); but the variable is the amount of money a campaign can spend on data-gathering of this type. Professional pollsters working on major campaigns play a critical and central role in determining strategy to be followed. They provide and analyze the data. Frequently they interpret what those facts mean in light of other campaigns in which they have participated (or are currently participating); they draw on their knowledge accumulated from a series of campaigns to devise new approaches based on their interpretations. (See Crespi 1988; 1989.)

2. *Media Consultants*

The campaign manager and the pollster also work closely with the media expert on a campaign. Again, various patterns are possible. Some large management firms take care of designing media strategies, making commercials, and buying time for campaigns. Some firms, primarily advertising agencies, specialize in political advertising and take care of other aspects of campaign management as well. Various patterns of interaction with pollsters are possible. Because media expenditures constitute such a high percentage of total campaign expenditures, the role of the media consultant is also central to most campaigns (Goldenberg and Traugott 1984, chap. 6; Pfau and Kenski 1990).

If the message of the campaign is to be carried by paid media, then the media consultant has to be involved not only in producing advertisements and commercials and buying time and space but also in setting strategies, in responding to different campaign situations, and in evaluating how the campaign strategies are or are not working. Goldenberg and Traugott (1984, 86) found that congressional candidates in 1978 spent nearly 60 percent of their total campaign budgets on media expenditures and advertising; these expenses included consultant fees and production as well as sheer advertisement purchases. Undoubtedly, similar patterns would be found for campaigns for statewide office. The percentage of total budgets spent on this category probably increases with the total budget of the campaign and has undoubtedly continued to increase since the 1978 study was completed (see also Diamond and Bates 1984; Pfau and Kenski 1990).

3. Fund-Raisers

Polling and media advertising are expensive. Million-dollar campaigns were cause for concern in the late 1960s; multimillion-dollar campaigns are commonplace today. In order to run campaigns of this magnitude, candidates must spend a good deal of time and effort on fund-raising. (The complex topic of campaign financing will be discussed in detail in chap. 11.) At this point it is sufficient to state that one important part of any campaign organization involves raising the money necessary to conduct the campaign and monitoring how that money is spent. This latter task necessitates complying with increasingly complex federal and state laws regulating the collection, disbursement, and reporting of all campaign finances.

Many campaigns now hire professionals to handle these tasks. Professional fund-raisers set a strategy for raising money and follow through on that strategy (Herrnson 1991). They must begin well in advance of the start of actual campaigning for two reasons. First, fund-raising requires a good deal of candidate time. It is difficult to convince a donor to make a major contribution if that donor cannot sit down and actually talk with the candidate. Second, most campaign expenditures require payment in advance. Few of those enterprises used to dealing with campaigns will do so on a credit basis; all too often campaigns end up with unpaid bills.

Therefore, candidates have to raise money in advance in order to start effective campaigning. A number of observers have commented that raising money early can have important strategic consequences for dissuading effective opposition (Goldenberg and Traugott 1984; Green and Krasno 1988; Jacobson 1990b; Jacobson and Kernell 1983; Sorauf 1984). This lesson is not lost on politicians. One group interested in assisting more women who are running for office has based its entire strategy of this premise. Many think that EMILY's List is named for its founder, but in fact it is an acronym for Early Money Is Like Yeast. The group supports female candidates early in the process so that those candidates will be able to demonstrate viability to others who might give them money later on.

DIRECT MAIL

A campaign technique through which voters are contacted by mail because of a campaign's prior knowledge concerning those voters' views.

One important technique for raising money—as well as for communicating campaign messages—is **direct mail**. This is a relatively new technique, first employed on a national level by the Republican party under Chairman Ray Bliss and perfected by Richard Viguerie, a kind of direct-mail guru who developed lists and raised money for a series of conservative candidates. Viguerie's success spurred others to copy his techniques, though none quite duplicated his early success in raising large sums of money. Today liberal and conservative candidates, as well as interest groups, use computer-generated lists of potential donors and/or potential voters. They appeal to these voters based on certain known characteristics or preferences. Although Viguerie's inflammatory techniques have not always been successful (in fact, declining response rates led him to cut back his efforts [Edsall 1986]), these techniques continue to reach many voters in each election cycle.

As a fund-raising tool, direct mail knows no political boundaries. Mailing firms appeal to potential donors throughout the country as they attempt to convince those who have donated to campaigns in the past that they should do so to similar campaigns now.

As a campaigning tool, direct mail is equally effective. Once lists have been developed, campaigns can direct "personalized" appeals to groups of voters who share certain characteristics. All environmentalists in a state might receive a mailing that stresses the candidate's record on environmental matters, and all members of the National Rifle Association might receive a mailing that describes the candidate's opposition to gun-control legislation. The environmentalist mailing will not mention the candidate's position on gun control, and the NRA letter will not mention environmental issues, lest anyone be offended. However, voters who are on both lists will receive both mailings and will have two reasons to support the candidate.

If a sufficient number of lists can be developed and effective appeals drafted, direct mail can be a most effective way to reach voters with a particular campaign appeal. Because the letters can be personalized by computer, direct mail can be a perfect surrogate for direct candidate contact. Direct-mail approaches are so prevalent today that few voters actually believe that the candidate has written directly to them. Despite this cynicism, however, voters respond positively to letters from candidates who share their political views.

4. Scheduling and Advance Work

Other parts of the campaign operation work to coordinate the use of candidate time. For instance, candidates for statewide offices, even in smaller states, frequently have more calls for personal time than they have time available. How to use the limited time of the candidate is not a trivial question. Every major campaign has one person—or even a staff of people—whose job it is to see that the candidate's time is used most effectively. Decisions on the use of candidate time are strategic decisions, not clerical decisions.

The scheduler must determine how much of a candidate's time is spent with what groups, how much in what areas of the district, how much with what kinds of activities. The scheduler must respond to the needs of all the others involved in the campaign, conserving that very scarce resource, the time of the candidate. And this task must be done in a way that ruffles as few feathers as possible and accounts for the idiosyncrasies of the individual candidate.

Once the scheduler has determined where a candidate will be on a certain day, others in the campaign make sure that the campaign day runs smoothly. In larger campaigns this often involves "advancing" a trip, that is, carefully running through an entire day's schedule, before the candidate makes a trip, to guard against slipups (Bruno and Greenfield 1971).

Candidates like to know who will greet them, what they should avoid discussing, how much time they are expected to spend at each event. Campaign managers want to be certain that the candidate gets as much political mileage out of each campaign stop as possible; the advance team must be concerned with details such as room size, crowd composition, and press accommodations.

Candidates want to be comfortable; they like to know where the microphone will be situated in a room and similar details. Some candidates are very particular about the details of overnight accommodations, travel arrangements, and arrangements for members of their family. One candidate for the U.S. Senate in the early 1980s insisted on calling his mother after every plane ride because she feared for his safety. The advance staff built the calls into his schedule, though today a cell phone would have eased their task. It is the responsibility of the advance team to see to it that all of a campaign day's details are arranged properly, no matter how trivial.

Frequently those who "advance" a trip are with the candidate when the trip takes place. If this is the case, they must have keen political judgment. The advance team is expected to know which people the candidate must be introduced to, record names of important people whom the candidate meets, and massage the political ego of the people with whom the candidate talks. Those on campaign advance teams often spend as much time with the candidate as anyone in a campaign. They have the responsibility of seeing to it that the candidate benefits as much from a campaign day as possible.

5. Press Relations

Another important campaign function involves establishing ongoing relations with the working press. The extent of press coverage varies significantly from campaign to campaign. The key variable in this instance is how important the individual campaign is for the geographic area covered by the various media. Thus a congressional race in Nevada is important for the print and electronic media in Las Vegas and Reno, since Nevada has only two representatives in Congress. On the other hand, the New York Times does not pay much attention to congressional races because more than two dozen members of Congress represent the metropolitan area served by the Times. The same is true for the electronic media in the New York area.

From a different perspective, press aides for Senate or gubernatorial candidates in smaller states have only a small number of media markets to worry about, and a relatively small number of political reporters. In California, Florida, Texas, or other large states, press aides must keep track of literally dozens of radio and television stations, daily newspapers, and weeklies. Candidates in larger states often attract national as well as local media. Handling the press is an important function, and a complex one as well.

Press aides to candidates in major campaigns do not function alone. Their job is to deal with the press, but they do not do so in a vacuum. Their relationships with the press go a long way toward structuring how the candidate is perceived, indeed in some cases if the candidate is perceived at all. Thus press relations are part of an overall strategy. Press aides work with the scheduler to increase the likelihood that the candidate's campaign day is covered by the media. The press staff works with the advance team to see to it that reporters have ready access to the candidate—or that they do not if that is what is called for. They work with the speechwriters to be certain that advance releases of the candidate's comments are ready for the press to review. The press aides work with the media consultant and the campaign manager to coordinate the press strategy with the overall strategy of the campaign.

6. Liaison to Party Organization and Organized Groups

Our understanding of how press aides function demonstrates the need for coordination among those working on a campaign. The same is true of the more traditional parts of the campaign discussed earlier, the work of the political party, the coordination of organized group activity, and the work of the field organization.

In any campaign, the campaign manager and the candidate must determine what effective role political party organization will play. However, even in those areas in which political party organization is not strong, someone in a campaign must have the responsibility of coordinating campaign efforts with those of the party leadership. Whatever party officials can do for a campaign to garner the support of their loyal followers is a plus. Whatever extra activities the party can undertake is a plus.

Whatever can be done to avoid alienating party regulars must be done. In some cases these are all important aspects of a campaign organization. Certainly this is the case in Illinois for statewide campaigns for the Democrats; the Cook County organization cannot be ignored, even by those who are not part of the organization. On the other hand,

Republicans in Maine do not receive much support from the formal party machinery, but each statewide and congressional campaign keeps in touch with party regulars to benefit from any supportive effort that might be forthcoming.

Another aspect of a large campaign organization coordinates the work of the organized groups that are supporting the candidate. This work involves a number of different problems. In some cases there must be coordination with the fund-raisers; in others, with direct mail; in others, with scheduling. At times it is appropriate to set up separate committees to demonstrate group support—Lawyers for Jones or Teachers for Miller; these efforts might require coordination with the press aide or with the media consultant. If organized groups aid a campaign by providing volunteers, their work should be coordinated with the field organization or with political party machinery. How each resource is used varies from situation to situation according to a number of intangibles, not the least of which is the strength of the candidate and the strategy and tactics that are to be employed.

7. Field Organizations

Finally, the field organization plays an essential role in almost any campaign organization. The campaign needs some way to reach out into the geographic area covered by the districts. Campaign managers talk about the need for a physical presence; voters need to know that there are real people behind a campaign. This physical presence takes the form of district offices, of volunteers on the street, of leaflet drops and brochures, of bumper stickers, buttons, and lawn signs.

Voters want to know that others support a candidate before they are willing do so as well. The field organization gives supporters the feeling of joining an ongoing organization. This is particularly important in statewide campaigns or in campaigns for Congress in geographically large districts. Much of this work is done by volunteers, the type of task that can be completed by those who want to demonstrate support for a candidate, to show the flag.

Some specific campaign tasks are also performed by this organization. Campaign managers like to be able to go door-to-door, to conduct the person-to-person campaign on a large scale that all of them feel is successful on a small scale. This kind of effort must be decentralized. It requires a large number of volunteers, each willing to give a significant amount of time.

Volunteer telephoning often is used as a substitute for door-to-door campaigning in sparsely populated areas, or even in more densely populated areas in which a sufficiently large door-to-door volunteer force cannot be recruited and trained. However, even if a set speech is written for the callers, it is difficult to monitor how many calls are made and what is said by various volunteers, especially since many volunteers prefer phoning from their homes to phoning from a central location. Thus volunteer telephoning tends to be somewhat unreliable.

As a consequence, many campaigns establish phone banks staffed by trained, paid workers and monitored by a professional staff person. These phone banks are much easier to control than volunteer efforts. Campaign managers can know how many calls are made in an evening, when a certain section of the district or state will be covered, what the response has been to particular appeals. The monitoring staff person can listen in on calls to gauge the effectiveness of the message that is to be delivered or the appeal of a particular telephone volunteer. Computerized systems are now in use to make these voter calls even more efficient. They represent the ultimate in depersonalized "personal" contact.[9]

III. OLD-STYLE POLITICS: A MORE PROMINENT ROLE FOR PARTIES

Look back at figure 8.1. The entire organization is directed toward getting in touch with as many voters as possible in as many effective and efficient ways as possible. Voters are informed about the candidate through the news media, through paid media, through sessions with the candidate, through mail, or through the campaign efforts of others. An efficient campaign organization will reach each prospective voter a number of times in a number of different ways; most of these appeals will be directed specifically at individual voters. Once voters have been informed about a candidate, they will be asked to support that candidate with their help, their money, and their votes. They will be asked, again and again, to help in whatever ways are possible. All the efforts of the campaign staff and organization, the professionals, the consultants, and the volunteers are aimed at this goal.

This campaign chart represents "new politics" because of the techniques used. Modern technology has, in fact, replaced older techniques that relied upon person-to-person contact and party allegiance. Now computers, not precinct committeemen, are used to identify and categorize voters, to analyze polling data, to monitor the progress toward reaching certain campaign goals.

Television and radio are used to reach large numbers of voters with messages that were carried by volunteers on foot in an earlier time. Direct mail allows for "personal" contact with significant numbers of voters. Campaign budgets have multiplied to amounts beyond belief even twenty years ago. Professionals are called in to monitor these huge organizations. No candidate can personally manage a major campaign; the two functions (candidacy and management) are separate, and each needs full-time function fillers for a big campaign. However, it is important to keep in mind that the job of the campaign in the modern era is not fundamentally different from what it was in the days before modern techniques changed politics.

Politics has changed at all levels. Remember the candidate for county supervisor described at the beginning of this chapter? He staffed the voter registration booth; he put up posters; he scheduled his own time. He was the one shaking the hands of voters at the fair, creating the media event by introducing the Senate candidate, probably with remarks that he himself had labored over. Why was *he* doing all these things himself? Where was *his* organization?

The answer probably is that he doesn't really have one. How many people can he expect to get excited about working for a candidate for county supervisor? How many people are likely to contribute large sums of money to candidates for county supervisor, clerk of courts, water district commissioner, even city council, school board, state representative, or state senate?

Think about the people who hold these offices in any community. Who are they? What do they do? For such low-visibility offices, do most people really care enough to become involved with active campaigning?

The answer for most of us for most of these offices is a resounding, "Who cares?" When we do care, the reasons are quite obvious. Most often the "organization" of candidates for local offices is made up of friends and neighbors, who are friends and neighbors first and become involved in politics secondarily.

A personal connection is enough to get someone involved in a campaign. If a neighbor asks for help, a conscientious citizen will probably help in that campaign. She probably won't become totally engrossed in a campaign and she is unlikely to make a large financial contribution. But she, like many people, will help.

Similarly, these campaigns often involve local issues. A parent who is concerned about a particular item on the school board's upcoming agenda, for instance, whether the junior high school should spend more money for football or start a girls' soccer program, might become involved in a campaign. Often local campaigns are the most intense because the issues strike closest to home. Issues and personalities are familiar. Neighbors work with and against neighbors.

But even when one is involved in these campaigns, the campaign is not of the same scale as a congressional or statewide campaign. With the exception of some of the very largest cities, candidates for city council or school board represent an approachable number of people. The candidate can personally touch those people. Large budgets are not necessary; surrogates are not necessary; complex organizations are not necessary. Furthermore, many of the important campaign functions that help one candidate help all candidates of the same party. Political parties play important roles.

A. Reexamination of the Role of Political Parties

This is not to say that local politics, campaigns for "less major" offices (*all* offices are major to the people seeking them), is a throwback to a time when political parties dominated our political scene. However, party plays a much more prominent role and the style of campaigning is much more susceptible to party organizational efforts than is the case in larger campaigns.

Candidates for state and local offices face the same strategic questions that other candidates face. Who are one's likely supporters? Who are those who might be convinced to become supporters? How can these people be convinced? What will draw supporters to the polls? However, these candidates face these questions in an environment, in most cases, in which the public has little awareness or concern about either the candidates or the offices they seek.

Most campaigns for state and local office involve candidates seeking to represent districts that fall within one county, the most common party organizational unit (Eldersveld 1982). County party activists are familiar with the offices and the candidates; and candidates need only deal with one party committee. Consequently, political party organizations work best in campaigns in districts for which the boundaries coincide with existing party structures.

Furthermore, party organizations work best at stimulating activity by those who are affiliated with the party. When candidates are looking for likely supporters, all other things being equal, voters who share party affiliation with them stand out as an obvious target. Think about your own decisions on voting. You are probably saying, "I don't vote for the party! I vote for the best candidate." Okay, now that you feel good about that, consider specific examples. You vote for the presidential candidate you think is best, for the candidate for governor, for U.S. senator, maybe even for representative in the House. After all, you are a political science student; you care about these things. But what about the candidate for registrar of deeds, for probate judge, for clerk of courts? Do you honestly know whom they are? Do you honestly know whom you think is the "best" candidate? How do you judge that? In a practical way, you need some other means to make a judgment. Party is often that voting cue. You might not be a "member" of one party or the other, but you probably have different feelings about the two major parties. And those feelings often determine votes for local office. Thus candidates are interested in party efforts to register copartisans and to get them out to vote on election day. Those are precisely the kinds of tasks that party organizations still perform quite well.

General election candidates for state and local office rarely have the funds to develop elaborate campaign literature or to purchase expensive media advertising. Party committees often distribute brochures listing all the candidates running under the party label; they are able to organize volunteers who distribute material for a variety of candidates; they will advertise (in a limited way) for all the candidates on the ticket. Again, individual candidates benefit from these activities. If a candidate could do all these things as an individual, that would be preferable. However, joint efforts by the party faithful are better than no efforts at all.

B. Local Campaigns in the Absence of Party

Campaigns using the party organization work well, if there is a party organization. How does a candidate run when the party organization is nonexistent or inactive, as is the case in many counties throughout the country? Or how does a candidate run if the opposition party is stronger in his or her district, making it necessary to appeal to those in the other party? In these cases it is necessary to return to the original form of "old politics," not party politics but person-to-person campaigning.

For some candidates, this is what politics is all about, getting to know those who live nearby. In city after city and town after town, evenings and weekends in the autumn see scores of candidates knocking on neighbors' doors. No kind of campaigning is more time-consuming, but none bears greater fruit.

If candidates are willing to devote the time, frequently they can cover an entire district. An early morning breakfast in a country store is more important for a candidate for sheriff than any advertisement the party will take out. Five minutes over coffee in an elderly man's apartment pays more dividends than literature distributed in a shopping center. Politics at these levels is intensely personal, and not very substantive. These kinds of politics also raise all sorts of questions about the functioning of our democracy. Why do we have such long ballots? Why are these kinds of positions filled by elections and not appointments? What does the electoral process mean in these cases?

IV. Do Campaigns Determine Who Wins Elections?

Earlier in this chapter conflicting theories about what determines the results of elections were discussed. One theory accounted for election results on the basis of aggregate economic conditions in the country. The second theory related electoral results to individual citizens' opinions about conditions in the country. Although these theories were developed to explain the results of congressional elections, they should cause anyone reading a chapter on general election campaigns to pause for a moment. Do campaigns—at whatever level—matter?

A. Lack of Competition in American Elections

The answer, simply put, is that they do. Jacobson and Kernell (1983) take some pains to demonstrate that the quality of a candidate is an important factor in determining the results of an election. The better candidates, identified as those who have previously achieved electoral success, are more likely to run credible campaigns and, therefore, are more likely to win. (For additional discussions of the importance of candidate quality, see Fowler and McClure 1989; Jacobson 1987a; 1987b; Maisel 1989; 1990a; for a different perspective on candidate quality, see Maisel, Stone, and Maestas 1999.) The problem analysts face is that there are not many of these better candidates running for office.

In the previous sections I described how campaign organizations are structured, how campaigns are run, what tasks are performed by whom in a campaign, what strategies and tactics are devised and how they are implemented. Actually, I have been describing how these things are done in well-run campaigns. For most campaigns, reality does not approximate this ideal. In district after district, in campaign after campaign, in year after year, candidates' names appear on ballots and then they are never heard from again. They lose. And they do not provide significant competition for the winner.

Most frequently they lose to incumbents. If no incumbent is running, they lose to the candidate of the dominant party in a particular locale. That they lose is less important than the fact that they never really run a campaign, that the voters are never really given a choice.

Simply put, without competitive campaigning by more than one candidate, the citizens of a district are denied the opportunity to choose. Even if two or more names appear on the ballot, electoral choice is effective only when the citizens are presented with candidates who appear serious to them. If this is not the case, the election goes by default.

B. Incumbent Advantage in U.S. House and State Legislative Races

For years political scientists have noted that incumbents running for reelection to the Congress have won in large numbers. Many explanations have been offered for the observed phenomenon of **incumbent advantage** (Cover 1977; Ferejohn 1977; Fiorina 1977a; 1978; Maybew 1974b). In 1978 it was possible, for the first time, to study this phenomenon in some depth, owing to the data provided by the National Election Study of that election. The analyses of that election were among the first to demonstrate what Jacobson (1981) has aptly called "the vanishing challengers" (see also Abramowitz 1981; Hinckley 1981; Maisel and

INCUMBENT ADVANTAGE

Advantages that current officeholders have in seeking reelection by virtue of the fact that they hold the office.

Cooper 1981; Mann and Wolfinger 1980). Whether measured in terms of dollars spent, voter perception, even voter recognition, challengers were basically invisible; incumbents won because no one knew who was running against them.

The extent to which incumbents hold an advantage in races for the House of Representatives surprises many casual observers. The data is presented in figure 5.3. In only six elections since World War II have fewer than 90 percent of those seeking reelection been reelected. In five of the last ten congressional elections more than 95 percent of the incumbents seeking to return to the House did so.

Scholars who have studied this phenomenon have identified many causes that clearly contribute to the advantage, but no single cause—or even most prominent cause—has emerged. A current examination looks at the supply side of incumbent advantage, seeking to identify why stronger challengers do not run for office (Jewell 1998; Moncrief, Squire, and Kurtz 1998; Stone et al. 1998; Stone, Maisel, and Maestas 1998; Williamson 1999). Although this research enterprise has not yet reached conclusion, preliminary results are encouraging.

State legislators seeking reelection also win virtually all of the time. Again, they do not seem to attract quality challengers (Jewell and Breaux 1988; see Calvert 1979, for an earlier but similar analysis of a group of twenty-nine states). Recent analysis by Ronald Weber, Harvey Tucker, and Paul Brace (1991) demonstrates that the number of **marginal seats** (i.e., seats in which contests are so close that either party has a legitimate chance of victory) and the number of contested seats in a group of twenty state lower houses declined between 1950 and 1986, though James Garand (1991) warns that a decline in marginality might not necessarily signal a decline in the likelihood of incumbent defeat (see also Jacobson 1987a).

MARGINAL SEATS

Seats in which either major party has a legitimate chance of winning.

One further piece of data concerning House elections and elections to state legislatures merits our concern. Lack of quality challengers to incumbents is cause for worry, considering the importance of competition in elections. But lack of any challengers at all is more troublesome. In many states large numbers of legislative seats go uncontested in every election. In eighty-six races in the 1998 congressional elections, one or the other of the two major parties did not field a candidate. As third-party candidates are almost never serious contenders in these races, that lack of opposition meant that nearly one-fifth of the Congress knew that they would return for the 106th Congress while the 105th was still in session and dealing with important issues. On those issues, the members without any opposition were totally free to ignore their constituents' views. One should not jump to the conclusion that those members did ignore constituent opinion, but it is undeniable that they were free to do so without any fear of electoral retribution.

C. Competition in U.S. Senate and Gubernatorial Races

Researchers who hypothesize that incumbent advantage is due to lack of quality challengers point out that incumbent U.S. senators, although frequently reelected, are not sent back to the Senate in anywhere near the same proportion as are House members. Incumbent senators are often challenged by well-known politicians who run impressive campaigns. The challengers spend significant amounts of money, are visible throughout the state, are recognized by large percentages of the voters, and are perceived in ways that demonstrated that their campaigns were effective. These are not new phenomena but were recognized at the same time that the advantages of House members were under exploration (Abramowitz 1981; Hinckley 1981). Figure 8.2 shows that there has been tremendous variation in the percentage of incumbent senators winning reelection.[10] In the 1998 midterm elections, for instance, only six of 401 incumbent representatives lost their reelection bids on November 3; but three of 32 senators seeking new six-year terms were denied return to the Senate.

Data on gubernatorial elections are less easily obtained than those on House and Senate elections (but see Jewell 1984). Figure 8.3 shows the success rates for gubernatorial challengers in recent elections. Not all incumbent governors are eligible for reelection because of state laws restricting the number of consecutive terms some governors may serve, and so the percentage of incumbents seeking reelection is not as large as it is for senators.[11] Nonetheless, the data still shows that governors seeking reelection lose more frequently than do members of Congress, seemingly in numbers more comparable to those for unsuccessful incumbent senators. In fact, the parallel to senators is quite close. Because of the prominence of the office in most states, many incumbent gover-

Figure 8.2 Incumbents Defeated in Senate Elections, 1946–1998.

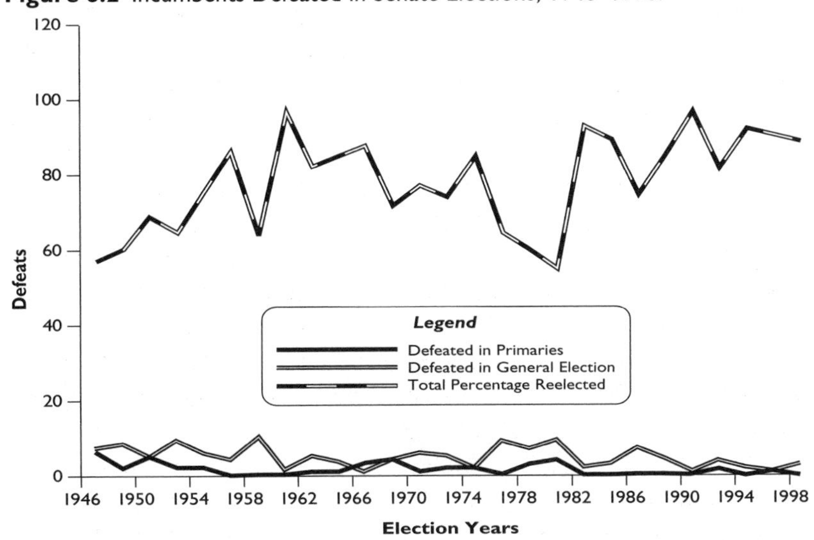

Source: Data from various Congressional Quarterly Service sources.

nors seeking reelection have attracted credible challengers. At times, elections are quite competitive and many incumbents lose; at other times, this seems less so. The variables at play seem to be peculiar to one election year and often to one election. Analysts were hard put to explain, for instance, why an anti-incumbent mood in the electorate in 1990 led to the defeat of more incumbent governors than in any other election in two decades, while only one incumbent U.S. senator was defeated and more than 96 percent of the House members seeking reelection were victorious (Addison 1990, 3838–3842).

D. Credible Competition in American Elections

What can be concluded from these facts? One obvious interpretation is that what has been happening at the congressional level has been happening at other levels as well. Incumbents are winning because challengers are poor campaigners (Jewell and Breaux 1988; Holbrook and Tidmarch 1991; Weber et al. 1991). When challengers run good campaigns, demonstrated in exceptional case after exceptional case, in state after state, incumbents can lose (Garand 1991). But good challengers appear too infrequently for too many important offices.

The lack of good challengers and good campaigns insulate incumbents in congressional races; in all probability, the same factors insulate those incumbents seeking reelection to other less visible and less attractive offices as well.

Campaigns do matter. The low number of credible campaigns for many offices, and the invulnerability of many incumbents because of the scarcity of these credible campaigns, points to a major flaw in the way in which our electoral system operates.

Figure 8.3 Electoral Successes of Incumbent Governors, 1980–1998.

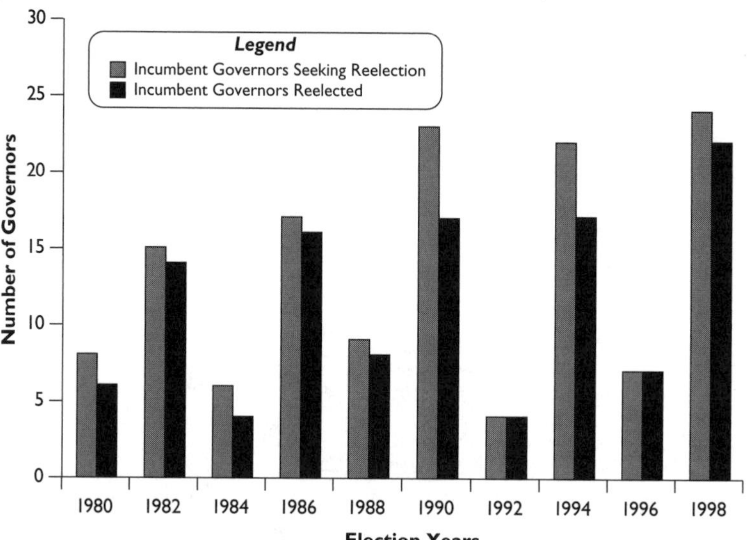

Source: Data from various Congressional Quarterly Service sources.

TERM LIMITS

Statutory limits on the number of successive terms an elected officeholder may serve.

Is this flaw correctable? Some feel the system has failed and that the only way to remedy the flaw is to change the system in a fundamental way. The means most often suggested is **term limits**. Those who advocate term limits argue that because incumbents cannot be beaten it is necessary to remove them from office by law, by limiting the number of terms they are permitted to serve. The term-limit movement spread widely in the country in the early 1990s; various term limitations for state legislators are now in effect in a number of states (recall table 1.3). Some states have attempted to impose term limits on members of their congressional delegation, though the constitutionality of such provisions has been challenged. A proposal for term limits for members of Congress was part of the Contract with America, though it did not achieve passage.

It is not our purpose here to debate the merits of the term-limits movement. Arguments have been made on each side of the issue. The question for this discussion is whether or not term limits would increase electoral competition. To this question, the answer seems clear. When term limits are imposed, competition is increased in the years when seats become open. That is, when a legislator is forced out of office because he or she is not legally eligible to seek reelection, a high level of competition is likely in that district.[12] We know from long experience that competition in congressional elections is strongest when seats come open due to death, retirement, or an incumbent leaving to seek another office. We would expect the same experience to follow if the seat became open when an incumbent was forced out by statute. And, in fact, early evidence from those states that have imposed term limitations on their state legislators seem to support this conclusion.

On the other hand, we also might expect *less* competition when a legislator is eligible to run for reelection. Here the reasoning of a potential candidate is quite different. Why should a potentially strong candidate run against an incumbent when he or she knows that that incumbent will shortly be forced to retire? The incentive to wait for an open seat is enhanced if it is known for certain when that seat will become open. Thus the effect of term limits on competition is most likely to be to increase competition in one election in every cycle (i.e., one in four, if the limit is four terms; one in six, if it is six terms, etc.), but to decrease competition or leave it unchanged in the other years. Whether this result is good or bad and (if it is judged to be beneficial) whether other results from the imposition of term limits merit such a change in the political system are value judgments, not matters that can be explored empirically.[13]

Short of such a fundamental change in the political system, is it possible to find other ways to enhance competition? What is necessary to run good campaigns? In major elections, the answer that is most often given is money (e.g., Gierzynski and Breaux 1990; 1991; Jacobson 1981; 1985–1986). A good campaign could be run, an incumbent could be seriously challenged, if the opponent's campaign were adequately financed. But this explanation may well beg the question. A challenger's campaign *would* be adequately financed if the challenger were viewed as serious. Serious challengers always appear when the risk of running for office is offset by the attractiveness of the office and the perceived chances of winning.

Can this circle be broken? Two answers seem possible. The congressional elections of the 1990s and the relationship between those elections and the legislative sessions that followed them provide hints of one answer. If the electorate becomes dissatisfied with incumbents, and this dissatisfaction is widely perceived, then challengers will emerge to give voice to this dissatisfaction.

Dissatisfaction was evidenced in the 1990 congressional elections, but it became apparent well after challengers had been selected. Despite the fact that in House elections the average incumbent's vote total fell by nearly 5 percent, 96 percent of the incumbents won. Of the twenty-five incumbent representatives whose vote total fell most sharply, over 14 percent in each case, twenty won reelection (Cook 1990). That election demonstrates the problem we are discussing. If quality challengers are not running, citizens cannot use the polls to express their views on the performance of those in power.

As the 1992 election approached, the public was voicing more dissatisfaction with members of Congress. The House bank scandal was in full bloom. Better challengers emerged; nineteen House members lost primaries and an additional twenty-four lost in the general election. In addition, sixty-five members did not seek reelection, the largest number in more than half a century. As a result, more than one in four members of the 103d Congress, sworn in January 1993, were new to the House.

The public expressed a different kind of dissatisfaction in 1994, clearly responding to the lack of progress on pressing problems, despite the fact that divided government had been ended with the Clinton victory and the return of a Democratic Congress two years earlier. The Republicans sought good candidates to challenge seemingly vulnerable Democrats. They ran as a team on the theme of implementing the Contract with America. And they won a major victory, gaining control of the House for the first time in four decades and regaining the majority status in the Senate that they had lost eight years earlier. Thirty-four incumbent House members and two incumbent senators were defeated in 1994—all Democrats defeated by Republicans. Republicans picked up eighteen House seats and six Senate seats because of partisan switches in open seats in that election as well. The Republicans in the House worked to pass the Contract, though they were thwarted on most items by a Democratic president and/or a Senate that was less enthralled with the items under discussion than were GOP House members.

In 1996 it was the Democrats' turn to field strong candidates. In the House particularly, they recruited and supported strong challengers to freshman Republicans. Although they did not win back majority control, despite retaining the White House, eighteen incumbent Republicans were defeated and many others had to fight off very serious challenges.

Finally, in the last election of the decade, incumbents emerged virtually unscathed. Why? The reason deals with strategic choices made by potential candidates once again. The most vulnerable Democrats had been defeated in 1994. The most vulnerable Republicans, especially of those first elected in 1994, had been defeated by Democrats in 1996. Most of those who remained were strong candidates for reelection. Most analysts viewed the 1998 election as a great victory for the Democrats because they held even in the Senate and picked up five seats in the House of Representatives, the first time a president's party had gained House seats since 1934 and only the second time since the Civil War. But the correct interpretation is that it was a victory for the incumbents—98.5 percent of the incumbents running on November 3, 1998 won reelection. Of the 401 incumbents seeking reelection, 316, or nearly 80 percent, polled more than 60 percent of the vote; that number includes the eighty-six who faced no major party opposition. Clearly this election was not one in which public dissatisfaction with the Congress was sufficient to draw out a large number of challengers to incumbents.

The second answer, clearly related to the first, may well be through a rejuvenation of political parties. Traditionally, as we have seen, political parties controlled access to the ballot. They controlled nominations. When they lost control over nominations, they also lost an important role in the recruiting process. In any case, we know very little about how individuals are recruited to run for office today (Canon 1990; Cotter et al. 1984; Eldersveld 1982; Gibson et al. 1985; Maisel 1991; Maisel et al. 1990; Seligman 1974; Snowiss 1966). We do know that many candidates are self-starters, that they themselves determine if and when they will seek office (Maisel 1986).

However, in the most recent elections, both national parties, through their congressional campaign committees, have begun to play a more active role in candidate recruitment at all levels (Adamany 1984; Bibby 1981; 1991). Jacobson and Kernell (1983) attribute unexpected Republican successes in the 1982 congressional elections to the fact that the Republicans ran a number of very attractive candidates. These candidates did not simply emerge; they were recruited and supported by the national party. The same was certainly true of Republican candidates in 1994 and Democratic candidates in 1996.

As has been typical of recent advances in party operations, Republicans have been way ahead of their Democratic counterparts in providing services for candidates for office. The Republicans have provided more money for their candidates, and they are able to help candidates raise money. In addition, they have been able to supply training and services to their candidates that the Democrats have not been able to match until most recently. This nationalization of congressional politics is an important trend to watch in the future (Herrnson 1988).

But more than that, the successful Republican efforts on the national level have set a precedent for both parties' state-level organizations to follow (e.g., Cotter and Bibby 1980; Cotter et al. 1982; 1984; Gibson et al. 1983; Huckshorn et al. 1986). For some years parties have been looking for a role to play in the era of new politics; that role may now be emerging. Changes in campaign techniques and in what is expected of candidates, in what is necessary to run for office, have made electoral office less appealing to many prospective qualified candidates and officeholders. The role of the party may well be to recruit these candidates and support their efforts so that elections in America can become more competitive, with incumbents not being guaranteed victory in every election.

As the national party staffs have moved into fund-raising and polling, into issue research and speechwriting, into strategy setting and media advising, state party organizations have seen opportunities to provide services as well. It is becoming more and more clear that parties have an increasing role to play if our electoral system is to become competitive at all levels of government.

V. THIRD PARTIES IN STATE AND LOCAL ELECTIONS

What is the role of "third parties" in a two-party system? Would it surprise you to know that as many as forty different parties ran at least one candidate for state or federal office in the 1998 general election? (These parties are listed in table 8.1.) Would you be surprised to learn that the Libertarian party ran candidates for the House of Representatives in 152 of the 435 districts across the nation? Does that sound like a two-party system to you?

The electoral system in the United States is described as a competitive two-party system because, all other things being equal (which in this case they usually are), only the Democratic or the Republican candidate for office in a partisan election anywhere in the United States has a realistic chance of winning. All one hundred U.S. senators are either Republicans or Democrats; 434 of the 435 representatives in the House of Representatives are affiliated with one of the two major parties; forty-eight of the fifty governors and more than 7,350 of the approximately 7,400 state legislators elected in partisan elections[14] ran under major party labels. In plotting strategy, most major party candidates only need to consider the candidacy of the individual running on the other major party's ticket.

But this is not always the case. An examination of the exceptions is a good way to come to an understanding of the general rule. Bernie

Table 8.1 "Third" Parties on the 1998 General Election Ballot

Alaskan Independence
American Constitution
American Heritage Party
American Independent
Concerned Citizens
Conservative
Cool Moose
DC Statehood
Freedom Party
Grass Roots
Green
Independence
Independent
Independent American
Legalize Marijuana
Liberal
Libertarian
Liberty Union
Marijuana Reform Party
Mississippi Taxpayers
Moderate
Natural Law
New Jersey Conservative
New Jersey Independent
Nonpartisan
Pacific
Peace and Freedom
Pro-Life
Pro-Life Conservative
Reform
Right to Life
Save Social Security
Socialist Workers
Term Limits
Umoja
Unity
US Taxpayers
Vermont Grass Roots

Source: Data from *The Washington Post* homepage: www.washingtonpost.com

Sanders (I-Vt.) is the only independent in the House of Representatives. Congressman Sanders, the former mayor of Burlington, has had a long and colorful career in Vermont politics. At one point he was the only avowed socialist mayor of any American city; his loyal band of followers was locally known as the Sandersistas, after the Nicaraguan socialist revolutionaries. When he ran for Congress, he drew support mostly from liberal Democrats; in the House he has caucused with Democratic members, who treat him as one of their own in awarding committee assignments. In fact, the Democrats have not run a candidate against Sanders, who has been reelected with relative ease since first winning his seat in 1990.

Angus King, the independent governor of Maine, came to office in a very different way. King entered politics as a Democrat, serving on the staff of William Hathaway, who represented Maine in the House from 1965 until 1973 and in the Senate from 1973 until 1979. Leaving politics and government service, King followed two careers simultaneously, as a very successful owner of a small business and as the host of a statewide television program examining Maine politics on the state's public television network. In 1994 he decided to run for governor. He made two key decisions: that he would run as an independent and that his campaign would be largely self-funded. Maine has had a long history of supporting independent candidates. Since James Longley was elected governor in 1974, every gubernatorial election has seen a serious "third-party" candidate (Maisel and Ivry 1998). At the time King sought office, the Democrats and Republicans were engaged in a bitter feud in the legislature; at one point state government had been shut down over a budgetary impasse. Partisan animosity had turned many citizens (and public servants) sour on the two major parties. King narrowly defeated the Democratic candidate, former governor and former congressman Joseph Brennan, who had run for one office or another for more than twenty years; he was the very personification of a professional politician. The Republican candidate was Susan Collins, an untested former senatorial aid.[15] King did not run against the two major parties so much as he ran as a conciliator, one who would work with leaders from both parties. For four years, he governed in that manner, gaining credit for economic recovery in the state. In 1998, he won reelection with 60 percent of the vote. Neither the Republican nor the Democratic candidate polled even one-third of his total.

But then there is the candidacy of Jesse "The Body" Ventura, who surprised virtually everyone by winning Minnesota's gubernatorial election as the Reform party candidate in 1998. Certainly some will claim that Ventura's victory reflects a resurgence in the Reform party, the true emergence of a national third party that will change the shape of American politics. Evidence to support this conclusion is very thin. Ventura won, in many ways, for the same reasons, though in a very different manner, that King won in 1994. The public was dissatisfied with the major party candidates, who were rather colorless, traditional, career politicians. They had a well-publicized alternative. Ventura, a former professional wrestler and radio talk-show host, was a character. His very physical presence drew attention. His name drew attention. His willingness to be outspoken, as he had demonstrated on his radio program, drew attention. His campaign gained momentum late; neither major party candidate was able to mount a significant reply to his advances.[16]

When King won in Maine and governed successfully for four years, he did so without forming a "third party." He dealt with the Democratic and Republican leadership in the Maine legislature and sought compromise. The citizens of Minnesota will watch carefully to see how Ventura governs and if, in 2000 when legislative elections are again held, Reform party candidates run and win election. That would represent a major advance for third-party candidacies, one not experienced when other non-major party candidates have been elected as state governors (see Bibby and Maisel 1998).

The exceptions are always interesting, but it is also important to look at the norm. It has already been noted that nearly forty parties ran candidates for Congress in 1998 and that the Libertarian party alone ran 152 candidates. What was the impact of these candidacies? By any measure, the impact was very limited. In only four of the 435 races for Congress did the winner poll less than 50 percent of the vote. That means, in only four races, if all of those who voted for the "third-party" candidate had voted for the losing candidate, would the losing candidate have polled enough additional votes to win the election? And of course the assumption that all who voted for the minor-party candidate would have voted at all, much less for one particular candidate, is difficult to justify.

But once again, it is valuable to look at cases in which the minor-party candidate might have had an impact. Let's compare experiences in two congressional districts in New Mexico. Two special elections were held for congressional seats from New Mexico during the 105th Congress. In each case, the Green party ran a candidate in opposition to the Republican and Democratic nominees. The Green party, which appeals to environmentalists and generally those who might be described as "counterculturalists," is stronger in New Mexico than in any other state.

In a special election in the New Mexico Third Congressional District in 1997, Republican Bill Redmond won the seat by a margin of 3 percentage points. The Green party candidate in that special election, Carol Miller, polled 17 percent of the votes. It is logical to conclude that many of her votes would have gone to the Democratic candidate, who shared many of her views, had she not been in the race. A similar result occurred in the special election in New Mexico held in July 1998. Republican Heather Wilson won the election with 44 percent of the vote, beating Democrat Phillip Maloof by 5 percent; the Green candidate, Robert Anderson, polled 14 percent, again with most of those votes logically coming from the Democrat.

In the 1998 general election, the field was exactly the same in the First Congressional District. Once again Wilson, now the incumbent, beat Maloof, this time by only 3 percent of the votes. Again, Anderson ran a strong third-party campaign, garnering 11 percent of the votes, more than enough to deny the Democratic candidate a chance for an upset. In the Third Congressional District, Miller also was the Green party candidate again in the 1998 election. In that election, however, there was a new Democratic candidate, Tom Udall, the state attorney general. The Udall name is well known in environmental circles in the southwest; his father, Stewart, had been a congressman from Arizona before serving as President Kennedy's secretary of the interior; his uncle, Mo, was a leading environmentalist during his own long congressional career. Tom Udall drew on his reputation as a defender of the environment. He appealed directly to Green party leadership not to undermine his campaign against Congressman Redmond. Although Miller remained on the ballot, about six weeks before the election, nine leaders of the Green party sent out a letter to their supporters asking them to support Udall over Miller. Their argument was that support for Miller would virtually ensure a victory for Redmond, a conservative Republican whose environmental record was such that he was among the dirty dozen identified by the League of Conservation Voters (see chap. 6) (Ayres 1998). In the November election Miller drew less than half of the support she had received only one year earlier; Udall was one of five Democrats to unseat incumbent Republicans in the off-year election.

These examples demonstrate both the potential and the problem for third-party candidates. They have the potential to force the major party candidates to take a stand on issues that are most important to their followers. But they also have the potential to divide the vote in such a way that the candidate they least favor wins. And they rarely have the opportunity to win an election. Thus, as campaigns draw to a close, third-party candidates face the argument that a vote for them is at best a wasted vote and at worst counterproductive. As the case of New Mexico's Third Congressional District demonstrates, that is an argument that can be decisive even for leaders of a relatively strong third-party movement.[17] The effectiveness of this argument is likely to restrict the importance of third parties in state and local elections for the foreseeable future.

VI. Politicians View the General Election

Recall the two candidates with whom we began this chapter. The candidate for county supervisor rearranged other aspects of his life so that he could concentrate on the county fair. For the Senate candidate, the campaign was her life. That defines a critical difference not only between the two individuals but also between the two jobs.

Think about candidates for different offices. At the more local levels, candidates serve in part-time positions and run limited campaigns to get there. Many of these candidates like campaigning. It is a different experience for them. They have the opportunity to meet a variety of interesting people, to observe how people live and what they do for a living, to talk to them about their concerns and about their opinions of government. Even when the campaign is over, they have the opportunity to serve, to work on some of the problems they have learned about, to make their community a better place in which to live. And they also have the opportunity to go back to a more normal kind of existence. They can have dinners with their families, spend weekends in the backyard, shop for groceries without shaking hands. The campaign is what they did for a while to win office; it is not their life's work and certainly not their life itself.

Contrast this normality with the existence—and I have chosen that word carefully—of a member of Congress from a marginal district. Members of Congress in this situation start one campaign the minute the last one ends. Many of them are at the plant gates the morning after an election, thanking those who voted for them and hoping that they will remember how much the candidate cared when voting time comes around again. Even those who do not start campaigning for reelection on day one of the new term are constantly campaigning. They come back to the district every weekend, if travel times make it possible. They continue with the same kinds of activities they did in the campaign: speaking to anyone who will listen, attending countless suppers, judging at county fairs. During the week they work hard in Congress, spending much of their time ensuring that their constituents are happy and will vote for them (Cain, Ferejohn, and Fiorina 1987; Fiorina 1978; Mayhew 1974). On weekends and during congressional recesses, they are back in the district. They know that if they work hard, they might be able to squeak out another term (Fenno 1978; Taggart and Durant 1985). But what about the rest of their lives—vacations, outings with their children or grandchildren, leisure reading?

Put simply, for many members of Congress, such things do not exist. They rarely see their children or spouses; there is no "rest of their lives." Their only enjoyment is politics. This picture should cause concern. Do we really want to be governed by a group of individuals who are willing to give up their lives to campaign full-time? Even if we are not concerned about the mental health of such individuals,[18] how much can they know about the problems facing their constituents, about the reality of ordinary day-to-day life for the majority of Americans?

Many have expressed concern that members of Congress represent a social and economic elite and cannot relate to the problems facing middle-class America. The problem may well be more serious than that. Many of today's politicians do not live a real life at all. Not only are they unrepresentative in terms of economic and social indicators, but they are even more unrepresentative in terms of their ability to understand the everyday problems Americans face.

Impressionistic evidence indicates that few members of Congress lead "normal" lives, even if normality is defined in as broad a way as is necessary, given today's heterogeneous world. Many are single and can imagine no time for a family; the divorce rate on Capitol Hill is very high. Few lead "normal" family lives. Competitive politics at this level has produced a group of officeholders unfamiliar with the daily experiences of most of the people they represent.

How do politicians react to this style of life? A number of responses are possible. Some politicians refuse to enter the arena. Every year political journalists speculate about likely candidates for office in a particular region. Every year some refuse to run; some say that they have enough to do where they are now; others are frank in saying that the sacrifices are not worth the honor.

Others immerse themselves in politics totally and then escape. In recent years many have been concerned about the number of members of Congress who are voluntarily retiring, a number that reached a modern record in 1992 (see, e.g., Cooper and West 1981). Many of these retirees state explicitly that they are leaving because the pressure to campaign is too heavy. Some of the best members of Congress have retired in recent years, often well before the age at which we might normally expect such officeholders to step down. Certainly we could list many reasons for such early retirements besides the exigencies of the two-year election cycle. However, as a matter of public policy, we must be concerned if some of the best officeholders feel that they cannot stay in office and serve because the electoral demands are too costly.

A third response is to avoid the pressure of constant election by seeking a different office. In 1998, eight members of Congress chose not to run for their old seats in order to seek seats in the Senate. One reason for taking this route is that senators face reelection every six years, not every other year. Senators campaign very hard in the two years before their term expires, but in the other four years they are able to concentrate on the policy-making aspects of their job (Fenno 1984). Another three left the House to run for governor, again a position with a longer tenure and one that seems more likely to have policy impact. Two years earlier, fourteen representatives left the House to seek seats in the Senate while one other ran for governor.

Not all members of Congress face difficult elections every two years. Some of these members have reached accommodations with their jobs that are not unlike the positions of senators or others who do not feel they must campaign constantly. Consider the career choice that Congressman Barney Frank (D-Mass.), one of those who faced no opposition in his 1998 reelection bid, was confronted with some years ago.

In 1984, when Massachusetts senator Paul Tsongas (D) decided not to seek reelection in order to spend more time with his family (he was diagnosed as having a serious illness), many speculated that Frank would be among the first in the race for the Senate seat. Frank is one of the more outspoken members of Congress; he won his seat in a hotly contested race when Father Robert Drinan (D-Mass., 1971–1981) was forced not to seek reelection by the papal decree that forbids Catholic clergy from engaging actively in politics. After the 1980 census Frank had to win reelection against Margaret Heckler (R-Mass., 1967–1983) in one of those few races every ten years in which, because of redistricting in states that have lost seats in Congress, two incumbents must face each other. The 1982 Frank–Heckler race was the most expensive race in the country. Political journalists conjectured that Frank, fresh from two extremely difficult campaigns, would view the six-year term of a senator as a panacea for all his ills.

Frank saw it differently:

> I've got the best job in the world. Look, I can build up a relationship with this district. I won't have another tough campaign for ten years, when they might fool around with reapportionment again.
>
> I go back to the district every other weekend. I enjoy it. I enjoy what I do there. I can live a normal life here [in Washington]. How many Senators ever live a normal life? They are always in the spotlight. I don't need that. (Frank 1985)

Frank is satisfied with his life in the House. He, like others who have gained the spotlight in the House of Representatives—men like majority leader Dick Armey (R-Tex.) and John Dingell (D-Mich.), the senior member of the Democratic Caucus, or the leaders of the House Judiciary Committee, Chairman Henry Hyde (R-Ill.) and ranking minority member John Conyers (D-Mich.)—have found the House to be a congenial home. In 1984 Frank had no desire to move on to the Senate. He was making the contributions he wanted to make in the House. He did not feel that the electoral pressure was burdensome because he had become comfortable with his district. Frank's subsequent electoral experience demonstrates his point. In May 1987, Frank revealed that he is a homosexual, becoming only the second member of the Congress at that time to publicly announce that he is gay. After having won reelection without opposition in 1986, Frank faced a challenger in 1988 but won the election with over 70 percent of the vote. In August of 1989 the *Washington Times* revealed that Frank was involved with a male prostitute whom Frank had hired as a household assistant. The House Ethics Committee investigated to determine if Frank had violated any House rules, particularly in response to a charge that Frank had used his influence as a member of Congress to have parking tickets fixed. Even after cries for his resignation and weeks of bad publicity, Frank was easily able to weather another serious challenge, winning the 1990 election by nearly 2 to 1. Massachusetts lost a seat in the House as a result of the 1990 census. But Frank was able to win easily in his reconfigured district and has had no difficulty since. His analysis of the difference between House and Senate seats, at least in his case, seems as prescient as it was nearly a decade and a half ago.

Thus politicians have a number of different ways of responding to general election pressures, from letting politics dominate their entire lives to opting out of the system. How they respond over a period of time is different, however, from how they view general elections in the short run.

The question of how politicians view elections can be approached in two ways. The first is affectively: what do politicians think about the prospect of campaigning? As was mentioned earlier in this section, this response varies from individual to individual and may vary as well from office to office and time to time. Many share the sentiments of an extremely successful politician who said, "I like lots of it, but not the door-to-door stuff. I feel I am imposing. People are awfully nice, but I feel their home should be their home, not a soapbox for my views." An opposite point of view is represented by former senator William Cohen (R-Me.; House, 1973–1979; Senate, 1979–1997), who routinely asked people if he could spend the night in their home while campaigning. Cohen figured that people really feel that they know you if they open their home to you and break bread with you in the morning.

Some politicians like talking to big contributors and impressing them with the importance of their being elected. Others, like the late senator (1949–1964; 1971–1978) and vice president (1965–1969) Hubert Humphrey (D-Minn.), found that asking someone for money was the most distasteful part of politics. Some enjoy appearing before large audiences and debating; others are more reticent and seek to have their records speak for themselves.

The list of variations could go on. All that can be said with certainty is that campaigning is a highly personal experience. Some find it totally rewarding in and of itself; others find it a necessary evil, withstood in order to attain or hold office.

The second way in which politicians view elections is in a strategic sense: what does this election mean to me? Can I win? What are the costs to me personally? Professionally? From this campaign? What are the costs if I win? What are the costs if I lose? What are the benefits if I win? What are the benefits if I lose?

Were politicians rational men and women in reaching these decisions, they would weigh the costs and benefits carefully and reach judgments based on that evidence. Jacobson and Kernell (1983) lay out this model of electoral decision making and defend it persuasively (see also Maisel et al. 1990; Brady, Maisel, and Warsh 1994). On the other hand, Maisel (1982; 1986) demonstrates that politicians do not always behave rationally in reaching decisions about their electoral future. Very often office seekers look at all the facts (e.g., the fact that over 90 percent of the incumbent members of Congress seeking reelection are successful) and make decisions:

> Given this caveat, however, some strategies followed by candidates in the general election reflect their view of this process in the short run. The objective of the election is not merely to win, but to win by a wide margin. If a title can be given to this strategy, it would be a

> "run-scared" strategy. No matter what the evidence says, no matter what one's instincts are, "run scared." Do not appear to be complacent; do not take anything for granted. Build the margin. Assure a big victory; it might frighten away opponents the next time. (Goldenberg, Traugott 1986; Jackson 1988; Krasno and Green 1988; Maisel 1990b)[19]

Analysts of elections and campaigns describe a rational process. They present a process in which politicians weigh alternatives, reach rational decisions, set appropriate strategies, allocate resources effectively, appeal to the voters persuasively, and evaluate their campaigns logically.

The difficulty with this description is that although the entire process viewed as a whole may be rational, individual politicians often act very irrationally. Two seemingly conflicting trends are in evidence. The first is represented by the incumbent member of Congress whose winning percentage has not fallen below 65 percent in ten years but is being confronted by one strongly organized group in his district on a particular issue. This politician "runs scared." All evidence from hundreds of campaigns for more than a decade indicates that as an incumbent he is safe. However, for a year he goes home every weekend, spending more time in the district than he has in years. He raises more money than has ever been spent on an election in his district. He employs a professional campaign staff and has it in place before any opposition has surfaced. He campaigns hard throughout the fall, despite the fact that his opponent is unknown and underfinanced.

The second trend could well be represented by his opponent. She believes that the group supporting her has widespread support throughout the district that will carry her to victory. All the evidence about incumbent safety does not deter her. She views this campaign through rose-colored glasses. Objective views of her chances do not mute her optimism. Her efforts are undeterred by the fact that she has little money and is not well known beyond the members of her group. She campaigns hard right up until the election, convinced that the justice of her cause will be sufficient to guarantee victory in the end.

The incumbent wins big. The process is understandable and rational in the overall picture. These two candidates and literally thousands like them campaigning for all sorts of offices all over the country have been acting irrationally. They have been caught up in an amazing exercise in self-deception. Politicians invest so much of themselves in campaigns that they cannot believe that their experiences are not unique.

The November campaigns are a critically important part of politicians' lives. For some, campaigns become too important. These politicians are not willing to put that much of themselves on the line and let others make a judgment about their merit. For others, the election is what their life is all about. Politics is not only a means to an end; it is an end in itself; campaigning becomes not only their life's work but also their life. For all, it is a deeply personal experience. At whatever level the campaign, the candidate is aware that fellow citizens are making a judgment of him or her. Few can view that process in a detached way as objective analysts. Most are caught up in the election as one of life's crises, which can only be experienced in the most personal of ways.

WEBSITES

The websites noted for chapter 7 pertain to the material is this chapter as well. In addition, many campaigns post their own websites during an election year, removing them after the election. These sites can usually be located under the candidate's name.

KEY CONCEPTS

candidate-centered	incumbent advantage	marginal seats
direct mail		term limits

DISCUSSION QUESTIONS

1. How do you decide which candidates you will vote for below the top of the ballot? Why are public officials such as registrar of deeds or judge of probate elected? What is you impression of our "long ballots"?
2. One recurring question about the way in which American campaigns are contested deals with issue content—even for the more salient races. What issues were discussed in the most recent elections in your hometown? What impact did they have on the outcome of the election? If you cannot name substantive issues that were discussed, why not?
3. How serious a flaw is it in our electoral system that so many offices are uncontested? Why should we worry about the lack of competition if incumbents are so popular that they always get reelected? Would you favor a system that allowed citizens to vote "none of the above" in an election, requiring the winner to receive a certain percentage of positive votes?
4. Should parties play a more or less prominent role in state and local elections? What should that role be? Why?

5. Do interest groups—through campaign contributions and influence over their members—play too prominent a role in American elections?
6. Candidate-centered campaigns are often dominated by political consultants—hired guns who travel from state to state and clearly have a great deal of influence over local politics because of their technical campaign expertise. Do you view their role as positive or negative? If positive, justify that evaluation. If negative, how can their function be performed without deleterious effects?

CHAPTER 9
Presidential Nominations

- I. The Post-1968 Reforms
  - A. The McGovern-Fraser Commission
  - B. The 1972 Nomination
  - C. Continuing Reform of the Process
    1. The Mikulski Commission
    2. The 1976 Nomination: Strategies under the New Rules
    3. The Winograd Commission
    4. The 1980 Nomination and the Hunt Commission
    5. The Fairness Commission and the 1988 Nominating Process
  - D. The Reform Movement: An Assessment
- II. Nominations under the Current System: 1992 and 1996
  - A. The 1992 Nominations
  - B. The 1996 Nominations
  - C. Toward 2000
- III. Strategic Considerations in the Contests for Nominations
  - A. The Political Calendar
    1. Front-loading the System
    2. Super Tuesday
    3. Filing Deadlines
    4. Strategic Implications of the Political Calendar
  - B. The Rules of the Game
    1. Proportional Representation versus Winner-Take-All Systems
    2. Superdelegates versus Influential Party Leaders
  - C. Strategic Use of Campaign Resources
    1. Office

The political year 1968 was a watershed in presidential nominating politics. That year, marred by the assassination of Robert Kennedy and Martin Luther King Jr., saw President Lyndon Johnson challenged within his own party and eventually withdrawing from the presidential contest and Vice President Hubert Humphrey, the advocate of the "politics of joy," nominated while the American public watched frustration on the convention floor and violence on the streets of Chicago. Events were set into motion that could not be reversed and that would fundamentally change the way in which presidential nominees are chosen.

Each nomination since 1968 has been played out under its own unique circumstances. Only by looking at these seven nomination processes individually, and then by attempting to generalize about the process, can one approximate an analytical understanding of how the Democratic and Republican party nominees are chosen. Only with a clear sense of the past can we make some judgments about future nominations.

This chapter will begin with a look back at the presidential nomination battles fought over the last three decades. Emphasis will be given to changes in the process that have implications for the current circumstances. Following that review, we will turn to an examination of the strategic questions that face potential candidates for major-party presidential nods. We will see that some of the important lessons from the past remain central as candidates look toward the year 2000 and beyond.

I. The Post-1968 Reforms

PRESIDENTIAL PREFERENCE PRIMARIES

Primary elections in which voters cast their votes for presidential candidates or for delegates who will support specified presidential candidates.

Democrats competed in fifteen **presidential preference primaries** in 1968. Senator Robert Kennedy won eleven of the primaries; Senator Eugene McCarthy won the other four. Vice President Hubert Humphrey, the heir apparent after President Johnson announced that he would not seek reelection, followed a political strategy in which he avoided confrontation with McCarthy and Kennedy. He did not announce his candidacy until deadlines for filing intentions to run had passed in all states. Humphrey backers won just over 2 percent of the primary vote; but, in 1968, votes in primaries did not convert directly to convention votes. For example, Senator McCarthy won nearly three-quarters of the votes in the

Pennsylvania primary; Vice President Humphrey garnered 80 percent of the Pennsylvania convention votes.

In 1968 primaries were seen as a tool used to influence party officials about electability; they were not a means to "win" a nomination. The conventional wisdom of party politicians was that the party bosses in the larger states had the power to control the nomination. They not only believed that this was true but also believed that this was as it should be. All of this was to change because of the 1968 Democratic Convention.[1] Needless to say, critics charged that the party was boss-controlled and claimed that the selection process was undemocratic and unfair.

A. The McGovern-Fraser Commission

Party leaders responded to this criticism; they saw the frustration of those who worked within the system. They saw the damage done to the party and the nation by the 1968 nominating process, which so obviously did not reflect the will of those who participated.

Shortly after the 1968 elections, Democratic national chairman Fred Harris appointed a commission to examine the nominating process. The Commission on Party Structure and Delegate Selection was to be chaired by South Dakota senator George McGovern, who had taken up the mantle of Senator Kennedy after his assassination. The McGovern Commission (which became known as the **McGovern-Fraser Commission** after the chairman resigned to run for president and was replaced by Congressman Donald Fraser of Minnesota) began by assessing the situation that existed in 1968. Their general assessment can be summarized succinctly: the "system" was disjointed across geographic lines; the procedures were unfair to many and undemocratic in the broadest sense of that term; the end result did not represent the views of many of those who participated.

MCGOVERN-FRASER COMMISSION

The first of a series of reform commissions that have restructured the way in which the Democratic party nominates candidates for president and vice president.

Some of the procedures revealed by the McGovern-Fraser Commission seem unbelievable from today's perspective. In two states (Georgia and Louisiana) governors appointed all members of the delegation. State committees appointed all or most of the national convention delegations in eight other states. So disorganized was the situation that no one really knew how the delegations were appointed in many other states. The usual explanation was that party officials met behind closed doors and reached secret accommodations. None of these revelations was surprising to the professionals in either the Democratic or Republican parties, however, for they made the decisions. From their point of view, that was how it should be done.

Research by the staff of the McGovern-Fraser Commission defined the philosophical issues that have structured the debate of the presidential nomination process since that time. On the one hand are party professionals who believe that the most important criterion for an effective process should be the selection of a nominee who can win the general election and govern the nation. They feel that those who have worked most closely with active politicians and know the political scene well can best make that judgment. On the other hand are those who believe that the process should be open and democratic and that the voters in a party should decide whom their nominee will be. The debate has gone back and forth and is often the backdrop for arguments over obscure sub-issues. But the question is fundamental: should the process be elite dominated or popularly dominated, should the outcome of the process be more important or the means by which that outcome was reached?

The final report of the McGovern-Fraser Commission, entitled *Mandate for Reform*, specified that nominating procedures must be changed to make the process *open, timely, and representative.* To the members of the commission and those who were distressed by the events leading up to Humphrey's nomination in 1968, these goals appeared to be at the heart of a democratic process and thus noncontroversial. However, the specific reforms that were suggested (and then accepted as mandatory for state parties for the 1972 nominating process by the Democratic National Committee) rocked the existing system so fundamentally that the ground has yet to settle.

Perhaps the most important guideline promulgated by the McGovern-Fraser Commission was to require that all state parties adopt procedures consistent with the principles it outlined. This requirement, with which states had to comply in order to be seated at subsequent national nominating conventions, changed the power structure within the Democratic party in a way that has not since been altered. The eighteen reforms stipulated by the McGovern-Fraser Commission led to the establishment of one nominating process, with the rules set at the national level by the national Democratic party. State parties had to adopt and publish written rules that complied with national guidelines.

The McGovern-Fraser guidelines shook party leaders badly. Read with the hindsight of seven presidential nominations, they seem to say nothing more than that the procedure should be open, democratic, and representative. Hardly radical notions. However, in 1970, many state party leaders thought it would be impossible to comply without drastically changing how they operated, as they looked toward the 1972 nomination.

Remember, in 1968 presidential preference primaries had been held in only fifteen states. In some of those states, such as Wisconsin, Oregon, and California, the primaries determined the delegations to the national convention. In many of the other states, such as New Jersey, Pennsylvania, and Illinois, the connection between primaries and convention delegations was less clear. And in thirty-five states, delegates were chosen through some appointive means. Often only the individuals making the appointments had any idea how they were decided. In Maine, in 1968, the delegation was reportedly chosen in a backroom at the Colby College gymnasium by Senator Edmund S. Muskie and a group of his friends.

For 1972, two procedures were permissible. States could run primaries, under a variety of permissible rules, but in any case with the result determining at least 90 percent of the state's delegation. Or the states could continue to keep delegate selection a matter for party regulars, selecting delegations through series of meetings of party members and regulars in a series of local party caucuses and conventions organized under the new guidelines.

The differences between primary elections and a caucus/convention system are important and should be made explicit. In a presidential preference primary, party members go to their local polling place and cast a ballot for their preference much as they do in a general election. In a caucus/convention system, party members go to a meeting; they all must come at the same time and stay for the duration of the meeting. At the meeting or caucus, those in attendance elect representatives to attend another meeting—usually at the county, congressional district, or state level—in proportion to the presidential preferences of those at the caucus. Those at the subsequent meeting (or perhaps a third-level meeting) elect the delegates to the national convention, again in proportion to the presidential preferences of those in attendance.

Does it sound complicated? Party leaders thought so. Many had preferred the caucus/convention system in the past because they could control the results. No public notices; no rules; no stated preferences. Just party leaders selecting themselves and their friends as convention delegates, fully understanding that they would be told for whom to vote by the party leaders, who really chose the nominees. But caucuses became more difficult to run under the new guidelines. In many states party leaders felt the procedures were too cumbersome to attempt. Twenty-two states opted to hold presidential preference primaries in 1972; 65 percent of the delegates were chosen in these primaries.

B. The 1972 Nomination

Imagine that you wrote the rules for a very complicated card game. If hand A were dealt, one set of rules applied; if hand B were dealt, another set of rules came into play; hand C would be played in a different way. Don't you think you would have an advantage the first time you played the game?

George McGovern resigned the chairmanship of the Commission on Party Structure and Delegate Selection after most of the work of that group had been finished. He resigned to run for president—under the new rules, his rules. McGovern chose as his campaign manager and chief strategist a young fellow named Gary Hart, who had been a key staff member of the McGovern Commission. They knew the rules and played them to their advantage.

The key strategy under the new rules was to organize at the grassroots and to compete everywhere. Convention delegates were actually selected in primaries and at caucuses, not by party leaders in secret meetings. The front-runner in 1972 was Maine senator Ed Muskie, who had impressed the party leaders as Humphrey's vice presidential running mate four years earlier. Muskie followed the old conventional wisdom. He lined up all the party leaders, the opinion leaders in the big states, behind him. Then he lost because they could not deliver. Hubert Humphrey entered the race late, as he had done in 1968, but this time he was too late; party leaders could not deliver for him either. Delegates selected in primaries and caucuses remained loyal to George McGovern, not to local party leaders.

Despite a concerted effort to derail McGovern's candidacy by those who had dominated previous conventions, the South Dakota senator went on to win the nomination in Miami. The process was not smooth. The openness of the process led to participation by activists interested in discussing controversial issues. The Democratic Convention showed the party for what it was, an amalgamation of differing and competing interests. All the warts were visible to the large national television audience.

GEOGRAPHIC REPRESENTATION

Representation based on the geographic area in which a person resides.

When McGovern lost the general election by a landslide to Richard Nixon, party leaders were quick to blame the new rules. McGovern had been an extremist; he might have been the candidate of women, youth, and minorities, but he was not the candidate of the traditional core of the party. He was not the candidate of the blue-collar, union Democrats. He certainly was not the candidate of the big-city Democrats. And he was not the candidate who would have been chosen by the party leaders who had dominated previous conventions.

DEMOGRAPHIC REPRESENTATION

Representation based on demographic characteristics such as gender, race, or age.

In fact, the rules neither gave McGovern the nomination nor caused his defeat. But it was easy to make a logical leap from McGovern rules to McGovern nomination to McGovern debacle. The rules did present something of a conflict between types of representation. As had always been the case, they called for **geographic representation**, specifying that states break delegations down to more local areas. They also called for **demographic representation**, at least of groups traditionally loyal to and underrepresented in the Democratic party—women, blacks, youth. And they called for representation by candidate preference. Individuals supported presidential candidates based on their views of critical issues; this last type of representation approximated, in the view of many, **ideological representation**.

IDEOLOGICAL REPRESENTATION

Representation based on how individuals stand on the issues under debate.

Critics claimed that the mixing of three kinds of representation, rather than the traditional reliance on geographic representation and domination by party leaders, led to the selection of a new kind of delegates. Delegates who were concerned with winning were replaced by issue-oriented delegates who cared more about specific matters of principle than electoral victory. This conclusion has been actively debated ever since (see Kirkpatrick 1976; 1978; Polsby 1983; Polsby and Wildavsky 1988; Ranney 1975; Sullivan et al. 1977–1978; Sullivan, Pressman, and Arterton 1976; Sullivan et al. 1977; Wayne 1988). Regardless of the merits of the debate, party leaders remained concerned about nominating rules, changing them after each subsequent presidential nomination.

C. Continuing Reform of the Process

1. The Mikulski Commission

The Mikulski Commission, named after the 1972 election by Democratic National Committee chairman Robert Strauss, was the first of the "reaction" reform commissions, that is, commissions created by the Democrats as a reaction to the previous year's rules.[2] If the regulars felt they could overturn the McGovern-Fraser reforms with the Mikulski Commission, they must have been gravely dissatisfied with the results. The commission made a number of concessions to party regulars, but the principles of reform were unchallenged. The major contributions of the Mikulski Commission were (1) the restriction of participation in the presidential nominating process to Democrats only, that is, outlawing the "open" primary and (2) the requirement that delegates be allocated proportionally among all contenders receiving at least 15 percent of the votes cast, that is, proportional representation according to candidate strength or, in the phrase employed by party rule makers, **fair reflection of presidential preference**. The legacy of these decisions persists in the nominating process today.

FAIR REFLECTION OF PRESIDENTIAL PREFERENCE

Delegates are chosen to each subsequent level of the presidential nominating process in proportion to the level of support they receive at a previous level.

However, while most of the new rules were left intact, state party leaders were given great leeway in interpreting them. The party and the press seemed tired of haggling and fighting over rules, and the 1976 nominating period proceeded without major incident.

2. The 1976 Nomination: Strategies under the New Rules

In 1976, thirty states held presidential preference primaries; 76 percent of the delegates to the convention were elected in these primaries. A number of Democrats joined the nominating battle, each eager to demonstrate he had learned the lessons of 1972.

Jimmy Carter, whose term as governor of Georgia expired in 1974, was out campaigning early. He and his chief campaign strategist, Hamilton Jordan, devised a simple, but most effective, strategy. Carter was going to campaign everywhere. Because of proportional representation, he would be guaranteed some delegate support from each state. He would have enough delegate support to be around at the end of the process.

NEW HAMPSHIRE'S "FIRST IN THE NATION" PRIMARY

The first primary held in every recent nominating season, so specified by New Hampshire state law that states that New Hampshire's primary is to be held at least a week in advance of that of any other state.

Others strategies were less well thought-out. Washington senator Henry Jackson thought that it would be difficult to differentiate himself from the field, because so many candidates were running in **New Hampshire's "first in the nation" primary**. He felt that he was well-enough known and that his candidacy was strong enough that he could afford to leave New Hampshire to others and to enter the fray after the field had been narrowed. This decision allowed Carter to campaign as the only moderate in a sea of liberals in the earliest test of strength. Positioning himself apart from the pack, Carter "won New Hampshire" with 28 percent of the vote. His picture smiled at the nation from the cover of *Time*. He went from near obscurity to the position of front-running moderate. The Jackson campaign never recovered.

An array of liberals all sought to emulate George McGovern's success in 1972. Morris Udall, congressman from Arizona, was able to separate himself from his fellow liberals but was never able to break through to win a big victory. Udall's campaign was marred by strategic mistakes and unfortunate luck. He wasted scarce financial resources in the early Iowa caucuses and, when the Federal Election Commission was sidelined by the Supreme Court's decision in *Buckley v. Valeo* (see chap. 11), he ran short of funds for later contests. His losses in Wisconsin and Michigan were each by less than 1 percent of the vote cast and stood as two of his six second-place finishes.

The final challenger to Carter's nomination in 1976 was California governor Edmund G. (Jerry) Brown Jr. Brown, like Jackson, entered the race too late. Brown did not realize that allotting delegates by proportional representation of candidate strength meant that Carter would continue to pick up additional delegates even if he lost primaries. Thus, despite the fact that Brown won the last round of primaries, he could not stop the inevitable Carter march to nomination. Even with his losses on the last day of primaries, Carter still picked up enough delegates to secure the nomination. The convention in New York was a Carter "love-in." The Carter majority was firmly in control of the party machinery.

3. The Winograd Commission

While the 1976 nominating season was under way, Democratic National Committee chairman Strauss appointed Michigan Democratic chair Morley Winograd as head of a new committee to look at the problem caused by the proliferation of primaries, an unintended consequence of the reforms. The regulars again wanted more control.

The 1976 convention called for another commission, in effect authorizing the extension of Winograd's group. However, the new commission was expanded to included representatives of the White House.

The not-so-hidden agenda of the commissioners loyal to President Carter was to assure that the 1980 rules hindered a challenge to the incumbent president.

Despite the fact that Jimmy Carter had been nominated under reform rules, the goal of his supporters was clearly to close the system, to move back from encouraging participation, competition, and an open system. The major contribution of the Winograd Commission was an attempt to shorten the "primary season" by restricting all primaries and first-round caucuses to a three-month period from early March to early June. This became known as the **window concept**, drawing an analogy from the space program in which a "window" of opportunity during which launches can be safely attempted is identified before each flight. Interestingly, exceptions were allowed for those states that had held caucuses or primaries before the opening of the window in 1976, most notably the early Iowa caucuses and the New Hampshire primary, which had provided the twin launch pads for Jimmy Carter's drive to nomination.

WINDOW CONCEPT

Analogous to the space program, in which a launch is only possible during a specified period of time, the concept that primaries and caucuses selecting delegates to presidential nominating conventions must be held between certain dates on the calendar.

Why restrict the time period? The stated rationale was to shorten the length of campaigns, but it was clear to all that candidates would still start campaigning years in advance of the first official event. The more logical reason was that it would be difficult for a challenger to gain the momentum needed to overcome an incumbent if all the events were closely packed.

Other proposals from the Winograd Commission also represented steps back from reform, designed instead to aid the president's drive for renomination and to increase the power of party regulars. The principle of fair reflection of presidential preference was not repealed, but it was diluted. The threshold of votes necessary in order to receive any representation was raised from 15 to 25 percent, as the campaign progressed.

As another step away from fair reflection, the Winograd Commission voted to allow **winner-take-all primaries**, if states created single-member districts. In a winner-take-all contest, the candidate with the most votes gets all of the delegates being contested. The winner-take-all primary at the state level had been eliminated by the McGovern-Fraser Commission; the justification was that such a system distorted the actual preference of those casting their votes. (See chap. 10 for a discussion of the winner-take-all aspect of the electoral college system.) In 1976 various states had run **loophole** primaries. The way around the prohibition of winner-take-all primaries was to have winner-take-all selection processes at the congressional district level. That loophole had been closed, over Carter campaign staff objections, by the 1976 convention's adoption of the report of the Rules Committee, which specified that no winner-take-all primaries would be permitted for congressional districts. The Winograd Commission created a new loophole, since it appeared that most of the single-member districts to

WINNER-TAKE-ALL PRIMARIES

Primary elections in which the plurality winner receives all of the delegates at stake.

LOOPHOLE

A way around the intent of a law or regulation.

be created would favor Carter. Jimmy Carter tried to take advantage of his incumbency to change the system to his advantage.

While the debates over the timing of the process, the cut-off level for fair reflection of candidate preference, and the prohibition or allowance of winner-take-all primaries seem esoteric at best, they consumed a great deal of energy because strategists saw clearly that changes in rules like these would impact the nominating process in important ways. These changes were victories for those who favored party elite domination of the nominating process over those who saw broad democratic participation as more important. President Carter, who had run as a party outsider in 1976, now dominated the party machinery. As the sitting president, he was the ultimate insider and sought to use the rules to maximize his chances for easy renomination in 1980. Discussion over rule reform always exists on two levels at the same time, a level of principle and a level of strategy.

4. The 1980 Nomination and the Hunt Commission

The relevant aspect of the 1980 nomination for the purpose of this review of procedural reforms is that Jimmy Carter won renomination despite the fact that by the time the Democratic National Convention ratified his renomination most party officials felt he was bound to lose the general election to Ronald Reagan. The response to this situation was predictable—another "reform" commission. The goals of this new commission, chaired by North Carolina governor James B. Hunt Jr., were simply to strengthen the party, increase the role of party regulars to help the party win elections, and ensure that the party could govern once in office (Crotty 1983, 88). What could be easier?

It could also be argued that this was the "reaction to the Jimmy Carter" commission. Carter had been the outsider who had won control of the party because of the openness of the rules. Once in office he had difficulty governing, in large part because he was an outsider. As the incumbent president, he controlled the party machinery and won renomination, despite the fact that other elected officials doubted he could win. Party leaders wanted to be certain that they, not some outsider, had more control.

The Hunt Commission reaffirmed many of the positions taken by previous commissions. First, it reasserted that the Democratic party nominating process should be open only to Democrats. The open primary was not to be used in any way for selecting delegates to the national convention.[3] Second, it examined the question of minority representation to national conventions, concentrating on the problem of underrepresentation of low-income Democrats. Although encouraging participation by these groups, it included no mandatory steps.

Third, it accepted the window concept, again arguing that a shortened period would shorten the campaign. The commission took this position despite the fact that such a position flew in the face of reality; candidates simply campaign for up to four years in order to be ready for the opening of the window. State after state devised systems to test strength before the window opens, so candidates fought the battles of Iowa, Florida, and Maine **straw polls**. The Hunt Commission again acquiesced to the desires of Iowa and New Hampshire party leaders but shortened the "prewindow" exception to two weeks for Iowa and one for New Hampshire.

STRAW POLL

An informal poll, frequently of attendees at off-year party conventions or at other party gatherings, in which preferences among potential presidential candidates are expressed.

The Hunt Commission took three positions that changed the 1980 rules for 1984. First, it unbound the delegates, returning to a commitment of "good conscience" as the constraint for whether or not delegates could switch from the candidate to whom they had been pledged. The justification for this change was that the 1980 nominating contest had shown that commitments made early in the nominating season were often made before the true circumstances of an election were known. President Carter secured enough delegates to ensure his renomination before the weakness of his candidacy had been revealed. The Hunt Commission change would have permitted delegates elected with pledges to support President Carter to switch at the convention if the circumstances warranted such action.

This change was more symbolic than real, however. Given the fact that presidential contenders can approve delegate candidates pledged to them and that delegate candidates are generally among the most committed supporters of the presidential candidates, it is highly unlikely that many would ever switch. The extent of this loyalty should have been apparent to the commission members. It had been demonstrated in delegate support for candidate positions on important rule controversies, including prenomination announcement of vice presidential selection at the 1976 Republican Convention and freeing of "robot delegates" at the 1980 Democratic Convention.[4] Nonetheless, some considered this an important issue, and the Hunt Commission reflected their concern.

Second, the commission relaxed the rules on proportional representation while maintaining that they were reaffirming the principle of fair reflection. Their logic was questionable, and the rules they created were more complex than any previously in existence. The result was a reinstitution of "loophole" primaries at the congressional district level in a number of states. This change, a concession to party officials, had a significant impact on the outcome of the 1984 Democratic nomination.

"ADD-ON" DELEGATES

Convention delegates added to the total a state normally would be allocated in order to accommodate certain party and elected officials

Finally, and most importantly, the Hunt Commission offered a proposal to increase significantly the impact of elected officials at the national convention. The Winograd Commission had increased state delegation size by allowing certain party officials to be "added on" to the slate elected. The Hunt Commission accepted the concept of **"add-on" delegates** but supplemented them with a new category of delegates, quickly dubbed **superdelegates**. These individuals were to be prominent party and/or elected officials, for example, governors, sen-

SUPER-DELEGATES

Delegates to the Democratic National Convention who hold their seats by virtue of their office, for example, members of congress, senators, and governors.

ators, or members of Congress who had played key roles at conventions before the reforms but whose participation levels had declined. The superdelegates were to come to the convention officially unpledged. The theory was that they would bring practical experience to the convention and help nominate a winning ticket should a situation such as the one that the Democrats faced in 1980 reemerge. Essentially they represented a compromise between those who wanted all delegates to be popularly elected and those who wanted more party elite influence.

The practice turned out to be quite different. In 1984, these delegates were selected quite early (in the case of congressional and senatorial delegates) and presidential contenders sought and received their endorsements. Most backed former vice president Walter Mondale. If nothing else, however, those most concerned with the elections could no longer claim that they did not have a vote or a stake in the process, and many officials were directly connected with the candidate selected (Mann 1985).

5. The Fairness Commission and the 1988 Nominating Process

In 1984, Walter Mondale benefited from the rules promulgated by the Hunt Commission. As mentioned, the superdelegates were chosen early and most of them favored Mondale. Moreover, Mondale did very well in those states that held loophole primaries, that is, winner-take-all or winner-take-more primaries.[5] As a result, Mondale had a higher percentage of delegates to the 1984 convention than his voting strength in the primaries or first-round **caucuses** would have dictated.

CAUCUSES

Meetings of party members at which presidential preferences are expressed and those representing preferred candidates are selected to reflect those views.

The losing candidates at the 1984 convention—Senator Gary Hart and Reverend Jesse Jackson—were upset by the advantage that the rules had given to Mondale. As a consequence, they called for a new reform commission, a so-called Fairness Commission, to examine what steps could be taken to respond to their complaints. The Mondale forces, magnanimous in victory at the convention, acceded to their request for a new study.

By the time the Fairness Commission began its work, a number of factors had changed. First, Mondale had been badly beaten in the presidential election. Second, Hart and Jackson had lost some of their concern for this particular part of the process. Third, Paul Kirk had become chair of the Democratic National Committee and was intent on strengthening the party. He viewed an increased role for party and elected officials as important in building a strong party.

The Fairness Commission finished its work by November 1985. According to commission chairman Donald L. Fowler, a long-time party activist from South Carolina, "There was a recognition that the 1984 rules worked pretty well and there was no reason to change a lot" (Cook 1986, 2158). The commission increased the number of party and elected officials who would be delegates to the 1988 Democratic National Convention, granting superdelegate status to all members of the Democratic National Committee (not just state party chairs and vice chairs as had been the case in 1984) and to 80 percent of the Democratic members of Congress (up from 60 percent in 1984). While the commission did lower the share of the vote that a candidate must receive in order to qualify for delegates to 15 percent from the 20 percent it had been in some states—a move in the direction favored by the Hart and Jackson forces at the 1984 convention—the ability of states to hold winner-take-all or winner-take-more primaries was reaffirmed. None of these was the kind of fundamental changes that the Hart and Jackson forces had originally sought.

In short, the commission adopted a strategic position, seeking to improve the chances that the 1988 Democratic nominee would emerge from the process of gaining the party's nod without hurting his chances of winning the general election. The goal for 1988 was to create a process that would bring more people into line behind the Democratic party candidate. New Hampshire and Iowa were permitted to keep their early dates for their primary and caucus, respectively; Wisconsin Democrats were even permitted to reinstitute their open primary, which had been ruled out some years earlier. No party obstacles were to stand in the way of Democrats being happy with the Democratic candidate.

However, while the party rules were not changed as a result of the 1984 nominating process, some states did alter their laws in ways that had a fundamental effect on the 1988 process. In 1984, the second Tuesday in March had been referred to in the press as **Super Tuesday**, because a large number of delegates were selected on that day. Many viewed the influence of the states holding primaries on that date (or caucuses within that week) as having been significantly increased. Mondale's victories in Georgia and Alabama allowed him to begin the process of turning back the tide that Hart had begun to mount in Iowa and New Hampshire.

SUPER TUESDAY

The Tuesday during the primary season on which the most delegates are chosen.

Southern politicians hit upon the strategy of concentrating their delegate selection processes early in the nominating season in order to maximize their influence. They felt that the voice of the South would be heard most loudly if the entire southern chorus sang at the same time. Thus southern state after southern state took the steps necessary to move its delegate selection process up to the second week in March 1988. This effort was led by influential southern governors like Robert Graham of Florida, Richard Riley of South Carolina, Mark White of Texas, and ex-governor Charles Robb of Virginia. Eventually twenty-one states—including fourteen southern or border states—chose convention delegates during this one-week period; more than a quarter of the delegates to the 1988 Democratic Convention and more than 35 percent of those elected to the Republican Convention were chosen during this single period.[6]

This change was as significant as any rule changes in recent years. Candidates and their strategists had to rethink how the early stages of the nominating process were to be organized. As with many "reforms," unintended consequences are often as apparent as intended consequences. For Democrats, the "winners" of the Super Tuesday sweepstakes were Mike Dukakis and Jesse Jackson as well as Tennessee senator Al Gore, who took up the mantle of the southern moderates. Clearly, devising a system to help Dukakis and Jackson was not what the southern governors pushing this change had in mind. For Republicans the clear winner was George Bush, who had more than 60 percent of the delegates needed to be nominated by the end of balloting on Super Tuesday. Again, Bush was not the candidate most reformers thought would have benefited from this change.

However, the reforms can be looked at in another way. The 1984 process in the Democratic party had produced a candidate who represented the mainstream of the party. He might have lost badly in November, and he might not have achieved the nomination with the ease he desired, but the process had avoided nominating an extremist or nominating an outsider. The election of 1988 was the first in twenty years in which an incumbent president was not eligible for reelection. Each party sought to nominate a candidate who could bring the faithful together to achieve victory in November. And each aptly did that. The process worked as theorists of political parties would want it to work. As Gerald Pomper (1989, 33) has written:

> To achieve victory, they seek politically adept but inoffensive candidates and pursue party unity by conciliating diverse factions, promoting agreement on public policies, and focusing party members' efforts on effective campaigns. . . . In nominating Michael Dukakis and George Bush, they chose two men who were experienced politicians with extensive records of public service, men who, if not stirring, were at least acceptable to tens of millions of their party's voters.

D. The Reform Movement: An Assessment

Compare the experience of the Democrats with that of the Republicans. We have just discussed four major reform commissions (and one minor one after 1988) in the Democratic party. The Republicans by contrast have been blissfully happy with their system. This is not to suggest that they have not had reform commissions. One was established at the behest of former president Eisenhower after the 1964 Republican Convention appeared on television. A second, the DO (Delegates and Organizations) Committee, established after the 1968 convention, was dominated by members of the Republican National Committee and dealt with no controversial matters. A third, the Rule 20 Committee, chaired by the late William R. Steiger, a moderate Republican congressman from Wisconsin (1967–1978), dealt with disclosing campaign expenditures by Republican candidates and with opening up the party to broader participation.

A number of factors distinguish Republican reform efforts from Democratic. First, Republicans, even when their nomination has been hotly contested, have not divided their party because of the nominating process. Each of the Republican nominees between 1968 and 1988 had a united party behind him once the convention had reached its decision.

Second, Republican "reforms" have been suggestions, not mandates. Philosophically the Republicans do not believe that the national party should dictate to the states. Certainly they do not believe that a committee of reformers should dictate procedures. The Republican party rules state clearly that the convention is the governing authority. Only the convention can change the rules. Thus any reform would have to be ratified by one convention to take effect in the process four years hence. As it is quite difficult to foresee the impact of some of these reforms, the lack of predictable detrimental political consequences has taken much of the sting out of Republican reform efforts.

However, the Republican process has changed significantly because some of the changes wrought by the Democrats have resulted in changes in state laws that also impact on the Republicans. Look at table 9.1. In 1968, sixteen states chose delegates to the Republican National Convention through the primary process, making up 34 percent of the delegates. By 1988, these numbers had changed to thirty-five states holding primaries and 77 percent of the delegates being chosen in that manner. The Democrats instituted the changes and caused states to change their election laws accordingly. Therefore, the Republicans were forced to follow suit. The Ford nomination battle in 1976, Reagan's in 1980, and Bush's in 1988 were fought and won under rules very different from those in effect when Barry Goldwater captured the heart of the Republican party in 1964.

The reforms begun in 1968 have fundamentally changed the ways in which the two parties nominate their presidential candidates. The conventional wisdom before 1968 was that party leaders in large states had the most influence over the nominations. The conventional wisdom by 1988 was that the process is open and that demonstrated success in attracting voters will be necessary in order to win. The delegates to the national conventions are now representatives of those who have participated in the process, not stand-ins for party bosses.

Party leaders and elected officeholders still retain influence, but the change in their role in the last forty years may provide a perfect example of the difference between influence and power. The strategic premises of presidential contenders in 1960 were not very different from those of 1948 nor for that matter from those of 1928. But since 1968, the situation has been one of continual flux. Winning in the

Table 9.1 Number of Presidential Primaries and the Percentage of Delegates Selected in Them, 1968–1996

	Democrats		*Republicans*	
Election Year	*No. of Primaries*	*% of Delegates*	*No. of Primaries*	*% of Delegates*
1968	17	38	16	34
1972	23	61	22	53
1976	29	73	28	68
1980	31	75	35	74
1984	234	61	23	54
1988	34	85	35	77
1992	40	87	39	84
1996	35	87	43	90

Source: Wayne 1996; 1996 data from Stephen Wayne.

reformed system involves mastering the rules, reading the political lay of the land, and learning the right lessons from the most recent contests, including lessons about the timing of primaries.

Critics claimed that the reforms after 1968 were harmful to the parties, particularly to the Democrats (Kirkpatrick 1976; 1978; Polsby 1983). By contrast, I would argue that the reform process, begun after 1968 but continuing for two decades, had a positive effect on the parties. Although party leaders can no longer dictate whom the nominees will be, the process involves many more people in the work of the parties and gives them a stake in the nominees. The process has evolved in such a way that party leaders themselves are now comfortable that successful nominees will emerge strengthened as candidates, not weakened, by the road taken to their nomination.

II. NOMINATIONS UNDER THE CURRENT SYSTEM: 1992 AND 1996

A. The 1992 Nominations

Thus in 1988 the system worked as it was designed. Party leaders looked at the results—and while the Democrats might have been dismayed by Dukakis's showing in the general election—they were satisfied with how he was nominated. The only rule changes for the 1992 process involved guaranteeing proportional representation of presidential preference for all states' systems, removing the vestiges of loopholes.

Once again, however, various states, worrying that they did not have enough influence, sought to move earlier in the process. Because a number of states have moved earlier in the process, and because some southern states have opted out of the early primary, the uniquely southern flavor of Super Tuesday has been diluted. In 1992, candidates for nomination faced a three-week period in March in which twenty-three states chose a total of over 1,700 convention delegates, nearly 40 percent of the total. This concentration of delegate selection had an important impact on the selection of each party's nominee.

President Bush should have been a shoo-in for his party's nomination. His popularity in the nation had peaked at over 90 percent after the victory in the Persian Gulf War. But Bush was challenged by conservative activist Patrick Buchanan, who claimed that the president was not living up to the legacy of Ronald Reagan. Buchanan attacked Bush for compromising with the Democrats on budgetary matters, for raising taxes, and for failing to take the lead on the conservative social agenda. Buchanan hoped to show Bush's vulnerability in the early states and then gain momentum from there. Buchanan struck a chord with some of the most conservative Republican voters and frightened President Bush into moving toward the right. However, despite providing evidence that Bush was vulnerable by holding him to just over 50 percent in the New Hampshire primary, Buchanan could not make real inroads toward the nomination because the president's organizational and financial advantages in the large number of primaries held on Super Tuesday overwhelmed Buchanan's insurgent efforts. Buchanan remained a candidate throughout the primary season and was an important factor at the Republican Convention in 1992. But his chances for victory, always slim, were reduced considerably by the large number of states in which delegate contests were all held on Super Tuesday.

The Democratic nomination contest in 1992 was complicated by the fact that President Bush seemed unassailable throughout much of 1991, when campaigns for the presidency are usually gearing up. Most of the Democrats thought to be the most serious contenders for their party's nomination opted not to run. One after another of the top candidates—Senators Bill Bradley from New Jersey, Lloyd Bentsen from Texas, and Jay Rockefeller from West Virginia; House majority leader Richard Gephardt from Missouri; New York governor Mario Cuomo; and 1984 and 1988 candidate Jesse Jackson—all announced that they would not seek their party's nod to oppose the president. Of those most often mentioned in 1991, only Arkansas governor Bill Clinton, thought by most to be an outsider among the top contenders, eventually declared his candidacy. Clinton was the candidate of the moderate wing of the Democratic party. A founder of the **Democratic Leadership Council (DLC)**, Clinton was one of the southern leaders who felt that the party had become too closely associated with unpopular liberal views to win a national election. He sought to give expression to that position through his candidacy.

DEMOCRATIC LEADERSHIP COUNCIL (DLC)

An organization of moderate Democrats formed in order to bring the party back from the liberal extreme toward the center.

Because the better-known candidates dropped out, Clinton rose to the top of the eventual field that included Senators Tom Harkin from Iowa and Bob Kerrey from Nebraska, former Massachusetts senator Paul Tsongas; former California governor Jerry Brown; and L. Douglas

Wilder, Virginia's first African-American governor. Clinton was considered the front-runner, if only because he was the candidate the others sought to beat. In New Hampshire, Clinton's campaign was nearly thrown off course when charges of marital infidelity were aired just before the primary. However, Clinton recovered and finished a very respectable second to Paul Tsongas, whose showing made him a serious contender. The other candidates were in serious trouble. Wilder dropped out even before New Hampshire, when his poll numbers never exceeded 2 or 3 percent, and he was unable to capture the support of Jesse Jackson's followers. Harkin and Kerrey fought for third in New Hampshire but finished well back of Tsongas and Clinton. Brown's somewhat quixotic campaign failed to catch fire.

Again for the Democrats the decisive moment occurred on Super Tuesday, March 10, 1992. On that day twelve states held their nominating contests. Clinton won decisively in seven of them; Tsongas won only in his native Massachusetts and in neighboring Rhode Island. By the end of that day, Clinton had amassed over seven hundred delegates; no other candidate was in striking distance. Following Clinton wins in Michigan and Illinois one week later, the battle was all but over. Brown did score an upset victory in Connecticut later in March, but the eventual outcome of the process was no longer in doubt. Party leaders may not have been comfortable with Bill Clinton—and many sought alternative candidates, none of whom emerged—but they had established a process that permitted the leading contender to vanquish his opponents quite early in the process.

B. The 1996 Nominations

Once again in 1996 the process had important consequences for the eventual choice of nominees. For President Bill Clinton, the nomination was assured when no prominent Democrats chose to oppose him. Early in 1995, on the heels of the Republican victory in the 1994 congressional elections and with investigations of potential scandals hounding his White House, it seemed likely that Clinton would be challenged within his own party. However, the president recovered in 1995, standing up to the Republicans over the government shutdown, defying conventional political judgment by sending American troops into action in Bosnia, and leading the nation in its response to the Oklahoma City bombing. Clinton appeared tough, seasoned, and "presidential." In addition he had accumulated a vast campaign war chest aimed as dissuading any potential challengers. None emerged.

The shape of the Republican primary field in 1996, as had been the case with the Democrats in 1992, was defined by the candidate who chose not to run. Retired army general Colin L. Powell Jr. captured the imagination of the nation and certainly of the nation's press in 1995.

Trial heat polls showed him running ahead of President Clinton, were he the Republican nominee. While not discouraging such attention, Powell did not declare his candidacy, nor did he reveal his party affiliation. Other Republicans, most notably Senate majority leader Bob Dole of Kansas, were off and running; but the nature of the campaign awaited Powell's decision. Finally, in November 1995, Powell made a dual announcement—that he was a Republican and that he would not seek the presidency in 1996. The GOP campaign then began in earnest.

Senator Dole, his party's nominee for the vice presidency in 1976 and an unsuccessful candidate for the presidential nomination in 1980 and 1988, organized early and raised a great deal of money. He was the clear leader, representing the establishment, the core of the Republican party. But his candidacy would not go unchallenged. Contenders included Texas senator Phil Gramm, who represented the more conservative segment of the Republican party on economic issues; 1988 candidate and television commentator Pat Buchanan, who again championed the social conservatives within the party; former Tennessee governor Lamar Alexander, who claimed that he was better able to beat Bill Clinton than the seventy-two-year-old Dole; and millionaire magazine publisher Steve Forbes, who had a rather simple message (advocacy of a flat tax) and ample personal funds with which to communicate it.

The process was very important in this contest. First, two states, Alaska and Louisiana, tried to preempt Iowa and New Hampshire by holding first rounds of their delegate selection processes even earlier than those in the traditional states. Most candidates ignored these contests, but Phil Gramm made a grave strategic error by predicting that he would do well in Louisiana, the state neighboring his native Texas. When he did poorly there and in New Hampshire, his campaign was essentially over. Buchanan nearly beat Dole in the Iowa caucuses and did beat him in New Hampshire; these states gave his campaign a boost and seemed to presage Dole's weakness. Alexander finished a strong third in New Hampshire, but his campaign never took off from there; how could he be better than Dole at facing Clinton if he could not beat Dole? Forbes was disappointed in his early showings but rebounded with victories in Delaware and Arizona, both in late February.

But then the Super Tuesday phenomenon reemerged. Fourteen states held caucuses or primaries between March 3 and March 5; six others held their contests on March 12. Bob Dole won every one of those contests.[7] In the Republican party, states can still opt for winner-take-all systems. At the beginning of March, Bob Dole had only twenty-seven delegates pledged to his candidacy; the other candidates had a total of over a hundred. By the middle of the month, Dole had 710 delegates; the others only 144. The nomination contest was over. The process had once again aided the front-runner to win the nomination early in the process and to enter the convention with a united party.

C. Toward 2000

In the year 2000, as in 1988, no incumbent will be seeking reelection. Once again the two major parties want a system that will permit their nominee to emerge with as little intraparty rancor as possible. There is little talk of changing the fundamental system that has been in place for the last four nominating cycles.

As in the recent past, various states are seeking to increase their influence over the party nominations. At their annual meeting in 1998, the secretaries of state of the various states (these are the officials in most states responsible for administering elections) discussed means of rationalizing the primary and caucus calendars. It seems unlikely that they will succeed in their efforts in time to affect the contest in 2000, however. Thus the calendar will be decided by various state legislatures acting in their own interests, or in a way thought to improve the chances of candidates favored by those controlling the legislatures.

In September 1998, the California legislature passed, and Governor Pete Wilson signed, legislation to move the California primary up to March 7, the first Tuesday in March. The chairman of the state Democratic Party, former state senator Art Torres, boasted that "California's shadow is now on the snows of New Hampshire's presidential primary" (Purdam 1998). Oregon and Washington are considering similar moves to create an early West Coast primary. New York has also set its primary for March 7.

While the calendars have not yet been determined, most observers feel that large numbers of states in various regions will cooperate to have their primaries on the same date, emulating the strategy that southern leaders first followed in 1984. The fear is that a number of regions might all decide to go for an early primary date, perhaps as early as March 7, the first eligible date, the date California has chosen. To deter this from happening, the Republicans have decided to award bonus delegates to states that hold their primaries late in the process, but it is unclear that the relatively small numbers of delegates so awarded would be enough of a deterrent.

The timing of the more than fifty separate nominating events remains troubling. For decades solutions have been proposed—starting with the window concept, but also including **regional primaries**, specifying a limited number of primary or caucus dates among which states must choose, even a one-day national primary—but no consensus has emerged. The lack of consensus follows directly from recognition that timing decisions are not neutral decisions as far as various candidates are concerned. If one candidate sees a particular calendar to his or her advantage, surely other candidates will feel disadvantaged. And the battle over timing will be renewed.

REGIONAL PRIMARIES

Arrangement through which a number of states in the same geographic region hold their presidential preference primaries on the same day.

If a number of states or regions opt for early primaries or caucuses in 2000, one of two scenarios seems likely. Either one or both parties might determine their nominee at this time, with one front-runner eliminating all others. Or no front-runner might emerge—again in one party or the other or both—and the eventual nominee(s) will be chosen by the much smaller number of voters whose states have opted for later primaries. In this latter scenario, it is not impossible that the conventions could play a real role in the nominating process, a situation that has not eventuated since the Republican Convention of 1976.

Merely raising these scenarios points to the importance of looking at how potential nominees run their campaigns to be the standard-bearer. The basic outlines of the system are known to all who participate, but strategic judgment (as well as context) often separates winners from losers.

III. STRATEGIC CONSIDERATIONS IN THE CONTESTS FOR NOMINATIONS

The nomination process is, by its very nature, complex. The goal for the two major parties at this stage is to winnow the field of potential presidents down from all those eligible to two—one Democrat and one Republican. What criteria are used? Obviously a principal concern is to find an individual qualified to hold the office, but that concern is for naught if the individual cannot win the general election. Thus the parties are looking for the individual who will be the best candidate and the best president. Those are separate jobs that call for different skills. Why would one think, for example, that the person who is best at campaigning on television or at raising money for a campaign would also have the skills necessary to negotiate with the leaders of other nations or to craft compromises that could be accepted by a Congress controlled by leaders of the other party? How should those skills be combined?

Perhaps a group of politicos reasoning together could arrive at the perfect mixture of skills and seek the best-qualified individual. But that is not the nature of our political system. The individuals selected are selected through a political process. More accurately, they are chosen through different political processes in each of the fifty states (and the District of Columbia and various other areas). And they are chosen by a large number of participants, each of whom is free to choose based on his or her own conception of how the choice should be made. It is small wonder then that the process is characterized most by complexity.

Presidential contenders must face a complex process, with uncertain dynamics. They do not control the order of events, though they do have some say in the importance they attribute to different events. They do not control others' perceptions of events. To a large extent they proceed by instinct; success or failure is often a function of the acuity of their political instincts and those of their advisers. Politicians as a group are firm believers in learning the lessons of the past. Given that, it is somewhat unbelievable how many politicians have learned the wrong lessons from even very recent experiences. But others have clearly benefited from understanding what happened to others facing similar situations. In the following sections, we will examine some of the strategic considerations facing today's would-be candidates as they try to decipher the presidential nominating process.

A. The Political Calendar

Perhaps the most important lesson that candidates and their staff must learn is that the calendar of events is critical to success or failure. Past examples cannot be followed if those examples are drawn from contests run with different calendars. Three concepts dominate calendar considerations under the current system. Each must be understood if appropriate and effective strategies are to be adopted.

1. Front-loading the System

FRONT-LOADING

The practice of holding primaries and caucuses near the beginning of the period in which such events are permitted.

Front-loading refers to holding a large number of primaries and caucuses, contests in which a significant number of delegates are selected, early in the political year. Rules in both parties call for all contests to select delegates to the national conventions, to be held between the first Tuesday in March and the first Tuesday in June of the presidential election year. New Hampshire and Iowa have traditionally been given exemptions from these rules, but only by one and two weeks, respectively. All other states must hold their contests in the window provided by party rules.

A number of states—and some political reformers—have felt that Iowa and New Hampshire have more influence on the process than they should. After all, the citizens in these states are not representative of either party's voters, nor of the nation as a whole. However, because they have been permitted to hold their contests first, when no other states compete for attention, candidates have spent an inordinate amount of time there. The media has devoted a disproportionate amount of attention to the contests in these states (Orren and Polsby 1987).

Partially in response to the prominence of Iowa and New Hampshire, and certainly as a means to increase their influence, a number of states decided to hold their primaries early in the 1984 nominating season. In part this strategy was an effort to help the Democratic front-runner, Walter Mondale. In part it was so these states could influence the process before it was over. The theory held that candidates, like Jimmy Carter in 1976, benefited from wins in Iowa and New Hampshire because they used the momentum gained from victories there to raise money and enhance their organizations before the next round of primaries. If the time between the first wins and subsequent primaries were reduced, the impact of the early contests would similarly be lessened. Candidates would have to be organized in the states whose contests followed closely on the heels of Iowa and New Hampshire, or they would not have time to wage effective campaigns. The result was the first movement toward front-loading the system.

In 1988, when southern politicians came together to organize a southern Super Tuesday primary, they chose an early March date as well. While they did not have the influence on the process they intended, as discussed earlier, they were able to see the impact of holding contests early. In 1992 nineteen states had held their primaries by the end of March, and first-round caucuses had been held in twelve others. In 1996 twenty-nine state held primaries by the end of March; all of the states that held caucuses had held their first round by that time. And, as already noted, there is evidence that a number of other states are moving in the same direction.

2. *Super Tuesday*

Super Tuesday was originally invented to give more influence to the South. However, changes in the political calendar have altered its influence. In 1992, March 10 was clearly Super Tuesday. Eight states held their primaries on that day—six southern or border states, plus Massachusetts and Rhode Island. In 1996, eight states held primaries on March 5—five New England states plus Georgia, Maryland, and Colorado. Seven states, with more delegates among them, held their primaries one week later.

Thus the concept of Super Tuesday is an evolving one. It is now closely linked with the concept of regional primaries. Regional primaries represent efforts by state officials to enhance the influence of a region by holding all of that region's primaries on one day—or within a week, if one includes the caucus states. Regional primaries hold an advantage for candidates as well. Because candidates want to appear in as many places holding primaries as possible, it is to their advantage to cluster primaries geographically, to cut down on travel time and costs. Also, because many media markets cross state lines, it is more possible to piggyback one's advertising budget if primaries in neighboring states, parts of which might well be in the same media market, are held on the same day.

3. Filing Deadlines

Each state specifies how a candidate wins a place on its primary ballot. In some cases the decision is made by a state official. In other cases the presidential candidates must file slates of proposed delegates. In still other cases the delegates themselves must file petitions to be on the ballot. The variety of requirements is almost endless. But each state, according to its own laws, specifies a certain date by which those who seek a place on the ballot must have fulfilled whatever requirements exist. **Filing deadlines** are a necessity so that ballots can be printed in advance of an election. But filing deadlines also have strategic implications. Anyone who does not meet a state's filing deadline cannot win delegates in that state. In 1984, for instance, Gary Hart was unable to gain the momentum he might have from his New Hampshire victory over front-runner Walter Mondale because Hart's campaign had failed to file delegate slates in many of the districts in Florida, a delegate-rich state whose primary followed shortly after New Hampshire's. A national campaign organization is important for a prospective presidential nominee in that someone can keep track of approaching deadlines and alert state campaigners, who are often rank amateurs, to their approach.

FILING DEADLINES
The dates by which candidates must fulfill whatever requirements exist to gain a place on a ballot.

4. Strategic Implications of the Political Calendar

Recent campaign experience has demonstrated conclusively that the political calendar has serious implications for campaign strategy. In 1992, for example, many of the first tier of Democratic candidates held back because they feared President Bush's strength as a candidate. Bill Clinton stepped into that void and became the front-runner. However, he looked like a flawed candidate, as his character and ethics were attacked during the New Hampshire primary. Many party leaders tried to urge one or more of those who had earlier decided not to run that it was time to step in. But it was too late to step in. By the time the New Hampshire primary was held, filing deadlines had passed in most of the states that would elect delegates in March and April. It was already too late to raise money and organize a campaign in those states that would hold primaries on the first two Tuesdays in March.

When Clinton stumbled again, at the Connecticut primary in late March, party leaders looked for an alternative. But the die was cast. Clinton had already amassed an insurmountable lead in delegates. Those familiar with the rules understood that he could not be beaten.

The concentration of many caucuses and primaries on the same day—whether it be Super Tuesday or Junior Tuesday, as the second most important day has come to be called—also has important implications. In the old system, when fewer states held primaries and they were spread out over the political calendar, it was possible for a candidate's organization to get by with a skeletal crew, moving key campaign operatives from one important primary state to another, after the first's contest had been held. However, under the new rules and calendar, a candidate to be successful must build a national organization from the start. If not, he will be overwhelmed by an opponent who has. Patrick Buchanan faced that harsh reality in 1992. He apparently did not learn from his loss to President Bush because he repeated the losing strategy in 1996. In that nominating contest, Bob Dole prevailed, despite poor showings in some of the earliest contests, because he had an organization that was strong enough to contest all of the primaries held in the first two weeks in March. No other candidate could do so. No other candidate survived that oppressive time on the political calendar.

B. The Rules of the Game

George McGovern's 1972 campaign will always stand as the example of a campaign that understood the rules and won because of how they were implemented. But in interesting ways that lesson has been repeated over and over again in the reform era. If there is a real lesson here, it is that campaign strategists ignore whatever rules are in effect at their peril. Although many rules were altered by state law changes in order to meet Democratic party mandates, there are still important areas in which the two parties' rules differ—with very significant consequences for the candidates.

1. Proportional Representation versus Winner-Take-All Systems

The Democratic party insists that delegates be apportioned according to the presidential preference of those voters participating in the process. While certain loopholes have been permitted, the basic concept of delegate strength reflecting proportional strength among the voters has been maintained. The Republicans, on the other hand, have not followed the Democrats' lead. They have maintained a system that permits states to run winner-take-all primaries should they choose to do so. Each system has strengths and weaknesses; decidedly each has strategic implications.

Consider the Democrats. If one is on the ballot in a system that gives delegates proportionately to the strength at the ballot box, a candidate can "lose" an election but still pick up delegate support. As the nominee is the person with a majority of the delegates, close losses can be important "victories." In 1976, Jimmy Carter ran everywhere. He picked up some delegates everywhere. Even when Democrats seemed to be tiring of Carter, as the primaries drew to a close, he picked up delegates. Few recall that Carter lost five of the last seven primaries. What is remembered is that he had guaranteed himself a majority of the delegates at the convention on the day the primary process ended. He did so by winning delegates in primaries that he lost. Similarly, in 1992 Bill Clinton continued to gain strength when he lost primaries, with the result that unexpected victories by Jerry Brown as the process wore on did not encourage new opposition. Savvy politicians understood that Clinton would win the nomination by attrition, even if not by acclamation. Thus they joined his bandwagon.

But proportional representation could work in another way, one much less beneficial to the front-running candidate. In recent contests the Democrats have had one leader and other candidates trying to make themselves into the one principal opponent. The leader has prevailed by successfully playing off other candidates against each other and amassing delegate support. Imagine a scenario in which there are two or three equally well-positioned candidates. Further, imagine that the front-loaded system persists. If two or even three candidates emerge from the early round of primaries in competitive positions, with enough money and organization to see themselves through the process, or if their resources are equally depleted (see section C, "Strategic Use of Campaign Resources," p. 292), then proportional representation might well mean that no one candidate can garner the support of a majority of the delegates before the convention. That scenario was envisioned by many before the Carter nomination in 1976, but it did not eventuate that year and has not since. However, serious strategists and analysts must consider the possibility as they plan a nominating campaign.

What about the Republicans? As mentioned earlier, the winner-take-all system proved to be a huge advantage for Bob Dole. When there is a front-runner with a strong financial and organizational base, a winner-take-all system allows that front-runner to dispense with pesky challengers quite easily. George Bush did it in 1992; Bob Dole did it in 1996. There is no question that the system benefits the leaders. It allows the eventual nominee to have more time to bring the party together, united behind his candidacy.

But what if the leader is not likely to be a winner in November? What if the early primaries reveal hitherto unnoted weaknesses or a lack of voter appeal? The same system makes it difficult to change course in midstream. And again, the Dole example is a good one. Bob Dole was the prohibitive favorite for the GOP nomination from the time that Colin Powell declared himself a noncandidate. But the Dole candidacy looked weak at many points in the early caucuses and primaries. As noted, the political calendar worked in his favor. But so too did the winner-take-all provisions in the rules of most states that held primaries in March 1996. In those primaries Dole never won more than two-thirds of the votes (albeit an impressive number) and on six occasions he won less than half of the votes, but in many states he won all of the delegates. The system exaggerated his strength and downplayed campaign weaknesses that would later become apparent.

2. Superdelegates versus Influential Party Leaders

Recall that the "add-on" delegates and the superdelegates were put back into the Democratic party process because influential party leaders and elected officials chose not to participate in the nominating process after the McGovern-Fraser reforms were implemented. These leaders refused to participate because they did not want their local reputations to be sullied by having backed a losing national candidate. Decisions not to back presidential candidates did not follow from lack of interest but rather from strategic considerations. Either an elected leader would beat some of his or her own constituents in a contest to be a convention delegate or he or she might lose. Neither was a good outcome. Thus many decided to opt out altogether; few party leaders were represented at the 1972, 1976, or even 1980 Democratic conventions.

The Republicans never faced the same problems. Because they allowed unpledged slates to run and because they did not require fair reflection of presidential preference, influential Republicans have continued to play a key role in their party's nominating process throughout the entire reform period. Most would argue that they have done so to the benefit of their party's candidates.

From the perspective of this discussion, what is important is the strategic differences that the two systems call for. The Republican process is not very different from what it has been in the past. Perspective candidates want party leaders and elected officials to support their candidacies. When Bob Dole was endorsed by New Hampshire governor Steve Merrill, political observers throughout the nation knew that Dole had an important ally in the first primary. The same could be said of Senator Alphonse D'Amato in New York, of Governor George Voinivich in Ohio, and of other influential Republican leaders. A presidential candidate is wise to spend his time courting those who have influence in their own states because they can frequently turn that influence into delegate support.

Democratic party leaders tend to hold back support. Their role is supposed to be that of a broker, to be certain that popular participation in the convention does not run away with the party. Thus the superdelegates were extremely important in helping Walter Mondale secure the party nomination in 1984; those who had worked closely with Gary Hart did not see him as presidential material. Similarly, superdelegates worked against Jesse Jackson in his two bids for the Democratic nomination. He won support from the Congressional Black Caucus (though not from all of its members), but he was not able to attract a wider following among the party leadership. Democratic campaigns for party leader and elected official support is more subtle than that in the Republican party. Each individual is courted for his or her own support, not because he or she can necessarily translate that support to a wider following.

On the other hand, the support of the superdelegates viewed as a whole is an important element in the democratic process. When selected superdelegates declared for Bill Clinton in 1992, they were essentially conceding him the race. Their support said that they knew whom the winner would be and that they wanted to be on his team.

The superdelegates and the party officials who have been added to state delegations have never played the brokering role that was intended for them. Again, however, that is not to say that a scenario could not eventuate that would necessitate that role. The brokered convention is a thing of the past according to most analysts. But if no nominee has a majority—or a near majority—of delegate support when a convention is called to order, no strategist and no contemporary analyst has a historical precedent to rely on to see what might happen. It seems very likely that the party elite would emerge as leaders in such a situation.

C. Strategic Use of Campaign Resources

Any serious candidate for president starts the campaign possessing certain resources. Others can be obtained. Still others must be done without. Campaign strategists are often in the business of resource management.

1. Office

The key resource to hold if one wants a presidential nomination seems to be the White House. Eligible incumbent presidents are normally renominated. Renomination may be semiautomatic, resembling coronations, as in the cases of Richard Nixon in 1972, Ronald Reagan in 1984, and Bill Clinton in 1996. Or renomination may require a battle, as was the case with Gerald Ford in 1976, Jimmy Carter in 1980, and George Bush in 1992.

These latter cases are particularly instructive. Gerald Ford nearly lost the nomination to Ronald Reagan in 1976. Ford was not very successful at using the office, largely because he had not become used to the office and had not had time to learn from it. Further, Ford had not earned the office through election; thus, he did not have the loyalty of legions of politicians who owed office to him, as does a president elected in his own right. However, it is doubtful that Ford ever could have competed with Ronald Reagan if he did not have his incumbency to rely on (Witcover 1977).

Carter used the White House to defeat Senator Kennedy. He played a Rose Garden strategy, claiming to be too busy to campaign, for as long as it suited him. At the same time he used the resources of his office—the pulpit from which to speak, cabinet officers to serve as surrogates, federal grants to remind voters of his service—to enhance his campaign. When the situation suited his political purpose, he emerged from the Rose Garden, campaigning with all the trappings of the office to which he had been elected (Germond and Witcover 1981).

As noted earlier, Bush was challenged by Patrick Buchanan, who claimed that as president Bush had not been a faithful successor in upholding Ronald Reagan's conservative agenda. Bush felt insecure about his own party base and was uncomfortable with the degree of strength Buchanan showed in some of the early primaries. Thus he responded to Buchanan, attacking him and positioning himself further toward the right on the political spectrum. Bush was able to use the power of his office to defeat Buchanan, but he was not secure enough in that power to dismiss him presumptively as others had done.

Other offices have also proved useful. The vice presidency seems to be something of a mixed blessing. Seven out of the last ten vice presidents have either succeeded to the presidency or sought that office themselves.[8] For Vice President Mondale his service under Jimmy Carter was something of a mixed blessing. He was considered an excellent vice president, gained a good deal of national exposure, and built a wide range of political contacts during his four years in office. However, he was also saddled with the legacy of a failed presidency and with defending policies for which he was not, in fact, responsible.

On the other hand, Vice President Bush, in 1988, had a tremendous advantage. His only problem was to convince Reagan supporters that he was not only a loyal lieutenant but also a worthy heir. That problem continued to plague him as president as well.

As Vice President Al Gore strives for the Democratic nomination in 2000, he will be able to draw on the allegiance of loyal Democrats who appreciate the hard work he has done for the party over an eight-year period, but he will also have to deal with the legacy of Bill Clinton and the residual consequences of the scandals, including fund-raising scandals in which Gore was involved, that plagued the Clinton presidency.

For some time the Senate was thought to be the incubator of presidential candidates. Twenty-five different senators have run for their party's presidential nomination since 1968 (see table 9.2). In 1980 Senator Howard Baker of Tennessee tried to parlay his prominence as Senate minority leader into a successful bid for his party's nomination. Senator Robert Dole did the same in 1988. Neither was successful. Baker found he was too busy in the Senate to campaign as effectively as those freed from day-to-day responsibility. Dole could not overcome the advantages that a sitting vice president had as heir apparent.

The Dole case may be most instructive. When he decided to seek his party's nomination again in 1996, Senator Dole was then the majority leader as Baker had been. Dole campaigned for a long period maintaining both positions. He hoped that the prominence of his role in the Senate would give him a public pulpit to compete with that of President Clinton. But when the Democrats in the Senate began to tie up his time with legislative haggling, Dole saw the Baker lesson more clearly. In May 1996 he announced that he would resign from the Senate to devote himself full-time to his presidential campaign. Dole's prominence in the Senate undoubtedly help him obtain the nomination, but it was impossible for him to continue to campaign and to hold his party's top Senate job as well. It is also important to note the experience of Jimmy Carter in 1976, Ronald Reagan in 1980, and Walter Mondale in 1984, all of

Table 9.2 Senators Seeking Their Party's Presidential Nomination, 1968–2000

1968
Robert F. Kennedy
Eugene McCarthy

1972
Vance Hartke
Hubert Humphrey
Henry Jackson
George McGovern
Edmund S. Muskie

1976
Birch Bayh
Lloyd Bentsen
Frank Church
Fred Harris
Hubert Humphrey
Henry Jackson

1980
Howard Baker
Robert Dole
Edward M. Kennedy

1984
Alan Cranston
John Glenn
Gary Hart
Ernest Hollings

1988
Joseph Biden
Robert Dole
Albert Gore
Gary Hart
Paul Simon

1992
Tom Harkin
Bob Kerrey

1996
Bob Dole
Phil Gramm
Richard Lugar
Arlen Specter

2000*
John McCain
Orrin Hatch
Bob Smith

*The field for 2000 has not been finalized at this time.

whom won presidential nominations while not holding other elective offices, as these seem to confirm Dole's perception.

On the other hand, Michael Dukakis won nomination in 1988 and Bill Clinton was nominated in 1992 while serving as state governors. Aren't the responsibilities of a sitting governor too burdensome to allow a race for the presidential nomination? Dukakis considered this question very seriously before deciding to enter the race. One key advantage he had was that Massachusetts is a heavily Democratic state; his party controlled the legislature, and his lieutenant governor was loyal to him. His top staff people could run the state government while he was campaigning (Black et al. 1988).

Bill Clinton faced a slightly different problem in that he had promised the citizens of Arkansas that he would serve his full term when he was reelected in 1990. But he was able to rationalize that his constituents would want him to take his best shot at the presidency and, like Dukakis, he did not face the burden of running a state in which a hostile opposition would take advantage of his absence (Ceaser and Busch 1993). The race would have been much harder for New York governor Mario Cuomo, who considered seeking the Democratic nomination in both 1988 and 1992. Cuomo was constantly bickering with his state's divided legislature over state policies. The Republicans in New York would have been anxious to argue over policies with an absent governor. Context is thus crucially important. Dukakis and Clinton, like Bush in 1988 and presumably Gore in 2000, could use their offices to their advantage, without worrying about constraints, but in today's complex world of governing, this situation may be more the exception than the rule.

2. *Money*

Running for a presidential nomination actually involves running more than fifty separate campaigns. The 1996 primary elections were held on fifteen different days, obviously with a number of primaries held on some of those days; first-round caucuses were held on six other days. Candidates had to monitor the selection of the individuals who would serve as convention delegates from the caucus states and many primary states as well as additional facets of the process. An enterprise this vast requires a complex organization, extensive travel by the candidate and staff, sophisticated information gathering and dissemination, and effective advertising. These require money.

Since the 1976 presidential nomination, all contenders for major-party nomination have been eligible for federal matching funds. (See chap. 11 for a detailed discussion of campaign financing in all elections.) In order to qualify for matching funds, candidates must meet certain minimal criteria, raising at least $5,000 in contributions of $250 or less in each of twenty states. After that, all gifts of $250 or less are matched from the Presidential Election Campaign Fund, provided that

Table 9.3 Spending by Candidates for Presidential Nominations, 1996

Candidate	*Federal Matching Funds*	*Individual Contributions Minus Refunds*	*Party Contributions Minus Refunds*	*Other Cmte. Contributions Minus Refunds*	*Candidate Contributions*	*Adjusted Campaign Total*
DEMOCRATS						
Clinton	$13,412,197	$28,285,108	$1,861	$40,580	$0	$42,489,548
LaRouche	$624,691	$3,058,562	$0	$1,000	$0	$3,684,253
REPUBLICANS						
Alexander	$4,573,442	$12,635,615	$0	$286,766	$9,583	$17,614,978
Buchanan	$9,812,517	$14,659,228	$0	$18,280	$0	$24,501,176
Dole	$13,545,770	$29,555,502	$1,000	$1,208,655	$0	$44,604,092
Dornan	$0	$297,511	$0	$1,000	$0	$346,885
Forbes	$0	$4,203,792	$0	$2,000	$1,000	$41,693,481
Gramm	$7,356,218	$15,880,676	$1,987	$400,879	$0	$28,791,502
Keyes	$892,436	$3,442,056	$501	$3,500	$2,500	$4,348,165
Lugar	$2,643,477	$4,803,612	$6,250	$129,015	$0	$7,769,383
Specter	$1,010,455	$2,284,901	$0	$158,791	$0	$3,490,295
Taylor	$0	$37,854	$0	$0	$3,342	$6,516,850
Wilson	$1,724,254	$5,285,889	$0	$242,349	$0	$7,363,215

(Continued)

OTHER PARTY						
Browne	$0	$1,112,482	$1,144	$100	$34,271	$1,147,997
Hagelin	$358,883	$700,085	$100	$0	$15,250	$1,124,318
Perot	$0	$82,781	$0	$0	$8,215,746	$8,298,527
Lamm	$0	$140,281	$0	$0	$5,000	$170,281
Democratic Subtotal	$14,036,888	$31,343,670	$1,861	$41,580	$0	$46,173,801
Republican Subtotal	$41,558,569	$93,086,636	$9,738	$2,451,235	$16,425	$187,040,022
Other Subtotal	$358,883	$2,035,629	$1,244	$100	$8,270,267	$10,741,123
Grand Total	$55,954,340	$126,465,935	$12,843	$2,492,915	$8,286,692	$243,954,946

Source: Federal Election Commission.

the candidate complies with certain overall and state-by-state spending restrictions and does not receive less than 10 percent of the vote in two consecutive presidential primaries in which he or she is running. When Steve Forbes decided to forgo federal funding and finance his own campaign in 1996, he became only the second candidate in twenty years to do so.[9] And as table 9.3 reveals, these candidates have spent a good deal of money.

Money as a resource for candidates provides opportunities and causes problems. First, in recent years, the ability to qualify for matching funds has become the first test of a serious candidacy. Candidates since 1984 tried to have the money needed to qualify for federal funds ready as soon as they announced.

Second, candidates had to raise early money in order to fund extensive campaigns in the early caucus and primary states.[10] Not only have they had to qualify for matching funds, but they have had to raise large amounts quickly. The record-shattering $36 million that George W. Bush reported on his June 30, 1999, FEC report caused many of his opponents to rethink their chances, as they knew they would have to have enough money in hand to compete throughout the primaries or they would not be able to compete at all. Whereas in the past a legitimate strategy was to concentrate on Iowa and New Hampshire and hope good showings there would lead to an infusion of the funds needed to contest later primaries, the front-loading of the calendar and the huge sums raised by President Bush and Bill Clinton in 1992, Bob Dole in 1996, and George W. Bush in 2000 have made raising early money essential for viability.

Beyond that, candidates have had to plan how to spend their money strategically because of the limitations to which they acquiesce when they accept public financing. Malbin (1985) has demonstrated that candidates spend a good deal of money before the year of the presidential nomination and that they spend a much higher percentage of the permitted limit in the early states than they do in later states. These decisions have consequences for later contests, since publicly funded candidates have accepted an overall limit in how much they will spend. As Walter Mondale nearly found out in 1984, too much money spent too early may leave too little to spend later when it is needed (Corrado and Maisel 1988; Maisel 1988). Even candidates who have been conceded the nomination rather early in the process, like Bill Clinton in 1992 and Bob Dole in 1996, have faced difficulties maintaining momentum going into the convention because they have run up against preconvention spending limits. In part the soft-money controversy in recent years has been the result of candidates' perceived need to continue spending after they have secured the nomination but before the conventions have been held (see chap. 11).

The last two election cycles have seen the first examples of extremely wealthy candidates funding their own campaigns. In 1991, first mentions of the potential candidacy of West Virginia's Democratic senator John D. Rockefeller IV was almost always accompanied by speculation that he would fund his own campaign. Certainly the Rockefeller wealth would have been sufficient to run as elaborate a campaign as was necessary, but most observers felt that if he did finance his own campaign effort, his wealth and not his experience or position on issues would have been the most frequent topic of discussion. In the 1992 general election H. Ross Perot turned the financing of his own campaign from a liability into an asset. Steve Forbes followed Perot's example in 1996, financing his own effort for the Republican nomination. Budgetary decisions by extremely wealthy individuals financing their own campaigns follow different strategic rules than do those by candidates who accept public funding. In the case of the self-financed candidates, two questions must be answered: (1) How much of their own wealth are they willing to invest in a campaign?—a question that must be reexamined as the fate of the campaign becomes clearer. (2) How will the public view revelations about the amount of money the candidate has spent on his own behalf?

In today's political world, money is a strategic resource that must be raised and then spent wisely. Candidate strategists must decide how to spend money, when to spend it, and where to spend it in order to assure that it is used most effectively. The ultimate goal is to win a majority of delegates to the national convention. Spending too much too early may not leave enough money to spend later. Or saving money for the end may result in poor early showings that doom a campaign. Small wonder that candidates and their managers spend much of their early time planning budgetary allocations.

3. The Media

In many ways the press makes the presidential nominating process work. How many average citizens are thinking about presidential politics over a year before an election, when the contenders are courting delegate candidates in Florida, Iowa, and Maine? Has the public begun to focus on the next election when scores of candidates and their staffs are trooping through the snows of New Hampshire? The answer is a resounding "No!" But the working press is gearing up.

Initially one or two reporters will accompany a candidate on a campaign swing. If a candidate is lucky or if a press secretary is extremely good, a television crew may cover part of a campaign trip. Particularly at the beginning of the primary process, free publicity is the key. Odd as it seems, presidential contenders are not necessarily well known to the general public. Consider the 1984 presidential nominating process that was discussed earlier. One obvious conclusion is that some of the large gap in early presidential preference polling between candidates Mondale and Glenn, on the one hand, and Hart, on the other, was a reflection of the number of voters who had heard of Senator Hart. However, with his good showing in the Iowa caucuses and his win in the New Hampshire primary, each of which was accompanied by significant publicity, both his name recognition and the number of voters selecting him as their choice for the nomination rose substantially.

In 1988, none of the candidates was really well known in the Democratic party, with Jesse Jackson the leader, again largely reflecting name recognition. In the Republican party, Vice President Bush led Senator Dole, again a reflection of the difference in how many people had any impression of them at all. As with the cases discussed earlier, these numbers changed drastically after the first caucuses and primaries and the media exposures wrought by those events.[11]

The experiences in 1992 and 1996 were similar. In 1992, Bill Clinton was able to separate himself from the field, but he had a long way to go to gain name recognition. Virginia governor Douglas Wilder dropped out when he understood that he had made no impact on the public's mind. In 1996 the image of Colin Powell, well-known, well-respected leader that he was, loomed over all of the potential candidates. While Bob Dole and Patrick Buchanan were more frequently recognized than the other candidates, the gap was still apparent.

The goal in the early stages of a campaign is to be mentioned. Television advertising cannot be effective without the public focusing on the campaign, and so candidates court press attention. They play to local media wherever they go; more important, they seek mention in the national press, some positive reference as a real contender.

These efforts can be spectacular successes or abysmal failures. At times a candidate's relationship with the press may make the candidate feel like a yo-yo on the end of a string. For example, consider John Anderson's campaign for the Republican nomination in 1980. Anderson was one of those congressmen who was widely respected in Washington but virtually unknown to the nation when he decided to forgo a difficult reelection campaign in Illinois in order to seek the presidency. Anderson was photogenic, articulate, and much too liberal for most of the activists in the Republican party. Most of all, he was good press. He understood that advocating gun control before the National Rifle Association would be regarded as newsworthy by the press (Robinson and Sheehan 1983).

In the early states in 1980 the media covered John Anderson like a rug. Ronald Reagan was not yet campaigning full-time; he never really did. The other Republicans were exciting neither the voters nor the media. Anderson was good copy. But after some early good showings, Anderson had to produce a victory. The press soon came to the hard truth. Anderson could not run successfully in the Republican party. That statement became the press line by the time of the Illinois primary in March. John Anderson could not win among Republicans; his chances for the nomination were downplayed in the press as much as they had been exaggerated earlier.

Anderson's roller coaster ride with the press at least gave him some national attention, the early exposure helping his eventual third-party campaign (chap. 10). Compare that experience to Reuben Askew's. Askew was the ex-governor of Florida who sought the Democratic nomination in 1984. Askew never became more than an asterisk in the polls. He tried to base an early appeal on his conservative stand on social issues, hoping that certain dedicated followers would support him and that that would distinguish him from the other candidates. What distinguished him was a brief trip to Maine and New Hampshire. The national political correspondent for a major newspaper decided to catch up with Askew, to see how he was doing. The reporter tried to call the local Askew headquarters; there was none. He called the national headquarters in Florida and asked for a local contact; there was none. He asked his Florida contact how to get in touch with the candidate; the contact didn't know. He asked where Askew was; his headquarters hadn't heard from him in days. The case of the missing candidate made news, but not the kind of news Askew counted on. His campaign was held up to a kind of ridicule from which it never recovered.

A third experience, that of Bruce Babbit from Arizona in the 1988 primaries, falls somewhere between these two. Babbit was not a main contender. He never made a real impact on the voting public. But he impressed the media who was following the candidates. In one of the New Hampshire debates, he called for everyone who believed that taxes needed to be raised to stand up. None of the other candidates did. They knew Babbit was right, but they would not take a politically unpopular "stand." The press loved it—and Babbit benefited from a couple of weeks' worth of good coverage. However, like Anderson, he failed because he could not transform that publicity into votes in a primary—still the sine qua non for electoral success.

As a final example, consider Bill Clinton in 1992. Clinton had a difficult press problem. In 1991 his candidacy began to be taken quite seriously by Washington insiders because most of the Democrats who were more prominently mentioned had decided not to seek the nomination. Washington journalists knew that Governor Clinton had a reputation in Little Rock as a womanizer. That reputation made the rounds of Washington cocktail parties, but it was never reported in nationally syndicated stories on the upcoming campaign. Then the accusations of Gennifer Flowers, first reported in a supermarket tabloid, hit the newsstands. The national press had to decide how to play the story. Media leaders decided that the story, once reported, had legitimacy; the pack of journalists on the presidential campaign trail followed. As the New Hampshire primary approached, the Clinton campaign was on the ropes. Clinton's response was again to use the media—this time an interview on *60 Minutes,* in which he and his wife talked about their marital difficulties and how they had worked them out. Clinton had gone around the intermediary of the journalists and used the media to communicate directly to the voters.[12]

His strategy was successful. His campaign halted what could have been a fatal plunge in his support.

Of course, the Clinton campaign stands as an example of another aspect of media as a "resource" for a campaign. The media portrays images of candidates to the public—for good or for ill. At times, as in the case with Gary Hart, media delving into a candidate's personal life can have devastating effects. At other times, the portrait can be much more positive. Candidates certainly understand that they are perceived by the public largely as they are portrayed by the media; they go to great lengths to be sure that the image that comes across is one with which they are comfortable.

Recent experience leads to the conclusion that a key to gaining early press attention is to do better than is expected or to make a more positive showing than early reports would have predicted. In this regard the Iowa caucuses and the New Hampshire primary—and how candidates are presented as these events unfold—have been very important (Orren and Polsby 1987). In 1972 George McGovern lost New Hampshire to Ed Muskie. But New Hampshire was the state next to Muskie's Maine, and Muskie should have won by more than he did. The press wrote the story as if Muskie had lost, and McGovern was on his way (Crouse 1973; White 1973).

In 1976 Jimmy Carter "won" New Hampshire with 28 percent of vote. Because he had come out on top and because this result was unexpected, Carter was pictured as a big winner; all the others were losers. His grin graced the cover of *Time* and *Newsweek*; he was on his way. That same year, President Ford edged Ronald Reagan in New Hampshire. Reagan had been expected to do very well in this conservative state; his campaign did not recover until the North Carolina primary, months later (Orren and Polsby 1987; Patterson 1980; Witcover 1977).

In 1980 George Bush took his turn at exceeding expectations. His "win" in Iowa, although again with much less than a majority, broke him out of a pack of Republicans chasing Ronald Reagan. It was Ted Kennedy who did not meet expectations. His poor showings in Iowa and especially in New Hampshire, billed as his neighboring state and not as the more conservative bastion it in truth is, all but nailed the lid on the coffin of a campaign that faltered from the start.

Gary Hart, who had engineered George McGovern's "upset" of Muskie in New Hampshire in 1972, returned to familiar territory in 1984. His strong showing in the Iowa caucuses served notice that his campaign was on the move. Despite internal campaign staff information that he would do very well in the New Hampshire primary, Hart played down his chances for success. And then when he won, again exceeding the press's predictions, more attention and cover stories followed.

Of course, the obverse of doing better than expectations is not to do worse than expectations. In 1988, as discussed earlier, both Dukakis's and Bush's managers worried about expectations. Dukakis had to prove that he was a national candidate in Iowa and then win in New Hampshire. His Super Tuesday strategy was based on demonstrating successes—even though he succeeded only in the carefully selected areas in which he chose to compete (Black et al. 1988). Bush had to recover in New Hampshire to cement the Super Tuesday landslide he had so carefully planned for. Once he met those expectations, the game was over for the other contenders (Runkel 1989).

In 1992, Senators Kerrey and Harkin had to prove that they could make some impact on primary voters; their struggle for third place in New Hampshire—behind Tsongas and Clinton—was a struggle for survival. When neither of them came within shouting distance of the leaders, the press began to sound the death knell for their campaigns. While they hung on to lose another round—it always seems difficult for candidates to accept when they have been "winnowed out" of the primary field[13]—their campaigns were essentially over when they did not meet minimal press expectations in New Hampshire.

Also in 1992 Patrick Buchanan's campaign was given a boost because he polled over 30 percent of the vote against an incumbent president. Certainly the press made that seem like a surprising total, and it caused concern in the Bush camp. A cautious analysis might have noted the conservative nature of the New Hampshire Republican party and the disparity between the resources Buchanan and Bush put into the effort, but the media are interested in a good political battle. As a group the journalists covering the campaign portrayed Buchanan's effort and his campaign as a stronger challenge to President Bush than they turned out to be.

The Gramm campaign ended almost before it started in 1996 because the Texas senator set expectations too high for early showings—in Louisiana and New Hampshire—and he failed to come close to his own predictions. On the other hand, the Dole campaign was able to hold expectations down and discount less-than-stellar showings in the earliest contests, focusing attention on the delegate-rich primaries in early March that were ripe for Dole's picking.

Surpassing expectations is not the only strategy for dealing with the media; demonstrating uniqueness—and thus newsworthiness—certainly works as well. In 1984 Jesse Jackson demonstrated that the press can be a crucial resource when used in this way. Jackson was newsworthy. He ran an entire campaign based on free media exposure. The press did not dare ignore him because he was the first serious black contender for a major-party nomination—that was news. He was articulate and controversial, and he was drawing large numbers of blacks to the polls—again, news. When he challenged his opponents, when he slept in the ghettos, when he traveled to Syria, when he did not disavow the support of the controversial Louis Farrakhan, when he ran well in the South, Jesse Jackson was news. He knew how to use the media. His rhetoric was made for television; his dynamism demanded action photos; his place in history commanded attention. Despite his total inability to draw financial support, despite the fact that his Rainbow Coalition never really materialized, Jesse Jackson stayed on page one. He stayed on the nightly news. Mondale, Hart, and Jackson. Hart, Mondale, and Jackson. But always Jackson, demonstrating the power of the press as a candidate resource (Barker and Walter 1989).

In 1988, Jackson's campaign took off from the spot at which his 1984 campaign had ended. Not only was he a serious candidate; he was a serious contender. He did not do well in the early rounds, though his strength in Maine surprised many. However, on Super Tuesday, he was clearly one of the winners.

Again, Jackson built a campaign without a great deal of money, gaining attention from the media because of the symbolism of his campaign and its successes. Jackson won where the intensity of his supporters turned into electoral success. Thus he did better in caucus states than in primaries. His most noteworthy success was in the restricted primary in Michigan, a primary that functioned more like a caucus. But the press was notably unanalytical in examining the Jackson successes; Jackson was succeeding beyond everyone's expectation. Dukakis, Gephardt, and Jackson. Dukakis, Gore, and Jackson. Dukakis and Jackson. Always Jackson (Black et al. 1988; Pomper 1989b; Runkel 1989).

The role of the press in the nominating process has received a great deal of critical attention. That attention has been deserved because the national media, print and electronic journalists alike, have not done a very good job of defining their role in this process. The nominating process itself has come under scrutiny because it is so easily manipulated by the press. (See Grassmuck 1985; Orren and Polsby 1987; Traugott 1985.) But reform is not the immediate province of candidates for party nominations. They are concerned with winning. In reaching for that goal, they must learn to use the press as a resource. Free media attention has made and broken many presidential campaigns.

While most of the attention has been given to the role of free media in the nominating process (Arterton 1984; Graber 1984a; Mathews 1978; Patterson 1980; Traugott 1985, as examples), relatively little attention has been paid to the role of media advertising at this stage of an election. In 1988, campaign managers had to plan carefully for Super Tuesday. The Gore campaign, as one example, tried to save most of its resources for the southern states on Super Tuesday, ignoring the early rounds in Iowa and New Hampshire.[14] The Gephardt campaign hoped that a win in Iowa would stimulate enough momentum to carry its candidate through New Hampshire—and that that victory would lead to the infusion of enough money to advertise widely on Super Tuesday. That did not happen. Bob Dole's strategy in 1988 paralleled Gephardt's; and it might have worked had he not failed to respond to Bush's last-minute attack on him in New Hampshire.

Dukakis and Bush planned all along for heavy media campaigns in the Super Tuesday states. Bush had organizational strength everywhere and enough money to overwhelm the others. Dukakis planned strategically, organizing in areas in which he could win—the northern and western states that were competing for press attention with the South on Super Tuesday and specific areas within the South in which his advisers thought he could do well—suburban areas with northern transplants, Hispanic areas, and so on. Dukakis and his advisers concentrated their efforts on specific congressional districts and media markets, knowing that they could not blanket the region and that they would lose to either Gore or Jackson in many areas. That advertising strategy was crucial to the degree of success that Dukakis enjoyed on Super Tuesday, a success that was duly reported in the free mass media (Black et al. 1988; Cook 1989; Runkel 1989; Pomper 1989b).

The impact of paid media strategies in the two most recent nominating processes is apparent. In 1992, all of the Democrats had to plan strategically when so many primaries were held in close succession. When the Tsongas campaign was "suspended," just prior to the Connecticut primary, the decision reflected the reality that he did not have enough money to compete on television, not that he was failing to get his message across. In that same round of primaries, Bush was able to vanquish Buchanan in part at least because his financial base—as well as his organizational base—overwhelmed those of his challenger.

In 1996, Steve Forbes used a media blitz to attack Dole in New Hampshire, but when the public reacted negatively to Forbes's using his money in that manner, he switched to a positive message to win primaries in Delaware and Arizona. As noted, the Dole campaign tried to lower expectations in the first round of caucuses and primaries. It worked hard, even before those first caucuses and primaries were held, to be certain that it could contest those after the first round. When primary after primary occurred on the same day, only Dole and Forbes had the financial resources to advertise widely enough to assure a good chance for victory in each state. Only Dole had an organization and a message that were resonating with the Republican rank and file.

D. Evaluating Nominating Campaigns

Nominating campaigns are difficult to assess. Viewed with 20/20 hindsight, one can easily see that the Muskie strategy was flawed; that the Carter strategy was brilliant; the Dole strategy, pragmatic and effective; and so on. The evidence again points strongly to the conclusion that politics is more art than science.

Some of the most effective members of Congress—Wilbur Mills of Arkansas, Fritz Hollings of South Carolina, Ed Muskie of Maine, Ted Kennedy of Massachusetts, Phil Gramm of Texas—proved to be poor presidential candidates. Skills are not always transferable. The corps of national campaign experts is very small, and these "experts" frequently learn the wrong lessons from their previous experience. New faces often have the clearest sense of how to attack the system—Hart as McGovern's strategist in 1972, Jordan for Carter in 1976, Jim Baker for George Bush in a losing effort in 1980, John Sasso for Michael Dukakis in 1988, James Carville for Bill Clinton in 1992.

All candidates show their strengths and weaknesses as they announce their candidacy. All understand the need for money, for an effective press strategy, for influential followers, for gaining and maintaining momentum, but few are successful in doing all these things. But the political terrain is difficult to read. In the preceding sections, many examples have been given that might seem to the reader at the turn of the century as if they are ancient history. Candidates have been mentioned of whom few reading these pages have heard. But presidential elections happen every four years. What happened in 1972 might be more than a quarter of a century ago, but it is only seven elections ago. If one is going to understand a process, as a student, a researcher, or a practitioner, it is necessary to study what history there is. New situations will arise in the year 2000, but they will not be totally without precedent; the precedents need to be understood for that reason. The process is so interesting precisely because those of us who are political analysts and members of the interested public can sit back and watch the contenders compete and test their strategies. We can know nearly as much about the past as do the strategists themselves. And we can judge the ways in which the campaigns are contested. Monday morning quarterbacks have no better process to kibitz about.

IV. The Conventions

The excitement was electric at the 1976 Republican Convention in the Kemper Arena in Kansas City. Betty Ford came in from one end and the band struck up the University of Michigan fight song, "Hail to the Victors!" Nancy Reagan entered from the other end; the band responded with "California, Here I Come!" The crowds cheered loudly as Ford and Reagan supporters tried to drown each other out. Television commentators tried to gauge support for the two candidates by the intensity of the cheering. The convention was as thrilling as any college football game.

The excitement of conventions stirs the emotions in those of us who love politics. But the broader question to be addressed is whether or not national nominating conventions decide anything at all anymore. After all, only Strom Thurmond (R-S.C.) among all active politicians has ever participated in a convention whose nominee was not known before the opening gavel sounded.

The first party conventions were held in the Jacksonian period in the nineteenth century (recall chap. 2). Conventions were places to which delegates came in order to make decisions, to choose the presidential nominees. In fact, nine times delegates have had to cast ten or more ballots in order to choose their party's nominees. In 1924, the Democratic National Convention in Baltimore took 103 ballots before finally settling on the nomination of John W. Davis, the last true favorite son to gain a major party nomination. But since 1952, every presidential nominee has been chosen on the first ballot cast at his party's convention.

Many observers felt that the Democratic rule change that calls for "fair reflection of presidential preference" would return decision-making power to the conventions. The argument went that many candidates going through a system that called for proportional representation of their popular support as delegate support would guarantee a situation in which no one candidate achieved a majority. However, that has not been the case. While I have suggested a scenario in which conventions could once again become decision-making bodies, recent history suggests that they have become little more than rubber stamps for decisions reached by primary and caucus voters. Some claim that they are nothing but celebratory events, opportunities for the party faithful to unite behind their nominee (Nelson 1996). The television networks seem to reflect this view as they provide fewer and fewer hours of live coverage (Kerbel 1998). The delegate selection process has worked in such a way that one candidate has a guaranteed first-ballot majority by the time the convention opens. Little else remains to be decided.

As much of the nation's attention still focuses on the nominating conventions every fourth summer, it is appropriate for us to examine whether this attention is warranted. If the conventions do not decide the nominee, what about the other decisions made in these political arenas (Davis 1983; Parris 1972; Shafer 1988; Sullivan et al. 1976; Wayne 1996; Polsby and Wildavsky 1997)?

National nominating conventions make four different kinds of decisions. In addition to deciding on the nominees for president and vice president, they rule on credentials disputes, changes in the party rules, and platform language.

A. Credentials Challenges

Credentials disputes are the most easily understood. In party rules and in the call to the convention, each party establishes the procedures through which delegates are to be chosen. In most cases no one challenges the delegates presenting themselves as representing a certain state. However, the procedures are not always simple. The political situations are not always unbiased, and challenges result. Each party appoints a Credentials Committee that hears challenges to proposed delegations and rules on the disputes. The report of the Credentials Committee is the first order of official business before the nominating convention.

While most credentials challenges are disposed of without major controversy, those that do attract attention are often critically important. Among the most noteworthy challenges was that of the Mississippi Freedom Democratic party in 1964 (White 1965). The appeal by Mississippi black Democrats, led by Aaron Henry, was instrumental in desegregating Democratic politics in the South.

The credentials battles at the 1972 Democratic Convention in Miami were more closely related to the impending presidential nominations and deserve a closer examination for what they say about the process. Recall that the 1972 nomination was the first conducted under the "reformed" rules. Many irregularities were in evidence. The results of a series of credentials challenges were to determine whether George McGovern, the clear front-runner, was going to be able to secure a first-ballot nomination or if the ABM forces (Anyone But McGovern) could derail his candidacy at the last moment.

The three most significant challenges dealt with South Carolina (where feminists felt too few women had been selected), Illinois (where McGovern forces charged that the Cook County organization of Mayor Richard Daley had not followed procedures for opening and publicizing caucuses), and California (where a winner-take-all primary had been given an exemption from the rules by the National Committee). On close votes, aided by an important procedural ruling from convention chair Lawrence O'Brien, McGovern delegates were allowed to replace anti-McGovern Daley delegates in Illinois and to hold all the delegates won in California. The result was that McGovern forces controlled enough votes to secure the first-ballot victory (White 1973). The decisions reflected the commitment of McGovern delegates to their candidate, a commitment that was more important than any commitment to the new reform principles. Many delegates cast conflicting votes, supporting the reforms in the case of the Illinois challenge but opposing them on South Carolina and California; they were supporting the position needed to secure McGovern's nomination in both cases.

B. Rules Disputes

The National Convention of each party is the ultimate rule-making authority for the national party.[15] Each party appoints a Rules Committee that examines proposed changes in party rules. In most cases party rules are sufficiently obscure and esoteric that few notice the workings of the Rules Committee. Often the real impact of rules changes will not be felt for four years; in the heat of an ongoing campaign, few are looking that far ahead.

On occasion, however, the work of the convention Rules Committee is seen as having immediate impact. In 1976, candidate Ronald Reagan tried a desperate ploy to wrest the nomination from President Gerald Ford. In an unprecedented move, Reagan announced, in advance of the convention, that he would choose Pennsylvania senator Richard Schweiker as his running mate if he were nominated for the presidency. Reagan's bold move was a reaching out toward the liberal wing of his party, toward those who felt he was too conservative. The battle was very close. Reagan hoped the needed delegates would swing to his side, but few budged.

As a second step in his strategy, Reagan sought a change on Rule 5 of the Republican Party Rules, requiring that prospective presidential candidates designate their choice for running mate in advance. Reagan hoped that this rule change would force President Ford into a choice that would cost him support from the followers of the hopefuls who were not chosen and give the nomination to Reagan. The ploy failed; the rule was not changed, although the vote on it was very close, and Ford secured the nomination (Pomper 1977, 18–27; Wayne 1988, chap. 5; Witcover 1977).

As mentioned above, the 1980 Democratic National Convention saw Senator Edward Kennedy try a similar tactic. The Democratic rules at that time bound delegates to vote for the candidate to whom they had pledged support for one ballot. (Some state rules extended that commitment even for subsequent ballots, if any were needed.) Though a majority of the delegates were pledged to President Carter, Kennedy felt that some might swing to him if they were unbound, since Carter's popularity had fallen to an all-time low. The binding rule had been part of an effort to guarantee that convention delegations reflected the views of the citizens who had chosen them. Kennedy ignored this rationale and attacked them as "robot delegates," seeking a rule change to allow them to "vote their consciences." The Kennedy effort failed and Carter was nominated (Shafer 1988, 193–196; Wayne 1988, chap. 5).

National political journalists have focused on the disputes described above as pivotal events in each of the cited conventions. In some sense they were, but in a more realistic sense the results were very predictable. Delegates to conventions choose which candidate they will support early on, and then they work hard for that candidate. They are seeking two goals. Their principal goal is to help their candidate secure the nomination. Their secondary goal is to be a delegate for that candidate and share in the candidate's success.

These individuals are not fooled by the intricacies of credentials or rules fights. The questions may be worded differently, but delegates know that the real question is: Which candidate for the presidency do you favor? Female McGovern delegates in 1972 voted against the challenge by South Carolina women because it would have hurt McGovern's chances (Weil 1973; White 1973). Liberal Carter delegates voted against Kennedy's proposed rule change because it would hurt their candidate. The most important factor to note in convention votes on credentials or rules fights is how closely the votes in these battles parallel the first-ballot votes for the presidential nomination. Though roll calls by individual delegates are not available, delegates are very aware of the impact these votes have on their favorite candidate's chances for nomination and vote accordingly. Put simply, the Carter delegates in 1980 were not robots; they were dedicated supporters of Jimmy Carter voting their consciences (Pomper 1981b, 25–32). In that sense, to the extent that one candidate has been guaranteed the nomination before the convention opens, credentials and rules fights are much less likely to assume importance.

C. Party Platforms

The party platforms are statements of the direction in which the two parties want our country to go. Their significance is frequently disputed, though Gerald Pomper (1982) demonstrated that they show real differences between our parties and that much of them are implemented and not forgotten. It is clear that they receive a lot of press attention at the time they are adopted.

The Democrats use the platform-writing process as a means to reach out to grassroots activists around the country. In many years, their platform committee, the composition of which reflects candidates' strengths, has turned into a traveling road show, seeking advice from Democrats around the country. The Republican platform committee, on the other hand, normally only meets in the convention city on the weekend before the convention itself. It is not a road show, but perhaps a sideshow before the main event.

Platforms serve different purposes for different individuals. For activists and ideologues they are often a means to gain a foothold into party dogma. For interest groups, they represent one way to gain support for particular views. For candidates, the platform process has served as a way to reach out to those in the party who did not support them.

Each candidate at a national convention has an extensive organization. Since the 1960 nomination of John F. Kennedy in Los Angeles (White 1961), each convention has seen increasingly sophisticated communications networks so that candidate organizations can reach their supporters on the floor. Each candidate sets up a "whip" organization so that delegates are instantly informed how they must vote on critical matters.

Credentials and rules disputes, which can determine who wins and loses, are seen as critical matters. The whips inform the delegates, and the delegates fall in line. At times the same is true of platform disputes. Thus, in 1988, the Dukakis campaign operatives allowed votes on the platform planks dealing with increasing taxes on upper-income families and pledging to forgo the first use of nuclear weapons, but they also assured that their candidate would not be saddled with a platform with which he was not comfortable (Pomper 1989b, 49–65). On the other hand, platform disputes are seen as matters of conscience more frequently than is the case of credentials or rules disputes. The delegates often are freed to vote as they choose. At times, as was the case with Jimmy Carter in 1980 and Walter Mondale in 1984, winning candidates concede platform disputes to their vanquished foes so that the losers have some pride with which to return home and thus they retain some enthusiasm for the party.

That is not to say that the platform-writing and -adopting processes are not important. Never was this more clearly demonstrated than in 1992. The entire Democratic platform-writing process was controlled by the Clinton campaign. The platform was drafted by a Clinton loyalist. The drafting committee was chaired by Clinton supporter Bill Richardson, a congressman from New Mexico and later Clinton Cabinet appointee. The supporters of Paul Tsongas and Jerry Brown were allowed their say at platform hearings and were permitted to offer amendments on the convention floor, but the result was preordained. The Clinton campaign wanted to present the image of a new Democratic party; the platform was one vehicle for doing this. Controlling the process throughout assured this goal and was thus considered to be very important.

At the other extreme, the Bush campaign lost control of the platform-writing process at the Republican Convention. The platform battle became a symbol of an intense ideological struggle being waged within the Republican party. To oversimplify, three camps, each claiming to be true conservatives, were in evidence. Bush represented the traditional conservatives in his party; these were fiscal conservatives, concerned with balancing the budget and deficit reduction. Buchanan fought for the soul of the Republican party on moral and value-related issues; his backers were engaged in a cultural war with those who had deserted traditional American values. Buchanan supporters controlled key positions on the platform subcommittees that dealt with valence issues such as abortion. Finally, lurking in the background were economic conservatives represented by Jack Kemp; they favored opportunity and growth policies, but they also supported the Buchanan definition on family values. The platform that emerged reflected the most controversial statement of conservative views, particularly on social issues. Many Republicans, particularly moderate Republicans from the Northeast, felt that it was a divisive platform, one that divided them from their own party. It certainly was not a centrist platform that could help President Bush in the November election.

It would be too much to argue that the differences between the two parties' platforms in 1992 determined the result of that very complex election (see chap. 10). However, one can surely claim that the

Republican platform in that year did go far toward defining the public's view of the GOP. In 1996, the Republican platform-writing process was much less complex. Bob Dole went so far as to claim that he had not read the platform when he accepted the nomination. Dole came from the same traditional conservative economic background that Bush represented. His party's platform took a very different view. In some ways, that was symbolized by his choice of Jack Kemp as his running mate. Dole and Kemp had publicly feuded over economic policies for much of the preceding four years. Kemp had gone so far as to endorse Steve Forbes for the Republican nomination, at a time when it seemed that Forbes's candidacy was doomed. But Dole chose Kemp, and Kemp muted his differences for a while. By the end of the campaign, however, it was clear that Kemp was voicing a new set of Republican ideas, ones more in line with the party's platform than with the views his running mate had expressed during nearly fifty years in public life.

Platforms, which do distinguish the two parties, clearly can still play a role in uniting a party for the November showdown or preventing party activists from coming together behind the nominee. They are important statements about party philosophy. Writing the platform is an exercise in defining a party. Controversy may or may not be apparent at a convention, but this part of the process remains critically important and should not be underestimated.

D. Vice Presidential Nominations

Vice presidential running mates for major-party candidates are officially nominated by the two parties' conventions. But the choices, of course, are made by the presidential candidate. The last presidential candidate to leave the choice of running mate to the convention was Adlai Stevenson, for whom the Democratic National Convention chose Tennessee's veteran senator Estes Kefauver over a young Massachusetts senator named John Fitzgerald Kennedy in 1956.

Today's presidential nominees know that the choice of vice president is a most serious undertaking. From a political standpoint, the vice presidential nominee can help or hurt the ticket. Certainly the nominee is evaluated in part on this choice, the first important decision he has to make after confirmation as his party's standard-bearer. In 1972, George McGovern's campaign suffered badly when it was revealed that his original choice, Thomas Eagleton, a senator from Missouri, had undergone shock treatment for mental depression. Under intense pressure, Eagleton eventually withdrew. McGovern faced the embarrassing situation of having to find a stand-in and of having a number of prominent Democrats turn him down before Sargent Shriver, President Kennedy's brother-in-law and the founding director of the Peace Corps, accepted McGovern's invitation.

But the choice is viewed as more than a political decision. The nominee is naming an individual who will be the proverbial "heartbeat away" from the presidency, should the ticket win. Since Harry S Truman succeeded to the presidency upon the death of Franklin Roosevelt in 1945, political leaders have been confronted with the seriousness of the vice presidential decision. Truman was picked for a variety of reasons, none of them clear at the time (Phillips 1966). What was clear was that he was not included in the Roosevelt inner circle as the president directed Allied efforts toward ending World War II. As an extreme example, Truman was only vaguely aware of the project to develop the atomic bomb when he became president. In a world in which the president of the United States is the most powerful single individual on earth, the choice of the person who is to succeed to the presidency should anything happen to the incumbent must be taken most seriously.

The process for choosing vice presidential candidates is not a formal one, but it has been a careful and organized one for each of the last seven elections. Candidate Jimmy Carter established a process that his successors as Democratic nominees have more or less followed since 1976. As it becomes clear that the nomination is in hand, each prospective nominee has asked a trusted adviser to begin to compile a list of possible running mates. These individuals are then screened in great detail, to make sure that none has any problems similar to that discovered with Senator Eagleton in 1972. The extent to which the names on the list have been public has varied from year to year. In part that is because being mentioned is a great political coup—and those seeking the nomination understand that they are involved in a political process. Eventually the list of many nominees is pared to a few, usually fewer than five. They are interviewed by the prospective nominee, again sometimes in secret and sometimes quite openly. The Republicans have not followed a process quite as formal as the Democrats, but their outline is basically the same.

The eventual decision rests with the nominee, but he consults widely, seeking opinions on the assets and liabilities of each of those under consideration. He wants to be certain that the nominee is someone he is comfortable with, personally, politically, and in terms of policy views. But he also wants to be certain that he chooses someone whom others respect—as a running mate, as a vice president, and potentially as a successor. When the choices have been announced, the nominee always hails his running mate as the person in the nation most qualified to assume the presidency should anything happen to the president. And in fact, the nominees chosen in recent years have been quite competent. When Bob Dole was chosen as Gerald Ford's running mate in 1976, he had as much or more experience in government as did Ford. The same could be said of Walter Mondale (Jimmy Carter's choice in 1976), George Bush (Ronald Reagan's choice in 1980), Lloyd

Bentsen (Michael Dukakis's running mate in 1988), and Al Gore (Clinton's 1992 choice).

Even the choices not on that list were experienced public servants. When Geraldine Ferraro was chosen by Mondale in 1984 and Dan Quayle by Bush in 1988, each was criticized for lack of experience. While it is certainly true that these choices were made for obvious political reasons—Ferraro for the symbolism of choosing the first woman, and Quayle for his appeal to a younger generation of Republican voters—each nominee had experience in Congress and a record of competence. The most recent vice presidential nominee, Jack Kemp, did not have as much experience as Bob Dole, but neither did anyone else, given the length of Dole's career. However, Kemp was a longtime member of Congress, a member of President Bush's cabinet, and a one-time contender for his party's presidential nomination—impressive credentials.

The vice presidential nominees are certainly chosen to aid the national ticket. In the past, they were often selected to balance the ticket—someone from a different wing of the party, from a different region of the country, with different types of experience. But the nomination of Al Gore surprised many on that count. Gore was from the same Democratic Leadership Council, moderate wing of the party as was Clinton; he, like Clinton, is a southerner; his is of the same generation, the same religion. The only way in which he "balanced" the ticket was that he had legislative experience in the national government, whereas Clinton had mainly executive experience in state government. Perhaps most important, Gore's life was very different from Clinton's, from his very traditional family to his service in Vietnam. Similarly, some were surprised by the choice of Jack Kemp, since he and Bob Dole had been openly critical of each other's views on economic policy making. However, Dole felt that Kemp served his needs, particularly his need to breathe some life into the campaign. Kemp was seen as having the charisma that Dole lacked—and his nomination was greeted enthusiastically by Republicans around the nation.

E. An Evaluation of the Conventions

The national television networks have cut way back on their television coverage of the recent nominating conventions. They did this because the excitement was gone—because the ratings were not there. Obviously, they have every right to make that judgment.

But they are wrong. Conventions are important events. They are times for partisans to share and to celebrate. That is newsworthy. They are "comings together," which is what "convention" really means. Republicans and Democrats around the country can share this via television, if they are permitted to do so.

Television journalists define news as controversy. Surely the last four conventions in each party lacked that. But the rhetoric of Mario Cuomo and Jesse Jackson and Pat Buchanan, the emotions caused by the nomination of Geraldine Ferraro, the depth of feeling for Bob Dole and Fritz Mondale and Paul Tsongas, the humanness of photographer and outgoing Senate leader Howard Baker, the degree of unanimity behind and pride in Ronald Reagan and George Bush in 1984 and Bill Clinton and Al Gore in 1996—these too were important news events. So were the delegates' reactions to those individuals and their performances, but also their emotional reaction to the American flag and the National Anthem. Television misses a major opportunity by focusing on journalists' interviewing journalists when the public really wants to experience the thrill of a convention vicariously.

Conventions have not been forums for decision making in recent years. That is not to say they will not again become so. Delegates will continue to be pledged and bound (by conviction) to their favorite candidates. If one candidate has gained majority support before the opening gavel, the "competition" will be a charade. But if this does not eventuate, we may once again see real decisions made by conventions.

We have already painted a scenario that would lead to the convention playing an important role in 2000. Others are free to hypothesize about how a convention faced with reaching important decisions would work, should the situation eventuate for either party in 2000. The frank answer is that we do not know. Could candidates control their delegates? Would demographic representation—of women, blacks, Hispanics—become more potent? Would interest groups come to the fore? Would impressive rhetoric win the day? We just do not know. The old keys—domination by a few bosses—no longer fit, but it is unclear if anyone has yet crafted the new ones.

In recent years Walter Cronkite, the very epitome of a network news anchor in the heyday of convention coverage, has nostalgically recalled conventions of another era, when the crowds and the demonstrations were important, when emotions swept the floor, when spontaneous excitement ruled the day. Conventions still have that potential. They are an important element of American politics and continue to deserve attention as potentially significant events, not as dinosaurs from another era. (See Polsby and Wildavsky 1988, chap. 3; Shafer 1988; Wayne 1988, chap. 5.)

V. POLITICIANS VIEW THE NOMINATING PROCESS

Frequently how one views a certain situation depends on whether or not one benefits from that situation. Junior members of congressional committees like the seniority system less than senior members do. Five-foot-eight-inch point guards favor a wider lane under the basket than do seven-foot centers. Such is human nature.

The same holds for how politicians view the nominating process. At one extreme perhaps is the Walter Mondale of 1976. After testing the presidential waters for a number of months, Mondale withdrew. The reason: "I simply do not want it enough. I cannot face a whole year of nights in Holiday Inns." The process was dehumanizing. It was too long and too boring, and, in Mondale's case that year, offered too little hope for success.

Sometimes the criticism of the process deals with the rules. Thus losing candidate Morris Udall in 1976 became an advocate for regional primaries, to restrict the amount of time and money spent traveling. Others have advocated a national primary. Of course that would favor well-known candidates and hurt those seeking to make a name for themselves. Obviously how one stands on a reform like that would depend on where one sits. What's progressive reform to some is unfair to others. Politicians' ultimate view of the nominating system—other than complaints about how arduous it is—relates to whether they are helped or hurt by it. Jackson was hurt by the rules so he cried for reform.

The nominating process will always be controversial. Politicians are vying for the highest office in our land. Those even considering the nomination are already successful politicians at some level. But the national arena is different. The breadth of this country, the diversity of her people, the accidents of history that have led to varying political traditions, the magnitude of the office sought, and the expectations that citizens have of presidential candidates, on the one hand, and presidents, on the other, combine to make the design of the perfect nominating system a pipe dream.

The process will always be long. But its length does not seem to bother the winning candidates. Bill Clinton thrived on it in 1992. Bob Dole had no complaints in 1996, even though he traveled the length and breadth of the North American continent over and over. The process will always be complex. It will always seem to favor some candidates over others. Some candidates will always be dissatisfied.

But the system can be viewed as successful if the citizens feel that the candidates have been tested fairly, in a variety of ways, under rules that were designed to be as fair as possible for all contenders. As the nation looks to the year 2000 nominations, knowing that once again no incumbent president will be running, citizens want a system that tests their next president. A candidate who is found wanting should not be chosen. If Al Gore cannot stand the heat of intense scrutiny of his role as vice president, if Texas governor George Bush cannot bring together a coalition on a variety of issues, if the other Democrats and Republicans who seek the nation's highest office cannot invigorate wide followings, they should not be chosen. The system gives legitimacy to the nominees. The concessions of losing candidates confirm that legitimacy, and the process moves on from there.

WEBSITES

http://www.democrats.org/
http://www.rnc.org

The websites of the two national committees have a good deal of information about the candidates, party rules, the nominating calendar, the party platforms, and similar matters. Various candidates for party nominations also maintain their own websites.

http://www.fec.gov/

The Federal Election Commission maintains up-to-date records of all candidate fund-raising and spending during the nominating phase of the electoral process.

http://www.cq.com/
http://cnn.com/ALLPOLITICS/

These sites mentioned in chapter 7 are also excellent for getting information on the presidential nominating process.

KEY CONCEPTS

"add-on" delegates
caucuses
Democratic Leadership Council (DLC)
demographic representation
fair reflection of presidential preference
filing deadlines
front-loading
geographic representation
ideological representation
loophole
McGovern-Fraser Commission
New Hampshire's "first in the nation" primary
presidential preference primaries
regional primaries
straw poll
Super Tuesday
superdelegates
window concept
winner-take-all primaries

DISCUSSION QUESTIONS

1. Do you think that the nominating process for presidential candidates goes on too long? How would you go about shortening it?
2. Some claim that the caucus system of selecting delegates to national nominating conventions is superior because it gives an advantage to those who care enough about the process to participate fully. Others claim that primary elections are a superior way to select delegates because more people participate. Does your state have primaries or caucuses? Which system do you favor? Why?

3. Turnout in presidential primaries is normally very low. Can you think of ways to stimulate more voter interest? Would your reforms be politically feasible?

4. This is a complex question, so think about it carefully. When you vote, you vote for one person only. Even if there are five candidates, in all nominating processes you get only one vote. What if a system were devised so that you could express your preference among all of the candidates running for your party's nomination, designating your first choice, second choice, and so on? Would you favor such a system? Such a system has in fact been devised and suggested—and a variation of it is used in caucus states. Why do you think it has not been more widely adopted?

5. Many reforms of the presidential nominating process have been proposed. One calls for having the conventions first and then holding a runoff primary between the two top finishers at the convention. How would you react to a system like that one?

6. Who is advantaged and who is disadvantaged in the presidential nominating system now in place? Given your answer to that question, how do you evaluate the system? If you were going to change it, which of the reforms discussed in this chapter—or others that you know of—would you favor?

CHAPTER 10

Presidential Elections

The Dole campaign seemed to march inexorably toward nomination in 1996. Everything went according to plan. Candidate Dole raised money, put together a superb organization, and dispatched his opponents with relative ease. The Republican nomination was his, as if finally bearing his party's mantle was his destiny. The campaign reached an incredible crescendo at the Republican National Convention in San Diego—*his* convention—in which his wife charmed the nation with a folksy address, his choice of running mate drew wide praise, and he himself made his best case to lead the nation.

And then it all fell apart. The Dole-Kemp general election campaign never found its message. The campaign was marked by missed opportunities. The candidate could not connect with the people and dropped further and further behind in the polls. Dole seemed to feel that he "deserved" to be president by virtue of his background, experience, and character; he could not understand why the nation seemed to disagree, to prefer the obviously tainted Bill Clinton. No part of the fall campaign ran as well as the well-oiled machine that had secured the nomination. The difference between the nominating campaign and the general election campaign could not have been more stark.

Well, yes it could. In 1984 the Mondale organization moved through the caucuses and primaries with nearly as much dispatch as did Dole's twelve years later. And if anything, the Mondale-Ferraro fall campaign was even more of a disaster than the Dole-Kemp effort. The Mondale campaign's difficulties were apparent for all to see on the very first day of the campaign, Labor Day 1984, as the Democratic presidential and vice presidential nominees paraded down empty streets in New York, marching in a Labor Day parade before the expected crowd of Democratic boosters had arrived. Similarly, the 1988 Dukakis general election campaign, in terms of strategy and execution, paled in comparison to the battle for the nomination; so too did the Bush campaign in 1992 (though many claimed his drive to nomination led to the difficulties in the fall).

Why were such experienced, seasoned campaign organizations plagued by these problems? Why were they not solved during primary contests? After all, much more is known about the general election than about the contests for a party's nomination. At the most rudimentary level, strategy can target voters who use party affiliation as a cue to evaluating candidates; the campaign's plan of action can be formulated with a single opponent in mind. Shouldn't there be fewer problems instead of more problems? These are the issues we will address as we look at how presidential election campaigns are run.

I. From the Convention to the General Election

Politicians at the national level spend a good deal of time complaining about the length of presidential campaigns. What they are really concerned with is the length of the campaign for nomination. For the candidates who win nomination, and for the advisers most closely involved with their campaigns, the break between the convention and the general election is almost seamless. They continue to campaign hard, to work on the same issues, to work at the same pace, with the same goal in mind. There is little time for relaxation or reflection.

What is lost in their fatigue is the realization that the general election is separate from the campaign for nomination. The opponent is different, the rules are different, the strategies are different, and the length of time one is campaigning is different. General election campaigns are in fact quite short. The party conventions are held in middle or late summer. The general election is held on the first Tuesday after the first Monday in November. The general election campaign is over in about three months.

In this short period of time, the candidates and their staffs must run a truly national campaign. The battle for the nomination involves a separate campaign in each state. Different states have different rules, and the political calendar extends through five months. The general election campaign is different on all counts. One of the most significant of these is that the campaign must reach its peak in every state throughout the entire nation on the same date. Whereas during the preconvention period it was possible to run separate campaigns in each state and to reuse human resources by switching staff from one state in which the primary or caucus had been held to another state in which the contest was upcoming, in the general election campaign the organization must cover the entire expanse of the nation at one time. The logistics of an operation on this scale exceed anything that first-time campaign organizations and staff have experienced.

Furthermore, the rules of the election contest make strategic planning intricate. The point in the general election is not simply to win a plurality of the votes. While vote maximization is desirable, in our presidential elections the winner is the candidate who is supported by a majority of the **electoral college**. Therefore, each state is, in some ways, a separate contest. Campaign strategists must determine into which states they should put how much effort. Because all states (except Maine and Nebraska) award the plurality winner of the popular contest in a state all of that state's **electoral votes**, strategists not only focus on large states but also have to determine which states are lost (and therefore not worth additional effort), which states are safe (making further effort superfluous), and which states are competitive (and therefore worthy of increased effort).[1] These estimates must be evaluated and reevaluated as the campaign progresses.

ELECTORAL COLLEGE

The indirect means through which U.S. presidents and vice presidents are chosen.

ELECTORAL VOTES

The actual votes cast for president and vice president by the electors, members of the electoral college, chosen for that purpose alone.

Candidates for the presidency are interested first in winning, but they are also interested in winning with a large mandate. Therefore, even apparent winners cannot coast. They must be aware of their opponent's strategies and must counter them effectively. They must take into account the mix of voters throughout the nation as they respond to the events of the day. They are uniquely aware of the complexity and the magnitude of the job that they are seeking. They have reached the point at which they are not just among those considered for the presidency, but are one of two individuals who will hold that job. They must be certain that the conduct of their campaign does not make governing more difficult.

In the remainder of this chapter, we will look at the campaigns for the presidency, from after the conventions to the November election. We will begin by examining campaign organization and planning and proceed to look at the strategies and **tactics** used in these most important contests. (On presidential elections generally, see Kessel 1988; 1992; Polsby and Wildavsky 1991; 1996; Wayne 1988; 1992; 1996; on specific campaigns see, e.g., Black and Oliphant 1989; Ceaser and Busch 1993; 1997; Drew 1981; Germond and Witcover 1985; 1989; 1993; Goldman and Fuller 1985; May and Fraser 1973; Moore 1981; Moore and Fraser 1977; Runkel 1989; Schram 1977; Simon 1998; White 1965; 1969; 1973; 1982; Witcover 1977.)

TACTICS
The specific techniques used to implement the overall strategic design.

II. Organizing for the General Election

The campaign organization for the general election must be much more extensive than that for the series of primaries and caucuses that lead up to a presidential nomination. A presidential campaign must be run in each state at the same time. Some aspects of the campaign are controlled in a centralized manner, but others are decentralized. Further, the magnitude of the tasks that can be handled centrally call for significant and sophisticated staffing.

A. Structuring the Campaign Organization

1. The Campaign Headquarters

A number of questions must be faced when a nominee and his closest advisers reassess their campaign organization after having been victorious at their national convention. A very basic question involves the location of the campaign headquarters. Should there be one national headquarters for the campaign? Probably yes. Where should it be located? Washington is the logical choice, but it is not the only choice. In 1992, for example, candidate Bill Clinton decided that his national headquarters would remain in Little Rock, Arkansas. For Clinton, Little Rock was a strategic choice. Like Jimmy Carter, the last southerner elected president, Clinton wanted to emphasize that he was not part of the old Washington crowd. While many "regular" Democrats and politicians who were old hands at presidential campaigns backed Clinton, they understood this decision. When Clinton ran for reelection as a sitting president in 1996, however, his headquarters was in Washington—another logical choice.

Most candidates have chosen Washington as their national headquarters, a decision dictated, in part at least, because Washington is the seat of government and also the home of the Democratic and Republican National Committees. But merely mentioning these committees raises another set of questions.

2. The National Committee

What should be the relationship between the candidate's personal organization and the staff of the national committee? This is not an easy relationship to work out. Obviously the national committee staff is a resource that a candidate should use. While the national committees remain officially neutral in the prenomination phase of the election, once the nominee has been chosen, the national committees are dedicated to helping their candidate win.

A number of patterns have become apparent. When an incumbent president is renominated, the national committee staff is often pretty much under his control before the nomination is secure. Thus in 1996 the Democratic National Committee and its staff were actively involved in the Clinton reelection campaign well before the conventions were held. In 1992, on the other hand, while Republican National Committee members and staff generally favored President Bush over Pat Buchanan, they had to maintain a semblance of impartiality because of the nature of their position. That neutrality is the exception when a sitting president is seeking reelection, not the rule.

But what if no incumbent president has a nomination in hand or an out-party nominee begins to organize for the general election? The long-standing tradition had been for the nominee to name his own people as officers of the national committee and for the national committee to get to work on the campaign. In 1972, for example, George McGovern named Jean Westwood, a loyal supporter from the state of Utah, as DNC chair, the first woman to hold that position, and she headed that organization during his unsuccessful effort to unseat Richard Nixon. But the tradition requires reexamination.

First, the two national committees are no longer the same. For some time the Republican National Committee has been better financed and more professionally run than its Democratic counterpart. The DNC has made significant inroads on the advantage that the Republicans gained in the late 1960s, but the gap between the two organizations remains appreciable. One aspect of this difference has been the extent to which the committees view themselves as independent.

The RNC, more than the DNC, has been likely to retain its prenomination chair and its independent role.

But as the Democrats worked to rejuvenate their organization, their party leaders showed an independent streak as well. For example, in 1984, Walter Mondale, assured of the Democratic nomination, sought to name Bert Lance, the chair of the Georgia State Democratic Committee, as chair of the Democratic National Committee. Lance was one of Mondale's most important supporters in the South and Jimmy Carter's friend, confidante, and first budget director (until he was forced to resign). But the Democratic National Committee had taken on a life of its own. DNC chair Chuck Manatt had worked hard at retiring the Democrats' debt, at increasing the professionalism of the DNC staff, at closing the gap between Democratic and Republican fund-raising ability, and at restoring some luster to the badly tarnished DNC image. Manatt's success had earned him the admiration, loyalty, and support of DNC members throughout the nation. Many members of the DNC were not willing to see Manatt unceremoniously dumped in favor of a political crony whose ethical standards had been publicly called into question. Vehement in their opposition to Lance, they forced Mondale to back down and announce that Manatt would stay on. Not only did one of the first attempts to structure the campaign fail, but while the DNC did work with the Mondale campaign, the DNC also remained, in fact as well as in theory, an independent organization.

In 1992, the situation worked in the reverse fashion, although again the independence of the party organization was demonstrated. Ron Brown, DNC chair, decided that one of his priorities should be to help whomever gained the party's presidential nomination emerge from the convention with the greatest possible opportunity to win the general election in November. Brown thus used his position as DNC chair to negotiate with those whom Bill Clinton beat on his road to the nomination. While the DNC staff stayed separate from Clinton's, the Clinton operatives saw the utility of the role that Brown was playing and urged that he stay on as chair throughout the campaign. He did, and resigned only after the election, when he accepted a position in the Clinton cabinet.

FEDERAL ELECTION CAMPAIGN ACT OF 1971

Reform of the way in which the financing of elections is regulated that was the precursor to the current legislation.

Other factors further complicate the relationship between the national committee and the candidate. The **Federal Election Campaign Act of 1971** (FECA) mandated that each candidate have a separate central campaign committee that is responsible for all spending during the campaign. (This is discussed at length in chap. 11.) Thus in 1972 the Nixon campaign set up the Committee to Reelect the President as a separate entity, a pattern that has been followed ever since. The roles played by the national committees have had to be pointedly separate from those played by candidates' central campaign committees.

One result in recent elections has been multiple campaign headquarters, a candidate's national headquarters and the national committee headquarters. The two national committees work for the presidential candidates as well as the entire ticket. However, since 1984 presidential campaigns for both parties have taken advantage of a loophole in the campaign finance legislation. Money raised by the national committees and spent on behalf of the entire ticket can be used in addition to the grants given the presidential campaigns from public financing. This money is the so-called **soft money**, meaning money outside of the limitations of the FECA, which has drawn so much attention in recent elections.

SOFT MONEY

Campaign money raised and spent but not regulated by limitations of the FECA.

How is this soft money raised? Really in two ways. First, the national committees have their own fund-raising operations. These groups work hard to raise money for the party, not only for party maintenance, but to use during the fall campaigns of the party's candidates. But, second, the presidential campaigns have extensive fund-raising operations in place during the primaries. Every winning nominee has a fund-raising organization in place with no candidate-related task, as the presidential campaigns are publicly funded. Thus, in each of the last four presidential elections, the nominees have essentially transferred their fund-raising operations to the national committees after the conventions, thus allowing the national committees to raise and spend more money on the fall campaign than they otherwise would have been able to do. As more and more soft money is raised by the parties by individuals loyal to the presidential nominee, the separation between party activities designed to help the entire ticket and those more helpful to the presidential nominee has blurred (chap. 11; Magleby and Holt 1999; Corrado et al. 1997; Alexander 1986; Alexander and Bauer 1991; Center for Responsive Politics 1985; 1989).[2]

However, during the second Clinton administration the DNC suffered because it did not maintain enough independence and distance from the Clinton reelection effort. The DNC was involved in and tainted by campaign-related fund-raising scandals that caused the Democrats to return vast sums of money raised to help in the 1996 campaign. One result of this scandal may well be a re-separation of the fund-raising and spending by the national committees and the presidential campaigns.

Certainly the national party chairs and the national committees and their professional staffs have a stake in electing their party's nominee to the White House. But party officials have other responsibilities as well—responsibilities to other candidates on the ticket.

Campaign headquarters are places in which decisions are made. Maintaining multiple headquarters makes some sense because different kinds of decisions can be made by national party committees, which are concerned with all candidates throughout the nation, and candidate organizations, which are only concerned about one office. Combining these offices made more sense when the only concern of the national committees was the presidential campaign. However, because of changes in federal law and committee expertise, this is no longer the case.

3. The Mobile Headquarters

But if the definition of campaign headquarters is where important decisions are made, then one must also consider the mobile nature of presidential campaigns in this era of crisscrossing the nation in a matter of hours. In a very real sense, the campaign headquarters is where the candidate is. Presidential campaigns travel in an airplane that is outfitted for the comfort of the candidate and the needs of his staff. In essence, the candidate's plane is a traveling office (Kessel 1984, 354; 1988, 131; 1992, 123-124). Those traveling with the candidate (not those in the permanent campaign headquarters) make many of the important strategic decisions, since decisions must often be made quickly. Thus candidates often insist that their most trusted advisers travel with them.[3] However, those on the plane can lose sight of the fact that many important decisions are not instantaneous, but rather require planning and staff work and must be made back in the more permanent headquarters.

Campaign managers face a dilemma. They know that managing a national campaign with a multimillion-dollar budget represents a major administrative challenge. To handle this task requires time for planning, staff assistance, and a complete organization. On the other hand, they need access to the candidate, and he needs their counsel on the road. Most managers divide their time between the permanent headquarters and the plane—the traveling headquarters of the campaign.

In 1992 the Clinton campaign came up with a new headquarters concept. While some of Clinton's principal advisers traveled with him, others, including strategist James Carville, typically remained behind in the Little Rock "war room." Carville was convinced that the Dukakis campaign in 1988 suffered from an inability to respond to the actions of the Bush campaign. He did not want to repeat that error. Thus, taking a page from military strategists, he organized a rapid response team in the Little Rock headquarters. These strategists were constantly in touch with what was happening throughout the nation as well as with the candidate and his wife, vice presidential candidate Gore and his wife, and others on the campaign trail. The successful Clinton pattern, although followed less dramatically in 1996, is likely to be emulated in campaigns to come.[4]

4. Division and Integration of Authority and Responsibility

Since a presidential campaign requires a tremendous amount of work, a large number of people, all of whom are quite powerful politically, is involved in organization and management. Authority is divided among the chair of the national committee, the campaign manager, the chair of the candidate's campaign committee, and perhaps others with similar titles. Each of these has access to the candidate; each came to the campaign with a certain power base; each hopes to leave with more power. Each definitely has a personal stake not only in the outcome of the campaign but in his or her own role in reaching that outcome.

In addition, various individuals assume authority over functional aspects of the campaign. They carve out their own space and either apply existing expertise or quickly develop expertise, so that they know the area in which they are working better than anyone else. In short, they make themselves indispensable. These individuals must be made to fit into the campaign organization. On the one hand, they are important cogs in a wheel that needs to be complete in order to function efficiently. On the other hand, they demand (and often require) a certain amount of autonomy. The juggling act is often difficult.

One test of a campaign organization is how well it all works together. With the stakes so high, for the candidate and for the individuals involved, with the time so short, and with the task so formidable, it is possible that integration of the campaign organization is never accomplished. A fragmented campaign often is the result of frustration when strategies are not working; that kind of fragmentation only compounds the problems that created it. Many who watched the 1984 Mondale campaign felt that fragmentation problems plagued that effort until the very last weeks. On the other hand, observers of the Dukakis campaign in 1988 felt that many of his problems came from an inability to listen to what his advisers said (Black and Oliphant 1989). The losing efforts by President Bush in 1992 and Bob Dole in 1996 both showed signs of leadership difficulties.

Perhaps the most interesting contrast in recent years has been between the 1988 Bush campaign, which appeared to be a unified organization—a group working together for a common goal—and his 1992 effort, one that often seemed to be in total disarray. In 1988 Lee Atwater and James Baker, who later became RNC chair and secretary of state respectively, made public assurances that all staff rivalries and jealousies were put on the back burner. By 1992, Atwater had unfortunately succumbed to brain cancer. Baker was reluctant to return to politics from his higher callings in government service. He was never able to control campaign rivalries nor to set **strategy** on a positive course. Of course, analysts can be guilty of exercising 20/20 hindsight. Winning campaigns always seem to have been well run and losing campaigns to have flailed about for direction. If things are going well, there is enough glory to share and enough spoils so that everyone can be rewarded. When things are going badly, the problems inherent in campaign organization are exacerbated as everyone looks for someone else to blame for the deteriorating situation. But to a certain extent these characterizations do in fact reflect reality.

STRATEGY
The overall design of a campaign.

B. Functions of a Presidential Campaign Organization

In simplest terms, the function of a presidential campaign organization is to carry the candidate's campaign for the presidency the length and breadth of the country. The structures adopted by various campaigns over the years to achieve this goal have had a number of similarities.

1. Grassroots Politics

The media lead observers to believe that candidates and their top aides take some time to rest after securing a presidential nomination. In fact, nothing could be further from the truth. They simply are engaged in a different type of activity that is less visible and that involves less travel and fewer speeches. But it is no less important. They are engaged in the task of building and cementing an organization that spans the nation, that draws in as many different types of people from different locales as is possible, and that is ready to jump into action, to perform the tasks necessary to campaign nationally, as soon as it is called upon. Bill Clinton and Al Gore demonstrated this most conclusively in 1992 when they set off on a six-state bus tour right after the convention.

These tasks involve the grassroots approach to politics. Friends and neighbors must be convinced to support the candidate. A campaign must be visible in area after area. There must be a feeling that it is right to support a candidate actively because many others are doing so. When the candidate or his running mate appears in an area, enthusiastic crowds must be in evidence. This enthusiasm breeds more enthusiasm, but the initial response does not occur spontaneously; it results from continuous activity on the part of the most active on board.

Geographic organization. Basic to any presidential campaign organization is a national campaign committee that stands at the pinnacle of a pyramid of more local geographically defined committees. That is, below the national level a campaign sets up regional committees, state committees, and local committees. One test of the strength of an organization is its ability to find individuals willing to lead and serve on all these committees. During the prenomination phase of the campaign, it is not at all uncommon for a campaign to have spotty coverage, including some areas in which no coterie of supporters emerges to run the campaign for a candidate. After the nomination, the task is to fill these gaps and to augment previously existing committees with important individuals who may have previously supported other candidates. Thus a state chair in a pivotal state may have to be wooed and courted to join the campaign; such negotiations take time, often the scarce time of the candidate himself. But this is a nontrivial task requiring organizational skills and tact. It is one of the first important tests for an organization after the nomination has been secured.

In establishing a national organization, a candidate and his campaign manager must remember a number of important factors. First, they must be cognizant of the role of party and of the relationship of the candidate's supporters to local party officials in various areas. In some cases the local committee for a presidential campaign will be the same as the local party committee. In other areas, such an arrangement would be counterproductive. Detailed political knowledge is the only basis for making such decisions. Having state and regional advisers who are attuned to the nuances of local politics is of greatest importance. In the elections since 1984, particularly the 1992 and 1996 races, the ability of the presidential campaigns to offer local committees financial assistance—from soft money channeled through the national committees—has been an important incentive for state and local party organizations to work for the presidential ticket. One key variable has been how much control the presidential campaign exerts over an area's coordinated campaign.

Demographic organization. Further, campaign organizers must beware of the trap of thinking only in geographic terms. An activist woman from Pittsburgh might well relate more closely to women's groups supporting a candidate than to the Pittsburgh party organization. Consequently, campaign organizers frequently set up a series of committees based on demographic characteristics that are parallel to those based on geographic location.

For these committees to work, a number of conditions must be met. Group members must have a sense of unity and a sense that there is a reason for them as a group, not just as individuals, to back one candidate. Second, a key leader of the group must be willing to take a visible position, heading that group's efforts on behalf of the candidate. The leader must be aware of the internal politics within the group and of the ways to unify that group behind one candidate. Finally, the communications network between the campaign organization and the group organization must be extremely sensitive.

Establishing parallel organizations with overlapping responsibilities always creates the possibility of conflict. Every woman, every black, every Hispanic, every Jew, every member of every group lives somewhere. Most of these individuals are members of more than one demographic group. Many are members of other self-defined groups, for example, labor unions, teachers, clergy. Their loyalty is often divided. They are undoubtedly part of a group for reasons other than electoral politics; members share a common interest but not necessarily a common political orientation. Group leaders in each group appeal for their support. These efforts, while all well intentioned, can work at cross-purposes. Gaining the benefits of group efforts without losing support because of intergroup conflict or conflict between group organizations and geographically defined committees defines another test of the strength of a candidate's overall campaign organization (Kessel 1984, 363; 1988, 131–136; 1992, 125–133).

Grassroots politics at the presidential level might seem to be a contradiction in terms, but that type of campaigning remains crucial. Building enthusiasm for a candidate at the grassroots is the most important function performed by many who work on that candidate's behalf. Without that effort, the work of the rest of the organization, to which we now turn, would be fruitless.

2. Staffing the Candidate's Plane

As mentioned earlier, one of the key decisions faced early in a campaign is deciding who should travel with the candidate. In many ways, the candidate's plane becomes a surrogate campaign headquarters. Many of the functions that are performed at a campaign headquarters for a local campaign are service functions for the candidate. It only seems logical that those who perform these tasks need to be near the candidate wherever he happens to be campaigning.

Press aides must accompany a candidate, since the press is traveling with him. Staffers charged with massaging the press to polish the candidate's image need to be along as well. Speechwriters are similarly needed in a candidate's traveling entourage. For some time journalists have been aware that every candidate for national office develops a set speech that is given at virtually every campaign stop along the way. "The speech" is an important part of a candidate's campaign arsenal, but it is not the only public address given during a campaign.[5]

"The speech" is modified in two ways. First, it is shaped and molded and improved along the way. Speechwriters come up with new lines for the candidate to try. If they receive a positive response, they are incorporated into the speech for future presentations. Less successful phrases or topics, or those that have lost their time value, are dropped. If the new parts of the speech do not receive the anticipated audience reaction, they are dropped as quickly as they are tried. Some candidates work hard at the details of their set speech. Most leave that to the wordsmiths, staffers traveling with the candidate who are responsible for his spoken word.

"The speech" reflects the basic themes of a presidential campaign. A candidate must speak to a specialized audience or on a detailed or technical topic almost every day. The set speech is not appropriate for these occasions, and the speechwriter is called for. Many have marveled at the ability of candidates for national office to speak authoritatively on a wide range of subjects. Their real skill is to present the words of others as if they were their own.

When a speech to a group with a particular interest is called for or a new policy statement must be outlined or a candidate must respond to an important event during the campaign, the candidate and his top advisers go over the general topic, refining the positions to be taken. The speechwriters then take over, converting some vaguely stated ideas into smooth-flowing prose that echoes the cadences and images thought to be unique to their candidate. If the speech is of particular significance, the candidate and top staff might review draft after draft, suggesting changes and calling for the amplification of some points or the downplaying of others. The candidate might even practice speeches that will be seen by large or influential audiences. Just as frequently, however, the candidate will give a speech he has seen only once. The true test for a candidate comes when he is asked to clarify points he has made in a speech that he has hardly had time to read.

Advance men and women make certain that a candidate's day runs smoothly. The plane carries logistical staff of various types. Campaigns employ teams of young staff members, many right out of college, whose job is to go into an area ahead of a candidate, plan all the logistics of the visit, and then remain for the candidate's visit in order to ensure that all goes as planned. Advance work has become an art, the art of knowing where a candidate should appear and when, the art of knowing which politicians to consult and which not, the art of knowing how to bring out the biggest crowd (or the crowd that appears the biggest), the art of assuring good visuals for the nightly news. (See Bruno and Greenfield 1971 for a description of advance work by an acknowledged expert.)

The work of the press aides is easier when the speechwriters and those concerned with the logistics of a presidential campaign are doing their job well. When they are not, however, decisions must be made about how a campaign can be turned around. In order to do this, most candidates want a group of their top advisers with them at all times. Access to the candidate means influence, and those who view themselves as important often want to be traveling with the candidate at all times.

Key political advisers and strategists are thus yet another element of the campaign plane staff. Everyone with important responsibilities on a campaign must decide whether those responsibilities can best be carried out on the road with the candidate or at the national headquarters. Senior campaign advisers, in consultation with the candidate, must determine who should have instant access to the candidate and on whose counsel the candidate wants to be most dependent. These decisions often change as a campaign progresses. In any event, the staff on the campaign plane must remain in constant communication with campaign headquarters.

3. *Staffing the Campaign Headquarters*

Two functions, research and public relations, are a part of every presidential campaign. Speechwriters, as mentioned earlier, perform one type of research necessary for a campaign to function smoothly. But more is expected of a presidential candidate than the ability to turn a quick phrase. Speechwriters draw on the research performed by an array of issue specialists.

Some of these people are paid staff, professionals who are working on detailed presentations of a candidate's views. Others are supporters of the candidate, or of his party, drawn into the campaign for a particular purpose. Recent campaigns have used task forces of experts drawn from universities, research think tanks, and the private sector to work on a candidate's position in a certain area. For instance, candidate Michael Dukakis often tapped former colleagues at the John F. Kennedy School of Government at Harvard for expert advice. Bill Clinton used many friends he had first met as a Rhodes Scholar in England and contacts he had made through that most impressive network. Most often a staff member coordinates the work of these groups and presents the material in a coherent way, ready for review by the candidate and his top staff and for eventual presentation to the public.

The general public is not very concerned about the details of the wide range of proposals presented by presidential candidates. However, one of the means that the press uses to assess the effectiveness of a campaign and the quality of a candidate is to evaluate the specific proposals floated by that candidate to handle the nation's problems. The press (as well as the most interested segments of the public) is also concerned about the quality of the individuals who are working for a candidate. A candidate's campaign advisers give some idea of the kind of people who will staff an administration should that candidate be elected. The press and the attentive public view these matters seriously. Their evaluation of the individuals who advise a candidate on issues plays an important role as the public arrives at an overall evaluation of that candidate. For all these reasons, presidential campaign organizations spend a good deal of time developing a corps of issue advisers to serve throughout the fall campaign.

Public opinion pollsters do an entirely different kind of research for presidential campaigns. Though the tasks and the methods are different from those researching specific policy issues, the results are put to surprisingly similar use. Public opinion polling has played an important role in presidential campaign politics at least since John Kennedy's campaign in 1960. However, as pollsters have become more sophisticated and as campaigns have become more sophisticated, that role has been changing.

Today every major-party candidate for the presidency employs a professional public opinion pollster throughout the campaign. Some firms have dominated the presidential campaign market in recent elections. Republicans have turned to Robert M. Teeter, who heads Market Opinion Research in Detroit, and the Tarrance Group of Alexandria, Virginia, most frequently. The Clinton presidential campaign relied heavily on Stanley Greenberg and Celinda Lake (Greenberg-Lake: The Analysis Group). Public opinion firms are engaged in many campaigns in any cycle, but securing a presidential campaign is their most important prize. Whereas pollsters once sampled public opinion a couple of times during a campaign, today that opinion is under scrutiny constantly. The latest polling technique involves a **rolling sample**: pollsters test public opinion continuously. They arrive at their latest judgments by replacing responses that are a couple of days old with ones coming in overnight, rolling over a third or a fourth of the sample each day. Thus the pollsters feel they can tell, on a day-to-day basis, how a campaign is moving, what appeals are working with what groups, and what ideas should be dropped.

ROLLING SAMPLE

Technique used by pollsters to gauge public opinion by continuously replacing one portion of the group they are polling each night with a newly selected group.

In addition, public opinion experts are now relying on **focus groups** to supplement their polling data. Focus groups are smaller groups of citizens taken to be roughly representative of some subpopulation. Their views on a particular subject are probed in depth by a public opinion analyst. Focus groups are typically employed to see how people are likely to react to a new campaign initiative or to a proposed commercial.

FOCUS GROUPS

Technique used by pollsters to explore deeper aspects of public opinion.

The pollster of today is, almost by definition, a major adviser to a candidate. The pollster tests the political waters on new ideas, gauges how the public will respond to new issue positions or to the candidate's response to an emerging crisis, and advises how a campaign can present the best image to the public. Major-party candidates for the presidency are too well known, and their positions are too well known, for any candidate to modify his or her views to fit the latest polling results. But that is not to say that these candidates are not capable of molding their views, shaping their position papers, and determining where to place their emphasis according to their pollsters' latest reading of the public's will.

Pollsters are still used for the traditional task of determining how a campaign is doing. It was Pat Caddell who told President Carter that he was about to be badly defeated as he finished his 1980 campaign. Similarly, shortly after his final debate with President Reagan, Walter Mondale was told by Peter Hart, his chief pollster, that he could not possibly win the presidential election. And it was President Reagan's chief pollster, Richard Wirthlin, who told the president that he had a chance to carry all fifty states in the same election.

But in the final analysis, knowing whether one is winning or losing is not very important unless one can do something about it. The increased sophistication of modern polling techniques has allowed pollsters to play a key role in political decision making precisely because they are the ones who can give the best indication of what is necessary to maintain or improve the fortunes of a campaign in progress.

But the press aides who travel with the candidate are not the only ones on a campaign concerned with public relations. They are only part of a larger public relations team. The public relations team works on many different levels. Press aides are concerned with the working press that covers the candidate on a day-to-day basis. This group includes the traveling press corps and the local media who covers the candidate when he or she visits their area (Adams 1982; Patterson 1980; Patterson and McClure 1976; Robinson and Sheehan 1983; Wayne 1988; 1992; 1996).

Others on the campaign are concerned with how the candidate is perceived by the press throughout the nation. The candidate on the road stimulates coverage in most of the nation's newspapers. The campaign headquarters staff concerned with press relations monitors this coverage and seeks means to assure that the campaign is perceived in the best light. Thus, staff members send out appropriate "press packages" to local newspapers; they talk with editors and publishers; they work to enhance the campaign's image by giving members of the press whatever will help them know the candidate better. Campaign managers are very concerned about the image a candidate portrays in the daily newspapers, on the nightly news shows on television, and in the weekly newsmagazines. Thus a good deal of effort goes into working with those responsible for the media (Adams 1982; Crouse 1973; Robinson and Sheehan 1983; chap. 12 discusses the role of the media in greater detail).

However, to an uncomfortable extent, how a candidate and a campaign are portrayed in the press is beyond the control of the campaign staff. Hard as they may work, the final decisions are made by those observing and interpreting their actions, not by campaign staff. On the other hand, the campaign organization has direct control over paid media. A crucial part of the public relations effort revolves around producing paid commercials for television and advertising for other media.

Ever since the 1952 and 1956 Eisenhower campaigns, advertising firms have played a key role in presidential campaigns. Many were scandalized that General Eisenhower was a "Madison Avenue" candidate. Yet by today's standards, the extent to which he relied on commercial advertising to create a favorable image seems paltry.

In modern presidential campaigns, the advertising executive is (again, almost by definition) a key political adviser. This situation was apparent for everyone to see in the 1968 campaign, although it started emerging in the 1950s and early 1960s. Richard Nixon was presented to the public in a carefully packaged manner, as chronicled in Joe McGinniss's popular book, *The Selling of the President 1968* (1969). McGinniss presented a picture of a presidential candidate who was marketed to the American people just as any commercial product is marketed. Just as with commercial marketing, the bad sides of the product were hidden from public view. Only the most favorable images, carefully screened, were ever seen by the buying (or rather, voting) public.

While the McGinniss book was clearly critical of the Nixon experience, more recent accounts have accepted the preeminence of media specialists as campaign advisers. Gerald Rafshoon carried this role to one logical extreme by accompanying Jimmy Carter to the White House in order to create the correct image for a president, just as he had for a presidential candidate. The transformation from media adviser for a candidate, creating paid commercials to garner necessary support, to media consultant for a president, staging walks down Pennsylvania Avenue on inauguration day or fireside chats in cardigan sweaters, seemed almost imperceptible as Rafshoon moved from a campaign payroll to a White House job. President Clinton, of course, was known for involving media consultants in deciding how he would present many situations to the American people.

David Garth, working for John Anderson (R-Ill., 1961–1981) in 1980, carried the role of media consultant to the other extreme. When it became apparent that the Anderson campaign could not build the kind of national organization necessary to run a full-fledged campaign throughout the nation, Garth assumed overall campaign direction. Essentially the Anderson campaign became a mass media campaign. Garth devised a media strategy that was aimed at creating a candidate image, raising money, convincing voters, and, in the most fundamental way, remaining viable.

Criticism of the media packaging of candidates was renewed in 1988. Roger Ailes, media adviser for the Bush campaign, structured a hard-hitting campaign that critics felt was short on substance and unduly negative. In order to picture Governor Dukakis as someone soft on crime, Ailes created a commercial that showed criminals in a revolving door, leaving incarceration unattended. The ad was a not too subtly veiled reference to the record of Willie Horton, a man convicted of murder in Massachusetts, who raped a woman while out on furlough under a program passed during the Dukakis administration. The ad seemed to go out of its way to provoke racial antagonism. The ad did not mention Horton specifically, but Bush's campaign operatives highlighted the Horton episode at every opportunity.

Other advertisements wrapped candidate Bush in the American flag and seemed to question Governor Dukakis's patriotism. Political analysts and media critics cried foul, but Bush campaign operatives defended their strategy as an appropriate way to highlight weaknesses in Dukakis's record (Germond and Witcover 1989). Perhaps more to the point, the Dukakis campaign let these commercials air unanswered throughout the first months of the campaign. While the methods of the Bush campaign advertising staff were questioned, the inability of Dukakis's counterparts to mount a counteroffensive has been raised as one of the main failings of that campaign. According to Christine Black and Thomas Oliphant, *Boston Globe* reporters who followed the Democratic campaign closely,

> the advertising failure was colossal, stupendous, dramatic, intricate, but also at times side-splitting, thigh-slapping, head-scratching. It was

> a failure that needed long and complex roots because it was far too gigantic to have been produced by one lone bumbler. To produce a failure this sweeping took scores of people, meetings, committees, plans, proposals, outlines. . . . Internal rivalry, a balky candidate, and some fatally flawed judgments kept it tearing at the increasingly tattered fabric that was Michael Dukakis's presidential candidacy. (1989, 234–259)

Criticism of the negativity of the 1988 Bush campaign might have led to a "kinder, gentler" George Bush in 1992, but the lack of a response from Dukakis in 1988 definitely led to increased preparedness by the Clinton staff four years later. In neither 1992 nor 1996 did negative campaigning play the role in the presidential election that it had in 1988, but that is not to say that the importance of the message portrayed through paid political advertising was in any way decreased.

The public relations aspect of a campaign cannot be devised in a vacuum. What the candidate is saying on the road, what issues the candidate chooses to emphasize, how the candidate is perceived in the press, and the themes of paid media commercials must all fit together in one harmonious package. The 1988 Bush campaign as a whole was seen as negative, emphasizing the symbols of patriotism but without substance. It was, however, a winning campaign. Bush emerged from being far back in the summer public opinion polls to holding a commanding lead by the time of the general election. Thus the Bush team portrayed a coordinated, effective message and the Dukakis team did not. The 1992 Bush effort was less focused and allowed Bill Clinton to emphasize that he was a new Democrat and to define the most important issue before the public—the state of the economy. In 1996 Bob Dole was unable to put forth a reason for the country to replace a popular president whose programs seemed to be creating prosperity at home and peace in the world. The job of coordinating and presenting a coherent message is the most important in the campaign. Its effectiveness is measured by public reaction, not by how critics respond to the way in which the message is portrayed (Buchanan 1991).

C. Directing the Campaign Organization

1. The Inner Core

In every modern presidential campaign, one individual has had the title campaign manager or perhaps campaign director; some campaigns include both. But it is essential to realize that the enterprise of running a national presidential campaign in such a short period of time is so monumental that no one person can have overall responsibility. In virtually every recent campaign the major-party nominees have surrounded themselves with an inner core of dedicated and trusted advisers who collectively have made the major decisions for the campaign.

Who are the individuals who constitute this core group? Typically they are the advisers who have served the candidate throughout his political career—his personal friends and his most trusted confidantes. For candidate Ronald Reagan in 1980, this group included Edwin Meese, who had served Reagan throughout his California governorship; Richard Wirthlin, who had polled for Reagan throughout his political career; William Casey, who had been a friend and adviser to Reagan for the better part of three decades; William Timmons, a Republican strategist who had been with Reagan since 1968; Stuart Spencer, a longtime California political consultant; and Michael Deaver, the aide who was personally closest to the Reagans.

President Carter's strategy group in that 1980 campaign was composed mainly of the same group of Georgians who had advised candidate Carter in 1976. The names were familiar. Hamilton Jordan, the White House chief of staff and campaign manager in both 1976 and 1980, and Jody Powell, the president's press secretary, had both been with Carter since his days as Georgia's governor. Charles Kirbo, a prominent Atlanta attorney, had been Carter's senior adviser throughout his career. Robert Lipshutz, issues coordinator Stuart Eizenstat, pollster Pat Caddell, and media consultant Gerald Rafshoon all retained positions of influence.

In 1988 the Bush inner core was headed by longtime friend James Baker. Baker had run Bush's unsuccessful campaign for the Republican nomination in 1980. He served in the Reagan administration as White House chief of staff and then secretary of the Treasury. But he left the administration to help orchestrate the general election campaign of his Texas neighbor. Bush and Baker worked closely throughout their careers; it was Baker whose instincts the candidate trusted most. But the team had other seasoned professionals whose political instincts were tested and proven: Lee Atwater, the political strategist; Robert Teeter, the pollster; Roger Ailes, the media guru; and Robert Mosbacher, the fund-raiser. All had experience in national campaigns; all were close to George Bush and were committed to his success.

Michael Dukakis had never run a national campaign before 1988. His inner core were those who had been close to him in Massachusetts. His campaign suffered from the loss of longtime political confidante John Sasso. He resigned during the primary campaign because of his role in releasing to the media some tapes of primary opponent Delaware senator Joseph Biden's speeches in which Biden assumed the words and even the life history of British Labour party leader Neil Kinnoch as his own without attribution, and then denied it (Black and Oliphant 1989, 59–70). But in some ways it is a testimony to the strength of Dukakis's inner core that his campaign survived the loss of his right-hand man. Dukakis relied on the advice of his old friend and neighbor, attorney Paul Brountas; his fund-raiser, Robert Farmer; Susan Estrich, the Harvard law professor who succeeded Sasso; and Sasso himself, who returned to the general election campaign in a less public but equally important role.

In 1992 President Bush relied on some of the same people who had worked with him in his earlier campaigns. But most agree that Atwater's death was a critical blow. Baker left the government to direct the campaign, but he was not as effective as he had been earlier. Most would agree that the 1992 Bush inner core followed the 1988 pattern but was less effective (Germond and Witcover 1993; Ceaser and Busch 1993; Nelson 1993; Pomper 1993).

On the other hand, the Clinton inner core in both 1992 and 1996 could not have been better tuned. Political strategist James Carville was at the center of both campaigns and was surrounded by talented loyalists. Communications director George Stephanopoulos, who went to the White House as press secretary, remained a pivotal figure. Pollsters Stan Greenberg and Celinda Lake (in 1992) and Mandy Grunwald (in 1996) worked well with the rest of the team. Despite some personal rivalries, media consultants Frank Greer and Dick Morris added important strategic voices. The contrast to Bush's campaign in 1992 and to Dole's in 1996 (that evidenced no clear strategy and no solid advisory core) was apparent (Ceaser and Busch 1997; Nelson 1997; Pomper 1997; Simon 1998).

The pattern of deriving a core group in this manner has been broken only once in recent campaign history. That exception proves the rule. In the 1976 Ford campaign, the inner circle was composed of individuals with important campaign responsibilities, but, on the whole, not people who were personally close to the president. The group was made up of five individuals whose goal was to retain the White House for the Republican party. Their loyalty was to that goal much more than to the individual whose campaign they were running.

Why did Ford not rely on longtime political advisers? Quite simply, Ford had little experience in national politics. He had had a very successful career in the House of Representatives, but congressional politics is local politics. He quickly discovered that his political cronies were out of their league in the national arena. His strategy then was to form a team of professionals to run the best campaign that experience could produce.[6]

The function of this core group, in any case, is to set the overall strategy and to coordinate all the aspects of the campaign in order to carry out that strategy. Typically members of this group who have specific areas of responsibility choose their own subordinates to monitor those areas. They in turn choose their own subordinates, and a network of campaign workers grows.

2. Expanding the Core

Expanding the campaign organization is a time-consuming task. Work in this area begins immediately after a nomination has been secured. Efforts are made to draw in party regulars who have worked for other candidates or remained neutral in the prenomination phase of the process. The party organization's role is defined, with an appropriate (but often second-level) loyalist in charge of that operation.

Once the vice presidential candidate has been named, his or her campaign staff must be melded with that of the presidential candidate. A number of different patterns have been seen. In some cases, as when Ronald Reagan chose George Bush in 1980, this entailed working the existing Bush staff into the Reagan organization. The vice presidential candidate came to the fall campaign with an experienced and proven staff ready to work.

But when Walter Mondale chose Geraldine Ferraro as his running mate in 1984 or when Bush chose J. Danforth Quayle in 1988, they did not have experienced staff ready to aid in the general election campaign. Ferraro's most recent political experience had been in the House of Representatives; her staff was not ready to undertake a national campaign. When Bush chose Quayle, he selected a junior, inexperienced politician. Bush wanted a fresh face, but the choice was not a happy one for the campaign. In addition to spending hour upon hour defending the choice, the Bush management team had to supply a complete staff for Quayle, not just to coordinate his efforts with the presidential candidate's but to assure that he did not have a negative impact on the campaign.

The contrast with other vice presidential choices on this score is instructive. When Governor Dukakis chose Texas senator Lloyd Bentsen, he was choosing an experienced and mature politician. To be sure, Bentsen had not run a national campaign, but he had seasoned staff members and contacts throughout the nation. The Dukakis staff coordinated with the Bentsen staff (Tad Devine, a key Dukakis aide who had been delegate selection coordinator during the prenomination phase of the campaign, moved over to run the Bentsen effort), but the Dukakis staff did not have to rely solely on its own staff members to take over total management of Bentsen's time.

Similarly, when candidate Clinton chose Al Gore in 1992 and Bob Dole chose Jack Kemp in 1996, each was selecting an old hand at national political campaigns. Each had run unsuccessfully for his party's presidential nomination in the past. Although neither had a staff in place, each had contacts throughout the nation on which to draw. These campaigns required the coordination and melding together of separate efforts, but neither needed the hand-holding and tight control that Ferraro and Quayle called for.

3. Co-opting the Losers

Finally, in working to establish a smoothly functioning organization for the general election campaign, strategists must find a way to bring into line key supporters of those who were defeated for the nomination. The ritualistic display of unity on the platform at the national convention must be converted into real support for the winning nominee. This is not an easy task.

Up until the most recent elections, Republicans have done this much more successfully than Democrats. Consider the lack of support for Hubert Humphrey by supporters of Eugene McCarthy or Robert Kennedy in 1968, the lack of support for Jimmy Carter by the supporters of Mo Udall in 1976 or the supporters of Edward Kennedy in 1980, or the lack of support for Mondale by supporters of Jesse Jackson in 1984 and for Dukakis in 1988, and contrast it to the more unified front presented by the Republican party for President Ford in 1976, despite a very narrow victory over Ronald Reagan at the Kansas City convention, or for Ronald Reagan in 1980, when his chief opponent for the nomination accepted the vice presidential nod, or for George Bush himself in 1988, when none of his opponents presented an obstacle to his unifying the party.

But the pattern clearly reversed itself in 1992. In that year, reflecting the efforts of DNC chair Ron Brown, defeated Democratic candidates came together behind Bill Clinton early in the process. All of those who dropped out before the convention came onto the Clinton bandwagon. Those who stayed through the convention—Tsongas and Brown—were given enough concessions at that celebration of Democratic party unity to avoid any continuing resentment.

The Republican Convention, which should have been a coronation of the incumbent president, was much more divisive. Pat Buchanan's followers argued vociferously for their view of the principles on which their party should stand. They forced concessions from the Bush campaign and left a picture of a divided party as the impression television viewers took from the convention.

In 1996 the Democrats were again united, with President Clinton and Vice President Gore facing no opposition. Although the convention nominating Bob Dole was not as divisive as the GOP gathering in Houston four years earlier, it did not have the enthusiasm a candidate would like to see from his followers.

These differing experiences reflect patterns in party development. Prior to 1992, the Democrats were badly divided, with liberals fighting with moderates for control of the party. In 1992, however, it was clear that the moderate wing of the party, many of whom had come together under the banner of the Democratic Leadership Council, was in control. By contrast, the Republican nomination contest represented a pitched battle for the heart of the party. President Bush was viewed as an accommodationist more concerned with pragmatic political decisions than with the conservative doctrines favored by the Buchanan loyalists. Although Bob Dole's conservative credentials were impeccable, he was viewed as part of the old guard; his nomination was an honor due to an old warrior, not a victory for new doctrinaire conservatives. However, whatever the cause, the ability or inability of an organization to unite all factions of a party behind the nominee has important consequences for the functioning of the general election campaign.

Building an organization is not glamorous work, but some of that work is public in nature. As the organization takes shape, press aides to a candidate let the political world know who will be working for the candidate and what they will be doing. If these events are given the correct kind of press treatment, the act of building an organization can also be a demonstration of strength and competence. If supporters of vanquished opponents join a candidate's ranks, then the candidate is seen as having brought the party together.

D. Setting a Campaign Strategy

The enormity of postconvention work cannot be overestimated. Certainly much of the organization was in place during the nomination battle, and the key advisers were all known. But the game has changed: the organization has to be expanded, the prenomination opposition must be absorbed, and, most importantly, the new opposition has to be assessed.

Not only is setting a campaign strategy not glamorous work, but also it is not done in public. While candidates appear to be resting after gaining the nomination, frequently they and their advisers are hard at work, devising a plan that will maximize chances of victory in November. The public is not privy to these plans, since their effectiveness would be limited if they were made known.

Chroniclers of recent campaigns have had access to some of these plans after the campaigns have ended (Caddell 1981; Drew 1981; Wirthlin 1981). Some are quite elaborate. The plan for Ronald Reagan's 1980 campaign filled two full volumes. Others have been little more than one-page outlines of what had to be accomplished. The sophistication of these plans says a good deal about the sophistication of the campaign organization. In fact, two sets of plans are put into motion. The first deals with the basic strategy of the campaign: What themes will be stressed? How will the candidate be portrayed? What issues will be spotlighted? Where will the necessary electoral votes be found? To whom will the candidate appeal? The second set of plans deals with tactics: How will the message be conveyed? What consideration will be given to **third-party candidates**, if any are relevant? When and how

THIRD-PARTY CANDIDATES

Candidates on the ballot representing any parties other than the two major parties.

will debates be structured? The tactical matters deal with how the strategic elements will be implemented.

III. Strategies for the General Election

Every campaign must deal with various types of strategies, and these can be categorized in a variety of ways. We will look first at geographic determinations. In this section the basic questions deal with how the campaign views the country. Where are the necessary votes likely to be found? From there we move to considerations of group dynamics. Just as the campaign organization must be built geographically and demographically, so too must strategies be set to appeal to specific groups as well as to specific regions. Finally, we will look at the way in which the candidate is to be perceived. What is the basic theme of the campaign? Why should citizens support this candidate and not the other one? What kind of person is the candidate? How has he demonstrated the qualities that Americans look for in a president? What will the candidate do once in office? What concerns are highest on his priority list? How does he respond to the issues of the day?

A. Geographic Determinations

POPULAR VOTE

Direct vote for a candidate as opposed to an indirect method such as the electoral college.

The basic goal of a presidential campaign is deceptively simple: garner 270 electoral college votes. Campaign strategists are all well aware that the **popular vote** is not the vote that counts in presidential elections. Each state has a number of electoral votes equal to the number of representatives plus the number of senators (always two) who represent that state in Congress. As mentioned earlier, in forty-eight states, plus the District of Columbia, the candidate who wins the plurality of the votes wins all of the electoral votes.[7] To win the presidential election, a candidate must win a majority of the electoral votes—270 electoral votes. If no one wins that number, the election is thrown into the House of Representatives for an election among the top three electoral vote recipients. Were such a contingency election to be held, each *state* would cast one vote—presumably cast according to the views of the majority of representatives from that state, though the procedures for such an election would be debated at the time. Again, a majority of the votes would be needed to win.[8]

In point of fact, the plurality winner in the popular vote has won a majority of the electoral votes in every election since 1888. No election has been decided by the House of Representatives since that of 1824. But on a number of more contemporaneous occasions, one or the other of those eventualities nearly occurred. In 1960, John F. Kennedy beat Richard Nixon by just over 100,000 votes out of nearly 70 million cast.

He won the electoral college vote with an electoral college plurality of eighty-four votes. If Nixon had carried Indiana by 350,000 votes, instead of the 220,000-vote margin he had, he would have been the popular winner but the electoral loser. In 1968, Alabama governor George Wallace's strategy called for winning enough southern states and their electoral votes to throw the election to the House. He intended to negotiate for concessions on key appointments at that point. Election analysts love to play the "what if" game. What if . . . only 20,000 votes had shifted in these states? What if . . . a third-party candidate had won these electoral votes? Campaign strategists lose sleep over just these matters. For them the key question then is where to win the necessary electoral votes.

Different campaigns have used different techniques to determine which states are secure (won), which are hopeless (lost), and which are marginal (possible). Increasingly, the techniques used to devise campaign strategies are more and more sophisticated, but sophisticated scientific precision is not a substitute for political judgment. As has been oft repeated, politics remains more art than science. Strategies must reflect changing political times, multiple perceptions of the stakes involved, and the chemistry of certain candidacies as well as the more stark realities of political analysis.

Perhaps the best way to understand geographic strategies is to look at the Clinton campaign in 1992. By 1988 the concept of an electoral college "lock" was part of the everyday parlance of political analysts. The "lock" referred to states that seemed to be safe for Republican presidential candidates in recent elections. Twenty-three states (with over two hundred electoral votes) have voted for the Republican candidate in every presidential election since 1968. If the states that supported only Jimmy Carter among the Democratic hopefuls in this period were added, considering them aberrations because of his southern candidacy, the safe Republican states contained more electoral votes than the number needed for victory—the Republicans had a lock on the election. Despite losing the 1988 election to George Bush, Michael Dukakis demonstrated to some that the Republican lock might be "pickable." He came close to winning in a number of states that had gone to the Republicans for many years.

The 1992 Clinton strategy grew of what he considered a desperate situation—he was running third behind President Bush and Ross Perot in the early spring. In order to have any chance of winning, he needed to find a combination of states to give him an electoral majority. His strategists started with states that had gone consistently to the Democrats, added those in which Jimmy Carter had shown that a southern Democrat (and eventually in this case, one with a southern running mate) could do well, and finally tacked on those in which Dukakis had done better than expected. California and New York—the two biggest electoral prizes with eighty-seven electoral votes between them—

were key to his strategy. By August both states appeared safe. The Clinton campaign could then put extra effort into other states—trying to secure what they thought were winnable states in the South, the far West, and New England and then concentrating major efforts on the industrial heartland—states like Ohio, Pennsylvania, and Michigan. The results of the election show the extent to which the strategy succeeded. In addition to New York and California and the traditionally Democratic states, he won four southern states, most of the far West, all of New England, and the rustbelt states of Pennsylvania, Ohio, Michigan, and Illinois (Ceaser and Busch 1993, 160–161; for discussions of geographic strategies in earlier campaigns, see Black and Oliphant 1989; Germond and Witcover 1989; Runkel 1989; Germond and Witcover 1985; Pomper 1985; Ranney 1985; Drew 1981; Jordan 1982; Moore 1981; White 1982; Schram 1977; Witcover 1977).

Of course, when an incumbent wins, he almost always follows his winning geographic strategy again in the next election. President Clinton did that in 1996, hoping to draw on the supporters he had attracted four years earlier. Figure 10.1 shows the extent to which his geographic winning coalition in 1996 paralleled that of 1992. Clinton lost only three states—Colorado, Georgia, and Montana, with a total of twenty-three electoral votes—that he had won in 1992; he picked up two states—Arizona and Florida with a total of thirty-three electoral votes—that he had not won in his first election.

What does it mean to follow a geographic strategy? Put simply, the question is one of campaign resources. A campaign has a limited amount of resources, no matter how those are defined—candidate and surrogate time, money for television, staff. All votes across the country are not of equal value. A campaign puts more resources into states (and therefore looking for votes) that are more competitive but where it

Figure 10.1 Geographical Coalitions in Presidential Elections, 1992 and 1996.

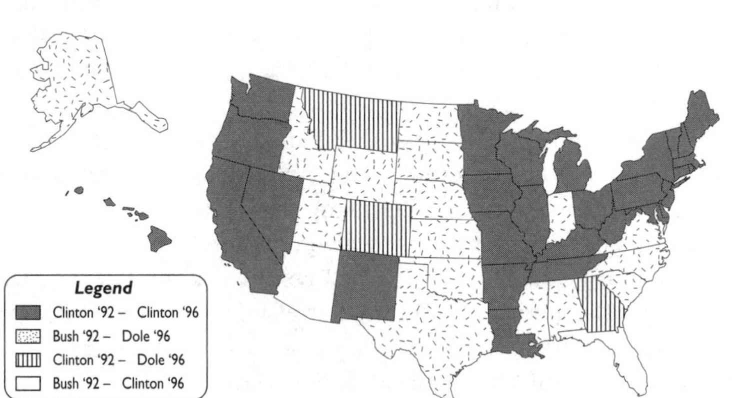

feels it has a chance. If a state is definitely won, then it will receive fewer resources—the candidate, the vice presidential candidate, and their wives will visit less often; less money will be spent on television. It does not matter by how much a state is won. There is no benefit in building up the margin of victory. What is important is that the state is in the win column and that its electoral votes are tallied. Conversely, if a state is lost, if there is no hope of winning the electoral votes, then it too receives fewer resources. It does not matter by how much it is lost, if it is lost. According to F. Christopher Arterton,

> The Clinton campaign used a sophisticated data-mapping operation to systematize its scheduling, media-buying, and get-out-the-vote operations. . . . Week by week, each media market was ranked in terms of the number of persuadable voters in the market weighted by the Electoral College votes and the perceived strategic importance of the states reached in that market. The resulting map . . . quickly revealed where the campaign needed to place its emphasis in travel, field operations, and media buys. (Pomper 1993, 87)

The goal is to concentrate efforts in winnable states in which the outcome is in doubt. Assessments of which states receive how much emphasis change over the course of a campaign. That is the nature of the dynamics of campaigning. But the theory that campaigns seek electoral votes and emphasize states that are winnable but not assured never changes.

B. Coalition Strategies

The election is contested in the states, but voters do not see themselves merely as citizens of states, and they do not receive campaign stimuli as citizens of states only. Thus another approach that campaign advisers use is to look at voters as people who can be grouped according to their views on politics and may logically be expected to either favor or oppose a certain candidate. Strategies using this premise are less explicit than those based on geography, but they are nonetheless important in campaign planning.

Let's look back to the 1980 campaign, as it demonstrates a clear example of this kind of strategy. Ronald Reagan's strategists knew that the conservative vote was assuredly in their column in 1980. No other candidate could "out-conservative" the record that the former California governor had established. On the other hand, Reagan was vulnerable from the center, with John Anderson and Jimmy Carter both appealing to the moderate element in the voting public.

The Reagan response to this perception was to mute some of his more conservative views and to appeal explicitly to the moderates and independents. He did this by denying some of the more outrageous charges against him, by concentrating on issues around which a consensus could be built, and by placing emphasis on moderate stands with which he was comfortable.

President Carter knew that he needed to capture the center away from Ronald Reagan and that he needed to cement the traditional New Deal coalition, much of which was leaving his camp for Reagan. The strategy was to base specific appeals to union members, to Jews, to Catholics, to blacks, and to women. He also planned to emphasize the differences between his views and those of Governor Reagan on foreign policy, hoping to depict Reagan as a dangerous reactionary who might lead us into an unthinkable war. The strategy was a wise one, but he was less successful in painting a frightening picture of Reagan than Reagan was in painting Carter as an incompetent.

Once again the 1992 and 1996 appeals of Bill Clinton serve as excellent examples. As mentioned earlier, Clinton's 1992 nomination marked a triumph for the Democratic Leadership Council, a group of mainly southern Democrats who were convinced that their party needed a new appeal. In their view, Democrats had based too much of their appeal of issues favored by relatively small minorities—blacks, gays, civil libertarians. While defending these groups involved important stands of principle, such actions also depicted the party as one defending the fringes and not concerned about the vast majority. Al From, the president of the DLC, argued that the Democrats could be true to their basic principles but still strive to appeal to a majority. He defined this group as suburban housewives, concerned with bread-and-butter issues, with the economy, with safety, with responsibility. Thus, in 1992, the Democratic platform stressed these issues; candidate Clinton never strayed from them in the campaign. To a large part they made him President Clinton.

TRIANGULATION

The effort to position oneself between extreme positions so as to draw support from both sides.

In 1996 the term **triangulation** came into common parlance. Political consultant Richard Morris, an old friend of Bill Clinton who had worked for both Democratic and Republican candidates, was brought into the White House for advice after Democrats were badly beaten in the 1994 midterm election. Morris's advice was simple. If Clinton positioned himself between liberal Democrats and conservative Republicans in Congress, he would be able to form a winning coalition. By "capturing the center," he would take potential voters away from the Republicans while losing no Democrats, as they would have no viable alternative to whom they could turn. The strategy, exemplified by passage of a conservative welfare plan, worked admirably. The Republicans screamed because Clinton was usurping their issues. But he did get credit for "Republican" programs passed on his watch. The Democrats were distraught because they were forced to abandon some cherished programs. But they had nowhere else to turn. And President Clinton was reelected with relative ease.

Polling data can tell strategists how they are perceived by groups of voters. Historical data also reveals how candidates from the two parties have done with various groups in previous elections. Just as it is possible to set targets for states by analyzing election returns, so too is it possible to set targets for groups by analyzing polling data. It is also possible to base some parts of a candidate's appeal on group loyalties. However, with few exceptions, group members do not live in concentrated geographic areas. Most campaign appeals go out through the mass media, which is by and large geographically based. Therefore, appealing to group loyalties as separate from geographic location is a difficult task for a campaign to undertake and is, in fact, a tactical matter to which we will return.

C. Issue Strategies

In one sense, events define the issues of a campaign. Jimmy Carter had to deal with the Iranian hostage crisis during his campaign for reelection, whether he wanted to do so or not. But in a very important way, the candidate sets the tone for a campaign. He does so by the force of his personality, by his statements about why he wants to be president and what he would do if elected, and by the concerns that he chooses to emphasize as he campaigns throughout the nation.

1. Campaign Themes

In 1992, President Bush was constantly criticized for not having "the vision thing." He never understood the term and never understood what was missing. In a very fundamental way, what was missing was any sense of why he should be reelected president of the United States. His campaign never had a theme. He never gave the citizens a sense of where he wanted to take the country.

Bush's two opponents in 1992, in very different ways, each adopted the same theme. Bill Clinton ran as an outsider, taking his cue from Jimmy Carter, who had run and won that way sixteen years earlier. He wanted to change the way things were done in Washington—to spark the economy, to end the gridlock of divided government and get things done, to rid Washington of those who had been there too long, personified by George Bush and his Republican colleagues who had run the executive branch for twelve years. He wanted to be the candidate for a new generation, the candidate who looked to make changes for the future. These variations on the change motif were symbolized by the theme song of the Clinton campaign, "Don't Stop Thinking about Tomorrow!"

H. Ross Perot was the ultimate outsider, stressing the change theme as no one had before. Perot wanted to "get under the hood and fix things." He wanted a whole different approach to government, his

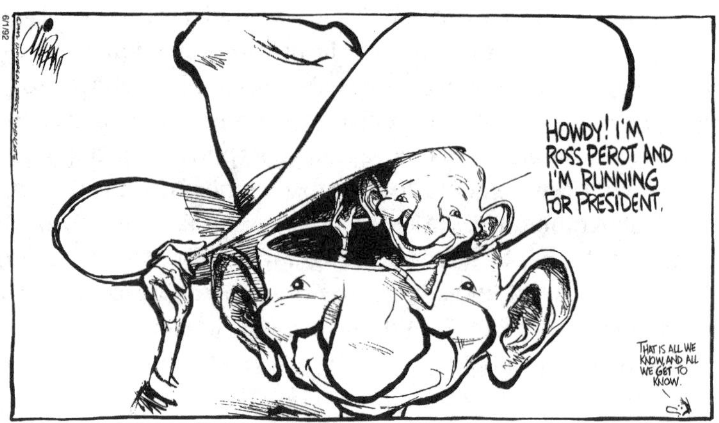

practical "down home" approach that had been so successful in business. There was nothing about Ross Perot, as a man, as a candidate, as a catalyst for new ideas, that did not say "change." He clearly struck a responsive chord with the American people. Before he dropped out of the campaign on the eve of the Democratic convention, his high poll showings suggested the extent to which his appeal was being heard. When he withdrew, those who had listened to his message turned toward Bill Clinton, the other change agent in the race. When Perot returned to the race, however, he was not able to recapture all of his former supporters. (See Ceaser and Busch 1993, 165.)

When a campaign begins, the opening theme needs to be presented often and forcefully. Candidates spend a great deal of time thinking about how to make their thematic statements most effectively. The messages conveyed in early speeches and television interviews, the ways in which those messages are delivered, the audiences to whom they are directed, the efforts made to disseminate them to the public. These are all part of a campaign's opening gambit. A candidate is most able to define his own message, to articulate his own theme, early in the campaign. After that, he often must respond to challenges from opponents and to events as they unfold.

Candidates must have a good deal of faith in their basic theme—in the ways in which they are presenting that theme to the nation. Their campaign is built on that foundation. But what if it is not working? Campaign strategies are not static; they are not set in cement. Situations change and the candidate must react. Pollsters, journalists, strategists, and the candidate all make assessments about "how it is going." All these observers see what is working and what is not. They know when it is time for a change, when it is time for a "strategic adjustment" (Kessel 1984, 314; 1992, 75-76).

Changes in the basic theme of a campaign are not easy to make. First, it takes some time to realize that all is not going as planned. With modern polling and with candidates sensitive to the "pulse of the people," feedback is constant. Still it takes some time to realize that a pattern of failure is appearing, that the campaign is not having its desired impact. Second, those who have made the initial decision about a campaign's theme, by and large, are the same ones who are assessing this new information. The team consensus about what should work was not easily arrived at. Consequently, it is not easily disrupted either. The more a candidate is invested in the theme, the harder it is to shift.

Changes during a primary campaign might be necessitated after a series of primary losses. Often, however, those losses presage the end of a campaign and any changes are fruitless. Similar changes in general election campaigns are much more difficult for a number of reasons. No events in a general election campaign are as decisive as a caucus or primary defeat to signal the need for change. The campaign team has experienced too much success together for the candidate to consider a change in senior advisers. Too little time remains before the November election to articulate a new theme and to sell it to the American people. Doing so might appear hypocritical. Finally, the advisers on board have given the situation the benefit of their best analysis, and thus it is unlikely they will come up with anything different.

Thus despite the fact that campaigns are not static events, major thematic adjustments are most difficult to make. More frequently, concerns are expressed and minor adjustments are made. Tactical decisions, not strategic decisions, are the order of the day. And the days slip by while these assessments and adjustments are being made. Soon it is time for the final push to election day. And by that time, as political scientist John Kessel has so aptly put it, "time's up" (Kessel 1984, 316; 1992, 76). Minor adjustments can be made, but, by and large, these are changes at the margin. The push to election day might be very important in a close election, but what one does in those last days cannot represent a major change in the themes that have been set out in advance.

In 1996, Bob Dole tried to change his basic theme as the campaign wore to a halt. In his case, he went from advocating his own cause to attacking Bill Clinton and the Democrats. He went from his own basic theme to attacks on Clinton's character. Presidential character is an important consideration as citizens decide which candidate to support. It is the second aspect of issue strategy.

2. Character as a Campaign Issue

Americans hold their presidents to a high standard. They want to respect their leader. The press examines candidates for party nominations in great detail, and those who are found wanting are often left by the wayside. But even among the survivors, character is an important issue. Americans vote for a party; they vote for a set of ideas; but they also vote for a person—someone they can trust to lead the nation.

To what kind of person do voters turn? George Bush had an idea. He had been "bred" to lead. He was the heir to a political family. He had the right pedigree. But more than that, he had the right résumé. He had volunteered for World War II at a very young age and had been shot from the sky. He had worked in his own business and succeeded in rugged west Texas. He had served in Congress, as chair of the Republican National Committee, as director of the CIA, as ambassador to China and the United Nations, as vice president. He knew the government. He had experience. He was a leader.

Bob Dole knew he had the character to be president. He had been a hero in World War II, suffering an injury that he carries with him as a badge of honor to this day. He came up the hard way, not from a privileged background but from small-town America, by virtue of his own hard work and skill. He too had served his party as national chair; he had run for vice president; he had a distinguished record in Congress, in both houses, capped off by his years as leader of the Republicans in the Senate. He was respected by his peers, who felt his time to be president had arrived.

Bush, in 1992, and Dole, in 1996, tried to make character a key campaign issue. And to a large extent they succeeded. Bill Clinton's character had been called into question during the 1992 primaries. His alleged marital infidelity was exposed to the nation and his veracity was questioned as he responded to inquiries about his draft status during the Vietnam War and about his use of marijuana. Bush played on concerns raised by these issues throughout the 1992 campaign, trying to divert attention from the "change" theme to one of fitness for office.

Clinton's character was assaulted throughout his first term in office. The Whitewater investigation, questions about firing workers in the White House travel office, the entire litany of charges that came under the purview of the Office of the Special Prosecutor, as well as the ways in which President Clinton responded to each allegation, caused people to remember his "Slick Willie" image. In the final hours of the 1996 campaign, Bob Dole turned up the heat on the character issue. He did not believe that the American people would really choose someone with Clinton's character flaws over him.

Bush and Dole clearly won the "character wars" in their respective campaigns against Clinton, but that one issue was not enough to offset others. There were aspects of character from which Clinton benefited, particularly his relative youth and his ability to appeal to minorities and others not from Main Street America. Clinton represented a new generation of American politician. That aspect of his character, while not offsetting the attacks leveled at him by his opponents—and the wounds he inflicted on himself—clearly aided his appeal in each election. His victories also demonstrated that character has many dimensions in a campaign, a lesson certainly not lost on candidates looking at future possible runs for the White House.

3. The Issues Raised during a Campaign

Candidates for the presidency must be responsive to the issues of the day. They attempt to emphasize those issues that work to their advantage and downplay those that help their opponents. At times, events dictate how issues will affect a campaign. At other times, candidate strategy concerning issue emphasis has most impact.

It is possible to generalize about these matters. When the nation is involved in a foreign crisis, international concerns tend to dominate the issue discussion during a campaign. If American soldiers, sailors, pilots, and marines are in harm's way, the citizenry focuses on these concerns. However, in times of peace, domestic issues, particularly the bread-and-butter issues relating to the economy, are more salient. The electorate's attention to these issues is broader than it is deep. Citizens care how the economy is affecting them personally, and they credit or blame the incumbent president for these effects. They are not sophisticated critics of particular economic policies; rather they evaluate results. Similarly, the views on other domestic policies, including controversial issues like affirmative action and abortion, are focused on an emotional level; citizens have general views on these policies but they do not want to examine programmatic details.

The 1992 and 1996 elections provide relevant examples of how issues play in presidential campaigns and of how they can be used for strategic purposes. As discussed earlier, President Bush was accorded record high poll ratings after the victory in the Persian Gulf War in 1991. He was so popular that many leading Democrats decided not to challenge him, thinking could not be beaten. However, when election time rolled around in 1992, the popular frenzy over the lightning-fast military victory had died down. Bush was given credit for his foreign policy success, but the electorate was less concerned about that aspect of presidential decision making than they were about the economy.

The Clinton campaign emphasized the economy. Recall the now famous sign on the desk of press secretary George Stephanopoulos: "It's the economy, stupid!" Candidate Clinton stressed the economy at every opportunity. He talked about the problems caused by the expanding deficit; he talked about the need to create more jobs, "to grow the economy." He talked about the failures of the Bush administration to handle the perceived recession. Other issues also worked to Clinton's advantage. The Republican Convention had been dominated by those stressing "family values." But the stridency of the debate made many uncomfortable; it seemed as if the Republicans wanted to dictate what values should be important to all citizens. The voters responded negatively to that kind of direction. On the other hand, Clinton talked about health care, education, and the environment—noneconomic domestic issues about which the public clearly cared. On each of those, his views reflected the concerns that citizens felt. Thus Clinton came out ahead of Bush on the issues strategy. The one area in which Bush had an advantage—foreign and military policy—was the one about which the people cared least.

Fast-forward four years. By 1996 the recession had ended. The deficit was receding and the budget moving toward balance. More people had jobs, and they were more confident that they would retain jobs in the future. The voters credited Bill Clinton for these improving conditions. Many economists' belief that the seeds for the economy's improvement had been planted in the Bush administration was irrelevant. It was irrelevant that Clinton's policies at times were forced on him by the Republicans, particularly after the election of 1994 and Republican commitment to the Contract with America. What is relevant is that the public credited President Clinton with these improvements. Bob Dole could not make an argument as to why he should be favored on the issues. The country was at peace, the economy was healthy, and people were optimistic. That left Dole with nothing to exploit but Bill Clinton's character flaws. In 1996, as in the 1998 midterm elections, when debate centered on the president's character, the voters clearly demonstrated that they were more concerned with their quality of life and their economic future than they were with assessments of the moral rectitude of the man sitting in the Oval Office.

D. The Strategic Use of Incumbency

The 1996 campaign points out the strategic importance of incumbency in presidential politics. One would think that incumbents would have enormous advantages in seeking reelection. We have already seen this advantage to be incredibly significant in the case of members of the House of Representatives. Think about the advantages an incumbent president holds. First, he has the power and prestige of the office at his beck and call. No one speaks for the nation as does the president. Even the most cynical political observer realizes that "Hail to the Chief" quickens the heartbeat of many Americans. When the president travels, he travels in *Air Force One,* with "United States of America" proudly emblazoned on its side. When the president speaks, the presidential seal adorns the podium. And presidents play their role to the hilt. The basic premise is that the incumbent is "our" president, and anyone else is a pretender to the throne.

Other advantages follow from this one. Whatever the president says or does is news. Thus an incumbent president is guaranteed front-page stories in the nation's press every day. More than that, his views are considered important and legitimate merely because they are the views of the president. Few are willing to put presidential statements under the same scrutiny as those of a mere challenger to office.

As well, presidential action shapes events. When a president travels overseas, he is the U.S. government negotiating with another power. When a challenger travels, he is gaining experience in foreign affairs. When a president signs a bill into law, the law goes on the books. When he vetoes legislation, Congress must address his veto. When a challenger says what he would do, there are no consequences. When a president says that he will not close an air force base or that he will push a public works project, the base remains open or the bridge is built. Citizens know too well the difference between wielding actual power and promising what might be done. Presidents for some time have used the advantages of their office to time grants, appointments, legislation, and travel for strategic political purposes.

Presidents do not have to prove that they are capable of handling the office or that they have the requisite background and experience; they have held the job for four years. What is better experience for being president than having been president?

Finally, incumbent presidents have a political organization in place. In most cases this is an organization that has already run and won a national election. But even in the case of incumbents who have succeeded to the presidency, the White House staff serves the president for political purposes as well as governmental purposes. Their job is to keep the president in a strong political position so that he can achieve his policy objectives (Neustadt 1976); one consequence of this job is to enhance his chances for reelection.

All these advantages would seem to make incumbent presidents seeking reelection invulnerable and thus Democratic challengers to George Bush were difficult to find in 1991. But three of our last five presidents have lost bids for reelection. President Clinton is the first Democrat to be elected twice as president since Franklin Delano Roosevelt. Among Republicans, only Dwight Eisenhower, Richard Nixon, and Ronald Reagan have achieved reelection in this century. The advantages in favor of incumbent presidents might appear to be strong, but their record of winning reelection is not unblemished.

Earlier in this century, Presidents Taft and Hoover lost bids for reelection, but these defeats are easily explained. Taft lost because former president Theodore Roosevelt ran as a third-party candidate, as the candidate of his famous Bull Moose party, and split the Republican vote, allowing Woodrow Wilson to win with less than a majority. Hoover lost because the voting public blamed him for the Great Depression. Each loss took place before the electronic media multiplied the advantages of incumbency.

Further, Truman won with great difficulty in 1948;[9] and Truman in 1952 and Johnson in 1968 each decided not to seek their party's nomination, in part at least because it seemed they would succeed in doing so only at great political cost. But only Ford, Carter, and Bush have lost in recent years. How can their cases be distinguished from Wilson, Eisenhower, Nixon, Reagan, and Clinton? It is a fact that all these presidents did seek renomination and did win reelection, all with relative ease.

However, there are commonalities among Ford, Carter, and Bush, with parallels to Truman (1952) and Johnson (1968), which are more revealing. For all the advantages of incumbency, one important consequence serves as a countervailing force. Incumbents are held accountable for what happens while they are in office, even if they do not cause those events. Truman and Johnson were president during unpopular wars (and the narrowness of Truman's earlier victory was caused by economic difficulties at home for which Truman was blamed).

Ford is an exception that can be explained because he was never elected to a national ticket, having been appointed to the vice presidency when Spiro Agnew resigned that position and succeeding to the presidency after Nixon stepped down under threat of impeachment. His short period in office was marked by continuing controversy over the Watergate scandal, his pardon of former president Nixon, and a recession in 1975. He did not have the opportunity to use the prestige of the office to build up his own reputation.

President Carter's problems also were caused by difficulties that arose during his presidency. The prestige of the nation was compromised as night after night the news programs emphasized that "America was held hostage" by a band of terrorists in Iran. The economy was floundering so much that challenger Reagan could ask citizens to examine whether they were better off than they had been four years earlier. The answer for most Americans was that they were not, and they evaluated President Carter accordingly.

Similarly, despite his foreign policy successes, President Bush was blamed for the recession that was being felt in 1992. His position was further hurt by the fact that he refused to recognize the recession and continued on a policy course that citizens felt was not working. The judgment of the voters can be cruel; their horizon is very short. That Bush's policies eventually proved effective did not counter the citizens' short-term view that their economic future was not bright.

The lessons for incumbents seeking reelection appear to be clear. The incumbency is a tremendous advantage in running for the White House if the first term has been a successful one and is perceived as such as it is ending. Only an incumbent can point to leadership ability, experience, and accomplishments in precisely the appropriate context. Only an incumbent can say to the American voting public, "Let's not rock the boat. Things are going well because of me. Why change?" The themes of "Let Us Continue," or "Reelect the President," or "Four More Years" can be complemented by a strategy of emphasizing the presidential character of the incumbent, by running a Rose Garden campaign in which the candidate is always seen as the president, not as a campaigner.

However, if the accomplishments are not there, if the country does not have a positive view of the way in which the incumbent has run the country, if the four years since the last election have been troubled ones, then the president is likely to be blamed. If the difficulties outweigh the accomplishments, the election is just as likely to be a referendum on the last four years and the outcome is not so likely to be a happy one for the individual in the Oval Office.

IV. TACTICS FOR THE GENERAL ELECTION

The distinction between strategies and tactics is often a subtle one. The *strategy* that a campaign adopts is its overall plan to convince voters controlling a majority of the electoral college that a candidate deserves support. The *tactics* are the day-to-day means used to implement that strategy. As an example, a strategic decision involves identifying areas of the country to be emphasized; a tactical decision would be how to carry the message to the specified areas. A strategy might dictate that a certain percentage of resources will be used to win over a certain ethnic group. Tactical decisions convert that strategy into action, laying out which resources will be used in which ways. This section will review four specific tactical considerations to which all campaigns must give attention—scheduling of the candidate and other campaign principles, the message that will be used in the paid media, the issues that will be emphasized, and the decisions concerning possible candidate debates.

A. Tactical Considerations of Where to Go

The most scarce resource in a presidential campaign, as with a campaign for state or local office, is the candidate's time. Strategic decisions about what areas of the country to stress dictate some tactical decisions about where the candidate should campaign.

But other factors must be taken into account as well. What image should be portrayed on the campaign trail? As an example, the Mondale campaign in 1984 decided that Mondale and vice presidential nominee Ferraro, the first woman nominated for a national ticket, should campaign together for much of the early campaign. They wanted to appear as a team, so that Mondale could draw on what some saw as Ferraro's charismatic appeal. This meant that the two of them could cover only half as many media markets in a day as would have been the case if they had traveled separately.

Similarly, in 1992, the Clintons and the Gores campaigned together for the first week after the convention. Instead of sending the four individuals to different campaign events, the tactical decision was to use joint appearances to create an image, an image of unity, of family togetherness, of relative youthfulness. These all were seen as ways to extend the strategic emphasis on changing generations and not doing politics in the old ways.

Other tactical decisions regarding candidate appearances deal with scheduling surrogates. Who should appear with the candidate? When? Who would be best for which areas? Or who would suffice in less important areas? The 1996 Dole campaign knew that it would only be able to use General Colin Powell on a limited number of occasions. How should this be done? The Clinton campaign had to make tactical decisions about appearances by and with Jesse Jackson. These tactical questions were aimed at implementing a strategy that determined where the candidate would have to do well in order to win.

Tactics, like strategies, can be changed over time. As some states become more marginal, as some campaigners gain in appeal or effectiveness, as specific situations warrant reconsideration, these tactical decisions can be reviewed. It is difficult to make broad strategic adjustments, but it is much less difficult to refine the strategies by changing tactics. Candidate and surrogate schedules require some advanced planning. However, they require neither the lead time nor the fundamental rethinking that changes in strategy necessitate.

B. Tactical Considerations of Media Use

Today it is a given in planning a presidential campaign that a large percentage of a campaign's budget will be spent on paid media. For example, in 1996 Bill Clinton and Bob Dole spent about half of the total money spent on their campaigns on paid media advertising. However, important decisions about how this money will be spent need to be made.

The general strategy of a campaign lays out how the campaign will appeal to the voters and how a candidate will be distinguished from his opponent. Tactical considerations include what specific messages will be emphasized on the media campaign at what times. Of particular importance is the opening message, for this sets the theme for a campaign. Just as important is the way in which candidates respond to changing situations. The 1988 election demonstrates the relationship between these messages and campaign strategy.

In 1988 the Bush strategy was brilliantly conceived and executed, even if controversial. The Dukakis campaign was unable to make a tactical adjustment until much too late. Governor Dukakis did not want to go negative, but he was seemingly incapable of responding to Bush's attack on his character. Only in the waning days of the campaign did he finally cut an ad in which he charged that Bush was inappropriately portraying his record. This tactical shift might have been successful had it come earlier, but when it came, most voters' impressions of the two candidates were already formed.

James Carville, Bill Clinton's chief strategist in 1992, learned the lessons of the Dukakis campaign. He set up the much publicized war room at the Little Rock campaign headquarters with the express purpose of being able to respond to anticipated negative campaign ads from President Bush. The tactic in this case was the ability to respond quickly with new, countering advertisements. Modern media technology allows campaigns to design, cut, and air commercials virtually overnight. Tactical responses necessitate that kind of decisive action.

C. Tactical Considerations of Which Issues to Discuss

The questions of what issues a candidate should discuss and what the emphasis of television ads should be are closely related. For example, when the Dole campaign decided to stress the character issue in the 1996 campaign, candidate Dole changed his basic speech to reflect this new reason for supporting his candidacy.

Right from the start, the content of the speech repeated at each stop by a candidate is a tactical expression of his basic strategy. The tactical aspects of the 1980 Reagan campaign have been used as models by candidates in succeeding elections. Reagan's strategy in 1980 called for disabusing voters of the notion that his views were out of the mainstream and that electing him would be dangerous. His early speeches emphasized that his views were not set in ideological stone and that he was willing to change. When President Carter was unsuccessful in his attempt to convince Americans that they had to be afraid of a Reagan presidency, the Reagan strategists knew that their tactic had worked. Poll results confirmed this assessment.

At that point, Reagan's tactics changed. His image was secure, so he could begin to attack Carter's image. He could begin talking about the four-year Carter record. The tactical decision was to switch to issues that reflected badly on Carter once Reagan's own image was secure in the minds of the voters. The final weeks of the campaign saw Reagan repeatedly asking one question, "Are you better off now than you were four years ago?" The tactic was to change the focus of the debate from Reagan's image to Carter's record. It was a most successful switch.

Recall the tactics used by the Clinton campaign that we have already considered. First, Clinton portrayed an image of an outsider, "the man from Hope," someone who wanted to change the way things were done. Once he had set that basic picture in the electorate's eye, he turned to the economy. His advisers reminded him over and over again to stay on message—and the message was that the economy was in trouble, that Bush did not have the answer, and that he would "grow the economy" and provide jobs for the American people. When Clinton was on the stump, when he was engaged in debates with his opponents, when he was interviewed on television, no matter what question was posed, he came back to the economy as the basic issue of the campaign—health care, education, and the environment to be sure, but always the economy.

In this case the tactical consideration is to be certain that the issues discussed by the candidate reflect the same concerns as those portrayed in television commercials. The basic strategy of theme and issues had been set; the tactic involved ways to portray that message forcefully and repeatedly to the voters.

D. The Tactics of Presidential Debates

EQUAL TIME PROVISION

Regulation requiring that regulated media provide an equal amount of time to any candidate in an election in which they have given time to another candidate.

Debates between (or among) presidential candidates have become a familiar part of the election process, but it was not always so. Until 1960 the television networks felt that they were restricted from presenting debates between the Republican and Democratic candidates for the presidency because of the **equal time provision**, which specified that if any candidate for an office was given free time on television, all candidates should be given equal time. The networks were concerned about how this applied to minor-party candidates. In 1960 Congress suspended the equal time provision to allow for the famous Kennedy–Nixon debates (Kraus 1962; see also Ranney 1979). These set one agenda for campaign tacticians for the future. Should a candidate seek (or accept) a series of debates with his opponent(s)?

The legal questions about the viability of debates have been ironed out, and the debates have now become a much anticipated, institutionalized part of presidential campaigning. Since 1988, the debates have been sponsored by the Commission on Presidential Debates, a privately funded, bipartisan organization headed by the chairs of the two major political parties.[10] But every four years the candidates still face tactical decisions regarding the debates, in these cases questions of how many debates will be held, when, under what format, and with what participants. Candidates also must decide on the tactics they will use during the debates themselves. Let's look at some recent experiences.

Michael Dukakis felt that there was no way he could lose in debating George Bush in 1988. For a number of years Dukakis had hosted the PBS television show *The Advocates.* He felt totally comfortable on television and totally comfortable in the debate format.[11] The Democrats thus wanted as many debates as possible; the Republicans, as few. The Democrats also wanted to assure that the vice presidential candidates debated.

The presidential candidates debated twice in 1988; the vice presidential candidates, once. The presidential debates were another lost opportunity for Dukakis. He was given plenty of material by his staff, but he never went after George Bush. Dukakis looked like the well-prepared, well-briefed technocrat; Bush looked human and funny. Dukakis won the debating points; Bush the hearts of the listeners. The most poignant moment came at the start of the second debate when Bernard Shaw of CNN asked Governor Dukakis, who opposed the death penalty, how he would respond if his wife Kitty were raped and killed. Dukakis responded mechanically, answering the question but never revealing any emotion. If Dukakis's goal was to connect with his audience, Shaw had flipped him a gopher ball, and he swung and missed. The debate came at a time when the Democratic campaign desperately needed a boost; instead it fell flat (Black and Oliphant 1989, 262–272, 282–296; Germond and Witcover 1989, 219, 251–254, 425–447).

The vice presidential debates, on the other hand, aided the Democrats and hurt the Republicans. Those who were preparing Senator Bentsen for this debate had noted that Dan Quayle frequently compared his background to President Kennedy's before he took office. When Quayle used the line in the debate, Bentsen pounced: "Senator, I served with Jack Kennedy. I knew Jack Kennedy. Jack Kennedy was a friend of mine. Senator, you're no Jack Kennedy." The lines were delivered so perfectly, so slowly, with such a measured rhythm that no one who heard them—least of all Dan Quayle—will ever forget them. Bentsen was the statesman who exuded confidence; Quayle was like a wounded puppy. The debate caused a momentary bump in the Dukakis-Bentsen polling numbers, but it had no lasting effect on the presidential election. It did, however, leave an indelible mark on Dan Quayle's reputation.

In 1992 the debates were held among three contenders—President Bush, Bill Clinton, and Ross Perot—and separately among their running mates. Perot's polling numbers were so high that there was no real question of excluding him from these nationally televised events.[12] One of the key questions in the "debates about the debates" dealt with format. President Bush was most comfortable with a formal arrangement, with set statements and responses, or with questions from journalists. Bill Clinton wanted a more open format. Perot seemed to be happy to be on the same stage, regardless of the format. In the debates that were held, Clinton's performance proved that his tactics were right. He excelled at the informal, town meeting debate in which citizens asked questions. He left his set position and walked out to the questioners. He communicated directly with his audience. President Bush seemed ill at ease and was caught checking his watch at one point.

In that debate the moderator ruled out questions of character as matters not of concern to the citizens in the audience. Again, this decision played to Clinton's tactical advantage, allowing him to stress the economy question. Clinton was also aided by a Perot tactic, a decision to concentrate his fire on Bush and on the job he had not done on the economy. The debates drew huge audiences, with an estimated 80 million people watching the first debate (Nelson 1997, 67). They clearly helped candidate Clinton in that he appeared as "presidential" as the incumbent he sought to unseat.

In 1996, because he was trailing badly in the polls, Bob Dole wanted as many debates as possible, and he wanted them as close to the election as possible—so that President Clinton would have limited time to recoup from any errors. President Clinton wanted as few debates as possible, and he wanted the town meeting format with which he was so comfortable. He did not want Ross Perot to participate. In this case his tactical consideration was simple. Perot was not doing well in the polls, but he was still something of a loose cannon whose behavior was unpredictable. Clinton's advisers knew where they stood. They did not want to allow anything to happen that they could not predict. Because President Clinton held all of the cards (i.e., Dole needed the debates and Clinton did not), Dole eventually conceded to Clinton on all format questions. The presidential candidates participated in two debates; the vice presidential candidates in one. Neither Dole nor his running mate Jack Kemp was able to dent the Clinton image effectively.[13]

The debates have become an accepted part of presidential campaigning. It is difficult to see how debates will not remain a permanent part of presidential campaigns. But they will also continue to raise tactical questions that all campaigns must address as they view ways to implement their strategies. And debates will have an impact, not necessarily a decisive impact, but surely one about which every campaign manager must be concerned.

V. Third-Party Candidates in Presidential Elections

The American party system has been described as a strong two-party system. Yet in five of the last thirteen presidential elections more than two parties have fielded candidates who have had a significant impact on the strategies of the major-party nominees (and perhaps on the outcome of the elections themselves).[14]

DIXIECRATS

Southern Democrats who walked out of the 1948 Democratic National Convention in protest over the party's civil rights plank and ran Strom Thurmond as their candidate for president.

In 1948 the Democratic party was split from the left (by former vice president Henry Wallace) and from the right (by the **Dixiecrat** walkout and the candidacy of Strom Thurmond).[15] Wallace ran a national campaign that attracted over a million popular votes but no electoral college votes. Thurmond ran a regional campaign that attracted slightly fewer voters to his cause but, because they were regionally concentrated, garnered thirty-nine electoral votes. Both of these candidacies were thought to hurt the Truman campaign and help his Republican opponent, New York governor Thomas Dewey. However, Truman still managed to win both the popular vote and a majority of the electoral college.

The 1968 campaign of Alabama governor George Wallace and the 1980 campaign of Illinois congressman John Anderson provide more recent examples of the potential impact of third-party efforts. Wallace left the Democratic party because he felt that the party was too liberal for his views and those of his followers. He attracted a disenchanted Democratic following. Originally political analysts thought that he would only appeal to racist southerners who remembered Wallace's defiance of Kennedy administration civil rights policies. However, during the course of the campaign it became clear that his appeal was to the more conservative elements of the Democratic party throughout the nation. In that way, he was drawing votes away from the Humphrey candidacy. On the other hand, because Hubert Humphrey was so unpopular in the South, the Wallace appeal in that segment of the country seemed to be drawing votes away from Richard Nixon; many white southern Democrats would have voted for Nixon before voting for a liberal pro–civil rights Democrat.

Each of the major candidates had to adopt a strategy for dealing with Wallace. They had to assess whether he was taking votes away from them or their opponent; they had to determine how they could minimize the impact on their voters. For Humphrey this meant an appeal to party loyalty in the North. For Nixon, it meant stressing his appeal to southern conservatives as a potential president who shared their views. The Wallace strategists had to find a way to stay viable in all areas of the country, to convince followers that a vote for Wallace was not a wasted vote.

In 1980 the "Anderson difference" sought to set candidate John Anderson apart from the Democratic incumbent and his Republican challenger by finding a middle ground between the two major-party candidates. Anderson had done well among a certain segment of Republicans in the primaries, but he could never capture the heart of the Republican party because he was viewed as too liberal on social issues. In running an independent campaign in the general election, Anderson wanted to attract voters who combined the orthodox Republican party view on economic matters with the Democratic party view on social issues. He carved a nice niche and exploited his personal strengths—intelligence, charisma, and rhetorical skills—and policy positions to maximize his support among those who disliked each of the other two candidates.

The Carter campaign viewed Anderson as more of a threat than did the Reagan campaign. The strategy of Carter's staff members against Anderson was clear. They belittled his campaign effort. First, they sought to ignore him and to convince the media to ignore him as well. They rejected any debate format that included Anderson, saying he was not really a factor in the campaign.

However, after Reagan agreed to debate Anderson and both received national attention for that debate, the Carter strategists decided to attack

Anderson head-on. They did not attack John Anderson the man or his ideas. Rather, they attacked the idea of a third-party candidacy. Their approach was to say, in essence, "John Anderson is a fine man with good ideas, but he is not going to win. If you really favor his ideas, vote for Carter, because his views are much closer to yours than are Reagan's."

Third-party candidates in American presidential elections frequently suffer a loss of support as election day approaches. Candidates win electoral votes only if they lead a state's ballot on election day, not if they do better than expected. Many voters realize that a protest vote for a third-party candidate is, in fact, a wasted vote, because that candidate will not win enough votes in their state to capture any electoral votes. Thus they are convinced that it serves their interest better to vote for whichever major-party candidate more closely reflects their views. It is difficult to know the extent to which the Carter strategy of dealing with the Anderson candidacy worked. It is clear, however, that Anderson's vote total on election day was much less than the percentages he was drawing in the polls a month earlier in the campaign.

The Anderson campaign demonstrates the problem faced by third-party candidacies. Without the base of political party support, a non-major party candidate has a difficult task demonstrating viability. To be viable, the candidate must remain visible throughout the campaign. The candidate must not fall too far behind in the polls. Television (both paid commercials and news broadcasts) must keep the candidate's name before the public, on a footing as nearly equal to those of the major-party candidates as possible. Such a campaign requires a good deal of money. The major-party candidates do not have to worry about having a critical mass of money with which to run their general election campaign. Their campaigns are funded out of the federal Treasury. But minor-party candidates must raise their own money (which will be repaid from the Treasury if they poll a certain percentage of votes). The financial burden is a heavy one. Many thought that burden too heavy for any minor-party candidate to overcome. However, H. Ross Perot gave lie to those sentiments in 1992.

Perot's 1992 campaign stands as the most successful challenge to major-party dominance of presidential politics since former president Theodore Roosevelt ran on the Bull Moose party ticket in 1912. Perot's appeal was unique. Rather than splinter off from one of the two major parties, Perot denounced them both. He claimed that he stood as an alternative to business as usual in Washington. Using simple "down home" language, Perot based his appeal on a simple premise: he had been fabulously successful in business and would do the same in running the government. He would not permit the kinds of sloppy business dealings that had been exhibited by the Democrats and the Republicans. He would butt heads and not permit partisan differences to obscure solutions to pressing problems. He was the pragmatist who could do it right.

His theme was clear and, despite its oversimplistic view of exceedingly complex problems with which the national government sought to deal, he struck a responsive chord. He also had one unique advantage over previous third-party candidates:[16] he was capable of and fully prepared to finance his own campaign. In fact, during the 1992 campaign Perot spent approximately the same amount of money as did the two major-party candidates. Financing was not an issue in this case.

Perot crossed the first hurdle—viability—by gaining access to the ballot in every state. That alone is no mean feat. Every state has its own requirement. Some are quite onerous, though challenges by previous third-party candidates have eased the burden somewhat. Still, the logistical problem of exploring legal statutes and meeting petition requirements by the deadlines that are imposed is a major one. Previous candidates have had to rely on volunteers to cross this hurdle. Perot was able to hire "volunteers" whenever he needed to do so.

Viability also involves continuous exposure. In this case, while Perot's money certainly helped, his genius for gaining the spotlight was equally significant. He first announced that he would explore the possibility of running on Larry King's CNN television show. King is a flamboyant host with a large following. He is not known as a hard interviewer. Perot appeared on King's show over and over, garnering free publicity not only from his appearance but also from the news stories that reported on his appearance.

His genius for attracting attention carried over into claim that he would only run if "the people" urged him to do so. They were to do this by calling his 800 line and volunteering to help in his campaign. He aptly named his organization United We Stand, clearly with the intent of implying a large following. And people did decide to follow him.

Perot pursued his campaign theme assiduously, never getting off message. His tactic was simple: to belittle his opposition and to pose solutions that everyone could understand. Whether or not those solutions were in fact practical, or if they were politically possible, mattered little to him or his followers. He implied that he would impose them on the system, seemingly ignoring the branches of government coequal to the one he sought to head. But again, none of this mattered. When Perot withdrew from the campaign in July, he was seen as running even with President Bush and Bill Clinton in most trial heat polls. When he reentered the campaign, he never quite achieved that position again, but he was always a strong contender.

Two other aspects of Perot's 1992 campaign should be noted. First, he was included in the presidential debates, and his running mate participated in the vice presidential debate. There is no question that his participation had an impact on how those debates were contested. There is also little question that he did not do as well as some thought he might in that medium. However, he concentrated his fire on President Bush, thus impacting the picture that the viewing public saw of the candidates. His mere presence on the stage gave credibility to his campaign.

INFOMERCIAL

Long television commercials, exemplified by those used by H. Ross Perot, that purport to provide voters with enough information to make informed choices.

Second, Perot essentially invented a new form of political media advertising, the **infomercial**. Perot bought half-hour blocs of time and went before the cameras to explain his program. Political experts derided his effort when he announced his plans, arguing that no one would watch. They were wrong. The audience tuned in to see what this new phenomenon in American politics was all about. As Perot stood before the cameras with his charts and diagrams, millions watched. Many accepted his points—and many more understood that the complaints he had about the way the system was functioning were valid, even if his solutions might not be.

Perot did not crisscross the nation. He did not have an elaborate national campaign structure. He followed virtually none of the techniques we have laid out as typical of presidential campaigns. He had a dedicated corps of volunteers and enough paid staff to use them effectively. And he went his own way. He frustrated traditional politicians who simply did not know how to react to him. And in the end, he had an impact, forcing the two major parties and their candidates to pay attention to his message and his followers.

After the 1992 campaign, Perot remained on the national stage. As an example, he debated Vice President Gore on the issue of the North American Free Trade Agreement (NAFTA), arguing that it would send American jobs to Mexico. But the major decision that he made was to transform his movement, United We Stand, into a political party, the Reform party. In so doing, he signaled that a new force was on the political horizon, and he frightened the major parties. Both sought to appeal to his followers. When his organization had a meeting in Texas, virtually every potential Republican candidate sought to address them. The administration sent representatives as well. The goal was to stem the tide toward a new party and to bring Perot's followers back to the Republicans or the Democrats.

Perot persisted and claimed that he did not want to run for president; of course, he had said he did not want to run for president in 1992, but that he was forced into it. In 1996 he set up an elaborate apparatus to nominate a Reform party candidate for president. However, none of those he sought as his candidate chose to run, and when former Colorado governor Richard Lamm did decide to seek the Reform party nod, Perot reentered the arena. Lamm was led to the slaughter. Perot had never relinquished control of the Reform party. It was too dependent on his financial largesse. He won the nomination at a convention that represented another first in American politics—a convention designed to meet in two different sites at two different times, again with the goal of gaining media exposure.

The 1996 Perot campaign never equaled the 1992 campaign. In many ways he seemed a caricature of himself, claiming that he did not want to run but showing every indication that he longed to have the attention once again. In 1996 Perot did not fund his own campaign; rather, he accepted the public funding that his effort in 1992 had earned. Accordingly, as his funding level was determined by the proportion of the major-party vote that he received, Perot was outspent. When he did not seem to be attracting as many supporters as he had earlier, he was excluded from the presidential debates, thus further marginalizing his candidacy. In the end, the 1996 Perot campaign stands as a third-party effort that had the potential to impact on the national race but never realized that potential.

The Reform party continues to exist. As mentioned in chapter 8, one of their number, Jesse "the Body" Ventura, was elected governor of Minnesota in a monumental upset in 1998. But the party ran only a limited number of candidates for office in the 1998 elections. It still remains to be seen whether this group, as a party, can come out from under the shadow of the figure who has dominated it throughout its existence.

In presidential elections, third-party candidates have been of three types. First, the minor-party candidates who run on ideologically pure platforms. Their goal is to express their views in the public forum. They expect to (and do) have little impact on the result of the election. But they play an important role by raising public debate on critical issues.

The second type of candidate represents a group that is splintering from one or the other of the major parties, or both. The Dixiecrats are a perfect example of this kind of third party. Generally, the major parties reabsorb these third-party candidacies after one election. Again, this happened after the 1948 election, as it did after Theodore Roosevelt's split from the Republicans in 1912. But as demonstrated in chapter 2, other scenarios are possible. If the major parties do not respond, then a new party can come into existence, replacing one or both of the major parties.

Perot represents a third type of third-party candidate—one based on the individual. As individuals frequently act as catalysts for a split from the major parties, it is difficult to be certain that this category is in fact distinct. Was George Wallace's campaign a split within the party or the effort of one man? Perot's case can be differentiated in two ways, however. First, he had no previous allegiance to either of the major parties; nor did many of his followers. He was appealing to those who were disaffected with politics as usual. Second, he institutionalized what had been personal by establishing the Reform party. What remains to be seen is whether this new institution can continue to exist, to organize, to run candidates for a variety of offices, to appeal to a significant following in the electorate, and to impact on the strategies of the other parties. If it can meet those tests, then it should be considered a new continuing force in American politics. (For further discussions of the significance of the Perot campaigns, see Black and Black 1993; Abramson et al. 1995; see also

Aldrich 1995; Abramson, Aldrich, and Rohde 1995; and Rosenstone, Behr, and Lazarus 1984.)

VI. POLITICIANS VIEW THE CAMPAIGNS

From a candidate's perspective, the key aspect of a presidential campaign is that it is totally consuming. If the incumbent president is running, he certainly has other duties to perform. But the emphasis is on winning reelection. The duties of the presidency are performed around the exigencies of the campaign. For the challenger (or if no incumbent is running), the campaign is everything. The race for the White House is the peak of any candidate's political career. There is no higher prize in the American system; no higher stakes exist.

Once the strategy is set and the active phase of the fall campaign begins, the two presidential candidates and their chief surrogates are on the road constantly. If the campaign is going well, then they continue what they are doing. If it is not going well, then they must figure out what to do with the feeling that they are not accomplishing their goals. But they cannot sit down and think about a new strategy. They must leave that to someone else. They simply do not have time. The candidate and his entourage can have input, but their fate is in the hands of the organization they have carefully molded over an extended period of time.

No campaign could demonstrate all these points more than the 1996 Dole campaign. Dole had campaigned for years for the Republican nomination. He had run for vice president twenty years earlier. He had headed his party's national committee; he had led his party in the Senate. But the prize he wanted was the presidency. He had sought his party's nomination in 1988 but had been denied. When he was nominated in San Diego in August 1996, it represented a dream fulfilled. But it really was only half a dream—the nomination but not the top prize. So his quest—and that of his loyal, dedicated, and talented wife—continued. It was their life.

After the second debate between the presidential contenders, the Dole strategists knew that their campaign was not going to stop the Clinton bandwagon. What was Dole's reaction? To campaign harder. To do a marathon ninety-six hours of nonstop campaigning from one end of the country to the other and back again as the campaign ended. Many saw Dole's finest hours as those of his last four days. At one level, he must have known that he was going to lose, but he decided that he would lose being himself, showing Americans the kind of individual they could have had as president, the differences between the man he was and the man they were choosing. He never slackened his pace; he never seemed discouraged. The campaign ended with his best effort.

And how did Dole respond to his devastating defeat? He made a very quick assessment of his political career and said that it had gone as far as it was going to go. Bob Dole had stood before the American people for his entire adult life; at the end he was seeking their mandate for leadership. They rejected his appeal. He was bitter about that verdict for a short period of time, but he accepted it and chose to move on to other pursuits.

Much the same can be said about the losing campaigns of Walter Mondale in 1984 and of Michael Dukakis in 1988. But we should recall the Dukakis case. After that campaign, the biggest price was paid by his wife, Kitty. His best friend, his constant companion, his most loyal supporter, Kitty Dukakis was more sensitive than was her husband to the criticisms from George Bush and to the judgments of the people. The campaign took a heavy toll on her mental health, one that took many months to overcome. The Dukakis family weighed the personal costs of a campaign heavily before they embarked on what the governor frequently described as a "marathon." But they seemingly were unable to imagine what those personal costs really would be.

The glare of public light was too much for Gary Hart and Joe Biden in the 1988 primaries; the emotional roller coaster was too much for Kitty Dukakis. In 1992, prospective candidate after prospective candidate was looking not only at political questions but also at personal questions when they decided to forgo a presidential race. Was the prize worth the cost to himself and those he loved? Certainly the Clintons must have asked that question on more than one occasion. Before the race for the White House in 2000, George W. Bush, twice-elected governor of Texas, a tested politician, looked at recent experiences and at the costs borne by his father and mother, in their successful and unsuccessful races. According to the *Washington Post,* Bush was concerned about the level of commitment involved in a presidential race. " 'All this business about me not wanting to put myself in the bubble [of news media scrutiny] is bull,' Bush said. 'I'm in the bubble. I was in the bubble in '94 and '98. . . . The question is whether Laura [his wife] and I want to make a lifestyle change' " (Balz 1998).

Consider the amazing tenacity of Thomas Dewey, of Adlai Stevenson, of Richard Nixon, and of Hubert Humphrey. How these men could receive the verdict of a nation regarding their candidacy and then come back to run again is difficult to comprehend. Each must have had a great sense of his own worth, of his ability to convince the nation that its decision had been in error, or of the inability of his strategists to convey the correct image and message. Nixon went on to victory and then disgrace and eventually, some feel, to resurrection as a wise man (others disagree). Humphrey died as the Happy Warrior, seemingly always ready to have another go at the nation's highest office.

For most, however, one unsuccessful campaign for the presidency is enough. A number of candidates have tried in the prenomination phase more than once, but few have come back from a losing general election campaign to try again. Why? Because of the effort involved, because of the finality of the decision, because once one has campaigned throughout the entire nation, once one has presented his best effort to the electorate, and once one has been rejected, that verdict is enough.

On the other hand, victorious presidential candidates want to have that experience again. Harsh personal attacks did not deter Bill Clinton from seeking reelection; George Bush's health did not deter him; Ronald Reagan's age did not deter him; Jimmy Carter's lack of popularity did not deter him. In the last seventy-five years, only Lyndon Johnson, saddled with an unpopular war and dissent within his own party, and Harry Truman, in much the same situation, did not run for reelection when they were eligible (and each of these had served more than one full term, having first succeeded to the presidency). Victory in a national election seems to have nearly aphrodisiac qualities. "If the public loved me once, they will love me again. And I owe it to them to give them the chance." That very personal reaction is the essence of a candidate's evaluation of a presidential campaign.

WEBSITES

http://www.democrats.org/
http://www.rnc.org/

The websites of the two national committees include a good deal of information about the candidates, the party platforms, and similar matters. Each campaign maintains its own website during an election year.

http://www.fec.gov/

The Federal Election Commission maintains up-to-date records of all candidate fund-raising and spending during the general election phase of the electoral process, including soft money expenditures.

http://www.cq.com/
http://cnn.com/ALLPOLITICS/

These sites mentioned in chapter 7 are also excellent for getting information on the presidential election as well. So too are the media websites listed in chapter 12.

KEY CONCEPTS

Dixiecrats
electoral college
electoral votes
equal time provision
Federal Election Campaign Act of 1971
focus groups
infomercial
popular vote
rolling sample
soft money
strategy
tactics
third-party candidates
triangulation

DISCUSSION QUESTIONS

1. What is your understanding of the electoral college system? Specifically, what difference does it make that our presidents are elected by the electoral college and not popularly? Do you think campaigns would be run differently were this not the case? How?

2. This chapter began by noting that in recent years many candidates' nominating campaigns have seemed to run more efficiently than their general election campaigns. How do you explain this? Can you think of ways in which candidates could assure that the transition from nominating politics to general election politics flowed more smoothly?

3. How can presidential campaigns pursue more than one strategy at the same time? What does that mean in terms of resource allocation? What are the conflicts that would arise in a dual-strategy campaign?

4. Do third-party candidates contribute positively or negatively to presidential campaigns? What distinguishes third-party candidates who seem to have an impact from those whose names merely appear on the ballot?

5. We have given little consideration to the role of political parties in this chapter, mostly because presidential campaign organizations run independently of the parties, as a result of federal campaign law. Do you think that this is appropriate? Or should parties play a more central role? One proposal would be to give public campaign funding to the national committees for the general election, not to the candidates. How would you evaluate that proposal?

CHAPTER 11

Campaign Financing

ISSUE ADVOCACY

Constitutionally protected advertisements that advocate a particular position on an issue of the day; thought to abuse spirit of law by implying support for or against a particular candidate.

FEDERAL ELECTION COMMISSION

The regulatory body charged with implementing the FECA.

MCCAIN-FEINGOLD BILL

Bipartisan campaign finance legislation proposed and debated in the last congresses of the 1990s.

1974 AMENDMENTS TO THE FECA

The significant changes to the 1971 FECA that structure most of campaign finance law today.

PUBLIC FINANCING

Any of the various schemes used to fund state or federal campaigns with taxpayer dollars.

After the much-publicized excesses in fund-raising techniques during the 1996 elections, campaign finance reform was given new impetus during the 105th Congress (1997–1998). The leaders of the campaign finance reform movement in the Senate, Senators John McCain (R-Ariz.) and Russell Feingold (D-Wis.), pushed hard for a bipartisan legislative package that would have banned the use of soft money and curbed **issue advocacy** commercials financed by outside interest groups. Soft money is money spent on federal elections that is not regulated by the **Federal Election Commission**. Issue advocacy advertisements are those in which the sponsoring organization typically takes a stand on an issue and implies that a certain candidate opposes that view. They are clearly aimed at affecting election returns, but, because they do not explicitly call for the election or defeat of a specific candidate, the Supreme Court has ruled that they do not come under the rubric of regulated expenditures because they constitute protected free speech.

The **McCain-Feingold bill** drew a great deal of media attention, but it too was defeated by a Republican filibuster led by Senator Mitch McConnell (R-Ky.), chair of the National Republican Senatorial Committee. In the House, the companion bipartisan legislation, cosponsored by representatives Christopher Shays (R-Conn.) and Martin Meehan (D-Mass.), passed after Republican pressure forced Speaker Newt Gingrich to bring a bill he opposed to the floor for an up-or-down vote.[1] But the "victory" in the House for the forces of reform was empty because the Senate took no action.

This reform effort was only the latest in a drive to fix the way in which we finance our elections, an effort that has lasted for more than three decades. A brief review will show how demoralizing the effort has been for those seeking cleaner campaigns.

In the 1960s, the focus of much of that concern was the extent to which the most visible campaigns in the nation were waged on television. In response to those concerns, the Federal Election Campaign Act (FECA) of 1971 was passed.

When Richard Nixon's reelection campaign in 1972 spent over $60 million, more than twice the amount spent on his 1968 campaign, analysts began to focus serious attention on the fact that the costs of campaigns were escalating out of sight. Congress passed the **1974 Amendments to the FECA** over President Nixon's veto. When parts of that act were found to be unconstitutional by the Supreme Court, Congress revised its provisions in 1976, implementing partial **public financing** for presidential primaries, complete public financing for presidential elections, and restrictions on the ways in which campaigns for Congress are financed. (These provisions are discussed in detail in section C, "The 1974 Amendments to the FECA," p. 378.) But concern with the escalating costs of funding American democracy and the appropriate sources of money to finance campaigns has continued unabated.

In the Ninety-fifth Congress (1977–1978), President Jimmy Carter made campaign finance reform his top priority; his administration's bill was given the prestigious designation HR 1. It went nowhere. In the next Congress, the House passed a bill limiting contributions by political action committees (PACs) (chap. 6), but the Senate took no action.

In every Congress from the 100th through the 105th, at least one major campaign finance bill drew significant attention. In the first Congress of the Bush administration, the House and Senate passed separate bills that called for voluntary limits on spending in congressional campaigns; the conference committee charged with ironing out the differences between the two bills never met. The subsequent Congress passed a compromise bill that provided partial public funding to candidates who complied with certain voluntary limits, and it restricted PAC contributions and the use of soft money. President Bush vetoed that legislation and the Senate upheld his veto.

President Clinton included campaign finance reform as an important part of his platform when he sought the presidency in 1992. In the first Congress during his administration the two houses again passed separate bills that dealt with voluntary spending limits and restrictions on PAC contributions and soft money. A Republican filibuster prevented the conference committee from convening.

After the Republicans took control of Congress in 1995, they attempted a new tactic. The Republican leadership proposed its own campaign finance reform package in the 104th Congress, a bill that would have made it more difficult for unions to raise money for their political action committees and would have restricted the amount of money a candidate could raise from outside his or her district or state. These provisions were seen as detrimental to Democratic candidates and were opposed by enough Republicans that the bill was not passed. Reform measures such as those proposed in the 103d Congress were also defeated in the House and in the Senate, where a Republican filibuster prevented a vote on passage. And that brings the story to the defeat of McCain-Feingold in 1998—a long, frustrating saga with few high points and little to show at the end.

Why all of this concern? Why have literally dozens of public-minded organizations, like the Pew Charitable Trust, the Brookings Institution, and the American Bar Association, in addition to those normally associated with this topic, like Common Cause, the Center for Responsive Politics, and Public Citizen, focused so much of their attention on campaign finance reform? Why have those who study U.S. elections made it one of the most heavily researched topics in their field?

Figure 11.1 depicts the rise in political spending for all campaigns in presidential years over the last four decades. The amounts seem staggering; the escalation is obvious. The costs of all elections in the United States have grown more than thirtyfold since 1952. Even if the figures are computed in constant dollars, the rise is startling, especially since the

Figure 11.1 Total Campaign Spending in Presidential Years.

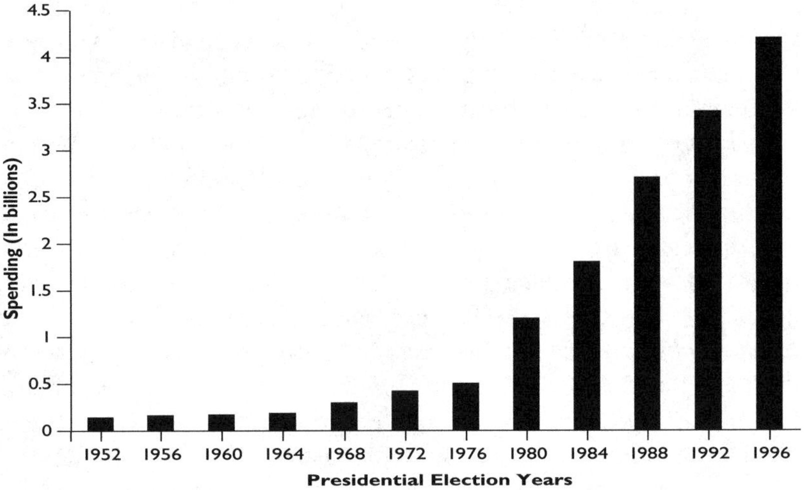

Source: Alexander and Corrado 1995 and estimates by Herbert Alexander.

number of votes cast has risen by only about 25 percent. The amounts spent on some individual races in 1998, such as the $34 million spent on the D'Amato-Schumer Senate race in New York State or the $6.9 million spent on the Sanchez-Dornan congressional race in California, are enough to move even the most laissez-faire observer to raise an eyebrow.

Two very real questions arise. First, does the rising cost of campaigns distort election outcomes in the direction of moneyed interests? Second, does undue influence accrue to those who give large sums of money to successful politicians' campaigns? That is, how do the escalation in campaign costs and the politicians' search for sources of money affect the government? These are the basic questions that have concerned reformers and the ones to which we turn in this chapter.

Politicians who have come of age in the last three decades might feel that these problems are of recent origin, brought on by the age of television and the consequent exponential rise in the cost of campaigns for major offices. But a little historical perspective is in order. Neil O. Staebler's political career spanned half a century. He served Michigan as a member of the state committee and its chair, as a national committeeman, and as a member of Congress (D, 1963-1965). He also served as a member of the Federal Election Commission. In short, his credentials as an observer of campaign financing practices are impeccable. According to Staebler,

> Money corruption has been present in politics for 170 or 180 years. We've been actively working at it since Teddy Roosevelt started back in 1907. But for sixty years practically nothing useful was done. A few acts were passed cosmetic in nature—and many of us in politics reached the point of despair. . . . Politics was very much the art of figuring out what you can get away with. (Alexander and Haggerty 1981, 13)[2]

I. THE CLIMATE FOR REFORM

However, it is apparent that certain types of excess, dramatized for the entire nation by television, provided the impetus for overcoming the inertia and despair of which Staebler complained. Concern over the cost of campaigns and the impact of media advertising reached a crescendo after the gubernatorial elections of 1966. Two of those elections stand out.

In Pennsylvania, millionaire Milton Shapp, an ambitious man with no previous political experience, decided that he wanted to be governor. He hired media consultant Joseph Napolitan to design an advertising campaign to sell "Shapp for governor" to the Pennsylvania voters. Napolitan spent millions of dollars to help Shapp win the Democratic nomination, though he lost the general election that year (Agranoff 1976, 9). In the next election, Shapp, again spending his own money quite heavily, became Pennsylvania's chief executive.

In neighboring New York State, incumbent governor Nelson Rockefeller was thought to be out of favor with his constituents as the 1966 election approached. He mounted a multimillion-dollar campaign, relying heavily on paid media to transform the Rockefeller image and the public perception of his tenure as governor. Governor Rockefeller's record was sold to the New York voters in the same way Madison Avenue sold soap products.

Other examples abound. Politics seemed to be leaving the realm of political parties and entering the suites of advertising executives. Those who could afford extravagant media campaigns won the privilege of governing us. In the 1968 presidential election, Richard Nixon outspent Hubert Humphrey by 2 to 1, and the nation was presented with a "new" Nixon, carefully packaged to rectify an unfavorable image that had emerged from the former vice president's first two decades in public life. Joe McGinniss's chronicle of that election paraphrased the well-known series of books by Theodore White (1961; 1965) with its title, *The Selling of the President 1968* (1969). Reformers found a more favorable climate for renewed attention to problems of campaign financing. Their concern was for the amounts of money being spent, the sources of those funds, and the campaign techniques purchased with those funds. In a basic way reformers were questioning if a truly representative gove rnment could be chosen through a system characterized by inequity among the contesting parties and openness only to those with access to huge sums of money.

Despite dissatisfaction with the system in existence, reform did not come easily. In the first place, those interested in changing the system had to be clear about what aspects they found objectionable and how they should be changed. Next they had to convince those in power, the very people who had reached office using the system that was being criticized, that change should occur. As has been oft stated, the rules of the game are not neutral: this truism is particularly apt for campaign financing rules. The lawmakers examining proposed changes have been most cognizant of the impact of potential reforms on their own careers.

In the remaining sections of this chapter, we will look at reforms in campaign financing since the 1970s. The examination of the solution put forth in the current campaign finance legislation will identify the problems that reformers sought to correct. Some of those problems are in the public eye today, nearly thirty years after the passage of the first of the major reform bills. The total costs of campaigns, the sources of campaign money and incentives for giving that money, and the impact of the ways in which money is raised and spent will be examined as a backdrop for an analysis of current reform proposals.

II. CAMPAIGN FINANCE REFORMS OF THE 1970S

A. Historical Background

A brief legislative history is in order. Before the 1970s, campaign financing for elections to federal office was regulated by a series of acts, none of which was rigorously enforced. President Theodore Roosevelt's efforts, referred to by Neil Staebler, were a response to the success that Republican boss Mark Hanna had in soliciting campaign money directly from corporations. The 1907 **Tillman Act** forbade corporate contributions to federal election campaigns. However, corporations remained active in financing political activity through indirect means, most notably election year "bonuses" to executives, which often found their way quickly to the appropriate campaign coffers, and through visible and generous contributions by well-known corporate presidents and chief executive officers.

TILLMAN ACT

Early twentieth-century legislation designed to curb political abuse by corporations.

The **Federal Corrupt Practices Act of 1925** was the principal means for regulating campaign financing before 1972. The 1925 act called for disclosure of receipts and expenditures by candidates for the House and the Senate and by political committees that sought to influence federal elections in more than one state. The law was silent about campaign activities by presidential and vice presidential candidates. But establishing a large number of committees supporting a particular candidate made it possible to circumvent the act. The multiple committees also made it nearly impossible to find out who was giving how much to a candidate and/or how much was being spent on behalf of a candidacy.

FEDERAL CORRUPT PRACTICES ACT OF 1925

The campaign finance act in place prior to the reforms of the 1970s; honored more in breach than practice.

The 1940 **Hatch Act** prohibited political activities by certain federal employees and set a limit on the amount an individual could donate to a candidate. The limit was meaningless, however, because the law was interpreted so as to allow contributions to a number of different committees all supporting the same candidate. According to James H. Duffy, for

HATCH ACT

Legislation aimed at preventing political abuse of and by federal employees.

two decades the counsel to the Senate Subcommittee on Privileges and Elections, "Money flowed through channels which were recognized as legal avoidance of existing acts" (Alexander and Haggerty 1981, 15).

The first major impetus for reform once campaigning entered the television age came from President Kennedy. Sensitized to the issue by claims that his father had "bought" the Democratic nomination for him, Kennedy appointed a bipartisan Commission on Campaign Costs that was charged with examining ways to reduce the costs of presidential campaigns and to finance necessary costs. The commission's recommendations, which were endorsed by Kennedy and his two immediate predecessors, Presidents Truman and Eisenhower, set the agenda for future reformers, though few of the recommendations were immediately enacted (President's Commission on Campaign Costs 1962). (For histories of campaign finance and reform efforts before 1970, see Heard 1960; Mutch 1988, chaps. 1-2; Overacker 1932; Sorauf 1988, 16-34; for a more journalistic account, see Thayer 1973.)

B. Federal Election Campaign Act of 1971

The first congressional response to pressure to reform campaign finance laws was the passage of an act regulating political broadcasts; however, this bill, which passed Congress in 1970, was vetoed by President Nixon.

In 1971 Congress regrouped and passed two significant pieces of legislation. The more comprehensive piece of legislation, the Federal Election Campaign Act, attacked three perceived problems. It dealt with the problem of extremely wealthy candidates "buying" their own elections by limiting the amount of money a candidate and/or the candidate's family could spend to win federal office. It dealt with the "Madison Avenue approach" to politics by placing a limit on media expenditures. And it dealt with the sources and uses of campaign funds by tightening the requirements for disclosure of receipts and of expenditures by candidates for federal office (Corrado 1991a; Sorauf 1988).[3]

Congress amended some of the provisions of this act after only the briefest experience. Other provisions were declared unconstitutional by the Supreme Court in ***Buckley v. Valeo*** (see section D). But the first important steps had been taken. Congress had identified some of the areas in need of attention—meaningful disclosure of campaign expenditures and receipts, the impact of media advertising, and the influence of personal wealth. These items were to remain on the agenda throughout the period of reform.[4]

The second piece of reform legislation passed in 1971 was the **Revenue Act** of that year. This law encouraged small contributions to political campaigns by allowing a tax credit or (alternatively) a tax deduction for limited contributions to campaigns. In addition, the Revenue

BUCKLEY V. VALEO

Supreme Court decision overturning certain aspects of the 1974 Amendments to the FECA that remains the ruling precedent for challenges to reform in campaign finance laws today.

REVENUE ACT

The 1971 law that encouraged small contributions to political campaigns through tax incentives.

TAX CHECK-OFF
The means through which citizens can contribute money to support the public funding of campaigns.

Act provided for a **tax check-off** to subsidize future presidential campaigns. The tax check-off has been used for the Presidential Campaign Fund, which has been used to fund presidential campaigns since 1976.

C. The 1974 Amendments to the FECA

The first election regulated under the provisions of the FECA of 1971 was the 1972 election, as key provisions of that law became effective in April 1972.[5] With considerable understatement one can conclude that the 1972 experience was not one that would convince reformers that all was in order. The unethical and illegal practices of the Committee to Reelect the President (and to a lesser degree of some of the Democratic campaigns in 1972) have been well documented, not only by the General Accounting Office (GAO) but also by two special prosecutors (Archibald Cox and Leon Jaworski), by the Senate Select Committee on Presidential Campaign Activities (the Ervin Committee), by the House Committee on the Judiciary as it considered impeachment proceedings in the summer of 1974, and by journalists and scholars too numerous to list.

The 1974 FECA amendments were legislated in response to the first experience under the FECA and to the increased urgency that many felt after the 1972 experience and Watergate. The 1974 act totally revised the 1971 FECA, fundamentally changing the ways in which campaigns in this country are funded (Corrado 1991b; Sorauf 1988).

The 1974 FECA amendments dealt with all federal elections. Presidential elections (including the prenomination phase) were to be publicly financed, at least in part. Candidates who accepted public financing also had to accept a cap on total spending, and so the runaway inflation on the cost of running for president was halted. While the cap on media spending for congressional elections that was imposed in 1971 was lifted, much stricter limits were placed on individual contributions ($1,000 to any campaign—primary, runoff, or general—in a single election, with a total cap of $25,000 to all campaigns in any one year) and PAC contributions ($5,000 to any campaign in a single election but with no cumulative limitation). Additionally, reporting and disclosure requirements were improved. Even the amount that an individual could spend on electoral activities independent of an organized campaign was limited. Finally, an independent, bipartisan Federal Election Commission was established to oversee the reporting and enforcement requirements of this act.

D. *Buckley v. Valeo*, 424 U.S. 1 (1976)

Shortly after the 1974 amendments became effective, a curious coalition of liberals and conservatives joined in a lawsuit challenging the constitutionality of the FECA. The law was attacked because it allegedly limited free speech and discriminated against presidential candidates of minor parties. The judicial branch of the government was asked to define the line between the guaranteed rights to free speech and free association, on the one hand, and the obligation of the polity to protect the integrity of elections, on the other.

In the case of *Buckley v. Valeo,* the Supreme Court ruled that some aspects of the 1974 act were unconstitutional while other provisions, deemed separable, were permitted to stand. With regard to the question of free speech, the Court held that limits on campaign expenditures, on **independent expenditures**, and on the amounts individuals could spend on their own campaigns restrained the interchange of ideas necessary to bring about social change and were therefore unconstitutional. The Court also struck down the way in which the Federal Election Commission was appointed, requiring that all appointments be made by the president with the advice and consent of the Senate.

INDEPENDENT EXPENDITURES

Money spent during an election near that is not coordinated with or controlled by a candidate's campaign.

At the same time, however, the Court permitted the disclosure and contribution limitations of the act to remain in place. In addition, the Court allowed other provisions of the law to stand if public funding was accepted: the limitations on the total amount to be spent on a campaign and the limitations on individual and group contributions (Gottlieb 1985; 1991; Lowenstein 1991a).

Buckley v. Valeo was handed down in the middle of the 1976 campaigns. The decision effectively closed down the Federal Election Commission and left many aspects of the funding of the 1976 presidential election in doubt. Those doubts were most serious for the candidates for the major parties' presidential nominations, as they had been counting on matching funds to finance their campaigns. Congressional and senatorial candidates also had to alter their financial planning.

E. The 1976 FECA Amendments

Despite the urgency felt by many of those involved, Congress took nearly four months to revise the FECA to comply with the Court's ruling. A number of controversial issues not dealt with in the challenge to the 1974 amendments were included in that debate, including the difficult question of public financing of congressional elections.

When the FECA was eventually revised in May 1976, the provisions for public funding of congressional elections were not included; however, other significant changes did become part of the campaign finance legislation. The 1976 amendments reconstituted the Federal Election Commission; they set limitations on the amounts individuals could give to PACs and to the national political parties; they restricted the proliferation of PACs established by one organization and the fundraising abilities of PACs; and they limited the spending by candidates for the presidency and the vice presidency if the candidates accepted public financing of their campaigns. A series of other changes that affected the reporting and disclosing of obligations of campaigns and the powers of the FEC were also included.

Again in 1979 Congress amended the FECA. However, recent amendments are mainly perfecting amendments, involving marginal changes as a response to experiences with the recent laws. As one example, state and local party committees have been allowed to contribute volunteer time to campaigns so that the grassroots approach to politics was not lost in the rush to reform. (See Adamany 1984; Aoki and Rom 1985; and Jacobson 1985–1986, among others, on the role of campaign finance legislation in the revival of political parties.)

F. Current Status of Key Issues

As a consequence of these laws, a number of issues have been settled:

1. Disclosure is accepted as a key element of campaign finance reform. Whatever is done must be opened to public scrutiny.
2. Large contributions to individuals' campaigns are suspect and therefore restricted. Gone are the days when a wealthy contributor can contribute $250,000 to one campaign (at least in federally regulated dollars, but see the discussion of soft money that follows).
3. On the other hand, individual candidates can spend what they want on their own campaigns, provided that they do not accept public funds for those campaigns. The right to express one's political beliefs includes the right to spend money to do so; this same logic extends to independent expenditures for political reasons, provided those expenditures are not coordinated with the efforts of a particular campaign.
4. Similarly, the concept of public financing has been accepted, at least by the Democrats; it has been applied to presidential elections and tied with a restriction on the amount of money to be spent in those elections.

Still, some old issues have not been settled and some new ones have appeared. No means have been found to control the amount of money spent on campaigns not funded by public money. The Court seemingly ruled that any such restriction must be tied to the acceptance of public funds. Many are still concerned about the sources of campaign funds for federal offices below the presidential level, particularly about the influence of political action committees. Others are concerned about the impact of finance regulations and of PACs on political parties. The issue of how finance regulation influences challengers' opportunities to unseat incumbents is never far from the minds of those concerned with further reform. Reformers remain concerned about the ways in which messages are conveyed to the voters—and look to campaign finance reform as a means to attack this problem. In recent election cycles, concern has grown about the influence of soft money, unlimited contributions that at this point in time are beyond the reach of federal regulators but are spent in such large sums as to have obvious impact on campaign outcomes. And the influence of issue advocacy advertisements, viewed by many as a loophole around restrictions on PAC activities, has received increased attention. It is to these and related issues that we turn in the remainder of this chapter.

III. THE COSTS OF DEMOCRACY

Recall figure 11.1. Just how concerned should we be with the amount of money being spent by political campaigns? What does it mean to say that Americans spent $4.2 billion on political elections in 1996? Is that too much or too little? Relative to what? In 1996 Philip Morris spent over $2.25 billion on advertising in the United States (*Advertising Age* 1997), and much of that was to convince the American people to buy products that the surgeon general of the United States has found to be hazardous to their health. No one complained very loudly. That is free enterprise.

The top 100 advertisers in 1996 spent over $39.97 billion; no one complained. If no one complains about the advertising budget of the tobacco industry or the $2.58 billion spent by Proctor and Gamble, the $2.38 billion by General Motors, the $1.26 billion by Walt Disney, the $1.24 billion by Pepsico, or the comparably staggering amounts by over a hundred other corporations that each spend over $200 million annually on advertising, more than was spent on the two presidential campaigns combined, why should we complain about the costs of maintaining a democracy (*Advertising Age* 1997)?

The simple answer seems to be that Americans feel that the escalation in campaign costs has been caused by increased use of electronic media to sell political candidates and that political candidates should not be promoted like cigarettes or soap products, automobiles or ketchup. The increases in campaign costs do not mean that we know more about our candidates (Buchanan 1991; but cf. Patterson 1980). The increased costs merely mean that the campaigns are telling us that they want us to know more frequently and in different ways.

A. Federal Elections

The concern about the rising costs of campaigns first focused at the presidential level, particularly after the elections of 1968 and 1972. Figure 11.2 shows the rapid rise in the costs of running for president and the disparity that existed between the two major parties before

Figure 11.2 Costs of Presidential General Election Campaigns.

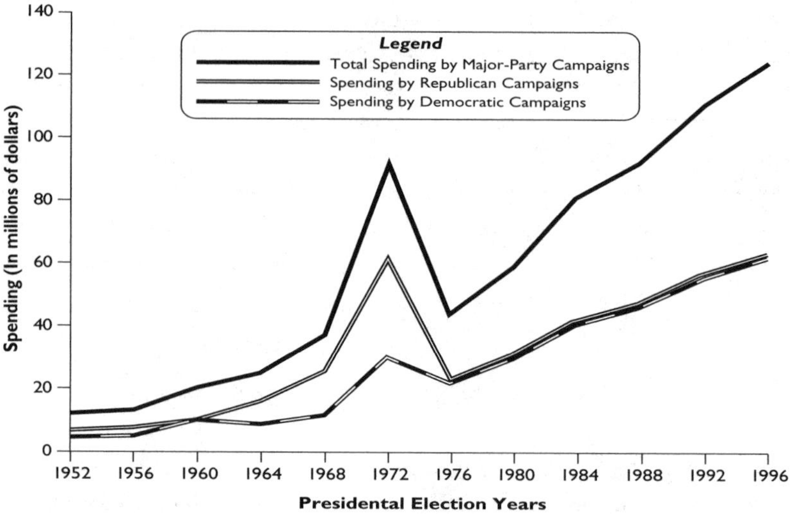

Source: Data from Federal Election Commission sources.

1976, the first election in which costs were contained through the use of public funds.[6]

It was commonly assumed that all of the increased spending was due to television advertising. This assumption was wrong, though the percentage of funds spent on radio and television advertising jumped from approximately 33 percent in 1952 to 50 percent in 1968 (Alexander 1976a, 28). In 1972, partly as a response to criticism of the 1968 campaign, the Nixon strategy called for spending far less on television and more on other forms of campaigning. The radio and television budget of the 1972 Nixon reelection campaign was only $54.3 million, compared with the $51.2 million spent on electronic media during his 1968 effort. Nixon as president used free media very expertly, emphasizing his service in office; this permitted a strategy of campaigning by other means, for example, direct mail.

Perception can dictate policy as much as reality does. One response to the 1972 campaign was the passage of public financing for the 1976 presidential election. The figures shown in figure 11.2 for the elections after 1976 reflect this change in policy. But those who financed campaigns in the past had to look elsewhere to spend their money in order to influence the political process. One of the results of this reallocation of political resources was the pattern of congressional and senatorial spending revealed in table 11.1.

No matter how these data are read, the same pattern is clear: increasingly large sums are being spent to finance campaigns. In 1974, the mean expenditure for all candidates for the House of Representatives was $53,384; in 1990, it was $325,145; in 1998, it reached $472,466. For incumbents the mean expenditure rose from $56,539 to $422,124 to $606,915 for the same years; for challengers to incumbents, from $40,015 to $134,465 to $238,739; thus the gap between incumbents

Table 11.1 Mean Congressional Campaign Expenditures: 1974, 1984, 1990–1998

	1974	*1984*	*1990*	*1992*	*1994*	*1996*	*1998*	*Percentage Increase, 1974–1998*	*Percentage Increase, 1984–1998*
House									
Expenditures:	$53,384	$241,313	$325,145	$408,240	$441,378	$516,852	$472,466	785	96
Incumbents	56,539	279,044	422,124	594,699	561,441	678,556	606,915	973	117
Challengers	40,015	161,994	134,465	167,411	240,188	286,582	238,739	497	47
Open-seat candidates	90,426	361,696	543,129	435,631	585,991	653,561	748,790	728	107
Democrats	53,993	237,732	355,862	462,897	487,493	472,313	426,969	691	80
Republicans	54,835	245,591	290,910	352,351	369,411	561,304	517,731	844	111
Senate									
Expenditures:	$437,482	$2,327,250	$2,592,163	$2,876,627	$4,000,274	$3,550,866	$3,484,927	697	697
Incumbents	555,714	2,539,929	3,582,136	3,852,428	4,691,617	4,236,694	4,645,166	736	736
Challengers	332,579	1,241,434	1,705,098	1,824,993	3,997,104	3,139,479	2,662,009	700	700
Open-seat candidates	401,484	4,976,051	1,599,792	2,938,871	3,006,247	3,310,759	2,671,279	565	565
Democrats	487,775	2,160,637	2,468,527	2,815,826	3,395,629	3,402,098	3,298,788	576	576
Republicans	382,343	2,499,417	2,719,546	2,939,218	4,604,919	3,695,126	3,671,066	860	860

Note: Includes primary and general election expenditures for general election candidates only.

Source: 1974–1996 data from Ornstein et al. 1998, tables 3-1, 3-3; 1998 data based on FEC sources.

and challengers has widened as well. For open seats, the mean expenditure rose from $90,426 to $543,129 to $748,790. The only number that has not constantly increased among all of these data is the amount spent by challengers for two election cycles. The decreases in those years reflect an awareness of the hopeless electoral situation in which challengers find themselves. In fact, only thirty-four House challengers spent more than the *average spent* by incumbents in 1990.[7]

In the Senate, the mean expenditure for all candidates went from $437,482 in 1974 to $2,592,163 in 1990 to $3,484,927 in 1998. For incumbents the mean expenditure surpassed $4.64 million in 1998; for challengers the mean was slightly more than half that amount, still a daunting $2.66 million. Only five seats were open in 1998; the mean expenditure in these races was $2.67 million. Because only one-third of the Senate is up for reelection in every election year, year-by-year comparisons can be misleading—especially open-seat data—as the same states do not necessarily have open seats. However, a look at table 11.1, which focuses on elections separated by six years (e.g., 1992 and 1998), when the same seats were contested (though recognizing that different seats were open), shows the extent to which campaign expenditures have continued to rise, with overall expenditures rising 50 percent between each set of elections.[8]

In 1974, only ten candidates for the House of Representatives spent over $250,000 on their campaigns, and none spent over $500,000. In 1990, the average incumbent spent nearly $400,000, and forty spent over $1 million each. By 1998, the average incumbent spent over $600,000, and the candidate who ranked fiftieth in amount spent on an election campaign, Helen Chenoweth (R-Idaho), spent over $1.3 million. The million-dollar campaign for the Senate was the exception in 1974; that amount was only spent in very expensive campaigns in very large states. By 1982 candidates in a state as small and as conservative in terms of spending as Maine contemplated million-dollar expenditures. By 1990, twenty-seven of the thirty-two incumbents seeking reelection spent at least $1 million. In 1998, all twenty-nine incumbents, eight of the ten candidates in open-seat races and thirteen challengers to incumbents, all spent more than $1 million. By every possible means candidates were raising and spending money. Politicians and the public expressed a good deal of concern about what it meant to spend these huge sums in attaining public office. Concern was expressed about the amounts being spent, regardless of where the money came from.

B. State and Local Elections

Campaign expenditure data for state and local elections are much less readily available than they are for elections at the federal level. Consequently, few analysts have examined state election financing. This paucity of analysis is caused by the magnitude of the task of gathering information on a variety of offices in the fifty states and is complicated because the data that can be gathered are often not comparable. Most states now require candidates to report campaign contributions and expenditures in some systematic way. However, no states have the resources to do the kinds of analysis that the FEC has done for federal elections.

Despite the limitations of the data available, some analysis has been undertaken. Those who study state and local elections have concluded that the same escalating campaign costs seen at the federal level are present at state and local levels.

In 1980 Herbert Alexander of the Citizens' Research Foundation estimated that $265 million was spent on state elections and $200 million on local elections (Alexander 1984, 104). A decade later he estimated that $540 million was spent on state elections and $365 million on local elections, an amount that constituted 45 percent of the total spent on all elections in 1990 (Alexander and Bauer 1991, 3).[9] After the 1996 campaigns, Alexander's estimates rose to $650 million for state elections and $425 million for local elections, just under 25 percent of the total amount spent. It should be remembered that more state and local elections are held in nonpresidential years than in presidential elections years and, further, that some of these elections (e.g., New Jersey's or Virginia's) are held in odd-numbered years.

Ruth S. Jones has examined costs of state legislative campaigns in a sample of states that do analyses of candidate reports. Her conclusions demonstrate that the campaign pattern for the House and Senate identified above is indeed repeated in state legislative races (Jones 1984, 174–180). In each of the states examined, the cost of the average legislative race increased significantly over the four campaigns she studied; Jones's data also show that the percentage of this increase varied from state to state, a pattern not unexpected given the differing nature of politics among the American states. Anthony Gierzynski and David Breaux, in examining the impact of money on state legislative races, gathered data from a different sample of states more recently. Their findings are similar; both are summarized in table 11.2. Looking at more recent examples, Michael Malbin and Thomas Gais concluded that

> Again, after controlling for inflation, total campaign expenditures in Kansas House elections grew by 66 percent between 1982 and 1992; in Kentucky House elections by 45 percent between 1981 and 1992; in Oregon House elections by 225 percent between 1982 and 1992; and in Maine Senate elections by 292 percent over the same period. (Malbin and Gais 1998, 15)

Jones also looked at sources of campaign funds. She found that most of the increase was from nonparty political organizations (1984, 186–187). While PAC activity at the state level has lagged behind that

Table 11.2 Average Cost of State House Races: Selected States and Years

State	*1974*	*1976*	*1978*	*1980*	*1986*
Arizona	$15,241	$35,844	$32,319	$60,778	—
California	—	—	93,572	—	$229,031
Colorado	5,385	8,219	12,280	17,403	25,920
Minnesota	8,256	9,694	11,813	15,882	—
Nebraska	—	—	7,365	—	30,013
Oregon	10,413	17,765	27,133	31,773	42,953

Sources: Jones 1984; Gierzynski and Breaux 1991.

at the federal level, it has not been far behind. States are now beginning to look at the implication of this infusion of PAC money into the political process at the state level and at its obvious implications for the increased escalation of the cost of running for state (and local) offices.

IV. Sources of Campaign Funds

While some people have a vaguely uneasy sense that campaigns in America cost too much, many more people are concerned about where the money for campaigns comes from and what strings, if any, are attached to political contributions. This type of concern led to the laws that prohibit individuals from contributing large sums of money to specific campaigns. The presumption is that these individuals do not act in a charitable manner but rather contribute huge sums in reward for past action and in hope of some later benefit. Although little empirical evidence supports the assumption of a link between contribution and "payoff," the general perception—if not the reality—is that few people give something for nothing.

Because both politicians and voters are still concerned about the sources of campaign funds, a good deal is known about the sources of funds for campaigns for federal office. In the sections that follow we will examine the five primary sources of money and the questions that accompany each funding base.

A. Sources of Campaign Contributions

The Federal Election Commission has changed the ways in which it categorizes the sources of campaign contributions to federal campaigns over the years, and thus comparison is not always possible. Generally, campaign funds come from the following sources: the candidate, other individuals (some of whom give larger and some smaller amounts), political action committees, political parties, and public financing (which is only available to presidential candidates for federal office and to some state and local candidates). While the ways in which these categories are analyzed have varied over the years, it is possible to discuss relative contributions with some historical perspective.

Gary Jacobson (1984) has studied what proportion of contributions to congressional candidates come from each of the identified sources. As is shown in table 11.3, the majority of contributions to both House and Senate candidates come from individual contributors. The amount that candidates contribute themselves was not reported between 1978 and 1986. For House candidates the amount contributed by candidates themselves tended to be just under 10 percent in the earlier period and much less than that more recently. There is wide variation, however, with some candidates financing much of their own campaigns while others contribute relatively little (Wilcox 1988). The same variations hold for Senate candidates, but because so few Senate elections are held in each election year, no pattern emerges. For instance, when John Heinz (R, 1973–1991) spent a large amount of his own money to win the Pennsylvania Senate seat in 1976, his expenditures raised the average for all Senate races in that year. When the amount that individuals donate to their own campaigns is estimated, it is clear that well over half of the money spent in congressional campaigns comes from contributions from other individuals, the amounts of which have been limited by the FECA since 1974.

One conclusion that could be drawn from table 11.3 is that restricting and disclosing contributions by individuals has solved most of the problem about the source of campaign funds. However, further study of these data clouds that relatively optimistic view. Two patterns have emerged since 1974. The clearest pattern is that the role of PACs has increased at a rapid pace (see chap. 6). Jacobson (1984, 40) has determined that the increase in PAC contributions from 1980 to 1982 was over 200 percent for both House and Senate races. By 1988 and 1990, PACs were contributing just under 40 percent of the money given to House campaigns, and their contribution level has stabilized just slightly below that level. More interesting, perhaps, is the fact the PACs continue to contribute nearly half of the money raised by House incumbents. Thus the fact that more contributions come from individuals than PACs does not allay the fears of those concerned about group influence.

In addition, the role of political party organizations has changed drastically over recent years (chap. 3). The data in table 11.3 only consider party contributions made directly to candidate campaigns. In 1982 and again in 1984, the Republican party spent a significant amount of money on behalf of congressional candidates independently of their campaign committees. In 1982 the Republican National Committee spent more than $200,000 on behalf of sixteen different Senate candidates; the Democrats spent that much for only one candidate. Table 11.4 shows that direct spending on behalf of candidates, particularly by the Republican party (but also by the Democrats), has

Table 11.3 Sources of Contributions to Congressional Campaigns: 1974, 1984, 1990–1998

	1974	*1984*	*1990*	*1992*	*1994*	*1996*	*1998*
			House Elections				
Average raised	$61,084	$240,722	$259,110	$248,278	$322,930	$326,048	$364,606
Percentage from:							
Individuals	73	51	45	49	52	55	53
Parties*	4	3	7***	5	4	4	4
PACs	17	39	42	38	37	35	37
Candidates**	6	6	5	9	8	7	6
			Senate Elections				
Average raised	$445,515	$2,273,635	$2,284,654	$1,302,865	$1,957,589	$1,560,652	$1,851,138
Percentage from:							
Individuals	76	68	65	66	59	63	62
Parties*	6	1	—	5	4	5	7
PACs	11	20	23	25	16	19	19
Candidates**	1	11	5	5	20	13	11
Unknown Souces	6	—	7***	—	1	—	—

*Does not include party expenditures on behalf of candidates.

**Includes candidates' loans unrepaid at time of filing.

***Includes contributions from unknown sources as party contributions.

Source: Data based on Federal Election Commission source.

Table 11.4 Party Contributions and Spending in Congressional Elections, 1986–1998 (in thousands of dollars)

Year	*Democrats*	*Republicans*
	HOUSE	
1986		
Direct Contributions	969	2,520
Spending for candidate	1,836	4,111
Total	$2,805	$6,631
1988		
Direct Contributions	1,198	2,650
Spending for candidate	2,800	4,163
Total	$3,998	$6,813
1990		
Direct Contributions	941	2,027
Spending for candidate	3,267	3,001
Total	$4,208	$5,028
1992		
Direct Contributions	1,235	2,198
Spending for Candidate	5,884	6,907
Total	$7,119	$9,105
1994		
Direct Contributions	1,501	2,037
Spending for candidate	8,455	8,852
Total	$9,956	$10,889
1996		
Direct Contributions	1,388	2,463
Spending for candidate	6,787	7,999
Total	$8,175	$10,462
1998		
Direct contributions	1,542	2,098
Spending for candidate	4,596	6,310
Total	$6,138	$8,408

continued

increased, while direct contributions by the parties to candidates have not been rising rapidly in recent years.

Federal Election Commission reports also make it possible to analyze contributions to presidential campaigns. Whereas the congressional data just presented totaled primary and general election contributions (for those candidates who competed in the general election), for presidential candidates the sources of funds for the prenomination and general election periods are reported separately because they are quite different.

In the prenomination phase of the presidential election, contributions come from three sources—individual contributions, PAC contributions, and federal matching funds. As table 11.5 shows, for the major-party candidates, PAC contributions play a more minor role in

Table 11.4 Party Contributions and Spending in Congressional Elections, 1986–1998 (in thousands of dollars) (*continued*)

Year	*Democrats*	*Republicans*
	SENATE	
1986		
Direct contributions	621	730
Spending for candidate	6,656	10,078
Total	$7,277	$10,808
1988		
Direct contributions	489	721
Spending for candidate	6,592	10,261
Total	$7,081	$10,982
1990		
Direct contributions	510	859
Spending for candidate	5,193	7,721
Total	$5,793	$8,580
1992		
Direct contributions	690	807
Spending for candidate	11,916	16,510
Total	$12,606	$17,317
1994		
Direct contributions	639	748
Spending for candidate	13,204	11,562
Total	$13,843	$12,310
1996		
Direct contributions	638	772
Spending for candidate	8,612	10,751
Total	$9,250	$11,523
1998		
Direct contributions	302	515
Spending for candidate	9,350	9,334
Total	$9,652	$9,849

Sources: 1986–1996 data from Ornstein et al. 1998, table 3-10; 1998 data based on FEC sources.

presidential nominating politics than they do in congressional elections. No candidates received even 10 percent of their contributions from PACs. The most recent FEC statistics combine political action committee money with other committee contributions. Much of the money listed in this category, and accumulated in these statistics, is in fact money transferred from other political committees, for example, a presidential campaign from the surplus in the successful senatorial campaign. Of course, political parties do not contribute to campaigns for nominations, so these sources of contributions are absent. In short, the sources of funds for the presidential primaries are basically individual contributions and public matching funds.

Table 11.5 Sources of Contributions for Presidential Primary Campaigns, 1992 and 1996 (in millions)

	Total	*Individual*	*PAC*	*Federal Match*
		1992		
Democrats				
Agran	$0.61	$0.33	$0	$0.27
Brown	9.42	5.18	0	4.24
Clinton	37.64	25.11	—	12.52
Harkin	5.68	3.07	0.49	2.10
Kerrey	6.47	3.91	0.35	2.20
LaRouche	1.60	1.60	0	0.10
Tsongas	8.10	5.06	—	3.00
Wilder	0.80	5.06	—	0.29
Republicans				
Buchanan	$12.21	$7.16	$0.02	$5.00
Bush	38.01	27.09	0.04	10.66
Duke	0.27	0.22	0.00	0.00
		1996		
Democrats				
Clinton	$41.74	$28.29	$0.04	$13.41
LaRouche	3.68	3.06	—	0.62
Republicans				
Alexander	$17.50	$12.64	$0.29	$4.57
Buchanan	24.49	14.66	0.02	9.81
Dole	44.32	29.56	1.21	13.55
Dornan	0.30	0.30	—	0.00
Forbes	4.20	4.20	—	0.00
Gramm	23.64	15.88	0.40	7.36
Keyes	4.33	3.44	—	0.89
Lugar	7.57	4.80	0.13	2.64
Specter	3.45	2.28	0.16	1.01
Taylor	0.04	0.04	0.00	0.00
Wilson	7.25	5.29	0.24	1.72

Sources: 1992 data from Alexander and Corrado 1995, table 2.4; 1996 data based on Federal Election Commission sources.

The prevailing myth is that public financing of the presidential general election erased the problems that caused the concern about sources of campaign contributions for that contest. That myth is not based in fact. Independent spending on behalf of the Reagan—Bush and Carter—Mondale campaigns played a major role in 1980. The Federal Election Campaign Act was designed to "level the playing field" in presidential elections; each campaign was supposed to spend the same amount of money. Each candidate received the same federal grant; each national committee was allowed to spend the same amount of money directly on each campaign. Still, the total amounts spent varied considerably.

During the 1980s, the major source of this variation was independent expenditures. Nearly $13 million was spent on behalf of the Reagan-Bush campaign (or against the Carter-Mondale campaign), and only $1.7 million on behalf of Carter-Mondale in independent expenditures. In 1984 the total spent by independent groups exceeded $17 million, the bulk of it being spent on behalf of the Reagan-Bush ticket. When the Supreme Court, in *Federal Election Committee (FEC) v. National Conservative Political Action Committee (NCPAC),* 470 U.S. 480 (1985), ruled that these expenditures could not be limited, it formalized a new, unregulated source of funding for the two major-party candidates' presidential campaigns. However, despite fears that the sums spent independently could skyrocket—and that they would cause an imbalance between the campaigns—the amount actually spent in 1988 declined to about $10 million, though the Republicans did hold a 3-to-1 advantage (Alexander and Bauer 1991, 82-85).

Since 1992, the major source of variation—and the major factor in the escalation of the total costs of presidential campaigns—has been soft money. In 1992, the Republicans raised nearly $50 million in soft money, compared to $36.3 million for the Democrats. In 1996, total soft money receipts reached $263.5 million, with the Republicans having an advantage of approximately $20 million over the Democrats. In nonpresidential election years, the totals have been lower but are escalating—and the GOP advantage has been maintained (fig. 11.3).

B. Individual Contributions

Although early reformers focused their attention on large contributions by individuals to campaigns, that concern has been tempered in the last decade. If the campaign finance reforms of the 1970s have been suc-

Figure 11.3 Political Party Soft Money Receipts, 1992–1998.

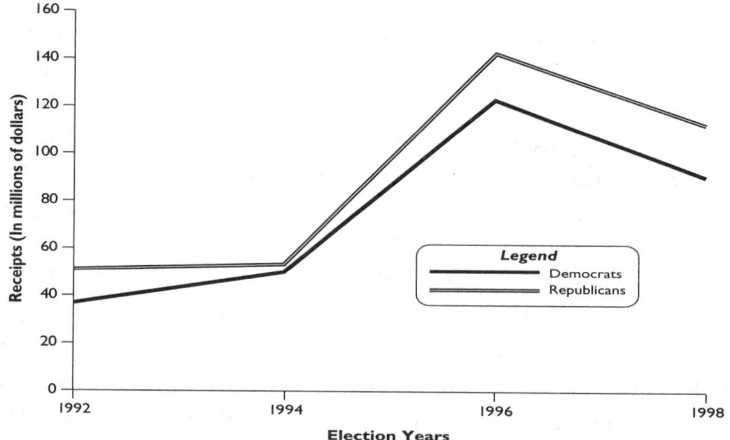

Source: Data from Federal Election Commission sources.

cessful in any one area, it has been in curbing very large contributions by wealthy individuals and thus limiting the alleged abuse caused by huge contributions.

Before the reforms, stories about extremely large contributions were legion, Most dealt with contributions to presidential campaigns because the costs of congressional and senatorial campaigns were lower and because data on the sources of funds for these campaigns were difficult to obtain.

However, the reformers' anxieties were not misplaced. In 1972 Stewart R. Mott contributed nearly half a million dollars to various Democratic presidential candidates in the prenomination phase of the campaign; he contributed over $800,000 to all campaigns in that year. In that same year, fifty-one multimillionaires contributed a total of over $6 million to political campaigns, more than $5.5 million to Republican candidates. While the number of Americans who contributed to political campaigns was nearly 12 million in 1972, nearly half of all money contributed to political campaigns in that year came in individual contributions of more than $500 (Alexander 1976a, chap. 4). Most of the 12 million gave contributions considerably smaller than that.

With the advent of the campaign finance reforms, the amounts that individuals could give to a single campaign and the total amounts that they could contribute were restricted (with the exception of contributions to their own campaigns and independent expenditures). The clear result of this change has been that large individual contributions play a smaller role in politics, and smaller contributions play a larger role.[10] These results are demonstrated in table 11.6.

The FEC data do not allow us to isolate small contributions, since setting a cap at $1,000 per election was deemed an adequate way to mitigate against undue influence by large contributors. A number of implications follow. First, as was intended in the reforms, large contributions are not the dominant means of raising campaign funds that they once were.[11] Second, as a result of the limits on large contributions, candidates must work at developing a broader base of smaller contributors in order to fill their campaign coffers. Candidates have had to develop new techniques for raising money. The Goldwater campaign of 1964 and the George Wallace campaign of 1968 demonstrated the power of direct mail as a tool for raising large amounts of money (and for cementing the allegiance of large numbers of voters). The techniques used in those campaigns have been emulated and improved upon by politicians throughout the land. Richard Viguerie, who was first to gain prominence as an expert in raising money through direct mail, became an important political figure in his own right. His skills and foresight gave conservative candidates a head start that took liberals years to overcome.[12] One clear impact of the efforts of direct mail fund-raisers has been to broaden the base of political donors in much

Table 11.6 Funding Sources for Congressional Candidates: 1974, 1984, 1994, 1996, 1998

	Amount Raised by Candidates and Party Expenditures on Behalf of Candidates (in millions)	Percentage Distribution				
		PACs	*Party (contributions and expenditures)*	*Individuals*	*Candidate to Self (contributions and unrepaid loans)**	*Other*
			House			
1974						
All candidates**	$45.7	17	4	79***	—	—
Democrats	23.9	22	1	77***	—	—
Republicans	21.7	10	7	83***	—	—
1984						
All candidates**	$203.8	36	7	47	6	5
Democrats	107.2	41	3	44	6	6
Republicans	96.6	30	11	49	6	5
1994						
All candidates**	$371.3	34	5	49	8	4
Democrats	196.7	43	5	43	5	4
Republicans	174.6	24	6	56	11	3
1996						
All candidates**	$460.7	33	4	53	6	4
Democrats	211.5	35	4	48	9	4
Republicans	249.2	30	4	57	4	4
1998						
All candidates**	$436.0	35	3	51	6	4
Democrats	190.8	38	3	49	6	4
Republicans	236.5	33	3	53	6	4

(continued)

			Senate			
1974						
All candidates**	$28.2	11	6	83***	n.a.	n.a.
Democrats	16.2	13	2	85***	n.a.	n.a.
Republicans	11.6	7	13	80***	n.a.	n.a.
1984						
All candidates**	$157.7	18	6	61	10	4
Democrats	73.1	18	6	56	16	4
Republicans	84.6	18	6	65	5	4
1994						
All candidates**	$291.7	15	8	54	19	4
Democrats	124.9	18	10	55	12	5
Republicans	166.7	13	6	53	24	4
1996						
All candidates**	$242.1	17	9	58	12	4
Democrats	116.2	13	8	59	16	4
Republicans	125.9	21	9	57	8	4
1998						
All candidates**	$265.9	18	7	58	11	7
Democrats	126.1	16	8	58	9	9
Republicans	139.8	19	7	57	12	4

*The FEC did not report candidate contributions to themselves separately.

**Major-party candidates only.

***Includes candidates' contributions to themselves, unrepaid loans, and individual contributions to $500.

Sources: 1974–1994 data from Ornstein et al. 1996 and 1998, table 3-9; 1998 data based on FEC sources.

the way the reformers desired. Third, candidates have looked elsewhere for funds, particularly to political action committees.

C. Political Action Committees

If large contributions from individuals are not so threatening as they were thought to be before the reforms of the 1970s, contributions from political action committees are more so. In fact, it can be argued that the "evils of PACs," for those who see such evils, are direct consequences of the reform movement. And as a consequence of recent experience, PAC reform has been highest on the agenda of campaign finance reformers.

Much has been written about PACs, and so it is important to understand clearly what is meant by a political action committee (recall chap. 6). As is not atypical when one scrutinizes commonly used terms, one finds that the term "political action committee" does not appear in the statutes of the federal government. However, the statutes do refer to political committees, which are distinct from either party committees or candidate committees. A political committee, according to the U.S. Code (26 U.S.C. 9001[9]) is "any committee, association, or organization (whether or not incorporated) which accepts contributions or makes expenditures for the purpose of influencing, or attempting to influence, the nomination or election of one or more individuals to Federal, State, or local elective public office."

MULTI-CANDIDATE POLITICAL COMMITTEE

Committee that supports more than one candidate for a federal office.

The U.S. Code further defines **multicandidate political committee**, a distinction that is important because these groups can contribute up to $5,000 to an individual campaign, whereas individuals are bound by a $1,000 limit. A multicandidate political committee is "a political committee which has been registered . . . for a period of not less than 6 months, which has received contributions from more than 50 persons, and, except for any State political party organization, has made contributions to 5 or more candidates for Federal office" (4 U.S.C. 441 [a]).

SEPARATE SEGREGATED FUND

The way in which a corporation or other entity must maintain a distinction between corporate funds and money raised and spent for political purposes.

Finally, political action committees, as we normally think of them, are separate from their parent or sponsoring organization (if there is one). Campaign finance legislation has long prohibited direct political contributions by labor unions or corporations; however, provisions have been made for establishing a **separate segregated fund** for political purposes. The law specifies how money for this fund may and may not be raised. Political action committees with parent organizations, then, are the committees set up to administer these "separate segregated funds" (Sorauf 1984a, chap. 1; 1991). The term "PAC" is thus commonly used to refer to a nonparty, noncandidate committee that funds more than one candidate and may or may not be affiliated with an established corporation, union, or interest group (Sabato 1985).

The Federal Election Commission identifies four major types of political action committees: labor, corporation, trade/membership/health, and nonconnected.[13] The first three types identified can be defined as multicandidate political committees that are administering campaign funds that have been raised from, but kept separate and segregated from, some parent organization, be that a labor union, a corporation, or a trade, membership, or health organization (such as the American Bankers Association or the American Medical Association). The nonconnected PACs tend to be ideological multicandidate political committees that have come together for specific political purposes and that do not draw on an established parent organization.

While their prominence is a recent phenomenon, political committees have been on the American political scene for some time. From the 1940s until its merger with the American Federation of Labor (AFL) in 1955, the Congress of Industrial Organizations (CIO) operated a separate fund to receive and dispense voluntary contributions from labor unionists to political campaigns. The AFL-CIO Committee on Political Education (COPE), established after the 1955 merger, has been described as "the model for virtually all political action committees" (Epstein 1980, 100). In the late 1950s and early 1960s some of the larger membership and trade professional organizations, like the American Realtors and the American Medical Association, formed political committees (Alexander 1979b, 559–566; Sorauf 1984a, 33).

However, the growth of PACs, an increase in the number of PACs (especially in the decade following the passage of the FECA of 1974) and in the magnitude of the role they play (as measured in the dollars they contribute), and the pattern of that growth are the phenomena that have caused most concern. The FECA amendments of 1974 put a more stringent limit on individual contributions than on contributions by multicandidate political committees. This followed naturally from the fact that reformers were more concerned about huge contributions by individuals than group contributions.

The 1974 amendments also lifted the restriction that had prohibited government contractors from setting up separate segregated political committees. The public financing of presidential elections, effective for the 1976 election, led PACs to switch their emphasis from presidential to congressional campaigns. But, because the viability of PACs under the FECA was initially unclear, there was only cautious movement toward establishing new PACs. This situation changed in 1975. The FEC, in response to an inquiry from the Sun Oil Company, issued an advisory opinion in which it informed Sun Oil that the corporation could legally establish a separate segregated fund for the purpose of contributing to political campaigns and that it could solicit voluntary contributions from its employees to support that fund. As a result of all these actions, many corporations decided to form PACs, and political action committees as a major force in funding congressional elections became a most visible aspect of electoral politics. Hundreds of other corporations eventually followed Sun Oil's lead (Epstein 1980).

Look back at table 6.2, which depicts the rapid growth of political action committees. The total number of PACs grew from slightly over 600 in 1974 to well over 4,200 by 1988. While the growth pattern has not been consistent since that time, in 1998 the 4,486 active PACs represented the highest total ever registered with the FEC. PAC expenditures during that period increased proportionally, from $12.5 million in 1974 to $159.2 million in 1988; they have continued to increase, passing $200 million in 1996.

It should be noted further that this growth has not been constant among the various types of PACs. Labor was very quick to see that PACs could increase their influence, and nearly all major labor unions organized political action committees. However, the number of labor PACs has never doubled the number that existed in 1974—and has declined in recent years. On the other hand, corporations were slower to realize the potential influence they could wield through PACs. But the number of corporate PACs eventually increased to far exceed that of labor unions, with major jumps coming after the **SunPAC** opinion and again during the Reagan administration. (See Eismeier and Pollock 1985a; 1985b; Malbin 1984a.) In the late 1980s growth also was seen in the nonconnected PACs, as more "political entrepreneurs" came to view this avenue as a viable way to increase political influence.

SUNPAC

The political action committee set up by the Sun Oil Corporation that tested the principle that corporations could establish PACs.

The growth in the number of PACs and the amount they contribute to political candidates, more specifically to congressional candidates, has led to a number of concerns. It is possible to classify these concerns in a number of different ways, but we will deal with four specific areas: the necessity of PAC support to secure electoral victory, the link between PAC support and legislative behavior, the ideological imbalance of present and future PACs, and the responsibility of PAC leaders to contributors.

1. The Influence of PACs on Electoral Outcomes

Some things are clear. Examining recent elections for the United States Congress shows that, by and large, winners spend more money than do losers. Although it is appropriate to be concerned about who gets money from each source, attention has been focused on PACs because PACs are contributing an increasingly large amount of money.

Table 11.7 shows PAC activity in recent House and Senate elections. Both the amount and the proportion of money contributed by PACs has been rising faster than the total amount spent on elections or the proportion coming from any other source.[14] This is particularly clear for House elections, in which PAC contributions reached nearly 40 percent of total expenditures in the early 1990s. In more recent years, however,

Table 11.7 PAC Contributions to Congressional Candidates by Party, 1990–1998

	Republican	*Democratic*	*Other*
1990			
Corporate	52.6%	47.4%	0.0%
Labor	6.9	93.0	0.2
Trade/membership/health	44.9	55.1	0.0
Nonconnected	35.7	64.2	0.1
Other	37.0	63.0	0.0
Total	36.9	63.1	0.1
1992			
Corporate	49.7%	50.2%	0.0%
Labor	4.8	94.6	0.5
Trade/membership/health	41.7	58.2	0.1
Nonconnected	36.9	62.8	0.2
Other	34.5	65.5	0.1
Total	97.8	1.8	0.5
1994			
Corporate	51.1%	48.8%	0.1%
Labor	3.9	95.7	0.4
Trade/membership/health	46.2	53.7	0.1
Nonconnected	40.0	59.8	0.2
Other	27.0	72.9	0.1
Total	37.4	62.4	0.2
1996			
Corporate	73.0%	26.8%	0.3%
Labor	6.5	93.0	0.5
Trade/membership/health	64.6	34.9	0.4
Nonconnected	59.7	39.8	0.5
Other	59.4	40.2	0.4
Total	53.5	46.1	0.4
1998*			
Corporate	66.3%	33.6%	0.0%
Labor	9.4	90.4	0.3
Trade/membership/health	59.9	40.1	0.1
Nonconnected	61.6	38.3	0.1
Other	52.6	47.3	0.0
Total	51.5	48.4	0.1

*Includes totals only through June 30, 1998.

Source: Data based on Federal Election Commission sources.

these percentages have decreased somewhat as PACs have concentrated more of their spending on independent expenditures. It is also clear from these data that virtually all successful candidates must raise a significant amount of money from political action committees. Incumbents are able to do this more easily than challengers. While PACs flirted with supporting more challengers in the early 1980s (see Eismeier and Pollock 1985b; 1986; Jacobson 1985–1986; Sabato 1985; Wright 1985), in the last decade PACs have typically given as much as 70 percent of their contributions to incumbents and less than 15 percent to challengers.[15] Ironically, money is more significant for challengers than it is for incumbents (Jacobson 1980, chap. 5). The key is whether challengers can attract enough money, including PAC money, to mount enough of a campaign to have a chance of victory. More and more they do not seem to be able to do so.

2. The Influence of PACs on Legislative Outcomes

Many committees are connected to specific groups that have a direct interest in legislative decision making. The funds may be separate and segregated, but the connection is there in the minds of all involved. One does not have to stretch one's imagination too far to see that the directors of the Amoco political action committee have certain views on issues affecting the oil industry or that those deciding on the allocation of funds from the Machinists Nonpartisan Political League care greatly about the level of governmental support for the aerospace industry.

The PAC leaders know this, and the candidates know this. Former Congresswoman Millicent Fenwick (R-N.J., 1975–1983) put it most succinctly: "That these groups influence voting is undeniable. 'I took $58,000. They want it,' was the explanation one colleague gave for his vote, bought by a number of donations from a number of groups of similar orientation" (quoted in Sorauf 1984a, 90).

Note the figure $58,000. It could just as easily have been $100,000. PACs are limited to contributions of $5,000 in a single campaign. The sum of $5,000 will not buy a great deal of influence in a campaign with a budget of $1.25 million. But if twenty groups with similar interests (e.g., oil or medical policy) each make maximum contributions, then the total impact may be significant. And that defines the concern. Many feel that PAC money does not directly buy influence; contributions, however, do buy access, and access can lead indirectly to influence.

On the one hand, PACs contribute to individuals likely to support their cause in any case, and individual PAC contributions are not significant in terms of the total amounts spent on campaigns. Incumbents have tremendous electoral advantages regardless of PAC actions or intentions, and incumbents face a wide array of pressures so that they cannot listen to PAC leaders only.

On the other hand, members of Congress do accept large amounts of money from groups of individuals with a direct stake in legislation. The total contributed by like-minded groups might well represent a sizable percentage of a candidate's campaign funds, and interest-group representatives are often quite overt in exercising pressure when key decisions are pending. There is, in the words of the Supreme Court, "the appearance of impropriety," which may well be as detrimental to the system as the reality.

Alleged PAC influence on legislation tarnishes the reputation of political action committees (Common Cause 1986; Drew 1983; Jackson 1988; Stern 1988). PAC supporters argue persuasively that citizens should have a right to associate with others of similar views in order to maximize the likelihood of having their views heard. PAC detractors point to the number of cases in which large PAC contributions have been funneled to incumbents facing no challengers as evidence that PACs are polluting the system by setting up an assumption that legislative behavior is for sale to the highest bidder. Political scientists have searched for evidence of PAC influence on legislative behavior, but their conclusion is that hard evidence of the corrupting influence of PACs is all but absent (Evans 1986; Frendeis and Waterman 1985; Grenzke 1989; 1990; Schroedel 1986; Wright 1985). In a very real sense, this debate has been the focus of reform efforts for more than a decade.

3. The Ideological Imbalance of Present and Future PACs

Labor leaders were among those most interested in writing legislation allowing for the formation of PACs in the early years of the 1970s reform movement. They saw tremendous advantages as they tried to exert influence over the electoral process.

However, these labor leaders were shortsighted, as the trends in the increases in PACs show. Labor PACs are as well organized and about as effective as they are likely to be. However, corporate PACs and trade association PACs have far outstripped those formed by labor unions in terms of number and influence. Now labor leaders, Democrats, and other liberals in this country worry that PAC influence will increasingly become conservative, business, and Republican influence.

This argument can be dealt with on two levels. First, table 11.8 shows that PACs have not given significantly more to Republicans than to Democrats. To the contrary, Democrats have received more than have Republicans, which to a certain extent can be explained by the fact that PACs have tended to support incumbents (table 11.9). The Democrats controlled the House (and the Senate except for the period between 1980 and 1986) for the first twenty years of experience under the FECA, the years for which we have reliable data. Since incumbents

Table 11.8 Growth of PAC Influence on Congressional Elections, 1984–1998

Year	*PAC Contributions (in millions)*	*Average Percent of House Receipts from PACs*	*Average Percent of Senate Receipts from PACs*
1974	$12.5	17	11
1976	22.6	22	15
1978	35.2	24	13
1980	55.2	28	19
1982	83.6	31	17
1984	105.3	36	18
1986	132.7	36	21
1988	147.8	40	22
1990	149.7	40	21
1992	179.4	36	21
1994	178.8	34	15
1996	201.2	25	16
1998	200.3	36	19

Source: 1974–1996 data from Ornstein et al. 1998, tables 3-9, 3-12; 1998 data based on FEC sources.

have received more PAC support, the Democrats benefited. Since the Republicans have regained control of Congress, PAC money has been split quite evenly between the two parties, reflecting the fact that nearly equal numbers of incumbents of both parties have been seeking reelection.[16]

At a more theoretical level, questions of the locus of power in the United States have long been debated. PAC influence is only one more manifestation of this question. Literally hundreds of PACs contribute to the most expensive campaigns for the House and Senate. Scholars would have to look long and hard to find the conspiracy linking these contributions. Size alone does not dictate specific kinds of influence. Our polity functioned under a system through which a few very wealthy individuals gave great sums to political campaigns in virtual anonymity. It is difficult to conclude that it cannot survive even a significant influx of PAC contributions made in the light of day.

4. The Lack of Accountability for PAC Decision Making

Even those who are not troubled by the supposed influence of political action committees have some concern over how decisions are made by PACs. Until very recently we knew little about how PACs functioned (but this is changing; see Sabato 1984b). The general assump-

Table 11.9 PAC Contributions to Congressional Candidates by Candidate Status, 1992–1998

	Incumbents	*Challengers*	*Open Seat*
1992			
Corporate	77.5%	8.8%	13.7%
Labor	60.5	18.7	20.8
Trade/membership/health	73.1	9.4	17.5
Nonconnected	59.3	18.3	22.4
Other	77.6	8.6	13.8
Total	70.7	12.1	17.2
1994			
Corporate	74.5%	7.6%	17.9%
Labor	66.9	14.3	18.8
Trade/membership/health	73.1	8.9	18.0
Nonconnected	60.5	15.7	23.8
Other	76.8	7.9	15.4
Total	71.1	10.3	18.6
1996			
Corporate	76.0%	6.2%	17.8%
Labor	50.6	28.4	21.1
Trade/membership/health	70.6	9.6	19.8
Nonconnected	54.8	21.3	23.9
Other	73.3	9.9	16.8
Total	66.2	14.1	19.8
1998*			
Corporate	91.0%	3.0%	6.0%
Labor	74.7	11.2	14.1
Trade/membership/health	87.0	4.5	8.5
Nonconnected	73.3	11.0	15.7
Other	90.5	3.5	6.0
Total	84.6	6.0	9.4

*Includes totals only through June 30, 1998.

Note: Figures may not add up to 100% due to rounding and contributions to other parties.

Source: Data based on Federal Election Commission sources.

tion has been that, with the possible exception of labor union PACs, members have very little influence over how their money is spent. Iowa Republican congressman Jim Leach has argued that

> groups seldom reflect the same collective judgment as all their members. More importantly, decisions for organizations frequently occur at the top not the bottom. . . . Individuals who control other people's money become power brokers in an elitist society. Their views, not the small contributors to their associations, become the views that carry influence. (Quoted in Sorauf 1984a, 96)

This concern is especially troublesome for nonconnected PACs, organizations that are often built around the reputation of one or two individuals and a mailing list. These PACs have been most active in influencing the electoral process through independent expenditures on behalf of, or in opposition to, a candidate. When only a few of these PACs spent significantly and their influence seemed to be waning, decision making was not a major concern (Alexander and Bauer 1991, 84–86; C. Nelson 1990). However, the potential to use these instruments to impact specific elections—without adequate input from contributors—remains high.

Those who support the activity of political action groups most often argue that PAC activity is nothing more than constructive collective activity. If this is so, then collective decision making is a logical correlate. The lack of accountability of PAC leaders to their "followings" will be a pressing reform issue for the agenda of the future.

5. PAC Influence: A Summary

The consequences of reform are often not immediately apparent to the reformers. Few involved in the campaign finance reforms of the early 1970s could have foreseen the rise in influence of political action committees. With more than two decades of experience, some of the same reformers are critically examining what their work has wrought. While the discourse often breaks down on partisan lines, the entire question seems to be one on which reasonable men and women can differ and the "prevailing view" is in flux.

In 1983, less than ten years after the FECA reforms were implemented, the Twentieth Century Fund convened the distinguished, bipartisan Task Force on Political Action Committees under the leadership of former senator and secretary of state Edmund S. Muskie. The task force concluded that the integrity of the system necessitated reforms, including a limitation on the amounts that candidates could receive from PACs, efforts to preclude collusion between those running campaigns and those making "independent expenditures," partial voluntary public funding, a strengthening of the roles of political parties in campaign finance, and an increase in the amount individuals can contribute to campaigns (Twentieth Century Fund 1984). But only six of the thirteen members of the task force agreed with the final conclusions without significant reservations. Three separate statements of views were filed, one by a well-known Democrat, one by a well-known Republican, and one by a noted academician. A problem was perceived, but no consensus existed on the solution.

Since that time, reformers have kept proposals for limiting PAC influence on the legislative agenda.[17] They have been countered by the position that PACs represent a legitimate form of political participation—and by the political position that PAC limitation must be accompanied by other reforms.

The growth of PACs and their apparent influence has given rise to a good deal of uncertainty. Many feel that PAC growth is a force in escalating the total costs of campaigns. But the experience with the 1970s reforms leads to caution. How will PAC influence shake out? What other factors and changes are likely to come into play? In this area, as in many others, significant reform requires a climate for action. To date such a climate has not existed.

D. Political Parties

Perhaps the most underrated item on the agenda for reform in campaign financing is the change in the role that the major political parties play in financing campaigns (Sorauf 1988, chap. 5; 1998).

The conventional wisdom in the 1970s was that parties did not play a major role in campaign finance. The Nixon campaigns of 1968 and 1972 raised substantial amounts of money independent of the Republican National Committee. The major financial effort on behalf of the Democrats was to retire the debts incurred by the Humphrey and Kennedy campaigns of 1968. The Democratic National Committee expended most of its fund-raising efforts in paying off debts, not in aiding candidates.

Congressional and senatorial campaigns did not cost the large amounts that are in evidence today. The national parties were not active in raising large sums for these campaigns; the state and local parties did not have sufficient resources to make significant differences.

However, as Gary Jacobson (1984, 49; 1985–1986), Frank Sorauf (1988, 127–149), Paul Herrnson (1995; 1998; 1998a), and others have shown, the biggest change in campaign financing since the 1980s has been the significant role played by the political parties, particularly the Republican party, on behalf of congressional and senatorial candidates and the efforts the Democrats made to match Republican efforts (Jackson 1988). (Recall table 11.4; see also Arterton 1982.)

The difference between Republican and Democratic party efforts in this regard has been particularly troublesome for Democrats. The Republicans have had much more money to spend on campaign functions than have the Democrats. This difference has been apparent at all electoral levels. The Republican National Committee spends money to provide in-kind services for candidates at reduced costs. They provide more funding so that, at the state and local levels, Republican organizations are stronger and better financed than their Democratic counterparts.

The 1980s saw the emergence of the Republican Senatorial and Congressional Campaign Committees as important forces in congressional politics. At each of these levels, the Republicans were much more active than Democrats and much more successful. Most discouraging for Democrats has been the fact that, despite Herculean efforts, the gap has not disappeared.

In the late 1980s then senator George Mitchell (D-Me., 1980–1995) and then congressman Tony Coelho (D-Calif., 1979–1989), who headed the Democratic Senatorial and Congressional Campaign Committees respectively, played important roles in their party's future. Their goal was to strengthen these committees so that they could compete effectively with their Republican counterparts (Jackson 1988). Each used the campaign committee experience as a takeoff point for a position in their party's formal congressional hierarchy. Their successors also see the importance of their role, both for their party's electoral chances and for their own political futures.

The path set by Mitchell and Coelho has been followed by their successors, and the Democrats, while still trailing the Republicans in party funding, have closed the gap. The disparity between Republican and Democratic party funding has clear implications for campaign finance reform. Frequently those who examine the various sources of campaign funds view their impact in isolation. Candidates for office look at all sources as a whole. Any reform that affects one will have a concomitant effect on the total available. While the Democrats had a comparative advantage in PAC funding, they were unwilling to look at reforms in that area so long as the Republicans retained their advantage in party funding. In a sense, reform was thwarted because each party had a comparative advantage it was unwilling to concede. As those comparative advantages shrink, the opportunity for reform presents itself once again (Gibson et al. 1983; 1985).

E. Soft Money: The Newest Loophole to Be Closed

Soft money has been referred to frequently in this chapter. In some ways, it has become the tail that wags the dog. So much soft money has been spent in recent campaigns (see table 11.8) that all of the restrictions on existing campaign finance laws seem useless. The 1996 presidential election has been held up as evidence of a system gone totally wrong. Some say it is evidence that no system exists at all.

What exactly is the nature of the soft money problem? Put in the most blunt terms, individuals and corporations can give as much as they want to campaigns through soft money. Even though these amounts are now reported, the result is that influence can be purchased, or at least can seem to be purchased, in much the same way as it was before the reforms of the 1970s.

And how serious is the problem? According to Public Disclosure, Inc., a watchdog group that monitors Federal Election Commission filings, the problem is out of hand. In the 1997–1998 election cycle, the amount of soft money given to political parties nearly doubled the amount reported in the last congressional off-year election, 1993–1994. The money did not come equally from all rungs of American society. Businesses gave over $105 million; trade associations gave an additional $13 million. By contrast, labor unions contributed only $8 million. Individual contributors were responsible for approximately $43 million, but think about who gives money in this way. Twenty-five individuals each gave at least a quarter of a million dollars; twenty-three of those were either chairmen, presidents, or CEOs of well-known corporations.

Why do these individuals give, and why do they give to the extent that they do? Direct linkages between motivation for giving and pending legislation are difficult to confirm, but the appearance of impropriety is not hard to imagine. During a Congress in which tobacco regulation and telephone access legislation were high on the legislative agenda, Philip Morris contributed $2.1 million in soft money and RJR Nabisco, $900,000; Bell Atlantic, MCI, and AT&T each contributed nearly $1 million. Cynical citizens were given a substantial amount of ammunition to fuel their concerns.

Given this level of spending, and the lack of restrictions in the current law and FEC regulations, it is small wonder that some reformers claimed that if Congress could get a hold on soft money spending and failed to do anything else, that would represent significant progress.

F. The Debate over Public Financing

The reformers of the 1970s proposed public financing as the way to take the taint of money out of politics. If political campaigns were funded by the mass public, politicians would not have to deal with those seeking to buy influence.

Since 1976, public financing has been an important part of presidential campaigns. During the prenomination phase of the presidential election, after reaching a qualifying plateau, candidates for the two parties' nominations receive matching funds for all contributions of $250 or less received from individuals. As figure 11.4 shows, candidates spent over $200 million in 1988 and 1996 in this phase of the campaign.[18]

Each major party is granted public funds to run its nominating convention ($12.36 million in 1996). Each party's nominee is granted public funds for running a general election campaign ($61.8 million each in 1996); other candidates for the presidency qualify for public funding according to the success they achieve.[19] As seen in table 11.10, the total cost to the public of running the 1996 presidential election exceeded $200 million.

Many reformers also feel that public financing should be applied to congressional elections. In 1977 a public financing bill was high on President Carter's initial legislative agenda. However, that bill, given the symbolic designation of H.R. 1, never emerged from the House Administration Committee.

The debate over public financing of congressional and senatorial elections is a heated one. Proponents say that public financing has worked for presidential elections and will do so at the congressional level as well. They hold that using public funds to finance elections is fairer, less susceptible to corruption, and, in the long run, the only way to reduce the costs of elections, especially given the Supreme Court ruling that only those who accept public financing can be restricted in the amounts they spend.

Opponents of public financing argue from a number of different points. Some argue that any public financing bill would automatically protect all incumbents because challengers must spend huge sums of money to overcome the advantages of incumbency. This argument is especially important in the House, as incumbents there are rarely defeated.

Others argue that public financing would be impossible to implement for congressional and/or senatorial elections because congressional districts (and even states) are so different that amounts of money needed to campaign effectively in different districts would vary substantially. They are further concerned about candidates who receive public funds when no serious challenger exists.

Still others argue that public funding would create opposition to popular incumbents where none now exists. Some incumbents are forthright enough to state that they will not support public financing because it is against their best interest. Others hedge this argument, stating that it is not in the interest of the nation to force people to pay for unwanted campaigns. Challengers and those eager to support competitive elections see this as an advantage of public financing because

Figure 11.4 Public Funding in Presidential Primary Campaigns, 1976–1996.

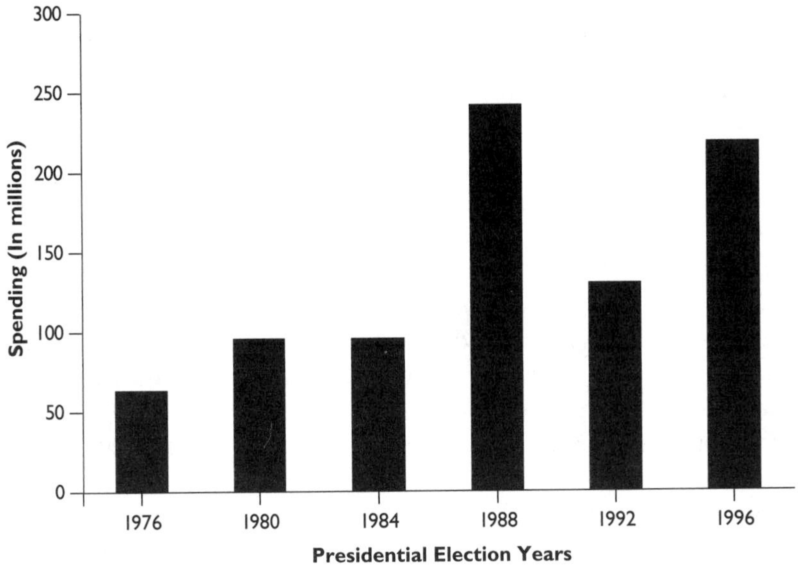

Table 11.10 Cost of Public Financing of the 1996 Presidential Election

Prenomination phase	
Democrats	$14,036,888
Republicans	$41,558,569
Other	$358,883
Subtotal	$55,954,340
Conventions	
Democrats	$12,360,000
Republicans	$12,360,000
Subtotal	$24,720,000
General Election	
Clinton–Gore	$61,800,000
Dole–Kemp	$61,800,000
Subtotal	$123,600,000
Total	$204,274,340

Source: Data based on Federal Election Commission sources.

it encourages competition. But the level of public funding must be sufficient so that challengers can run credible campaigns. There is significant disagreement about what that level of funding is—and whether it is the same from district to district for House elections.

There are other points to consider as well. Should people be forced to pay for the campaigns of candidates they oppose? Can fair competition ever be imposed through law? Is there anything wrong with the current situation? And if not, why change it?

It should also be noted that twenty-three states have some form of public financing for some state offices or for political parties; fifteen of those states fund candidates at some level (Malbin and Gais 1998, 53, table 4-1; Alexander and Eberts 1986; Jones 1980; 1984; Noragon 1981; Sorauf 1988, 286). Some states allocate public funds to the political parties. Other states allocate public funds directly to candidates for office. And some states, to both. State experiences vary widely in the amounts of money involved, in their methods of dispensing the funds, and in assessing the ways in which public financing has worked. The different public financing programs have provided interesting laboratories for those interested in public policy formation (Malbin and Gais 1998, chap. 4).

This area of reform continues to interest those concerned about the costs of running for office and the influence of those supporting candidates. How quickly action is taken (and if it is ever taken) in a particular state varies with the political climate experienced by decision makers in that state.

V. Politicians View Campaign Financing

Many years ago, Congressmen Al Swift (D-Wash., 1979–1995) and Bill Thomas (R-Calif.) addressed a conference sponsored by the Citizens' Research Foundation, an organization that has been at the forefront of election financing for nearly four decades. They disagreed on many particular aspects of what is desirable but came to the same conclusion about the likelihood of campaign finance reform. According to Swift, "The issues of campaign finance reform inherently affect partisan politics. There will be winners and losers. These issues are particularly difficult when one house is controlled by one party with Priorities X, and the other house is controlled by the other party with List Y [which was the case at the time of the conference]."

Thomas's conclusion about the motivations of those seeking reform was similar: "What's motivating people who are opposed to PACs is something that is basic and totally American—politics. All they are concerned about is who gets what? When? And how?"

And those are precisely the issues. Politicians view campaign finance reform from the position of winners and losers, of where they stand now. Politicians are not generally in the business of creating the perfect world; they want to create the best world within the very practical limits that they see. Again, Congressman Swift summarized this view: "I think that public financing would be a good solution to much of the problem that we see, but I also happen to believe that we have enough to do in the Congress and that chasing chimeras is not very productive. . . . No legislation can emerge from our subcommittee which will pass the full House and which would pass the Senate. So, seeing no use in spinning our wheels, we move on to other topics."

These statements, voiced more than ten years ago, accurately describe the situation that exists as we approach the twenty-first century. Campaign finance reform falls into the realm of political reality. Despite the fact that campaign finance reform has been high on the political agenda for some years, no action has been taken.

Many reformers felt that the abuses in how the 1996 presidential campaigns were financed rose to the level of scandal that would establish the climate for significant reform (Corrado et al. 1997; Citizens' Research Foundation 1997; Kassebaum and Mondale 1998; Task Force on Campaign Reform 1998). A bipartisan group of House freshmen, headed by Republican Asa Hutchinson (Ark.) and Democrat Tom Allen (Me.) introduced one reform bill, a mild measure aimed at limiting the amount of soft money spent and calling for increased disclosure of independent expenditures. They felt that their bill significantly improved the current law and would prove to be passable.

Those who had suggested wider-ranging reform in an earlier Congress came back with a more ambitious package. The McCain-Feingold bill—and its House counterpart, the Shays-Meehan bill—sought (1) to impose limits on expenditures in congressional and senatorial elections by giving candidates incentives to comply with those limits, (2) to reduce the influence of special interest groups, (3) to close tightly the soft money loophole, (4) to curtail the influence of independent expenditures, and (5) to define in a much more restricted manner issue advocacy advertisements that are protected by First Amendment guarantees.

The Clinton White House, reeling under charges that the president's 1996 campaign had violated the spirit if not the letter of the existing law, called for passage of serious campaign finance reform. But Republican leaders opposed all of these reform efforts. Speaker Gingrich kept the House bills off the floor. Majority leader Lott allowed Senate consideration but knew that filibusters would prevent action. Public pressure, however, was mounting for some congressional attention to be devoted to the problem. In the spring of 1998, Speaker Gingrich conceded that he would allow a vote on campaign finance reform. In August, a significantly watered-down version of Shays-Meehan

EXPRESS ADVOCACY

Advertisements taking a position on issues or controversies, a constitutionally protected right.

passed the House. Its major accomplishment was to ban soft money and to redefine **express advocacy** (chap. 12).

A companion piece was debated in the Senate. Despite numerous efforts to rewrite the bill to make it palatable to more senators, proponents could not garner the sixty votes needed to invoke cloture. Thus campaign finance reform failed once again. The reason pertains to the very basic nature of politics. On this issue members have philosophical differences to be sure, but more importantly, they see the stakes differently. While many in the country are offended by the way in which elections are currently run, no consensus has emerged as to which problems must be treated—and no one has successfully traversed the obstacles involved in sorting out the ways in which the various reform proposals relate to each other.

When asked about the evils of PAC money, Barney Frank (D-Mass.) was noncommittal. PAC money in the abstract was of no interest. But, "If my opponent takes no PAC money, I'll take no PAC money. Heck, if he makes no speeches, I'll make no speeches." The point is clear. Incumbents win most of the time unless they give their

opponent some advantage. They are not likely to change the system to their own disadvantage. No nonincumbents would favor changing the system to incumbents' further advantage, and so the system has remained in place.

That is not to say that reform is dead. In the 1998 election two very different states—Arizona and Massachusetts—each passed fundamental campaign finance reform calling for public funding of state campaigns. Citizen activists, led by Ellen Miller of Public Campaign, maintain that they can keep pressure on Congress but also have an impact by passing fundamental reform at the state level. This tactic has been successful in smaller and medium-sized states, but it has yet to be proven in larger states, where more money is often involved. But just as politicians vote for their own interest when this issue reaches the legislature, so too do they watch with concern as their constituents clearly express preferences for a reformed system.

WEBSITES

http://www.fec.gov/

The Federal Election Commission website is the most important for understanding campaign finance. The site presents information on campaign finance laws and data and analysis of recent experiences. All candidate, party, and PAC filings are available on-line.

http://www.brook.edu/gs/campaign/cfr hp.htm

The Brookings Institution's website provides a good deal of unbiased information on campaign finance-related matters. This site also includes a discussion group dedicated to exploring issues such as those raised in this chapter.

http://www.crp.org/

The Center for Responsive Politics provides analysis of recent campaign finance data and information about ongoing campaigns. This is an advocacy group favoring significant reform of the current process.

http://www.publicampaign.org/

Public Campaign is a reform group that has proposed various successful state-level reforms that include public financing of state elections.

http://www.usc.edu/dept/CRF/

The Citizens' Research Foundation is a forty-year-old nonpartisan group dedicated to providing information to the public about the ways in which campaigns are financed. It has been responsible for a set of books examining campaign finance practices in each of the recent presidential elections.

http://www.followthemoney.org/

The National Institute on Money in State Politics provides information to reporters, scholars, and citizens interested in campaign finance practices in the various states.

KEY CONCEPTS

1974 Amendments to the FECA
Buckley v. Valeo
express advocacy
Federal Corrupt Practices Act of 1925
Federal Election Commission
Hatch Act
independent expenditures
issue advocacy
McCain-Feingold bill
multicandidate political committee
public financing
Revenue Act
separate segregated fund
SunPAC
tax check-off
Tillman Act

DISCUSSION QUESTIONS

1. With so many activists interested in campaign finance reform, how do you explain the fact that no major reform bill has passed Congress since 1974?
2. What is the best evidence that campaign finance reform is needed? What is the best evidence that the current system should not be changed in any fundamental way?
3. Discuss the advantages and disadvantages of public financing of presidential elections. Do these same points apply equally to congressional elections? In what ways does the financing of congressional elections differ from presidential elections?
4. Hard money is regulated and disclosed. Soft money is disclosed but not regulated. Do recent complaints about soft money disprove the theory that we can rely on disclosure to keep the campaign finance system aboveboard? If so, why isn't public disclo-

sure of financial sources enough to allow the public to hold politicians accountable?

5. What is wrong with spending lots of money in congressional elections? In fact, should we want more money to be spent so that we could know more about those who seek to govern us?

CHAPTER 12

The Media and the Electoral Process

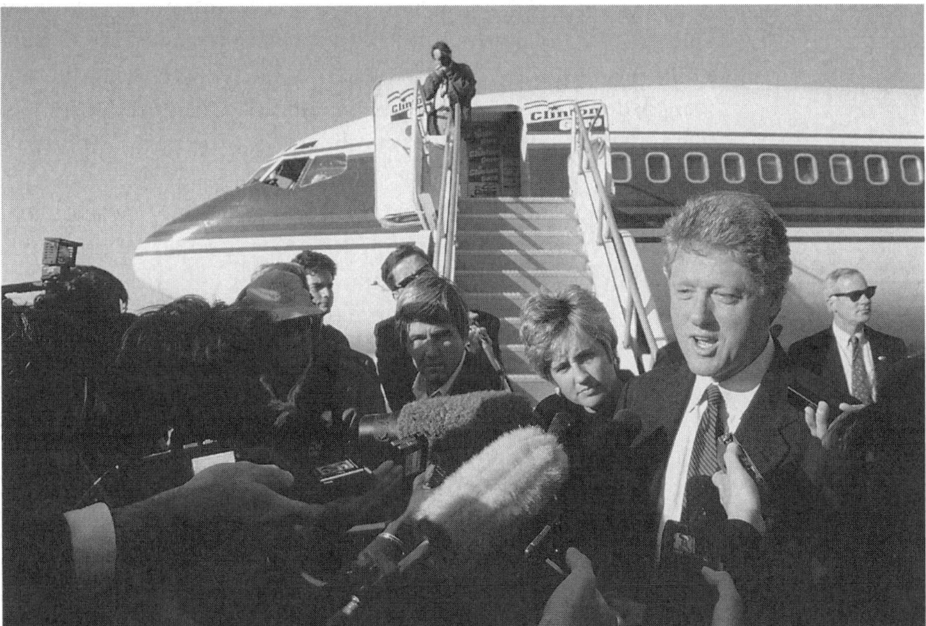

How many of the candidates for president in 1996 did you see? I do not mean "see" as in seeing on television. I mean "see" as in seeing face-to-face in person, whether across a room, in an auditorium, or even at a football stadium. I do not want to be too restrictive in my definition.

Let's go back a step. How many of the candidates for governor, U.S. senator, or even member of Congress in 1998 in your state did you see (same sense of the word)? One? Well, if you didn't see these people often enough to form an opinion about them and their views, then how did you learn about them? Where did your political information come from?

A century ago the answer to that question would have been easy. Citizens did not know much about candidates for office. But they did know about political parties. And candidates were candidates of political parties. Today, campaigns are candidate centered. Citizens proudly claim that they vote for the candidate, not the party. How do they find out about the candidate?

The short answer is that they find out from "the media." But that very answer begs the question. What do we mean by "the media"? How are political messages communicated through the media? How effectively does this institution serve our democracy?

I. The Media in the Contemporary Context

Sixty years ago, newspapers dominated the mass media that affected American politics. Citizens learned the news of the day through their daily papers; in major cities, often, more than one newspaper competed for the public's attention. Newspapers lost their primacy with the emergence of television. By the late 1950s television sets had saturated the American landscape. Over 90 percent of American homes had televisions; many had more than one.

Twenty years ago, three major networks—ABC, CBS, and NBC—dominated television broadcasting. According to Nielsen Media Research ratings, nearly three out of every five homes watched one of the major networks during prime viewing hours in 1979 (Samuelson 1999, A23). In 1998, the three major networks captured only about one quarter of the market. Even if the newer networks such as Fox are added in, the number does not reach a third. It's not that the total amount of television viewing has decreased but rather that citizens are turning to cable or satellite outlets, means of viewing that were available to only a small minority at the time of the ratings first cited (Samuelson 1999, A23).

What has been the effect of these changes on the impact of the mass media on politics? Put simply, it is more difficult to cut through the noise. Twenty years ago, politicians had a pretty good idea of what sources their constituents would turn to for news. National politicians were concerned about the major networks. Statewide, politicians tried to garner national media attention, but they concentrated on local outlets, television stations, and major newspapers. Local politicians lowered their sights again, hoping for some television coverage but trying to ensure that the local press covered them adequately.[1]

Today's politicians try to find an audience wherever it might appear. The political elite might tune in to *The News Hour with Jim Lehrer* or spend time watching C-SPAN or CNN. Certainly many still watch the network newscasts and read the major newspapers. But others pay less attention to the news—and politicians must find their targets "where they live." Thus presidential candidate Clinton appeared on MTV in 1992. Thus an increasing number of candidates have launched their own websites and use the Internet for communicating with constituents as well as for campaigning. Thus political consultants worry about where to communicate a message as much as about what message is to be communicated.

Twenty years ago—the date is arbitrary, for the process has been changing over time—reporters covered the news. Increasingly today, candidates for office take actions in order to be covered by the media. No clearer example can be found of this phenomenon than the national nominating conventions.

In the 1960s, presidential nominating conventions were major events on television. The networks competed with each other to provide the best "gavel-to-gavel" coverage. They were concerned about what was going on at the podium, what decisions were being made in the hall, and who was having what influence.

At the 1964 Republican National Convention, when nominee Barry Goldwater chided his vanquished moderate opponents that "extremism in the defense of liberty is no vice," the networks reported that his selection marked a defining moment for his party. The drama at the site of the convention, San Francisco's Cow Palace, was presented "live" for the entire nation to watch. Few who watched would forget the late John Chancellor's exit line as he was forcibly removed from the convention floor, "This is John Chancellor, NBC News, somewhere in custody!"

When the Democratic National Convention in Chicago broke into chaos in 1968, the networks covered the disorder as a major news event. Again, few who watched would soon forget the delegates barred from the floor, the protestors beaten outside delegate hotels, or the religious slur shouted by Chicago mayor Richard Daley at Connecticut senator Abraham Ribicoff, who was decrying the violent tactics of the Chicago police. The events were real; the reporting was real; the news was real.

But the parties could not stand the criticism. Internal schism, they felt, should not be viewed by potential voters. Not atypically, the Republicans learned this lesson before the Democrats. In 1972, Democratic nominee George McGovern accepted his party's nomination with a truly great speech, which was heard by nearly no one because it was delivered long after most people had gone to bed. Convention business had dragged on—viewed in all of its untidiness by a large television audience—and McGovern was not afforded his finest hour until well past midnight. By contrast, the Republican convention of that year was scripted down to the minute to guarantee that the viewing audience saw only what the party officials wanted them to see and saw it when they wanted it to be seen. President Nixon's renomination was as carefully orchestrated as a royal coronation, down to the minutest detail (Davis 1996, chap. 13).

It didn't take the Democrats long to learn the lesson of careful planning from the Republicans; their conventions came to be as carefully scripted as their opponent's. Once national nominating conventions were widely anticipated events with huge television audiences, but by the time George Bush and Michael Dukakis were nominated in 1988, fewer than one in five households bothered to watch. The major networks abandoned the gavel-to-gavel coverage of which they had been so proud only a few short years earlier, leaving such coverage to C-SPAN, CNN, and PBS.[2] Even when the networks were on the air, they covered the podium only selectively, preferring to air their own versions of what was going on.

Network disenchantment with the extent to which the conventions had become a showcase for the parties as opposed to news reached a new height in 1996. Ted Koppel had moved his *Nightline* television show to California, the site of the Republican National Convention. After one night, he picked up stakes and returned to New York with the disclaimer, "There is no news here."

Coverage of the national conventions demonstrates two points. First, politicians try to use the media to "make the news" they want. Second, media coverage is no longer cast broadly; it is now cast narrowly. Each media outlet is aware of its audience and programs accordingly. Thus the major networks reduced their coverage of the conventions, but the more news-oriented cable networks continued theirs. The media context for politics as we enter the twenty-first century is an extremely complex one. Politicians try to structure the ways in which they appear on **free media** outlets; they continue to use **paid media** in ways to present their message as they define it in a way most likely to impact the intended audience. The distinction between free media and paid media continues to be important.

FREE MEDIA

Media exposure that a candidate receives without having to pay for it, for example, coverage in newspapers or on television news shows.

PAID MEDIA

Media exposure that a candidate's campaign pays for and thus controls.

II. Free Media: Journalists' Presentations of Candidates and Campaigns

A. The Varieties of Free Media

There was a time when anyone who heard the phrase "free media" would have a pretty good sense of what was meant. In the early days of the republic, free media referred to pamphlets and early newspapers, the so-called **penny press**, that printed news for all to read. Frequently the news was slanted in one political direction or another because many of the early presses were controlled by persons having specific political agendas.

PENNY PRESS

Newspapers and leaflets in the early years of the republic, so named because they sold for a penny.

As the country grew and as technology advanced, free media came to mean newspapers, many of which were parts of national or regional chains, and eventually newsmagazines. In the first half of the twentieth century radio and television—network and local—were added to the media mix. When free media was discussed in the context of political parties and elections, it meant news as covered in the free media.

In the contemporary context both the media and the ways in which political messages are communicated have changed. To be sure, the media still include newspapers and magazines, radio, and television. But none of these is the same as it was even a few decades ago. For instance, the number of newspapers—and the number of communities served by more than one major paper—has shrunk dramatically. In addition, the instant newspaper, *USA Today*, serves a national audience in a way vastly different from that done by any competitor. News is condensed and homogenized in a way that makes many more traditional newspaper professionals uncomfortable.

More and more specialized magazines are filling part of the news picture. Whereas once "newsmagazine" meant *Time*, *Newsweek*, *U.S. News & World Report*, and a couple of opinion monthlies, today the number of magazines has expanded greatly. Many aim at narrow readership and are not at all hesitant to voice their views. *Modern Maturity*, the magazine for members of the American Association of Retired Persons, reaches millions with each issue. Although the readership of magazines put out by other groups tends to be smaller, their influence on public policy matters may well be greater.

Changes in television have already been noted. The trend is clear. Major network audiences are falling and cable audiences are growing. Cable networks aim at particular audiences. The news that they provide, if any, is also aimed at those audiences—youth, women, religious people, sports enthusiasts, and so on.

As a result, how citizens receive their news has changed. As recently as a decade ago, news was conveyed mainly on news shows, nightly news broadcasts, and the occasional television magazine, such as *60 Minutes*. The nightly news broadcast continues and the number of newsmagazines has greatly increased. News stations now dot the dial. There is more news available than any one person can digest. But many people choose not to avail themselves of these sources.

TALK SHOWS

Radio (and occasionally television) broadcasts in which the format consists of a host, often with guests, interacting with the audience either in person or via telephone and expressing views on the issues of the day.

For what news they get, they turn to other sources. **Talk shows**, on radio as well as on television, provide much of the political information that reaches many people. These shows provide a forum for citizens (and often opinionated hosts) to inform and misinform each other. Opinion replaces action as the message communicated. Balance is almost never a goal and is rarely achieved.

Entertainment programming informs the public as well. At one extreme you see President Clinton playing his saxophone on the *Arsenio Hall Show*. But more importantly, you see political humor as one of the most common media on late-night television. For many, the image of our political leaders is the image portrayed on *Saturday Night Live*, *Politically Incorrect*, or the Leno and Letterman shows.

These media are similar in that they reach broad audiences and are not controlled by politicians. They are different in terms of citizen involvement. If a citizen chooses to tune in to a radio talk show because he or she agrees or disagrees with the host, that represents a political decision. If, on the other hand, a viewer is given a clear message by an entertainer when the viewer's goal was to listen to comedy, not to be involved in a political dialogue, that is a very different kind of activity. Yet both are a critically important part of today's political context.

From this perspective, it is interesting to consider the Internet as a medium through which citizens learn about politics. There is no question that use of the Internet and citizen exposure to the Internet are rapidly growing. Between 1995 and 1998, the use of the Internet expanded five times (Samuelson 1998, 26). Campaigns now routinely use websites to communicate with their supporters. Candidate biographies and issue positions are posted for all to read; some candidates have even begun to attack their opponents on the web (Ranney 1998, E1). But the question remains: Who reads this material? Surfers tend to visit websites that appeal to them. Those interested in politics might well look at a candidate's home page, but those more interested in science fiction are likely to surf in another direction. According to Mark Mellman, a Democratic political consultant, "On TV, you decide you want to watch 'Seinfeld,' and you got our ad. The problem is that not many people want political information. When you go to the Web, you have to want to go to a political site. . . . The truth is as a tool of political communication, the Internet today is of marginal value, but increasing value" (Ranney 1998, E1). That is, the Internet remains a media source with untapped, but also unexplored, potential.

One further point can be made concerning the varieties of free media. Newsgathering techniques are generational as well as interest specific. Those who came of political age before the recent rapid changes in the media environment, the pre-baby boom generation, tend to keep up on the news and to go to a variety of sources for their information. Only one-third of those who have come of political age in the last decade follow politics closely; they tend to rely on a very different set of sources. Politicians have to keep these differences in mind as they determine how to work with various news providers (Samuelson 1998).

B. The Role of the Free Media

Perhaps there is another way to view the role of the free media in political contexts. Rather than look at the number of media and the ways in which they communicate information, perhaps we can concentrate on the role that they should be playing in electoral theory. That is, what is it we hope free media do in order to make our political processes function more effectively?

1. Informed Consent of the Governed

A representative democracy rests not just on the consent of the governed but on the **informed consent of the governed**. The role that the media should play in our political system is to permit those who choose our elected officials to do so in an informed way. That answer, however, oversimplifies a complex situation. As noted earlier, one important question deals with how much information citizens need to make an informed judgment. That obviously reflects on what kind of information we should expect the media to provide.

INFORMED CONSENT OF THE GOVERNED
A minimal requirement for an effectively functioning representative democracy.

Let's look at the question from a slightly different perspective. The media are an intermediary institution in our system. That is, they link other important actors; in the case we are interested in, they link those seeking elective office (including those currently holding office) with those who will make the electoral choice. In an earlier era, political parties performed this role for almost all offices. Today, many citizens reject the automatic link between themselves and political parties, even if they assume the link between parties and candidates. The media fill that void.

But we still need to explore what kinds of information should be provided. Should citizens only be concerned about candidates' policy positions? Should they be concerned about personalities? Should they be concerned about personal lifestyle, about "youthful indiscretions,"

and families? Do the media have an obligation to provide all of this information? In what form? The briefest answer is that the media can be expected to provide the information that citizens seek.

How that definition is reached still poses difficult questions. For instance, I claimed earlier that the media today do provide virtually any information that a citizen could want about officeholders and candidates for office. But the citizen must play an active role in finding that information. On the other hand, information that may not be relevant to citizens' needs reaches many "automatically." Certainly in recent years the media have delved more deeply into highly personal aspects of candidates' lives than was true in the past. Many complain that they are learning things that they do not need to know, that candidates' private lives should remain just that, private. Some claim that this kind of intrusive media information changes the political scene by discouraging strong candidates.

Speaking before an informal meeting of senators during the heat of the Senate trial on the impeachment of President Clinton, former president George Bush echoed this view: "I worry too about sleaze, about excessive intrusion into private lives. I worry about once great news organizations that seem to resort to tabloid journalism, giving us sensationalism at best and smut at worst" (Dewar 1999, A16).

On that very same day, President Bush's daughter-in-law Laura, wife of Texas governor George W. Bush, one of the front-runners for the 2000 Republican nomination, told a group of journalists in Austin that she was very reticent to have her husband seek the presidency owing to the loss of privacy such a campaign would entail (Neal and Duggan 1999, A8).

Why do the media insist on presenting stories that cause these concerns? Simply put, because the public buys them. They sell newspapers and magazines; they increase Nielsen ratings. The public expresses its desires in a number of ways. The media react to the cash register, to the public's demonstrating its real desire by what it purchases.

2. *Window on the Candidates*

The media should play other roles as well—and these too may be controversial. As noted already, it is impossible for every citizen to see every candidate. But many voters want to "experience" the candidates they are supporting or opposing. The media should let them have this experience. These windows should be free from outside manipulation; they should be free from candidate manipulation. And in searching for this lack of interference, controversy arises. It is clear that candidates know when the media are covering them—and they act accordingly. It is thus difficult for the media to provide a clear picture. In the most recent electoral cycles, C-SPAN has played this role probably as well as it can be played, following candidates for various offices for extended periods of time, making it more difficult for candidates to perform for the camera in ways different from how they act when not under such scrutiny.

3. Referee between Candidates

We have all seen campaigns in which candidates get involved in a " 'He said . . .,' 'No, I didn't' " kind of dispute. In recent years these battles have often been fought through competing television advertisements. A relatively new role for the media is serving as a referee in these battles and thus raising the chances that candidate advertisements will be honest. During the 1988 presidential campaign, the record of Democratic candidate Michael Dukakis as governor of Massachusetts was attacked in a series of negative ads that many observers felt unfair. Following suggestions by veteran campaign watchers David Broder of *The Washington Post* and Ken Bode, host of Public Television's *Washington Week in Review,* largely as a result of this experience, many newspapers and television stations took on the role of monitoring political advertisements for truthfulness, so-called **"adwatch" campaigns**. "For the first time in most places, a referee in the form of political reporters showing up in the campaign arena with the savvy to call fouls and a voice that's being heard [is present]. A game with a referee is a different kind of game" (Monroe 1990, 6).

ADWATCH CAMPAIGNS

Efforts by newspapers and some television stations to monitor political advertising for accuracy.

Adwatches "force campaigns to issue extensive documentation *before* the ad is aired—instead of waiting until the other side has complained" (Alter 1992, 37). Adwatches have even spread to small-town newspapers. Most feel that their impact has been positive, reducing the likelihood of campaign ads being false or misleading (Milburn and Brown 1997). However, some scholars argue that adwatches have not had the desired effect of making voters less favorably disposed toward those whose advertisements are most severely criticized (Ansolabehere and Iyengar 1995). That the referee's role in the rough-and-tumble of political campaigns is an appropriate one for the media, however, is now well accepted.

C. The Actual Role That the Media Play

It should come as little surprise that analysis of the role that the media actually do play in the political process differs significantly from the role observers theoretically feel that they should play. Much of the work on this topic has looked at presidential campaigns and the role that the media have played in them, but the findings apply almost as directly to campaigns for other offices in which candidates must rely on the media to communicate with potential voters (see Iyengar and Reeves 1997; Norris 1997; Davis 1996; Seib 1994). Based on this work, it is possible to characterize the role actually played by the media in modern campaigns according to a number of different categories.[3]

1. The Great Mentioner

Earlier in this chapter I referred to Texas governor George W. Bush as a front-runner for the Republican presidential nomination in the year 2000. Governor Bush became a front-runner before he announced his candidacy for the White House or even formed an exploratory committee. How did he get to be a front-runner? The press dubbed him one. To be sure, Governor Bush has enormous political assets—his name and family connections, his ability to raise money, and his popularity in a large state. But he was not the only Republican governor reelected in 1998, and many of the others were not "mentioned" as leading contenders for their party's nomination.

Thus one role that the press has come to play is to raise some potential candidates above others in the months before a campaign really starts. This kind of mention can give momentum to a nascent campaign, whereas the lack of such recognition can stop a campaign in its tracks. One key to a candidate's being taken seriously is having his or her name recognized by large numbers of citizens. Early preference polls are often nothing more than name recognition polls. Candidates who do not do well in them are not taken seriously by influential politicians. Thus the media role at this early stage is a most critical one.

2. Image Creator

Think for a moment about what you know about any major political figure, other than those of whom you have some detailed knowledge. How did you acquire that image? Where did it come from? The simple answer is that most images of that type are media created.

In 1988, when no major Democratic candidates came forward to seek their party's presidential nomination, the candidates who did run were dubbed the "seven dwarves" by the media. That image—lack of stature—stuck, despite the fact that the field included men who were prominent in their states and in Congress. In 1984, Walter Mondale was characterized as the candidate of Big Labor and other Democratic-leaning interest groups; Gary Hart was the candidate of new ideas. Each picture was oversimplified but widely accepted.

PACK JOURNALISM

The phenomenon of all journalists covering an event following the lead of one of their colleagues instead of pursuing their own angles on the story.

The press has the ability to portray such an image because members of the press tend to read each other's writing, talk with each other, and follow each other's lead. The concept of **pack journalism**, in which "one reporter's story becomes every reporter's story" (Seib 1994, 60–61), has been expounded for more than twenty years (see Sabato 1991; Crouse 1973; Thompson 1973). Although reporters strive for independence, the news of the day is often dictated by the schedules set by the campaigns themselves. Events are planned in order to create good visual effects for television and to meet deadlines for the print media. Candidates rush from event to event; so too must those covering them. As a result there is little time for reflection, and stories tend to be similar from one reporter to the next. When one reporter comes up with a new, apt way of describing a candidate, with a new image, it is not long before others adopt it. And those images tend to stick. Do you think this is an exaggeration? Which presidential candidate is so challenged he cannot even spell "potato"?

3. Expectation Setter

Commentator after commentator, as well as media critic after media critic, has pointed to the role that the media play in setting expectations for candidates at various early stages in campaigns.

When looking at presidential campaigns, the media note how much money each candidate raises at the times of various Federal Election Commission reports. They comment on candidate performance in debates vis-à-vis their opponents. They examine poll results, noting who is doing better than predicted and whose ratings are not so high. And, most importantly, they lay out in advance how each candidate is likely to do in an upcoming primary and weigh that candidate's performance and standing in the polls in terms of how well he or she fared in comparison to those expectations. State and local media play similar roles in the campaigns they cover. And evaluations of expectation meeting are important as a campaign progresses.

EXPECTATION GAME

The strategy of setting expectations of performance low so that results will be viewed in a favorable light.

Merely look at the **expectation game** and the New Hampshire primary (chap. 9). In 1968, President Johnson won that primary, but he did not do nearly as well as he had been expected to do; shortly thereafter he withdrew from the race. In 1972, Maine Democratic senator Edmund S. Muskie won the primary, but his margin was low; his campaign never recovered. In 1976, former Georgia governor Jimmy Carter won the Democratic primary, exceeding expectations; his campaign took off. In 1980, former California governor Ronald Reagan met expectations for a victory in the Republican primary, after having done poorly in the Iowa caucuses; the serious challengers to his nomination lost their momentum. In 1984, Colorado senator Gary Hart upset front-runner Walter Mondale, who had been Carter's vice president; a tight campaign followed for many months because Hart had exceeded expectations and Mondale had failed to reach them. In 1988, Kansas senator Bob Dole failed to do as well as had been predicted; his campaign never seriously challenged that of Vice President George Bush again. In 1992, Patrick Buchanan exceeded expectations and President Bush did not meet them in the Republican primary; Buchanan gained the momentum needed to carry his campaign to his party's convention. Finally, in 1996, Senator Dole did meet expectations in New Hampshire and his Republican challengers failed to so do; his march to nomination went smoothly from then on.

Where did the expectations come from? From the media—often prodded by candidates who tried to set low standards for themselves so that they could exceed these standards. But in each case, the popular view of the expectations—and of whether they were met or not—was put forth by the media covering the campaign.

4. Issue Identifier

The media determine what is important in a campaign. That is, they determine which of the items that candidates mention are transmitted to the public. Every candidate for a major office discusses a large number of issues during a campaign. All develop position papers. All give speeches on many topics. All make a sincere attempt to tell the public what they stand for.

However, detailed issue discussion is not "good news." The media determine what the agenda for the public will be. The agenda might well be the personal characteristics of a candidate. It might be how competing candidates stand on contentious issues. It might be which candidate in a primary election is likely to poll better in the general election.

In primary elections the agenda is very frequently related to the game of politics, not to the business of governing. That is, the journalists covering a campaign are concerned about who is likely to win, what techniques are in use to push a campaign forward, what groups or key individuals favor which candidates. Even in general elections, the media frequently concentrate more on the nuts and bolts of the campaign than they do on differences among candidates. Consequently, that is what the public knows about the campaign. That is what is discussed over the watercooler, at the mall, on the subway, at the dinner table. Citizens are more likely to view campaigns in terms of the latest poll results, debate strategy, or advertising gambits than they are to know about substantive differences in candidates' stands on key issues, since citizen knowledge reflects media presentation.

5. Field Narrower

FIELD WINNOWER

Playing the role of eliminating some candidates from a multicandidate competition.

When all of these roles are combined, one result is that the press plays an important role in narrowing multicandidate fields. This role, also known as **field winnower**, has long been recognized in presidential primaries (Barber 1978) and is just as apparent in statewide and other highly visible primaries.

When the media stop mentioning a candidate, when the image associated with a candidate is an unflattering one, when a candidate does not meet expectations, or when the agenda discussed in the media excludes issues raised by a candidate or his or her role in a campaign, a signal goes out that that candidacy has lost viability. This role is an important one in primary campaigns, particularly in presidential primary campaigns, in which it is necessary to present the public with a set of choices with which it can cope. But this role is not necessarily one that the media are best suited to play.

In primaries below the level of the presidency, this role is often played either by political parties in a formal way (when state laws or party rules permit it; chap. 7) or by party leaders in an informal way. Some candidates are supported by party regulars; others are not. Some find encouragement from those who typically fund campaigns; others cannot raise money. While these "winnowers" are not always part of the formal process, they have a certain legitimacy within the process. Below the presidential level, the extent to which the media have assumed this role varies from state to state. As at the level of presidential nominations, the extent to which the media's playing such an important role is accepted often depends on the perspective of the person evaluating the process. Not surprisingly, those who are "winnowed out" tend to be less satisfied than those who are "winnowed in."

6. Campaign Critic

The media have also assumed the role of critic, judging the performance of those seeking office. Some patterns have become clear in recent elections.

First, the media tend to view themselves as watchdogs of the public good. Thus they are particularly vigilant in observing and commenting on the character and performance of individuals who are likely to be elected, or who are serious contenders to be elected. Much of what is reported is negative. Rarely does one read a story that is full of praise for all aspects of a front-running candidate's qualities (Davis 1997, 187–189). On the other hand, underdog candidates are often afforded much kinder treatment. In 1992, when Texas billionaire H. Ross Perot was seeking the presidency, the press treated him as something of a darling early in the campaign season. He was photogenic, funny, willing to take controversial stands, and he was polling better than was expected. However, once Perot started to receive serious consideration from voters, the press turned more critical, raising questions about his electability and the extent to which his solutions were more simplistic than the problems they addressed (Germond and Witcover 1993).

Of course, the result of this kind of treatment has a certain impact not only on the campaigns but also on the public officials subsequently elected. Winners appear in a less favorable light than do losers, who frequently emerge from elections as sympathetic figures. Certainly this kind of media treatment contributes to public cynicism.

7. Documentor of Elections

It is also true that the media play the role of documenting elections for the public. That is, we know what happens in an election because the media tell us.

In some instances, this role is played because the election events themselves take place on or in front of the media. Thus debates among or between candidates for many offices are aired on and closely covered by the various media. The public has the opportunity to observe these events as they happen, to read transcripts, to absorb analysis, or to follow others' reactions.

In other instances, the role involves media documentation of what is happening. Media polls tell the public how the various campaigns are doing. Whereas media polls were intermittent during the elections of the 1960s, by the 1990s national and statewide polls were so frequent that individual voters began to wonder how so many polls could be published without their opinions having been sought.[4] These polls have proven accurate as predictors of outcomes to be sure, but they are also important to provide an understanding of which voters are supporting which candidate and for what reasons.

These polls have also been criticized. In most recent presidential elections, pollsters have known the results well in advance of the actual voting; for instance, President Clinton's lead over Senator Dole was so large in 1996—and his lead in so many states was so overwhelming—that his reelection was assured well before election day. Critics claim not only that these polls remove the drama from a campaign but also that they deflate turnout and may impact elections lower on the ballot. Although they may be documenting one election, they can alter the results of another. The media have been sensitive to this charge—changing the ways in which they use exit polls on election night, as one example—but they also feel an obligation to provide such information about a campaign as they are able to garner.

Analyses by political journalists document campaigns in other ways as well. As controversy has swirled around political advertisements, the media have begun to monitor these attempts to influence the public. **Adwatch campaigns** seek to ensure that advertisements are accurate and not deceptive. Other journalists have also begun to report on strategy used in designing advertisements.

In the 1998 midterm elections, newspaper after newspaper and television special after television special commented on what various campaigns were doing and why they were doing it. In the closing days of that campaign, the Republicans launched a $10-million ad blitz in selective districts, seeking to link Democratic candidates to President Clinton and the scandal surrounding him. As soon as the ad campaign began, journalists wrote about what the Republicans were trying to do, where they were doing it, and what the Democrats' likely reaction was going to be (Associated Press 1998; Berke 1998; Connolly 1998); CNN and C-SPAN did much the same thing, and the campaign was featured on the network nightly news shows.

In these and other ways, the media ensure that the public knows what is happening in an election. But the line between "news" and "analysis" can blur in these circumstances. The media are certainly a documentor of what is happening during an election; but in playing that role, they become a participant as well.

D. An Assessment of the Role of Free Media

It is clear that the role that the free media play in the electoral process differs from theories propounded about it by political scientists. Two questions remain: Why is it different? Is this good or bad?

1. Why Do the Media Play the Roles They Do?

No journalist feels compelled to play a role dictated by electoral theories. That should go without saying. Journalists follow the dictates of their profession. They cover stories. They write about events in what they perceive to be an even-handed way.

But their efforts are by necessity constrained. They must meet deadlines. They can only cover so many campaigns in so much detail. They have limited access to some sources. They must be aware of the costs to their owners of their efforts. Publishers and editors, and executives in electronic media outlets, are concerned about audience share.

Many journalists would like to cover every aspect of a certain campaign in great depth. But they must also cover other campaigns. They must compete for space in their newspaper or time on the air. They must be certain that their stories are accurate and fair, that one candidate is not advantaged over another. Thus they follow certain patterns. Their access is dictated largely by campaign staff. Their ability to file complete stories is compromised at times by deadlines. They compete with fellow journalists covering a campaign, but they also do not want to be too far away from what most of their colleagues are saying, for fear that they will be proven wrong or that they will have missed the "real story."

In short, media coverage of campaigns evolves the way it does because of the norms of the journalists' profession, the demands of their employers, and the constraints on their efforts. Just as all candidates do not run their campaigns as they would were there no limits on what they could do, so too are journalists limited. And the cumulating of this limitation is the role that the media as a whole play. It is not a designed role; it is an evolved role. And thus it is one that must be accepted as part of the system. Marginal changes can be wrought. Individual journalists can do their job well or less well. Innovations such as adwatch campaigns can alter the performance in sometimes significant ways. But fundamental change is not likely to be forthcoming in a system whose parameters are so clearly set by a variety of forces over which they have little control.

2. *How Should We Evaluate That Role?*

In a sense, it does not matter how the role is evaluated because it is largely inevitable. But the media do have an impact on campaigns. Is it good or bad? By what standards should that impact be judged?

In general, the answer is that the media role contributes positively to the electoral process as long as that role is played openly, honestly, and fairly. But that final caveat is not an empty one. One important factor to note concerning the media's coverage of elections is the number of media markets that are dominated by one particular provider of information.

One example should suffice to demonstrate how this can be a problem. For years, the *Manchester Union Leader* has dominated media coverage of campaigns in New Hampshire. The paper, which circulated statewide, is unabashedly conservative, not just Republican but ultraconservative Republican. The editor of the paper frequently writes front-page editorials trumpeting personal views. The paper treats politicians with whom it does not agree with disdain, often preventing them from getting their message through to the public. In that case, the media does not serve the public and the electoral process. Certainly, on a statewide basis, the influence of the *Union Leader* has been unusual, but even its influence in New Hampshire has diminished. However, in local communities, many of which are served by only one newspaper and for which television is not really a viable source of local election news, the problem persists.

With that exception noted, however, the electoral process is quite well served by the free media. Given constraints, the media cover campaigns quite well. Citizens can get what information they need. Journalists look carefully at how they practice their own craft and seek to correct obvious flaws. Thus, for instance, the major networks now routinely rotate reporters among various campaign assignments so that no reporter becomes too close to one campaign and loses objectivity. Campaigns attempt to get the best publicity that they can—for that is the nature of their enterprise—but they also permit journalists to do their job. And the public picks and chooses what it watches and reads, as another example of citizens participating in the process to the extent that they desire to be involved.

III. PAID MEDIA: THE CANDIDATE PROVIDES THE MESSAGE

The difference between free media and paid media could not be more stark. With free media, candidates put their best face forward, but someone else communicates the message to the public. There is an intermediary—the journalists who determine how the message will reach the public. With paid media, candidates determine their message and pay to communicate it directly to potential voters. No intermediary. Straight shot. In this section, we will explore who produces paid advertisements for political campaigns (and what types of advertisements they produce); we will then look at controversies surrounding the ways in which paid media impact political campaigns. We will conclude by looking at the impact of paid media on the electoral process.

A. Types of Paid Media

Paid commercials for political campaigns in this country come from three sources—candidates and their campaigns, the political parties, and interest groups. In fact, the producers of these advertisements are frequently paid consultants to the candidates, parties, or groups; but the message is determined in conjunction with strategies set by campaign committees.

Broadly speaking, political advertisements fall into two categories—**spot advertisements** and longer advertisements. The spots are equivalent to the ads used by commercial enterprises to sell their products or services (Diamond and Bates 1984). They tend to be short—always under one minute in length—colorful, and polished. The longer commercials, most recently known as infomercials, are often thirty minutes in length or even longer. Some believe that H. Ross Perot invented infomercials for his presidential campaigns, but in fact their history is much longer. Many of the original television commercials were longer attempts by candidates to explain their campaigns to the citizens. These messages were shortened because consultants felt that viewer attention span was too short, that citizens turned off longer commercials and sought entertainment television. Perot resurrected the genre to great effect, as Nielsen ratings demonstrated that citizens were willing to spend the time to become informed.

SPOT ADVERTISEMENTS

Short paid political advertisements that must simplify a message to conform to a ten-, twenty-, or thirty-second time frame.

What purposes are served by political advertisements? The purpose clearly depends on the candidate—and the state of his or her candidacy (Seib 1994). For candidates who are not well known to the public, early in a campaign the purpose of ads is to improve name recognition, essentially to prove that a candidacy is viable. For statewide campaigns and even for congressional campaigns, this kind of advertising can be quite expensive. Quality ads must be produced and repeated over and over in order to make an impression on prospective voters. Of course, incumbents, who have by definition run in the past, do not need to spend money in this way. However, incumbents often run biographical ads early in a campaign to cement a positive image in the public's mind.

POSITIVE ADS

Political advertising that stresses the record of the sponsoring candidate, not that of his or her opponent.

NEGATIVE ADS

Political advertising that points to perceived flaws in the record of the sponsoring candidate's opponent.

Once a candidacy has achieved viability, advertisements are used for one of two purposes. Either they are intended to convince citizens to vote for the candidate or they are designed to denigrate an opponent.[5] These ads have been characterized as **positive ads** or **negative ads**, though there is a great deal of disagreement about how these terms should be defined.

Positive ads state the case for a candidate. The goal is to convince the public that the candidate is the right person for the job, that he has the right qualities to do the job effectively, that he is on the right side of the crucial issues. Negative ads try to convince voters that they should vote against the sponsoring candidate's opponent. Some feel that all negative ads have a deleterious effect on the system; this view will be discussed later. At this point, let it suffice to state that all negative ads are not alike. Most analysts would claim that it is perfectly legitimate for a challenger to point to his or her opponent's record in office and to question whether citizens approve of that record. Most would also agree that it is inappropriate to distort that record or to present it in a confusing manner. But what about raising questions about a candidate's moral fitness for office? Some claim that such personal matters should not be part of the political discourse. Others claim that they are at the heart of a candidate's qualifications for office. No consensus exists on this point. In addition, disagreement exists on how all of these points can or should be made.

The purpose of ads that are run during the heat of a campaign is to ensure that the voters consider the views of the candidate sponsoring the ads. In so doing, paid commercials create an impression of the candidate and go a long way toward setting the agenda for a campaign. As was pointed out in chapter 8, candidates coordinate their media message with the message they are transmitting throughout the campaign.

Infomercials, such as those sponsored by Ross Perot, are a special case of political advertising. Their strength is that they give a candidate sufficient time to explain his or her position on often complex matters. By necessity viewers gain a different kind of impression of a candidate than they would from a thirty-second spot. It is difficult to maintain a false image when speaking to a television audience for half an hour or more.[6]

A number of candidates have seen the advantage of longer presentations, but they do not want to spend the money that such exposure on television costs. They have found a solution to this dilemma through the production of campaign videos. Through this medium they can discuss their issues in great detail; campaign videos also have the advantage that they can be targeted to specific audiences. Generally a campaign will mail or distribute videos to those with interests in certain topics; thus, they can avoid fallout from those not interested in one issue or another. While videos distributed in this way do not reach an audience as large as that reached by television infomercials, they have proven to be a successful technique and will be used more and more as Internet technology makes widespread distribution more feasible.

Paid political advertisements have become the principal means through which candidates for national and statewide office, and those for other offices with large constituencies, communicate with the voters. They are used because candidates have found them to be effective. There is no more effective means of creating name recognition. Once a campaign is under way, advertisements have been shown to work most effectively at reinforcing existing loyalties (Ansolabehere and Iyengar 1995, 64ff.). They help candidates focus a campaign on the issues they want to discuss. And they allow candidates to raise questions about their opponents, questions that often impact undecided voters. But, as noted earlier, paid media raise a number of questions concerning how the American political process functions. We turn to them next.

B. Controversies Caused by the Use of Paid Media

At least three separate controversies are connected with the use of paid media in political campaigns. The first involves the question of balance—of whether it is fair if one candidate dominates the political discussion because his or her campaign has been able to raise much more money than opponents' campaigns. That question was considered in chapter 11. But two important controversies remain to be explored. In the following sections we will examine the questions surrounding negative advertising and those raised by so-called issue advocacy advertisements.

1. Negative Advertising

As noted earlier, no consensus exists on the question of negative advertising. While most agree that it is appropriate to raise questions about an opponent's record, most also agree that the practice of attacking an opponent can, at times, go too far. The controversy in the use of paid advertising relates to negative **attack ads** that are either personal in nature or presented in a way that invites criticism as unfair, deceptive, or in other ways inappropriate in political discourse.

ATTACK ADS
Political advertisements that attack the sponsoring candidate's opponent, often on personal and not political grounds; viewed by many as contributing to citizen cynicism.

Washington Post media commentator Howard Kurtz examined this issue in an analysis of advertising in a series of statewide campaigns during the 1998 election cycle. Kurtz's article appeared under the headline, "Attack Ads Carpet TV, Spinning the Issues; Distortions Rule the Airwaves; Attack Ads Carpet TV as Issues Are Swept Away."[7] In that article, which focused on campaigns in California, Florida, Georgia, New York, and Texas, Kurtz concluded that

> America is again being carpet-bombed by political ads, many of them fiercely negative. . . . The themes vary from race to race, from education to the environment to health care to gun control, but many of [them] oversimplify and distort the opponent's record. (Kurtz 1998, A1)

In Maryland in 1998, "voters [witnessed] the most sustained assault of negative political advertising in state history" (Wilson 1998, A1), with several hundred ads appearing on Baltimore and Washington television stations each week.

Why do candidates engage in negative advertising? The answer is quite simple. They believe—and they have evidence from recent electoral experience—that such techniques are effective. They work. The point is to win, not to be a nice guy. Thus Mary Crawford, communications director of the National Republican Congressional Committee, justified her party's $10-million advertising blitz linking votes for Democratic candidates to the scandals surrounding President Clinton in 1998: "The challenge in this environment is to acknowledge [the scandal's] existence and to pivot the issues that we want to focus on" (Burke 1998). "The president's scandal is on the very top of the minds of the public, particularly as it turns its attention to the election. . . .To ignore it is as if you're ignoring a dead horse in the middle of the table" (Connolly 1998).

But there is also counter evidence, and a clear recognition that relying on negative advertising can backfire. "Political analysts say hostile advertising can be risky in Maryland, where political debate is generally restrained compared with the shrill name-calling of New York or the racial overtones of North Carolina campaigns" (Wilson 1998).

Similarly, in Michigan, the concern was that negative ads had gone too far: "They can make a heroine out of [the attacked candidate]. Whenever a negative ad pushes the line too far, a negative ad can backfire and make the victim the hero" (Hoffman 1998).

Some Republicans considered the 1998 attack ads aimed at the president during the last week of the congressional elections unnecessarily risky. Ralph Reed, a conservative Republican consultant, expressed the view that "people who are going to vote Republican because of their distaste for the personal conduct of the president made that decision some time ago" (Associated Press 1998).

Those sharing this view feared that voters would react negatively to the advertising campaign and stay home or, alternatively, that it would invigorate Democrats, who were ignoring the election because they were angry at the president, to turn out to vote because of their equal revulsion toward the Republican campaign. The results of the

1998 midterm elections, in which hotly contested districts targeted for the Republican attack ads broke in favor of the Democrats, seemed to confirm the accuracy of these fears.

Strategists have debated the efficacy of negative attack ads in terms of their contribution to electoral outcomes, but others are concerned about their broader impact on the electoral process. One line of argument holds that the negativity of campaigns has kept qualified citizens from seeking elective office (Maisel, Stone, and Maestas 1999). Another concern is that citizens have turned off to political process because they view it as unnecessarily negative. Iyengar and Ansolabehere (1995, 101, 107–110) have demonstrated that positive political advertisements encourage people to vote, whereas negative advertisements reduce voter turnout. According to their analysis, citizens exposed to relentless negative advertising aimed at candidates they favor find that "dropping out may be easier than switching to the attacker" (Iyengar and Ansolabehere 1995, 109–110).

Negative advertising is not likely to go away. The right of candidates to press their political cause as they see fit is a fundamental aspect of freedom of speech; it is unimaginable that the content of political advertising would be restricted in a way that would survive a legal challenge on constitutional grounds.

That certainty has not deterred reformers from seeking a means of ameliorating the impact of negative attack ads. One proposal that has been seriously floated requires candidates who name their opponents in a political advertisement to do so themselves; that is, any negative attack on an opponent must come from the attacking candidate in his or her own words. The theory behind this reform is that it is more difficult to make outlandish statements personally than it is to do so through a third party, or through clever media presentations.

Whether this or any similar reform effort could pass either Congress or a state legislature, and whether it would pass a constitutional challenge, is highly debatable. However, the mere existence of proposals such as this one suggests that the issue of negative advertising is of enough concern to keep efforts to restrain such practices high on reformers' agendas.

2. *Issue Advocacy Advertisements*

Political groups have used a variety of means to further their policy agendas (chap. 6). One technique used by wealthier groups on critical issues has been to advertise to the public, seeking to gain popular support for their positions. In 1994 opponents of President Clinton's health care reform package ran a very successful set of commercials—the "Harry and Louise" commercials, named after the characters portrayed in the ads—that were given credit for turning public opinion against the president's plan.

Noting the success of the "Harry and Louise" commercials, a number of interest groups decided to tie their issue concerns to particular candidacies in the 1996 election. In so doing, they were taking advantage of a judicial interpretation that the right of groups to advertise on behalf of issues with which they were concerned was constitutionally protected and could not be restricted by campaign finance regulations as long as the advertisements did not explicitly call for the election or defeat of a particular candidate.

Organized labor was the first to exploit this interpretation of the law. In 1996 they ran a $35-million campaign targeting particular Republican candidates running for reelection to the House of Representatives. Entering the relevant media markets very early in these campaigns, the labor advertisements were successful in raising doubts in voters' minds about their representatives in Congress. Later in the campaign, a coalition of business groups including the National Federation of Independent Businesses and the National Association of Manufacturers countered the labor campaign with a multimillion-dollar effort of their own, targeted at the same contested districts.

The Annenberg Public Policy Center studied these 1996 advertisements. They noted that 87 percent of these "issue" ads mentioned an individual candidate by name and that the tone of these ads was significantly more negative than the tone of candidate ads in the same districts (Broder and Marcus 1997, 6). They also noted that between $130 million and $150 million was spent on such ads during the 1996 congressional elections.

The extent of this kind of advertising and the fact that it was concentrated in a relatively small number of districts raised concerns. Those who were interested in restricting soft money (chap. 11) also felt that issue advocacy ads had to be limited, lest those who contributed through soft money merely divert their funds to this technique. Thus redefining "issue advocacy" has become an important part of campaign finance reform legislation.

However, two factors have lessened those concerns somewhat. First, no unanimity exists as to how effective the barrage of 1996 issue ads was. Second, partially in response to this uncertainty, the number of such ads and the amount spent on them in the 1998 cycle decreased dramatically. In part, both of these results followed from the fact that issue advocacy advertisements by one side in a campaign were often followed by an equal volume of issue advocacy ads on the other side in the same campaign. Candidates felt that their own voices were being drowned out, and the groups sponsoring the ads were unsure that their investments were wise. In part, issue advocacy ads for candidates in 1998 were restrained because of the furor over the president's sex scandal and the feeling that attention directed to that topic would offset any other advertising campaign.[8]

However, in 1998, as in 1996, one concern was that those issue advocacy campaigns that did target particular campaigns often outspent the candidates themselves. New Jersey Republican congressman Frank Pallone was attacked in a series of ads sponsored by Americans for Job Security. These ads warned Pallone to "keep his hands off of Social Security." The Americans for Job Security advertising campaign against Pallone spent approximately twice as much as he was able to spend on his own campaign. In total that group spent more than $20 million in a select number of districts across the nation (Marcus 1998).

Thus, while the level of concern about issue advocacy advertisements might have abated somewhat with the 1998 experience, there is no indication that the fundamental controversy has lessened. Any reform efforts in the foreseeable future will have to account for the impact of these advertising efforts on campaigns throughout the nation.

C. Impact of Paid Media on Election Campaigns

Obviously modern campaigns have spent such a high percentage of their resources on paid media advertising because candidates, campaign managers, and consultants feel that such expenditures pay electoral dividends. At the most basic level, campaigning through the media allows a candidacy to reach the largest possible audience with a message that is designed by the campaign strategists, not interpreted by journalists. But it is possible to be slightly more explicit, to be clear about what effects campaign commercials are designed to produce.

1. Intended Consequences of Paid Media Campaigns

Campaign strategists have at least four separate goals for paid media campaigns. The first goal is to establish a positive image for the candidate. If the candidate is an incumbent, that image is of a hard-working, effective public servant. If the candidate is a challenger, the goal is to depict the candidate as one who can do the job well. If the candidate is not well known, the first aspect of this strategy is merely to create name recognition. Tactics vary. Some candidacies stress personal characteristics: he is a family man who is loyal to his friends. Others emphasize connections between the candidate and the electorate: she went to high school here and has always lived here; she knows our people. Still others might talk about job qualifications: she has been successful on the city council and will be a great representative in Sacramento. But whatever the tactic, the strategic premise is to build a positive image. Typically commercials of this type run early in a campaign.

The second goal is to set the agenda for the campaign. Through saturating the airwaves with commercials, campaigns hope to affect how the potential voters see the entire campaign. If all commercials talk about local issues, voters are likely to think of the candidate and the campaign in those terms. If the paid media stress a candidate's work in Washington or in a state capital, those issues are likely to be at the forefront. The discussions may be very concrete (i.e., about specific legislation) or diffuse (i.e., about the state of the local economy), but the goal is the same—to concentrate public attention on items that play well for the candidate sponsoring the ads and put his or her candidacy in the most positive light.

The third goal of a campaign is to reinforce the loyalties of party members and others who should logically support a candidate. These ads often link the candidate to popular figures in the same party; congressional candidates appear with the governor or senator of their party to remind voters where their loyalty should lie. One strategy in any campaign is to protect one's base, to be sure that those who are your most likely supporters turn out to vote. Paid media is used to further this effort.

Finally, some (many observers would say most) campaigns use paid media to attack their opponents. Even critics of negative advertising admit that it is appropriate for a candidate to point to flaws in the record of his or her opponent. A challenger has to provide a reason for replacing the incumbent. As discussed above, the question here revolves around the specific points that are attacked and the way in which the message is presented. From a strategic point of view, the goal is clear—to convince voters that there are reasons not to vote for one candidate—and presumably therefore to vote for the other candidate.

2. Unintended Consequences of Paid Media Campaigns

The simple word "presumably" in the last sentence defines the major unintended consequence of paid media campaigns. As more and more campaigns have become more and more negative, voters have turned off to the process. Rather than switch support from one candidate to another, they have decided to stay out of the process altogether, to march away from the ballot box (Ansolabehere and Iyengar 1995, 101–110). One clearly unintended consequence of extensive paid media campaigning is voter rejection of the messengers because they reject the message. Candidates who have turned away from negative advertising have done so for a number of reasons. Clearly one of those is increasing evidence that the costs of such efforts may well have begun to exceed the benefits.

IV. Politicians View the Media

Without meaning to belittle politicians, one could say that their relationship to the media resembles that familiar lament of Kermit D. Frog, "You can't live with 'em; you can't live without 'em." Politicians complain frequently about how unfairly they are treated in the media, about how difficult it is to talk about issues, about how paid advertising presents distorted images, about how they wish they could talk about issues at length, not in sound bites.

But their actions tell another story. Virtually every politician in Washington has a press secretary whose job is to guarantee that the politician is seen frequently in the media, particularly in the media that serves the elected official's constituents. Every campaign has a press secretary who is charged with the care and feeding (in two senses of that word) of journalists covering the campaign. Candidates treat the press well so that journalists are inclined to treat them favorably; and they want to influence the substance of the stories that are reported. Every campaign for a major office hires political consultants to design and place advertisements. Few candidates fret about the length of the ads, only about their effectiveness. None of the examples described herein sound like politicians who cannot stand the media.

And, of course, the reason is the other side of the equation. They cannot live without them. And this is not all bad. After all, elected officials and candidates for office need to communicate with large numbers of citizens. Mass media—free and paid—are the only effective means of doing this. Journalists, in legitimately and professionally pursuing their craft, cover politicians. Politicians have a clear stake in trying to influence what is said so that their message is heard as they intend it to be delivered. Advertisements do not produce themselves. Candidates, if they want to win, have an obligation to work with professional media consultants who can produce effective ads. There is nothing evil in any of this.

The problem that thoughtful politicians really worry about is balance. What happens when the press reaction to one set of circumstances impacts another? Examples abound. Potential candidates worry about private matters from their past being raised during campaigns. Some even decide not to run for office, based on such worries (Maisel, Stone, and Maestas 1999). Officeholders worry that principled positions taken forcibly on one set of salient issues might well define their image for some time to come. Thus the Republican senators who sided with the Democrats on campaign finance reform during the 105th Congress were concerned that they would be branded as party mavericks. Senator John McCain, a generally conservative Republican, differed from his co-partisans not only on campaign finance reform but also on holding the tobacco industry to account for the dangers of its products. He was derided by the tobacco industry in a series of ads aimed at defeating proposed legislation that would expose them to more regulation. McCain had to be concerned that his prominence on that issue would hinder his campaign for the presidential nomination in 2000 (Balz 1998a).

But in essence, politicians also realize that those examples make the point precisely. The media is an important part of politics, but it is one only partially controlled by politicians themselves. They must accept that constraint if they are going to enter the public arena. The positive contributions of the media to our polity were considered so important that the press was given a uniquely privileged position in the Constitution. Nothing in our political experience since the founding has led even the harshest critic of the media to think that the judgment of the founders regarding the sanctity of a free press should be questioned.

WEBSITES

http://appcpenn.org/

The Annenberg Public Policy Center at the University of Pennsylvania analyzes media usage during election campaigns. It maintains an ongoing study of issue advocacy advertising as purchased by more than seventy organizations.

Most media outlets have their own websites. Among those of prominent national media are:

New York Times	**http://www.nyt.com**
Washington Post	**http://www.washingtonpost.com**
Wall Street Journal	**http://wsj.com**
ABC News	**http://www.abcnews.go.com**
CBS News	**http://www.cbsnews.com**
Interactive	**http://www.cnn.com** CNN
MSNBC	**http://www.nbcnews.com**

KEY CONCEPTS

adwatch campaigns
attack ads
expectation game
field winnower
free media
informed consent of the governed
negative advertising
pack journalism
paid media
penny press
positive ads
spot advertisements
talk shows

DISCUSSION QUESTIONS

1. One of the most difficult problems facing news providers is to balance news broadcasts with wide audience appeal against those that provide more information but might not be attractive to viewers. How do you evaluate the balance struck by the electronic media in your local area? On the national scene? Is your evaluation of print media the same or different from your evaluation of electronic media?

2. What is the difference between negative advertising and attack advertising? Is it possible to portray the negative aspects of a candidate's career without resorting to attack advertising?
3. When President Eisenhower's campaign used the first television ads, many feared that we would be selling candidates for office like soap products. Nearly fifty years and millions and millions of dollars of televised campaign advertising later, this means of communicating with the public is an accepted form of campaigning. Should it be? Would we be better off if no television advertising were permitted? What might replace it?
4. What do you see as the future of the Internet as a campaign tool? How extensively will it be used? For what purposes? With what kind of impact?

CHAPTER 13

The Party in Government

Let's begin by considering a number of facts. When Maine reelected Angus King as governor in November 1998, he became the first person who was neither a Democrat nor a Republican to be reelected as a state governor in this century. In fact, when King was first elected in 1994, he was only the sixth person not running as the candidate of one of the major parties to be chosen as his state's chief executive.

When the 106th Congress convened in January 1999, 434 of the 435 members of the House of Representatives and every one of the hundred senators was either a Republican or a Democrat.[1] Not only the U.S. Congress but also forty-nine of the fifty state legislatures are organized along party lines by the Republicans and the Democrats.[2] Fewer than one-tenth of 1 percent of the nearly 7,500 state legislatures in those forty-nine states are independents or members of non-major parties.

PARTISAN
Referring to a political party.

Most judicial posts in the states, as well as those in the federal government, are filled by executive appointment followed by legislative confirmation. That is, **partisan** Democrats or Republicans make these appointments and approve them. The vast majority of appointments made by recent presidents and governors have been judges who share their partisan affiliation. Most of the state judges who are not appointed to the bench are elected in partisan elections; they run for judge as the candidate of either the Republican or the Democratic party.

Cabinet-level positions in the federal government and in the various state governments are filled by executive appointment, again, with legislative confirmation. Once again the norm is for the president and the various governors to appoint members of their own political party. Once it was routine for presidents to have at least one member of the opposing party in his cabinet (Fenno 1959), but when President Clinton named former Maine senator William Cohen, a Republican, as secretary of defense, he was lauded for reaching out to the opposition in recognition of Republican gains in congressional elections.

Clearly, government in the United States—at the federal level and in the fifty states—is organized along two-party lines. Party plays a critical role in nominating candidates for office and in running various aspects of campaigns, as I have shown in earlier chapters in this book; it also plays a most significant role in organizing the government.

At the same time, however, we must recognize, again as has been demonstrated in earlier chapters, that the major political parties in the United States are loose coalitions of politicians and citizens from differing constituencies, with varying allegiances to the party label and the party philosophy, but generally more alike than different. Furthermore, unlike their European counterparts in parliamentary democracies, American parties operate in a context of separation of powers, which means that they cannot necessarily serve as a unifying element at any level of government, much less from the federal level to the states or across state lines.

And thus, we are faced with a dilemma. Political parties are the single most important, dominating element in organizing the government of the United States and of the various states, but they do not control the entire process. More than half a century ago, E. E. Schattschneider (1942, 1), a preeminent theorist of political parties, wrote:

> When all is said, it remains true that . . . the parties are unable to hold their lines on a controversial public issue when the pressure is on. Th[at] condition . . . constitutes the most important single fact concerning the American parties. He who knows this fact, and knows nothing else, knows more about American parties than he who knows everything except this fact. What kind of party is it that, having won control of the government, is unable to govern?

The question that Schattschneider posed remains as relevant now as it was at the beginning of World War II. It is the question to which we turn in this chapter. We will begin by considering the concept of party in government; it is important to understand what role party can play in government in order to assess the role that it actually plays in the United States. We will then turn to an examination of the role that political parties actually play in organizing and structuring the functioning of the legislative and executive branches of the U.S. government. As elsewhere in this text, we will focus on the national government but will refer to state governments at appropriate times.

I. THE CONCEPT OF PARTY IN GOVERNMENT

In his classic text *Politics, Parties, and Pressure Groups* (1964), V. O. Key Jr., his generation's most prominent analyst of American politics, divided his discussion of party into the party organization, the party in the electorate, and the party in government. The basis for that division was the classic notion that partisans, once elected to office, should be able to implement the programs on which they ran. That notion is an old and revered one in the study of the American polity.

When Woodrow Wilson wrote *Congressional Government* in 1885, his notion was that parties should be strong enough to govern. His well-known complaint about committee government was in essence Wilson's way of lamenting the lack of strong parties controlling Congress. He was distressed by the absence of strong party leaders in the Congress he analyzed (1885, 76). His solution: "The great need is, not to get rid of parties, but to find and use some expedient by which they can be managed and made amenable from day to day to public opinion" (1885, 79–80). Woodrow Wilson, the political observer and analyst, and Woodrow Wilson, the scholar, was a "small d" democrat; his view was that strong parties were the best mechanism through which a democracy could convert public opinion into policy alternatives.

Sixty-five years later, the Committee on Political Parties of the American Political Science Association prescribed stronger parties in its influential report *Toward a More Responsible Two-Party System* (1950), a report frequently referred to as the Schattschneider Report (after the committee's chair). Again the complaint was familiar. American parties were too weak to form a link between the electorate and the elected. Parties did not stand firmly on issues; candidates did not feel bound to implement party programs once in office. Essentially the norm that was espoused was a parliamentary system—programmatic parties, strong leaders, compliant followers, party-dominated legislative decision making. And American parties were found lacking.

Writing in the early 1960s, political historian James MacGregor Burns noted with alarm that our political parties were causing a *Deadlock of Democracy* (1963). Burns claimed that the American government was unable to address pressing problems because four "political parties" were constantly struggling with each other—the congressional Democratic party, the congressional Republican party, the presidential Democratic party, and the presidential Republican party. He felt that each of these stood for different policies and represented a different base of constituent support. The deadlock in policy making followed from these factions, each with its own power base in the government, struggling with each other.

Burns's work countered David Truman's analysis of political parties in yet another classic work, *The Congressional Party* (1959). Truman's analysis centered on the relationship between congressional parties and the White House. Essentially he argued that parties in Congress behaved differently when the White House was controlled by their party than they did when a member of the opposite party was the president. He further noted that parties behaved differently in the majority than they did in the minority. Political scientists have continued to examine the functioning of the political parties as organizers of the government in these terms.[3]

Political analysts of the contemporary Congress have tended not to view parties as critically important to an understanding of the national legislature. In fact, a study by Melissa Collie (1986) revealed that political scientists publishing in the leading scholarly journals up through the mid-1980s all but ignored parties as significant to understanding the legislative process. The conventional wisdom held that changes in electoral politics and the congressional reforms of the 1970s had stripped parties of (1) their ability to influence the behavior of legislators and thus (2) their ability to shape policy. In short, the conventional wisdom held that the party in government deserved little attention.

In the last decade, that conventional wisdom has been revisited. This reexamination stemmed from earlier work, most of it historical in nature. In a seminal article on congressional leadership, Joseph Cooper and David Brady (1981) noted the importance of context in examining the ways in which Speakers of the House have led their body; they focused particularly on the rules of the House and on the role of political parties—on changes in each and the interplay between them. Brady, writing alone and with a series of coauthors, spent a number of years studying party behavior in the House. His astute analysis of the historical importance of party voting and of the variables that have influenced the strength of partisanship in Congress has been critical to our understanding of when party is most important in the legislative context. (See, e.g., Brady 1988; 1990; Brady, Cooper, and Hurley 1979; Brady and Ettling 1984; Brady and Sinclair 1984; Collie and Brady 1985; Cooper, Brady, and Hurley 1977.)

David W. Rohde (1991), drawing on the theory developed earlier, questioned the view that parties are insignificant to an understanding of the workings of Congress. Rohde demonstrated that political parties made a significant comeback in recent sessions of the House of Representatives; he also analyzed the context and contrasted the House with the Senate. Others have followed his lead, looking at the mechanisms developed by party leaders to enhance their influence (see Sinclair 1989; 1997; 1998).

Much of this analysis of party in government has dealt with partisanship in the House of Representatives, the more party-sensitive of the two houses of Congress (cf. Sinclair 1997 for a recent study on the Senate). Other analysts have looked at the partisan role that the president plays, though frequently their studies have dealt mainly with the president as a leader of Congress, as an agenda setter, and as a leader of his copartisans in Congress (Bond and Fleisher 1990; Edwards 1980; Edwards and Wayne 1990; Wayne 1978). And there has also been a start in analyzing the partisanship of recent presidents in making policy-level appointments (Mackenzie 1990; 1998).

The model implicit in studies that stress the importance of party in government is essentially a parliamentary model, that is, a government structured so that the individual who leads a party in the election is the same person who leads that party in government. In a parliamentary system such as the one in Great Britain, of course, the party leader is a member of the legislature as well as the prime minister. Our political system, with its legislative and executive powers separated, is quite different. Legislators' electoral bases are distinct from that of the president—though presidential elections are held on the same day as House and Senate elections (only one-third of the Senate, however, is up for election in any one year). And, of course, neither the president nor any of his top administrative officers are members of the legislature.

Pre-1950 discussion of party in government generally assumed that most citizens cast votes for candidates of either one party or the other and, consequently, Congress and the White House were controlled by the same party. Such control was in fact the norm for much of the nation's history. However, for a variety of reasons (see chaps. 4, 7;

Jacobson 1990c), the presumption that the president's party will control Congress has been reversed in the last half-century. Between 1953 and 2001, the same party has controlled the presidency and both houses of Congress for only sixteen years: one-third of the time. Divided government has become the norm for the national government.

Less often recognized is the extent to which divided government has existed in the states as well. Figure 13.1 shows the extent to which the situation in the states has come to parallel the one in Washington. (See Fiorina 1996 for an important discussion of the causes and consequences of divided government in the states.) Whereas once most states fell under unified control, following the 1998 election in fifteen states the Republicans controlled both houses of the legislature and the governorship; in ten states, the Democrats had similar unified control; but in the remaining twenty-five states control of state government was divided in one way or another.[4]

With divided government has come a clearer realization that party members in the legislature might not always share the views of their copartisan in the White House (Rohde 1991, 138–151; recall the earlier discussion of Truman 1959). Thus party in government is something of an evolving concept. The remaining sections of this chapter deal with the structural organization of the parties in government and with the impact of party as an organizing element in the national government.

II. Party as the Organizing Element of the U.S. Congress

Today congressional observers take for granted that the major political parties are quite elaborately organized to coordinate their work in

Figure 13.1 Partisan Division of State Governments, 1954–1998.

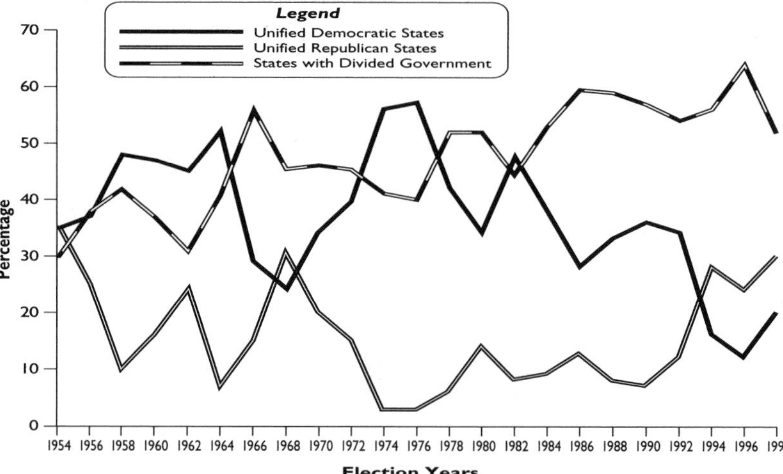

Source: Data from Various Congressional Quarterly Service Sources.

Congress. In fact, however, the development of party structures in Congress is a rather recent phenomenon. Article 2, Section 2, of the Constitution mandates that the House of Representatives elect its own Speaker, and from the earliest days of the Republic, Speakers have always been partisan leaders of that body (Peters 1990). But no other congressional or party officers are mentioned in the Constitution. From its first session the Senate has chosen a president pro tempore to serve in the chair in the absence of the vice president (whom the Constitution designates as the president of the Senate); twenty-four senators served as president pro tem in the first ten Congresses, and the position was viewed as more honorific than powerful. The roles of **majority leader** and **minority leader** (and **majority whip** and **minority whip**, their assistants) did not appear until late in the nineteenth century in the House and after the first decade of the twentieth century in the Senate. Institutional development of the organizational support for these leaders followed slowly (Sinclair 1983).

MAJORITY LEADER

The floor leader for the majority party in a legislature.

MINORITY LEADER

The floor leader of the minority party in a legislature.

MAJORITY WHIP

The majority party official in a legislature charged with aiding the floor leader, informing members of party positions, tracking the intentions of individual members, and attempting to persuade reluctant members to follow the party stance (when appropriate).

MINORITY WHIP

The minority party official in a legislature charged with aiding the floor leader, informing members of party positions, tracking the intentions of individual members, and attempting to persuade reluctant members to follow the party stance (when appropriate).

REPUBLICAN CONFERENCE

Name of the organization of all Republicans in the House of Representatives and the Senate.

A. Organization of the House of Representatives

With the exception of those who have most recently received their doctoral degrees, every political scientist writing on Congress today was educated and until 1994 observed the House of Representatives under the control of the Democrats only. The Democratic party assumed majority control of the House after the 1954 election and did not surrender that control for forty years. Thus, when most political scientists were writing about "majority party leadership in the House," they were really writing about Democratic majority party leadership in the House. All of that changed with the election of 1994 and the ascension of Newt Gingrich (R-Ga.) to the speakership in January 1995.

Officially an officer of the entire House, Speakers have been party leaders virtually since the inception of the role. Speakers are elected by the entire House. However, the vote for Speaker, the first vote in each new Congress, turns out to be a strict party-line vote. Each party's caucus (i.e., a meeting of all party members) nominates a candidate for Speaker. All the Republicans vote for their candidate; all the Democrats for their candidate. Because the Republicans have been in the majority since the 1994 election, Gingrich's nomination by the **Republican Conference** (as the caucus of all Republicans is officially called) has been tantamount to election.[5]

1. Republican Organization under Gingrich

Let us begin with a look at the Republican organization under Speaker Gingrich. But first, some background information. The fact that the Republicans had continuously been in the minority and had often tried unsuccessfully to pass programs promulgated by a president of their own party affected the Republican party in the House (Jones 1970; Ripley 1967).

Gingrich's predecessors. One obvious impact of Republican minority status was on the career of a succession of minority leaders. After the Republican party did poorly in the 1958 midterm elections, minority leader Joseph Martin, who had been his party's leader in the House since before World War II, was challenged and defeated by Charles A. Halleck (R-Ind., 1935–1969), who claimed that the party needed new, more forceful leadership and a new image if it was ever to achieve majority status. Six years later, after another Republican electoral debacle in 1964, Halleck was challenged and replaced by Gerald Ford, who represented Grand Rapids, Michigan, in the House from 1949 until he was named to succeed Spiro Agnew as vice president in 1973. Like Halleck before him, Ford claimed that new leadership was necessary if the Republicans were to overcome their position as the minority in the House.

Ford in turn was succeeded by John J. Rhodes (Ariz., 1953–1983). The minority status of the Republicans continued. Rhodes's leadership style, like that of Ford and also of Martin, was to attack the Democrats publicly on occasion but to work with Democratic leaders in Congress cooperatively in private. This style rankled a group of younger, more ideologically conservative Republicans at the time when Ronald Reagan assumed the presidency. Rhodes eventually decided to retire rather than try to manage the conflict within his own party. His successor, Robert Michel (Ill., 1957–1985), was a more effective minority leader, castigating the vociferous Speaker Jim Wright (D-Tex., 1957–1989) for overt partisanship. But Michel, like his predecessors, tempered his actions as he continued to work from a minority position. His increasingly conservative troops wanted more forceful leadership.

For thirty years, through the leaderships of Martin, Halleck, and Ford, the second-ranking Republican in the House, the minority whip, had been Leslie Arends (Ill., 1935–1974). However, even as whip, Arends was not a dominating figure in the Republican hierarchy. He was a loyal supporter of whomever the leader was, even that succession of leaders who overthrew their predecessors. The Republican whip's job had become largely routinized. For most of this period the Republican party presented a united front, and thus the whip organization did not have to concern itself much with persuading members to do what they would have done in any case.

Arends was succeeded by Michel, who used the job as a springboard to party leadership by building ties with both Rhodes's supporters and the more conservative junior Republicans. He transformed the minority whip's job to one that gained importance as a possible launching pad for advancement. When Michel became minority leader in 1983, Trent Lott (Miss.) won election as whip. Lott had headed the Republican Conference and was the first of the new breed of southern conservative Republicans to step into a party leadership position. But Lott did not plan for his career to be in the House; he gave up a safe seat and his leadership role to run successfully for the Senate in 1988.

Lott was followed briefly by Richard Cheney (Wyo., 1979–1989), who had served as chief of staff in the Ford White House. Cheney switched to the legislative branch and was rising rapidly in the party's leadership hierarchy. Many viewed him as "the future" of the House Republican party, perhaps as a future Republican Speaker. But just as suddenly as he had switched from service in the Ford White House to running for Congress, in 1989 he switched branches again, resigning his seat and leadership position to accept President Bush's nomination to serve as secretary of defense. Michel endorsed the candidacy of his friend and Illinois neighbor Edward Madigan (1973–1991) to succeed Cheney. The membership, however, had other ideas. Despite Michel's popularity as leader, they chose the acerbic Newt Gingrich, an outspoken conservative and the leading critic and nemesis of deposed Speaker Jim Wright, as minority whip. Pressure from Gingrich and the more vocally conservative wing of the party that he represented led Michel to announce his retirement after the 103d Congress.[6]

Gingrich's leadership team. Gingrich assumed effective leadership as the Republicans fought the 1994 campaign. He is credited with formulating the idea of a **Contract with America**, a pact on which all Republican candidates would stand. It was Gingrich who gathered all of the Republican candidates for the House on the steps of the Capitol, had them sign the Contract, and proclaimed that they would guarantee a vote on the issues in the Contract within the first hundred days of the 104th Congress. And it was Gingrich to whom the new members of that Congress, now in the majority for the first time in forty years, looked to for continued leadership.

CONTRACT WITH AMERICA

Campaign pledges made by Republican candidates for the House of Representatives prior to the 1994 election.

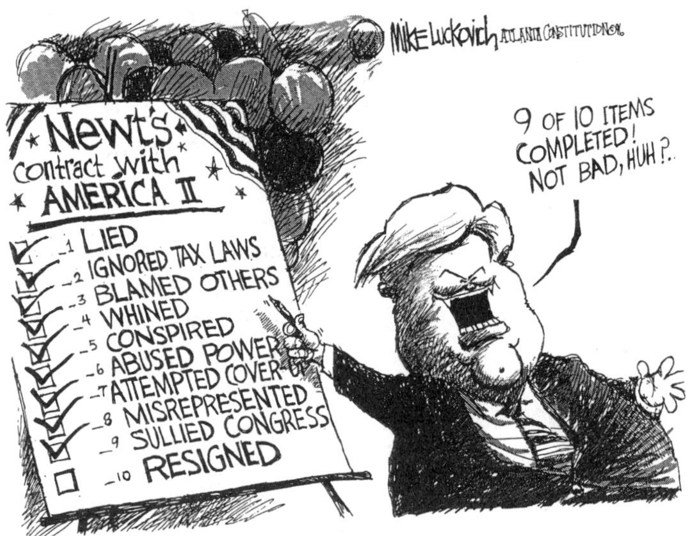

Not only did Gingrich become the Speaker of the House at the beginning of the 104th Congress, but he also brought with him an entire leadership team. Dick Armey of Texas became the new majority leader; if Gingrich conceived the Contract with America, Armey was its primary draftsman. He is a true doctrinaire conservative on the issues that defined the Republican party as it presented itself to the public for the 1994 election. He was one of those least happy about compromises that House Republicans had wrought with those in the Bush White House, much less with conservative Democrats.

The rest of the leadership team—Tom DeLay (Tex.), the minority whip; John Boehner (Ohio), the chair of the Republican Conference; Bill Paxon (N.Y.), the chair of the National Republican Congressional Committee; Chris Cox (Calif.), chair of the Policy Committee—were all Gingrich loyalists. No room was left for dissenters within the party.

Gingrich also moved quickly to consolidate his power by fitting the Republican organization to meet his needs. The whip organization, made up of members appointed by DeLay (but all acceptable to Gingrich), is composed of a chief deputy whip (who is considered part of the leadership's inner circle), thirteen deputy whips, and forty assistant whips. That organization, built on a model developed by the Democrats some years earlier (see in following paragraphs), is the most extensive in the history of the House. Using sophisticated computer and communications technology, the whip organization can contact every Republican member in a matter of minutes, guaranteeing efficient scheduling and the maximization of Republican support for party proposals.

Primary power, including the power to make committee assignments, was given to the Steering Committee. That committee, headed by the Speaker, is composed of members of the leadership team plus seven selected committee chairs. Gingrich and Armey have enhanced voting power in committee deliberations.

The Policy Committee is composed of forty members, including the Speaker and all of his leadership team. Twelve of Gingrich's most trusted allies were appointed to both committees when the Republicans took over control. (Fig. 13.2 depicts the formal leadership structure in the 106th Congress.) The importance of this structure becomes obvious when it is compared with what preceded it. No contrast can be clearer than if one looks at the process through which Republican members are appointed to standing committees.

No aspect of the organization of the House is more important to members than the committee appointment process. Members' prestige within the institution, their ability to pass legislation that is most important to them, and their opportunities to serve their constituents are all determined by the standing legislative committees to which they are assigned (Fenno 1973). Prior to the election of 1994, Republican assignments were made by a Committee on Committees that was composed of the senior member of each state's delegation, for those states

Figure 13.2 Party Leadership in the House of Representatives, 106th Congress.

Republicans	
Speaker of the House	Dennis Hastert (Ill.)
Majority Leader	Dick Armey (Tex.)
Majority Whip	Tom DeLay (Tex.)
Conference Chairman	J. C. Watts (Okla.)
Vice Chairman	Tillie Fowler (Fla.)
Secretary	Deborah Pryce (Ohio)
National Republican Congressional Committee Chair	Thomas M. Davis III (Va.)
Policy Committee Chairman	Christopher Cox (Calif.)
Democrats	
Minority Leader	Richard Gephardt (Mo.)
Minority Whip	David Bonior (Mich.)
Caucus Chairman	Martin Frost (Tex.)
Vice Chairman	Robert Menendez (N.J.)
Democratic Congressional Campaign Committee Chair	Patrick Kennedy (Mass.)
Policy Committee Chair	Gephardt
Steering Committee Chair	Gephardt
Co-chair	Steny Hoyer (Md.)
Leadership Advisory Group Chair	Gephardt

that had Republican members. Most of the work was done by an Executive Committee made up of the senior members of that group, with each region of the nation guaranteed representation. Votes were allotted according to the number of Republican members elected from each region. Ranking minority members of the committees (and the Republicans had been in the minority for forty years) were the members with the longest service on the committees; seniority was not violated.

Under Gingrich, the Steering Committee, which he dominated, made committee assignments. Furthermore, the Steering Committee recommended committee chairs to the Republican Conference. In 1995, seniority was violated in three different instances to guarantee that Gingrich loyalists were in key committee positions.[7] The result was not only a leadership team but also a cadre of committee chairs who were loyal to Gingrich and dedicated to the same conservative cause that drove him.

Gingrich clearly understood the need to solidify his organizational power base if he wanted to implement the Contract with America. One item in the Contract dealt with term limits. To demonstrate that he was true to the principle of rotating those in power, Gingrich insisted that committee chairs serve only three terms in office. He also limited the term of the Speaker, but his limit was to be four terms, not three. He would have a major influence on the next set of committee chairs as well as those whose initial appointment he oversaw.

He also stripped committee chairs of some of their powers—control over their own budgets, over staff allocations, and over the scheduling of events. He and his lieutenants assumed those powers, seen as necessary to move legislation through the congressional process. Similarly, Gingrich supervised aggressive use of the House rules in order to assure the timing of legislation that came to the floor. He also instituted the use of leadership task forces to move legislation through committees that might be recalcitrant.

The picture is a clear one—a dominating Speaker and a compliant party. Gingrich assumed powers that were more evident than those of any Speaker of the House since "Czar" Joe Cannon (R-Ill., 1873–1891; 1893–1913) was deposed in the famous Revolt of 1910 (Gallaway 1961; Peters 1990; Sinclair 1998). And under his leadership, at the beginning of the 104th Congress, party rule dominated. In fact, every item on the Contract with America did come out of committee and was voted on by the House within the promised hundred days. If the Contract items did not all become law, it was because of recalcitrant Democrats and a less committed group of Senate Republicans, not because of any lack of effective leadership by Speaker Gingrich and his allies.

The abortive revolt of 1997. To be sure, Gingrich's power did not remain absolute. In July 1997, a mere two and a half years after the Republicans returned to power after forty years in the wilderness, a group of dissidents plotted against the leader who had brought them to the promised land of majority status. (See Connolly, Broder, and Balz 1997 for a thorough description of the Republican insurrection.)

The first hundred days of the 104th Congress marked the high point of Gingrich's party leadership. From that point on, the reality of how difficult it is to institute party government set in. In the winter of 1995–1996 Gingrich and the Republicans were blamed by the public for the shutdown of the federal government. The Republicans insisted on cuts to balance the budget and would not permit the passage on continuing resolutions to allow the government to function until a new budget was passed. Gingrich seemed petulant when he complained that he would not negotiate with President Clinton out of anger at the seat he was assigned aboard *Air Force One* on the trip to attend the funeral of Israeli prime minister Rabin.

Speaker Gingrich was forced to spend a good deal of time responding to charges that he had violated congressional ethics. In the 1996 elections, not only was President Clinton reelected but the Republican majority in the House was pared to a mere eleven seats. Talk of an emerging Republican hegemony was silenced. Shortly after the new Congress convened, Gingrich was reprimanded by the House for ethics violations and was forced to pay a $300,000 fine. His poll ratings continued to decline as he suggested various ways of paying off that debt. He no longer seemed the invulnerable foe of a weakened president; rather, he sought compromises with President Clinton on a number of important items. According to press reports, there was dissatisfaction among the conservative ideologues who had looked to Gingrich as their leader. His own leadership team felt that he was acting on his own, without consulting them as he had in the past (Connolly, Broder, and Balz 1997, 6).

Gingrich was able to fight off what nearly developed into a full-blown coup attempt. In part he was successful, it seems, because those plotting against him could not agree on who should replace him as Speaker. Those interested in the job fought each other, and Gingrich was the beneficiary. In the end Gingrich met with the conference and noted that he had heard the voices of dissent and would respond. Congressman Paxon, once high on the list of Gingrich loyalists but actively courted by the dissidents as a potential successor to Gingrich, was removed from the leadership team (and eventually decided not to seek reelection). He was the only victim of the movement against the Speaker. The other leaders remained on board, but they are certainly viewed with less of an unwavering eye than in the past.

The end of the Gingrich speakership. Speaker Gingrich was successful in fighting off earlier challenges to his leadership, but he was not able to survive the Republican electoral debacle in 1998. Gingrich was blamed for setting the strategy that led to the Republican party's losing seats in the midterm election, the rarest occurrence for the party not controlling the White House in the sixth year of a president's administration. Shortly after the election, Appropriations chair Robert Livingston announced that he was considering a challenge to Gingrich. The Speaker saw the handwriting on the wall and announced that he would not seek reelection. Though a number of other Republicans floated their own candidacies for Speaker, Livingston clearly had the votes committed to be elected.

But there was a slip between the commitments and the votes. Even as he was being hailed as the healer of Congress and the new GOP leader, Livingston was forced to admit to an extramarital affair. In December 1998 Republicans were adamant that President Clinton was unfit for office because he had an extramarital affair and lied about it under oath. Thus Livingston conceded to pressure from his own conference and withdrew his candidacy. Like Gingrich, he also announced that he would resign from the House.

For a brief period congressional Republicans were in disarray, but they quickly came together behind the candidacy of Dennis Hastert (Ill.), who was elected Speaker without opposition from any other Republican and assumed the gavel at the beginning of the 106th Congress. Majority leader Armey was reelected after some opposition—and after he had to give up his own ambition to succeed Gingrich. Majority whip DeLay was also reelected and seemed to have become the leader of the most conservative faction within the party. Thomas M. Davis III (Va.) was chosen to head the National Republican Congressional Committee, replacing Gingrich ally John Linder, who was also blamed for the 1998 electoral loss.

An evaluation of Republican House organization. The Republican House leadership and party organization at the century's end have been fascinating for students of parties and Congress to observe. The basic question raised by the election of 1994—Newt Gingrich's ascension to the speakership and consolidation of power under his leadership, and the Republican experience under his stewardship as Speaker—relates to whether party government is possible in the United States. And the answer seems to be that it is not.

Political parties are strongest in a legislative setting when members must rely on the parties to be reelected and for their own power within the legislature. Parties are also strongest when they are homogeneous and capable of enacting their programs. These elements seemed to be in place when Gingrich took office. He and his closest advisers understood what structural elements had to be in place in order to use the opportunity presented to him effectively. Thus, he consolidated the party organization under his rule; he placed his loyal followers in position of power; he skipped over those who did not share his policy views.

But the illusion that the House of Representatives can be run like the House of Commons was a momentary one. Basic elements work against that kind of party control. First, members have their own agendas. They are independently elected and must rely on their own records, not the party record, to be reelected. When the party takes actions to which their constituents object, they will desert the party.

Second, the House is not the government. Passage in the House is not akin to implementation of policy. In order to accomplish concrete goals, House leaders must negotiate with those in the Senate and with the president. When there is disagreement, compromise, not recalcitrance, is called for. Gingrich first lost power when he felt that his "mandate" to implement the Contract overrode these basic provisions of a constitutional system based on separation of powers and checks and balances. Ironically, he further lost power within his own conference when he did give recognition to the constraints of separation of powers and compromised with the president. He lost the consensus within his own party when the old lines that led to Gingrich's rise to power—the division between those who saw the need to compromise and those who preferred confrontation—reemerged.

Third, leadership in a setting like the House of Representatives must be personal and not institutional in nature. Gingrich needed to work with members of his conference, not set himself above them. For many of the same reasons that he was effective at gaining his leadership position, he has not been effective at retaining it. He acted on impulse without fearing those he offended. Those who had been without power for a long time saw such actions as a means to an end—getting back in the majority. But once in the majority, they wanted a leader who considered all of their views, who consulted with them, who was not off on his own agenda. And there, finally, Speaker Gingrich seems to have fallen flat.

The true test of the Republican organization and how it leads the House may well be found in what follows Gingrich. Hastert is viewed as a team player, a conciliator, the athletic coach that he once was. But he faces the difficult task of resolving conflicts between the true-believer conservatives and those more anxious to reach accommodation with the Democrats and their president.

In addition, committee chairs who are forced to give up their leadership positions after the 106th Congress because of party-imposed term limits have begun to jockey for new positions of influence. Some look forward to taking over other committees as their seniority puts them in line for new posts. The issue is not so much who retains or gains power but rather how the Republicans reach these decisions. It seems clear that they will not be made by one person, as they were for all intents and purposes after the election of 1994. The pattern that eventually emerges will say a good deal about party organization in the future.

2. The Democrats in the Minority

The other way to obtain a clear picture of party organization in the House is to look at the Democrats in the minority. In 1995 the Democrats stood as a shocked but chastened party, having lost what they thought was theirs by right—majority status. And they lost it in a most ignominious way, surprised by someone who not only was their nemesis but had no respect for the institution they had led for four decades. And they lost their leader, Speaker Tom Foley, in the process.

But a loss like that can also be viewed as an opportunity. What did the Democrats learn from their loss? How did it translate into organizational terms?

Democratic leaders. Perhaps the place to start this discussion is by noting that, to this point, Democratic leaders in the House for the entire twentieth century have viewed service in the House as the capstone of their career. Progressive ambition to a future Democratic leader in the House of Representatives has been progression within the party hierarchy in Congress, not "rising" from the House to some other office (Schlesinger 1966).

The current Democratic leader, Richard Gephardt, was first elected to the House in 1976. He worked his way up the party hierarchy before becoming minority leader in 1995. However, it should also be noted that Gephardt has tried to keep his feet on two career ladders. In 1988, he was a candidate for the Democratic nomination for president; he toyed with running again in 1992 but decided against such a race. From 1996 on, he has been viewed as the most likely challenger to Vice President Gore for the year 2000 Democratic nomination. However, after the Democrats' victory in 1998, Gephardt decided that he would rather try to become Speaker by helping the Democrats recapture the House in 2000 than fight for his party's presidential nomination. That announcement was viewed as a sign that Democrats feel they have a real chance to recapture the House after only six years of Republican control.

Gephardt's predecessor, Thomas S. Foley from Washington, had served in the House for a quarter century before his election as Speaker in 1989; he had served as chair of the Agriculture Committee (1975–1981), majority whip (1981–1987),[8] and majority leader (1987–1989). His predecessors, Jim Wright (Tex., 1954–1989; Speaker 1987–1989) and Thomas P. (Tip) O'Neill Jr. (Mass., 1952–1987; Speaker 1977–1987), had served thirty-three and twenty-five years, respectively, before their elections as Speaker. Each of these men—and their immediate predecessors as well—served as majority leader before ascending to the speakership; the path through the majority whip position is also followed but less commonly.

DEMOCRATIC CAUCUS

Name of the organization composed of all Democrats in the House of Representatives and in the Senate.

The Democrats have developed a fairly routine path of succession. Leaders are developed and prove themselves through service to the House and to the membership. Although the party has staged heated contests for election to other leadership posts, candidates for the top position have routinely been nominated and renominated by the **Democratic Caucus** without opposition (Peabody 1976).

Powers of the Democratic leaders. Gephardt's predecessors, of course, served as Speaker of the House, since the Democrats controlled the majority throughout their tenure as party leaders. In seeking an understanding of party in government, therefore, it is important to see how their powers evolved—and ultimately how Speaker Gingrich's reach for power reflected that evolution.

The story is, in fact, a complex one, involving competing centers of power. For our purposes, it makes sense to examine the period of Democratic hegemony in the House, not just the unbroken forty-year period of rule but the period from the election of 1932 on.[9] For the first half of that period, party leaders shared power with, and often were at the mercy of, committee leaders in the House. Committee chairs were chosen strictly by seniority; the Democratic member who had served longest on a committee was the chair (Hinckley 1971).

In the 1970s, a group of younger members, frustrated by the seniority system and their inability to pass legislation important to them and their constituents, initiated a period of reform aimed at restructuring power in the House. The reform movement took power away from the committee chairs and spread it more evenly among the members. The reform era was marked by the reinvigoration of the caucus, the empowerment of rank-and-file (and thus junior) members of Congress, and the decentralization of power to subcommittees and their leaders (Oleszek 1989; Ornstein 1975; Rohde 1974; 1991, chap. 2; Sheppard 1985; Smith and Deering 1990).[10]

Part of that reform saw the first efforts aimed at reinvigorating centralized party leadership, as party leaders were seen as more likely to be responsive to rank-and-file members than were committee chairs. More power was given to the Democratic Steering and Policy Committee (which has recently been divided into two committees), and the Speaker was given more control over that committee. Thus Steering and Policy became the committee that recommends committee assignments for all House Democrats and subcommittee chairmanships for the important Appropriations Committee. It is the committee that examines party priorities and helps set strategy.

The committee's membership is important. Steering and Policy is very much the party leader's committee; he is the chair. The whip is the vice chair, and the caucus chair is the second vice chair. Other party leaders have seats on this committee because of the offices they hold—the chief deputy, the chair of the DCCC, the vice chair of the caucus. Twelve rank-and-file members are elected to the committee by fellow Democrats, based on region of the country. The minority leader himself appoints nine additional members; these members, along with the members of his leadership team, assure his dominance over the committee. It is equally important to note that the ranking members of the four most powerful committees in the House—Appropriations, Budget, Rules, and Ways and Means—are also members of the committee. These ex-officio memberships are clear recognition of the continuing importance and power of committee leaders in the modern Congress.

During the last years of Democratic party rule in the House, Speakers O'Neill and Wright claimed more power than their predecessors had possessed. For example, they had the power to appoint (with caucus approval) the Democratic members of the powerful Rules Committee. They had also been given the power to refer bills to more than one committee, either simultaneously or sequentially, and other controls over the flow of legislation (Bach and Smith 1988; Collie and Cooper 1989). Thus the clear trend was for the Speaker to become more of a true party leader, and party and House rules were shifting to give him the potential to exercise leadership powers in an effective way. Gingrich's changes at the beginning of the 104th Congress can thus be seen as long steps in a progression, but steps that clearly had precedents in the actions of his Democratic predecessors.

The Democrats' leadership team. The second person in the Democratic hierarchy is the whip. We have seen that in 1980 Tom Foley was the last Democratic whip appointed by the Speaker and the majority leader. As part of reform efforts to democratize the House, the whip is now elected by the caucus.

The first elected whip was Tony Coehlo (D-Calif., 1978–1989). Coehlo's election says a good deal about the connections among party in government, party organization, and party in the electorate. Coehlo had sought and received appointment as chairman of the Democratic Congressional Campaign Committee in 1980. The DCCC had never been a base of power in the House; indeed, it seemed only a poor imitation of its Republican counterpart. But Coehlo saw potential and grabbed it. He raised unprecedented sums of money by emulating the methods of the National Republican Congressional Committee and reminding political action committees of which party controlled the House. He won the DCCC chair (and thus himself) a position in the House leadership hierarchy by virtue of the increasingly important role that the DCCC played in maintaining majority status. Although he could not match the NRCC's dollar totals, he built a first-class operation and earned the admiration of (and accumulated political IOUs from) those whose campaigns he supported (Jackson 1988). When the whip's seat opened, with Foley's ascent on the leadership ladder, Coehlo was ready. He drew on his reputation, called in his chits, and won the election.[11]

The Democratic whip in the House now heads an extensive supporting organization. (This section draws heavily on Rohde 1991, 82–93; Ripley 1964; 1967; Sinclair 1983.) The whip organizations in Congress developed out of the intense partisan conflict in the late nineteenth century. By the time of the New Deal, however, the sectional and ideological conflicts within the Democratic party also required attention. Under Speaker Rayburn, the majority whip was assisted by a phalanx of regional whips. Rayburn's leadership style was so personal, however, that he rarely relied on the whip system. While the regional whips could potentially gather information, their capability to perform this function and to have it as an important part of leadership's role was never developed.

Regional whips were either appointed by senior Democrats in a region or elected by the members from that region; they did not owe loyalty to the party leader. In fact, they were never included in the leadership structure; and at least during the Kennedy and Johnson administrations (when New Frontier and Great Society programs split the party on ideological and regional grounds), they often did not support the party leader's policy preferences.

Much of this rebellious individualism changed during the Nixon administration, when the majority Democrats saw the need to organize in opposition to Republican policy initiatives. First, the whip organization was enlarged, with the creation of the position of chief deputy whip and with the addition of three deputy whips and the first at-large whips, representing the Women's Caucus, the Black Caucus, and the class of newly elected members. Then the visibility of the office was enhanced when the whip and the chief deputy whip were given ex-officio seats on the Steering and Policy Committee. The whip organization began to play the role of persuading members to support the party as well as that of informing House members of the leadership's intentions and desires and informing the leadership of the members' reactions to those positions.

The most significant changes in the whip organization have occurred in the period since Foley took over as the whip. An additional deputy whip was added, and the number of at-large whips was increased to fifteen. By the time Foley left the whip office, he was supported by seven deputy whips and thirty-two at-large whips. The whip organization had come to include one-fourth of the Democratic membership of Congress. By the time Coehlo resigned, *his* organization included 40 percent of the members of the caucus.

The whip organization under David Bonior in the 106th Congress is composed of four chief deputy whips, twelve deputy whips, forty-five assistant whips, twenty-four regional whips, and the ranking member of the Rules Committee as an ex-officio whip, still about 40 percent of the Democratic members. The organization is heavily involved in disseminating and gathering information and conducting frequent whip polls. It is also involved more and more in persuading members to follow the position of the leadership, a task made somewhat easier by the initiation of so many members into the leadership and by the now nearly regularized position of standing in opposition to the Republicans in the majority. The Democratic pattern of inclusion has been an important one for increasing party loyalty.

The organization below the whip is also important to note. The party leader chairs the Policy Committee and cochairs the Steering Committee (with Congressman Steny Hoyer [D-Md.]). The Steering Committee has much of the power of the old Steering and Policy Committee, including the power to make committee assignments; it is dominated by the leader and members of his or her team. The Policy Committee is small and includes none of the leadership cadre other than Gephardt. The DCCC chair, Congressman Patrick Kennedy (D-R.I.) in the 106th Congress, has remained part of the leadership team and is seen as critical to the electoral success of the party. Generally, the pattern has been to show a willingness to work with all Democrats. This reflects the history of the party in Congress, a history of a party divided along sectional lines. But it also reflects a recognition that inclusion is a better strategy than intraparty confrontation for achieving cohesion.

The Democratic leadership structure: A summary. Changes in the structure of the Democratic party leadership in the House have reflected changes in the role of the party in the government. Once Speakers had to rely heavily on their relationships with powerful and independent committee chairs—those who owed their positions to the safety of their seats and to their seniority on their committees, not to the party or to the Speaker—to pass legislation. Then for a time power was seemingly fragmented, and no one appeared to be able to formulate a party position in the House. During the last years of Democratic rule, however, the Speaker stood atop a party hierarchy that had the potential to present party positions effectively and to induce allegiance from rank-and-file members. In the minority, the Democrats have given every indication that they are satisfied with the structure they developed and that they would continue that structure should they regain majority status. However, they have also demonstrated that power within their party is a balancing act—a recognition that party leadership is important, that committee leaders must be recognized for their expertise and longevity in the House, and that neither of these groups can stray too far from the views of the rank-and-file members, or changes will be exacted in the powers given to each. This balance is one that the Republicans are currently struggling to reach.

B. Party Leadership in the Senate

For very good reasons, party as an organizing element is more important in the House than it is in the Senate. First, the Senate is a smaller body. Senators know most other senators, not just members of their state delegation, their committee, or their party. Senate staff members know other staff members. A body of a hundred people is manageable; one of 435 is not.

Second, senators tend to see themselves as powerful individuals who are able to attract media attention, are listened to for their special expertise, and are to be deferred to because of their prominence. Senators are less likely to follow party line because it is party line. They are less likely to defer to others because of institutional prerogatives, and they are more likely to build alliances with like-minded people with whom they have worked. As noted in chapter 9, the Senate is now seen as the incubator of presidential candidates. At any time as many as 10 percent of the senators are, either actively or with a few confidantes, exploring their options of running for the White House. In the Senate they want to be seen and heard; they want to make a difference; they are not interested in toeing the party line. While the House is structured in such a way as to permit majorities to work their will in almost all circumstances, individual incentives and institutional differences make clear that this is not the case in the Senate (Rohde 1992).

In addition to, or perhaps because of, these reasons, the Senate is a less partisan body than is the House. The aisle that separates Democrats from Republicans in the House of Representatives is a true gulf. Few cross it, and those who do are viewed with suspicion. The same simply is not true in the Senate. Leaders work more closely together; senators work closely with members of the other party. Friendships and alliances cross party lines. (For an analysis of the differences between the House and Senate in terms of the size of the two bodies, the electoral environments, the prominence of the members, and the partisan contexts, see Baker 1989a.)

The differences between the two houses of the national legislature lead to very real differences in the roles played by the parties in the two houses. In many ways, the differences between the parties in the House and the parties in the Senate are more significant than party differences between the Democrats and Republicans in the Senate itself.

1. The Senate Republicans

In May 1996, Senate majority leader Bob Dole announced that he was resigning his seat in the Senate, and thus his leadership position, to devote full time to his campaign for the presidency. Thus ended a distinguished and remarkable legislative career.

Dole had been the Republican leader in the Senate since 1985. He was majority leader for one Congress, minority leader for four, and then majority leader once again for most of another Congress. Dole, like his predecessor, Howard H. Baker Jr. (R-Tenn.), found it difficult to run for president at the same time as he managed the Senate majority. Also like Baker, he eventually found that his talents were more attuned to the pace of life in the Senate than to that of a presidential candidate. Some of the same traits can be seen in Dole's successor, Trent Lott of Mississippi, and in recent Democratic leaders, especially George Mitchell of Maine and the current minority leader, Tom Daschle of South Dakota.

What are those traits? What defines Senate leadership? Senate leaders must be managers and persuaders. They must cajole and coax. They must be patient and tolerant. They must be willing to negotiate and to compromise. And their role is restricted by the rules and traditions of the Senate.

The most important norm is to defer to the desires of individual senators. Thus the Senate schedule is changed to accommodate an individual senator who cares about a particular vote but cannot attend the Senate session on a certain day. Senatorial "holds" on key appointments are recognized and dealt with. Each individual senator is dealt with as a powerful individual, not simply as a vote that can be counted on.

The most important rule to be considered is the rule permitting unlimited debate. That rule means that the Senate majority leader cannot move legislation through the body if forty-one senators oppose it. Mere majorities will not suffice. It is necessary to obtain sixty votes on controversial legislation—the number needed to break a **filibuster**. Consequently, the leader must of necessity deal with his or her counterpart in the other party—no party has had enough votes to break a filibuster on its own—and the leader must, of necessity, deal with the most difficult individuals in the body, those most likely to stand on firmly on their own issues.

FILIBUSTER

Exercising the right to unlimited debate in the Senate; used literally "to talk a bill to death."

Who is likely to do this? In the past we have seen that Senate leaders tend to be men who are willing to suppress their own egos and desires to those of the body. Baker, son-in-law of one Senate leader and son of another legislator, fit that mold. So too did Dole, the war hero patriot who returned to public service as the highest calling. Each won leadership positions in the Senate because of his work with other members of that body. They earned the respect of their colleagues and were rewarded by promotion to positions of leadership. Ironically, each also sought the presidency, in part at least because of his success within the Senate and the respect that he had earned. That different skills were needed for the two tasks did not seem apparent to them, nor to others at the time they declared their candidacy.

Lott might well fit the same mold. A smooth southern gentleman, Lott was viewed as a legislative leader in the House, in which he rose to the position as minority whip, before leaving that body to run for the Senate. In the Senate, Lott quickly moved up the party ladder, serving as whip under Dole.[12] As leader, he has played his role to mixed reviews. A staunch ideological conservative, Lott has been a strong spokesperson in opposition to the White House and to compromise. However, he has also seen the need to compromise in order to move forward the legislative agenda. He accepted the same compromises in early 1997 that caused Speaker Gingrich difficulty within his own party but did not suffer the same consequences.

The structure of the Republican organization, depicted in figure 13.3, is less important than the structure in the House. Most Republicans can find a spot on a party committee should they seek one, but the committees themselves are less important in the Senate. Again this follows from the individualistic nature of the institution. Each senator can have his or her say on every issue, should he or she desire to do so.

What is important to note is the individuals who lead the Senate Republicans in the 106th Congress. Each Senate leader is an ideologue, and none represents the moderates in the party. Each is willing to toe the conservative line, not out of commitment to party loyalty but because of firm personal belief. The moderate Republicans in the Senate, fewer in number than they have been in many years, are clearly removed from any power within the institution.

However, the Senate is a small place, and the Republican majority is quite thin. Obviously, the Republicans have a vested interest in maintaining unity against the Democrats on key issues. One of the tests of Lott's leadership will be his ability to hold his coalition together while the members seek to oppose President Clinton on policy initiatives with which they disagree. A good test of this was the series of votes on campaign finance reform described in chapter 11.

2. The Senate Democrats

Tom Daschle is only the fifth Democratic party leader in the Senate in the last half-century. Lyndon Johnson served from 1953 until he became vice president in 1961. Mike Mansfield (Mont.) led the Democrats

Figure 13.3 Party Leadership in the Senate.

Republicans	
President Pro Tempore	Strom Thurmond (S.C.)
Majority Leader	Trent Lott (Miss.)
Assistant Majority Leader	Don Nickles (Okla.)
Conference Chairman	Connie Mack (Fla.)
Secretary	Paul Coverdell (Ga.)
National Republican Senatorial Committee Chairman	Mitch McConnell (Ky.)
Democrats	
Minority Leader	Tom Daschle (S.Dak.)
Assistant Minority Leader	Harry Reid (Nev.)
Caucus Chairman	Daschle
Democratic Senatorial Campaign Committee Chairman	Robert Torricelli (N.J.)
Vice Chair	Patty Murray (Wash.)
Policy Committee Chair	Daschle
Co-chair	Byron Dorgan (N.Dak.)

as the majority leader from 1961 until he retired in 1977. Robert C. Byrd (W.V.) succeeded Mansfield and served as the party leader—in majority and minority—until he decided not to continue as leader (though remaining in the Senate as president pro tempore for a time and as chair and then ranking minority member of the Appropriations Committee) after the 1988 elections.

Byrd was eased toward retirement as leader because of dissatisfaction among the Democratic senators about the image he portrayed. Byrd, though never a member of the old Senate establishment, is clearly a child of "old-style" politics. He became leader because of his ability to work hard, to serve the members, to exploit the intricacies of Senate procedure. But he never was capable of—or interested in—developing a media personality with which his colleagues were comfortable.

The Democrats lost their majority in the Senate in a Republican landslide in 1980. They regained majority status in 1986; Mitchell had served as chair of the Democratic Senatorial Campaign Committee for that election. In addition, Mitchell had proved to his colleagues during the televised Iran-Contra hearings that he could use the media to convey their message to the public. Many of the newer members were, moreover, not so deeply enamored of life in the Senate as was Byrd. They wanted to be able to lead personal and political lives apart from the Senate, and Byrd showed no inclination to accommodate them.

Mitchell's election was viewed as an upset by most media analysts.

He beat two more senior and well-established Democrats, Bennett Johnston (La.) and Daniel Inouye (Hawaii). He won by proving to members that he could be the kind of leader they wanted, one capable of combating the Republican in the White House, concerned about the legitimate demands of the members, and dedicated to including more Democrats on his leadership team.

Mitchell shocked virtually everyone by announcing his retirement from the Senate in 1994. He had been touted as a possible Supreme Court nominee earlier in the 103d Congress but remained in the Senate to lead the unsuccessful fight for health care reform. Many assumed that he would stay in the Senate until another opening on the Court arose, when President Clinton would reward him for his diligence and his loyalty. But Mitchell opted for private life.[13]

Tom Daschle had been promoted by Mitchell to serve as cochair of the Democratic Policy Committee. This appointment was viewed as Mitchell's way of sharing power and of rewarding those who were loyal to him in the leadership balloting. Daschle first came to the Senate in 1986 as part of the class of new Democrats Mitchell had been active in recruiting and supporting when he served as chair of the DSCC. Daschle ran to succeed Mitchell, defeating Wendell Ford (Ky.), who had been (and remained) party whip. Daschle's appeal was similar to Mitchell's, though his stature was considerably less. Daschle represented a new, moderate image for the Democratic party. He stated that he wanted to carry on where Mitchell left off. As the party had once again lost majority status, Daschle's colleagues felt that his image was more likely than Ford's to appeal to the nation's voters. Daschle's first year as leader was not a strong one, as he struggled to emerge from under Mitchell's shadow. As he grew in the role, however, he came to reflect a brand of steady, non-headline seeking but strong advocating leadership to which his colleagues could relate.

In the Johnson, Mansfield, and Byrd days, the leadership of the Democratic party in the Senate was centrally controlled. The leader chaired all party committees and kept most decisions close to his vest. Mitchell's first move as majority leader was to expand the powers of the Policy Committee and to name Daschle as cochair. Four other senators were named vice chairs on this committee of twenty. The new majority leader asked Inouye, the popular senior member he had defeated, to chair the party's Steering Committee, which makes Democratic appointments to the legislative committees. He also named Wyche Fowler (Ga.) as assistant floor leader. He took whatever steps he could to expand the leadership team.

Daschle has pointedly followed the same model. He retained Ford, whom he had defeated, as whip. He named Harry Reid of Nevada as cochair of the Policy Committee; when Ford announced his retirement, Reid moved up to the second position in the party hierarchy, now called assistant minority leader. Daschle's leadership team originally included Bob Kerrey of Nebraska, one of the senators who has already shown interest in presidential campaigning, as chair of the campaign committee. Kerrey was replaced in the 106th Congress by Robert Torricelli of New Jersey; Patty Murray, reelected in 1998 in Washington State, serves as vice chair of the DSCC. Like Mitchell, Daschle wants his party leadership group to be inclusive, not exclusive. Virtually every Democratic senator serves on one party committee or another; many serve on more than one. Daschle works hard to include all relevant actors in each political discussion. But it is also clear that this Senate leadership team is dominated by the Democratic Leadership Council, the moderate wing of the party. Nowhere in the leadership are the most visible and vocal liberals such as Kennedy, Moynihan, or Boxer speaking for the party in this Senate.

3. The Muted Role of Party Leaders

This rather brief discussion of Senate party leaders leads back to the question of why partisanship—and particularly partisanship in the roles of party leaders—is less prominent in the Senate than in the House. To a great extent this difference follows directly from the rules of the two bodies.

It is true that the parties "organize" the Senate (e.g., make committee assignments), the leaders are not given the powers and resources that House leaders hold. The majority leader is responsible to schedule floor debate and to provide leadership for his party's positions, but he is not given the tools to do so without significant cooperation from his colleagues.

In fact, the only advantage the party leaders have over other senators is that they will be recognized first when a number of senators are seeking recognition. Beyond that, the norms and the rules of the Senate give resources and power to individual senators, not to institutional officers. Senators have multiple committee assignments and are rarely discouraged from speaking on areas outside of their committees' jurisdictions. Individual senators can hold the floor indefinitely, exercising their right to filibuster a bill. As the Senate does not have a powerful Rules Committee to schedule floor debate, the flow of legislation onto the floor is arranged through unanimous consent decrees, which the party leadership negotiates in consultation with committee leaders and other concerned senators. Any senator can upset scheduling agreements arranged by party leaders by objecting to these unanimous consent decrees.

Rules such as these mean that the job of the majority leader is really that of a negotiator. He must confer with his allies constantly to be certain that they are all on board. He must work closely with the minority leader to be certain that the other party will not disrupt agreed-upon arrangements. Individual egos must be stroked; individual personalities taken into account; individual agendas accommodated. (On these aspects of the role of the majority leader, see Sinclair 1990.)

Trent Lott's role as majority leader has been to define the line that the Republican party must walk between adhering to ideological principles even if it means obstructing the programs put forth by a Democratic president and compromising on those principles in order to arrive at some legislation that can be passed. By and large, he has walked this tightrope successfully, enhancing his own prestige as a leader, muting conflict within his own party, confronting President Clinton and the Democrats in the Senate when necessary, and working with them when possible.

Tom Daschle's job as minority leader has been difficult as well. He has had to defend an embattled president and his programs without being able to mount a strong position in the Senate, due to his party's status in the minority. He has not been as visible a leader as Mitchell was, but that follows logically from the fact that Mitchell led a majority in the Senate, often in opposition to a Republican in the White House. Thus Daschle's role has been quieter and more inside the Senate. His successes have been less visible, as often the president, not his party in the Senate, has been given credit for victories that have been won.

III. The Impact Of Party on Congressional Behavior

PARTY UNITY VOTES

Votes on which a majority of one party votes against a majority of the other party.

PARTY UNITY SCORES

The percentage of times that an individual legislator votes with his or her party on those votes in which a majority of one party votes against a majority of the other party (party unity votes).

PARTY COHESION SCORES

The absolute difference between the percentage of a party voting for an issue and the percentage voting against it.

This discussion of the organization of the two parties in the national legislature and some of the politics involved in that organization may be interesting, but the more vital questions about party in government relate to whether the parties structure the behavior of their copartisans in the legislature. Remember that the model employed as a "goal" is a parliamentary model, a system in which party discipline is enforced by strong party leaders. In this text I have given many reasons why the American electoral system differs from a parliamentary system, most notably the decentralized nature of political parties, the independence of the nominating system, and the personalization of campaigning and appeals to the voter. In this section we turn briefly to how the federal legislators elected through this system respond to the legislative choices that confront them.

Political scientists use three different measures of party voting. First, **party unity votes** are votes in which a majority of the Democrats voting cast their votes on one side of an issue and the majority of Republicans on the other side.[14] **Party unity scores** are the percentage of times that an individual legislator votes with his or her party on party unity votes.[15] **Party cohesion scores** are the absolute difference between the percentage of a party voting for an issue and the percentage voting against it. Thus, if every Democrat voted aye on a particular vote while 75 percent of the Republicans voted nay and 25 percent voted aye, that would be a party unity vote (a majority of Democrats voting on one side and a majority of Republicans on the other). That vote would be included in a computation of the legislators' party unity score; the party cohesion score for the Democrats on that vote would be one hundred points (100 to 0), and for the Republicans fifty points (75 to 25). Systems in which party structures legislative decisions tend to have more party unity votes, higher party cohesion scores, and higher party unity scores.

Figure 13.4 depicts the percentage of party unity votes in the House and Senate for the last forty-five years. Even from these very rudimentary data, a number of conclusions follow. First, the number of party unity votes fell during the middle years of this period, but just as significantly, partisan voting has made a comeback in more recent years. The percentage of party unity votes has been at or near a majority of all votes in both houses of Congress since the beginning of the second Reagan term, with the sole exception of the Senate in 1989. The extent to which voting in Congress was on a partisan basis was most notable in the first year after the Republicans regained majority status in 1994. The extent of partisanship in 1998 reverses a noticeable downward trend that began after the extremely contentious first session of the 104th Congress.

Figures 13.5 and 13.6 reveal the truly remarkable extent to which party voting has again become an important factor in Congress, and they give some clues to the reasons. First, claiming that party voting is not important is difficult when the average party unity scores of Democrats and Republicans in both houses of Congress have been above 75 percent for the last decade. The Republican party, always assumed to be the more

Figure 13.4 Party Unity Votes in Congress, 1954–1998.

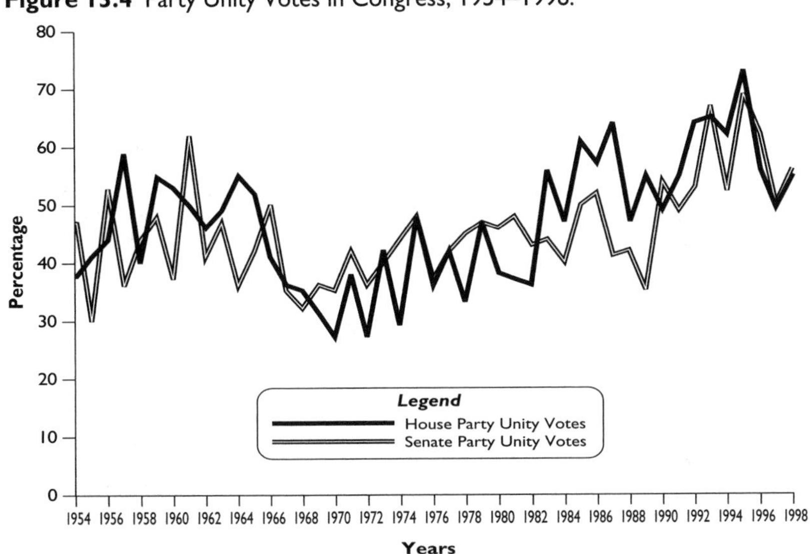

Source: Data from various Congressional Quarterly Service sources.

Figure 13.5 Party Unity Scores in the House, 1954–1998.

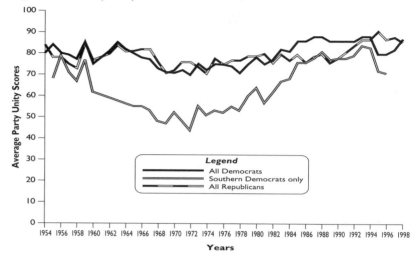

Source: Data from Various Congressional Quarterly Services sources.

ideologically homogeneous, has shown remarkable unity throughout the period under study, but most particularly in the most recent years.

Democratic party scores declined in the mid-1960s and into the 1970s, particularly in the House of Representatives. However, David Rohde (1991, 50–58) has demonstrated that much of the decline in the Democratic party scores was in fact a decline in the party unity scores of southern Democrats. The Democratic scores rebounded—to astoundingly high levels—during the Reagan administration. The average scores of northern Democrats never fell below 80 percent during this entire period. They peaked during the Bush years and remained remarkably high until the Congress following the election of 1994. Even then, with south-

Figure 13.6 Party Unity Scores in the Senate, 1954–1998.

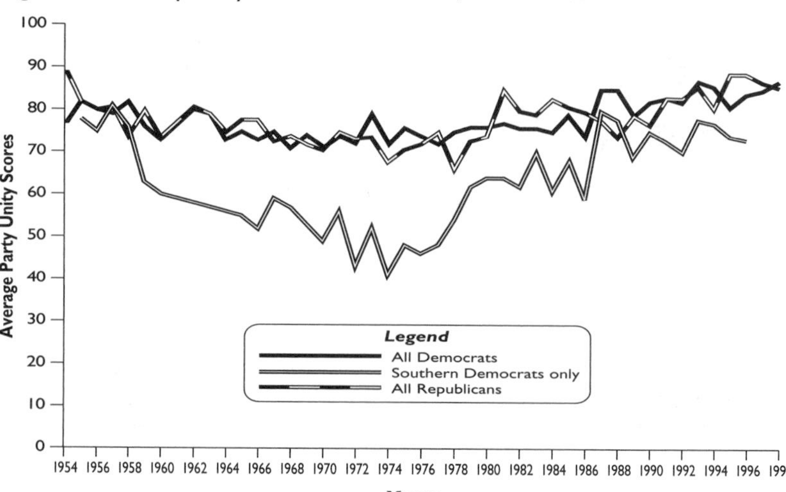

Source: Data from various Congressional Quarterly Service sources.

ern Democrats again showing lower scores, the party as a whole had a cohesion rate of 80 percent; it rebounded again as the party found its voice after the 1996 election. It is interesting to note that the Democrats have supported President Clinton's policies by voting cohesively both when they were in the majority and when they became the minority.

Note that this discussion of party in government in Congress has related party unity and party cohesion to presidential administrations. The concept of party in government implies a unified government. As has been mentioned many times, the norm for the American polity in recent decades has been divided government. The question then becomes: With whose party in government are we to be concerned—that of the legislative leaders or the president's? And how do they relate?

What is clear from this analysis, and from any study of policy making in the United States, is that the two are clearly interrelated, despite the separation of powers and their separate electoral bases. Political analysts are virtually unanimous in agreeing that presidents play the primary role in setting the congressional agenda (Fisher 1985; Jones 1988b 1988c; Kingdon 1984; Light 1983). Analysts of congressional behavior have explained how the parties function relative to the president's program. *Congressional Quarterly* computes **presidential support scores** and **presidential opposition scores** annually. It also notes how often the president succeeds and how often he fails on key votes. Party performance is analyzed in terms of legislators' support for a president of their own party or opposition to a president of the other party, clearly implying that the president defines the issues on which the parties might or might not divide.

PRESIDENTIAL SUPPORT SCORES

Percentage of times a legislator votes with the position of the president on those votes on which the president has taken a public stance.

PRESIDENTIAL OPPOSITION SCORES

Percentage of times a legislator votes against the president's position in votes on which the president has taken a public stance.

The analysis in this section, drawing on the contextual theory argued most forcefully by Cooper and Brady (1981) and Rohde (1991), implies that an analysis of party in the legislature is more complex than that.

> Thus, analysts saw, united government increased partisanship, while divided government reduced it. Yet there are other possibilities. Rather, the impact of party control on the two branches is conditional. . . . *If*, under united government, the president's proposals reflect the views of the dominant faction in the majority party, and *if* the majority party is relatively homogeneous on major issues and the minority party does not have incentives to go along, then the result will be a fairly partisan pattern of support. . . . In the case of divided government, *if* parties are internally divided, and *if* the president does not push radical departures from the status quo, and *if* the administration's inclination is to compromise a significant share of the differences with congressional Democrats, . . . then partisanship should be muted. (Rohde 1991, 140)

In addition, this analysis demonstrates that congressional parties in the 1990s are stronger than they were twenty years ago. Rohde (1991) is right in his analysis that the reforms of the 1970s have rejuvenated the parties and their leaders, even if that reaction was somewhat delayed. But it is also clear that party leadership—and as a consequence the extent of partisanship in Congress—is a function of personality as well as context and rules. Nothing could reveal this personality quotient more dramatically than the transfer of power from the highly partisan Speaker Jim Wright to the more accommodating Tom Foley (Sinclair 1990). And finally, looking at both Democratic and Republican congressional leaders, we can simply comment that leaders only lead as far and as fast as their followers want them to.[16] Leadership has its privileges to be sure, but rank-and-file members still exert those independent judgments that constrain leadership prerogatives.

IV. The President as a Leader of Party in Government

Much of the previous discussion has dealt with the president as a force in determining the direction taken by his party's members in Congress. The president is the most visible symbol of his party in the government. It is the *president's* program that is presented to Congress. It is the *president's* budget that Congress responds to. The members of the *president's* cabinet defend the *president's* proposals in hearings on Capitol Hill. In the current context no one talks about the Democratic policy agenda; it is the Clinton policy agenda. Commentators do not discuss the Democrats' response to a bill concerning the International Monetary Fund; they discuss President Clinton's response. Thus the first way in which the president serves as a leader of his party in government is in defining issues—and this action goes a good way toward defining his relationship with Congress.

But the agenda-setting role is not the only one played by presidents. Leadership involves convincing supporters to follow as well. Thus part of the role of the president is to convince his copartisans in Congress to follow his lead. Presidents can do this through *persuasion,* that is, convincing legislators to vote as the president wants, or through *conversion,* that is, by convincing them to want the same things the president wants (if they did not want these things before). An additional role played by presidents is as leader of an administration, an administration he largely staffs. This section will explore first the role the president plays in leading Congress, following on the previous discussion of the party in Congress, and then the partisan role the president plays in leading his administration.

A. The President as Leader of His Party in Congress

1. The Presidential Role in Setting the Parties' Agendas

The key to understanding the importance of the president's role in setting the congressional agenda is to note differences in how that role is played. When President Kennedy was elected in 1960, for instance, he won by a very narrow margin. His party had delicate majorities in Congress, and the conservative branch of his party controlled many of the key posts in Congress. Consequently, despite his call for a New Frontier, he went very slowly in proposing major changes to Congress.

By way of contrast, after his landslide election in 1964, an election in which his party also made huge gains in congressional majorities, Lyndon Johnson proposed sweeping reforms in his Great Society legislation. Those proposals energized the Democrats, particularly the liberal Democrats, and most particularly the newly elected liberal Democrats, many of whom believed that they had ridden into the House on Johnson's coattails. Similarly, the scope of Johnson's legislative initiatives stimulated reaction from the Republicans, enhancing the role of party for them as well.

Or to cite another example, contrast the experience of Democratic president Jimmy Carter with that of his Republican successor, Ronald Reagan. When Jimmy Carter became president in 1977, his agenda was tied closely to the role for government that he had developed as a governor in Georgia. He wanted to streamline government; he wanted to cut costs. Carter's "ideology" was difficult to pin down. He was a liberal idealist on some issues, advancing the cause of human rights and halting nuclear proliferation to name two, but he was something of a conservative on others. He had not been the presidential candidate of the liberals in Congress—many of them had backed Mo Udall—and his program invoked neither strong united support from the Democrats nor strong united opposition from the Republicans (see Jones 1988c.)

On the other extreme, Ronald Reagan won a landslide victory with a campaign in which he espoused a series of extremely conservative policy alternatives. He advocated a conservative agenda. The question of whether his landslide represented the voters' mandate for his policy views—a proposition that is highly dubious in light of public opinion surveys both on how voters decided and on how they stood on the issues—is irrelevant. What is relevant is that Reagan perceived the election as a mandate to go forward with at least some of these programs. His party, which regained control of the Senate in the election of 1980, was strongly behind him. Even Speaker O'Neill and many southern Democrats initially agreed with the president's view of the election and did not oppose the fiscal cuts he proposed in his first Congress. Reagan set the agenda; his party gladly embraced it and the Democrats were too impressed with his victory to offer much resistance.

Rohde (1991, 138–144; see also Jones 1988b) and others have demonstrated that a president's agenda has a direct impact on partisanship in Congress. But his ability to lead his own party—and either to win support in the other party or to coalesce opposition—changes over the course of an administration, as the president's power waxes and wanes. The Reagan experience demonstrates this aspect of a president's role as party leader as well. After the Democrats did well in the 1982 midterm elections, their willingness to oppose the president rose markedly. House Democrats' support of positions put forth by President Reagan, as reported by *Congressional Quarterly*, fell from 46 percent in the first session of Congress after his election in 1980 to 30 percent in the first session after the midterm election of 1982. They fell even lower during his second term, when Reagan's standing was shaken by the Iran-Contra affair.

And, of course, the Clinton experience supports this contention as well. Republican support of Clinton's initiatives fell from 39 percent in the first session after his election in 1992 to 22 percent after the 1994 midterms. Clinton's own party members continued to back their leader, unifying as a minority to defend traditional Democratic programs from an assault at the hands of the new and vigorous Republican majority. But Democratic party unity was shaken in the second term because of the scandals surrounding the president. As impeachment hearings were debated and then set on the eve of the 1998 midterm, commentators bemoaned the president's inability to lead his own party in Congress, as he focused on saving his presidency. Clearly the president's party held together on impeachment votes, in the House at the end of the 105th Congress and in the Senate at the beginning of the 106th. But the true test of Clinton's ability to continue to lead his party will come in the postimpeachment period.

Four decades ago Richard Neustadt described presidential power as the "power to persuade" in his seminal book on the presidency (Neustadt 1960; 1976). Neustadt's description is as accurate at the dawn of the twenty-first century as it was when the country moved to the New Frontier. A president can lead his party in the Congress only as long as he can persuade legislators that following his lead is in their best interest. A president with a strong electoral mandate—or the perception of such a mandate—can set the nation's agenda and lead his party effectively. A president who appears weak in the polls or who is preoccupied with scandal cannot exert that kind of leadership.

2. *Presidential Means of Working with Congress*

Not surprisingly, the president's ability to serve as party leader for his copartisans in Congress is in part a function of how well he works with Congress. The first organized efforts at congressional liaison are generally traced to the Eisenhower administration, though some would say that the role really goes back at least as far as Thomas Jefferson (Young 1966). Lawrence F. O'Brien, who built a congressional liaison staff in the Kennedy years, is often given credit for institutionalizing this staff function within the White House staff. But the sheer existence of an office and the effective functioning of that office are two different things.

Once again a clear example comes from the Carter administration. Carter was elected to the presidency as an outsider. He campaigned as an outsider; the voters liked the fact that he was an outsider; he refused to "play the Washington game." But working with Congress is inherently "playing the Washington game." Carter's chief of staff, Hamilton Jordan, often seemed to go out of his way to insult the new Speaker of the House, Tip O'Neill. The presidential assistant in charge of liaison with Congress was Frank Moore, a Carter loyalist from Georgia who had few contacts on Capitol Hill and little knowledge of how the system worked.

The result was a disaster. Carter and his party's leaders in Congress seemed almost at war. Given this background, that Democratic party unity scores did not soar when a Democrat recaptured the White House is unremarkable. The ability of a president to muster support for his programs from his own party's members of Congress is a function of both the program and his efforts to work with Congress—and the latter seems to be as much a function of personality as it is of policy.

Other presidents have been much more successful. Presidents use every means at their disposal to persuade legislators to go along with their views. They can persuade by the power of the argument, by their logic, by their expertise, by the quality of the programs put forward, and by the skills of those they appoint. But they also can persuade by going the extra mile to help members of Congress of their party—by attending the fund-raiser, by asking a senator to join the delegation to an international meeting, by such simple things as inviting a member's family to a White House function or to sit with the First Lady during the State of the Union Address. Friendships and favors, politics and policy all blend together to define ways in which presidents work to lead Congress.

3. The President as Party Leader in Congress: A Summary

Thus, in the final analysis, the president's ability to lead his party in Congress is a function of politics and personality. America's is *not* a parliamentary system. We do not elect presidents and give them a mandate to push their policy alternatives through Congress. Congress is a separate branch of the government. Representatives and senators have separate electoral bases from the president. Divided government has become almost a norm, certainly not an exception. Therefore, the ability of the president to lead his party in Congress will depend on his popularity, the majority or minority status of his party in Congress, the fit between his views and those of the majority of the members of his party in Congress, the perceived need or desire to compromise on the part of all concerned, and the mix of the personalities involved. A president can be a party leader, but nothing in our system guarantees that he will play that role, much less that he will play it effectively.

B. The Role of Party in the President's Administration

The final aspect of party in government that requires explication is the role of the party in staffing a president's administration. Partisan control of presidential appointments is often discussed in terms of the spoils system, which reached its height during the Jacksonian party system: "To the victor goes the spoils." When a party captured the White House, its followers received jobs and the followers of the losing party lost jobs. The spoils system was deeply embedded in American politics. It was, for example, the glue that held traditional political machines in place.

However, in terms of federal employment, the spoils system was undercut by the civil service system. Before the passage of the Pendleton Act, which created the civil service system in 1883, none of the roughly 100,000 civilian employees of the federal government was covered by a merit system. By 1920, roughly four-fifths of the civilian employee force for the federal government was so covered—and that number has not changed dramatically since (Mackenzie 1998, 322). However, the expansion of the functions of the federal government left a great many patronage jobs. Contrary to popular belief, most of those jobs were not in Washington. Rather they were out in the states, in post offices, in court houses, and they were appointments controlled by local party leaders, not by national party leaders.

Presidents nevertheless had a number of positions to fill. Throughout the first half of the twentieth century, presidents, lacking alternative means, relied heavily on the party machinery to suggest people to fill these positions. The Eisenhower administration marked a turning point in this process.[17] Eisenhower had few ties to the Republican party; in fact he had never even voted before his own presidential election in 1952. His appointees had few ties to the party. For the first time a centralized personnel function was established in the White House, with the creation of a special assistant for personnel management. This position was continued in the Kennedy and Johnson administrations. The object was to make certain that congressional and party leaders did not oppose a nominee for an appointive position, but the recruitment process was separated from the party. As Dan H. Fenn Jr., who assisted the Kennedy administration on personnel matters, concluded, "The kind of people we were looking for weren't the kind of people who were active in party activities" (quoted in Mackenzie 1998, 329).

In recent years the centralization of the personnel function in the White House Office has become institutionalized with the establishment of the Presidential Personnel Office. The key component of this operation, developed in the Nixon administration and expanded ever since, has been the implementation of a recruitment function. Recent presidents have set up an organization to staff and to maintain their administrations. They have not relied on other existing organizations to find people to serve in appointive positions. The key elements have become the ability to do the job, and ideological and personal loyalty to the president.

At the same time, as recent presidents have increasingly exercised personal control over the appointment process, more positions in public employment are being protected from partisan politics. Thus the role of party is doubly diminished: the president has fewer positions to fill, and the party has a diminished role in advising the president on how those that do exist should be filled.

What does this tell us about the president's role as the leader of his party in this sense? Interestingly, it probably reveals very little. When more appointments were available, and when they were made by party, party leaders rarely suggested a potential appointee based on his views on issues and ability to serve the president in that way. Indeed, appointments were offered to those who had served the party in an electoral sense. The president may have benefited from this activity indirectly, but the appointee's political activity was usually at the state or local level, not the national level.

In recent years, with personalized campaigning, presidents have developed their own following—loyalists who have worked with the president earlier in his career or on his campaign, men and women who share policy views and visions with the president. In this sense the president is the leader of his administration but the party plays a greatly diminished role (Mackenzie 1998).

V. POLITICIANS VIEW THE PARTY IN GOVERNMENT

Much of the discussion to this point says a great deal about how politicians view the party in government. Generally speaking, if the party is saying and doing what politicians want to be said and done and if backing the party seems to be in their own interest, then they are all for the party in the government. If party leaders are not taking those views, then opposition mounts.

Perhaps the best proof of this hypothesis is seen in the Republican party in the 102d Congress. As that Congress convened in 1991, Republican Conference chairman Jerry Lewis of California was challenged by Carl Pursell from Michigan. At every level the issue concerned how the party should be led. On the surface, questions were raised about loyalty. Lewis felt that the Republican party in the House should back its president: "If we are not going to support the president when that office gives us an opportunity to affect policy, . . . the entire leadership of the minority party needs to be reviewed" (Hook 1990, 3997).

Pursell felt that the Republican leader in the House should listen to his membership; if the members are more conservative than the president or want to go in a different direction, so be it. As one of Pursell's followers said, "If you are elected by the Conference, your loyalty is to the Conference" (Hook 1990, 3998).

At another level, the Lewis–Pursell contest drew clear distinctions between the style of minority leader Bob Michel and the style of minority whip Newt Gingrich. Gingrich was the leader of the Conservative Opportunity Society, the group of young ideologues intent on forcing the agenda of the Congress to the right. He was proud of his reputation for attacking Democrats, especially Speaker Jim Wright, with a confrontational and combative style. Michel's style was quieter, more accommodationist. He competed with the Democrats, fought hard when he thought partisanship was dominating a discussion, but also believed that compromise was necessary to achieve results. Gingrich had attacked President Bush when he felt the president had strayed from conservative policies. Michel's style was to criticize the president in private but support him in public.

And in the background of the fight for Conference chair was one abiding reality: Gingrich wanted to succeed Michel as Republican leader; so did Lewis. Lewis beat Pursell easily, but his victory was pyrrhic for those who favored an accommodationist style of leadership. Gingrich was not even challenged in his bid for reelection as whip. And when Michel announced his retirement, it was the combative Gingrich, not the accommodationist Lewis, to whom the party turned.

But as we have seen, the debate over Gingrich as party leader continues. He has had towering successes to be sure. But his popularity with the public and his ability to continue to lead his party and the House were called into question. He put down one challenge but eventually had to resign. So the debate between politicians who see their role as confronting ideologues and those who see their role as working within the party goes on. The debate is unlikely to be resolved permanently, but movement toward one side or the other will be affected by political context and personalities involved.

WEBSITES

http://www.house.gov
http://www.senate.gov

The House of Represenatives and the Senate each maintain a website with links to various members and leadership offices.

http://www.cq.com

Congressional Quarterly Service provides a wealth of information on the current Congress. *CQ* provides the party unity and opposition and presidential support and opposition scores as well as roll call votes and summaries of all legislation.

http://www.hillnews.com
http://www.rollcall.com

The two newspapers covering the Hill, as well as the major national media outlets cited after chapter 12, also cover the role of party in government by showing how the parties take positions on various substantive issues.

KEY CONCEPTS

Contract with America
Democratic Caucus
filibuster
majority leader
majority whip
minority leader
minority whip
partisan
party cohesion scores
party unity scorces
party unity votes
presidential opposition scores
Presidential support scores
Republican Conference

DISCUSSION QUESTIONS

1. To what extent do you believe that your representatives should vote in Congress along party lines as opposed to supporting what they perceive to be the views of their constituents? Where should their own consciences enter into their decision-making equations?
2. When Republicans gained majority status in Congress after the 1994 election, they argued that they did so based on the Contract with America. Yet they were unable to implement the various proposals on which they had campaigned. How do you explain their failure to pass legislation for which they claimed to have an electoral mandate?
3. Discuss the fact that active involvement in party matters seems to matter little to newly elected presidents as they select cabinet and subcabinet appointees.
4. How would you define the relationship between party in government and party in the electorate (or party organization)? Do you think this relationship is as it should be? Or should the connections be more formal?

CHAPTER 14

Conclusions: The Role of Political Parties at the Dawn of the Twenty-first Century

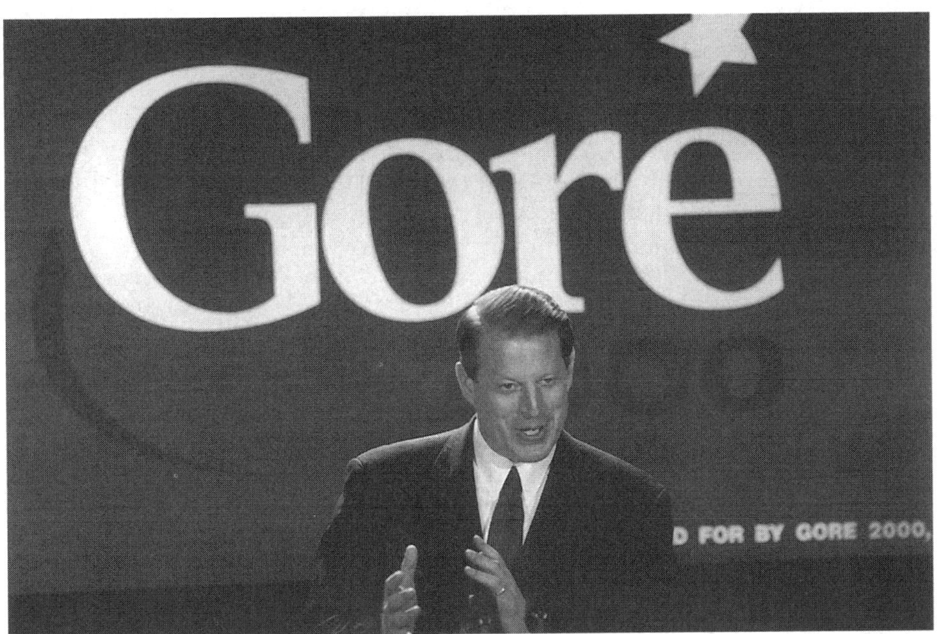

Modern political parties were in their infancy at the dawn of the nineteenth century. They were dominating the American political landscape at the dawn of the twentieth century. What can be said of them as we enter not only a new century but also a new millennium?

To this point, I have examined the historical development of political parties and the electoral process, and the context in which they currently exist, from an empirical point of view. That is, I have analyzed the role played by parties in nominations and elections, explored why elections have been decided as they were, described the processes and explained how variations in processes influence results. Then we looked at the implications of some of the aspects of those processes and of institutional linkages for politics and for governance.

In this final chapter, we move from empirical analysis to evaluation. Specifically, we look at how well the electoral process and political parties within that process play the roles that have been assigned to them in the American system of government.

I. The Role of Elections

Recall Professor Finer's definition of the role that elections must play if a democracy is to function effectively:

> The real question . . . is not whether the government deigns to take notice of popular criticisms and votes, but whether it can be voted out of office or forced by some machinery or procedures to change its policy, above all against its own will. (Finer 1949, 219)

In the most theoretical terms, the answer to Professor Finer's question with regard to the American system is that the government can be forced to change its policies against its own will; the government can be voted out of office. But in an empirical sense, is that what elections mean in the United States? Do elections today give the citizenry a chance to decide on the course of action that their government will take? This question is more easily posed than answered.

A. The Context of Federalism

It should come as no surprise that the answer to the basic question will vary depending upon whether one is analyzing federal, state, or local elections. Once again we must be alert not to generalize about the electoral process in the United States, when the process at the federal level is different from that at the state level (and states differ significantly from each other), and the processes in the various states are different from those in localities throughout the country.

I. Presidential Elections

Presidential elections have come closest to meeting the criterion set forth above. The American public has shown that it is willing and able to remove presidents when the policies of the government have consequences that displease the citizenry. And, of course, it has shown that it will retain presidents and policies with which it is in agreement. A number of linkages are implied in that conclusion.

First, we assume that the policies of the president and those of the government are the same. We know this assumption to be false in part because separation of powers necessitates that nearly all policies are the result of compromise. But we also know that the public makes this linkage even if it is not in fact accurate.

Second, we assume that the consequences of governmental policies were the ones desired or at least foreseen when those policies were implemented. Again, we know that this linkage is partial at best. For example, the success or failure of an administration's agricultural policies is dependent on the weather, advances in technology, and the actions of other nations as well as on the wisdom of the policies put forth. Again, however, we know that the public holds the president accountable for the consequences of his actions, not for the intentions of those actions, and so the assumed linkage has the effect hypothesized.

Third, we assume that all citizens view all policies in the same way and vote accordingly. Again, we know that this linkage is not complete. From the time of Madison, American politicians have recognized and dealt with the diversity of interests throughout this land. Even in landslide presidential elections approximately two out of every five voters support the losing candidate. In any election those supporting any candidate do not all do so for the same reasons. But, once again, a perfect linkage is not necessary. What is necessary is for a critical mass of citizens to express dissatisfaction with the policies (either general or specific) of an administration and to translate those feelings into support for another candidate.

Given the standard stipulated above, a number of the presidential elections discussed in chapter 10 meet the criterion of serving as an appropriate expression of the views of the citizenry in opposition to the actions of the government. In the election of 1992, as the most recent example, the Clinton campaign emphasized "the economy, stupid." The voters agreed with the Democratic candidate that the Republican incumbent had not been successful in economic terms. Candidate Clinton portrayed himself as an agent of change; the public chose him on that basis.

The elections of 1932, 1952, 1960, 1968, 1976, and 1980 all can also be interpreted as examples of elections in which citizens chose to change the direction of policy. Obvious differences exist among these examples. The election of 1932 is described as a critical election in which public attachment to the major political parties underwent major changes. In 1952 and 1968, dissatisfaction with the policies of incumbent administrations was strong enough to convince Presidents Truman and Johnson not to seek reelection. The nominees of their parties were unable to dissociate themselves sufficiently to avoid defeat. In 1976 and again in 1980 sitting presidents lost to challengers whose campaigns emphasized the policies that were in place. In each case, the public chose to replace a government holding policies of which it disapproved.

The elections of 1964, 1972, 1984, and 1996—elections in which incumbents were reelected—can be seen as cases in which the public said, in effect, that it preferred policies enacted by the sitting president to those proposed by the challenger.[1] In the first three elections, in 1964, 1972, and 1984, challengers proposed truly radical changes in the policies in place—and those radical changes were rousingly rejected (Converse, Clausen, and Miller 1965; Miller et al. 1979; Wayne 1984; Shanks and Miller 1990). In the 1996 election, as we have already seen, Republican candidate Dole attacked President Clinton on issues of character as much as policy; the public voted to stay the course with a president whose policies had proven to be popular.

In each of these cases, the claim that the electorate expressed its views on the policies of the day through the ballot box can be supported. Presidential elections are highly salient. Although incumbents have some advantages and it can be argued that the "right" issues are not discussed and that the electorate lacks requisite sophistication, the argument can also be sustained that presidential elections fulfill the role they were designed to play in American politics. As we look to the election of 2000, it seems likely that once again the electorate will have a choice between ratifying the policies passed by a retiring president (as they did in 1988) or signaling that it is time for a change of course (as was the case when President Eisenhower retired in 1960).

2. Congressional Elections

What about elections to other federal offices—to the Senate and the House of Representatives—when the campaigns, the candidates, and the issues are not as visible to the public as they are in presidential elections?

In these cases, the findings are mixed. In chapters 7 and 8 I presented a good deal of evidence demonstrating incumbent advantages in House elections. Senate incumbents have fewer advantages—and challengers have greater assets—but recent Senate elections suggest that incumbents in those races are not without strengths. Do these elections serve to link the views of the public with the policies of the government? Or are incumbents so protected as to erase the connection between elections and outcomes that Professor Finer defines as necessary? Or is voter satisfaction with incumbent representatives for whatever reason sufficient cause to evaluate the electoral process positively?

Elections in individual districts and/or states do not seem to demonstrate the prescribed connection. Yet there are a few cases in which key issues have led to the defeat of an incumbent and thus indirectly to a representative's reflecting the views of constituents in a different manner. For instance, the defeat of Congresswoman Marjorie Margolies-Mezvinsky (D-Pa., 1993–1995), who cast the deciding vote in favor of President Clinton's budget and tax package in 1993, is generally attributed to that vote. She had barely won election in 1992 in wealthy Montgomery County. In 1994 she lost to the same Republican candidate, John Fox, who used the vote over and over in the campaign to show that Margolies-Mevzinsky opposed tax cuts, an unpopular position among voters.

But more frequently incumbents seeking reelection are sent back to Washington. Over 90 percent of House incumbents seeking to return are successful in election after election. In 1998 that percentage reached 98.5. Senators too are rarely defeated. And when incumbents do lose, more frequently personal scandals, not stands on policies, play a key role in those defeats.

However, the case that elections allow the electorate to hold its representatives accountable can still be made in a number of less direct ways. First, look at the role of interest groups and their use of soft money (chap. 11; Magleby and Holt 1999). Groups tend to invest heavily in campaigns in competitive congressional districts when the major party candidates differ on the issues that the groups feel are most critical. Organized labor, business and industry groups, environmentalists, those on both sides of the abortion issue, and those favoring term limits are all obvious examples of groups that strive to hold representatives accountable for their actions in Washington. Even when these groups are not successful in defeating incumbents, they often define the issue agenda for a campaign, with two consequences: (1) voters do in fact have an opportunity to focus on key issues and to express their preference and (2) representatives often moderate positions in order to accommodate the views of more of their constituents. Whatever one concludes about the role of soft money in campaigns—an issue of great controversy—it is difficult not to see that campaign spending of this type raises the issue content of certain campaigns.

The second argument in favor of the proposition that congressional elections serve the purpose of holding representatives accountable for their actions rests on observing the results of these elections at the macro level, that is, looking at all elections held in one year together rather than at individual elections separately. There is a good deal of evidence that these elections reflect the views of the voters, at least on the major economic issues of the day (Jacobson and Kernell 1983; Tufte 1973; 1978). At times when there has been massive public discontent with governmental policies, changes wrought on the composition of the legislature as a result of congressional elections have been sufficient to lead to changes in those policies (Brady et al. 1988). The election of 1966, generally interpreted as a reaction to excesses in social welfare policies passed by the so-called Great Society Democrat-dominated Eighty-ninth Congress, is one clear example of this linkage. Certainly it could be argued that the election of 1994, in which Republicans regained control of both houses of Congress for the first time since 1954, had the same impact.

3. State and Local Elections

While most states now see some level of two-party competition, as was demonstrated in chapter 1 (see also Bibby et al. 1983; Jewell and Olson 1982; 1988; Holbrook and Van Dunk 1993), one party or the other still has a decided advantage in statewide elections in many states. Moreover, in legislative districts in virtually every state, true two-party competition remains the exception, not the rule (Crotty 1985, chap. 8). How can citizens effect policy change if the result of the election will have virtually no impact on who governs?

Local elections have the same types of problems that state elections have, only more so. Many localities are now and have been for some time dominated by one political party or the other. We read often about the strength of the Democratic party organization in Cook County, Illinois, the area including and surrounding Chicago. In the city of Chicago, Democratic party nomination is all but tantamount to election. Other organizations are not as strong as that in Cook County, but one-party rule in local elections remains very common (see Gibson et al. 1985; Schlesinger 1985).

4. Nonpartisan Politics

Even more common than one-party rule in local governing units is nonpartisan government. This text has dealt only with partisan elections because those are the elections that see the most competition in the American system. Yet nonpartisan elections merit comment.

Nearly two-thirds of U.S. cities with a population of over 5,000 hold nonpartisan elections to determine who will hold local offices (Crotty 1985, 105). The movement toward nonpartisan government was part of Progressive era reforms; advocates of nonpartisan local government feel that running a local government should be more like administering a business than playing partisan politics. Frequently they cite the corruption and the inefficiency of partisan politics. "There is no Republican and no Democratic way to clean a street."

On the other hand, those concerned with democratic control over the means of governing have not been overly impressed with the experience of nonpartisan elections. Critics contend that nonpartisan elections tend to draw fewer voters because citizens do not care who wins these elections and because elections without the cue of party often confuse voters. The voters are less informed about the issues than is the case in partisan elections. Fewer races are competitive in the sense of close elections; in fact, in many races only one candidate runs. The advantages of incumbency are increased over those in even heavily one-party areas with partisan elections, since the opposition is deprived of its chance to organize.

The end result is less serious, less issue-oriented campaigning, more domination by those with well-recognized names, an increase in domination by single-issue groups that have the ability to mobilize their supporters, and generally less representative and less accountable government.

If the goal of reformers was to establish a system in which democracy functions more effectively, and if democracy for this purpose is defined as a system in which the views of the voters on policy matters are converted into government policy, then nonpartisan elections represent a regressive step. Only someone who believes that local government involves only administration, with no policy implications, can view the results of the nonpartisan movement as a movement toward more democracy. Given the nature of citizen concerns about local issues, about education and crime and growth policies, as well as about street repair and garbage collection, that argument is difficult to sustain.

B. Voters and Elections

In evaluating the effectiveness of elections, it is also important to look at how voters are deciding for whom they will vote. *The American Voter* model stipulated that most voters used political party as a cue in determining their electoral choices during the decade of the 1950s. *The Changing American Voter* analysis revealed that issue orientation was more important in determining vote than had been the case when the earlier study was undertaken. *The New American Voter* argued that the importance of the concept of party identification should not be underestimated, even as we approach the twenty-first century and many voters view politics cynically.

But more needs to be known than that party or issue orientation is the most important cue for voting. Specifically, in an age of changing technology and changing campaign techniques, we are concerned with how voters gain the information that helps them determine how they will vote. In the 1950s—and for some time before—we believe that voters cast their votes largely on the cue of party and that party affiliation was determined by influences such as parental partisanship and group pressures. If party is a less important cue today, how do citizens learn what candidates stand for?

1. Television as a Source of Political Information

Television is the news source most relied on by the American voting public. For more than three decades approximately two-thirds of those responding to the National Election Studies surveys conducted by the Center for Political Studies of the Survey Research Center at the University of Michigan have responded that television is their most important source for political information. Nearly 90 percent rely on television to some extent. Although newspapers are listed as one source by approximately 75 percent of respondents, only about 20 percent consider newspapers their primary source. (See, e.g., Adams 1982; Patterson 1980; Ranney 1990; Robinson and Sheehan 1983.) In 1998 polls conducted by the Pew Research Center for the People and the Press, the number who relied on television had fallen to about 75 percent, but television was still the medium most frequently mentioned.

What are the implications of this reliance on television? Television is a visual medium and emphasizes stories that can be presented visually. A number of earlier chapters discussed the media's emphasis on campaign-oriented stories: Who is gaining? Who is losing? What are the various strategies, and how are they working?

Doris Graber has studied television coverage of presidential elections for some years. Her conclusions support the commonly held view that television presents the news and covers campaigns in a simplified manner. In every election that she studied, save that of 1968, the media in general and television journalists in particular presented stories on campaign events more than analyses of domestic politics, foreign affairs, economic policy, or social problems (Graber 1980; 1982; 1984a; 1984b; 1989; 1990; see also Buchanan 1991; Crouse 1973; Patterson 1980; Robinson and Sheehan 1983).

During the election of 1968 the war in Vietnam as a news event and as an issue received more coverage than did campaign events. However, this may well be the exception that proves the rule. Vietnam was a news issue that could be covered visually. That was the first war that was telecast live into America's living rooms. As a news story, it had the ability to capture the attention of the viewing audience.

But compare the coverage of the war in Vietnam with television coverage of the major economic policy crises that have dominated the governmental agenda in recent years. How many times can the network news anchors show bar graphs that describe the growth of the federal debt? How many times can they depict the federal budget with pie charts? These economic issues—and the important issues of domestic politics, foreign affairs, and social problems—are complex problems that do not translate easily into two-minute spots on the network news (Graber 1980; see also Kerbel 1998; Buchanan 1991; Gans 1979). Yet these are undoubtedly the important issues of the day. And television, which cannot and does not cover these issues very well, is the medium most relied on by the voting public for its political information. The necessary conclusion is that voters are deciding based on a grossly oversimplified view of the important issues of the day.

2. Television as a Source of Information about State and Local Issues

The previous discussion has dealt with national news events and presidential elections because that is the only context that has been studied in depth by social scientists. It does not take much intuition, however, to extend this discussion to the state and local contexts. Think for a moment about the quality of news coverage in local newspapers and on local television news broadcasts. Let us assume for the moment that most citizens gain their political information about events at the state and local level from television, just as they do for events at the national level.[2]

The average local news program spends nearly as much time on weather and sports as it does on all news. The news segment frequently carries one story about national news and at least one human interest story. Then, of course, there is the obligatory story about the latest local disaster—fire, murder, automobile accident. But how often is there in-depth coverage of a state house hearing on workers' compensation, of a city council debate on zoning ordinances, of a school board discussion on resource allocation? When state and local elections are held, how often are the candidates seen on local television?

Example after example could be mounted, but the point would remain the same. It should be emphasized, however, that all the blame does not rest with television journalists (nor with newspaper reporters, for much the same argument would apply to most local papers). In point of fact, they are faced with a nearly impossible task. Local journalists for all media have very few resources with which to cover a vast amount of material. They do not have large staffs or large budgets; they have limited space and/or time; they have many localities and issues to cover.

And they are under tremendous pressure to draw an audience. It is difficult to imagine how most issues that face state and local governments—or most issues that distinguish candidates for state and local offices—could be covered in a way that would excite the public. Yet if newspapers do not sell and if television broadcasts do not achieve high ratings, the business end of these enterprises fails and the public is even less well served (Kerbel 1998; Berkman and Kitch 1986; Gans 1979). As a consequence, local journalists do what they can to cover state and local government and politics; in most instances what they can do is very little. And again, very little is what the public is left to rely on in making its decisions!

C. An Evaluation of the Electoral Process as a Means of Choosing Those Who Govern

The purpose of this section has been to evaluate the electoral process we have described as a means of selecting representative governments in the United States. What we have found is that the extent to which the elections serve as a vehicle for public expression of views of issues varies according to the salience of the election. We could also add that the American voting public represents barely a majority of American citizens and that those who do vote are not representative of the country as a whole. (Recall chap. 4.) Each of these conclusions is exaggerated as we progress from the presidential election through the federal system down to local elections.

Furthermore, we have found that most Americans rely heavily on television as a source of information about political events, yet television is not a very apt medium for supplying in-depth information and analysis. Once again, this is even more true for local elections than it is for more visible national elections.

The process discussed at some length throughout this book advantages some and disadvantages others. In electoral terms, the advantage clearly lies with incumbents, with those whose names are well known, and with those who have (or have access to) large amounts of money. For those trying to influence policy through the electoral process, money seems to be the most relevant resource. Those with fewer resources, those challenging the status quo, and those less advantaged in American society are those least advantaged by the electoral system. (Recall chap. 11.)

In an earlier era, parties served to offset this balance somewhat. Decrying the decline of political parties, Walter Dean Burnham characterized them as "the only devices thus far invented by the wit of Western man which with some effectiveness can generate countervailing collective power on behalf of the individually powerless against the relatively few who are individually—and organizationally—powerful" (Burnham 1970, 133).

Burnham's point was that political parties serve many functions in the American system, not the least of which is to help new and less advantaged groups "make it" in American society.

But parties seem to have lost much of their influence over the electoral process. They have been replaced by candidate-centered campaigns, by media messages, by interest-group domination, by low voter turnout, by increased apathy, and, it could be argued, by a governing elite more concerned with maintaining power, and with using office to maintain power, than with using the offices to which they have been elected to benefit the greater number in American society. Polls show a cynicism among the public that reflects this view. In the concluding section we will look at the role of political parties at the approach of the millennium.

II. THE ROLE OF POLITICAL PARTIES

In an earlier edition of this book, the concluding section discussed efforts by party professionals to rejuvenate party organizations. As noted in chapter 3, the Republican party, under Chairman Bill Brock, began an effort to revitalize the party beginning in the late 1970s. The Democratic party followed suit, starting in the early 1980s. Today both national party organizations are staffed with campaign professionals, skilled at aiding their copartisans with all aspects of electioneering (see Herrnson 1998a; for a similar discussion of state party organizations, see Bibby 1998).

But the role of parties in elections remains in doubt. To what extent do candidates or does the electorate depend on political parties? For what purposes? How do these participants see the role of parties? It is to these questions—and to the role that the Republican and Democratic parties are likely to play in the elections in the first decade of the twenty-first century—that we now turn.

A. The Parties in the Modern Election

The most apt description of elections at the end of the twentieth century is that elections had become "candidate centered." Let's be certain we understand what that term means. Candidate-centered campaigns are to be distinguished from party-centered campaigns. The major political parties have lost control of their own candidates.

Why? Three reasons stand out. First, parties lost control of the nominating process. The major cause for this change was the advent of the direct primary system. Although state law and state party rules vary, the norm is that party organization cannot be involved in determining who will be the party's nominees. In a sense, that is ludicrous on its face. A well-meaning reform, aimed at restoring intraparty democracy and lessening the influence of party bosses making decisions out of public view, essentially removed political parties' raison d'être. Parties exist to run candidates who will carry forth the programs supported by party adherents into government. The primary system removed from party control the selection of candidates whom party officials feel could carry out that task. From a practical point of view, the imposition of primary elections as the principal way of nominating candidates meant that those candidates had to set up their own organizations, separate from the party organization, in order to run a primary campaign. This requirement went a long way toward focusing campaigns on candidates and not parties.

Obviously the impact of this reform was not felt everywhere in the nation at the same time. Some states adopted the primary system essentially as a means of weakening political parties—and that effect was felt. In other states, party organizations resisted and developed coping mechanisms, preprimary endorsements as one example. At the national level, party organizations remained important in determining presidential nominees until after the 1968 reforms. But certainly by the end of the century, the role of party in the nominating process had been reduced from a once prominent position to a much lesser one, everywhere in the nation. Variation still exists, but a pattern is clear.

The second reason for the replacement of party-centered campaigns with candidate-centered campaigns relates to campaign techniques. Parties were strongest when the most valuable resource in a campaign was manpower. Party organizations, often building on material incentives, could command the troops who would go door-to-door and bring the voters to the polls. Men and women literally worked hour upon hour to turn out the loyal voters, many of whom were also committed to the party because of material benefits that they had received.

With the advent of television advertising and of computer-generated, targeted direct mail, the role of dedicated, loyal campaign workers diminished. These techniques required skilled professionals to design campaigns and money to pay for them. Political party organizations responded to this changing environment, but they did so in competition with others who could also provide these resources. Candidates could hire their own consultants and raise their own money. Party organization became one of many players in a game orchestrated by candidate organizations.

Related to this second reason is the third reason—the role of money in modern campaigns. Here the question is not just the amount of money that is needed, but the ways in which money can be raised. Under the provisions of the Federal Election Campaign Act, political parties are restricted in the amounts of money they can give directly to a campaign; they compete with others, mostly interest groups, in the money they can contribute in other ways (chap. 11).

The last point deserves further elaboration. Parties have essentially become one of a class of participants in modern elections. How is this class defined? They are actors in the electoral arena who have a stake in the outcome of an election but are not directly part of the campaign. Chris Arterton (1982, 135) and others have commented that parties have become little more than superPACs. The Pew Charitable Trust–funded examination of soft money in the 1998 electoral process lumped together party money and interest-group money as "outside money." The study concluded that soft money had played such a major role in competitive races in 1998 that those races could be classified as "interest group centered" more than candidate centered (Magleby and Holt 1999).

But to a certain extent that analysis misses the point about the role that parties could play in modern election campaigns, even given the decline in their influence. Candidates view parties as a source for money (but in actuality this seems only to be the case in competitive elections) but are concerned that party soft money coming into a campaign can take control of the campaign away from them.[3] Citizens view parties skeptically, attesting that they are looking to support the candidate, not the party. And parties have played into both of these roles, viewing them almost as inevitable.

In 1998, however, some party organizations began to look back to traditional roles, though implementing them in new ways. The concern in state after state in 1998 dealt with voter turnout. Parties in states as geographically and culturally different as Oregon, California, and South Carolina saw that their best role might well be to increase turnout among their partisans—to use their soft money to run "get out the vote" drives. Some of these were almost traditional GOTV drives, similar to those run in the heyday of party organizations. But much more frequently they were targeted, sophisticated get-out-the-vote drives using modern techniques to increase turnout among specific segments of the population thought to favor their candidates. The South Carolina party worked hard to turn out African-American voters, and the election of Governor Jim Hodges and the reelection of Senator Ernest Hollings were directly related to those efforts.

Campaign finance legislation remains highly controversial. But as long as parties can raise and spend soft money, they will continue to exploit this gap in regulation. More interesting than the existence of this money is concern over how it is spent. If it is spent merely to add "noise" to political communication, then the parties are not contributing positively to the electoral process. However, if it is spent to define a party stake in the process, to stimulate those who should be party supporters to participate and to back party candidates, then a much more positive role emerges. Despite a good deal of concern over how the 1998 elections were run, some positive signs in this direction were detectable.

B. Parties' Appeal to the Electorate

The most interesting debate about the role of political parties in the twenty-first century may not be the debate about how parties try to influence elections but rather the debate about how the two parties define themselves.

For much of the last half of the twentieth century this debate was fought within the Democratic party. The Democrats had two wings—a conservative wing and a liberal wing. The conservative wing was largely southern; the liberal wing was largely northern. The liberals were dominant nationally, but the conservatives controlled southern states; the liberals needed their support to win presidential elections and to pass legislation in Congress. Frequently, that support was not forthcoming and Democrats lost.

Late in the 1980s, Democrats began to move away from the two extremes toward the center. Philosophically, this movement was defined as "the third way," not all government and not all private sector, but a third way, a partnership, a sense that government largesse came with personal responsibility. These views were voiced by the Democratic Leadership Council and served as the basis for President Clinton's successful campaign for election in 1992 and reelection in 1996. Liberals complained that the DLC was throwing away fundamental Democratic principles in order to win elections. "New" Democrats countered that they were true to those principles and voicing them in a way that resonated with the American electorate. As the Clinton administration drew to a close, some still complained that he ran as a Democrat but governed like a Republican. But more Democrats accepted his successes in electoral terms and in policy terms. The positive side of the Clinton legacy may well be defined as his ability to unite his party around an agenda that appealed to most voters.[4]

Meanwhile the Republicans seem to be moving in the other direction. A party that had been united under Ronald Reagan as the conservative alternative to radical Democrats, a party that had brought blue-collar Democrats into its fold, split over the definition of true conservatism.

Never was this more clear than during the 1998 elections and the debate over the impeachment of President Clinton. Essentially the Republican party is divided into three camps, each fighting for control (chap. 9).

The social conservatives feel that the party should define its principles clearly and stick to them. That group pushed hard for impeaching President Clinton. They thought that the election of 1998 should be fought over the issue of the president's character and were responsible for the last-minute Republican campaign blitz aimed at the president. Despite the fact that that blitz did not result in electoral success and was viewed as a failure by many, they remained committed. According to Gary Bauer, former head of the Family Research Council and a candidate for the Republican presidential nomination in 2000, Republican candidates "bailed out on social issues. . . . We just ran one of the least ideological campaigns in years and none of us feel [sic] very good" (Balz and Broder 1998). His views were echoed by Randy Tate, executive director of the Christian Coalition:

> If the 106th Congress does not immediately take up pro-family, conservative issues and talk about them, not just for one day, but day in and day out, if they don't do these things, things will get worse before they get better for them [GOP congressional leaders]. (Balz and Broder 1998)

These views were reflected in the words of the House managers of the impeachment trial and in the actions of those Republicans who prolonged that trial, to the detriment of their party's standing with the public, long after the eventual outcome was apparent. When one Democratic leader was asked why the Republicans were acting in a manner that seemed certain to hurt them at the polls, he replied, "Tom DeLay would rather be the Minority Leader of 190 committed Republicans than Whip for a majority that is not ideologically pure."

Congressman Chris Shays has a very different view. According to Shays, the disproportionate influence of the religious and social conservatives is causing serious problems for the party. "As soon as my leaders started to jump when the Christian Coalition and Gary Bauer and others said jump, we lost a lot of voters" (Mitchell 1998).

Economic conservatives, by contrast, are concerned that the conservative Christian agenda not dominate party thinking in terms of the issues about which they care most. Congressman Rick Lazio (R-N.Y.), in reviewing the 1998 election, concluded, "I think the party has the best cohesion when it talks about fiscal issues" (Mitchell 1998).

The third wing of the party might be called pragmatic conservatives. Looking at the electoral debacle of 1998, former congressman Steve Gunderson (R-Wis.) concluded, "I really see this as a clarion call from the nation to bring the political parties back to the pragmatic governing center. . . . It's a wonderful warning to my party between now and the year 2000" (Balz and Broder 1998). Marshall Wittman of the Heritage Foundation discussed the victories of Republican governors in key states in 1998 in the same terms. "I think that the lesson of the election is that sharp-elbowed conservatism doesn't work and what they offer is a new paradigm of compassionate conservatism" (Balz 1998b).

An airplane with three wings cannot fly. A political party with three wings, struggling against itself, will have difficulty defining an electorate to which it can appeal. The year 2000 Republican nomination is viewed as a fight for the heart and soul of the party. In some ways, it is also a fight to define the two-party system in the years ahead. If, on the one hand, Republicans insist on ideological purity, be it social conservatism to the exclusion of all else or economic conservatism to the exclusion of all else, they will be defining a losing coalition, just as the Democrats did thirty years ago. In that case the first decade of the new century will see an effort for the Republicans to redefine a competitive position. If, on the other hand, more pragmatic Republicans emerge victorious from the 2000 convention, the first decade of the new century will be one in which two parties struggle to capture the center of the nation's ideological spectrum. In that case, the unanswered question will revolve around the reactions of disappointed ideologues.

C. The Tone of Twenty-first Century Politics

One further question about the future of American politics in the decade ahead remains to be discussed. Citizens and politicians alike have become increasingly distressed about the tone of the political debate.

Evidence of this dissatisfaction is rampant. Citizens respond to poll questions that they are cynical, that they do not like the tone of campaigns, that they will not vote because of how candidates come across. Potential candidates decide not to run, in part at least because they do not want to face the negativity of a campaign and because they do not want to be associated with that negativity. Those in office decry the lack of civility among officeholders as they go about the nation's business.

Friends of Texas governor George W. Bush (R) were asked what factors he was considering, in the fall of 1998, as he decided whether or not to enter the Republican presidential nominating contest:

> It's not the past as much as [Bush saying], "I don't really want to put up with this."
>
> He is seriously enjoying the quality of his own life right now and enjoying the quality of the politics he's practicing, which is bipartisan and aimed at getting things done. I think the question for him is, "Is there anything I can do differently to change the [political] environment." (Balz 1998c)

The Annenberg Public Policy Center Issue Advocacy Advertising Reports conclude that express advocacy advertisements are distinctly more negative than candidate advertisements—and their role in competitive campaigns is on the rise (Magleby and Holt 1999, 27). All of these factors point in one direction, a negative one. The health of the polity and the efficacy of the roles played by the electoral process and political parties within that process depend on citizen commitment to America's democracy. Cynical reactions to negative campaigns that depress turnout and lower the probability that those who might best lead the nation will even enter political life are a cancer on the body politic. At various points in this text, possible reforms have been examined. None can be more important than reform in the way politicians practice their craft and journalists report on it so that citizen apathy and distrust can be converted into active involvement.

III. CONCLUDING REMARKS

It is of more than passing interest to some that the political scientists who are vocal advocates for stronger political party organizations have themselves been active in politics (Bill Crotty, David Price, Tom Cronin, Bob Huckshorn, John Bibby, Kay Lawson, Larry Longley, Paul Herrnson, and this author, to name a few). That link is not coincidental. Those who become involved in the political process are acutely aware that many citizens simply do not care. They are also aware that policies pursued by government officials often have direct and immediate impact on those citizens. Further, it is difficult to know how the people feel on lots of issues, certainly in advance of the time at which decisions must be made. Politicians hear from the citizens who are most concerned, but not from a wide variety of citizens.

So the search begins for a mechanism to involve more people in the political process, particularly in the electoral process because it is the vital link between the citizens and their government. And the institution of party readily stands out. For all its imperfections, so vividly described by political analysts and journalists of all types, party remains the vital linking institution. When parties are weak, the linkage role of the electoral process is not played well. When they are strong, a possibility exists that representation and accountability will follow. Other institutions—the media, interest groups—have tried to pick up the slack, but they have done so without notable success. And thus we are drawn back to the conclusion that if political parties did not exist, someone would have to invent them. Since ours already exist, we should get on with the work of making them function more productively.

Notes

Chapter 1

1. The Seventeenth Amendment to the Constitution was ratified in 1913. Prior to that time, U.S. senators were elected to the Senate by members of the state legislatures.
2. Feinstein's decision may well have been prescient. Checchi, the former chairman of Northwest Airlines, spent approximately $40 million of his own money in the Democratic gubernatorial primary. Congresswoman Jane Harman, who was encouraged to enter the race by Feinstein after she demurred, spent nearly half that much, again most of it family money. They finished second and third respectively to Lt. Gov. Gray Davis, who himself spent nearly $10 million, an amount that would have been a record in a primary election had it not been so far exceeded by his two opponents.
3. As each state has two U.S. senators, this provision means that senatorial elections are held in roughly two-thirds of the states and not in the other states during each national election.
4. In *Baker v. Carr*, 369 U.S. 186 (1962), the Court ruled that Tennessee's legislative districts, which had not been redrawn since 1901, despite major demographic changes in the state, violated the constitutionally guaranteed rights of those citizens living in highly populated areas because they were less well represented than those living in less densely populated areas. This ruling set a precedent for changes in districts throughout the country and led to a series of rulings on how districts could legitimately be drawn (Perry 1991).
5. Some states have also attempted to impose limitations on the number of terms their representatives and senators can serve in Congress, but these efforts have been deemed unconstitutional.
6. This "double election" was permissible only because of the precedent set when Lyndon Johnson ran for vice president under John F. Kennedy in 1960 and simultaneously sought reelection to the Senate. The state legislature passed a special law in 1960 to permit Johnson to seek both offices and it applied to Bentsen as well. The law has since been repealed.
7. These numbers include the eight Louisiana members of Congress who faced reelection in that state's unique nonpartisan primary held in September.
8. Most of the prominent elections in the United States are partisan elections, that is, contests between nominees of political parties. However, when all contests for office are considered, including local contests for positions such as city council, selectman, and

even less prominent positions, such as trustee of the local library, nonpartisan elections outnumber those in which party is involved. This text will only deal with partisan elections, though a wide variety of those will be mentioned.

9. The distinction between independent candidacies and third-party candidacies is an important one and will be discussed in chapters 8, 10, and 11. In Anderson's case the situation was further complicated because his designation on the ballot differed from state to state. See Bibby and Maisel (1998).
10. Anderson eventually decided that he would not run in 1984, preferring to build the organizational base for his "party," a task that proved fruitless.
11. Party systems are described, classified, and criticized in many scholars' works, for example, Chambers and Burnham (1975), Sartori (1976), and Sundquist (1983).
12. Silbey (1991; 1998) applies a very different definition of party system, emphasizing the centrality of parties to the electoral process. See chapter 2.
13. The Holbrook and Van Dunk (1993) index is not included because they only measure degree of competitiveness and are not concerned with which party has an advantage. Thus their index itself is not directly relevant here, though their criticism of other measures is.
14. Richard Fenno (1978, chap. 1) writes at length of how politicians judge public opinion and about the ways in which they reach their judgments. Jacobson (1980, 108) suggests that this process might well be a natural act, even for seemingly safe incumbents.
15. And even the necessity of party nomination does not apply in some states for some offices. Although Nebraska's state legislature is the only such body with nonpartisan elections, Louisiana has a "nonpartisan" primary for Congress and statewide offices. See chapter 7.
16. Some state party organizations have on occasion been so opposed to the national candidate that they have denied him a place on the ballot. This happened throughout the South to Harry Truman in 1948 and in two states to John Kennedy in 1960. State party organizations placed the names of Strom Thurmond (1948) and Harry Byrd (1960) on the ballot instead of those of the national standard-bearers. The problems of ballot access for even these nominees pales in comparison to those faced by "independent" candidates like George Wallace in 1968 or John Anderson and Barry Commoner in 1980. However, ballot access rules for independent and minor-party candidates were changed considerably as a result of the legal as well as political battle fought by Ross Perot in 1992.
17. For a further discussion of soft money and funding of presidential campaigns, see chapters 10–11.

CHAPTER 2

1. The best description of the history of party organization per se in America is found in Mayhew (1986).
2. I am indebted to David Brady for pointing out this piece of electoral trivia to me.

3. Much of this and the following sections draw heavily on Sundquist (1983). I unapologetically offer this statement as acknowledgment of the debt that all of us owe to Sundquist's impressive scholarship.
4. Mayhew's (1986) discussion of traditional party organizations is particularly important on this point.
5. Pomper (1973, 104) describes the 1896 election as a "converting," not a realigning, election because the same party maintained majority status although the electoral coalition changed.
6. Others would argue that Axelrod's analysis is flawed in that it fails to incorporate geography. For example, blacks might not have made as significant a contribution to the New Deal coalition nationally as they did in some specific and important geographic areas.
7. It should be noted that membership in these groups is overlapping. Thus Catholic union members who live in one of the twelve largest metropolitan areas would be counted in all three groups.

CHAPTER 3

1. It should be noted that all "machines" are not necessarily alike. The southern Democratic machines of Long and Talmadge are clear examples of very personal organizations, which emerged largely because of the powerful demagogic appeals of their leaders. See Steinberg (1972) and Williams (1969).
2. Roraback was the most powerful figure in Connecticut politics from the early 1910s until the New Deal; he remained the most important Republican in the state until his death in 1937. The Democrats took over the state in the 1930s; Bailey took over leadership of the state committee in 1946 and built a powerful organization that persisted until his death in 1975.
3. To a large extent what the political science community knows about state-level organizations—and what the remainder of this section draws on—comes from the Party Transformation Study conducted by Cornelius P. Cotter, James L. Gibson, John F. Bibby, and Robert J. Huckshorn about a decade ago, and by a subsequent confirming study conducted by the Advisory Commission on Intergovernmental Relations. Those interested in pursuing this topic further are directed to Bibby (1990); Bibby et al. (1983); Conlan, Martino, and Dilger (1984) for the Advisory Commission Study; Cotter and Bibby (1980); Cotter et al. (1984; 1989); Gibson, Cotter, Bibby, and Huckshorn (1983; 1985); Huckshorn (1991); and Huckshorn, Gibson, Cotter, and Bibby (1986).
4. I am indebted to Paul Herrnson for reminding me that party endorsement can be the "kiss of death" in some states and in areas of other states. Democrats in Massachusetts and New York have been made painfully aware of this in recent years.
5. To be technically accurate, the national conventions stand atop the pyramid. However, the conventions come together only once every four years, and the national committees are the ongoing symbols of the national party organizations.
6. The addition of representatives from American Samoa, the District of

Columbia, Guam, Puerto Rico, and the Virgin Islands brings the total membership of the RNC to 165. From 1952 to 1968, the RNC membership reflected Republican voting strength in the most recent elections; this scheme was abandoned with a return to the principle of state equality after the 1968 election.

7. These at-large members and two additional vice chairs were added to the DNC in 1988, primarily to include the followers of unsuccessful presidential candidate Jesse Jackson.
8. The RNC also has an Executive Committee that includes the Executive Council and the officers of auxiliary organizations, e.g., the Young Republican National Federation, the National Republican Heritage Council (ethnics), the Republican Labor Council, and Republican elected officials' organizations and others whose activities the RNC is trying to coordinate with its own. The Executive Committee is advisory to the chair and has no formal powers within the party.
9. Usage here follows the *Rules of the Republican Party*, adopted by the Republican National Convention in New Orleans, August 16, 1988.
10. Pennsylvania's Democratic governor Robert R. Casey, after some delay, appointed Harris Wofford to replace Heinz until the time of the special election. The Democratic State Committee nominated Wofford as its candidate in that special election, by acclamation, on June 1, before Judge Cahn's ruling. The relatively unknown Wofford was considered an underdog to Thornburgh. Any delay in the special election was to Wofford's advantage, as it gave him more time to spread his name throughout the state.

CHAPTER 4

1. To demonstrate just how close elections can be, consider the New Hampshire election for the U.S. Senate in 1974. In the race between Congressman Louis Wyman, the Republican nominee, and John Durkin, the Democrat, Wyman was first thought to be the winner, by 355 votes. After a recount, Durkin was declared the winner by *ten votes* out of nearly 300,000 cast. Many ballots were challenged by both sides as having been improperly cast. After seven months of dispute, the decision was made to have a new election, as no fair way could be determined to ascertain who had really won. Durkin won the special election but served only one term before losing to Warren Rudman by the "overwhelming" margin of 17,000 votes.
2. Arguments over the extension of the Voting Rights Act were effectively ended on June 23, 1982, when the Voting Rights Act was extended an additional twenty-five years.
3. Currently, one must be a resident for thirty days within a state to be eligible to vote in a presidential election. About half of the states have month-long residency requirements for state and local elections; Arizona, with its fifty-day requirement, is the only state that requires more than one month; the rest have no specified time of residency required. Additionally, criminals and those deemed mentally incompetent are prohibited from voting in all states.
4. This debate also points to the cumulative way in which a discipline in-

forms itself. A careful review of this literature reveals concern with normative questions, with pragmatic consequences of those normative questions, and with methodological controversies over how to answer the important questions posed.

5. The 1988 Florida Senate race, cited earlier in this chapter, also illustrates the difficulty in providing simple explanations for complex phenomena. Supporters of Democrat MacKay also claim that the form of the ballot used in this particular race might well have resulted in some of their potential supporters leaving the Senate election blank on their ballots. Although the Democrats did not complain about the ballot form before the fact, this post hoc explanation of the high "drop-off," i.e., people who voted in the presidential election at the top of the ballot but not the senatorial election further on down, demonstrates how difficult it is to determine the exact cause of failure to vote.
6. Some claimed that people would take advantage of a holiday to travel or vacation and that the effect would therefore be the exact opposite of that desired.
7. The National Election Study stopped asking these questions after 1988 and thus the data end at that point.
8. We also know that there is a problem in distinguishing voters from nonvoters in surveys. Typically survey data overrepresent actual voters by as much as 20 percent. Citizens are not anxious to admit they do not vote. (See Gant and Luttbeg 1991, 84–86; Hill and Luttbeg 1980, 79–80; Sigelmam 1982.)
9. Verba and Nie do not ask similar questions and thus do not identify this group.
10. Milbrath (Milbrath and Goel 1977, 15) made distinctions among protesters by race and other factors; however, this is not a major part of his finding and might well be peculiar to the situation in Buffalo in the late 1960s.

CHAPTER 6

1. This information is available at *http://www.fec.gov*.

CHAPTER 7

1. Certainly, how politicians view career progression can change during an individual's career as a result of political decisions or personal decisions. See Stone, Maisel, and Maestas (1998) and the work evolving from the Candidate Emergence Project.
2. I am indebted to Larry Sabato for information on Virginia politics. It should also be noted that a number of states use party conventions either for endorsing purposes (see section III.A.2 or for building solidarity within the party.
3. When a majority is required to win a nomination or an election, the winner must poll one half plus at least one of the votes cast. When a plurality is required, the winner is the candidate who polls more votes than any

other candidate, even if that number is considerably less than half. Some systems require that a plurality winner must have received a certain percentage of the total votes cast or a runoff between the top two (or perhaps among the top three) finishers is held to determine the winner. See section III.C. "Who Wins."

4. To further demonstrate the variety of state experiences, the Democratic party charter in Massachusetts requires that a candidate receive 15 percent of the vote at the convention to appear on the primary ballot; despite the fact that this provision is *not* in state law, the Massachusetts courts have upheld the provision, so that it has the same impact as if it were law. (See Jewell and Olson 1988, 97.)
5. For some endorsed candidates, avoiding the label as the candidate of the party "bosses" is more difficult than it is for others. The 1998 Democratic candidate for governor of Connecticut was Barbara Kennelly, who was the candidate of the party leaders. She is also the daughter of the most well-known Connecticut Democratic leader of the current era, John Bailey, who served not only as Connecticut party chair but also as chair of the Democratic National Committee during the Kennedy administration.
6. Due to a court ruling, the Louisiana nonpartisan primary was held on the date of the general election in 1998, November 3. If any candidates did not win a majority on that date, a runoff would have been held. However, all seven district elections were settled with a majority winner on November 3.
7. Each of the major parties failed to nominate a candidate in one congressional district.
8. It is worth noting that Cunningham drew only 6 percent of the vote against the immensely popular Rangel.
9. These states are Connecticut, Kentucky, Maine, Maryland, Nebraska, Nevada, New Hampshire, New Jersey, New Mexico, New York, and Oklahoma.
10. These states are Arizona, Colorado, Delaware, Florida, Iowa, Kansas, Massachusetts, North Carolina, Ohio, Oregon, Pennsylvania, Rhode Island, South Dakota, West Virginia, and Wyoming.
11. These states show the difficulty and futility of attempting to classify the wide variety of state systems into a small number of categories. Carr and Scott (1984) and Jewell and Olson (1988) classify these states as having open primaries because of the ease with which one can vote in either party's primary. However, Carr and Scott (but not Jewell and Olson) place Rhode Island in the category of open primary state, despite the fact that the state maintains party enrollment lists and prospective primary voters must change three months before a primary if they wish to participate in a primary of a party other than the one in which they last voted. This is clearly more restrictive than the rules in some of the other states Carr and Scott classified as closed.

    The states that require party registration of this type are Alabama, Arkansas, Georgia, Illinois, Indiana, Mississippi, Missouri, South Carolina, Tennessee, Texas, and Virginia.
12. The open primary states are Hawaii, Idaho, Michigan, Minnesota, Montana, North Dakota, Utah, Vermont, and Wisconsin.
13. The Louisiana primary, in which all candidates appear on one ballot, is a variation of the blanket primary. It differs in that the result carries over to

the general election if any candidate polls a majority of the primary votes. See section III.A.

14. Orchestration of a concerted effort to nominate the weakest opponent for Lundgren would still be very difficult.
15. In 1989 North Carolina amended its runoff primary law to lower the threshold to 40 percent. Furthermore, the second-place finisher must request a runoff. In 1992, in the newly created majority minority first district, Walter Jones, the only white candidate in a six-person field, led the primary field with 38 percent of the vote. The runner-up, Eva M. Clayton, won the primary runoff with 55 percent of the vote, beating Jones by 8,000 votes. Three of the primary candidates openly endorsed Clayton. Jones was on the defensive for most of the campaign, accused of trying to thwart black political aspirations. He denied this and yet tried to get on the ballot the following November as an independent, an action deemed illegal under North Carolina law.
16. This controversy has carried over to the 2000 census. The Census Bureau wanted to conduct the entire census using sampling techniques that they claimed would increase the accuracy of the count. Others disagreed, arguing that the Constitution called for an actual enumeration. The Supreme Court sided with the latter position and ruled that the 2000 census must be conducted using an actual count of citizens for reapportionment and using a sampling technique for determining the population for other purposes, e.g., the allocation of funds to states for various program redistricting purposes. The decision did present the Census Bureau with the option of using a sampling technique for determining the population for other purposes, e.g., the allocation of federal funds among the states.
17. The means of redistricting is set by state law. Some states have special commissions for the purpose. Often the courts are a last resort if the political institutions cannot resolve conflicts.
18. Provision calling for a runoff election if no nominee polls 40 percent of the primary vote. This provision was struck down by a federal court that accepted the argument that the runoff provision unfairly discriminated against minorities and thus violated the Constitution and the Voting Rights Act. However, that decision was reversed by the circuit court of appeals. Similarly, the Arkansas runoff primary provision was struck down by a three-judge panel of the court of appeals but reinstated by the entire court sitting *en banc.* I am indebted to Charles Bullock for these examples.
19. It should also be noted that there are fewer Republican primaries than Democratic primaries for similar offices in similar states. This phenomenon deserves further study.
20. Party officials—county chairs, state and county committee members, ward and precinct leaders, and the like—are frequently not well known. Why they seek and accept such positions is a most interesting question, the answer to which varies significantly from locale to locale and individual to individual. In any case, one of the principal responsibilities they undertake is to assure that their party is represented on the general election ballot.
21. One could make the subgroup smaller still. Primary contests could be divided into those involving serious opposition and those in which the opposition is marginal or frivolous. Candidates have a sense of this distinction in advance, but analysts have trouble determining who is serious and who

is frivolous until some additional information is added, e.g., how much money a candidate can raise, what kind of organizations or endorsements a candidate can attract, etc. Because these judgments are essentially subjective, this differentiation will not be pursued in this discussion.

22. It should be noted that ten or more incumbents were defeated in primaries in 1982, 1972, and 1962 as well.
23. Fitzgerald won the Republican primary and went on to beat Senator Moseley-Braun in the general election, the only senatorial challenger to beat an incumbent Democrat. However, most analysts feel that Senator Moseley-Braun's performance in office and a scandal from which she had to defend herself in the campaign's closing days had more to do with her defeat than did Fitzgerald's ideological purity.

CHAPTER 8

1. Before we proceed any further, we should recognize that this assumption is, in all likelihood, not supportable. Few politicians really understand the process into which they are entering; even experienced politicians make decisions about campaigns in spite of information that would lead a rational person to another conclusion (Hershey 1984; Maisel 1982; 1986).
2. Exceptions to this generalization include a politician's race for office in order to increase name recognition and visibility for a future race and/or a politician's willingness to run a seemingly futile race in order to assure that a respectable candidate is fielded. The candidate in the latter instance earns many IOUs from the party.
3. Obviously one key factor is whether one must give up a current office to run for another office. In most cases this is so, but exceptions exist. For example, as noted earlier, five states hold state elections in odd-numbered years and thus terms for state legislature do not expire when congressional elections are held.
4. The candidate is not an incumbent. Incumbents have all faced this problem at some point—when they first sought the office. They are now in the position of a candidate seeking to stay in the same office. By and large, their campaign tactics were dictated by what worked well the last time.
5. This discussion does not deal with financial contributions by organized groups. These contributions are often critical for campaigns. However, they are used to pay for campaign techniques that in turn substitute for candidate time or otherwise transmit the candidate's message. These techniques and the entire question of campaign financing were discussed briefly in chapter 6 and will be returned to in chapter 11.
6. The role of third-party candidates in state and local elections will be discussed in detail.
7. In areas with strong party organizations, party volunteers still carry "sample ballots," urging supporters to vote for all candidates in their party. This technique is particularly effective in areas dominated by one party or the other, or in areas in which the organization can effectively target households in which their supporters live (Hicks 1998).
8. There is a growing literature on campaign consultants. See, as examples,

Johnson-Cartee and Copeland 1997; Medvic and Lenart 1997; Petracca 1989; Shea 1996; Sabato 1981.

9. Computerized telephone messages have been used in many campaigns. However, campaign organizers must be sensitive to citizens' dissatisfaction with obviously impersonal attempts to contact them. This technique has recently been abandoned in many parts of the country for this reason.
10. As is always the case with data concerning U.S. Senate elections, it is necessary to interpret percentages with great caution. Although percentaging among 435 House elections make good sense, presenting percentage data when the total number involved is generally less than thirty can lead to misinterpretation. The number of incumbent senators seeking reelection in any campaign is small enough that analysis of individual races is often most appropriate.
11. The very small numbers involved in some years is the reason that I have presented raw numbers rather than percentages. Following the logic in note 10, above, percentaging would be even more likely to lead to misinterpretation because of the very few cases examined.
12. The caveat that increased competition is not likely in strong one-party areas needs to be added, though it is rarely raised by those arguing for term limits.
13. It is worth noting that the momentum for term limits seems to have abated. After they captured majority status in the Congress in 1994, the Republicans attempted to pass a constitutional amendment mandating term limits, as they had promised in the Contract with America. That amendment did not pass; it was opposed by a significant number of Republicans. As the 2000 congressional elections approach, Republican representatives first elected on the Contract face the inevitability of the self-imposed three-term limit on which they originally campaigned. Many have had second thoughts but are faced with a dilemma—to leave the House or to risk giving an opponent a campaign issue, the broken term-limit promise.
14. Nebraska's state legislature differs from those in all of the other states in two regards. First, legislators are elected on nonpartisan ballots, i.e., they do not run under a party label. Second, the legislature has only one house; it is unicameral, not bicameral, as are the other state legislatures as well as Congress.
15. As noted earlier, in 1996 Collins and Brennan again faced each other, in a race to succeed retiring Senator William Cohen. Collins won that race, perhaps finally ending Joseph Brennan's long, and at times illustrious, career in Maine electoral politics.
16. In Ventura's case, the Minnesota campaign finance law, which restricted the amounts the major-party candidates could spend, worked in the Reform party candidate's favor. He was unable to secure loans to spend money until late in the campaign. By the time Ventura was viewed as a serious candidate and had money to advertise, his opponents had already committed most of their money. Thus the playing field tilted to his advantage. I am indebted to former Congressman Bill Frenzel of Minnesota for this insight into his home state's politics.
17. State law can make a difference in the impact of third-party candidacies. In New York State, as discussed in chapter 7, candidates can run on more than one party label at the same time. If that is the case, their *total* vote is the

one that is counted, i.e., their votes on different labels are added together. In that situation, third parties use the leverage of either giving or refraining from giving an extra line on the ballot as a means to convince candidates to adopt certain policy positions. To counter the influence of third parties, or in some cases to supplement that influence, many candidates run as "independents" as well as on party lines, in the same election. Although the "independent" label might appear oxymoronic, candidates believe that some voters will support them on that label, rather than as a candidate of a party, in order to show lack of support for the parties themselves.

18. One defeated congressional challenger has concluded, "No one can win a congressional seat unless he is willing to campaign full-time twice, knowing that he will lose the first time. Anyone who is willing to do that must be crazy." The reader can draw his or her own conclusion about what that statement says about successful congressional candidates.
19. A corollary of this strategy is that a candidate whose chances do not appear strong must look for how events could break so that he or she would have a chance. He or she seeks the positive interpretation. More votes mean a "symbolic" (if not an actual) triumph, and enhanced credibility for future campaigns.

CHAPTER 9

1. Much of this discussion focuses on the Democratic party because most recent reform efforts have been made by Democrats. Republicans have been more satisfied with their procedures but have had to change as well because many of the reforms implemented by the Democrats involved changes in state laws affecting both parties.
2. The post-1972 commission was originally an effort to bring labor back into the fold of the Democratic party. Leonard Woodcock, president of the United Auto Workers, was originally named as the commission chair; Barbara Mikulski, a little-known Baltimore city council member, was named as vice chair. Woodcock resigned, and the leadership role fell to Mikulski. As she has subsequently demonstrated in her congressional career, the fiery Mikulski proved an able and independent leader, not at all what Democratic National Chairman Robert Strauss had in mind when he named her.
3. As a result of this decision, ratified by the Supreme Court in *Democratic Party of the United States v. Wisconsin*, 450 U.S. 107 (1980), Wisconsin and other states hold "beauty contest" open primaries that have no role in determining the composition of the state's delegation to the national convention; the delegations are chosen through a caucus-convention system.
4. When Senator Kennedy challenged President Carter in 1980, he claimed that delegates pledged early in the process to Carter were nothing but "robots" by the time of the convention, unable to exercise independent judgment. The Kennedy campaign forced a vote on a rules change that would have freed the delegates to vote their conscience. However, on that vote the Carter delegates held firm, demonstrating that they were not mere robots but rather true Carter loyalists.
5. The ingenuity of state party officials to devise rules and systems to their benefit seems unbounded. In 1984 some states used a system in which the

plurality winner of a primary was given a bonus delegate (or more) for winning the primary while the remaining delegates were allocated in accord with the presidential preference of those voting. These primaries were thus dubbed "winner take more."

6. Once again this change wrought by Democratic party officials in the various states had an impact on the Republican nominating process, even though the Republicans played little role in its implementation. Changes in state law, even if pushed by only one party, affect both.
7. Missouri held its caucuses on March 9; Buchanan in fact edged Dole in those caucuses, though the estimated turnout was only 10,000 (Stanley in Nelson 1997, 22).
8. Of the others, one resigned in disgrace (Agnew), one was an appointed vice president who had earlier sought the presidential nomination of his party (Rockefeller), and one is running in 2000 (Quayle).
9. John Connally, former governor of Texas who became famous when he was shot in the motorcade with President Kennedy and later switched to the Republican party (serving as President Nixon's secretary of the Treasury), did so in 1976. Connally felt that his only chance for success was to outspend and thus outadvertise all his opponents. He felt, correctly, that he could raise a good deal of money from his Texas oil friends and the big-business connections he had cemented during his tenure as Treasury secretary. He was wrong in believing that he could parlay that money into a successful campaign. When Connally withdrew from the race, he had won only one delegate who, when interviewed on television at the Republican National Convention, was kiddingly referred to as the "$6,000,000 delegate."
10. Many candidates in recent years have campaigned extensively before the time when they announced their candidacy and/or federal funds have became available. The money that some candidates have used has been raised by independent candidate-sponsored political action committees. These PACs have raised and spent significant amounts of money, giving a platform to the candidate, staffing a nascent organization, and preparing for a major campaign. For example, Walter Mondale's PAC was called the Committee for the Future of America; Ronald Reagan's, Citizens for the Republic; Howard Baker's, the Republican Majority Fund; and Ted Kennedy's, the Fund for a Democratic Majority. See Corrado (1992). Virtually all of those considering a campaign for the presidency in the year 2000 had established leadership PACs in 1998 or early 1999. For example, Vice President Gore's PAC was called Leadership '98; former New Jersey senator Bill Bradley's, Time Future Inc.; former vice president Dan Quayle's, Campaign America; and former Tennessee governor and secretary of education Lamar Alexander's, Campaign for a New American Century.
11. Early poll results also have an impact on the ability to raise money. When Michael Dukakis approached his principal fund-raiser, Robert Farmer, to ask if enough money could be raised to wage a viable campaign, Farmer first assured the governor that it could be done—he added the caveat that he had never raised money for someone who stood at 1 percent in the polls before (Black et al. 1988).
12. The Clinton campaign used another extremely effective technique in the 1992 primary campaign, again seeking to communicate directly with the voters. The campaign mailed approximately 30,000 campaign-produced

videotapes to potential undecided voters in order to rebut personal attacks on the candidate. Polling results showed that those who in fact viewed these positive biographical tapes voted overwhelmingly for Clinton (Arterton 1993).

13. In point of fact, candidates often stay in one round of primaries after they know they have no chance of winning because the functioning of the federal financing of presidential primaries makes it in their interest to do so.
14. There is some evidence that the Gore campaign unsuccessfully attempted a most sophisticated "exceed expectations" strategy. While claiming that he had pulled out of Iowa and New Hampshire to concentrate on southern states, Gore in fact spent some time and expended a good deal of organizational and financial resources in New Hampshire. Apparently he was hoping for a better-than-anticipated New Hampshire finish with consequent press attention benefiting his Super Tuesday campaign in the South.
15. By any definition this is true in the Republican party. As mentioned earlier, in recent years the Democrats have permitted the National Committee and/or specially appointed commissions to change rules between national conventions. Whether these commissions in the DNC can overrule specific votes at a national convention is still in question.

CHAPTER 10

1. In Maine the winner of the First Congressional District's popular vote receives one electoral vote, the winner of the Second Congressional District's popular vote receives one electoral vote, and the winner of the entire state receives two electoral votes. Since this provision has been in effect (1976), Maine has delivered all of its electoral votes to the same candidate every time. Nebraska switched to a similar system for 1992, with the similar result of no splits in electoral vote allocation through 1996.
2. The amounts raised and spent in this manner are discussed in chapter 11.
3. Even in an age of virtually instantaneous communication, candidates want the physical proximity of their closest advisers. Bill Clinton and Al Gore have been the exceptions among presidential and vice presidential candidates in that they have been comfortable with the technological innovations in telecommunications and computers that many feel will lessen the need for advisers to travel with candidates.
4. The drama of the 1992 Clinton campaign experience was captured in the film *The War Room,* released in 1994.
5. "The speech" is as much a part of the arsenal of candidates when they are seeking the nomination as it is after they are nominated. In January 1988, *The New York Times* ran a series in which the set speeches of those seeking the nomination were reprinted. Similar series have appeared in various newspapers across the nation in each subsequent campaign.
6. I am indebted to Anthony Corrado, who has correctly pointed out to me that one advantage Republicans have had in recent presidential campaigns is that they have been able to rely on campaign professionals experienced in presidential campaigns. No group parallel to that assembled to run the Ford campaign—many of whom were active before and would be active again, for Reagan and Bush—has emerged within the Demo-

cratic party. Rather, each Democratic campaign seems to bring in new campaign consultants who must relearn the lessons of the past.

7. Recall note 1 in this chapter.
8. The general procedure for the contingency election is spelled out in the Constitution, in Article 2 and in the Twelfth and Twenty-second Amendments. The specific procedures to be used in the House would be determined by the rules adopted by the House at that time. In a curiosity that has given pause to many analysts, the president would be elected by the House, but the vice president would be chosen by the Senate. In this age of divided government, it would theoretically be possible for the two individuals so chosen to be from different political parties.
9. The 1948 election was the first time Truman had run for president on his own, but he had served all but a few months of the fourth term to which President Roosevelt had been elected in 1944.
10. The Commission on Presidential Debates took over this role from the League of Women Voters, which had sponsored presidential debates in 1976, 1980, and 1984.
11. All of the presidential contenders in 1988—and all of those since then—have become debate veterans. During the primary campaign seasons all of the candidates of the two parties have participated in a large number of debates, with the exception of President Clinton, who was unopposed for his party's renomination.
12. In 1980, one of the key questions was whether third-party contender John Anderson should be included in the debates. The sponsoring organization, the League of Women Voters, ruled that if he were above 15 percent in the polls, he would be included. President Carter refused to participate in one debate in which Anderson took part, feeling that allowing Anderson to appear with the other candidates would give his campaign a legitimacy that would hurt Carter in the long run. Although the audience for the Reagan–Anderson debate was small, the two took turns attacking the absent Carter and essentially forced him to reverse tactics and participate in later debates.
13. The Commission on Presidential Debates determined, on the advice of an expert panel, that Ross Perot could not possibly win the presidential election and therefore did not have to be included in the debates. Perot went to court to try to get this decision reversed, but he was rebuffed. The inclusion or exclusion of non-major–party candidates from debates sponsored by a private organization set up by the two major parties remains an issue of contention. Perot argues, with some evident legitimacy, that no one can be a serious contender who is not included in these debates; therefore the reasoning on which he was excluded is essentially circular. At the same time, it must be noted that these debates would lose their impact if all minor-party candidates were included. Thus the dilemma continues to exist.
14. In addition, a series of minor-party candidates have qualified for the ballot in some states in virtually every modern presidential election. The role of minor-party candidates in American politics is an interesting one, particularly in historical perspective, but these candidates do not have significant impact on either the strategies of the major-party candidates or the outcome of the general election. For those reasons only, they are not dealt with in greater length in this text. (See Bibby and Maisel 1998; Mazmanian 1974.)

15. Students should note that Strom Thurmond, who ran as the Dixiecrat candidate for president from his position as Democratic governor of South Carolina, is the same Strom Thurmond, who more than half a century later, represents South Carolina in the Senate, as a Republican. He is one of the few American politicians who has successfully switched parties and continued in office.
16. I have been using the term "third-party candidate" to refer to any candidate other than one of the two major-party candidates. In fact, the individuals under consideration have been, more often than not, independent candidates, not third-party candidates, because the labels under which they ran were not those of political parties that meet the definition used throughout this text.

CHAPTER 11

1. The recent history of campaign finance reform can be traced through many of the sources mentioned in this chapter (see Mutch 1988; Corrado et al. 1997) and is summarized in Clymer 1998.
2. For more nearly four decades the research into campaign finance practices and reform has been dominated by a small group of political scientists. Alexander Heard of Vanderbilt University set the agenda for much of the work in this area (see Heard 1960). Since 1960 Herbert Alexander, director of the Citizens' Research Foundation, has gathered and analyzed more data on the financing of federal elections than anyone would have thought possible (see Alexander 1971; 1976; 1979a; 1979b; 1980; 1983; 1991; Alexander and Bauer 1991; Alexander and Corrado 1995; Alexander and Haggerty 1987; Citizens' Research Foundation 1997). This quotation is taken from the report of one of the conferences on campaign finance reform, which have been sponsored by CRF and directed by Alexander. Since the Federal Election Commission has been gathering data, more political scientists have begun to look systematically at the ways in which American elections are financed (see particularly Corrado et al. 1997; Corrado 1993; 1995; Jacobson 1980; 1991; and elsewhere; Magleby and Nelson 1990; Malbin 1984b; Mutch 1988; Sabato 1989; Sorauf 1988). Relatively little work has been done on elections at the state or local level, largely because the experiences differ so widely from state to state and data are difficult to gather (but see Gierzynski and Breaux 1991; Gierzynski 1992; Jones 1984; 1991; Malbin and Gais 1998).
3. Thc congressional response dealt only with candidates for federal office (and thus would not have impacted on the Shapp or Rockefeller campaign discussed previously) because of perceived limitations of congressional jurisdiction. Various states responded in different ways at different times (Alexander 1976a; Jones 1984; 1991).
4. It should also be noted that this law did have a significant impact on campaign finance practice. Despite the fact that the Government Accounting Office, which was assigned enforcement responsibilities for presidential campaign compliance with this law, had very little time to gear up for its new role, that office did investigate and prosecute some major violations of the law, including the "laundering" of campaign

funds by President Nixon's Committee to Reelect the President during the 1972 campaign.

5. It should be noted that the public financing of presidential elections, called for in the 1971 act, was not to go into effect until the 1976 election; this provision was part of the agreement necessary to prevent a veto of the legislation by Richard Nixon, who was, of course, a candidate for reelection in 1972.
6. These data should be interpreted with some caution because it is frequently unclear which expenditures are and are not reported in "official" reports.
7. These data do not deflate the averages by including uncontested seats. The data used in this discussion are drawn from FEC reports on the elections over this period. These data, for the period from 1974 to 1990, have been summarized in various sources, including Malbin (1984b) and Ornstein et al. (1998).
8. It should be noted that total spending for Senate campaigns in 1990 and 1996 was less than those in 1988 and 1994, respectively. These figures clearly reflect the fact that elections in some states are more expensive than those in others and that different states had open seats in each of those years.
9. Ruth Jones, an expert on the cost of state and local campaigns, feels that Alexander's estimate is low; on this topic scholars must speculate because of the lack of systematic data. Election officials in a majority of states do not publish aggregate figures on receipts and expenditures for those offices (Sorauf 1988, 288).
10. This rosy conclusion should not be accepted casually. In point of fact, a small number of individuals still manage to give large sums of money, much of it to the political parties in soft money. In addition, wealthy individuals often play the role of broker, bringing their wealthy friends in contact with candidates they support in order to add significantly to those candidates' war chests.
11. Although this effect cannot be seen in the most recent years, because the data are not reported in this fashion, the limit on the size of contributions has remained in place and thus the percentages from large contributors in the more recent elections should not be very different from that reported earlier.
12. By the mid-1980s, the success of some of the more conservative direct-mail fund-raisers had begun to wane. Liberals, using similar techniques, made significant headway in cutting what had been a distinct conservative advantage. See Edsall 1986.
13. It also lists cooperative PACs and PACs for corporations without stock, but these two categories together constitute fewer than 5 percent of all political action committees, in terms of number of committees and/or amounts contributed.
14. The one apparent exception is in 1990, but the total spending went down slightly because of the particular mix of Senate seats contested in that year, as compared with those in 1988.
15. The remaining money, of course, went to candidates in open seats.
16. When the Republicans controlled the Senate, between 1980 and 1986, there was some evidence that PACs were giving more to the Republicans than to the Democrats. Upon careful scrutiny, it was revealed that this

finding reflected the larger number of incumbent Republicans than Democrats whose seats happened to be contested in the years studied (Magleby and Nelson 1990, 82, table 5-3).

17. See Corrado et al., eds. 1997; League of Women Voters 1997; Citizens' Research Foundation 1997; Task Force on Campaign Reform 1998; Kassebaum, Baker, and Mondale 1998.
18. In 1988, neither party had an incumbent running, so both parties had spirited primary campaigns. In 1992, President Bush was challenged by Patrick Buchanan, but the campaign was not one in which large sums were spent. In 1996, though he was without a challenger in his own party, President Clinton spent extensively to jump-start his reelection effort. The Republicans also had a spirited campaign in that race.
19. For example, H. Ross Perot received $29 million in 1996, which is just under half of what the major-party nominees received; the amount was determined because he had received just under half of the average major-party vote in 1992.

CHAPTER 12

1. Radio has never had the same impact on politics that newspapers and television have had, though local politicians do spend a good deal of time trying to be certain that their views are aired on that medium as well.
2. In fairness, it should be noted that the two parties' nominees were known well in advance of these conventions. Thus, even in the absence of party orchestration, there would have been very little drama.
3. What follows draws heavily on Davis 1996, though similar categories have been used in other earlier works. See, for example, Barber 1978.
4. In fact this very question has been asked of many pollsters. Sampling techniques allow pollsters to obtain accurate assessments of the mood of the nation (always within a specified margin of error) by asking questions to relatively few citizens (under 1,500). The same is true for polling within the various states.
5. The discussion to this point deals with candidate advertisements. Party advertisements have similar goals, either for one candidate or for a group of candidates running under the party label. Interest-group advertisements are somewhat more complex and are discussed in section III.B.
6. A variation on paid advertising is the use of advertising that is paid for by the public. Proposals to restrict campaign spending using publicly provided advertising have been around for some time, but none has been implemented in the United States. It is unclear how the form of these ads would or would not vary from those currently in use.
7. The cited headlines reflect both the initial appearance of the article and its continuation inside the newspaper.
8. It should be noted that the total amount spent on issue advocacy advertising in the 1997–1998 period more than doubled that spent in 1995–1996, according to the Annenberg Public Policy Center. However, much of the money spent in 1997–1998 was directed at legislative initiatives such as the tobacco bill and the regulation of telephone access charges, both decided well in advance of election campaigns (Marcus 1998).

CHAPTER 13

1. Congressman Bernard Sanders (I-Vt.) is the only member of the 106th Congress who was not elected as the candidate of one or the other of the major parties. Independents and third-party representatives and senators have been so rare in the modern Congress that most "political junkies" can name them all.
2. Nebraska stands as the exception. The Nebraska legislature, which has only one house (i.e., it is unicameral), is composed of members elected in nonpartisan elections; the party affiliation of candidates does not appear on the ballot for these offices.
3. Similarly, some political scientists have continued to discuss the functioning of political parties in normative and/or prescriptive ways, whereas others have remained more purely analytical.
4. Nebraska, with its nonpartisan legislature, and Maine and Minnesota, with their non-major-party governors, are included in the states with divided government.
5. The losing candidate for Speaker becomes the minority leader. Richard Gephardt (D-Mo.) was the Democrats' nominee for Speaker at the beginning of the 106th Congress; he became minority leader. If Democrats regain control of the House and Gephardt remains a member, it is likely that he will be selected as Speaker. In the election of 1994, Thomas Foley (D-Wash., 1965–1994), Speaker of the House in the 103rd Congress, was beaten in his own bid for reelection, the first sitting Speaker to lose a reelection bid since the Civil War. In the two "most recent" instances in which party control in the House had switched hands prior to 1994 (when the Republicans took control for the Eighty-third Congress, after the 1952 election, and then the Democrats regained control for the Eighty-fourth and subsequent Congresses after the 1954 election), the two party leaders, Sam Rayburn (D-Tex., 1913–1961; Speaker 1940–1947; 1949–1953; 1955–1961) and Joseph W. Martin Jr. (R-Mass., 1925–1967; Speaker 1947–1949; 1953–1955), merely switched positions.
6. The reelection of Jerry Lewis (Calif.) as Republican Conference chairman in 1990 stands as an example of pressure within the party caused by Gingrich's ascension to a leadership position. Lewis's career was typical of a moderate Republican accommodationist who worked his way up the party ladder, serving as chairman of the Research Committee and the Policy Committee before his election as conference chairman in 1988. He saw himself as a future leader. Lewis's view included the party working closely with the White House and with conservative Democrats when that is necessary. He was challenged by Carl Pursell of Michigan. Pursell was backed by Gingrich, who saw Lewis as an obstacle in his own bid to succeed Michel as party leader. But Pursell differed from Lewis mainly over style. He believed that the minority party in the House should be an independent force, not reliant on the White House, even a Republican White House, for policy leadership. In the final vote, members of the Republican Conference narrowly reelected Lewis. The vote showed support for minority leader Michel but gave notice that the Gingrich forces were to be reckoned with (Hook 1990).
7. The Republicans appointed Robert Livingston (La.) as chair of Appropria-

tions, although he was only fifth in line in terms of seniority. In addition Henry Hyde (Ill.) and Thomas Bliley (Va.) were appointed chairs of Judiciary and Commerce, respectively, each leapfrogging over Carlos Moorhead (Calif.), who had been the ranking Republican on each committee in the 103d Congress.

8. When Foley became whip after the Democrats' electoral debacle of 1980, an election that cost his predecessor John Brademas (Ind., 1959–1981) his seat in Congress, the whip was appointed by the Speaker and majority leader. A party rule change now calls for whips to be elected by the Democratic Caucus, a practice used in the selection of Foley's successors, William H. Gray III (Pa., 1978–1991) and the current minority whip, David E. Bonior (Mich.).
9. The Democratic domination of the House was only broken for two brief periods, 1947–1949 and 1953–1955, in that entire time span.
10. Conventional wisdom held that one of the unintended consequences of these reforms was the disaggregation of power to so many junior members (many of them subcommittee chairs) that it was impossible to lead the House. For reasons that Rohde (1991, chaps. 4, 6) astutely points out, party leaders were also given new powers, but they did not effectively exercise their new powers for some time.
11. Coehlo became whip at the remarkably young age of forty-three. He seemed destined for a rapid rise up the leadership ladder—and a long career atop that ladder until he was forced to resign from Congress in 1989 because of allegations that he had used his office and influence inappropriately.
12. One of the interesting asides on Senate politics involves the competition between Lott and his fellow Mississippian Thad Cochran. Lott and Cochran have competed since their college days at the University of Mississippi. They were among the first Republicans elected to the House from Mississippi since the resurgence of the Republican party in the South. Cochran preceded Lott to the Senate and has also sought a leadership role, but he has had to settle for the chairmanship of the Republican Conference as his state colleague reached a higher rung on the leadership ladder. Should Lott leave his position, Cochran would be an obvious candidate to succeed him.
13. Of course, Mitchell's post-Senate life has been anything but private. When Warren Christopher resigned as secretary of state, Mitchell was considered for the position but was passed over for Madeleine Albright. He served as President Clinton's personal envoy to negotiate a peace in Northern Ireland, a task that he relished and performed admirably. For a time he was widely rumored to be the leading candidate to become Commissioner of Baseball. According to many stories, he was warned that the job held no power and that he would have to negotiate with twenty-six spoiled millionaires. Mitchell's reported reply was that would be a large reduction in the number he had to deal with in the Senate.
14. These votes are distinguished from non-party unity votes and consensual votes. Consensual votes are those in which over 90 percent of those present vote for or against a particular issue (Rohde 1991, 51); see also Collie (1986) for a slightly different definition of universalistic votes. Nonparty unity votes are the rest.

15. Party opposition scores, a concept not employed in this discussion, are the percentage of times an individual legislator votes against his or her party on party unity votes. This score is not the residual of party unity scores only because of differences caused by absences.
16. In fact, a good argument can and has been put forth that increases in party unity scores are more a function of the nationalization of political parties (thus muting the impact of southern representatives on Democratic scores) and of party members genuinely sharing views of policy matters than they are of any increased role play by party leaders in Congress.
17. Much of what follows draws heavily on the work of my colleague G. Calvin Mackenzie, especially "Partisan Presidential Leadership: The President's Appointees" (1998).

CHAPTER 14

1. It could be argued that the election of 1988 is another example of this kind of election. In that election, the voters elected a president of the same party as a retiring incumbent. This election is generally interpreted as a reaffirmation of the Reagan legacy, though definitions of that legacy vary. Even with that caveat accepted, the election of George Bush, Ronald Reagan's vice president and designated heir, as Reagan's successor reinforces the point that presidential elections can serve as an effective means to allow citizens to express their view of the policies of the day (Jones 1988a; Pomper 1989a; Shanks and Miller 1988).
2. Although this assumption is untested in the professional literature, it seems reasonable. One piece of evidence comes from a Pew Research Center Poll conducted right after the 1998 election in which voters responded that they had obtained much more of their information about the election from local news broadcasts than had been the case in 1992 or 1996, when presidential elections were being held.
3. Recall from chapter 11 that parties can give money to campaigns in two ways: direct hard money contributions or soft money. Hard money contributions are given to the candidate's campaign committee and are spent as that campaign wishes. Party committees can also spend money independently of a campaign, but that money must be hard money as well. Finally, party committees can issue advocacy advertisements that benefit a campaign; those expenditures can be totally in soft money and must, of course, not only be independent of the candidate's campaign but must not expressly call for that candidate's election of the opponent's defeat. Candidates worry that this kind of advertising by political parties, just as by interest groups, can take control of campaign strategy out of their hands.
4. In 1972 Democratic nominee George McGovern's nomination represented the victory of the liberal wing of the party; his overwhelming defeat in the general election led to a reaction against extreme candidates. McGovern had been dubbed the candidate of "amnesty, acid, and abortion," and the Democratic party was associated with social extremism. The other way to view the Clinton legacy is that he converted the image of the party to a more centrist one, often adapting policy positions previously held by Republicans and making them his own.

References

Abramowitz, Alan I. 1980. "A Comparison of Voting for U.S. Senator and Representative in 1978." *American Political Science Review* 74: 633.

Abramowitz, Alan I. 1981. "Party and Individual Accountability in the 1978 Congressional Election." In *Congressional Elections,* edited by L. Sandy Maisel and Joseph Cooper. Beverly Hills: Sage.

Abramowitz, Alan I., and Kenneth J. Cribbs. 1989. "Don't Worry, Be Happy: Evaluations of Senate and House Incumbents in 1988." Paper presented at the annual meeting of the American Political Science Association, Atlanta, Ga.

Abramowitz, Alan I., Ronald B. Rapoport, and Walter J. Stone. 1991. "Up Close and Personal: The 1988 Iowa Caucuses and Presidential Politics." In *Nominating the President,* edited by Emmett H. Buell Jr. and Lee Sigelman. Knoxville: University of Tennessee Press.

Abramowitz, Alan I., Ronald B. Rapoport, and Walter Stone. 1991a. "Do Endorsements Matter? Group Influences in the 1984 Democratic Caucuses. *American Political Science Review* 85: 193-204.

Abramowitz, Alan I., and Kyle L. Saunders. 1998. "Ideological Realignment in the U.S. Electorate." *Journal of Politics* 6: 634-653.

Abramowitz, Alan I., and Jeffrey Segal. 1991. "Throwing the Bums Back In: The 1990 Congressional Elections." Paper presented at the annual meeting of the Midwest Political Science Association, Chicago.

Abramson, Paul R., and John H. Aldrich. 1982. "The Decline of Electoral Participation in America." *American Political Science Review* 76: 502.

Abramson, Paul R., John H. Aldrich, Phil Paolino, and David W. Rohde. 1995. "Third Party and Independent Candidates in American Politics: Wallace, Anderson, and Perot." *Political Science Quarterly* 110: 347-367.

Abramson, Paul R., John H. Aldrich, and David W. Rohde. 1982. *Change and Continuity in the 1980 Elections.* Washington, D.C.: Congressional Quarterly Press.

Abramson, Paul R., John H. Aldrich, and David W. Rohde. 1995. *Change and Continuity in the 1992 Elections.* Rev. ed. Washington, D.C.: Congressional Quarterly Press.

Abramson, Paul R., John H. Aldrich, and David W. Rohde. 1998. *Change and Continuity in the 1996 Elections.* Washington, D.C.: Congressional Quarterly Press.

Achen, Christopher H. 1989. "Prospective Voting and the Theory of Party Identification." Paper presented at the annual meeting of the American Political Science Association, Atlanta, Ga.

Adamany, David. 1984. "Political Parties in the 1980s." In *Money and Politics in the*

United States, edited by Michael J. Malbin. Washington, D.C.: American Enterprise Institute/Chatham House.

Adamany, David, and George E. Agree. 1975. *Political Money.* Baltimore, Md.: Johns Hopkins University Press.

Adams, William C. 1982. "Media Power in Presidential Elections: An Exploratory Analysis, 1960–1980." In *The President and the Public,* edited by Doris A. Graber. Philadelphia: Institute for the Study of Human Issues.

Adler, Bill, ed. 1964. *The Kennedy Wit.* New York: Citadel.

Adrian, Charles, and Oliver Williams. 1959. "The Insulation of Local Politics under the Nonpartisan Ballot." *American Political Science Review* 53: 1052.

Advertising Age. 1997. "100 Leading National Advertisers." http://www.adage.com

Agranoff, Robert. 1972. *The Management of Election Campaigns.* Boston: Holbrook.

Agranoff, Robert. 1976. *The New Style in Election Campaigns.* Boston: Holbrook.

Aistrup, Joseph D. 1996. *The Southern Strategy Revisited.* Lexington: University of Kentucky Press.

Aldrich, John. 1980. *Before the Convention: Strategies and Choices in Presidential Nomination Campaigns.* Chicago: University of Chicago Press.

Aldrich, John. 1995. *Why Parties? The Origin and Transformation of Political Parties in America.* Chicago: University of Chicago Press.

Aldrich, John, and Richard G. Niemi. 1990. "The Sixth American Party System: The 1960s Realignment and Candidate-Centered Parties." Unpublished manuscript, University of Rochester, New York.

Alexander, Herbert E. 1971. *Financing the 1968 Election.* Lexington, Mass.: Lexington Books.

Alexander, Herbert E. 1972. *Money in Politics.* Washington, D.C.: Public Affairs Press.

Alexander, Herbert E. 1976a. *Financing Politics: Money, Elections, and Political Reform.* Washington, D.C.: Congressional Quarterly Press.

Alexander, Herbert E. 1976b. *Financing the 1972 Election.* Lexington, Mass.: Lexington Books.

Alexander, Herbert E. 1979a. *Financing the 1976 Election.* Washington, D.C.: Congressional Quarterly Press.

Alexander, Herbert E. 1979b. *Political Finance.* Beverly Hills: Sage.

Alexander, Herbert E. 1980. "The Impact of the Federal Election Campaign Act on the 1976 Presidential Campaign: The Complexities of Compliance." *Emory Law Review* 29: 315.

Alexander, Herbert E. 1983. *Financing the 1980 Election.* Lexington, Mass.: D. C. Heath.

Alexander, Herbert E. 1984. "Making Sense about Dollars in the 1980 Presidential Campaigns." In *Money and Politics in the United States: Financing Elections in the 1980s,* edited by Michael J. Malbin. Washington, D.C.: American Enterprise Institute/Chatham House.

Alexander, Herbert E. 1986. *"Soft Money" and Campaign Financing.* Washington, D.C.: Public Affairs Council.

Alexander, Herbert E. 1991. "Financing Presidential Campaigns." In *Political Parties and Elections in the United States: An Encyclopedia,* edited by L. Sandy Maisel. New York: Garland.

Alexander, Herbert E., and Monica Bauer. 1991. *Financing the 1988 Election.* Boulder: Westview.

Alexander, Herbert E., and Anthony Corrado. 1995. *Financing the 1992 Elections.* New York: Sharpe.

Alexander, Herbert E., and Mike Eberts. 1986. *Public Financing of State Elections: A Data Book on Tax-Assisted Funding of Political Parties and Candidates in Twenty States.* Los Angeles: Citizens' Research Foundation.

Alexander, Herbert E., and Brian A. Haggerty. 1981. *The Federal Election Campaign Act: After a Decade of Political Reform.* Washington, D.C.: Citizens' Research Foundation.

Alexander, Herbert E., and Brian A. Haggerty. 1987. *Financing the 1984 Election.* Lexington, Mass.: Lexington Books.

Alger, Dean E. 1989. *The Media and Politics.* Englewood Cliffs, N.J.: Prentice-Hall.

Allsop, Dee, and Herbert F. Weisberg. 1988. "Measuring Change in Party Identification in an Election Campaign." *American Journal of Political Science* 32: 996.

Almond, Gabriel A., and Sidney Verba. 1965. *The Civic Culture.* Boston: Little, Brown.

Alston, Chuck. 1990. "Contest Raises Hard Questions about How NRCC Uses Funds." *Congressional Quarterly Weekly Report* 48: 4000.

Alston, Chuck. 1991. "One Chamber's View of Reform Is Anathema in the Other." *Congressional Quarterly Weekly Report* 49: 1727.

Alt, James E. 1994. *The Impact of the Voting Rights Act on Black and White Voter Registration in the South.* Princeton, N.J.: Princeton University Press.

Alter, Jonathan. 1992. "The Media Mud Squad." *Newsweek,* October 29, 37.

American Political Science Association, Committee on Political Parties. 1950. "Toward a More Responsible Two-Party System." *American Political Science Review* 64.

Andes, Gary J. 1985. "Business Involvement in Campaign Finance: Factors Influencing the Decision to Form a Corporate PAC." *PS: Political Science and Politics* 18: 213.

Ansolabehere, Stephen, Roy Behr, and Shanto Iyengar. 1993. *The Media Game: American Politics in the Television Age.* New York: Macmillan.

Ansolabehere, Stephen, and Shanto Iyengar. 1995. *Going Negative: How Political Advertisements Shrink and Polarize the Electorate.* New York: Free Press.

Anthony, Susan B., and Ida Husted Harper, eds. 1902. *The History of Woman Suffrage.* Vol. 4. Indianapolis: Hollenbeck.

Aoki, Andrew L., and Mark Rom. 1985. "Financing a Comeback: Campaign Finance Laws and Prospects for Political Party Resurgence." Paper presented at the annual meeting of the American Political Science Association, New Orleans.

Appleton, Andrew M., and Daniel S. Ward. 1997. *State Party Profits: A Fifty-State Guide to Development, Organization, and Resources.* Washington, D.C.: Congressional Quarterly Press.

Arsenau, Robert B., and Raymond E. Wolfinger. 1973. "Voting Behavior in Congressional Elections." Paper presented at the annual meeting of the American Political Science Association, New Orleans.

Arterton, F. Christopher. 1978a. "Campaign Organizations Confront the Media-Political Environment." In *Race for the Presidency,* edited by James David Barber. Englewood Cliffs, N.J.: Prentice-Hall.

Arterton, F. Christopher. 1978b. "The Media Politics of Presidential Campaigns: A Study of the Carter Nomination Drive." In *Race for the Presidency,* edited by James David Barber. Englewood Cliffs, N.J.: Prentice-Hall.

Arterton, F. Christopher. 1980. *Media Politics: The News Strategies of Presidential Campaigns.* Lexington, Mass.: D. C. Heath.

Arterton, F. Christopher. 1982. "Political Money and Party Strength." In *The Future of American Political Parties,* edited by Joel L. Fleishman. Englewood Cliffs, N.J.: Prentice-Hall.

Arterton, F. Christopher. 1984. "Campaign Organizations Confront the Media-Political Environment." In *Media Power and Politics,* edited by Doris A. Graber. Washington, D.C.: Congressional Quarterly Press.

Arterton, F. Christopher. 1993. "Campaign '92: Strategies and Tactics of the Candidates." In *The Election of 1992: Reports and Interpretation,* edited by Gerald M. Pomper. Chatham, N.J.: Chatham House.

Asher, Herbert B. 1980. *Presidential Elections and American Politics: Voters, Candidates, and Campaigns since 1952.* Rev. ed. Homewood, Ill.: Dorsey.

Asher, Herbert. B. 1992. *Polling and the Public: What Every Citizen Should Know.* 2d ed. Washington, D.C.: Congressional Quarterly Press.

Associated Press. 1998. "Democrats Assail Republicans for Attack Ads." October 28.

Austin, Erik W., Jerome M. Clubb, William H. Flanigan, Peter Granda, and Nancy H. Zingale. 1991. "Electoral Participation in the United States, 1968–86." *Legislative Studies Quarterly* 16: 145.

Axelrod, Robert. 1972. "Where the Votes Come from: An Analysis of Electoral Coalitions, 1952–1968." *American Political Science Review* 66: 11.

Ayres, Drummond. 1998. "Political Briefing: Greens Abandon One of Their Own." *New York Times,* September 29. On-line edition.

Bach, Stanley, and Steven S. Smith. 1988. *Managing Uncertainty in the House of Representatives: Adaption and Innovation in Special Rules.* Washington, D.C.: Brookings Institution.

Baker, Ross. K. 1989a. *House and Senate.* New York: Norton.

Baker, Ross K. 1989b. *The New Fat Cats: Members of Congress as Political Benefactors.* New York: Priority Press Publications/Twentieth Century Fund.

Balz, Dan. 1991. "The Democrats' 50-State Dash to Nomination." *Washington Post National Weekly Edition,* June 10–16, 11.

Balz, Dan. 1998a. "The Question about John McCain." *Washington Post National Weekly Edition,* July 13, 11.

Balz, Dan. 1998b. "GOP Governors Look to Wield Stronger Hand in Party Affairs." *Washington Post,* November 16, A4.

Balz, Dan. 1998c. "Bush Derides Talk He Fears 2000 Run." *Washington Post,* October 18, A1.

Balz, Dan. 1998d. "Bush Derides Talk He Fears 2000 Run." *Washington Post,* October 15, A1.

Balz, Dan, and David Broder. 1998. "Shaken Republicans Count Losses, Debate Blame." *Washington Post,* November 5, A1.

Banfield, Edward C., and James Q. Wilson. 1963. *City Politics.* Cambridge: Harvard University Press.

Barber, James David. 1978. *The Race for the Presidency: The Media and the Nominating Process.* Englewood Cliffs, N.J.: Prentice-Hall.

Barker, Lucius J. 1988. *Our Time Has Come: A Delegate's Diary of Jesse Jackson's 1984 Presidential Campaign.* Urbana: University of Illinois Press.

Barker, Lucius J., and Ronald Walter, eds. 1989. *Jesse Jackson and the 1984 Presidential Campaign.* Urbana: University of Illinois Press.

Barone, Michael, and Grant Ujifusa. 1981. *The Almanac of American Politics.* Washington, D.C.: Barone.

Barone, Michael, and Grant Ujifusa. 1983. *The Almanac of American Politics.* Washington, D.C.: Barone.

Barone, Michael, and Grant Ujifusa. 1985. *The Almanac of American Politics.* Washington, D.C.: National Journal.

Barone, Michael, Grant Ujifusa, and Douglas Matthews. 1972. *The Almanac of American Politics.* New York: Dutton.

Barone, Michael, Grant Ujifusa, and Douglas Matthews. 1973. *The Almanac of American Politics.* New York: Dutton.

Barone, Michael, Grant Ujifusa, and Douglas Matthews. 1975. *The Almanac of American Politics.* New York: Dutton.

Barone, Michael, Grant Ujifusa, and Douglas Matthews. 1977. *The Almanac of American Politics.* New York: Dutton.

Barone, Michael, Grant Ujifusa, and Douglas Matthews. 1979. *The Almanac of American Politics.* New York: Dutton.

Bartels, Larry M. 1985. "Expectations and Preferences in Presidential Nominating Campaigns." *American Political Science Review* 79: 804.

Bartels, Larry M. 1988. *Presidential Primaries and the Dynamics of Public Choice.* Princeton, N.J.: Princeton University Press.

Basehart, Harry, and John Comer. 1991. "Partisan and Incumbent Effects in State Legislative Redistricting." *Legislative Studies Quarterly* 16: 65.

Baumer, Donald C. 1990. "Senate Democratic Leadership in the 101st Congress." Paper presented at the annual meeting of the American Political Science Association, San Francisco.

Beeman, Richard R. 1991. "Republicanism in the First Party System." In *The Encyclopedia of American Political Parties and Elections,* edited by L. Sandy Maisel. New York: Garland.

Bennett, Stephen E. 1990. "The Uses and Abuses of Registration and Turnout Data." *PS: Political Science and Politics* 23: 166–71.

Bennett, Stephen E., and David Resnick. 1991. "The Implications for Non-Voting for Democracy in the United States." *American Journal of Political Science* 34: 771–803.

Berelson, Bernard, Paul F. Lazarsfeld, and William N. McPhee. 1954. *Voting.* Chicago: University of Chicago Press.

Berke, Richard L. 1998. "New Republican Advertising Blitz Centers on President's Sex Scandal." *New York Times,* October 28, A1.

Berkman, Ronald, and Laura Kitch. 1986. *Politics in the Media Age.* New York: McGraw-Hill.

Berry, Jeffrey M. 1977. *Lobbying for the People.* Princeton, N.J.: Princeton University Press.

Berry, Jeffrey M. 1989. *The Interest Group Society.* Glenview, Ill.: Scott, Foresman.

Beyle, Thad L. 1983. "Governors." In *Politics in the American States,* edited by Virginia Gray, Herbert Jacob, and Kenneth N. Vines. 4th ed. Boston: Little, Brown.

Bibby, John F. 1981. "Party Renewal in the National Republican Party." In *Party Renewal in America,* edited by Gerald Pomper. New York: Praeger.

Bibby, John F. 1986. "Party Trends in 1985: Constrained Advance of the National Party." *Publius* 16: 79.

Bibby, John F. 1990. "Party Organization at the State Level." In *The Parties Respond: Changes in the American Party System,* edited by L. Sandy Maisel. Boulder: Westview.

Bibby, John F. 1991. "Republican National Committee." In *Political Parties and Elections in the United States: An Encyclopedia,* edited by L. Sandy Maisel. New York: Garland.

Bibby, John F. 1998. "State Party Organizations: Coping and Adapting to Candidate-Centered Politics and Nationalization." In *The Parties Respond,* edited by L. Sandy Maisel. 3d ed. Boulder: Westview.

Bibby, John F., Cornelius P. Cotter, James L. Gibson, and Robert J. Huckshorn. 1983. "Political Parties." In *Politics in the American States,* edited by Virginia Gray, Herbert Jacob, and Kenneth N. Vines. 4th ed. Boston: Little, Brown.

Bibby, John F., and Thomas M. Holbrook. 1996. "Parties and Elections." In *Politics in the American States: A Comparative Analysis,* edited by Virginia Gray and Herbert Jacob. 6th ed. Washington, D.C.: Congressional Quarterly Press.

Bibby, John F., and L. Sandy Maisel. 1998. *Two Parties or More?* Boulder: Westview.

Binkley, Wilfred. 1963. *American Political Parties.* 4th ed. New York: Knopf.

Black, Christine, Andrew Blake, John Aloysius Farrell, Thomas Oliphant, and Joan Vennochi. 1988. "The Road to Nomination." *Boston Globe,* May 8, 9, 10, 11, p. 1.

Black, Christine M., and Thomas Oliphant. 1989. *All by Myself: The Unmaking of a Presidential Campaign.* Chester, Conn.: Globe Pequot Press.

Black, Earl, and Merle Black. 1987. *Politics and Society in the South.* Cambridge: Harvard University Press.

Black, Gordon S., and Benjamin D. Black. 1993. "Perot Wins: The Election That Could Have Been." *Public Perpective* 4: 15–16

Bloom, Howard S., and H. Douglas Price. 1975. "Voter Response to Short-Run Economic Conditions: The Assymmetric Effect of Prosperity and Recession." *American Political Science Review* 69: 1240.

Bolingbroke, Lord. [1841] 1976. *The Works of Lord Bolingbroke.* Philadelphia: Carey and Hart. Cited in Giovanni Sartori, *Parties and Party Systems: A Framework for Analysis.* New York: Cambridge University Press.

Bond, Jon R., Cary Covington, and Richard Fleisher. 1985. "Explaining Challenger Quality in Congressional Elections." *Journal of Politics* 47: 510.

Bond, Jon R., and Richard Fleisher. 1990a. "Assessing Presidential Support in the House II—Lessons from George Bush." Paper presented at the annual meeting of the American Political Science Association, San Francisco.

Bond, Jon R., and Richard Fleisher. 1990b. *The President in the Legislative Arena.* Chicago: University of Chicago Press.

Bone, Hugh A., and Austin Ranney. 1976. *Politics and Voters,* 4th ed. New York: McGraw-Hill.

Born, Richard. 1985. "Partisan Intentions and Election Day Realities in the Congressional Redistricting Process." *American Political Science Review* 79: 305.

Boyd, Richard W. 1981. "Decline in U.S. Voter Turnout: Structural Explanations." *American Politics Quarterly* 9: 133.

Brady, David W. 1988. *Critical Elections and Congressional Policymaking.* Stanford, Calif.: Stanford University Press.

Brady, David W. 1990. "Coalitions in the U.S. Congress." In *The Parties Respond: Changes in the American Party System,* edited by L. Sandy Maisel. Boulder: Westview.

Brady, David W. 1993. "The Causes and Consequences of Divided Government: Toward a New Theory of American Politics." *American Political Science Review* 87: 189–195.

Brady, David W., Charles S. Bullock III, and L. Sandy Maisel. 1988. "The Electoral Antecedents of Policy Innovations: A Comparative Analysis." *Comparative Political Studies* 20: 395.

Brady, David W., Joseph Cooper, and Patricia A. Hurley. 1979. "The Decline of Party in the U.S. House of Representatives, 1887–1968." *Legislative Studies Quarterly* 4: 381.

Brady, David W., and John Ettling. 1984. "The Electoral Connection and the Decline of Partisanship in the Twentieth Century House of Representatives." *Congress and the Presidency* 11: 19.

Brady, David W., L. Sandy Maisel, and Kevin M. Warsh. 1994. "An Opportunity Cost Model of the Decision to Run for Congress: Another Contributor to Democratic Hegemony." Paper presented at the annual meeting of the American Political Science Association, New York.

Brady, David W., and Barbara Sinclair. 1984. "Building Majorities for Policy Change in the House of Representatives." *Journal of Politics* 46: 1033.

Brady, David W., and Joseph Stewart Jr. 1986. "When Elections Really Matter: Realignment and Changes in Public Policy." In *Do Elections Matter?* edited by Benjamin Ginsberg and Alan Stone. Armonk, N.Y.: Sharpe.

Bridges, Amy. 1984. *A City in the Republic: Antebellum New York and the Origins of Machine Politics.* New York: Cambridge University Press.

Broder, David S. 1971. *The Party's Over.* New York: Harper and Row.

Broder, David S. 1986. "Campaign Time: Away We Go." *Washington Post National Weekly Edition.*

Broder, David. 1998. "Key Republican Primaries to Focus on Right's Appeal." *Maine Sunday Telegram,* March 8, 3C.

Broder, David, and Ruth Marcus. 1997. "The Debate Over 'Issue Ads,' " *Washington Post National Weekly Edition,* September 29, 6.

Brody, Richard A., and Benjamin I. Page. 1972. "Policy Voting and the Electoral Process: The Vietnam War Issue." *American Political Science Review* 66: 979.

Brunell, Thomas L., and Bernard Grofman. 1998. "Explaining Divided U.S. Senate Delegations, 1788–1996: A Realignment Approach." *American Political Science Review* 92: 391.

Bruno, Jerry, and Jeff Greenfield. 1971. *The Advance Man.* New York: Morrow.

Buchanan, Bruce. 1991. *Electing a President: The Markle Commission Research on Campaign '88.* Austin: University of Texas Press.

Buell, Emmett H., Jr., and James W. Davis. 1991. "Win Early and Often: Candidates and the Strategic Environment of 1988." In *Nominating the President,* edited by Emmett H. Buell Jr. and Lee Sigelman. Knoxville: University of Tennessee Press.

Buell, Emmett H., Jr., and Lee Sigelman. 1991. *Nominating the President.* Knoxville: University of Tennessee Press.

Bullock, Charles S., III. 1988. "Regional Realignment from an Officeholding Perspective." *Journal of Politics* 50: 553.

Bullock, Charles S., III, David W. Brady, and James E. Anderson. 1983. *Public Policy in the 1980s.* Monterey, Calif.: Brooks/Cole Publishers.

Bullock, Charles S., III. 1977. "Explaining Congressional Elections: Differences in Perceptions of Opposing Candidates." *Legislative Studies Quarterly* 2: 295.

Burke, Edmund. 1976. "Thoughts on the Cause of the Present Discontents." In *The Works of Edmund Burke*. Vol. 3. Boston: Little, Brown. Cited in *Parties and Party Systems: A Framework for Analysis,* edited by Giovanni Sartori. New York: Cambridge University Press.

Burnham, Walter Dean. 1970. *Critical Elections and the Mainsprings of American Democracy*. New York: Norton.

Burnham, Walter Dean. 1975. "American Parties in the 1970s: Beyond Party?" In *The Future of Political Parties,* edited by Louis Sandy Maisel and Paul M. Sacks. Beverly Hills: Sage.

Burnham, Walter Dean. 1982. "Shifting Patterns of Congressional Voting Participation." In *The Current Crisis in American Politics,* edited by Walter Dean Burnham. New York: Oxford University Press.

Burnham, Walter Dean. 1991. "Critical Realignment: Dead or Alive?" In *The End of Realignment,* edited by Byron E. Shafer. Madison: University of Wisconsin Press.

Burns, James MacGregor. 1963. *The Deadlock of Democracy: Four-Party Politics in America*. Englewood Cliffs, N.J.: Prentice-Hall.

Butler, David, and Bruce E. Cain. 1991. *Congressional Redistricting: Comparative and Theoretical Perspectives.* New York: Macmillan.

Caddell, Patrick H. 1981. "The Democratic Strategy and Its Electoral Consequences." In *Party Coalitions in the 1980s,* edited by Seymour Martin Lipset. San Francisco: Institute for Contemporary Studies.

Cain, Bruce E. 1984. *The Reapportionment Puzzle.* Berkeley: University of California Press.

Cain, Bruce E. 1985. "Assessing the Partisan Effects of Redistricting." *American Political Science Review* 79: 320.

Cain, Bruce E., and David Butler. 1991. "Redrawing District Lines: What's Going On and What's at Stake?" *American Enterprise* 2: 28.

Cain, Bruce E., John Ferejohn, and Morris Fiorina. 1987. *The Personal Vote: Constituency Service and Electoral Independence*. Cambridge: Harvard University Press.

Cain, Bruce E., D. Roderick Kiewiet, and Carole Uhlaner. 1991. "The Acquisition of Partisanship by Latinos and Asian Americans." *American Journal of Political Science* 35: 390.

Caldeira, Grogory A., and Samuel C. Patterson. 1982. "Contextual Influences on Partisipation in U.S. State Legislative Elections." *Legislative Studies Quarterly* 7: 359.

Caldeira, Grogory A., Samuel C. Patterson, and Gregory A. Markus. 1985. "The Mobilization of Voters in Congressional Elections." *Journal of Politics* 47: 490.

Calvert, Jerry W. 1979. "Revolving Doors: Volunteerism in State Legislatures." *State Government* 52: 174.

Campbell, Angus. 1960. "Surge and Decline: A Study of Electoral Change." *Public Opinion Quarterly* 24: 397.

Campbell, Angus, Philip E. Converse, Warren E. Miller, and Donald A. Stokes. 1960. *The American Voter*. New York: Wiley.

Campbell, James. 1989. "The Cross-Pressured Partisan." Paper presented at the annual meeting of the American Political Science Association, Atlanta, Ga.

Canon, David T. 1990. *Actors, Athletes, and Astronauts: Political Amateurs in the United States Congress.* Chicago: University of Chicago Press.

Canon, David T., Michael Alvarez, and Patrick J. Sellers. 1990. "Contesting Senate Primary Elections: 1972–1988." Paper presented at the annual meeting of the Midwest Political Science Association, Chicago.

Carmines, Edward G., and James A. Stimson. 1989. *Issue Evolution.* Princeton, N.J.: Princeton University Press.

Carmines, Edward G., John P. McIver, and James A. Stimson. 1987. "Unrealized Partisanship: A Theory of Dealignment." *Journal of Politics* 49: 376.

Carr, Craig L., and Gary L. Scott. 1984. "The Logic of State Primary Classification Schemes." *American Politics Quarterly* 12: 465.

Carter, Jimmy. 1982a. *Keeping Faith: Memoirs of a President.* New York: Bantam.

Carter, Jimmy. 1982b. *Public Papers of the President.* Washington, D.C.: U.S. Government Printing Office.

Cassel, Carol A., and Robert C. Luskin. 1988. "Simple Explanations of Voter Turnout." *American Political Science Review* 82: 132.

Catt, Carrie C., and Nettie R. Shuler. 1969. *Woman Suffrage and Politics.* Seattle: University of Washington Press.

Cavanagh, Thomas E. 1979. "Changes in American Electoral Turnout, 1964–1976." Paper delivered at the annual meeting of the Midwest Political Science Association, Chicago.

Cavanagh, Thomas E. 1981. "Research on American Voter Turnout: The State of Evidence." Paper prepared for the Conference on Voter Participation, Washington, D.C.

Ceaser, James, and Andrew Busch. 1993. *Upside-Down and Inside-Out: The 1992 Elections and American Politics.* Lanham, Md.: Rowman and Littlefield.

Ceaser, James, and Andrew Busch. 1997. *Losing to Win: The 1996 Election and American Politics*. Lanham, Md.: Rowman and Littlefield.

Ceaser, James W. 1982. *Reforming the Reforms.* Cambridge: Ballinger.

Center for Responsive Politics. 1985. *Soft Money: A Loophole for the '80s.* Washington, D.C.: Center for Responsive Politics.

Chambers, William N. 1963. *Political Parties in a New Nation: The American Experience, 1776–1809.* New York: Oxford University Press.

Chambers, William N. 1975. "Party Development in the American Mainstream." In *The American Party Systems: Stages of Political Development,* edited by William N. Chambers and Walter D. Bumham. 2d ed. New York: Oxford University Press.

Chambers, William N., and Walter D. Burnham, eds. 1967. *The American Party Systems: Stages of Political Development.* New York: Oxford University Press.

Charles, Joseph. 1956. *The Origins of the American Party System.* Williamsburg, Va.: Institute of Early American History and Culture.

Cigler, Alan J., and Burdett A. Loomis, eds. 1983. *Interest Group Politics.* Washington, D.C.: Congressional Quarterly Press.

Citizens' Research Foundation. 1997. *New Realities, New Thinking: Report of the Task Force on Campaign Finance Reform.* Los Angeles, Calif.: Citizens' Research Foundation, University of Southern California.

Clark, Peter, and Susan Evans. 1983. *Covering Campaigns: Journalism in Congressional Elections.* Stanford, Calif.: Stanford University Press.

Clem, Alan L. 1976. "The Case of the Upstart Republican: The First District of South Dakota." In *The Making of Congressmen: Seven Campaigns of 1974,* edited by Alan L. Clem. North Scituate, Mass.: Duxbury.

Clymer, Adam. 1998. "The Nation: Campaign Finance: The Lateral Pass." *New York Times,* August 9, News of the Week in Studies, sec. 6.

Cohen, Jeffrey E., Michael A. Krassa, and John Hamman. 1991. "The Impact of Presidential Campaigning on Midterm U.S. Senate Elections." *American Political Science Review* 85: 165.

Cohen, Richard E. 1984. "Many Are Skeptical about Jackson's Dual Primary Argument." *National Journal* 922.

Collie, Melissa. 1986. "New Directions in Congressional Research." *Legislative Studies Section Newsletter* 110: 90.

Collie, Melissa P., and David W. Brady. 1985. "The Decline of Partisan Voting Coalitions in the House of Representatives." In *Congress Reconsidered,* edited by Lawrence C. Dodd and Bruce I. Oppenheimer. 3d ed.. Washington, D.C.: Congressional Quarterly Press.

Collie, Melissa P., and Joseph Cooper. 1989. "Multiple Referral and the 'New' Committee System in the House of Representatives." In Lawrence C. Dodd and Bruce I. Oppenheimer, eds., *Congress, Reconsidered,* edited by Lawrence C. Dodd and Bruce I. Oppenheimer. 4th ed. Washington, D.C.: Congressional Quarterly Press.

Commission on Party Structure and Delegate Selection. 1970. *Mandate for Reform.* Washington, D.C.: Democratic National Committee.

Committee on Political Parties of the American Political Science Association. 1950. *Toward a More Responsible Two Party System.* New York: Rinehart.

Common Cause. 1986. *Financing the Finance Committee.* Washington, D.C.: Common Cause.

Congress and the Nation. 1981. Washington, D.C.: Congressional Quarterly, Inc.

Congressional Quarterly Almanac. 1971–1984. Washington, D.C.: Congressional Quarterly, Inc.

Conlan, Tirnothy, Ann Martino, and Robert Dilger. 1984. "State Parties in the 1980s: Adaption, Resurgence, and Continuing Constraints." *Intergovernmental Affairs* 10: 6.

Connolly, Ceci, and Terry M. Neal. 1998. " 'Get Out the Vote' Heard Coast to Coast." *Washington Post,* November 3, A1.

Connolly, Ceci. 1998. "GOP Spends Millions on TV Ads Attacking President's Conduct," *Washington Post*, October 28, A5.

Converse, Philip E., and Richard G. Nierni. 1971. "Nonvoting among Young Adults in the United States." In *Political Parties and Political Behavior,* edited by Williarn J. Crotty, Donald M. Freeman, and Douglas S. Gatlin. 2d ed. Boston: Allyn and Bacon.

Converse, Philip E., and Roy Pierce. 1987. "Measuring Partisanship." *Political Methodology* 11: 143.

Converse, Philip E., and Warren E. Miller. 1969. "Continuity and Change in American Politics: Parties and Issues in the 1968 Election." *American Political Science Review* 63: 1083.

Converse, Philip E., Aage R. Clausen, and Warren E. Miller. 1965. "Electoral Myth and Reality: The 1964 Election." American *Political Science Review* 59: 321.

Converse, Philip E., Angus Campbell, Warren E. Miller, and Donald E. Stokes. 1961. "Stability and Change in 1960: A Reinstating Election." *American Political Science Review* 55: 269.

Cook, Rhodes. 1986. "Democrats Alter Rules Slightly in Effort to Broaden Party Base." *Congressional Quarterly* 44: 2158.

Cook, Rhodes. 1989. "The Nominating Process." In *The Elections of 1988,* edited by Michael Nelson. Washington D.C.: Congressional Quarterly Press.

Cook, Rhodes. 1990. "Most House Members Survive, But Many Margins Narrow." *Congressional Quarterly Weekly Report* 48: 3798–3800.

Cook, Timothy E. 1990. "Thinking of the News Media as Political Institutions." Paper presented at the annual meeting of the American Political Science Association, San Francisco.

Cooper, Joseph, and David W. Brady. 1981. "Institutional Context and Leadership Style: The House from Cannon to Rayburn." *American Political Science Review* 75: 411.

Cooper, Joseph, and William West. 1981. "The Congressional Career in the '70's." In *Congress Reconsidered,* edited by Lawrence Dodd and Bruce I. Oppenheimer. 2d ed. Washington, D.C.: Congressional Quarterly Press.

Cooper, Joseph, David W. Brady, and Patricia A. Hurley. 1977. "The Electoral Basis of Party Voting: Patterns and Trends in the U.S. House of Representatives, 1887–1969." In *The Impact of the Electoral Process,* edited by Louis Maisel and Joseph Cooper. Beverly Hills: Sage.

Copeland, Gary W. 1983. "Activating Voters in Congressional Elections." *Political Behavior* 5: 391.

Corrado, Anthony J. 1991a. "Federal Election Campaign Act of 1971." In *Political Parties and Elections in the United States: An Encyclopedia,* edited by L. Sandy Maisel. New York: Garland.

Corrado, Anthony J. 1991b. "Federal Election Campaign Act Amendments of 1974." In *Political Parties and Elections in the United States: An Encyclopedia,* edited by L. Sandy Maisel. New York: Garland.

Corrado, Anthony J. 1992. *Creative Campaigning: PACs and the Presidential Selection Process.* Boulder: Westview.

Corrado, Anthony J. 1993. *Paying for Presidents: Public Financing in National Elections.* New York: Twentieth Century Fund Press.

Corrado, Anthony J., and Charles M. Firestone. 1996. *Elections in Cyberspace: Toward a New Era in American Politics.* Washington, D.C.: Aspen Institute.

Corrado, Anthony J., and L. Sandy Maisel. 1988. "Campaigning for Presidential Nominations: The Experience with State Spending Ceilings, 1976–1984." Paper presented at the annual meeting of the Western Political Science Association, San Francisco. Occasional Paper nos. 88–84, Center for American Political Studies Harvard University, Cambridge.

Corrado, Anthony J., Thomas E. Mann, Daniel R. Ortiz, Trevor Potter, and Frank J. Sorauf, eds. 1997. *Campaign Finance Reform: A Sourcebook.* Washington, D.C.: Brookings Institution.

Costikyan, Edward N. 1980. *How to Win Votes: The Politics of 1980.* New York: Harcourt Brace Jovanovich.

Cotter, Cornelius P., and John F. Bibby. 1980. "Institutional Developments of Parties and the Thesis of Party Decline." *Political Science Quarterly* 1: 95.

Cotter, Cornelius P., James L. Gibson, John F. Bibby, and Robert J. Huckshorn. 1982. "Party-Government Linkages in the States." Paper delivered at the annual meeting of the American Political Science Association, Washington, D.C.

Cotter, Cornelius P., James L. Gibson, John F. Bibby, and Robert J. Huckshorn. 1984. *Party Organization in American Politics.* New York: Praeger.

Cotter, Cornelius P., James L. Gibson, John F. Bibby, and Robert J. Huckshorn. 1989. *Party Organization in American Politics.* 2d ed. New York: Praeger.

Cotter, Cornelius P., and Bernard C. Hennessy. 1964. *Politics without Power: The National Party Committees.* New York: Atherton.

Coval, Michael. 1984. "The Impact of the 1980 Election on Liberal Political Organization." Honors project presented at Colby College, Waterville, Me.

Cover, Albert D. 1977. "One Good Term Deserves Another: The Advantages of Incumbency in Congressional Elections." *American Journal of Political Science* 21: 523.

Covington, Cary, Richard Fleisher, and Jon R. Bond. 1985. "Explaining Challenger Quality in Congressional Elections." Paper presented at the annual meeting of the Midwest Political Science Association, Chicago.

Cox, Gary, and Samuel Kernell, eds. 1991. *The Politics of Divided Government.* Boulder: Westview.

Cox, Gary W., and Scott Morgenstern. 1993. "The Increasing Advantage of Incumbency in the U.S. States." *Legislative Studies Quarterly* 18: 495.

Cox, Gary W., and Scott Morgenstern. 1995. "The Incumbency Advantage in Multimemember Districts: Evidence from the U.S. States." *Legislative Studies Quarterly* 20: 329.

Crespi, Irving. 1988. *Pre-election Polling: Sources of Accuracy and Error.* New York: Russell Sage Foundation.

Crespi, Irving. 1989. *Public Opinion, Polls, and Democracy.* Boulder: Westview.

Crosby, Stephen. 1998. Personal correspondence with author, September 2.

Croteau, David, and William Hoynes. 1994. *By Invitation Only: How the Media Limit Political Debate.* Monroe, Me.: Common Courage Press.

Crotty, William J. 1968. "The Party Organization and Its Activities." In *Approaches to the Study of Party Organization,* edited by William J. Crotty. Boston: Allyn and Bacon.

Crotty, William J. 1978. *Decision for the Democrats: Reforming the Party Structure.* Baltimore, Md.: Johns Hopkins University Press.

Crotty, William J. 1983. *Party Reform.* New York: Longman.

Crotty, William J. 1985. *The Party Game.* New York: Freeman.

Crotty, William J. 1986. *Political Parties in Local Areas.* Knoxville: University of Tennessee Press.

Crotty, William J., and John S. Jackson III. 1985. *Presidential Primaries and Nominations.* Washington, D.C.: Congressional Quarterly Press.

Crotty, William J., and Gary C. Jacobson. 1980. *American Parties in Decline.* Boston: Little, Brown.

Crouse, Timothy. 1973. *The Boys on the Bus.* New York: Ballantine.

Cunningham, Noble E. 1957. *The Jeffersonian Republicans.* Chapel Hill: University of North Carolina Press.

Cunningham, Noble E. 1965. *The Making of the American Party System, 1789 to 1809.* Englewood Cliffs, N.J.: Prentice-Hall.

Dahl, Robert. 1961. *Who Governs? Democracy and Power in an American City.* New Haven: Yale University Press.

Daley, Steve, and Roger Worthington. 1989. "Senior's Wrath Stings Lobby Protests over Catastrophic Care Law Targets AARP." *Chicago Tribune,* September 3, 1.

Darcy, R., and Sarah Slavin Schramm. 1977. "When Women Run against Men." *Public Opinion Quarterly* 41: 1.

Davidson, Roger H. 1989. "The Impact of Agenda on the Post-Reform Congress." Paper presented at the annual meeting of the American Political Science Association, Atlanta, Ga.

Davidson, Roger H., ed. 1992. *The Post-reform Congress.* New York: St. Martin's.

Davis, James W. 1983. *National Conventions in an Age of Party Reform.* Westport, Conn.: Greenwood.

Davis, Richard. 1996. *The Press and American Politics: The New Mediator.* 2d ed. Upper Saddle River, N.J.: Prentice-Hall.

Dawson, Richard E., and James A. Robinson. 1963. "Inter-Party Competition, Economic Variables, and Welfare Policies in the American States." *Journal of Politics* 25: 265.

Dennis, Jack. 1966. "Support for the Party System by the Mass Public." *American Political Science Review* 60: 600.

Dennis, Jack. 1978. "Trends in Public Support for the American Party System." In *Parties and Elections in an Anti-Party Age,* edited by Jeff Fishel. Bloomington: Indiana University Press.

DeVries, Walter, and Lance Tarrance Jr. 1972. *The Ticket-Splitter: A New Force in American Politics.* Grand Rapids, Mich.: Eerdmans.

Dewar, Helen. 1999. "Senate Democrats Seek an Early Vote on Articles." *Washington Post,* January 21, A1, A16.

Diamond, Edwin, and Stephen Bates. 1984. *The Spot: The Rise of Political Advertising on Television.* Cambridge: MIT Press.

Dionne, E. J., Jr. 1988. "Michigan G.O.P. Snarled in Uncertainty." *New York Times,* B4.

Dodd, Lawrence C., and Sean Q. Kelly. 1990. "The Electoral Consequences of Presentational Style." Paper presented at the annual meeting of the American Political Science Association, San Francisco.

Donovan, Beth. 1991. "Deadlines Not Always Met When Stakes Are High." *Congressional Quarterly Weekly Report* 49: 1776.

Downs, Anthony. 1957. *An Economic Theory of Democracy.* New York: Harper and Row.

Drew, Elizabeth. 1979a. *American Journal: The Events of 1976.* New York: Random House.

Drew, Elizabeth. 1979b. *Senator.* New York: Simon and Schuster.

Drew, Elizabeth. 1981. *Portrait of an Election: The 1980 Presidential Campaign.* New York: Simon and Schuster.

Drew, Elizabeth. 1983. *Politics and Money: The New Road to Corruption.* New York: Macmillan.

Duverger, Maurice. 1951. *Political Parties.* New York: Wiley.

Edsall, Thomas B. 1986. "Conservative Fund-Raisers Hit Hard Times." *Washington Post.*

Edsall, Thomas B. 1988. "The Reagan Legacy." In *The Republican Legacy,* edited by Sidney Blumenthal and Thomas Byrne Edsall. New York: Pantheon.

Edsall, Thomas B., and Ceci Connolly. 1998. "The GOP Is Coming Apart at the Seams." *Washington Post National Weekly Edition,* April 6, 13–14.

Edwards, George C., III. 1980. *Presidential Influence in Congress.* San Francisco: W. H. Freeman.

Edwards, George C., III. 1989. *At the Margin: Presidential Leadership of Congress.* New Haven: Yale University Press.

Edwards, George C., III, and Stephen J. Wayne. 1990. *Presidential Leadership: Politics and Policy Making.* 2d ed. New York: St. Martin's.

Ehrenhalt, Alan, ed. 1984. *Politics in America: Members of Congress in Washington and at Home.* Washington, D.C.: Congressional Quarterly Press.

Ehrenhalt, Alan. 1991. *The United States of Ambition: Politicians, Power and the Pursuit of Office.* New York: Times Books.

Eisenstein, James. 1991. "Pennsylvania's 1990 Legislative Elections: From Virtually No Competition to Low Competition." *Comparative State Politics* 12: 36.

Eismeier, Theodore J. 1985. "The Microeconomy of PACs." Paper presented at the annual meeting of the American Political Science Association, New Orleans.

Eismeier, Theodore J., and Philip H. Pollock III. 1984. "Political Action Committees: Varieties of Organization and Strategy." In *Money and Politics in the United States,* edited by Michael J. Malbin. Washington, D.C.: American Enterprise Institute/Chatham House.

Eismeier, Theodore J., and Philip H. Pollock III. 1985a. "The Microeconomy of PACs." Paper delivered at the annual meeting of the American Political Science Association, Washington, D.C.

Eismeier, Theodore J., and Philip H. Pollock III. 1985b. "An Organizational Analysis of Political Action Committees." *Political Behavior* 7: 192.

Eismeier, Theodore J., and Philip H. Pollock III. 1986. "Strategy and Choice in Congressional Elections: The Role of Political Action Committees." *American Journal of Political Science* 30: 197.

Eldersveld, Samuel J. 1964. *Political Parties: A Behavioral Analysis.* Chicago: Rand McNally.

Eldersveld, Samuel J. 1982. *Political Parties in American Society.* New York: Basic Books.

Entman, Robert M. 1989. *Democracy without Citizens: Media and the Decay of American Politics.* New York: Oxford University Press.

Epstein, Edwin M. 1980. "Business and Labor under the Federal Election Campaign Act of 1971." In *Parties, Interest Groups, and Campaign Finance Laws,* edited by Michael J. Malbin. Washington, D.C.: American Enterprise Institute for Public Policy Research.

Epstein, Leon D. 1967. *Political Parties in Western Democracies.* New York: Praeger.

Epstein, Leon D. 1986. *Political Parties in the American Mold.* Madison: University of Wisconsin Press.

Epstein, Leon D. 1989. "Will American Political Parties Be Privatized?" *Journal of Law and Politics* 5: 239.

Epstein, Leon D. 1991. "The Regulation of State Political Parties." In *Political Parties and Elections in the United States: An Encyclopedia,* edited by L. Sandy Maisel. New York: Garland.

Erie, Steven. 1988. *Rainbow's End: Irish-Americans and the Dilemmas of Urban Machine Politics, 1840–1985.* Berkeley: University of California Press.

Erikson, Robert S. 1981. "Why Do People Vote? Because They Are Registered." *American Politics Quarterly* 9: 259.

Erikson, Robert S., Thomas D. Lancaster, and David W. Romero. 1989. "Group Components of the Presidential Vote, 1952–1984." *Journal of Politics* 51: 337.

Evans, Diana. 1986. "PAC Contributions and Roll-Call Voting." In *Interest Groups and Politics,* edited by Allan Cigler and Burdett A. Loomis. Washington, D.C.: Congressional Quarterly Press.

Federal Election Commission. 1991a. "1990 Congressional Election Spending Drops to Low Point." Press Release, February 22, 1991.

Federal Election Commission. 1991b. "PAC Activity Falls in 1990 Elections." Press Release, March 31, 1991.

Feigert, Frank B., and Pippa Norris. 1989. "Candidate Recruitment and Government Popularity in Special and By-Elections: The United States, Canada, Britain, and Australia." Paper presented at the annual meeting of the American Political Science Association, Atlanta, Ga.

Fenno, Richard F., Jr. 1959. *The President's Cabinet.* New York: Vintage.

Fenno, Richard F., Jr. 1972. "If, as Ralph Nader Says, Congress Is 'the Broken Branch,' How Come We Love Our Congressmen So Much?" Paper presented for discussion at the Harvard Club, Boston.

Fenno, Richard F., Jr. 1973. *Congressmen in Committees.* Boston: Little, Brown.

Fenno, Richard F., Jr. 1978. *Home Style: House Members in Their Own Districts.* Boston: Little, Brown.

Fenno, Richard F., Jr. 1984. *The United States Senate: A Bicameral Perspective.* Washington, D.C.: American Enterprise Institute for Public Policy Research.

Fenno, Richard F., Jr. 1990. *The Presidential Odyssey of John Glenn.* Washington, D.C.: Congressional Quarterly Press.

Ferejohn, John A. 1977. "On the Decline of Competition in Congressional Elections." *American Political Science Review* 71: 525.

Ferejohn, John A., and Randall Calvert. 1984. "Presidential Coattails in Historical Perspective." *American Journal of Political Science* 28: 127.

Ferejohn, John A., and Morris P. Fiorina. 1974. "The Paradox of Not Voting: A Decision Theoretic Analysis." *American Political Science Review* 68: 525.

Finer, Herman. 1949. *The Theory and Practice of Modern Government.* New York: Holt.

Finkel, Steven E., and Howard A. Scarrow. 1985. "Party Identification and Party Enrollment: The Difference and the Consequence." *Journal of Politics* 47: 620.

Fiorina, Morris P. 1973. "Electoral Margins, Constituency Influence, and Policy Moderation: A Critical Assessment." *American Politics Quarterly* 1: 479.

Fiorina, Morris P. 1977a. "The Case of the Vanishing Marginals: The Bureaucracy Did It." *American Political Science Review* 71: 166.

Fiorina, Morris P. 1977b. "An Outline for a Model of Party Choice." *American Journal of Political Science* 21: 618.

Fiorina, Morris P. 1978. *Congress: Keystone of the Washington Establishment.* 4th ed. New Haven: Yale University Press.

Fiorina, Morris P. 1981. *Retrospective Voting in American National Elections.* New Haven: Yale University Press.

Fiorina, Morris P. 1990. "An Era of Divided Govemment." In *Developments in American Politics,* edited by Bruce Cain and Gillian Peele. London: Macmillan.

Fiorina, Morris P. 1992. *Divided Government.* New York: Macmillan.

Fiorina, Morris P. 1996. *Divided Government.* 2d ed. Boston: Allyn and Bacon.

Fishel, Jeff. 1973. *Party and Opposition: Congressional Challengers in American Politics.* New York: McKay.

Fishel, Jeff. 1977. "Agenda Building in Presidential Campaigns: The Case of Jimmy Carter." Paper presented at the annual meeting of the American Political Science Association, Washington, D.C.

Fishel, Jeff. 1985. *Presidents and Promises.* Washington, D.C.: Congressional Quarterly Press.

Flanigan, William, and Nancy Zingale. 1983. *Political Behavior of the American Electorate.* 5th ed. Boston: Allyn and Bacon.

Foner, Eric. 1988. *Reconstruction: America's Unfinished Revolution, 1863–1877.* New York: Harper and Row.

Formisano, Ronald P. 1974. "Deferential-Participant Politics: The Early Republic's Political Culture, 1789–1890." *American Political Science Review* 68: 473.

Foster, James C., and Susan M. Leeson. 1998. *Constitutional Law: Cases in Context.* Upper Saddle River, N.J.: Prentice-Hall.

Fowler, Linda L. 1979. "The Electoral Lottery: Decisions to Run for Congress." *Public Choice* 34: 399.

Fowler, Linda L. 1980. "Candidate Perceptions of Electoral Coalitions: Limits and Possibilities." Paper presented at the Conference on Congressional Elections, Houston, Tex.

Fowler, Linda L. 1982. "How Interest Groups Select Issues for Rating Voting Records of Members of the U.S. Congress." *Legislative Studies Quarterly* 7: 403.

Fowler, Linda L. 1989. "Candidate Recruitment and the Study of Congress: A Studies Essay." Paper presented at the Conference on Elective Politicians, Institute of Politics, Kennedy School of Government, Harvard University, Boston.

Fowler, Linda L., and Robert McClure. 1989. *Political Ambition: Who Decides to Run for Congress.* New Haven: Yale University Press.

Franklin, Charles H. 1984. "Issues, Preferences, Socialization, and the Evolution of Party Identification." *American Journal of Political Science* 28: 459.

Franklin, Charles H., and John E. Jackson. 1983. "The Dynamics of Party Identification." *American Political Science Review* 77: 957.

Fraser, Steve, and Gary Gerstle, eds. 1989. *The Rise and Fall of the New Deal Order, 1930-1980.* Princeton, N.J.: Princeton University Press.

Freed, Bruce F. 1978. "Political Money and Campaign Finance Reform, 1971-1976." In *Parties and Elections in an Anti-Party Age,* edited by Jeff Fishel. Bloomington: Indiana University Press.

Frendeis, John P., James L. Gibson, and Laura L. Vertz. 1990. "The Electoral Relevance of Local Party Organization." *American Political Science Review* 84: 226.

Frendeis, John P., and Richard Waterman. 1985. "PAC Contributions and Legislative Behavior: Senate Voting on Trucking Deregulation." *Social Science Quarterly* 66: 401.

Friedman, Paul A. 1990. "Environmental Action's Dirty Dozen of 1990." *Environmental Action Magazine* 22: 16.

Frymer, Paul. 1994. "Ideological Consensus within Divided Government." *Political Science Quarterly* 109: 287-312.

Gais, Thomas L., Mark A. Peterson, and Jack L. Walker. 1984. "Interest Groups, Iron Triangles, and Representative Institutions in American National Government." *British Journal of Political Science* 14: 161.

Galloway, George B. 1961. *A History of the House of Representatives.* New York: Crowell.

Gans, Curtis B. 1990. "A Rejoinder to Piven and Cloward." *PS: Political Science and Politics* 23: 175.

Gans, Herbert J. 1979. *Deciding What's News.* New York: Random House.

Gant, Michael M., and Norman R. Luttbeg. 1991. *American Electoral Behavior.* Itasca, Ill.: F. E. Peacock.

Garand, James C. 1991. "Electoral Marginality in State Legislative Elections, 1968-86." *Legislative Studies Quarterly* 16: 7.

Geer, John G. 1989. *Nominating Presidents: An Evaluation of Voters and Primaries.* Westport, Conn.: Greenwood.

Geer, John G. 1991. "Critical Realignments and the Public Opinion Poll." *Journal of Politics* 53: 434.

Gelman, Andrew, and Gary King. 1990. "Estimating the Electoral Consequences of Legislative Redistricting." *Journal of the American Statistical Politics* 85: 274.

Germond, Jack, and Jules Witcover. 1981. *Blue Smoke and Mirrors: How Reagan Won and Why Carter Lost the 1980 Election.* New York: Viking.

Germond, Jack, and Jules Witcover. 1985. *Wake Us When It's Over: Presidential Politics of 1984.* New York: Macmillan.

Germond, Jack W., and Jules Witcover. 1989. *Whose Broad Stripes and Bright Stars? The Trivial Pursuit of the Presidency, 1988.* New York: Warner Books.

Germond, Jack, and Jules Witcover. 1993. *Mad as Hell: Revolt at the Ballot Box, 1992.* New York: Warner Books.

Gibson, James L. 1991. "County Party Organizations." In *Political Parties and Elections in the United States: An Encyclopedia,* edited by L. Sandy Maisel. New York: Garland.

Gibson, James L. 1991a. "Institutional Legitimacy, Procedural Justice, and Compliance with Supreme Court Decisions: A Question of Causality." *Law and Society Review* 25 (August): 631-635.

Gibson, James L., Comelius P. Cotter, John F. Bibby, and Robert J. Huckshom. 1983. "Assessing Party Organizational Strength." *American Journal of Political Science* 27: 193.

Gibson, James L., Cornelius P. Cotter, John F. Bibby, and Robert J. Huckshom. 1985. "Whither the Local Parties?: A Cross-Sectional Analysis and Longitudinal Analysis of the Strength of Party Organizations." *American Joumal of Political Science* 29: 139.

Gibson, James L., John P. Frendreis, and Laura L. Vertz. 1989. "Party Dynamics in the 1980s: Change in County Party Organizational Strength, 1980-1984." *American Journal of Political Science* 67.

Gienapp, William E. 1987. *The Origins of the Republican Party, 1852-1856.* New York: Oxford University Press.

Gienapp, William E. 1991. "The Formation of the Republican Party." In *The Encyclopedia of American Political Parties and Elections,* edited by L. Sandy Maisel. New York: Garland.

Gierzynski, Anthony . 1992. *Legislative Party Campaign Committees in the American States.* Lexington, Ky.: University of Kentucky Press.

Gierzynski, Anthony, and David Breaux. 1990. "It's Money That Matters: The Role of Campaign Expenditures in State Legislative Primaries." Paper presented at the annual meeting of the American Political Science Association, San Francisco.

Gierzynski, Anthony, and David Breaux. 1991. "Money and Votes in State Legislative Elections." *Legislative Studies Quarterly* 16: 203.

Ginsberg, Benjamin, and Alan Stone, eds. 1986. *Do Elections Matter?* Armonk, N.Y.: Sharpe.

Ginsberg, Benjamin, and Martin Shefter. 1985. "A Critical Realignment? The New Politics, the Reconstituted Right, and the Election of 1984." In *The Elections of 1984,* edited by Michael Nelson. Washington, D.C.: Congressional Quarterly Press.

Glaser, James. 1996. *Race, Campaign Politics in Realignment in the South.* New Haven: Yale University Press.

Glazer, Amihai, Bemard Grofinan, and Marc Robbins. 1987. "Partisan and Incumbency Effects of the 1970s Congressional Redistricting." *American Journal of Political Science* 30: 680.

Goldenberg, Edie N., and Michael W. Traugott. 1980. "Campaign Effects on Voting Behavior in the 1978 Congressional Elections." Paper presented at the annual meeting of the American Political Science Association, Washington, D.C.

Goldenberg, Edie N., and Michael W. Traugott. 1984. *Campaigning for Congress.* Washington, D.C.: Congressional Quarterly Press.

Goldenberg, Edie N., Michael W. Traugott, and Frank R. Baumgartner. 1986. "Preemptive and Reactive Spending in U.S. House Races." *Political Behavior* 8: 3.

Goldman, Peter, and Tony Fuller. 1985. *The Quest for the Presidency, 1984.* New York: Bantam.

Goldman, Ralph M. 1990. *The National Party Chairmen and Committees: Factionalism at the Top.* Armonk, N.Y.: Sharpe.

Gosnell, Harold. 1939. *Machine Politics: Chicago Model.* Chicago: University of Chicago Press.

Gottlieb, Stephen E. 1985. "Fleshing Out the Right of Association: The Problem of the Contribution Limits of the Federal Election Campaign Act." *Albany Law Review* 49: 825.

Gottlieb, Stephen E. 1991. *"Buckley v. Valeo."* In *Political Parties and Elections in the United States: An Encyclopedia,* edited by L. Sandy Maisel. New York: Garland.

Graber, Doris A. 1980. *Mass Media in American Politics.* Washington, D.C.: Congressional Quarterly Press.

Graber, Doris A. 1982. *The President and the Public.* Philadelphia: Institute for the Study of Human Issues.

Graber, Doris A. 1984a. *Mass Media and American Elections.* Washington, D.C.: Congressional Quarterly Press.

Graber, Doris A. 1984b. *Media Power in Politics.* Washington, D.C.: Congressional Quarterly Press.

Graber, Doris A. 1989. *Mass Media in American Politics*. 3d ed. Washington, D.C.: Congressional Quarterly Press.

Graber, Doris A. 1990. *Media Power in Politics*. 2d ed. Washington, D.C.: Congressional Quarterly Press.

Grassmuck, George, ed. 1985. *Before Nomination: Our Primary Problem.* Washington, D.C.: American Enterprise Institute for Public Policy Research.

Gray, Virignia, and Herbert Jacob. *Politics in the American States: A Comparative Analysis.* 6th ed. Washington D.C.: Congessional Quarterly Press.

Gray, Virginia, Herbert Jacob, and Robert B. Albritton. 1990. *Politics in the American States: A Comparative Analysis.* 5th ed. Glenview, Ill.: Scott, Foresman/Little, Brown.

Green, Donald, and Jonathan Krasno. 1988. "Salvation for the Spendthrift Incumbent: Reestimating the Effects of Campaign Spending in House Elections." *American Journal of Political Science* 32: 884.

Greenstein, Fred I. 1970. *The American Party System and the American People.* 2d ed. Englewood Cliffs, N.J.: Prentice-Hall.

Greenstein, Fred I., and Frank B. Feigert. 1985. *The American Party System and the American People.* 3d ed. Englewood Cliffs, N.J.: Prentice-Hall.

Grenzke, Janet. 1989. "PACs in the Congressional Supermarket: The Currency Is Complex." *American Journal of Political Science* 33: 1.

Grenzke, Janet. 1990. "Money and Congressional Behavior." In *Money, Elections, and Democracy: Reforming Congressional Campaign Finance,* edited by Margaret Latus Nugent and John R. Johannes. Boulder: Westview.

Grofman, Bernard, ed. 1990. *Political Gerrymandering and the Courts.* New York: Agathon.

Gugliotta, Guy. 1998. "Going Where the Money Is." *Washington Post National Weekly Edition,* July 6, 12.

Hadley, Charles D. 1985. "Dual Partisan Identification in the South." *Journal of Politics* 47: 254.

Hamilton, Alexander, John Jay, and James Madison. 1981. *The Federalist.* New York: New American Library.

Hargrove, Erwin C., and Michael Nelson. 1985. "The Presidency: Reagan and the Cycle of Politics and Policy." In *The Elections of 1984,* edited by Michael Nelson. Washington, D.C.: Congressional Quarterly Press.

Hawley, Willis D. 1973. *Nonpartisan Elections and the Case of Party Politics.* New York: Wiley.

Heard, Alexander. 1960. *The Costs of Democracy.* Chapel Hill: University of North Carolina Press.

Herrnson, Paul S. 1988. *Party Campaigning in the 1980s.* Cambridge: Harvard University Press.

Herrnson, Paul S. 1989. "National Party Decision-Making, Strategies, and Resource Distribution in Congressional Elections." *Western Political Quarterly* 42: 301.

Herrnson, Paul S. 1990a. "Campaign Professionalism and Fundraising in Congressional Elections." Paper presented at the annual meeting of the American Political Science Association, San Francisco.

Herrnson, Paul S. 1990b. "Reemergent National Party Organizations." In *The Parties Respond: Changes in the American Party System,* edited by L. Sandy Maisel. Boulder: Westview.

Herrnson, Paul. 1991. "Campaign Professionalism and Fundraising in Congressional Elections." Unpublished manuscript, University of Maryland.

Herrnson, Paul S. 1995. "Potential Research Policies for Political Science." *PS: Political Science and Politics* 28: 492–494.

Herrnson, Paul S. 1998. *Congressional Elections: Campaigning at Home and in Washington*. 2d ed. Washington, D.C.: Congressional Quarterly Press.

Herrnson, Paul S. 1998a. "National Party Organizations at the Century's End." In *The Parties Respond,* edited by L. Sandy Maisel. 3d ed. Boulder: Westview.

Herrnson, Paul S., Ronald G. Shaiko, and Clyde Wilcox. 1998. *The Interest Group Connection: Engineering, Lobbying, and Policymaking in Washington.* Chatham, N.J.: Chatham House.

Hershey, Marjorie R. 1974. *The Making of Campaign Strategy.* Lexington, Mass.: D. C. Heath.

Hershey, Marjorie R. 1984. *Running for Office: The Political Education of Campaigners.* Chatham, N.J.: Chatham House.

Hershey, Marjorie R., and Darrell M. West. 1983. "Single Issue Politics: Pro-Life Groups and Senate Campaigning in 1980." In *The Changing Nature of Interest Group Politics,* edited by Allan Cigler and Burdett A. Loomis. Washington, D.C.: Congressional Quarterly Press.

Hess, Stephen, and Michael Nelson. 1985. "Foreign Policy: Dominance and Decisiveness in Presidential Elections." In *The Elections of 1984,* edited by Michael Nelson. Washington, D.C.: Congressional Quarterly Press.

Hicks, Jonathan P. 1998. "Efforts to Get Voters to the Polls Are Feverish for Both Sides," *New York Times,* November 2, on-line edition.

Hill, David B., and Norman R. Luttbeg. 1980. *Trends in American Electoral Behavior.* Itasca, Ill.: F. E. Peacock.

Hill, David B., and Norman R. Luttbeg. 1983. *Trends in American Electoral Behavior,* 2d ed. Itasca, Ill.: F. E. Peacock.

Hinckley, Barbara. 1971. *The Seniority System in congress.* Bloomington, In.: Indiana University Press.

Hinckley, Barbara. 1980a. "The American Voter in Congressional Elections." *American Political Science Review* 74: 641.

Hinckley, Barbara. 1980b. "House Reelections and Senate Defeats: The Role of the Challenger." *British Journal of Political Science* 10: 441.

Hinckley, Barbara. 1981. *Congressional Elections.* Washington, D.C.: Congressional Quarterly Press.

Hoffman, Kathy Barks. 1998. Negative Ads Hurt Turnout—Or Increase It," *Detroit News,* October 17, on-line edition.

Hofstadter, Richard. 1969. *The Idea of a Party System.* Berkeley: University of Califomia Press.

Holbrook, Thomas, and Charles Tidmarch. 1991. "Sophomore Surge in State Legislative Elections." *Legislative Studies Quarterly* 16: 49.

Holbrook, Thomas, and Emily Van Dunk. 1993. "Electoral Competition in the American States." *American Political Science Review.* 87 (December): 955–963.

Hook, Janet. 1990. "Republican Contests Reflect Election Woes, Party Rift." *Congressional Quarterly Weekly Report* 48: 3997.

House, Ernest R. 1988. *Jesse Jackson and the Politics of Charisma: The Rise and Fall of the PUSH/Excel Program.* Boulder: Westview.

Hrebenar, Ronald J., and Ruth K. Scott. 1990. *Interest Group Politics in America.* Englewood Cliffs, N.J.: Prentice-Hall.

Huckshom, Robert J. 1976. *Party Leadership in the States.* Amherst: University of Massachusetts Press.

Huckshorn, Robert J. 1985. "Who Gives It? Who Got It? The Enforcement of Campaign Finance Laws in the States." *Journal of Politics* 47: 773.

Huckshorn, Robert J. 1991. "State Party Leaders." In *Political Parties and Elections in the United States: An Encyclopedia,* edited by L. Sandy Maisel. New York: Garland.

Huckshorn, Robert J., James L. Gibson, Comelius P. Cotter, and John F. Bibby. 1986. "Party Integration and Party Organizational Strength." *Journal of Politics* 48: 977.

Huckshorn, Robert J., and Robert C. Spencer. 1971. *The Politics of Defeat: Campaigning for Congress.* Amherst: University of Massachusetts Press.

Hume, David. 1976. "The Philosophical Works of David Hume." In *Parties and Party Systems: A Framework for Analysis,* edited by Giovanni Sartori. New York: Cambridge University Press.

Hurley, Patricia A. 1989. "The Senate, Representation, and Recruitment to the Presidency." Paper presented at the annual meeting of the American Political Science Association, Atlanta, Ga.

Idelson, Holly. 1990. "Governors Find Re-Election a Trickier Proposition." *Congressional Quarterly Weekly Report* 48: 45.

Inglehart, Ronald, and Avram Hochstein. 1972. "Alignment and Dealignment of the Electorate in France and the United States." *Comparative Political Studies* 5: 343.

Iyengar, Shanto, and Richard Reeves. 1997. *Do the Media Govern? Politicians Voters, and Reporters in America.* Thousand Oaks, Calif.: Sage.

Jackman, Robert W. 1987. "Political Institutions and Voter Turnout in Industrial Democracies." *American Political Science Review* 81: 405.

Jackson, Brooks. 1988. *Honest Graft.* New York: Knopf.

Jackson, Brooks. 1990. *Broken Promises: Why the Federal Election Commission Failed.* New York: Priority Press Publications/Twentieth Century Fund.

Jackson, John E. 1975. "Issues, Party Choices, and Presidential Votes." *American Journal of Political Science* 19: 161.

Jackson, John S., Barbara Leavitt Brown, and David Bositis. 1982. "Herbert McClosky and Friends Revisited: 1980 Democratic and Republican Party Elites Compared to the Mass Public." *American Politics Quarterly* 10: 158.

Jacob, Herbert, and Kenneth Vines, eds. 1971. *Politics in the American States: A Comparative Analysis.* Boston: Little, Brown.

Jacob, Herbert, and Kenneth Vines, eds. 1976. *Politics in the American States: A Comparative Analysis.* 2d ed. Boston: Little, Brown.

Jacobson, Gary C. 1980. *Money in Congressional Elections.* New Haven: Yale University Press.

Jacobson, Gary C. 1981. "Congressional Elections, 1978: The Case of the Vanishing Challengers." In *Congressional Elections,* edited by L. Sandy Maisel and Joseph Cooper. Beverly Hills: Sage.

Jacobson, Gary C. 1983. *The Politics of Congressional Elections.* Boston: Little, Brown.

Jacobson, Gary C. 1985a. "Congress: Politics after a Landslide without Coattails." In *The Elections of 1984,* edited by Michael Nelson. Washington, D.C.: Congressional Quarterly Press.

Jacobson, Gary C. 1985b. "Parties and PACs in Congressional Elections." In *Congress Reconsidered,* edited by Lawrence D. Dodd and Bruce I. Oppenheimer. 3d ed. Washington, D.C.: Congressional Quarterly Press.

Jacobson, Gary C. 1985–1986. "Party Organization and Distribution of Campaign Resources, Republicans and Democrats in 1982." *Political Science Quarterly* 100: 603.

Jacobson, Gary C. 1987a. "The Marginals Never Vanished: Incumbency and Competition in Elections to the U.S. House of Representatives, 1952–1982." *American Journal of Political Science* 31: 126.

Jacobson, Gary C. 1987b. *The Politics of Congressional Elections.* 2d ed. Boston: Little, Brown.

Jacobson, Gary C. 1989. "Strategic Politicians and the Dynamic of House Elections, 1946–1986." *American Political Science Review* 83: 773.

Jacobson, Gary C. 1990a. "Divided Government, Strategic Politicians, and the 1990 Congressional Elections." Paper presented at the annual meeting of the Midwest Political Science Association, Chicago.

Jacobson, Gary C. 1990b. "The Effects of Campaign Spending in House Elections: New Evidence for Old Arguments." *American Journal of Political Science* 34: 334.

Jacobson, Gary C. 1990c. *The Electoral Origins of Divided Government: Competition in U.S. House Elections, 1946–1988.* Boulder: Westview.

Jacobson, Gary C. 1991. "Financing Congressional Campaigns." In *Political Parties and Elections in the United States: An Encyclopedia,* edited by L. Sandy Maisel. New York: Garland.

Jacobson, Gary C. 1992. *The Politics of Congressional Elections,* 3d ed. Boston: Little, Brown.

Jacobson, Gary C. 1996. *The Politics of Congressional Elections*. 4th ed. New York: Longman.

Jacobson, Gary C., and Samuel Kernell. 1983. *Strategy and Choice in Congressional Elections.* New Haven: Yale University Press.

Jewell, Malcolm E. 1998. Political Party Recruiting of State Legislative Candidates." Paper presented at the annual meeting of the American Political Science Association, Boston.

Jewell, Malcolm E. 1984. *Parties and Primaries.* New York: Praeger.

Jewell, Malcolm E., and David Breaux. 1988. "The Effect of Incumbency on State Legislative Elections." *Legislative Studies Quarterly* 13: 495.

Jewell, Malcolm E., and David Breaux. 1991. "Southern Primary and Electoral Competition and Incumbent Success." *Legislative Studies Quarterly* 16: 129.

Jewell, Malcolm E., and David M. Olson. 1982. *American State Political Parties and Elections.* Homewood, Ill.: Dorsey.

Jewell, Malcolm E., and David M. Olson. 1988. *Political Parties and Elections in American States,* 3d ed. Chicago: Dorsey.

Johnson-Cartee, Karen S., and Gary W. Copeland. 1997. *Inside Political Campaigns: Theory and Practice*. Westport, Conn.: Praeger.

Jones, Charles O. 1970. *The Minority Party in Congress*. Boston: Little, Brown.

Jones, Charles O. 1981a. "The New, New Senate." In *A Tide of Discontent: The Elections of 1980 and Their Meaning,* edited by Ellis Sandoz and Cecil C. Crabb Jr. Washington, D.C. : Congressional Quarterly Press.

Jones, Charles O. 1981b. "Nominating Carter's 'Favorite Opponent': The Republicans in 1980." In *The American Elections of 1980,* edited by Austin Ranney. Washington, D.C.: American Enterprise Institute.

Jones, Charles O. 1988a. "Ronald Reagan and the U.S. Congress: Visible-Hand Politics." In *The Reagan Legacy,* edited by Charles O. Jones. Chatham, N.J.: Chatham House.

Jones, Charles O. 1988b. *The Trusteeship Presidency: Jimmy Carter and the United States Congress.* Baton Rouge: Louisiana State University Press.

Jones, Charles O., ed. 1988c. *The Reagan Legacy.* Chatham, N.J.: Chatham House.

Jones, Charles O. 1989. "Presidents and Agenda Politics: Sustaining the Power of Office." Paper presented at the annual meeting of the American Political Science Association, Atlanta, Ga.

Jones, Ruth S. 1980. "State Public Financing and the State Parties." In *Parties, Interest Groups, and Campaign Finance Laws,* edited by Michael J. Malbin. Washington, D.C.: American Enterprise Institute for Public Policy Research.

Jones, Ruth S. 1984. "Financing State Elections." In *Money and Politics in the United States: Financing Elections in the 1980s*, edited by Michael J.Malbin. Washington, D.C.: American Enterprise Institute for Public Policy Research.

Jones, Ruth S. 1991. "Financing State Campaigns." In *Political Parties and Elections in the United States: An Encyclopedia,* edited by L. Sandy Maisel. New York: Garland.

Jordan, Hamilton. 1982. *Crisis: The Last Year of Carter's Presidency.* New York: Putnam.

Just, Marion R., W. Russell Neuman, and Ann N. Crigler. 1989. "Who Learns

What from the News: Attentive Publics versus a Cognitive Elite." Paper presented at the annual meeting of the American Political Science Association, Atlanta, Ga.

Kassebaum Baker, Nancy, and Walter Mondale. 1998. "House Passage of Campaign Finance Reform." Washington, D.C.: Aspen Institute's Policy Program on Campaign Finance Reform.

Kayden, Xandra. 1978. *Campaign Organization.* Lexington, Mass.: D. C. Heath.

Kayden, Xandra, and Eddie Maye Jr. 1985. *The Party Goes On.* New York: Basic Books.

Kazee, Thomas A. 1979. "The Decision to Run for Congress: Challenger Attitudes in the 1970s." Paper presented at the annual meeting of the Midwest Political Science Association, Chicago.

Kerbel, Matthew Robert. 1998. *Remote and Controlled: Media Politics in a Cynical Age.* 2d ed. Boulder: Westview.

Kernell, Samuel. 1977. "Presidential Popularity and Negative Voting: An Alternative Explanation of Midterm Congressional Decline of the President's Party." *American Political Science Review* 71: 44.

Kessel, John H. 1968. *The Goldwater Coalition: Republican Strategies in 1964.* Indianapolis: Bobbs-Merrill.

Kessel, John H. 1972. "The Issue in Issue Voting." *American Political Science Review* 66: 459.

Kessel, John H. 1980. *Presidential Campaign Politics: Coalition Strategies and Citizen Response.* Homewood, Ill.: Dorsey.

Kessel, John H. 1984. *Presidential Campaign Politics: Coalition Strategies and Citizen Response.* 2d ed. Homewood, Ill.: Dorsey.

Kessel, John H. 1988. *Presidential Campaign Politics: Coalition Strategies and Citizen Response.* 3d ed. Homewood, Ill.: Dorsey.

Kessel, John H. 1992. *Presidential Campaign Politics: Coalition Strategies and Citizen Response.* 4th ed. Homewood, Ill.: Dorsey.

Kessel, John H., John M. Bruce, and John A. Clark. 1990. "Advocacy Parties: A Stable Feature of American Politics." Paper presented at the annual meeting of the American Political Science Association, San Francisco.

Kessel, John H., John A. Clark, John M. Bruce, and William G. Jacoby. 1989. "I'd Rather Switch Than Fight: Lifelong Democrats and Converts to Republicanism among Campaign Activists." Paper presented at the annual meeting of the American Political Science Association, Atlanta, Ga.

Key, V. O., Jr. 1955. "A Theory of Critical Elections." *Journal of Politics* 17: 3.

Key, V. O., Jr. 1956. *American State Politics.* New York: Knopf.

Key, V. O., Jr. 1959. "Secular Realignment and the Party System." *Journal of Politics* 21: 198.

Key, V. O., Jr. 1964. *Politics, Parties, and Pressure Groups.* New York: Crowell.

Key, V. O., Jr. 1966. *The Responsible Electorate.* Cambridge: Harvard University Press.

Kinder, Donald R., and P. Roderick Kiewiet. 1979. "Economic Discontent and Political Behavior: The Role of Personal Grievances and Collective Economic Judgments in Congressional Voting." *Journal of Political Science* 23: 495.

King, Anthony, ed. 1990. *The New American Political System.* 2d ed. Washington, D.C.: American Enterprise Institute Press.

King, Gary. 1989. "Representation through Legislative Redistricting: A Stochastic Model." *American Journal of Political Science* 33: 787.

Kingdon, John W. 1984. *Agendas, Altematives, and Public Policies.* Boston: Little, Brown.

Kirkpatrick, Jeane Jordan. 1976. *The New Presidential Elite: Men and Women in National Politics.* New York: Russell Sage Foundation.

Kirkpatrick, Jeane Jordan. 1978. *Dismantling the Parties.* Washington, D.C.: American Enterprise Institute for Public Policy Research.

Kirschten, Dick. 1985. "An Uncertain Transition." *National Journal* 17.

Knack, Stephen. 1995. "Does 'Motor Voter' Work? Evidence from State-Level Data." *Journal of Politics* 57: 796–812.

Kramer, Gerald L. 1971. "Short-Term Fluctuations in U.S. Voting Behavior, 1896–1964." *American Political Science Review* 65: 131.

Krasno, Jonathon S., and Donald Philip Green. 1988. "Pre-empting Quality Challengers in House Elections." *Journal of Politics* 50: 920.

Kraus, Sidney. 1962. *The Great Debates: Kennedy vs. Nixon, 1960.* Bloomington: Indiana University Press.

Kurtz, Howard. 1998. "Attack Ads Carpet TV, Spinning the Issues," *Washington Post*, October 20, A1.

Ladd, Everett Carll, Jr. 1978. "The Shifting Party Coalitions-1932–1976." In *Emerging Coalitions in American Politics,* edited by Seymour M. Lipset. San Francisco: Institute for Contemporary Studies.

Ladd, Everett Carll, Jr. 1982. *Where Have All the Voters Gone? The Fracturing of America's Political Parties.* 2d ed. New York: Norton.

Ladd, Everett Carll, Jr. 1991. *The American Polity: The People and Their Government.* New York: Norton.

Ladd, Everett Carll, Jr., and Charles D. Hadley. 1975. *Transformations of the Amelican Party System.* Rev. ed. New York: Norton.

Lamb, Karl A., and Paul A. Smith. 1968. *Campaign Decision-Making: The Presidential Election of 1964.* Belmont, Calif.: Wadsworth.

Lamis, Alexander. 1984. "The Runoff Primary Controversy: Implications for Southern Politics." *PS: Political Science and Politics* 17: 782.

Lane, Robert E. 1959. *Political Life.* New York: Free Press.

Laver, Michael, and Kenneth A. Shepsle. 1990. *Divided Government: America Is Not Exceptional.* Cambridge: Center for American Political Studies, Harvard University.

Lawson, Kay. 1976. *The Comparative Study of Political Parties.* New York: St. Martin's.

Lazarsfeld, Paul F., Barnard Berelson, and Hazel Gaudet. 1944. *The People's Choice: How the Voter Makes Up His Mind in a Presidential Campaign.* New York: Columbia University Press.

League of Women Voters. 1997. "5 Ideas for Practical Campaign Finance Reform." Unpublished typescript.

Leighly, Jan. 1996. "Group Membership and the Mobilization of Political Participation." *Journal of Politics* 58: 447.

Lemann, Nicholas. 1985. "Implications: What Americans Wanted." In *The Elections of 1984,* edited by Michael Nelson. Washington, D.C.: Congressional Quarterly Press.

Lengle, James I. 1981. *Representation of Presidential Primaries: The Democratic Party and the Post-Reform Era.* Westport, Conn.: Greenwood.

Lengle, James I., and Byron E. Shafer. 1980. *Presidential Politics.* New York: St. Martin's.

Leuthold, David A. 1968. *Electioneering in a Democracy: Campaigns for Congress.* New York: Wiley.

Light, Paul C. 1983. *The President's Agenda.* Baltimore, Md.: Johns Hopkins University Press.

Light, Paul C., and Celinda Lake. 1985. "The Election: Candidates, Strategies, and Decisions." In *The Elections of 1984,* edited by Michael Nelson. Washington, D.C.: Congressional Quarterly Press.

Longley, Lawrence D. 1989. "Changing the System: Anticipated versus Actual Results in Electoral and Legislative Reform." Paper presented at the annual meeting of the American Political Science Association, Atlanta, Ga.

Lowenstein, Daniel Hays. 1991a "Campaign Finance and the Constitution." In *Political Parties and Elections in the United States: An Encyclopedia,* edited by L. Sandy Maisel. New York: Garland.

Lowenstein, Daniel Hays. 1991b. "Legislative Districting." In *Political Parties and Elections in the United States: An Encyclopedia,* edited by L. Sandy Maisel. New York: Garland.

Lowi, Theodore J. 1985. "An Aligning Election, a Presidential Plebiscite." In *The Elections of 1984,* edited by Michael Nelson. Washington, D.C.: Congressional Quarterly Press.

Luntz, Frank I. 1988. *Candidates, Consultants, and Campaigns.* Oxford: Blackwell.

Mackenzie, G. Calvin. 1991. "Partisan Presidential Leadership: The President's Appointees." In *The Parties Respond: Changes in the American Party System,* edited by L. Sandy Maisel. Boulder: Westview.

Mackenzie, G. Calvin. 1998. "Partisan Presidential Leadership: The Presidents' Appointees." In *The Parties Respond: Changes in American Parties and Campaigns,* edited by L. Sandy Maisel. 3d ed. Boulder: Westview.

MacKuen, Michael, Robert S. Erikson, and James A. Stimson. 1989. "Macropartisanship." *American Political Science Review* 77: 957.

MacNeil, Neil. 1981. "The Struggle for the House of Representatives." In *A Tide of Discontent: The 1980 Elections and Their Meaning,* edited by Ellis Sandoz and Cecil C. Crabb Jr. Washington, D.C.: Congressional Quarterly Press.

Magleby, David, and Marjorie Holt, eds. 1999. *Outside Money: Soft Money and Issue Ads in Competitive 1998 Congressional Elections.* Provo, Utah: Brigham Young University.

Magleby, David B., and Candice J. Nelson. 1990. *The Money Chase.* Washington, D.C.: Brookings Institution.

Maisel, Louis. 1975. "Party Reform and Political Participation: The Democrats in Maine." In *The Future of Political Parties,* edited by Louis Maisel and Paul M. Sacks. Beverly Hills: Sage.

Maisel, L. Sandy. 1982. *From Obscurity to Oblivion: Running in the Congressional Primary.* Knoxville: University of Tennessee Press.

Maisel, L. Sandy. 1986. *From Obscurity to Oblivion: Running in the Congressional Primary.* 2d ed. Knoxville: University of Tennessee Press.

Maisel, L. Sandy. 1988. "Spending Patterns in Presidential Nominating Campaigns, 1976–1988." Paper presented at the annual meeting of the American Political Science Association, Washington. Occasional Paper no. 88, Center for American Political Studies, Harvard University, Cambridge.

Maisel, L. Sandy. 1989. "Challenger Quality and the Outcome of the 1988 Congressional Elections." Paper presented at the annual meeting of the Midwest Political Science Association, Chicago.

Maisel, L. Sandy. 1990a. "Congressional Elections: Quality Candidates in House and Senate Elections, 1982–1988." Paper presented at the Back to the Future: The United States Congress at the Bicentennial Conference at the Carl Albert Congressional Research and Studies Center, the University of Oklahoma, Norman.

Maisel, L. Sandy. 1990b. "'The Incumbency Advantage." In *Money, Elections, and Democracy: Reforming Congressional Campaign Finance*, edited by Margaret Latus Nugent and John R. Johannes, Boulder: Westview.

Maisel, L. Sandy, ed. 1990c. *The Parties Respond: Changes in the American Party System.* Boulder: Westview.

Maisel, L. Sandy, ed. 1991. *Political Parties and Elections in the United States: An Encyclopedia.* New York: Garland.

Maisel, L. Sandy. 1993. *Parties and Elections in America: The Electoral Process.* New York: McGraw-Hill.

Maisel, L. Sandy, ed. 1998. *The Parties Respond.* 3d ed. Boulder: Westview.

Maisel, Louis, and Joseph Cooper, eds. 1977. *The Impact of the Electoral Process.* Beverly Hills: Sage.

Maisel, L. Sandy, and Joseph Cooper. 1981. *Congressional Elections.* Beverly Hills: Sage.

Maisel, L. Sandy, Linda L. Fowler, Ruth S. Jones, and Walter J. Stone. 1990. "The Naming of Candidates: Recruitment or Emergence." In *The Parties Respond: Changes in the American Party System,* edited by L. Sandy Maisel. Boulder: Westview.

Maisel, L. Sandy, and Elizabeth J. Ivry. 1998. "If You Don't Like Our Politics, Wait a Minute: Party Politics in Maine at the Century's End," *Polity.* Supplement to the winter issue.

Maisel, Louis, and Paul M. Sacks, eds. 1975. *The Future of Political Parties.* Beverly Hills: Sage.

Maisel, L. Sandy, Walter J. Stone, and Cherie Maestas. 1999. "Re-evaluating the Definition of Quality Candidates: Evidence from the Candidate Emergence Study." Paper presented at the annual meeting of the Midwest Political Science Association, Chicago.

Malbin, Michael J. 1980. *Parties, Interest Groups and Campaign Finance Laws.* Washington, D.C.: American Enterprise Institute for Public Policy Research.

Malbin, Michael J. 1981. "The Conventions, Platforms, and Issue Activists." In *The American Elections of 1980,* edited by Austin Ranney. Washington, D.C.: American Enterprise Institute for Public Policy Research.

Malbin, Michael J. 1984a. "Looking Back at the Future of Campaign Finance Reform: Interest Groups and American Elections." In *Money and Politics in the United States: Financing Elections in the 1980s,* edited by Michael J. Malbin. Washington, D.C.: American Enterprise Institute for Public Policy Research.

Malbin, Michael J., ed. 1984b. *Money and Politics in the United States: Fi-*

nancing Elections in the 1980s. Washington, D.C.: American Enterprise Institute for Public Policy Research.

Malbin, Michael J. 1985. "You Get What You Pay for, but Is That What You Want?" In *Before Nomination: Our Primary Problem,* edited by George Grassmuck. Washington, D.C.: American Enterprise Institute for Public Policy Research.

Malbin, Michael J., and Thomas L. Gais. 1998. *The Day after Reform: Sobering Campaign Finance Lessons from the American States*. Albany, N.Y.: Rockefeller Institute Press.

Mann, Thomas E. 1985. "Elected Officials and the Politics of Presidential Selection." In *The American Elections of 1984,* edited by Austin Ranney. Durham, N.C.: Duke University Press.

Mann, Thomas E., and Norman J. Ornstein. 1981. "The Republican Surge in Congress." In *The American Elections of 1980,* edited by Austin Ranney. Washington, D.C.: American Enterprise Institute for Public Policy Research.

Mann, Thomas E., and Raymond E. Wolfinger. 1980. "Candidates and Parties in Congressional Elections." *American Political Science Review* 74: 617.

Marchant-Shapiro, Theresa, and Christopher H. Achen. 1990. "Do Party Elites Pick Better Presidential Candidates Than Primary Voters?" Paper presented at the annual meeting of the American Political Science Association, San Francisco.

Marcus, Ruth. 1998. "Issue Advocacy Ads Less of an Issue." *Washington Post,* October 23, A1.

Masters, Marick F., and Gerald D. Keim. 1985. "Determinants of PAC Participation among Large Corporations." *Journal of Politics* 47: 1158.

Mattei, Franco, and Richard G. Niemi. 1991. "Unrealized Partisans, Realized Independents, and the Intergenerational Transmission of Partisan Identification." *Journal of Politics* 53: 161.

Matthews, Donald. 1978. "Winnowing. The News Media and the 1976 Presidential Nominatinos." In *Race for the Presidency,* edited by James D. Barber. Englewood Cliffs, N.J.: Prentice-Hall.

May, Ernest R., and Janet Fraser. 1973. *Campaign '72: The Managers Speak.* Cambridge: Harvard University Press.

Mayhew, David R. 1974a. *Congress: The Electoral Connection.* New Haven: Yale University Press.

Mayhew, David R. 1974b. "Congressional Elections: The Case of the Vanishing Marginals." *Polity, 6,* 295.

Mayhew, David R. 1986. *Placing Parties in American Politics.* Princeton, N.J.: Princeton University Press.

Mazmanian, Daniel A. 1974. *Third Parties in Presidential Elections.* Washington, D.C.: Brookings Institution.

McCarthy, Michael. 1997. "Inside the Beer Industry's Political Machine." *Wall Street Journal,* August 18, B1.

McClain, Paula D., and Joseph Stewart Jr. 1995. *Can We All Get Along? Racial and Ethnic Minorities in American Politics.* Boulder: Westview.

McClain, Paula D., and Joseph Stewart Jr. 1999. *Can We All Get Along? Racial and Ethnic Minorities in American Politics.* 2d ed. Boulder: Westview.

McFarland, Andrew S. 1984. *Common Cause.* Chatham, N.J.: Chatham House.

McGinniss, Joe. 1969. *The Selling of the President, 1968.* New York: Trident.

McKibben, Gordon. 1989. "AARP Takes One in the Chin in Congress." *Boston Globe,* October 15, A1.

Medvic, Stephen K., and Silvio Lenart. 1997. "The Influence of Political Consultants in the Congressional Elections." *Legislative Studies Quarterly* 22: 61.

Mendelsohn, Harold, and Irving Crespi. 1970. *Polls, Television, and the New Politics.* Scranton, Pa.: Chandler.

Mezey, Michael L. 1989. "Congress within the United States Presidential System." Paper presented at the annual meeting of the American Political Science Association, Atlanta, Ga.

Milbrath, Lester W. 1963. *The Washington Lobbyists.* Chicago: Rand McNally.

Milbrath, Lester W., and M. L. Goel. 1977. *Political Participation: How and Why Do People Get Involved in Politics?* Chicago: Rand McNally.

Milburn, Michael and Justin Brown. 1997. "Adwatch: Covering Campaign Ads." In *Politics and the Press: The News Media and Their Influence,* edited by Pippa Norris. Boulder: Lynne Rienner.

Mileur, Jerome. 1991. "Party Renewal." In *Political Parties and Elections in the United States: An Encyclopedia,* edited by L. Sandy Maisel. New York: Garland.

Miller, Arthur H. 1978. "The Majority Party Reunited? A Comparison of the 1972 and 1976 Elections." In *Parties and Elections in an Anti-Party Age,* edited by Jeff Fishel. Bloomington: Indiana University Press.

Miller, Arthur H., and Warren E. Miller. 1977. "Partisanship and Performance: 'Rational' Choice in the 1976 Presidential Elections." Paper presented at the annual meeting of the American Political Science Association, Washington, D.C.

Miller, Arthur H., Warren E. Miller, Aldern S. Raine, and Thad E. Brown. 1976. "A Majority Party in Disarray: Policy Polarization in the 1972 Election." *American Political Science Review* 70: 753.

Miller, Arthur H., and Martin P. Wattenberg. 1985. "Throwing the Rascals Out: Policy and Performance Evaluations of Presidential Candidates, 1952–1980." *American Political Science Review* 79: 359.

Miller, Warren E. 1985a. "The Election of 1984 and the Future of American Politics." Paper presented at the Thomas P. O'Neill Jr. Symposium on Elections in America, Boston College, Chestnut Hill, Mass.

Miller, Warren E. 1985b. "Participants in the Nominating Process: The Voters, the Political Activists." In *Before Nomination: Our Primary Problem,* edited by George Grassmuck. Washington, D.C.: American Enterprise Institute for Public Policy Research.

Miller, Warren E. 1990. "The Electorate's View of the Parties." In *The Parties Respond: Changes in the American Party System,* edited by L. Sandy Maisel. Boulder: Westview.

Miller, Warren E. 1991a . "Party Identification." In *Political Parties and Elections in the United States: An Encyclopedia,* edited by L. Sandy Maisel. New York: Garland.

Miller, Warren E. 1991b. "Party Identification, Realignment, and Party Voting: Back to Basics." *American Political Science Review* 85: 557.

Miller, Warren E. 1992. "The Puzzle Transformed: Explaining Declining Turnout." *Political Behavior* 14.

Miller, Warren E. 1998. "Party Identification and the Electorate of the 1990s."

In *The Parties Respond,* edited by L. Sandy Maisel. 3d ed. Boulder: Westview.

Miller, Warren E., Arthur H. Miller, and Edward J. Schneider. 1980. *American National Election Studies Data Sourcebook, 1952–1978.* Cambridge: Harvard University Press.

Miller, Warren E., and Teresa E. Levitin. 1976. *Leadership and Change: Presidential Elections from 1952 to 1976.* Cambridge: Winthrop.

Miller, Warren E., and J. Merrill Shanks. 1982. "Policy Directions and Presidential Leadership: Alternative Interpretations of the 1980 Presidential Elections." *British Journal of Political Science* 12: 266.

Miller, Warren E., and J. Merrill Shanks. 1996. *The New American Voter.* Cambridge: Harvard University Press.

Miller, Warren E., and Donald S. Stokes. 1963. "Constituency Influence in Congress." *American Political Science Review* 57: 45.

Miroff, Bruce. 1980. "Presidential Campaigns: Candidates, Managers and Reporters." *Polity* 12: 667.

Mitchell, Alison. 1998a. "1998 Candidates Advertise Early and Expensively," *New York Times,* April 4, A1.

Mitchell, Alison. 1998b. "Just Whose Party Is It? A G.O.P. House Divided." *New York Times,* November 12, on-line edition.

Moberg, David. 1998. "Grass-roots Politics in Comeback—With Winning Results." *Boston Sunday Globe,* A11.

Moncrief, Gary F. 1990. "The Increase in Campaign Expenditures in State Legislative Elections: A Comparison of Four Northwestern States." Paper presented at the annual meeting of the American Political Science Association, San Francisco.

Moncrief, Gary F., Peverill Squire, and Karl Kurtz. 1998. "Gateways to the Statehouse: Recruitment Patterns Among State Legislative Candidates." Paper presented at the annual meeting of the American Political Science Association, Boston.

Monroe, Bill. 1990. "Covering the Real Campaign: TV Sports." *Washington Journalism Review,* October 6, 6.

Moore, Jonathan. 1981. *The Campaign for President: 1980 in Retrospect.* Cambridge: Ballinger.

Moore, Jonathan, and Janet Fraser, eds. 1977. *Campaign for President: The Managers Look at 1976.* Cambridge: Ballinger.

Morehouse, Sarah McCally. 1980. "The Effect of Preprimary Endorsements on State Party Strength." Paper presented at the annual meeting of the American Political Science Association, Washington, D.C.

Mutch, Robert E. 1988. *Campaigns, Congress, and Courts: The Making of Federal Campaign Finance Laws.* New York: Praeger.

Nader, Ralph. 1965. *Unsafe at Any Speed: The Designed-In Dangers of the American Automobile.* New York: Grossman.

Napolitan, Joseph. 1972. *The Election Game and How to Win It.* Garden City, N.Y.: Doubleday.

Neal, Terry M., and Paul Duggan. 1999. "Concerns in Bush Household." *Washington Post,* January 21, A8.

Nelson, Candice J. 1990. "Loose Cannons: Independent Expenditures." In *Money, Elections, and Democracy: Reforming Congressional Campaign*

Finance, edited by Margaret Latus Nugent and John R. Johannes. Boulder: Westview.

Nelson, Michael, ed. 1985. *The Elections of 1984.* Washington, D.C.: Congressional Quarterly Press.

Nelson, Michael, ed. 1989. *The Elections of 1988.* Washington, D.C.: Congressional Quarterly Press.

Nelson, Michael, ed. 1993. *The Elections of 1992.* Washington, D.C.: Congressional Quarterly Press.

Nelson, Michael, ed. 1997. *The Elections of 1996.* Washington D.C.: Congressional Quarterly Press.

Neumann, Sigmund, ed. 1956. *Modern Political Parties: Approaches to Comparative Politics.* Chicago: University of Chicago Press.

Neustadt, Richard E. 1976. *Presidential Power: The Politics of Leadership with Reflections on Johnson and Nixon.* New York: Wiley.

Nie, Norman H., Sidney Verba, and John R. Petrocik. 1976. *The Changing American Voter.* Cambridge: Harvard University Press.

Nie, Norman H., Sidney Verba, and John R. Petrocik. 1979. *The Changing American Voter.* Enl. ed. Cambridge: Harvard University Press.

Niemi, Richard G., and Larry M. Bartels. 1985. "The Efficacy of Registration Drives." *Journal of Politics* 4: 1212.

Niemi, Richard G., and M. Kent Jennings. 1991. "Issues and Inheritance in the Formation of Party Identification." *American Journal of Political Science* 35.

Niemi, Richard G., and Simon Jackson. 1991. "Bias and Responsiveness in State Legislative Districting." *Legislative Studies Quarterly* 16: 183.

Niemi, Richard G., Simon Jackson, and Laura R. Winsky. 1991. "Candidacies and Competitiveness in Multimember Districts." *Legislative Studies Quarterly* 16: 91.

Niemi, Richard G., and Herbert F. Weisberg, eds. 1976. *Controversies in American Voting Behavior.* San Francisco: Freeman.

Niemi, Richard G., and Herbert F. Weisberg, eds. 1984. *Controversies in Voting Behavior.* 2d ed. Washington, D.C.: Congressional Quarterly Press.

Niemi, Richard C., and Herbert F. Weisberg, eds. 1993. *Controversies in Voting Behavior.* 3d ed. Washington, D.C.: Congressional Quarterly Press.

Niemi, Richard G., Stephen Wright, and Linda W. Powell. 1987. "Multiple Party Identifiers and the Measurement of Party Identification." *Journal of Politics* 49: 1093.

Noragon, Jack L. 1981. "Political Finance and Political Reform: The Experience with State Income Tax Checkoffs." American *Political Science Review* 75: 667.

Norpoth, Helmut. 1987. "Under Way and Here to Stay: Party Realignment in the 1980s?" *Public Opinion Quarterly* 51: 376.

Norris, Pippa, ed. 1997. *Politics and the Press: The News Media and Their Influence.* Boulder: Lynne Rienner.

Nugent, Margaret Latus, and John R. Johannes, eds. 1990. *Money, Elections, and Democracy: Reforming Congressional Finance.* Boulder: Westview.

Obey Commission. 1977. *Final Report of the Commission on Administrative Review.* United States House of Representatives, David R. Obey, Chairman, 95th Congress. Washington, D.C.: Government Printing Office.

Oleszek, Walter J. 1989. *Congressional Procedures and the Policy Process.* 3d ed. Washington, D.C.: Congressional Quarterly Press.

Oppenheimer, Bruce I., James A. Stimson, and Richard W. Waterman. 1986. "Interpreting U.S. Congressional Elections: The Exposure Theory." *Legislative Studies Quarterly* 11: 227.

Ornstein, Norman J. 1975. "Causes and Consequences of Congressional Change: Subcommittee Reforms in the House of Representatives." In *Congress in Change,* edited by Norman J. Ornstein. New York: Praeger.

Ornstein, Norman J., Thomas E. Mann, and Michael J. Malbin. 1990. *Vital Statistics on Congress, 1989–1990.* Washington, D.C.: Congressional Quarterly.

Ornstein, Norman J., Thomas E. Mann, and Michael J. Malbin. 1992. *Vital Statistics on Congress, 1991–1992.* Washington, D.C.: Congressional Quarterly.

Ornstein, Norman J., Thomas E. Mann, and Michael J. Malbin. 1998. *Vital Statistics on Congress, 1997–1998.* Washington, D.C.: Congressional Quarterly.

Ornstein, Norman J., Thomas E. Mann, Michael J. Malbin, Allen Schick, and John F. Bibby. 1985. *Vital Statistics on Congress, 1984–1985 Edition.* Washington, D.C.: American Enterprise Institute for Public Policy Research.

Ornstein, Norman J., and David W. Rohde. 1978. "Political Parties and Congressional Reform." In *Parties and Elections in an Anti-Party Age,* edited by Jeff Fishel. Bloomington: Indiana University Press.

Orren, Gary R. 1985. "The Nomination Process: Vicissitudes of Candidate Selection." In *The Elections of 1984,* edited by Michael Nelson. Washington, D.C.: Congressional Quarterly Press.

Orren, Gary R., and Nelson W. Polsby. 1987. *Media and Momentum: The New Hampshire Primary and Nomination Politics.* Chatham, N.J.: Chatham House.

Overacker, Louise. 1932. *Money in Elections.* New York: Macmillan.

Page, Benjamin I. 1978. *Choices and Echoes in Presidential Elections: Rational Man and Electoral Democracy.* Chicago: University of Chicago Press.

Parker, Glenn R., and Suzanne L. Parker. 1989. "Why Do We Trust Our Congressman and Does It Matter?" Paper presented at the annual meeting of the American Political Science Association, Atlanta, Ga.

Parris, Judith. 1972. *The Convention Problem.* Washington, D.C.: Brookings Institution.

Patterson, Kelly D. 1996. *Political Parties and the Maintenance of Liberal Democracy.* New York: Columbia University Press.

Patterson, Samuel C. 1984. "The Etiology of Party Competition." *American Political Science Review* 78: 691.

Patterson, Samuel C., and Gregory A. Caldeira. 1983. "Getting Out the Vote: Participation in Gubernatorial Elections." *American Political Science Review* 77: 495.

Patterson, Thomas E. 1980. *The Mass Media Election: How Americans Choose Their President.* New York: Praeger.

Patterson, Thomas E. 1990. *The American Democracy.* New York: McGraw-Hill.

Patterson, Thomas E. 1994. *Out of Order.* New York: Vintage Books.

Patterson, Thomas E., and Richard Davis. 1985. "The Media Campaign: Struggle for the Agenda." In *The Elections of 1984,* edited by Michael Nelson. Washington, D.C.: Congressional Quarterly Press.

Patterson, Thomas E., and Robert D. McClure. 1976. *The Unseeing Eye: The Myth of Television Power in National Politics.* New York: Putnam.

Peabody, Robert L. 1976. *Leadership in Congress: Stability, Succession, and Change.* Boston: Little, Brown.

Perry, H. W., Jr. 1991. "Racial Vote Dilution Cases." In *Political Parties and Elections in the United States: An Encyclopedia,* edited by L. Sandy Maisel. New York: Garland.

Peters, Ronald M., Jr. 1990. *The American Speakership: The Office in Historical Perspective.* Baltimore, Md.: Johns Hopkins University Press.

Petracca, Mark P. 1989. "Political Consultants and Democratic Governance." *PS: Political Science and Politics* 22: 11.

Petracca, Mark P., and Pamela A. Smith. 1989. "Please Don't Bring Back My Party to Me." Paper presented at the annual meeting of the American Political Science Association, Atlanta, Ga.

Petrocik, John R. 1987. "Realignment: New Party Coalitions and the Nationalization of the South." *Journal of Politics* 49: 347.

Petrocik, John R. 1989. "Issues and Agendas: Electoral Coalitions in the 1988 Election." Paper presented at the annual meeting of the American Political Science Association, Atlanta, Ga.

Petrocik, John R., and Frederick T. Steeper. 1987. "The Political Landscape in 1988." *Public Opinion* 10: 41.

Pfau, Michael, and Henry C. Kenski. 1990. *Attack Politics: Strategy and Defense.* New York: Praeger.

Phillips, Cabell B. H. 1966. *The Truman Presidency: The History of a Triumphant Succession.* New York: Macmillan.

Pitney, John J., Jr. 1990. "Republican Party Leadership in the U.S. House." Paper prepared for the annual meeting of the American Political Science Association, San Francisco.

Piven, Frances Fox, and Richard A. Cloward. 1988. *Why Americans Don't Vote.* New York: Pantheon.

Piven, Frances Fox, and Richard A. Cloward. 1989. "Governmental Statistics and Conflicting Explanations of Nonvoting." *PS: Political Science and Politics* 22: 172.

Piven, Frances Fox, and Richard A. Cloward. 1990. "A Reply to Bennett." *PS: Political Science and Politics* 23: 172.

Polsby, Nelson W. 1981. "The Democratic Nomination." In *The American Elections of 1980,* edited by Austin Ranney. Washington, D.C.: American Enterprise Institute for Public Policy Research.

Polsby, Nelson W. 1983. *Consequences of Party Reform.* New York: Oxford University Press.

Polsby, Nelson W., ed. 1971. *Reapportionment in the 1970s.* Berkeley: University of California Press.

Polsby, Nelson W., and Aaron Wildavsky. 1984. *Presidential Elections.* 6th ed. New York: Scribner.

Polsby, Nelson W., and Aaron Wildavsky. 1988. *Presidential Elections.* 7th ed. New York: Scribner.

Polsby, Nelson W., and Aaron Wildavsky. 1991. *Presidential Elections.* 8th ed. New York: Scribner.

Polsby, Nelson W., and Aaron Wildavsky. 1996. *Presidential Elections.* 9th ed. New York: Scribner.

Pomper, Gerald M. 1972. "From Confusion to Clarity: Issues and American Voters, 1952–1968." *American Political Science Review* 66: 415.

Pomper, Gerald M. 1973. *Elections in America.* New York: Dodd, Mead.

Pomper, Gerald M. 1975. *Voter's Choice: Varieties of American Electoral Behavior.* New York: Dodd, Mead.

Pomper, Gerald M. 1977. "The Nominating Contests and Conventions." In *The Election of 1976: Reports and Interpretations,* edited by Gerald M. Pomper. New York: McKay.

Pomper, Gerald M. 1980. *Party Renewal in America.* New York: Praeger.

Pomper, Gerald M., ed. 1981a. *The Election of 1980: Reports and Interpretations.* Chatham, N.J.: Chatham House.

Pomper, Gerald M. 1981b. "The Nominating Contests." In *The Election of 1980: Reports and Interpretations,* edited by Gerald M. Pomper. Chatham, N.J.: Chatham House.

Pomper, Gerald M., ed. 1985. *The Elections of 1984: Reports and Interpretations*. Chatham, N.J.: Chatham House.

Pomper, Gerald M., ed. 1989a. *The Election of 1988: Reports and Interpretations.* Chatham, N.J.: Chatham House.

Pomper, Gerald M. 1989b. "The Presidential Nominations." In *The Election of 1988: Reports and Interpretations,* edited by Gerald M. Pomper. Chatham, N.J.: Chatham House.

Pomper, Gerald M., ed. 1993. *The Election of 1992.* Chatham, N.J.: Chatham House.

Pomper, Gerald M., ed. 1997. *The Elections of 1996: Reports and Interpretations*. Chatham, N.J.: Chatham House.

Pomper, Gerald M., with Susan S. Lederman. 1980. *Elections in America.* 2d ed. New York: Longman.

Poole, Keith T., and R. Steven Daniels. 1985. "Ideology, Party, and Voting in the U.S. Congress, 1959–1980." *American Political Science Review* 79: 373.

Porter, K. H. 1918. *A History of Suffrage in the United States.* Chicago: University of Chicago Press.

Powell, G. Bingham. 1986. "American Voter Turnout in Comparative Perspective." *American Political Science Review* 80: 17.

President's Commission on Campaign Costs. 1962. *Financing Presidential Campaigns.* Washington, D.C.: Government Printing Office.

Price, David E. 1984. *Bringing Back the Parties.* Washington, D.C.: Congressional Quarterly Press.

Prysby, Charles. 1989. "Congressional Elections in the American South." Paper presented at the annual meeting of the American Political Science Association, Atlanta, Ga.

Purdam, Todd S. 1998. "California Moves Its Presidential Primary to Early March." *New York Times,* September 29, on-line edition.

Quirk, Paul J. 1985. "The Economy: Economists, Electoral Politics, and Reagan Economics." In *The Elections of 1984,* edited by Michael Nelson. Washington, D.C.: Congressional Quarterly Press.

Rakove, Milton L. 1975. *Don't Make No Waves . . . Don't Back No Losers.* Bloomington: Indiana University Press.

Ranney, Austin. 1962. *The Doctrine of Responsible Party Government: Its Origins and Present State.* Urbana, Ill.: University of Illinois Press.

Ranney, Austin. 1968. "The Representativeness of Primary Electorates." *Midwest Journal of Political Science* 12: 224.

Ranney, Austin. 1975. *Curing the Mischiefs of Faction: Party Reform in America.* Berkeley: University of California Press.

Ranney, Austin. 1979. *The Past and Future of Presidential Debates.* Washington, D.C.: American Enterprise Institute for Public Policy Research.

Ranney, Austin, ed. 1981. *The American Elections of 1980.* Washington, D.C.: American Enterprise Institute for Public Policy Research.

Ranney, Austin. 1983. *Channels of Power.* New York: Basic Books.

Ranney, Austin, ed. 1985. *The American Elections of 1984.* Durham, N.C.: Duke University Press.

Ranney, Austin. 1990. "Broadcasting, Narrowcasting, and Politics." In *The New American Political System,* edited by Anthony King. 2d ed. Washington, D.C.: American Enterprise Institute Press.

Ranney, Austin, and Leon D. Epstein. 1966. "The Two Electorates: Voters and Nonvoters in a Wisconsin Primary." *Journal of Politics* 28: 598.

Rapoport, Ronald B., Walter J. Stone, and Alan I. Abramowitz. 1991. "Do Endorsements Matter? Group Influence in the 1984 Democratic Caucuses." *American Political Science Review* 5: 193.

Reed, Adolph L., Jr. 1986. *The Jesse Jackson Phenomenon.* New Haven: Yale University Press.

Reichley, James. 1985. "The Rise of the National Parties." In *The New Directions in American Politics,* edited by John E. Clubb and Paul E. Peterson. Washington, D.C.: Brookings Institution.

Reichley, James. 1992. *The Life of the Parties.* New York: Free Press.

Reiter, Howard L. 1985. *Selecting the President: The Nominating Process in Transition.* Philadelphia: University of Pennsylvania Press.

Riordan, William L., ed. 1963. *Plunkitt of Tammany Hall.* New York: Dutton.

Ripley, Randall B. 1964. "The Whip Organizations in the United States House of Representatives." *American Political Science Review* 58: 561.

Ripley, Randall B. 1967. *Party Leaders in the House of Representatives.* Washington, D.C.: Brookings Institution.

Ripley, Randall B. 1990. "Congress and the President: Stability and Change." Paper presented at the annual meeting of the American Political Science Association, San Francisco.

Robinson, Michael, and Margaret Sheehan. 1983. *Over the Wire and on TV.* New York: Russell Sage Foundation.

Roche, John P. 1961. "The Founding Fathers: A Reform Caucus in Action." *American Political Science Review* 55.

Rohde, David W. 1974. "Committee Reform in the House of Representatives and the 'Subcommittee Bill of Rights.' " *Annals* 411: 39.

Rohde, David W. 1989. "Democratic Party Leadership, Agenda Control, and the Resurgence of Partisanship in the House." Paper presented at the annual meeting of the American Political Science Association, Atlanta, Ga.

Rohde, David W. 1991. *Parties and Leaders in the Post-Reform House.* Chicago: University of Chicago Press.

Rohde, David W. 1992. "Electoral Forces, Political Agendas, and Partisanship in the House and Senate." In *The Postreform Congress,* edited by Roger H. Davidson. New York: St. Martin's.

Roll, Charles W., Jr., and Albert H. Cantril. 1972. *Polls: Their Use and Misuse in Politics.* New York: Basic Books.

Rosenstone, Steven J., Roy L. Behr, and Edward H. Lazarus. 1984. *Third Parties in America: Citizen Response to Major Party Failure.* Princeton, N.J.: Princeton University Press.

Rosenstone, Steven J., and Raymond E. Wolfinger. 1978. "The Effect of Registration Laws on Voter Turnout." *American Political Science Review* 72: 27.

Rothenberg, Stuart. 1983. *Winners and Losers: Campaigns, Candidates, and Congressional Elections.* Washington, D.C.: Free Congress Research and Education Foundation.

Royko, Mike. 1971. *Boss: Richard Y. Daley of Chicago.* New York: Dutton.

Runkel, David B., ed. 1989. *Campaign for President: The Managers Look at '88.* Dover, Mass.: Auburn House.

Sabato, Larry J. 1981. *The Rise of Political Consultants: New Ways of Winning Campaigns.* New York: Basic Books.

Sabato, Larry J. 1985. *PAC Power: Inside the World of Political Action Committees.* New York: Norton.

Sabato, Larry J. 1988. *The Party's Just Begun: Shaping Political Parties for America's Future.* Glenview, Ill.: Scott, Foresman.

Sabato, Larry J. 1989. *Paying for Elections: The Campaign Finance Thicket.* New York: Priority Press Publications/Twentieth Century Fund.

Sabato, Larry J. 1991. *Feeding Frenzy: How Attack Journalism Has Transformed American Politics.* New York: Free Press.

Salmore, Stephen A., and Barbara G. Salmore. 1985. *Candidates, Parties, and Campaigns.* Washington, D.C.: Congressional Quarterly Press.

Samuelson, Robert J. 1998. "No More Media Elite." *Washington Post National Weekly Edition,* July 13, 26.

Samuelson, Robert J. 1999. "Network Fadeout." *Washington Post,* January 13, A23.

Sartori, Giovanni. 1976. *Parties and Party Systems: A Framework for Analysis.* Cambridge: Cambridge University Press.

Schattschneider, E. E. 1942. *Party Government.* New York: Holt, Rinehart, and Winston.

Schattschneider, E. E. 1960. *The Semisovereign People.* Hinsdale, Ill.: Dryden.

Schlesinger, Joseph A. 1966. *Ambition and Politics: Political Careers in the United States.* Chicago: Rand McNally.

Schlesinger, Joseph A. 1985. "The New American Political Party." *American Political Science Review* 79: 1152.

Schlozman, Kay L., and John T. Tierney. 1986. *Organized Interests and American Democracy.* New York: Harper and Row.

Schneider, William. 1981. "The November 4th Vote for President: What Did It Mean?" In *The American Elections of 1980,* edited by Austin Ranney. Washington, D.C.: American Enterprise Institute for Public Policy Research.

Schneider, William. 1988. "The Political Legacy of the Reagan Years." In *The Republican Legacy,* edited by Sidney Blumenthal and Thomas Byrne Edsall. New York: Pantheon.

Schram, Martin. 1977. *Running for President, 1976: The Carter Campaign.* New York: Stein and Day.

Schroedel, Jean Reith. 1986. "Campaign Contributions and Legislative Outcomes." *Western Political Quarterly* 39: 371.

Schuck, Peter H. 1987. "The Thickest Thicket: Partisan Gerrymandering and Judicial Regulation of Politics." *Columbia Law Review* 87: 1325.

Seib, Philip. 1994. *Campaigns and Conscience: The Ethics of Political Journalism.* Westport, Conn.: Praeger.

Seliginan, Lester. 1974. *Patterns of Recruitment: A State Chooses Its Law-Makers.* Chicago: Rand McNally.

Shafer, Byron E. 1983. *Quiet Revolution: The Struggle for the Democratic Party and the Shaping of Post-Reform Politics.* New York: Russell Sage Foundation.

Shafer, Byron E. 1988. *Bifurcated Politics: Evolution and Reform in the National Nominating Convention.* Cambridge: Harvard University Press.

Shafer, Byron E. 1991. *The End of Realignment? Interpreting American Electoral Eras.* Madison: University of Wisconsin Press.

Shaffer, Stephen D., and George A. Chressanthis. 1990. "Accountability in U.S. Senate Elections: Implications for Governance." Paper presented at the annual meeting of the American Political Science Association, San Francisco.

Shanks, J. Merrill, and Warren E. Miller. 1989. "Alternative Interpretations of the 1988 Election: Policy Direction, Current Conditions, Presidential Performance, and Candidate Traits." Paper presented at the annual meeting of the American Political Science Association, Atlanta, Ga.

Shanks, J. Merrill, and Warren E. Miller. 1990. "Policy Direction and Performance Evaluation: Contemporary Explanations of the Reagan Elections." *British Journal of Political Science* 20: 143.

Shanks, J. Merrill, and Warren E. Miller. 1991. "Partisanship, Policy, and Performance: The Reagan Legacy in the 1988 Election." *British Journal of Political Science* 21: 129.

Shea, Dan. 1996a. *Campaign Craft: Strategies, Tactics, and the Art of Political Campaign Management.* Westport, Conn.: Praeger.

Shea, Daniel M. 1996b. *Campaign Craft: The Strategies, Tactics, and Art of Campaign Management.* Westport, Conn.: Praeger.

Sheppard, Burton D. 1985. *Rethinking Congressional Reform.* Cambridge: Schenkman.

Shribman, David. 1999. "National Perspective." *Boston Globe,* February 16, A3.

Sigelman, Lee. 1982. "The Nonvoting Voter in Voting Research." *American Journal Political Science* 26: 47.

Sigelman, Lee, Philip W. Roeder, Malcolm E. Jewell, and Michael A. Baer. 1985. "Voting and Nonvoting: A Multi-Election Perspective." *American Journal of Political Science* 29: 749.

Silbey, Joel H. 1990. "The Rise and Fall of American Political Parties." In *The Parties Respond: Changes in the American Party System,* edited by L. Sandy Maisel. Boulder: Westview.

Silbey, Joel H. 1991. *The American Political Nation, 1838–1893.* Stanford, Calif.: Stanford University Press.

Silbey, Joel H. 1998. "From 'Essential to the Existence of Our Institutions' to 'Rapacious Enemies of Honest and Responsible Government': The Rise and Fall of American Parties, 1790–2000." In *The Parties Respond,* edited by L. Sandy Maisel. 3d ed. Boulder: Westview.

Simon, Roger. 1998. *Show Time: The American Presidential Circus and the Race for the White House.* New York: Times Books.

Sinclair, Barbara. 1983. *Majority Party Leadership in the U.S. House.* Baltimore, Md.: Johns Hopkins University Press.

Sinclair, Barbara. 1989. *The Transformation of the U.S. Senate.* Baltimore, Md.: Johns Hopkins University Press.

Sinclair, Barbara. 1990. "The Congressional Party: Evolving Organizational, Agenda Setting, and Policy Roles." In *The Parties Respond: Changes in the American Party System,* edited by L. Sandy Maisel. Boulder: Westview.

Sinclair, Barbara. 1997. *Unorthodox Lawmaking*. Washington, D.C.: Congressional Quarterly Press.

Sinclair, Barbara. 1998. "Evolution or Revolution? Policy-Oriented Congressional Parties in the 1990s." In *The Parties Respond,* edited by L. Sandy Maisel. 3d ed. Boulder: Westview.

"Six Decades of Gallup Polling." 1997. *Public Perspective* 8, no. 3 (April-May).

Smith, Gregg W. 1990. "Party Organizations and Voter Turnout: The 1988 Elections." Paper presented at the annual meeting of the American Political Science Association, San Francisco.

Smith, Steven S., and Christopher J. Deering. 1990. *Committees in Congress.* 2d ed. Washington, D.C.: Congressional Quarterly Press.

Snowiss, Leo M. 1966. "Congressional Recruitment and Representation." *American Political Science Review* 60: 627.

Sonenshein, Raphael J. 1990. "Can Black Candidates Win Statewide Elections?" *Political Science Quarterly* 105: 219.

Sorauf, Frank J. 1980. *Party Politics in America.* Boston: Little, Brown.

Sorauf, Frank J. 1984a. "Political Action Committees in American Politics: An Overview." In *What Price PACs?* New York: Twentieth Century Fund.

Sorauf, Frank J. 1984b. "Who's in Charge? Accountability in Political Action Committees." *Political Science Quarterly* 99: 591.

Sorauf, Frank J. 1988. *Money in American Elections.* Glenview, Ill.: Scott, Foresman.

Sorauf, Frank J. 1990. "Political Organizations: Concepts and Categories." Paper presented at the annual meeting of the American Political Science Association, San Francisco.

Sorauf, Frank J. 1991. "Political Action Committees." In *Political Parties and Elections in the United States: An Encyclopedia,* edited by L. Sandy Maisel. New York: Garland.

Sorauf, Frank J. 1998. "Political Parties and the New World of Campaign Finance." In *The Parties Respond,* edited by L. Sandy Maisel. 3d ed. Boulder: Westview.

Sorauf, Frank J., and Paul A. Beck. 1988. *Party Politics in America.* 6th ed. Glenview, Ill.: Scott, Foresman.

Southwell, Priscilla, and Justin Burchett. 1997. "Survey of Vote-by-Mail Senate Election in the State of Oregon." *PS: Political Science and Politics* 30 (March): 53–58.

Sparks, Jared, ed. 1840. *The Writings of George Washington.* Boston: F. Andrews.

Spitzer, Robert J. 1987. *The Right to Life Movement and Third Party Politics.* Westport, Conn: Greenwood.

Squire, Peverill, Raymond E. Wolfinger, and David P. Glass. 1985. "Residential Mobility and Voter Turnout." Paper presented at the annual meeting of the American Political Science Association, New Orleans.

Squire, Peverill, Raymond E. Wolfinger, and David P. Glass. 1987. "Residential Mobility and Voter Tumout." *American Political Science Review* 81: 45.

Stanley, Harold W. 1985. "The Runoff. The Case for Retention." *PS: Political Science and Politics* 18: 231.

Stanley, Harold W., William T. Bianco, and Richard G. Niemi. 1985. "A New Perspective on Partisanship and Group Support over Time." Paper presented at the annual meeting of the American Political Science Association, New Orleans.

Stanley, Harold W., William T. Bianco, and Richard G. Niemi. 1986. "Partisanship and Group Support over Time: A Multivariate Analysis." *American Political Science Review* 80: 969.

Stanley, Harold W., and Richard G. Niemi. 1989. "Partisanship and Group Support." Paper presented at the annual meeting of the American Political Science Association, Atlanta, Ga.

Stanley, Harold W., and Richard G. Niemi. 1990. *Vital Statistics on American Politics.* 2d ed. Washington, D.C.: Congressional Quarterly Press.

Stein, Robert M., and Patricia Garcia-Monet. 1997. "Voting Early but Not Often." *Social Science Quarterly* 78 (September): 657–672.

Steinberg, Alfred. 1972. *The Bosses.* New York: Macmillan.

Stern, Philip M. 1988. *The Best Congress Money Can Buy.* New York: Pantheon Books.

Stewart, Charles, III. 1990. "Responsiveness in the Upper Chamber: The Constitution and Institutional Development in the Senate." Paper presented at the annual meeting of the Midwest Political Science Association, Chicago.

Stewart, John G. 1991. "Democratic National Committee." In *Political Parties and Elections in the United States: An Encyclopedia,* edited by L. Sandy Maisel. New York: Garland.

Stokes, Donald E., and Warren E. Miller. 1962. "Party Government and the Saliency of Congress." *Public Opinion Quarterly* 26: 531.

Stone, Walter J., L. Sandy Maisel, and Cherie Maestas. 1998. "Candidate Emergence in U. S. House Elections." Paper presented at the annual meeting of the American Political Science Association, Boston.

Stone, Walter J., L. Sandy Maisel, Cherie Maestas, and Sean Evans. 1998. "Candidate Quality in U.S. House Elections: Candidate Emergence in the 1998 Elections." Paper presented at the annual meeting of the Midwest Political Science Association, Chicago.

Stone, Walter J., Ronald B. Rapoport, and Alan I. Abramowitz. 1989. "The Reagan Revolution and Party Polarization in the 1980s." Paper presented at the annual meeting of the American Political Science Association, Atlanta, Ga.

Stone, Walter J., Ronald B. Rapoport, and Alan I. Abramowitz. 1990. "Candidate Perception among Nomination Activists: A New Look at the Moderation Hypothesis." Paper presented at the American Political Science annual meeting, San Francisco.

Sullivan, Denis G., Robert T. Nakamura, Martha Wagner Weinberg, F. Christopher Arterton, and Jeffrey L. Pressman. 1977–1978. "Exploring the 1976 Republican Convention." *Political Science Quarterly* 92: 531.

Sullivan, Denis G., Jeffrey L. Pressman, and F. Christopher Arterton. 1976. *Explorations in Convention Decision Making: The Democratic Party in the 1970s.* San Francisco: Freeman.

Sullivan, Denis G., Jeffrey L. Pressman, F. Christopher Arterton, Robert T. Nakamura, and Martha Wagner Weinberg. 1977. "Candidates, Caucuses, and Issues: The Democratic Convention, 1976." In *The Impact of the Electoral Process,* edited by Louis Maisel and Joseph Cooper. Beverly Hills: Sage.

Sullivan, Denis G., Jeffrey L. Pressman, Benjamin I. Page, and John J. Lyons. 1974. *The Politics of Representation: The Democratic Convention, 1972.* New York: St. Martin's.

Sundquist, James L. 1983. *Dynamics of the Party System: Alignment and Realignment of Political Parties in the United States.* Rev. ed. Washington, D.C.: Brookings Institution.

Sundquist, James L. 1988. "Needed: A Political Theory for the New Era of Coalition Government in the United States." *Political Science Quarterly* 103: 613.

Sussman, Barry. 1984. "How Can Labor Ties Hurt Mondale if Americans Cherish Unions?" *Washington Post National Weekly Edition* 1: 20.

Taggart, William A., and Robert F. Durant. 1985. "Home Style of a U.S. Senator: A Longitudinal Study." *Legislative Studies Quarterly* 10: 489.

Tarrance, V. Lance. 1978. "Suffrage and Voter Turnout in the United States: The Vanishing Voter." In *Parties and Elections in an Anti-Party Age,* edited by Jeff Fishel. Bloomington: Indiana University Press.

Task Force on Campaign Reform. 1998. *Campaign Reform: Insights and Evidence*. Princeton, N.J.: Woodrow Wilson School of Public and International Affairs, Princeton University.

Texeira, Ruy. 1987. *Why Ameticans Don't Vote.* New York: Greenwood.

Teixera, Ruy. 1993. *The Disappearing American Voter*. Washington, D.C.: Brookings Institution.

Thayer, George. 1973. *Who Shakes the Money Tree?* New York: Simon and Schuster.

Thompson, Hunter. 1973. *Fear and Loathing: On the Campaign Trail '72.* New York: Quick Fox.

Thurber, James A. 1991. *Divided Government.* Washington, D.C.: Congressional Quarterly Press.

Thurber, James A., and Candice J. Nelson. 1995. *Campaigns and Elections American Style.* Boulder: Westview.

Timpone, Richard. 1998. "Structure, Behavior, and Voter Turnout in the United States." *American Political Science Review* 92: 145–158.

Tolchin, Martin, and Susan Tolchin. 1971. *To the Victor . . . Political Patronage from the Clubhouse to the White House.* New York: Vintage Books.

Tolchin, Susan J. 1996. *The Angry American: How Voter Rage Is Changing the Nation*. Boulder: Westview.

Traugott, Michael W. 1985. "The Media and the Nominating Process." In *Before Nomination: Our Primary Problem,* edited by George Grassmuck. Washington, D.C.: American Enterprise Institute for Public Policy Research.

Truman, David B. 1951. *The Governmental Process.* New York: Knopf.

Truman, David B. 1959. *The Congressional Party: A Case Study*. New York: Wiley.

Tufte, Edward E. 1975. "Determinants of the Outcomes of Midterm Congressional Elections." *American Political Science Review* 69: 312.

Tufte, Edward E. 1978. *Political Control of the Economy.* Princeton, N.J.: Princeton University Press.

Twentieth Century Fund. 1984. *What Price PACs?* New York: Twentieth Century Fund.

Usher, Douglas L. 1998. "Party Institutions and Issue Activist Strength." Unpublished manuscript, Cornell University.

Uslaner, Eric. 1981. "Ain't Misbehavin': The Logic of Defensive Issue Voting Strategies in Congressional Elections." *American Politics Quarterly* 9: 3.

Verba, Sidney, and Norman H. Nie. 1972. *Participation in America: Political Democracy and Social Equality.* New York: Harper and Row.

Verba, Sidney, Kay Lehman Schlozman, and Henry Brady. 1995. *Voice and Equality: Civic Voluntarism in American Politics.* Cambridge: Harvard University Press.

Walker, Jack L. 1983. "The Origins and Maintenance of Interest Groups in America." *American Political Science Review* 77: 390.

Walters, Ronald W. 1988. *Black Presidential Politics in America: A Strategic Approach.* Albany: State University of New York Press.

Waterman, Richard W., Bruce I. Oppenheimer, and James A. Stimson. 1991. "Sequence and Equilibrium in Congressional Election: An Integrated Approach." *Journal of Politics* 53: 372.

Wattenberg, Martin P. 1981. "The Decline of Political Partisanship in the United States: Negativity or Neutrality?" *American Political Science Review* 75: 941.

Wattenberg, Martin P. 1984. *The Decline of American Political Parties, 1952–1980.* Cambridge: Harvard University Press.

Wattenberg, Martin P. 1986. *The Decline of American Political Parties, 1952–1984.* Cambridge: Harvard University Press.

Wattenberg, Martin P. 1989. "The Hollow Realignment Continues: Partisan Change in 1988." Paper presented at the annual meeting of the American Political Science Association, Atlanta, Ga.

Wattenberg, Martin P. 1990a. "And Quayle Too: Examining the Electoral Effect of Vice Presidential Candidates." Paper presented at the annual meeting of the American Political Science Association, San Francisco.

Wattenberg, Martin P. 1990b. *The Decline of American Political Parties, 1952–1988.* Cambridge: Harvard University Press.

Wattenberg, Martin P. 1991a. "Dealignment in the American Electorate." In *The Encyclopedia of American Political Parties and Elections,* edited by L. Sandy Maisel. New York: Garland.

Wattenberg, Martin P. 1991b. *The Rise of Candidate-Centered Politics: Presidential Elections of the 1980s.* Cambridge: Harvard University Press.

Wattenberg, Martin. 1994. *The Decline of American Political Parties, 1952–1992.* Cambridge: Harvard University Press.

Wattenberg, Martin. 1996. *The Decline of American Political Parties, 1952–1994.* Cambridge: Harvard University Press.

Wayne, Stephen J. 1978. *The Legislative Presidency.* New York: Harper and Row.

Wayne, Stephen J. 1981. *The Road to the White House: The Politics of Presidential Elections.* New York: St. Martin's.

Wayne, Stephen J. 1984. *The Road to the White House: The Politics of Presidential Elections.* 2d ed. New York: St. Martin's.

Wayne, Stephen J. 1988. *The Road to the White House: The Politics of Presidential Elections.* 3d ed. New York: St. Martin's.

Wayne, Stephen J. 1992. *The Road to the White House: The Politics of Presidential Elections.* 4th ed. New York: St. Martin's.

Wayne, Stephen J. 1996. *The Road to the White House, 1996*. New York: St. Martin's.

Weber, Ronald, Harvey Tucker, and Paul Brace. 1991. "Vanishing Marginals in State Legislative Elections." *Legislative Studies Quarterly* 16: 29.

Weil, Gordon L. 1973. *The Long Shot.* New York: Norton.

Wekkin, Gary D. 1984. "National-State Party Relations: The Democrats." *Political Science Quarterly* 99: 45.

West, Darrell M. 1990. "Television Advertising in Nomination Politics." Paper prepared for the annual meeting of the American Political Science Association, San Francisco.

White, Theodore H. 1961. *The Making of the President, 1960*. New York: Atheneum.

White, Theodore H. 1965. *The Making of the President, 1964*. New York: Atheneum.

White, Theodore H. 1969. *The Making of the President, 1968*. New York: Atheneum.

White, Theodore H. 1973. *The Making of the President, 1972*. New York: Atheneum.

White, Theodore H. 1982. *America in Search of Itself: The Making of the President, 1956–1980*. New York: Harper and Row.

Wilcox, Clyde. 1988. "I Owe It All to Me: Candidates' Investments in Their Own Campaigns." *American Politics Quarterly* 16: 266.

Wilcox, Clyde. 1996. *Onward Christian Soldiers? The Religious Right in American Politics*. Boulder: Westview.

Williams, T. Harry. 1969. *Huey Long*. New York: Knopf.

Williamson, Jonathan. 1999. "Supply-Side of Southern Politics: Candidate Quality and Candidate Emergence in House Elections." Paper presented at the annual meeting of the Midwest Political Science Association, Chicago.

Wilson, James Q. 1962. *The Amateur Democrat*. Chicago: University of Chicago Press.

Wilson, James Q. 1973. *Political Organizations*. New York: Basic Books.

Wilson, Scott. 1998. "Negative Ads Fill the Air in Maryland; Unprecedented Hostility Marks the Governor's Race." *Washington Post,* October 27, A1.

Wilson, Woodrow. 1885. *Congressional Government*. Boston: Houghton Mifflin.

Winebrenner, Hugh. 1983. "The Evolution of the Iowa Precinct Caucuses." *Annals of Iowa* 46: 618.

Winebrenner, Hugh. 1985. "The Iowa Precinct Caucuses: The Making of a Media Event." *Southeastern Political Review.*

Wirthlin, Richard B. 1981. "The Republican Strategy and Its Electoral Consequences." In *Party Coalitions in the 1980s,* edited by Seymour Martin Lipset. San Francisco: Institute for Contemporary Studies.

Witcover, James. 1977. *Marathon: The Pursuit of the Presidency, 1972–1976*. New York: Viking.

Wolfinger, Raymond E., and Steven J. Rosenstone. 1980. *Who Votes?* New Haven: Yale University Press.

Wright, Gerald C., Robert S. Erikson, and John P. McIver. 1985. "Measuring State Partisanship and Ideology with Survey Data." *Journal of Politics* 47: 469.

Wright, John R. 1985. "PACs, Contributions, and Roll Calls: An Organizational Perspective." *American Political Science Review* 79: 400.

Young, James. 1966. *The Washington Community*. New York: Harcourt, Brace and World.

Zuckman, Jill. 1990. "Thirty-Year High in Partisanship Marked 1990 Senate Votes." *Congressional Quarterly Weekly Report* 48: 4188.

Index

About the Author

L. Sandy Maisel is the William R. Kenan Jr. Professor of Government at Colby College in Waterville, Maine, where he has taught courses in American government for nearly three decades. He is the co-author of *Two Parties—Or More: The American Party System* (1998) and the author of *From Obscurity to Oblivion: Running in Congressional Primaries* (1986). He is also editor and co-author of ten other books, including *The Parties Respond: Changes in American Parties and Campaigns* (3d ed., 1998) and *American Political Parties and Elections: An Encyclopedia* (1991). For the last five years Maisel has been the series editor for the Dilemmas in American Politics Series; he has also served on the editorial board of five different political science journals. Former president of the New England Political Science Association and chair of both the Legislative Studies and the Political Organizations and Parties organized sections of the American Political Science Association, Maisel was the Philippine Centennial Distinguished Fulbright Lecturer in Manila, the Philippines, in 1998 and a Guest Scholar at the Brookings Institution in Washington, D.C., in the spring of 1999. He is currently engaged in research exploring decision making by those who consider running for political office.